Knock:
The Virgin's Apparition in Nineteenth-Century Ireland

Knock:
The Virgin's Apparition in Nineteenth-Century Ireland

Eugene Hynes

CORK UNIVERSITY PRESS

First published in 2008 by
Cork University Press
Youngline Industrial Estate
Pouladuff Road, Togher
Cork, Ireland

British Library Cataloguing in Publication Data

Hynes, Eugene.
  Knock : the Virgin's apparition in nineteenth-century
  Ireland.
  1. Mary, Blessed Virgin, Saint--Apparitions and miracles--
  Ireland--Knock. 2. Knock (Ireland)--Religious life and
  cutoms. 3. Knock (Ireland)--Religion--19th century.
  4. Catholic Church--Ireland--History--19th century.
  5. Religion and sociology--Ireland--Knock.
  I. Title
  232.9'17'094173-dc22

  ISBN–13: 9781859184400 hbk
  ISBN–13: 9781859184639 pbk

Typeset by Tower Books, Ballincollig, Co. Cork
Printed by Gutenberg Press, Malta

www.corkuniversitypress.com

For Sandy, Mary and
Michael

Contents

List of Illustrations

Acknowledgements

This book could not have even been started without the help of many others in getting access to sources. The Interlibrary Loan Department at Kettering University has been a Hogwarts in producing a succession of wizards: Joyce Keys, the late Meg Wickman and now Bruce Deitz have long worked their own brand of magic in tracking down hard to locate materials. Grace Mulqueen and her staff at Knock Museum have always been helpful and responsive to my inquiries. I thank Grace especially for sending me a copy of the Byrne typescript of Daniel Campbell's memoir, and Caroline Naughton for her help in procuring the cover illustration. Paul Carpenter, John Carty, Sr Theresa Delaney, Jim Donnelly, Stella Duffy, John Gallagher, Ivor Hamrock, Mary Heimann, Fr James Hodkinson, SJ, Sr Theresette Hunting, CSJP, two Marys (my sister and my daughter), Anne Kane, Brian Keary, Fr Brendan Kilcoyne, Clodagh Kingston and Eithne Massey at Dublin City Library and Archives, Thomas McGrath, Leo McNamara, John Moulden, Nollaig Ó Muraíle, Frank Naughton, the late Sr Catherine O'Connor, CSJP, Fr John O'Connor, OSA, Ash Rehal, Tony Varley, and Linda Wicks all helped me get my hands on some important sources, provided information themselves, or answered questions I had. I thank Joan Donnelly for the photograph of the Temperance Medal. I have benefited from the feedback Angela Bourke, Michael Carroll and Jim Donnelly each gave me on separate chapters. Catherine Coughlan, Maria O'Donovan and Sophie Watson made dealing with Cork University Press more joyful than drudgery. In thanking all of these, it goes without saying that nobody but myself is responsible for the errors of fact or interpretation that doubtless remain in my work.

Material from the National Folklore Collection, University College Dublin, is published with the kind permission of the Director.

Preface

The Virgin Mary had come to Ireland. That was what respected newspapers reported very early in 1880. On August 21 1879, in a poor rural village in the western county of Mayo, over a dozen people saw a bright silvery-white light outside the gable of the local Catholic church and within the light the Virgin Mary, St Joseph and a third figure they identified as St John the Evangelist. Some of the seers saw an altar, a lamb and a cross. Angels' wings surrounded the altar. According to the reports, the apparition persisted for several hours but the life-size figures did not speak or move. The place where the vision appeared remained dry even though both the surrounding area and the witnesses were drenched by the heavy rain that fell continuously during the episode. An investigation by a panel of priests had concluded that the witnesses' testimony was satisfactory.

Even before newspaper coverage began, the story of what had happened had spread by word of mouth and local people had made the site a place of pilgrimage. The media reports brought throngs of pilgrims from farther afield, but after a busy few years, fewer and fewer people came until a revival in the 1930s again turned Knock into a major pilgrimage site. In the second half of the twentieth century, Knock became a national and international centre of devotion. A visit by Pope John Paul II in the centenary year of 1979 both recognised and consolidated Knock's place as one of the world's premier Marian shrines.

Most accounts of the 1879 apparition are what might be called devotional, produced by people for whom it was a miraculous manifestation of divine power. Such believers understand the vision as supernatural in origin and thus beyond human explanation. In contrast to believers' accounts, some writers then and later dismissed the occurrence as meaningless superstition, delusion or fraud. Few social scientists have devoted much attention to the episode. In contrast to all these, in this work I examine the timing, location and content of the apparition by reference to the cultural, economic and socio-political context in which it occurred. To understand any apparition we have to understand those people who believe either their own experience or the claims of others that they have encountered some transcendent reality. In the early chapters I describe different pieces of what I argue was a coherent picture of local religious life, and in later chapters I examine how these fit together. As well as describing what was happening locally around the time of apparition, I seek to look as much as possible through the eyes of local people in Knock in the preceding decades to explain the insiders' experiences in 1879. Without impugning the honesty of the seers, I will argue that the vision embodied in microcosm many of the central conflicts and struggles within the Irish Catholic church and especially among its local members of the time; further, that we can explain how it both expressed and transcended these conflicts.

We can also use the apparition at Knock to contribute to debates among historians on how best to explain changes in nineteenth-century Irish Catholicism. Understanding the Knock case provides more than just another case study of local significance. It contributes to the recent upsurge in scholarly attention to popular religion and especially to the study of Marian apparitions in nineteenth-century Europe as exemplified by Ruth Harris' study of Lourdes, David Blackbourn's of Marpingen and Cheryl Porte's of Pontmain.[1] Some students of religious change have tended to stress local factors as key: what made people develop, adapt or retain their religious understandings and practices. Others emphasise the impacts of outside forces, often the missionary efforts of organised churches. This 'top-down' approach is exemplified in the scholarly study of nineteenth-century Irish Catholicism by the so-called 'devotional revolution thesis' developed by historian Emmet Larkin. Consideration of the Knock episode and the Larkin thesis, in light of each other, leads to insights into the comparative benefits and limitations of both the top-down and bottom-up approaches that have wider application.

In the small-scale study of Knock and its apparition, I observe processes of global significance. Folklore stories from pre-apparition Knock are not merely of local importance. The great religions of the world, universal in their claims and often in their reach, had origins that were local to some particular time and place, and their stories were oral stories. Alan Dundes summarised this important recognition in the title of one of his recent books, *Holy Writ as Oral Lit*. A fine-combed investigation of the sense-making processes observable in the 'little traditions' has deep implications for understanding the same processes on far bigger stages.

A Short Note on my Perspective

Social scientists come to their research topics from diverse starting points. Historian Ruth Harris, a self-described secular Jew, was led to study the history of devotion in Lourdes in an effort to understand something that initially turned her off, what she saw as the anachronistic superstitions of people she knew. She began to comprehend and to be impressed by their faith while participating as a helper on a pilgrimage for the sick, though she did not come to share their belief that the Virgin had come to earth. My relationship with Knock has had a very different trajectory but my ending point is very similar to Harris'. I was born in 1948 on a farm in east Galway, and I grew up in an atmosphere of Catholic faith that went beyond belief to unquestioned certitude. Several times in the late 1950s and early 1960s I travelled on pilgrimage to Knock. My father would engage one of the two local men who had cars to drive the nearly fifty miles to Knock, a service they provided for neighbours on many a summer Sunday. I remember these trips mainly for the car-sickness that I invariably suffered, which the rest of the family reminded me about for months afterward. But I also recall moments at Knock: being caught up in a stream of big people slowly circling the apparition church, a dense throng of pilgrims with different groups at different points in praying the rosary; at the edge of a crowd being able to hear the booming sound, but not understand the words of some sermon or prayer over a public address system; people pushing to fill bottles of holy water from the taps, as we did before driving home; invalids on stretchers sheltered by rubber sheets from a drizzling rain. On at least one occasion we were joined on the trip by my Aunt Katie, my father's sister visiting home from her job as a nurse in England. After she retired in the 1970s, Katie would become a Handmaid at Knock Shrine, for years giving the same kinds of services to the sick that Ruth Harris offered to Lourdes pilgrims.

As a student of sociology in graduate school in America in the early 1970s I was learning to see as an outsider what I knew as an insider. Among a wide variety of theorists I read, Emile Durkheim probably influenced me most early on. I knew he had been criticised for downplaying conflict within society but his suggestion that, despite their evident differences, all religions were true though not in the way that their faithful followers believed, made sense to me. One day, taking a break from analysing data for my dissertation on a completely different topic, I encountered David Miller's article on Irish mass attendance in 1834 and Emmet Larkin's already famous 'The Devotional Revolution in Ireland, 1850–1875'.[2] These articles shocked me. I had grown up with the remembered history of Irish Catholics suffering religious persecution through the Penal Laws and sheltering fugitive priests from priest-hunters. It went without saying that they would attend mass when free to do so. By showing that high mass-attendance rates date from the mid-nineteenth century, long after the Penal Laws, Larkin's argument shattered a whole understanding I had taken for granted. The more I read his article, however, the more convinced I became that he was wrong in explaining what he had undoubtedly identified. He did not mention what I saw as important, things as the ordinary Catholics rather than the bishops or even Rome understood them. My first article on religion was a response to Miller and Larkin.[3]

Over the years I occasionally returned to deeper thinking about Irish Catholicism, usually provoked by what some historian had written or stimulated by some insightful study elsewhere. In 1989, I published an essay taking stock of the research literature on the devotional revolution and out-lining what I saw as gaps in our understanding.[4] The more I tried to make sense of Catholicism in nineteenth-century Ireland, the more it became clear to me that I had to understand Knock as a social scientist as well as an insider. Like Everest, Knock was just there, and if I could not explain what had happened I did not understand the people or their religion or society. In the early 1990s, when I mentioned to my mother that I was thinking of doing such a study, I learned much that helps to focus some key issues. She told me that she had first gone to Knock sometime around 1940, perhaps for the big National Pilgrimage/Prayer to keep Ireland safe from the impending war. She cycled five miles to catch a specially arranged bus, but the bus driver took a wrong road out of Tuam, got lost and did not get to Knock on time for the key events. Her most vivid memory of the day was of going miles down some dusty road and having to turn back. While travel became easier in the 1960s and later, my mother grew less enthusiastic about attending. The more Knock was 'improved', the less it appealed to her. The original exposed gable of the apparition church was first railed off, then enclosed in glass and finally the church itself was dwarfed by the monster basilica built in the 1970s. My mother was sure that the woman who gave birth in a stable would feel out of place amid all the grandeur. Moreover, the posh new settings made it impossible to imagine the poverty into which the Virgin had come in 1879. The lesson is that there is a distinction to be made between believers and promoters.

My mother also told me another story: Knock wasn't all that different or special. I thought that the epidemic of moving statues of the mid-1980s in Ireland had indeed cast Knock in a new light, but that was not what my mother pointed to. Rather, the Virgin Mary had appeared to my mother's own grandmother. The old woman on her death-bed described to those around her the Virgin appearing on the curtains in the room along with the woman's son, who had emigrated to America, and the son's wife and two children whom the dying woman had never met. The son and his wife and children had all died in the flu pandemic after World War I, but the Virgin had let the dying woman see them all and she knew they were in heaven. My mother heard all this from the mouths of people who were present in the room.

If I had heard this story at some earlier point I had forgotten; it certainly was not one my mother dwelt on. Maybe the fact (which she mentioned) that I visited back in Ireland every year or two, along with my own wife and two children, was enough of a contrast with her grandmother's experience that she recalled this story when I brought up the subject of Knock. By that time, I knew that probably the foremost anthropologist student of the topic, William Christian, was convinced that apparitions were relatively frequent but that the vast majority were not reported or publicised. Christian had written books on apparitions in late medieval Spain and in the past century. In the intervening centuries, he believed, those who had seen apparitions learned to keep quiet about them for the very good reason that they stood to be investigated by the Inquisition for working with the devil. Perhaps my mother had kept quiet about the apparition in her own family during the decades that Knock was presented as Ireland's one and only apparition.

I also knew that psychologists were familiar with the phenomenon of dying people's reports of seeing lights and had explained this as due to distortion in perception resulting from progressive oxygen-deprivation in the brain. Anthropologists, historians and others had added the insight that survivors of near-death experiences 'saw the light' in different ways, shaped by their different cultures. In medieval Europe, for example, the dying who revived to tell of the light recounted visions of the terrible fires of hell, while in modern western societies most people experience the light as divine and their dying as being welcomed into a comforting loving presence. My great-grandmother's vision would fit that pattern with the recognition of what was culturally and psychologically central for her as she died. She was separated from not only her son but his whole family whom she had never even met. That horrendous emotional void in her life was the suffering that the Virgin came to end. For my mother, the Virgin came to comfort the afflicted, like her grandmother and the poor people in Knock in their desperate time. When I later checked as many of 'the facts' of the case as I could, I learned that most of the dying woman's children had gone to America and that this particular son and his wife and children had indeed all died there, but before World War I, not in the Great Flu after it. Was there any way to reconcile insider and outsider accounts of what had happened around my great-grandmother's deathbed? Memory and reality, truth and falsity, were not easily grasped or disentangled, but certainly any analysis that reduced everything to mere biochemical changes in the brain would be telling only one of numerous possible stories, and not the most important one for the vast majority of people.

Social scientists are in no position to determine whether or not supernatural personages appear in this world; what is beyond doubt is that people claim to have encountered the divine or supernatural realm in many different ways, and that their claims are given more or less credence in different times and places. The challenge to social scientists is to explain the social circumstances and social processes that make claims to seeing apparitions or having other encounters with the supernatural more or less likely and more or less credible. Those who open my book to see if the Virgin 'really' visited Knock will be disappointed since I do not address that question, and anybody who thinks I have discredited the supernatural nature of the apparition understands neither religious faith nor social science.

As a sociologist, I have drawn ideas from many of the classic early theorists and from a wide range of more recent approaches, so my work does not fall easily into some recognisable camp or research tradition. While seeking to thickly describe things as they seemed to insiders' eyes[5] I have found political scientist James C. Scott's ideas about what he calls 'the weapons of the weak' very helpful.[6] There's an earthy proverb from Ethiopia, 'When the great lord passes, the wise peasant bows deeply and silently farts'. Peasants bow low when the occasion requires it, but they know they're doing something else while they ostentatiously bow. And when they do create a stink, they do so in a way that makes it hard to detect the guilty party. Even if the local lord smells that something is amiss, without a lot of unbecoming sniffing he cannot get to the bottom of things. The lords may see or want to notice only the bowing and the peasants may want to recall only the simultaneous farting, but only among themselves and certainly not for the benefit of the lords. How then are later researchers to get evidence of the silent fart, never mind understand what was going on? James Scott, who quoted this proverb at the start of his book, took hundreds of pages to analyse the subtle ways the underdogs of the world respond to domination by the elites, but the peasants summed it up in one sentence. Wise peasants, indeed.

In nineteenth-century Mayo, the landlord/tenant and Catholic priest/laity relationships can each be usefully interpreted in Scott's terms of interactions between superordinates and subordinates, the behaviours that were publicly visible to all (the open script), those which were hidden by each side from the other (their hidden transcripts), and, most interestingly, those activities like the peasant's bow which were in front of all but not understood in the same way by all participants. These behaviours look the same to outsiders but insiders see them differently. It is important, however, to recognise that the priest/laity and landlord/tenant relationships were interconnected within the total social milieu which also included a multitude of other relationships. In either arena, what the underdogs did or said in front of the powerful was no sure guide to their beliefs. Back-stage behaviour in one theatre might well be on-stage at another time or in another theatre. Moreover, both these relationships changed greatly over the course of the century and so did the relationship between them. We can be certain that the Ethiopian proverb was told among peasants rather than by great lords, peasants who do know what's going on but who convey that knowledge cryptically. We have to decipher the meanings of the cryptic evidence available to us about the world of the wise peasants in Mayo.

If I give prominence to questions of language-use and the production of meaning, it is due to the nature of the questions I address and to the type of evidence Irish historians have neglected, not because I see language as central. Indeed, I agree with sociologist Erving Goffman,

> All the world is not a stage — certainly the theatre isn't entirely. (Whether you organize a theatre or an aircraft factory, you need to find places for cars to park and coats to be checked, and these had better be real places, which, incidentally, had better carry real insurance against theft.)[7]

Moreover, in this post-modern age, when critics claim that objectivity is impossible and all accounts are equally valid or invalid, I respond that, of course, objectivity is impossible but it does not follow that all accounts are equally plausible or that we should cease trying to develop better explanations of social phenomena. What Marvin Harris, an ecological-materialist anthropologist, wrote about his field is true also of sociology and history:

> The most productive intellectual response to the exposure of biases, hidden agendas, and lack of certainty . . . is not to adopt paradigms that from the outset promise even greater biases, more cryptic agendas, and total uncertainty. Rather, it is to work within scientific paradigms to reduce biases, expose hidden agendas, and decrease uncertainties.[8]

While thinking as a sociologist, in my writing I have as much as possible avoided using specifically sociological jargon. When I felt the need to clarify ideas or to elaborate on some non-central issue, I have done so in endnotes so as to leave my narrative accessible to non-specialists. My concern with insiders' encounters with other worlds could result in convoluted writing if I were to constantly add 'allegedly', 'so-called', 'was reported to', or similar terms to descriptions of what they said happened. Like Paolo Apolito in a similar context, in choosing a simpler writing style I trust that readers will not arbitrarily decide I believe insiders' claims.[9]

1

What Daniel Campbell Remembered

Daniel Campbell had many reasons to pay attention in 1880, when he read in a newspaper about a supernatural apparition in Knock the previous August. He was a labourer in the heart of England's industrial Black Country but he had spent over the first twenty years of his life in Knock. He had come to England over three decades earlier and had not stayed in touch with people at home. Now, however, the Virgin's appearance had made his birthplace famous and with parochial pride he wrote down all that he thought worthy of being recorded about the Knock of his day. In his cramped handwriting, Campbell filled a notebook of 120 pages, stressing that he could add much more information if necessary and he would be happy to assist two well-known Catholic writers of the day if they wanted to write a book on Knock.[1]

In the opening chapters, I rely heavily on Campbell to understand the religious landscape of Knock in the pre-famine era. I will argue later that some important elements of the world he described stayed intact and in some ways grew in strength in the period up to the famous 1879 apparition. If we are to understand that episode from the standpoint of those involved, we must comprehend their cultural world, and Campbell's memoir is indispensable in any attempt to penetrate that world and understand it from within. While I also use a wide variety of other sources, we are fortunate to have Campbell's evidence about popular religion. It is the only insider's account we have from pre-famine Knock and one of the few anywhere in pre-famine rural Ireland that gives a poor layperson's perspective on religion. The nature of the available sources means that these people's voices are rarely heard.[2] Extended first-hand accounts of popular religion by poor insiders in the pre-famine period are rare, and Campbell's is unique in the degree of its freedom from the constraints of the time and the social circumstances it describes.

Campbell was born in the parish of Knock in the mid- to late 1820s and left in the late 1840s, but the precise dates are unclear. At the end of his memoir, he tells us he was baptised in 1825, naming the priest who performed the ceremony. Moreover, he remembered being about five years old when a new church at Knock was dedicated. That building had a cornerstone bearing the date 1828, presumably the year construction was begun, and most likely it was a year or two before the building was completed and formally blessed and opened. Assuming the dedication took place in 1830 and Campbell's memory is accurate, he would have been born in 1825.[3] However his recorded ages in the censuses of 1851, 1861, 1871 and 1881 indicate he would have been born anytime from 1826 to 1828. We can plausibly suggest but not prove that Campbell's census claim in 1851 to being twenty-four years old and hence born around 1827 is more accurate than his claim thirty years later in his memoir that he was baptised in 1825. Campbell wrote that 'I have been a stranger to Knock and its people since 1848' and that he 'came to this country (England), 1849'.[4] Presumably, he did not emigrate directly but rather left Knock in 1848 and went to England the following year. Regardless of the precise dates, it is fair to say that Campbell was in his early to mid-twenties when he left home in the late 1840s.

Even though it would be another three decades before he wrote it, if we learn how to read it properly Campbell's memoir is an excellent guide to pre-famine Knock. He was a native with an insider's understanding of the life and culture and yet his time and his experience abroad gave him the physical and psychological distance necessary to become consciously aware of and to articulate what insiders would take for granted and not see as needing explication, like fish taking for granted the water all around them. His years in England also gave Campbell the freedom to speak his mind unthreatened by landlords or other local power-wielders. In addition, the primarily oral communication pattern of the society in which he grew to adulthood provided him with stories that were still with him decades later. The 1841 census recorded over 85 per cent of Mayo Catholics as illiterate but as Kerby Miller has pointed out, in the pre-famine period, 'strictly speaking, Irish country people were not illiterate but preliterate: through the oral medium they transmitted a rich, robust traditional culture,'[5] and it was this culture that informed Campbell's memory. Campbell's work is important for *what* he tells us directly but also for *how* he tells us; his mode of narrating his memoir embodies the conventions of storytelling from pre-famine Knock which were still important in the late 1870s. In describing this important source, I am also sketching the way stories were told in Knock up to and including the time of the apparition. While Campbell wrote his memoir in English, his first language, Irish, quite obviously shaped many of his constructions, for example, he refers to a landlord who 'was made a peer of'.[6]

Campbell by his own account did not maintain contact with people in Knock after he left[7] and this is true even in the case of his own relatives. Reporting on the 1879 apparition, newspapers in 1880 mentioned that at one point some of the apparition witnesses visited a house where an old woman was dying. This woman was Campbell's aunt, yet he did not know of her death until he read about it in the paper over six months after the event.[8] Campbell's lack of direct first-hand knowledge of post-famine Knock enables us to be confident that what he recalled actually refers to the pre-famine or famine period and was not conflated or confused in his mind with what might have been the situation later.

As we would expect from an insider, Campbell demonstrates an intimate familiarity with the local situation in Knock. He notes parish and barony boundaries as well as distances between local landmarks, and describes what was visible from particular hilltops or along a particular roadway. He specifies the location of many named fairy forts. Such places, like 'hedges, fields, houses and wells, the ruined monasteries and castles: these were available for any eyes to see. But to see them is not what it was to inhabit the place. The landscape does not speak to strangers'.[9] The landscape did speak to Campbell and his knowledge is not limited to the physical landscape. He remembers the unseen underground passages between the fairy forts. And the human social landscape speaks to him as well; indeed for him the social and the physical landscapes of Knock are intimately intertwined. Throughout his memoir, whenever he mentions particular persons or events he locates them in specific places. Thus, the local fairywoman was 'Mary Meegh or Mrs Moran, wife of Anthony Moran of Lower Oughteboy, within half a mile of Balina Costolo'.[10]

Since I rely on what he wrote three decades after he left Knock, it is necessary to inquire into the nature of Campbell's memory. This is not a straightforward process, however, because even though he wrote his memoir, he relied on memory techniques characteristic of an oral culture. On one level, he has an excellent memory. For one example, he distinguishes between the two Catholic archbishops who lived during his Knock years, Archbishop Kelly who dedicated the new church in Knock sometime after 1828 and Archbishop MacHale who succeeded him in 1834 and who later confirmed Campbell. Campbell also reports a neighbour telling his father during the 'Blessed Straws' episode that 'Bishop MacHale' was coming down the road. Though Campbell admits that 'it is as long [ago] as I can remember',[11] his reference to MacHale as bishop rather than archbishop is in fact accurate. Though Campbell did not know it, what he described was one event in a countrywide 'chain prayer' in June 1832, when MacHale was coadjutor bishop in the neighbouring diocese of Killala and not yet Archbishop of Tuam, the diocese in which Campbell was living. Campbell's good memory is also evident in his recall of election songs from a campaign in 1836 when he was at most eleven years old.[12] However, his memory is informed by the stories he recalls and it is important to keep in mind that these have their own characteristics as knowledge. His mind was not a blank slate on which impartial information and facts were etched and we should not expect his memoir to be like a phone directory in cataloguing explicit agreed-upon facts.

Some social scientists have seen a clear distinction between evidence derived from orally transmitted stories (unreliable and distorting), and that based on written documentation (supposedly fixed and more trustworthy). Although they would not state it so baldly, the research of most Irish historians makes that point clearly. An exception to the rule for historians is Guy Beiner, probably significantly an outsider from Israel. Using the National Folklore Collection archives in Dublin in the 1990s he found it 'most amazing' that during the long hours he spent there over the years, 'apart from a couple of stray passersby' he could not recall meeting other historians. As Cormac Ó Gráda put it, 'The gap between the *pietas* of the Irish folklorist toward the oral record and the scepticism of the historian is very wide indeed'.[13] Others dismiss the 'soft evidence' of qualitative materials as opposed to the supposed hard facts that can be counted.

However, such simplistic dichotomies cannot be defended. Some researchers, including Chris Morash in his study of the use of 'icons' such as the grass-stained mouths of corpses or the 'walking spectre' in descriptions of the famine, have recognised that written material can be 'transformed in the process of textual transmission'.[14] Even 'hard data' rarely are as unambiguous as initially appears. For one example, different historians interpret statistics on the number of tenants evicted during the famine years very differently. Even if researchers could agree on the numbers of evictions, which they cannot come close to doing even when they work with the same official published figures,[15] they would still be unable to describe what being evicted meant to those involved. Of course, landlords and tenants interpreted evictions in different ways.[16] Scally notes that while tenants claimed that eviction meant 'casting them and their large families to perish houseless by the ditchside', those actually evicted 'rarely travelled far from their former homes . . . relying on the obligatory help of kin . . . to absorb them into even deeper poverty'.[17] Just as aggregate data do not speak for themselves, so also the documented 'facts' in individual cases need to be interpreted;[18] written records, 'these artefacts of the past, filed away and forgotten, [may] preserve lies and misinformation'.[19] More generally, even when no deliberate lying is involved, 'documents . . . are often orality recorded',[20] and the historian who relies on them needs to understand their oral origins.[21]

Since the Campbell memoir is largely composed of stories, we should not expect it to be always factually accurate in every detail. We should not expect only precise literal facts but should recognise stories as having symbolic dimensions, and also recognise that Campbell and Knock people of his day could and routinely did use language in many figurative ways. Their stories embody culturally salient understandings.

> Story telling . . . assumes a certain repertoire of associations and responses on the part of the audience. . . [The teller or writer] derived his notions of meaning from his culture just as naturally as he drew air from the atmosphere around him.[22]

His 'insider as stranger' perspective enabled Campbell to describe everyday Knock beliefs and behaviour. In addition, Campbell goes further to establish his credentials as a credible witness in the eyes of his readers. He writes that of the ordinary Knock people, there were very few about whose families he could not give information, a claim backed up by the details he provides about the ancestry, marriage connections and extended kinship ties of many people. Moreover, Campbell is careful to be as precisely factual as possible. At one point, he estimates that there were 'at least 10,000 persons' in the combined parishes of Knock and Aghamore in his time. The 1841 census recorded a population of 10,916. This figure had increased since the 1820s when Campbell was born and was likely to decline before Campbell left in 1848. Thus on the one figure that we can double check against other data, Campbell is close to the mark with what he presents as his estimate. This is not to suggest that Campbell's estimate is a second-best guess as compared to the accurate census figure. In fact, there are good reasons for believing that the population of Mayo was systematically under-recorded in the 1841 census.[23] That Campbell, without benefit of an enumeration and based only on his memory over three decades later, was able to give a very good estimate of the population surely indicates how well-informed he was.

Campbell's memory is good precisely because he grew to manhood in a setting that valued and relied upon oral knowledge. His account carries numerous marks of his having grown up in such a milieu. In telling of incidents and people, for example, he often makes use of direct speech from the persons involved. Good examples include 'Oh John make haste, Bishop MacHale is coming down the road with his carriage full of straw', 'I'm only a Protestant for a living', and 'Oh, Fr Pat, did you know the relationship that existed between them? She is his wife's sister'.[24] In this last example, Campbell could not have directly heard what was one priest's comment to another priest in private. What he narrates is a remembered anecdote rather than a personal memory but it is remembered because it was originally cast in a memorable form suitable for retrieval from an orally informed memory. Even in cases where he does not use quotation marks to set direct speech apart, Campbell uses grammatical forms that show him recalling the actual spoken words. For example, in his narrated dramatic re-enactment of an encounter between the priest and a man who had married his dead wife's sister, Campbell writes that the priest 'told him send the woman away,'[25] rather than 'the priest told the man to send the woman away'. For a reader, quotation marks provide a visual signal as to whether speech is direct or not, but in an oral culture the speaker's voice has to convey that meta-information. That is the voice that Campbell uses here.

The sociologist, Basil Bernstein, has described different linguistic 'codes', different ways that people use language. In what he calls the restricted code, each speaker implicitly assumes that his or her audience already shares what the speaker knows, believes and thinks, and speakers therefore feel no need to provide detailed explication, elaboration or qualification of their statements.[26] A close-knit community would rarely require speakers to explain themselves to people with very different understandings. In the same account of a priest confronting an adulterer, Campbell has two consecutive sentences as follows, 'But he concealed the relationship. But he did marry them.' The 'he' is a different person in the two sentences. The referent of a personal pronoun is precisely the type of shared understanding that people in a densely interconnected community can take for granted and not need to spell out. Two sentences later, still not having used a noun to identify the subject of the sentence, Campbell writes, 'And the writer of these lines saw him marry parties in his father's house'. From the context, we understand that 'him' is the priest, but is 'his father's house' the house of the priest's father or of Campbell's father? Could this phrase be understood metaphorically to refer to the parish chapel, the house of God who was the priest's father? The answers can be provided only by entering Campbell's community of interpretation. Campbell seems completely unaware of potential confusion on the part of readers who did not share his consciousness.[27]

Describing the area around Ballylongford in north Kerry in which his mother grew up early in the twentieth century, historian Richard White wrote that 'life in Ballylongford was lived as annotated text. Things happened; they were described and commented on . . . In a place so poor, there was nothing to share but talk'.[28] Things were similar elsewhere. On the Blasket Islands, there was even a special term for the pervasive discussion, relating of stories and gossip that Peig Sayers' translator rendered as 'whisper-lisper'.[29] It is clear that what Angela Bourke wrote about the illiterate in South Tipperary in the 1890s was even more the case for Knock peasants before the famine. 'Theirs was an oral culture, its knowledge stored in human memory, in retrievable form, in stories of human action. They used vivid imagery and repetition to make facts, techniques, and ideas memorable'.[30] Campbell's stories comprise maps of the local social landscape and if we learn how to read them, they can guide us as we explore its various dimensions. It would be difficult to find a better illustration of the fact that 'the story of one's individual life depends on the larger stories of the community to which one belongs. That community, in turn, crystallizes around a stock of common narratives revivified in stories'.[31]

Campbell's memory for words is clear and he intersperses reported conversation with narrative; what he writes is often less a summary of information about some topic and more a dramatic re-enactment of conflicts. His memoir is full of set piece confrontations, including ones between Archbishop MacHale and Members of Parliament, between the priest and the fairywoman, between the factions of proselytisers and their opponents, between the priest and the man who married his dead wife's sister, between Anthony Welsh and John Flatley. The stories he recounts, like fairylore as discussed by Angela Bourke, are elements in a 'pre-modern database' with a 'built-in retrieval code' in the form of dense details of social connections and specific physical-spatial locations.[32] Campbell frequently traces a personal link to persons who feature in his stories. This is not just a rhetorical device to dramatise the effect by heightening the verisimilitude of the story.[33] To a person who comfortably consults written information, an account of two priests discussing an irregular marriage is interrupted by the observation that one of the priests had baptised the writer decades earlier. This inserted detail at best seems irrelevant, and at worst, it diverts attention from the point of the story. We need to remind ourselves, however, that a society dependent on written materials has other ways to access information that is already recorded and stored. In an oral culture, in contrast, the speaker is not only telling something but also remembering it for later; in such a context 'tradition is something that exists nowhere but in its flexible embodiment in memory and in current cultural life'.[34] This detail was just one more peg on which to hang other memories and other stories, all related to and by the speaker. Campbell's account of a miraculous cure during a station is embedded in a long series of remembered facts:

> Mrs. John Stanton of Knock [was] daughter of Edmund Morley of Carramore who owned or occupied the farm opposite the church of Knock when Fr Henry Bourke was PP – before the present church was built the present house of Revd. Archdeacon Cavanagh was built, for her and her husband, with 10 or 12 acres of land, and was given to her as a marriage-portion. She lived in it at the time of the miracle. My mother, who was sister to the above-named Mrs. Stanton and also daughter to Edmund Morley, lived with her sister after her father's and mother's death until she married out of the house . . .[35]

Such dense details of history, kinship, biography and local geography are so many triggers for the memory, pegs on which to hang recollections and connect them into coherent narratives. The references to specific places such as farms, houses and church buildings root the account in the local landscape and these in turn are connected to specific individuals, characteristically identified by their kinship linkages to others, including the author, and to events in the lives of these people. Finally, all of these are embedded in a locally significant temporal framework: 'When Fr Henry Burke was PP — before the present church was built' and 'at the time of the miracle'. To tell stories, to relate them, was mentally and then verbally to connect relevant persons, places and events, to relate them, to what was already familiar. Every person, place or event mentioned in one story was likely to feature also in perhaps numerous other stories which could then be recalled and 'related'. In this way, as ordinary people recognised, 'tarníonn sgéal céad sgéal anuas' (one story brings a hundred stories).[36]

As far as Campbell's memoir incorporates folklore it provides the historian with the benefits of such evidence while at the same time avoiding two significant shortcomings of more usual Irish folklore material. First, Campbell himself determined what went into the memoir and so we do not have to be concerned with questions of partiality among collectors, such as those later employed by the Irish Folklore Commission, who followed their own biases and responded to various pressures to which they were subject.[37] Campbell's memoir also avoids one other bias present in many folklore sources: the strategically selective way informants told stories to collectors. In the next chapter, it will become clear how serious a problem this is in the case of collectors like Lady Gregory. Finally, that Campbell did not publish his memoir meant that it was not subjected to the demands of the marketplace in the form of publishers and readers with their own predilections. True, he did indicate his willingness to help others who might want to publish a book on Knock. Obviously, he had not been in contact with such would-be writers. He saw his role as a provider of information, information that had been stored in his memory for decades. Perhaps the lay Catholic-born 'insider' who was the best-known and produced the most widely published accounts of popular pre-famine Irish religion is William Carleton. Scholars disagree about how much market considerations and his early evangelical Protestant patrons influenced his depictions of Catholicism and perhaps even his conversion to Protestantism.[38] But there can be no similar debate about whether Campbell shaped or skewed his memoir to fit the needs of his patrons or publishers; his memoir remains unpublished.

Another significant advantage of using Campbell's memoir as opposed to more usual kinds of folklore evidence is that we can determine the precise period that Campbell recalls. Often in folklore, 'the past' is very vaguely specified and history is commonly telescoped.[39] Such accounts tell us more about the time and place of their telling than about 'the past' they report. Campbell's memoir, however, differs because of two significant factors. First, he was absent from Knock for three decades before he wrote and therefore we can be certain that he did not conflate the things he remembered from the Knock of his youth with the situation there in the post-famine period. His concern was to describe and explain the Knock he knew. Second, he was a contemporary participant or eyewitness to many of the most important situations he describes and did not rely on stories passed down to him through the generations and thus subject to the 'chronological confusion' characteristic, for example, of the folklore about the Great Famine collected a century after the event.[40] What he did rely upon was a specific way of remembering so that when he did use folklore, it serves as evidence of the Knock of his day, not of some earlier uncertain past. Campbell recalled two episodes of collective behaviour — the 'Blessed Straws' episode of 1832 that I examine in chapter 4 and the 'strike' against the priests of 1842–43, discussed in chapter 3 — that extended beyond Knock and that we can document from other sources; in both cases Campbell tells us he did not know their extent. Moreover, he names the priests who, we know from other sources, served in Knock during his young years.

At one level, Campbell writes straightforwardly, relying on grammatically simple and direct sentences with verbs in the active voice and indicative mood. He employs tangible, concrete images and he rarely uses allusive language. His interest is in 'just the facts'. Yet his stories are only simple on the surface. They are dramatic accounts of important conflicts as he remembered them and they are replete with internal connecting references at multiple levels.

Campbell has a staunchly Catholic perspective but in no way can he be assumed to be merely a carrier who gave voice to an assumed communal consensus. Some early advocates of using oral accounts as historical evidence assumed that the folk were united in cultural beliefs and that individual members were similar products of their shared cultural moulding who differed only in being better or worse informants about what the 'real story' was in a given society. Such scholars implicitly denied that persons had their own individual interests or made their own choices about what to remember and relate. Campbell's view is discernibly lay but of what he called the 'religious portion of the congregation', supportive of priests. He was a layman but a clerical partisan. His perspective can be compared with that of another insider who gave an account of Catholicism in nineteenth-century rural Ireland, Hugh Dorian, who produced a memoir of Inishowen in northern Donegal. Dorian wrote after the Land War, beginning in 1879, had challenged and broken the power of the landlord ascendancy. Campbell wrote in the early days of the Land War and even though the events of those opening months were centred in Mayo, indeed not far from Knock, Campbell completely ignores the whole land issue. His deliverer was Archbishop MacHale, not Gladstone, Davitt or Parnell. Like Dorian, Campbell identified with the suffering people and at times was an amused critic of the gullible peasantry. But rather than blaming outside agitators as Dorian did for manipulating the locals into trouble, Campbell blames both their own naivety in seeking help from the fairywoman and the weaknesses of locals as well as nefarious outsiders who instigated proselytism in Knock. Campbell was anything but self-deprecating. Several times he refers to his expert knowledge of his subject and ostentatiously gives precise data on, for example, the amounts paid to the priests and the population of the parish. He recognised that outsiders might see fairylore as 'romance' but still he described it, even if he had a condescending attitude toward it. However, he defends priests and what he considers true Catholicism. At times he vacillates between establishing his own credibility and shielding those he criticises from the stigma of unfavourable comment, as in his discussion of the local man who married his dead wife's sister (page 43–4 below), but he has no hesitation in naming the several members of the local Flatley family who became proselytising Protestants. While many observers and some members of small rural communities ideologically deny intra-community conflict, Campbell does acknowledge in-fighting but then constructs one side as really 'not Knock' people. Further, he makes micro-distinctions among the Catholics, between those who attend mass and those who do not, and (among the former), the 'religious portion of the congregation' and the rest. And he recognises class differences among the Catholics in everything from their diet to how they travel to mass and whether or not they have pews to sit on there.

Plan of the Book

The following chapters will seek to disentangle several threads in the fabric of religion in pre-famine Knock that in reality were closely woven together. I have not attempted to provide a total picture of the religious scene but have rather concentrated on those aspects that prove important in enabling us to understand the later apparition. Chapter 2 sketches features that were common to Knock and most other similar rural areas and which have been described elsewhere by contemporaries or by later researchers. They include beliefs and practices related to the fairies, holy well devotions, and house-stations. I also examine the Stations of the Cross, a devotion that most researchers assume arrived only later. Chapter 3 examines the popular belief in the non-canonical supernatural powers of the priest. Chapter 4 takes up events and features that were episodic and/or perhaps unique to Knock, such as a 'chain-prayer' response to a cholera outbreak, electoral conflict with the ascendancy class, a 'strike' against the priests, and conflict with proselytisers. Chapter 5 considers the public reputation of Archbishop John MacHale, a centrally important figure in Knock and far beyond. Each of these four chapters stands alone but their greater importance lies in how they connect. Later in the book, I will indicate how these topics all fit together into a coherent picture of local religious life that provides the indispensable backdrop for understanding the 1879 apparition. In chapter 6, I document low mortality in the famine decade of the 1840s in Knock and evaluate later 'scientific' explanations of the reasons for this. I also present an insider explanation and interpret its significance. Finally, I offer a critique of the devotional revolution paradigm preparatory to examining the local religious scene. Chapter 7 is devoted to the religious scene from the 1840s' famine to the apparition of 1879 and documents both 'new' practices and considerable continuity with the pre-famine era. Chapter 8 examines the local scene just at the time of the apparition as much as possible from the perspectives of insiders. I document pervasive challenges to the taken-for-granted authority structures in most of the central areas of social life. In religion, the authority of both priest and bishop had been defied and their behaviour questioned as never before; in the social and economic realms, the authority of the landlord was confronted and made problematic by the Land War; in the family realm, for many different reasons the main family of seers, the Beirnes, were just then at a crisis point in their familial authority pattern. Chapter 9 is devoted to the apparition of August 1879 and is largely concerned with how that was understood and reported. Chapter 10 draws evidence and interpretations from the earlier chapters to construct an interpretation of the Knock apparition that addresses questions of what the witnesses saw, why they saw these things, when and where they saw them, who the witnesses were and why these people, and how local lay people, priests, various popularisers, and others responded. In chapter 11 I draw some wider conclusions.

2

Local Worlds

Knock is the name of both a rural parish in the south-east part of County Mayo in western Ireland and of a 'village' where some roads intersected within that parish. While the parish had legally defined borders, there was no administrative recognition of the village. How many houses it contained depended on how far along the roads any particular commentator chose to count the scattered dwellings. In 1880 most reporters counted only about half a dozen houses. The 'cnoc' or hill that gave the place its name was no great eminence but rather a slight elevation in a bleak, almost treeless[1] landscape. As in the rest of nineteenth-century rural Ireland, the people of the parish rented land from landlords but in Knock the farms were extremely small. Small plots when combined with the poor boggy soil and the absence of non-agricultural jobs meant abject poverty. To earn the rent, many men travelled to England to work as harvest labourers.[2] This seasonal migration was already well established in the pre-famine years; in the post-famine era most households sent at least one member on such a trip and perhaps most men participated. Before the apparition spread its fame, there was little reason for anyone other than locals to care or even know about Knock. However, the apparition occurred there rather than somewhere else, and if we want to understand that apparition we have to understand the local scene. In this and the following chapters I describe the religious beliefs and practices of the local people in Knock in the pre-famine years, concentrating on those features that prove important in understanding the context within which the 1879 apparition occurred.

Fairylore

Many earlier writers on nineteenth-century Irish Catholicism, myself included,[3] made the mistake of simply adopting the official church's definition of what constituted the practice of Catholicism. This standard set out certain minimum requirements of which the most important were attending mass on Sundays and holy days and making one's 'Easter duty' by confessing and receiving communion in a defined time after Easter each year. People

11

who met these criteria were 'practising' Catholics. However, people who did pilgrimages around local holy wells were also practising their Catholicism and people who made sure to be away from fairy forts before darkness fell were also practising this faith. Most Knock people did all of these, seeing no discordance. Campbell's father led the congregation in the Stations of the Cross after mass and also participated without a second thought in distributing straws to ward off cholera. Local religious beliefs, attitudes and behaviours were different from but overlapped with the canonically official versions. Many different threads were woven together to form the fabric of religious life and one very central strand concerned fairies.

Fairylore and associated behaviour was pervasive in pre-famine Knock as it was throughout the whole country.[4] Campbell devoted one paragraph to mass attendance but four to fairies and another two to the local fairywoman and by his own admission, his account of fairylore is incomplete. There is no reason to doubt the existence, in the Knock of his day, of beliefs and practices related to the little people widely described elsewhere and documented there in later decades. One classic compilation of fairylore, Diarmuid MacManus' *The Middle Kingdom*,[5] originally written in the 1930s, takes much of its material from the area around the author's birthplace in Killeadan, a parish adjacent to Knock. Campbell writes that 'Knock was a favourite place for these good people' and he names several specific fairy forts in townlands near his birthplace.[6] Fairylore was literally grounded in the local landscape. Throughout the whole country, local sites, usually called forts, were identified as the habitations of the fairies. An informant for the 1937–38 Schools Folklore project told a pupil in the Knock girls' school that 'there was not a townland in the country[side] that had not three or four forts,' and that people still believed there were fairies in them.[7] The usual estimate is that there were thirty to forty thousand such sites throughout the country.[8]

The ubiquity of fairylore poses a challenge to social scientists. Descriptions and listings of fairy beliefs are numerous but for the most part these fail to explain why people held those beliefs. It is as if researchers present fairylore as a worldview that people accepted merely because that is what they had always believed; that it was traditional, passed on from earlier generations in the normal processes of socialisation. People got their beliefs from their parents' generation, who got it from their parents, and so on, ad infinitum. Some writers have seen the fairy world as a relic of some long superseded cultural system, a mish-mash of almost arbitrary and often bizarre elements that presumably once were part of a coherently integrated whole. Others denigrate the fairy faith as primitive superstition. The problem with all of these perspectives is that they fail to explain what the people did and what they believed about fairies. They fail to explicate the relationship between fairylore and social arrangements. Rather than as survivals of earlier religious systems, however, fairylore must be understood as an element of the specific social arrangements and mental worlds where it is found. Even though the extant culture at any moment consists of different elements, each one of which has its own history, we have to understand how the people use the ensemble of elements we are studying.

Angela Bourke has developed the implications of this view in her study of the case of Bridget Cleary who was burned to death in 1895 in Tipperary by relatives who believed her to be a changeling.[9] Fairylore provides a language, or more accurately is a language, for talking about the focal concerns of specific groups of people. The issues that preoccupy the minds of people of course vary with their social circumstances as well as their cultural beliefs. In a community of Puritans in seventeenth-century Massachusetts, who believed themselves to be a small group of God's elect in a universal battleground between God and the devil, and who felt their community threatened by various factors, anxiety manifested itself in a fear that local people had been possessed by the devil, a fear that when corroborated by evidence convincing to the faithful led to the conviction that the devil had especially targeted their community. All this was the background to the Salem witch trials and executions of the 1690s. Analogous fears from earlier community crises in Salem led to the so-called 'Antinomian Controversy' of the 1630s, when internal critics of the role of ministers were suppressed or exiled, and to the repression of Quakers in the 1650s. In different decades of the century, followers of Mary Hutchison, Quakers or witches were identified for punishment for violating the values of the community. Each crisis produced its characteristic 'deviants' whose public punishment revivified the community's commitment to the transgressed values.[10] Bourke's study makes clear that Bridget Cleary was killed, not because of fairylore but because of the disruptions in gender, household, familial and other arrangements that Bourke so brilliantly delineated. If the belief was virtually universal and unquestioned that fairies sometimes abducted healthy people and substituted frail, sickly changelings, and moreover that such fairy changelings could be made to tell the truth by the threat of fire, how can we explain that, as far as can be documented, the burning of Bridget Cleary by people who suspected she was such a changeling, was the only killing of an adult? At least part of the answer is that the issues of culturally appropriate gender roles in the family and the local community were heightened at that time and place for the people involved in the case. Some issues such as fear of death are probably universal but the relative importance and salience of other concerns varies with lots of social factors. The burning issues of one day are not those of all days.

While this is not the place to provide a complete analysis of the nexus between social structure and fairylore, Campbell's account from Knock does provide significant insight into the connection between fairy beliefs and practices and contemporary social arrangements.[11] He recalls the occasions when people consulted the fairywoman.[12] They involved issues crucial in their own particular situation:

> [F]or the purpose of keeping the fairies away from themselves or their friends, or perhaps to give some person overlooked by the evil eye or a red-headed man or a black-eyed woman, or, as the case might be, to restore the butter that was stolen from the cow's milk on May Day by some ill disposed person, or it might be the sow did not take to the litter of bonaveens [piglets] as she ought to, or perhaps the hens began to crow or the cock crew at the wrong time, which would be a sure sign of bad luck.[13]

What all the concerns and problems in this list have in common is that they are specific to given individuals, ignoring for the moment Campbell's significant inclusion of 'or their friends' with 'themselves'. ('Friends' in this context meant relatives, persons connected through ties of kinship, an illustration of the significance of this principle for organising social interaction and constructing social identity.)

It is precisely in dealing with problems in one's own situation that fairy-intervention was invoked as explanation and perhaps resorted to in search of a remedy. Why did a particular individual's butter not come in the usual churning? Why did one's sow not care for her young as other sows did? The concern with churning the milk to make butter reflected the importance of food in the household and the unpredictability, given the available technology, of getting butter.[14] Charms and magical words and actions helped to ensure a good outcome,[15] but a poor outcome provided an occasion for resentment of a more lucky or successful neighbour who might be cast as suspect. Poor persons, often old women, or others who lacked social power could easily become scapegoats. Fairylore was a measure of more or less hidden resentment of others and of aggression against them.[16] As a 'hidden transcript' of the underdogs of society, fairylore bore the hallmarks of the weapons of the weak.[17] Precisely because it was an 'available narrative' it could be availed of but it did not have to be. If it was resorted to, it was done in a way that made retribution difficult. Moreover, fairylore, like folklore in general, was particularly appropriate in an oral culture. Fairy stories, as stories, functioned as 'cognitive tools' and as 'knots in a rope of memory'[18] that was further tied to the local physical landscape to which the fairies were linked by the identification of forts. Individual stories of fairies might well be dismissed as bizarre, but their logic emerges when the whole corpus of tales is considered. Fairylore was a component of a localistic worldview where the multiple linkages of person, place and event provided a reticulated skein of stories, fairy and otherwise, that in their expression comprised and ongoingly constructed the shared worlds of the people.

People consulted fairylore in search of solutions to their problems within a context of communal relations encompassing both cooperation and inevitable conflict. Fairylore was an integral part of a social life that was localistic and particularistic and, importantly, where resources were limited. The vulnerable poor were not the only possible targets of accusations of using fairy power. Individuals who lacked cultural credibility for whatever reason could also be targeted, and among the most important were those who might seek their own individual advantage. Just as the poorest might be successfully accused by neighbours, more 'successful' persons might be held to communal standards by the strategic use of fairy stories, of asserted beliefs in the powers of fairies. Both kinds of deviants stood accused of stealing what rightfully belonged to others or to all. The fairies discouraged individualistic achievement at the expense of neighbours or of the communal good.[19]

One historian wrote that 'an ambitious tenant who tried to hire labourers to drain a waterlogged field for pasture could find himself thwarted by his neighbours' conviction that the fairies would take vengeance on the community if their swampy habitation was disturbed'.[20] But perhaps the neighbours found in fairylore a useful tool to frustrate anyone who would exploit common resources for selfish gain. Some anthropologists have emphasised that peasant society was one where people operated on the assumption that one person could gain only if someone else lost out, that they held to 'a theory of limited good' and therefore the organised collectivity operated through various social mechanisms to ensure that no one person benefited more than others from the available resources.[21] As William Allingham put it in a famous poem

> Up the airy mountain,
> Down the rushy glen,
> We daren't go a-hunting
> For fear of little men.

Lady Wilde noted that

> The fairies . . . hold in great contempt the minor virtues of thrift and economy, and, above all things, abhor the close, hard, niggardly nature that spends grudgingly and never gives freely. Indeed, they seem to hold as their peculiar mission to punish such people, and make them suffer for the sins of the heart and niggard hand hard.[22]

Why there was disapproval of such 'minor virtues of thrift and economy' becomes comprehensible when we consider how the local economy was organised.[23] In Campbell's Knock as in most of Mayo at the time, access to land was organised in a system called rundale. While tenants or groups of tenants rented land from landlords, the actual use of the land was communal and arranged in ways designed to maintain either equal access to shared resources or access to land proportional to what a family contributed in rent. Land was typically recognised as good, poor or somewhere in-between. Each of these three categories was subdivided into perhaps very small plots that were then distributed among all the co-tenants with care taken to ensure that everyone had a number of plots of good, bad and in-between land.

Moreover, the plots were re-allocated among families after a given number of years.[24] While in theory, 'co-operation and equity were among the guiding principles' of the rundale system,

> every tenant considered himself entitled to a portion of each various quality of land in his townland, and the man who had some good land at one extremity, was sure to have some bad at the other, and a bit of middling in the centre, and bits of other quality in odd corners, each bounded by his neighbour's property, and without any fence or ditch between them. Fights, trespasses, confusions, disputes, and assaults were the unavoidable consequences of this system.[25]

The Devon Commission in 1843 heard that the bulk of the petty sessions court cases in Mayo arose from squabbles about subdivision and rundale.[26] This built-in potential for conflict in the system[27] was exacerbated by the resentments of those who felt unfairly treated in the re-distribution of plots. Moreover, according to the critics, the system discouraged any type of individual improvements in land or crops because the benefits would go to others.[28] Indeed, the arrangements of fields and households 'was the seething breeding grounds of every Irish vice,' according to a Donegal landlord's agent in the 1840s.[29] Many who advocated 'improvements' in agriculture, by encouraging individual enterprising farmers, repeated similar charges. Whether they realised it or not, the innovations these people championed threatened the very foundation of the claimed communal solidarity. This egalitarian and communal ideology had never been perfectly practised of course, but in Campbell's time, it was under intense pressure from population growth and subdivision of holdings and 'a contending ethic of commerce and individualism'.[30] Of course, the end of the rundale system did not result in the end of conflict among neighbours. With the decline in the ideology of communal egalitarianism that accompanied it, however, it is plausible that there was less need for an indirect and hidden method to express communal disapproval of the 'virtues' of individualistic acquisitiveness. Other things being equal, a long-term decline in rundale would result in an initial increased resort to fairylore to defend the traditional ideological egalitarianism, followed by a long-term decline in fairylore as rundale was eradicated.

One particular fairy story collected in Mayo in 1952 provides an unusually explicit statement of the argument I have suggested. The linkages among communal solidarity, the use or misuse of common resources, condemnation of acquisitiveness, and extended family ties are manifest. My analysis is thus not just an outsider explanation of fairylore but one that resonates with insiders' understandings. This is a summary of the story: To escape persecution for trapping hares on a landlord's property, a man called Micheál a Craith along with his wife and baby daughter seeks refuge in a remote seaside townland. Besides sharing their food, to help the man the local tenants 'give him a place to plant a little on the commons of the townland'. There, he 'made a ditch and a big garden'. (Left unstated here is that this act violated two social understandings: first, individual plots in a rundale system did not have ditches to mark boundaries between neighbours, and, second, the 'big' garden indicates that the man had taken more than the 'little' offered, and thus his deviance was compounded. Insiders would immediately understand what was implied.) The couple are determined to have their own potatoes, 'so we won't have to be running to ask this person or that person for a little can of potatoes', and the man sets about 'greedily' collecting seaweed to fertilise the new garden. Meanwhile, local women tell the wife that the ditch and garden are on a fairy path and she tells her husband, 'I think . . . that they are all against us . . . because we have built the ditch, that we are getting in their way'. The couple ignores several warning signs from the fairies. Staying too late one evening getting seaweed at the shore, Micheál is caught in a mist on his way home and led astray. He is brought before a council of the fairies. There, a leader tells him, '[your wife] explained to you that all the tenants were against you . . . for she thought that they were greedy for the land'. The leader tells him to flatten the ditch to allow the fairies, especially their weaker ones, easy traverse along their pathway. ('We have weak people with us', says he, '— children — and we don't like them to be climbing'). If he refuses, Micheál will be punished, and if his wife resists knocking down the ditch, it is she who will be punished. The fairies remind Micheál that he is the only one of his name in the townland but promise him that if he complies with their demands, he will 'have many descendants in the townland who will always be seen in big families'. On his release, Micheál and his wife do comply and knock down the ditch. Their garden 'bears fruit a hundred-fold'. Nine months later the woman has twin sons, and over the generations their name becomes numerous in the townland, sons, of course, continuing the family name unlike the couple's daughter.[31]

Not far beneath the surface of this tale is the suggestion that depending on neighbours is preferable to selfish striving toward self-reliance. It is easy to imagine how sharing what one has with those worse off, such as giving to poor beggars, would be praiseworthy; but accepting help is also neighbourly, perhaps even more so, a notion that we moderns in a very different cultural milieu find difficult to grasp. Accepting help from others is what makes one a neighbour for it creates obligations that tie the parties together in a chain of reciprocal expectations. 'Reciprocity rather than generosity is the engine of mutual assistance'.[32] Even the fairies, following the council, recognise Micheál's need for food after his day's work collecting seaweed but tell him, 'but we won't give it to you . . . for if we gave you the food you would have to come with us', and promise to take away his hunger using some other method. Rather than turn their backs on the newcomers from outside, the townland residents shared their food with them, incorporating them into the community. In an interdependent community, even the poorest have claims on the resources available. The community of fairies looked out for the welfare of all its members. But Micheál and his wife sought independence rather than accept temporary dependence upon or interdependence with their new neighbours, until the fairies intervened to secure access for their smallest and weakest members.[33] The story is both a product of thinking and talking about communal relationships and a model for such relationships.[34] His wife's statement to Micheál that 'they are all against us' is ambiguous only on the surface: are 'they' the fairies or the residents in the townland? The ambiguity disappears when we realise that 'they' are one and the same, both at the same time.

In discussing one particular fairy fort that was used as a children's burial ground, Campbell writes

> I remember one or two of our neighbours' [children] being buried there who happened to die at night or were smothered by the mother. It was a good excuse. The fairies took them by night, and some old woman or some person heard the child crying with air as the fairies were carrying it away.[35]

Campbell here suggests infanticide for which fairy abduction would provide a 'good excuse' that would be communally validated by other people's reports of the child's crying while being carried away. It is worth emphasising that *others* reported the baby crying while being carried away by the fairies: these others admitted[36] no doubt about either the reality of fairy abduction or the credibility of their neighbours who reported it. In fact the two beliefs were mutually reinforcing. For members of the community, the reality of fairies was proven because the pervasive belief in them was validated both by experience (including knowing of dead babies) and by conversation with credible others in their interpretive community. Each new episode provided corroboration for similar assumptions which were woven into the cultural fabric and sustained by the normal processes of social interaction and cultural transmission.[37] And it was not just on occasions of infant death that fairy belief was taught by conversation. Throughout the country, young boys were considered more susceptible than girls to fairy abduction and so steps were taken to protect them. A widespread strategy was to dress boys in girls' clothing to fool the fairies, a practice recalled in 1930s' Knock,[38] and so the lessons of fairy belief were literally as close as their skin for young boys, and as visible as the clothes children wore for everyone else. Fairylore was their second skin.

Infanticide is documented among the poor of Mayo as well as elsewhere in the post-famine period[39] and certainly cannot be ruled out in the desperate poverty of the pre-famine era. Maxwell reports the execution of a woman in west Mayo for the murder of her daughter's illegitimate child.[40] Even without infanticide, infant mortality was undoubtedly high. Other types of fairy-belief could be used in ways that led to the deaths of children even if not through active infanticide. For example, Lady Gregory recounts a case where a sick child was not cared for because the family, believing that one person might have to die, sought treatment for the sick father. ('If one had to die, they wanted it to be the child'.)[41] As is clear from what Campbell wrote, fairy-beliefs could be used to explain the deaths of children in a manner that absolved others from blame.[42] Campbell's reference to 'one or two' of his neighbours' children being buried in the fairy fort suggests that a given baby's identity was not highly individuated in the consciousness of people. As has been widely documented elsewhere, where death is common and infant mortality, especially, is high, there is little time for attention to the uniqueness of individual life.

It is important to realise that people's belief in fairies did not inexorably determine their behaviours. While admitting that 'it is impossible to be sure how much genuine popular belief' lay behind fairylore, Sean Connolly has argued that some behaviours such as avoiding fairy forts and not removing certain bushes, 'cannot be seen as anything other than manifestations of serious and deeply held beliefs'.[43] But the link between belief and behaviour is not a mechanistic one. While Campbell wrote that 'people did not like to intrude on forbidden ground', he also reported that farmers grew crops in one fort: 'it was tilled regularly every year'.[44] The fairylore consisted of what one researcher has called 'more or less believable narratives',[45] and another scholar concluded

> That there were times when belief was manipulated is evident from the ethnography and it should be noted that, although the categories were available, whether or not they were used depended upon situational and social factors and/or personal choice. The peasantry should not be seen as dominated by their own beliefs.[46]

Besides showing how fairylore was available to provide socially and culturally acceptable accounts of the deaths of infants, Campbell's memoir indicates a popular attitude toward fairies that is short of absolute certainty. He recounts how one young man exposed the fairywoman as fraudulent:

> On one occasion a young man went to consult her about his wife. He told her he thought she was overlooked or an evil eye bewitched her. So she fainted as usual and told him that his wife was already with the fairies and she would have great trouble to restore her to him. But by complying with her directions and paying the usual fee the wife would be as well as ever in a few days. She told him the description of the person that bewitched her — but the best of it all was: he had no wife and was never married![47]

Even though this story indicates some popular scepticism about the fairywoman's power, Campbell also documents the types of things people in Knock did that are consistent with the widely documented beliefs about the fairies. As was common throughout the country, people in Knock left the fairy forts undisturbed, their reported underground passages unexplored, and then made sure to be away from the forts before nightfall.[48] They believed in fairies enough to provide a clientele for the fairywoman, and they shared the widespread belief that the fairies sometimes abducted children and substituted frail, sickly changelings who wasted away and died.[49] Campbell also calls the fairies 'the good people,' a common precaution taken not to offend them precisely because their goodness could not be taken for granted.

To measure such stories against a yardstick of objective 'truth' or 'rationality' is to fall into a simpleminded, distorting analysis. When Campbell calls the fairies 'the good people' for example, does this mean that the fairies were 'good'? Does it mean that he believed they were good? That the people of Knock believed they were good? That they claimed they were good? Does it mean that fairies existed? The answers to these questions must be sought among the people and their construction of what was real for them. To think about the 'truth' of fairy stories, Angela Bourke has usefully proposed a 'dimmer-switch' rather than 'on/off' switch analogy. Such stories are neither 'true' nor 'not-true' but rather more- or less-true depending on the situation. Similarly, in his study of traditional oral narratives about the Cailleach, an archetype figure with supernatural powers, but often portrayed as a flesh-and-blood old woman living in the area of the story-telling, Gearóid Ó Crualaoich wrote that 'there was an ambiguous "operational" belief in their truth' and they 'were told as if they *were* true'.[50] Just as with more canonically recognised faiths — as has been said, there are no atheists in foxholes — fairylore was more or less believable and compelling depending on social circumstances, pressures, and opportunities.[51] One woman with an extensive repertoire of fairylore had attitudes ranging from 'firm belief — through uncertainty and fluctuation of belief — to a state of total disbelief' about various component elements of that lore, according to a researcher who interviewed her repeatedly in the 1970s and 1980s.[52] In addition, if one person could hold such divergent attitudes, within any group there was very likely to be an even greater range of views.

At the end of the nineteenth century, W. B. Yeats noted that 'the sceptic' about fairylore was always present.[53] Early in the twentieth century, after hearing several men recount their experiences with fairies, Lady Gregory asked the brother of one of her informants, a labourer, for his views; his response records the folk scepticism that unfortunately never made it into many collections of fairylore.[54] Of his brother's visions, the labourer said,

> Old he is, and it's all in the brain the things he does be talking of. If it was a young man told us of them we might believe him, but as to him, we pay no attention to what he says at all.

Warming to his theme, the man continued to debunk the claims of the others. That one of them saw 'queer things' was understandable given that he didn't go to bed 'quiet and regular'. Another man had too much to drink:

> There's another man, one Doran, has the same dreams and thoughts as my brother, and he leaves pieces of silver on the wall; and when they're took . . . it's the fairies! But myself I believe it's the boys do be watching him.[55]

Persons with views like this were unlikely to be sought out by collectors from the Irish Folklore Commission!

Different social situations provide different opportunities for fairylore (as for any cultural beliefs) to be validated by conversation with others and by experience. Truth, in these tales, is not reducible to a binary category of yes or no. To suggest otherwise is to do injustice to the evidence we have as social researchers and, beyond that, to do injustice to the people we claim to be seeking to understand.

Stations at Local Sacred Sites

Several important threads in the fabric of religious life are suggested by the word 'stations', which Campbell uses in three different ways to refer to three different phenomena. Campbell's terminology was widely used. Did the people perceive some common underlying dimension beneath the surface diversity?

People participated in pilgrimages to local outdoor holy sites where they performed religious rituals. Sociologist Michael Carroll argues that these 'rounding rituals' were the main religious rituals for Irish Catholics for centuries.[56] Typically, they involved people doing multiple circuits around some landscape feature, often but not always a holy well. The pilgrims progressed, often barefoot, and sometimes on their knees. The circuits, together with their associated prayers and ritual behaviours were called stations, and often a full pilgrimage or station consisted of a number of constituent stations or of a station repeated a given number of times. These outdoor pilgrimage sites were common but not nearly as common as fairy forts. Many writers repeat a figure of 3,000 for the holy wells in the country,[57] and there were other pilgrimage sites that lacked wells.

The nature of these pilgrimages is best grasped by describing one particular station, the so-called 'Great Station of Balla', a regionally important site a dozen miles from Knock. A 'not unsympathetic' traveller in 1825 wrote that 'a continuous stream of penitents wound its way round the beaten circuit' there on Garland Sunday, a stream which he estimated to total 20,000 pilgrims that day.[58] Relying on this traveller whom he does not identify, a 1930s' local historian described the scene:

> The devotional exercises of the pilgrims were performed around an altar in the old cemetery and round the tower conjointly, and around the

sacred spring of St Patrick, and the old tree which flung its branches over the house and canopied the holy well. Eleven times each pilgrim encompassed tower and altar on bare knees . . . ending and beginning . . . . with seven Paters, seven Aves, and the Creed. Having kissed devoutly an ivory crucifix, the penitents proceed by the well-trodden pathway to St Patrick's well, pausing on the way to pray before a stone cross. He then circled the well and the tree, with the same prayers before and after as at the cemetery. The final act of devotion . . . was to go through the small house covering the well, and he usually took some of the water with him.[59]

This station site included a well and a tree, two elements very commonly found at such holy places. It is worth noting that the prayers involved, Pater, Ave and Creed, were orthodox. Carroll compiled evidence that priests often said mass at these stations.[60] We also know from both the Catholic Archbishop of Tuam and Protestant critics that priests sometimes assigned a pilgrimage as a penance in confession,[61] so, to that extent, the stations can be seen as orthodox. Recent studies of the practices show that all social classes of Catholics attended and participated.[62]

Holy wells and other local sacred sites were specialised, in that people attended them either on specific days of the year, or in search of particular favours such as cures for the specific maladies they had. Thus, one holy well might have a cure for blindness and another site a cure for broken bones. There were stations also on locally significant days, such as the celebration of local saints' days.[63]

Many of the accounts we have of holy wells and other such sites are by outsiders, often hostile or at best unsympathetic.[64] However, one available insider account, though indirect and second-hand, does tend to show that the boundaries between holy well rituals and fairy-practice could be unclear. The eighteenth-century antiquary, Charles O'Conor, pressed an old man who visited wells in Roscommon to

> state what possible advantages he expected to derive from the singular custom of frequenting in particular such wells as were contiguous to an old blasted tree or an upright unhewn stone and what the meaning was of the yet more singular custom of sticking rags on the branches of such trees and spitting on them . . . his answer, and the answer of the oldest men, was that their ancestors always did it: that it was a preservative against *Geasú-Draíocht*, i.e. the sorceries of the druids: that their cattle were preserved by it, from infections and disorders; that the *daoine maithe*, i.e. the fairies, were kept in good humour by it: and so thoroughly persuaded were they of the sanctity of those pagan practices that they would travel bareheaded and barefooted from ten to twenty miles for the purpose of crawling on their knees round these wells, and upright stones and oak trees westward as the sun travels, some three times, some six, some nine, and so on, in uneven numbers until their voluntary penances were completely fulfilled.[65]

We would very much like to know what O'Conor meant by 'pressed' here, and how the old man interpreted the questioning. How 'strategic' was his response? Did he know of O'Conor's antiquarian interests and perhaps tell him what (he thought) he wanted to hear?

Campbell mentions several kinds of stations and there is every reason to believe that Knock had the same variety and ubiquity of holy sites as elsewhere. Whether there was any feature unique to Knock is impossible to say. What is clear is that throughout the country, sites were arranged in a hierarchy of importance with most sites only of local significance, and others drawing pilgrims from wider regions, and some few places such as Croagh Patrick or Lough Derg being important nationally. We might speculate that the 'pious pilgrim' that Campbell refers to was on his way to or from some regional site such as Balla or even Croagh Patrick itself. Harbison suggests that a set of sites in Mayo, including Aghagower, Turlough, Meelick and Balla were all links in Tóchair Phádraig, a chain of pilgrimage sites whose ultimate destination was Croagh Patrick.[66] Many other experts disagree that Balla was on the *tóchar*.[67] However, Campbell provides no evidence on this point. His concern and focus is the local scene, the here and now of his day in Knock, and the 'tochair' or causeway was significant mainly centuries earlier, before roads were available. It is noteworthy, however, that the Balla holy well was earlier fully endorsed by the clergy. There was a stone slab on the site with an inscription, in Latin, 'We fly to your protection, O Mother of God. The parish priest of Mary's well at Balla had me (i.e. the slab) affixed here, 25th March 1696'.[68]

One station Campbell does describe took place in the old church or graveyard and which, at least for one miracle cure he recalled, took place on Good Friday, probably not a coincidence:

> (His) aunt and (his) mother went to visit a corp-house, or where a person was dead, and it was reported that the person died of a fever. My aunt went to cry as was the custom, but when she approached the corpse she took a sudden fright and was struck dumb and remained so for many weeks until the next Good Friday, when my mother asked her to accompany her to the old church or burying ground where the people used to perform the Stations at the time. So they went and performed the Stations, but before half the Stations were performed, my aunt had the use of her speech as well as ever, and both my mother and aunt returned home thanking and glorifying God.[69]

Just how common and taken-for-granted stations were can be inferred from the fact that Campbell feels no need to spell out what this one involved — 'so they went and performed the Stations' — and refers to it only as the setting for the miracle that he recounts. As he remarks, not only was this station/practice traditional but the cure was not likely to have been the first miracle there 'or else they would not go there for the purpose' of seeking cures. The people were not surprised by the eruption of the sacred into their everyday reality. For them, the other world was near and the boundaries between it and the here and now mundane world were permeable.

Campbell's account of his aunt's miraculous cure is one expression of the prevailing faith in the proximity of the other world. The story is given verisimilitude by the particulars: the cure was of a named person, with a known relationship to the narrator, on a specific occasion, suffering from a particular ailment, which she contracted while engaging in other specified activity.[70] While the particulars matter to those directly involved, the healing associated with the station is what is remembered and retold later.

The miracle can also be understood within a larger ecology of the sacred, including the claims of a centralising, institutional church committed to the promotion of orthodoxy. The aunt had lost her voice when she had engaged in 'keening' at a funeral. The official church authorities had condemned that practice for centuries[71] and the woman's loss of speech, had it been permanent, might be seen as divine justice in service to this canonical teaching. However, the people ignored the official teaching and continued the keening, seeing such dramatically ritual mourning as prayer.[72] Only for deaths of babies was keening omitted in Campbell's time.[73] In a triumph of the local, the loss of the woman's speech was reversed when she went on a station in a local churchyard on Good Friday. While the day and site were sacred to both the local people and the official church authorities, what she did there was sacred only in the popular understanding. The recollection of her cure there is testament to the people's own faith in their local sacred rituals, even contrary to the official ones. In fact, keening women and those who supported them could appeal to higher authorities, as it were, to reject official ecclesiastical condemnation. They could, and did, quote the Bible against the church bans, and an old Mayo woman pointed out the Blessed Virgin Mary herself had called women to keen over her Son.[74]

A few years before Campbell, in his youth, was hearing and remembering stories about such cures as his aunt's, in the east of the country there was a well publicised wave of other miracles. These were associated with a German priest, Alexander Emmerich, Prince of Hohenloe, and practically all of them occurred during mass.[75] If these can be read as manifest proofs of the efficacy of the mass-centred devotionalism that was spreading more quickly in the east of the country, — and the idea of direct supernatural intervention to make miraculous changes was endorsed at the time by both Archbishop Murray of Dublin and Bishop Doyle of Kildare and Leighlin, and can be best understood as moves in the so-called Bible War[76] — in Knock and presumably elsewhere in the west around the same time, the reported miracles served local as opposed to central sacred powers. The most famous of the miracles associated with Hohenloe occurred on 10 June 1823 when Maria Lalor, a woman who had lost her speech as a child, had her voice restored during a mass which had been arranged for the precise time when the German priest was saying mass elsewhere.[77] That the miracle cure in both the Lalor and the Campbell cases involved the restoration of a woman's voice is probably no coincidence; the memory of the latter might well have been constructed in conversation with reports of the former.[78] However, there was resistance to the official church also in the east, as we will see in the case of the distribution of ashes to escape the wrathful curses of Bishop Doyle.

Another type of religious event, also called a station, was the celebration of local patron saints' days or 'patterns'. More accurately, patron days usually had their own specific stations or religious rituals such as pilgrimages. In addition, the pattern was an occasion for amusements and festivities bearing no religious aspect at all, a 'combination of ritual observance and boisterous celebration' as historian Sean Connolly put it.[79] Campbell makes no mention of the religious features of the pattern held each year on 24 June, the feast of Knock parish's patron, St John the Baptist. He could have assumed that the religious component went without saying, but more likely the drinking and secular recreation was uppermost in his mind, since he refers to cut heads and bleeding noses acquired in battles between faction fighters. The priest too was concerned with the non-religious behaviour and attempted to min-imise trouble by refusing to allow tents providing secular goods or amusements to be erected near the church. Presumably, if the tents or huck-sters' stalls were undesirable near the church, in his mind, the activities they housed were not likely to be highly desirable at a distance. What is reflected here is the priest's attempt to chart out space, centred on the parish church, which would be free from profanation by the secular activities associated with the pattern, and his implicit toleration of behaviours further away that he probably would have preferred not to exist. It reflects the priest's own sense of his limited power over his parishioners. If he was the shepherd, his flock were not docile sheep.[80]

Station Masses

The word 'station' also refers to masses held in private houses. Catholic lay people were irregular in attending mass and often ignored the official church requirement of doing one's 'Easter duty' of confessing their sins and receiving communion. Meanwhile, priests devoted time each year to saying mass in private houses throughout the parish. The neighbours were expected to attend the mass in some designated house nearby, to receive the required sacraments and to pay the priest. Houses were chosen in different areas for these stations so that, over a season, the whole parish was supposed to be visited. In Campbell's Knock, the circuit of station masses around the parish took nine to ten weeks in spring and again before Christmas.[81] The people had until June 29 to complete their Easter duty. Far from having existed from time immemorial, stations in this sense developed in the second half of the eighteenth century, according to one recent historian.[82]

Relying largely on a story by William Carleton, Carroll sees station masses as occasions for status display by the 'strong farmer' class emerging in the eighteenth century.[83] Priests probably justified them as opportunities to bring the sacraments to their parishioners who were not predictable church-goers, especially to provide times for them to do their Easter duty. In addition, they likely saw them as necessary to collect money for their own support. In contrast, there is evidence that lay people wanted to be able to confess in church, presumably without having to pay any fees. An anonymous letter handed to a curate near Kiltimagh adjacent to Knock around January 1843, not once but twice included 'confess at the chapel' in a list of demands made on the priests, and a similar document being distributed nearby in County Sligo repeated that specific demand.[84] Campbell gives us the lay, not the priest's perspective.[85] In Knock, the sacramental and the pecuniary aspects of the priest's involvement seem to have been combined in the book that the local priest, Fr Pat O'Grady, carried with him even if they were separated in his mind. At least this is what was uppermost in Campbell's recollection. At the stations, the priest

> always carried his book with him which contained the names of each householder, and after Mass he called the name of each householder, and each man came forward that was present and paid his 1/1, which cleared himself and his family for half a year. If they did not answer, the priest put 'A' down opposite the name, which showed he was absent and did not attend to his duties. And also he could see at a glance how many times he absented himself, and how much money he owed the priest — 2/2 per year. And he always reckoned up the absentees and how much money they owed him, and [he] always gave the absentees a good scolding for not complying with their religious obligations, and also for not paying the priest's salary.[86]

Throughout the country, especially among the poor, priests were condemned as grasping and acquisitive. Swords suggests that stories of avaricious priests probably spread in the eighteenth century when a growing number of clergy sought support from an increasingly impoverished population.[87] A likely contributing factor was the growing commercialisation of the countryside that was both cause and consequence of a more individualistic acquisitive orientation that threatened the harmonious communal solidarity that existed at the level of ideology if not in practice. Nationally, the first documented demonstration of popular hostility to priestly levies was in Cork and Kerry during the 1780s.[88] In Mayo, resentment of priests' avarice was sufficiently intense and widespread as to find expression in proverbs. 'When will the crow speak?' was one proverbial question whose answer was 'when priests lose their greed', while a list of things impossible to find in the country included 'four priests who are not greedy'.[89]

Campbell's account documents a similar attitude to priests. According to him, it was frequently alleged that several weeks of good meals was part of a priest's dominant motivation for holding station-masses. 'The priest always expected to be provided with a good breakfast and dinner, and they (sic) were not tea totallers (sic) either'.[90] Such meals nearly every weekday for eighteen to twenty weeks per year, if nothing else, substantially reduced the priest's cost of feeding himself. Moreover, decades later Campbell recalled[91] that people used to say that if you did not like to defray the expenses of entertaining the clergy you should treat the parish Clerk (who selected the precise household for the station) to half a pint of punch, and some other person in the village would have the pleasure of receiving and entertaining the priests for that half-year.

Fr O'Grady's book in which the same 'A' marked both neglect of one's religious duty and failure to pay the priest, marks one step in the regulation and control of the laity by the priest. The individual could not evade surveillance: the priest came to his or her locality and all householder names were publicly called; their dues and 'duties' commingled, conflated and publicly noticed; and absentees given 'a good scolding'.

Stations of the Cross

Campbell tells us he learned to read the Irish Stations of the Cross at Knock and that he 'sometimes assisted at and read in my turn when a boy, for my father always conducted the Stations of the Cross which were performed every Sunday before or after Mass by most of the congregation'.[92] While his explications of fairylore and of the priest's behaviour at station-masses are consistent with what many other observers have recorded, it has been suggested that Campbell was mistaken about the Stations of the Cross. This devotion is supposed to have been introduced to the area by an Austrian Redemptorist priest at a priests' retreat held in Tuam, the diocesan seat, in August 1854, six years after Campbell left Knock. Is Campbell, the insider, simply wrong, misremembering and conflating events in his later life with his earlier? Alternatively, even worse, is he deliberately mis-stating the facts to make himself and his father or his home parish look good? Following Emmet Larkin, Hoff and Yeates[93] write that the Stations of the Cross had 'not attracted' the Irish before the famine. In light of this array of experts, we might suspect that Campbell is wrong, whether deliberately or otherwise.

Many years later, Fr Joseph Prost, who was in charge of the priests' retreat, wrote down his memory of what had happened in Tuam in 1854:

> To begin with I preached the Way of the Cross, according to St Alphonsus, whereupon the archbishop said: 'This devotional service is beautiful.' And I answered: 'Yes, it would be even more beautiful if it were celebrated in a festive manner.' He said: 'How so?' So I told him he should authorise me to choose the most honourable priests to carry the cross accompanied by two candle-bearers, and that all the priests would follow in procession. Then I wanted to have a priest with a good voice to pray out loud and with clearness. The archbishop must conclude the procession in mochetta and mozzetta with two assistants. Then we should sing a verse of the *Stabat Mater* between each station.

> Furthermore, we should let the people participate in this devotion.
>
> The archbishop liked this and ordered that it should be done on the following day. The archbishop was delighted, and the people looked on with great wonderment. The archbishop translated the *Stabat Mater* into Irish that night and had copies made of it so that it could be sung in Irish.[94]

However, this is not proof that the devotion was not practised before that. Researchers seem to have taken absence of evidence for its presence as evidence of its absence. As a visiting missioner, Prost could not be expected to have detailed local knowledge; his ignorance of local history is manifest in his wrongly attributing the building of Tuam's Catholic cathedral to Archbishop MacHale[95] who had merely dedicated the building that had been built by his predecessor. Prost himself said of the cathedral building 'the Stations of the Cross were in the church but the devotion there was not much practiced'.[96]

Campbell's memory on the Stations of the Cross seems unreliable, because the devotional revolution paradigm has shaped how researchers have interpreted evidence. Emmet Larkin in his original 1972 article on the revolution developed a long list of practices, including the Way of the Cross, that he claimed spread in the post-famine period as part of the new devotionalism.[97] Seeing this new regime as a coherent syndrome, researchers do not expect to find evidence of the Stations of the Cross earlier, and when they do find such evidence they overlook it, or in the absence of evidence they simply assert the absence of the devotion, or they interpret ambiguous evidence to fit the paradigm. As noted, two writers list the Stations of the Cross among newly emphasised post-famine devotions, on Larkin's authority.[98] In his history of the diocese of Kilmore, Daniel Gallogly compiles a list very like Larkin's of new devotions and, like Larkin, he includes the Way of the Cross. In his review of Gallogly's book, Larkin cites this as supportive of his own 1972 claim. A few pages after his list of supposedly new devotions in the post-famine years, however, Gallogly reproduces an 1826 diagram of a chapel in Kilmore diocese in which the Stations of the Cross are clearly marked.[99] Such is the self-reinforcing power of a dominant paradigm to fit evidence to the pigeon-holes that it provides and ignore contrary information.

Fortunately, we have independent evidence definitively showing that the Stations of the Cross were performed in the region long before Prost gave his retreat and even long before Campbell, and long before the impact of the devotional revolution, if we follow Larkin's timeframe for that. The Stations of the Cross devotion is recorded in Galway City in the early nineteenth-century and from County Roscommon and the Athlone area in the eighteenth.[100] Campbell's statement that he learned to read the Irish Stations of the Cross while in Knock indicates the availability of written versions, almost certainly manuscripts. Several eighteenth-century Irish language manuscript copies of the *Via Crucis* have survived, one or another of which could easily have been available in the Knock area. Half a century ago Ó Cuív printed one such manuscript that had been transcribed near Athlone.[101] His interest was largely in regional dialect development of the Irish language so he concentrated on philological aspects of grammar and vocabulary in the work, but the text and Ó Cuív's study of it provide evidence useful for our purposes. Though it was transcribed in 1772, the manuscript is a copy, probably modified, of a work that Ó Cuív argues was probably composed some time earlier at the Franciscan community at Kilconnell, in the east of County Galway. Moreover, the text contains evidence of vernacular versions of the Stations of the Cross prior to the influence being felt in Ireland of the decree of the pope in 1731. Versions of the Way of the Cross were found throughout the Catholic world but they varied in many particulars. In an attempt to standardise them, Pope Clement XII promulgated an orthodox teaching that, among other things, fixed the number of stations at fourteen. Internal evidence in the manuscript printed by Ó Cuív shows that earlier vernacular versions had twelve stations, but that two more were added later.[102] Therefore we can conclude that before 1772 the influence of Roman decrees was detectable in Irish-language Stations of the Cross, in areas that supposedly saw the devotion introduced only after the 1840s' Great Hunger.

Another surviving Irish-language manuscript describing the devotion was written in County Roscommon in 1794–98, while a third, also composed near Athlone, has been dated to between 1789 and 1818.[103] Both east Galway and Roscommon counties adjoin Mayo very close to Knock, and based on this geographical proximity, in Knock there could easily have been manuscripts copied from, or similar to, the Roscommon texts or the one printed by Ó Cuív. Yet another possibility is that a printed book in Irish was brought to Knock from Ulster by Catholic refugees, of whom Campbell's father was one. Despite its English title, *The Spiritual Rose,* the book in question was an Irish-language translation of Catholic devotional works popular in England. It first appeared in Monaghan in 1800 and there were subsequent editions in 1825, 1835 and likely 1819 and perhaps other years also.[104] Among the devotions included and listed in a long subtitle were *Meditations and Prayers adapted to The Holy Way of the Cross.*[105] Near the turn of the twentieth century, Douglas Hyde found a copy of this book in Mayo;[106] there is no doubt that another copy *could* have been in pre-famine Knock.

Campbell refers to the *Irish* Stations of the Cross,[107] the one in which his father led the congregation. Apparently well informed, at the time he wrote, about orthodox Catholic teaching, Campbell recognised the difference between the vernacular Irish version and the continental version deriving from St Alphonsus that Fr Prost was promoting.[108] MacHale recognised the vernacular version as widespread and long established, as he made clear in a preface to the translation which he published some years after the Prost retreat.[109] He was an enthusiast for the Irish language, yet he chose to provide a new translation from Latin in lieu of encouraging the existing Irish language devotion familiar to Campbell, or available in other manuscripts. MacHale's publication of a translation of the St Alphonsus version shows his sponsorship of the more standardised, Rome-centred, hierarchically endorsed version. We find a similar pattern in MacHale's publication of Gaelic translations of prayers around death 'sanctioned by the church in the Roman ritual', while prayers for just this occasion were extremely common in Irish, and in his translations of other English devotions and prayers common in his day.[110] Such translations show MacHale to be as taken as everyone else with the orthodoxy and standardisation involved in the devotional revolution.[111] The Stations of the Cross installed in Tuam Cathedral perfectly captured MacHale's twin concerns of promoting Rome-endorsed practices and protecting the Irish language: their inscriptions were in Irish.[112] Rather than producing an overnight translation, as Fr Prost wrote, MacHale possibly built on the one that had been done by his nephew, Ulick Bourke, while a student at the diocesan seminary in Tuam from 1846 to 1849. That Bourke did this translation is itself evidence of his interest in the devotion, which most likely reflected the views of his uncle.[113]

Campbell's father led the congregation in the Stations of the Cross before or after mass. While the priest celebrated station masses in people's homes, here we have a devotion led by the laity in the chapel. Even there, this lay devotion was a communal activity with a 'leader' who was 'assisted' by others who 'read in turn'. The identification of priestly activities with the church building was not clearly established. This was merely one spatial expression of the pervasive co-mingling of the sacred and the secular that was so characteristic of the people's lives and minds.

In the absence of more evidence, it would be rash to guess how common the Stations of the Cross devotion was in the pre-famine rural west of Ireland. It may well have been rare and Knock an exceptional case but we cannot so conclude. In his story, 'The Battle of the Factions,' William Carleton described a rural pre-famine church apparently in his native county of Tyrone. According to him,

> *It is usual*, on Sundays, for such of the congregation as are most inclined to piety, to genuflect at the first of these pictures [of the Fourteen Stations of the Cross hung inside the church], and commence a certain number of prayers to *it*; after the repetition of which, they travel on their knees along the bare earth to the second, where they repeat another prayer peculiar to *that*, and so on, till they finish the grand *tower* of the interior.[114]

Like Mayo, Tyrone was outside the Catholic heartland that Larkin identified as the centre of the devotional revolution and where, allegedly, the Stations of the Cross spread only later. Elsewhere, in 'The Tithe-Proctor', Carleton describes some members of the congregation doing the stations in a county Limerick chapel before the priest arrived to say mass. The description is incorporated in an account of an historical event that took place in 1808, though Carleton acknowledges taking liberties with the chronology in the interests of making his story more interesting.[115] As noted, MacHale described the vernacular Irish devotion as 'widespread and long established' in introducing his Irish translation of the *Stabat Mater*.[116] Since the Stations of the Cross devotion was associated with Franciscans, possibly it could have been established in the Knock area through the Carmelite friary which existed for centuries at Ballinsmale, on the road between Knock and the town of Claremorris.[117] However, since these congregations were among the orders of Friars whose 1750 'undoing' in Ireland by Rome was at the instigation of the Irish bishops,[118] reports of the devotion, especially where the friars were most reduced such as in Mayo, are unlikely to be found in episcopal correspondence or Roman curial archives. Using such sources as bishops' and priests' requests to Rome to have indulgences granted for performing the Stations of the Cross, and reports of the installation of stations in churches in the nearby diocese of Achonry, Swords[119] does indeed show that such reports are almost exclusively post-famine and indeed cluster in the 1870s. However, such sources are apt to miss anything similar to what Campbell described in Knock or what Carleton characterised as 'usual' and MacHale as 'widespread and long established'. In Roman archives, the Stations of the Cross are mentioned in at least one other place in the archdiocese of Tuam before the Prost retreat, in an 1847 letter.[120] In Wexford, in south-eastern Ireland, the Austrian missioner had been warned that the Stations of the Cross were looked upon as a service for the poor and not for educated or scholarly persons.[121] If the same was true for Tuam, perhaps the 'great wonderment' of the people that he remembered was not at the devotion or even at the elaborate ceremonial liturgy, but at the participation in and hence endorsement of their humble devotion by the assembled clergy, including the archbishop. Perhaps, in the people's eyes, the clergy were following the laity rather than the other way round.

The fact that the Stations of the Cross devotion was to be found in pre-famine Knock does not mean that it continued unchanged in the following decades. There are two reasons to expect that it changed. In the shift from Irish to English as the vernacular, significantly, prayers were among the cultural elements least likely to be passed down in translated form.[122] This is largely due to the nature of the original Irish-language prayers; intended and honed for repeated use in an oral context they incorporated layers of literal and symbolic meanings and typically used a stylised often metrical idiom that was not easily translated. At the end of the nineteenth century, Douglas Hyde in collecting the poems of the Connacht poor, found such a large number dealing with religion and piety that he devoted two large volumes to them: '(P)rayers put in a setting of poetry, "melodious paidirs", and short petitions composed in metre were very numerous.'[123] Hyde frequently encountered informants who could fluently recite prayers in Irish but were unable to explain the meanings of (often-archaic) words they contained or even to distinguish the words they were praying. Unsurprisingly, then, most prayers were lost in the language shift and we would expect the vernacular Stations of the Cross, even though 'read', perhaps to suffer a similar fate. Moreover, the mode of participation in any devotion can vary over time as well as between different persons and different places. The communal praying of the Stations familiar to Campbell was one mode. Another mode, the practice of individuals engaging in silent prayer and contemplation of the steps in the Way of the Cross implied a different type of spirituality, one where the individual believer was central. In Knock, this possibly came later, after Campbell's day. A man born in 1915 not very far from Knock was sometime in his teens given the Stations of the Cross as penance in confession. He didn't know what that meant and 'hadn't the nerve to ask' the priest.[124] Nevertheless, the communal mode did survive as well. At least the bishop of Achonry informed Rome in 1918 that it was customary during Fridays in Lent.[125]

3

The Role and the Power
of the Priest

The Catholic priest had no monopoly on access to the sacred yet he was a centrally important person in the life of the people. Some scholars claim that Irish peasant Catholicism centred on visits to holy wells or pilgrimages to local sacred places and hence was relatively free from clerical control.[1] However, in administering the sacraments associated with individual rites of passage the priest was indispensable. Campbell adumbrated the priest's tasks as 'baptisms, marriages, deaths and confessions'.[2] The first three were rites of passage in people's social status and identity while confession, according to the church, marked a spiritual turning point. Even the Knock fairywoman wanted to have her children baptised and herself churched,[3] and a man who lived with his sister-in-law so wanted the priest to bless his 'marriage' that he deceived the priest about the woman being his dead wife's sister.[4]

While he does indicate popular dissatisfaction with the amount of money required by the priest,[5] Campbell never reports any sceptical questioning of his essential role, except by proselytisers whom Campbell regards as not part of the Knock community. Indeed, he explicitly 'relate(s) another true story' as a 'warning to those who do not believe in the power given to Catholic priests'.[6] However, the priest's canonically recognised powers were buttressed in the popular mind by non-canonical ones. The priest had special power; his was a sacred person. The people understood the priest's role differently from the one canonically sanctioned by the ecclesiastical authorities.

Evangelical Protestants critical of a whole catalogue of popular Catholic practices argued that

> the ground-work of all these superstitions is a persuasion of the miraculous power with which the priest is believed to be endowed, and from which it follows, as a necessary consequence, that every thing which the priest tells is to be believed, and every thing which he enjoins or recommends is to be done.[7]

If only the story were so simple! Of course, priests were unable to suppress a whole range of behaviours that we know they opposed. Faction-fighting, drinking, keening at wakes, 'superstitions' of all kinds and many other things all came in for clerical condemnation to various degrees, but the people more or less ignored what the priests said. Moreover, what the Protestants labelled superstition depended on some standard for what constitutes orthodox belief and practice. That, in turn, presupposed some authoritative institution to determine what is canonical. Such an unquestioned power structure and authority did not exist. Doubtless, the Evangelicals would still have been critical if the Catholic laity had in fact paid more attention to the priests.

The County Down-born clergyman, W. H. Maxwell, visiting Mayo around 1830, recounted the story of a man who said he had been with the fairies and 'received a sound horse-whipping from the priest, for attempting to abuse the credulity of the peasantry, by detailing the fairy revels in which he alleged he participated'.[8] Of course, fairylore did not disappear. The same visitor reported that Catholics in Mayo regarded an oath sworn on the priest's vestments as more powerful than one on the evangelists. What are we to make of all this?

There is no simple way to decipher the meaning of the stories about the extraordinary powers of priests that are attested to by many sources from different perspectives. Some of the issues that need to be taken into consideration will become apparent by examining the most extreme among such claims, such as the priests' supposed power to turn people into animals or even to raise the dead.[9] In discussing stories of priests' curses bringing negative consequences to cruel landlords, one researcher remarks that

> The unbelieving landlord is hardly likely to be moved by such threats. By contrast, the credulous peasant has his belief in the miraculous powers of the clergy exemplified and underlined in a further, for him, critical sphere of his life. Thus to the extent that beliefs condition behaviour, it is the relationship between priest and people that is being shaped by such peasant perceptions of the awesome nature of clerical powers, rather than that of landlord and peasant.[10]

However, this is far too simple. Even if priests' curses brought no immediately obvious punishments to landlords, peasants' belief that they might sometime do so served to buoy them, keeping their hopes alive and helping them sustain a sense of their own moral superiority. More importantly, this claim assumes that peasants are captives of their beliefs, that what they say is exactly what they mean, and that behaviour can then be predicted from their expressed beliefs. None of these links can be assumed. To better understand why this is so, imagine a scene that was not just a possibility but a probability in nineteenth-century rural Ireland. Some landlord tells tenants that they will have to pay more rent. The tenants are reluctant to agree but cannot risk open defiance, so instead they assert that if they comply the priest will curse them and perhaps turn them into animals. The tenants know that the landlord believes them to be ruled by a clerical tyranny and play on that belief to shield themselves from the new demands.

The landlord will be unable to enforce his will without confronting the united tenants who have now changed the topic of discussion from rent to eternal salvation. This is a simple example of one of the widest used 'weapons of the weak'[11] found whenever there are underdogs, which is to say to some extent in virtually every social context. If the landlord later wrote about the benighted tenants credulously ascribing powers to priests to change people into animals, should a social scientist regard this as evidence of the credulity of the peasants, or of the credulity of the landlord? Even if the landlord suspects the whole claim is a façade, the tenants still may gain what they wanted all along, the rollback of the increase in rent, and will have no interest in confirming the landlord's suspicions. Researchers should not fail to recognise possible strategic uses of their 'beliefs' about priests by poor lay people.

The example just discussed was a hypothetical one. In the nature of the case, we cannot expect to find straightforward descriptions of similar situations where the underdog participants have every reason to disguise their intent and create an apparently plausible alternative reading of their behaviour.[12] The premier scholar of such phenomena called them 'hidden transcripts' for good reason.[13] Asenath Nicholson, an American woman bible-reader who travelled throughout Ireland in 1845, concentrating on visiting the poorest of the poor wrote, 'I find in all Ireland the labouring classes, when I first speak to them, are ever praising their master', but knew enough not to take these claims at face value. Familiar as she was with the American slave system, she recognised the parallels in situations where a whipped slave stayed silent before a stranger for fear that the master might hear, and the Irish scene where the poor will 'make an imperious landlord an angel to a stranger' for fear of retribution.[14] Citing several other travellers' accounts, Kerby Miller noted that in pre-famine Ireland, 'the country people's true feelings were expressed in a language few outsiders could understand'.[15] In addition, numerous writers painted a picture of the Irish peasants 'addicted to lying and prevarication', as one of them put it.[16] What we need to recognise in this behaviour is not a pathology of personality but the strategic use of 'the weapons of the weak' available to the underdogs of society. They did not believe that deception was dishonesty. Indeed, folklore accounts presented a 'rather ambivalent attitude to truthfulness' in that lying, even under oath, was accepted provided one had a good, non-selfish reason. Even Christ's apostles were reported as counselling the hiding of the truth in the interest of protecting the Saviour.[17]

George Rooper, a visiting English sportsman, reported in the 1870s that a local 'servant', Larry, he had hired in Mayo to accompany him on a hunting trip, refused to eat a ham sandwich because it was Friday and gave as his reason that the priest would know if he did. The Englishman is so perplexed that he repeats the story twice in his book, and concludes that 'it is very strange how a naturally clever race, as the Irish peasantry without question is, persists in giving the priesthood credit for supernatural knowledge'.[18]

Rather than taking the servant's claim at face value, as the Englishman did, we should be alert to the dynamics of resistance to domination. After all, Larry's conscience may well have told him that it was wrong to eat meat on Friday. It is evident that observing the Friday abstinence was important to his self-identity, to his view of himself as a Catholic. This is not surprising since the Friday observance was a distinguishing mark of Catholics.[19] Moreover, Larry's identity as a *Gael* likely became more salient in this situation precisely because he had to interact with the *Gall* who had hired him. However, it is likely that Larry was rarely called upon to explain or defend his beliefs, and so had no elaborate vocabulary or stock of arguments available to do so when he encountered someone with different opinions. In contrast, Rooper was articulate enough to write several books. In addition, Larry was being paid in some way for his service to the hunting party, and so had good reason to keep his employer happy. It is entirely possible that he decided that engaging his sporting hirer in discussion about his beliefs could only subvert their working relationship. The sportsman might well get angry, but even if he did not, his powers of language about questions of religion were likely to be overwhelming. Employers and servants cannot discuss things as men of equal standing. In short, Larry had nothing to gain and some payment to lose by engaging in a theological discussion. What better way to both keep his job and maintain his self-respect by refusing the ham sandwich than by changing the subject and saying the priest would know? In addition, without explicitly claiming it, Larry's refusal of the meat, rather than his verbal response, allowed him to maintain a sense of moral superiority over the Friday meat-eaters regardless of their worldly standing. Rooper was blind to the effects of Larry's servant status on his freedom to speak his mind and was left wondering at how strange were these Mayo peasant beliefs, but historians should not be as easily befuddled. Even Larry's statement, that the priest would learn he ate meat, does not necessarily imply he believed the priest to be omniscient; it could be Larry's way of saying he would feel compelled to confess the sin to the priest, his way of upholding the value of truth-telling. Alternatively, Larry might have anticipated telling his family and friends what he had done and having his revelations reach the priest's ears through the usual processes of conversation. Finally, we cannot assume with Rooper that what Larry said is exactly what Larry believed. The whole episode, as reported by Rooper, says as much about the writer's cultural blindness and his arrogant inability to doubt his own superiority, as it does about Larry's credulity. Accounts like his construct a 'mythical portrait of the colonized',[20] especially since we now have only Rooper's version of the situation. We are not surprised to see this stereotype repeated by other representatives of the colonising power.[21] While we do not know what Larry felt or said in his circle of intimates, we can be confident that it would not be exactly what he said to Rooper's face.

When we examine some accounts of priestly power to turn people into animals we can indeed detect evidence of how people used such beliefs strategically. In claiming that peasants' beliefs in priestly power reduced their own (vis-à-vis priests) rather than the landlords' power, Liam Kennedy noted that the Countess of Fingall 'placed on record her astonishment on being told by a Connemara peasant in the 1890s of the power of the local priest to turn men into goats'.[22] The Bishop of Ohio in 1834 noted in his journal that he got a letter from a woman called Ogier requesting him 'to pray for the resurrection of her most amiable nephew, John Louis Ogier, from the grave!'[23] It has been suggested that Ogier was of Irish background but there were French-, German- and English- as well as American-born Catholics in the area. Even if Ogier was Irish we cannot take the bishop's perplexity as evidence of Irish immigrant belief. One wonders how much the Countess of Fingall or the Bishop of Ohio could decipher what poor Irish people really believed.

A different writer whose opinions are more easily documented is Matilda Houston, the wife of a Scottish sheep farmer who acquired a very large tract of land in south-west Mayo and lived there from a few years after the famine to the 1870s. Vehemently hostile to priests, Mrs Houston wrote of the poor being afraid of 'being metamorphosed in another world into goats, reptiles and especially into *hares*' by them.[24] She considered the people 'benighted priest-ridden' and ascribed priests' animosity toward landlords to the difficulty they had in getting money from peasants who paid rent to the landlords.[25] In her book, Houston returns repeatedly to her theme of a spiritual terror wielded by the priests. Even though she describes episodes that document some of the ways the poor tenants, who were dispossessed to clear the Houston tract, furtively resisted, such as the surreptitious poisoning of work dogs and juries' refusal to convict sheep-stealers, and she considered herself living where 'untruthfulness is the rule and honest speaking the exception', apparently she never suspected that stories of priests turning people into animals could be anything other than incontrovertible evidence of the priests' sustaining peasant credulity for their own interests.[26]

Clearly, there was talk of priests' power to change people into animals. Even priests themselves could use the idiom, as is clear in several cases where priests cursed persons who voted 'wrongly' at elections, threatening to turn them into goats, 'puckaunes' or 'amphibious animals'.[27] However, people could use the idiom in various ways; people spoke the language, the language did not speak them. For one example, to indicate the depth of public outrage over Judge Keogh's extremely unpopular verdict in the celebrated 1872 Galway election case, a Waterford priest wrote to Archbishop Kirby of the Irish College in Rome, the de facto agent of most Irish bishops:

> A very steady and religious man said to a priest in Waterford a few days ago 'I wish I were a priest for one half hour and to have Judge Keogh in my power. I would "read over him"* and turn him into a goat and leave him so all his life.'
> *(that is the prayers of the Church) thus the people express it.[28]

Allowing for only a literal meaning of this statement unjustifiably precludes a wide range of possible figurative readings. Social scientists would not expect either the writer or the recipient of this letter to have only literal understandings of their scriptures. By ignoring the symbolism involved in language, researchers blind themselves to the transcendent in the religious beliefs and practices shared in a community, regardless of whether these beliefs and practices are promoted, permitted or prohibited by some powerful institutional organisation with its own canon and orthodoxy.

A different example is provided in a ballad, 'Father O'Flynn', that became well known in the late nineteenth century, apparently especially among Irish immigrants in America. One verse is as follows:

> Don't talk of your Provost and Fellows of Trinity,
> Famous forever at Greek and Latinity,
> Dad and the devils and all at Divinity
> Father O'Flynn'd make hares of them all!

Far from being a poor Irish Catholic, the author of this, Arthur Percival Graves (1846–1931), born to the Church of Ireland Bishop of Limerick and his Scottish wife, was a graduate of Trinity College and spent almost all his adult life in England. The words may be useful evidence of Graves' bemusement but it does not follow that the people who sang this song understood anything more by it than a statement of affection for their priests, perhaps combined with the wished-for triumph of Catholicism in the battleground where Trinity College was a bastion of Protestantism and the ascendancy. What better way for Graves to defend his alma mater than to amusingly condescend to its critics.

Even in a story told by a hostile Protestant, the peasants do not automatically believe priests.[29] To coerce a man to vote for a particular candidate, a priest allegedly threatened to turn the man's unborn child into an animal. While the man did not believe the threat, his pregnant wife did and thus the priest successfully forced the man to cast an unwilling vote for the priest's choice. Surely, such a story tells us much more about the author than about peasant views and even such a writer acknowledged that husband and wife could hold different beliefs.

When we finally encounter an insider's account of this supposed unquestioned priestly power, the outcome is very different. In this story, a woman sought the help of a priest in preventing her husband from wasting their money on drink. The priest threatened to turn the drunkard into a mouse by midnight if he entered a pub. While the narrator says that the man 'believed he [the priest] had the power when he wanted', significantly, however, the threat was ineffective. If the man did indeed believe, his behaviour belied his belief. He could not resist the temptation and went to the pub. Tottering home later, he was too drunk to see the clock and so asked his wife what time it was.

'Mary', says he, 'what time is it?'
'What time do you think?' says she. 'It's a few minutes off midnight.'
'Mary', says he, 'if you see me getting wee and hairy . . . put out that bluddy cat.'[30]

This is the end of the narrative. Sober, the man hesitated but eventually overcame his doubts and went to the pub. It is only when he was drunk that the man could not put the priest's threat out of his mind.[31] For the audience, and importantly this is an account told among peers rather than strategically to some powerful superior or outsider,[32] the question of the priest's ability to make the man into a mouse is left open-ended and the story ends with the equivalent of the punch-line of a joke. Would the audience be left in terror or in laughter? Is not the whole tale an elaborate joke, a parody of the well-known genre of priest stories?

As in the case of the fairylore already discussed, such tales as these need to be recognised as moments in an ongoing conversation.[33] They are neither true nor not-true; rather their truth-value depends on innumerable variables in each given situation. The power to transform humans into animals was an available narrative (the Waterford priest did not need to spell out what it meant for the Roman official Kirby, but he did explain the phrase 'read over him'), it was an idiom that could be drawn on to make a wide range of statements. Even if individual tellers or hearers of any particular story did not believe it — it's doubtful if any priest who loudly threatened to change a recalcitrant voter into a frog actually believed he could do so[34] — there were probably others who were not quite sure of the answer. Enormous and mysterious powers were undeniably ascribed to priests beyond those defined by official ecclesiastical teaching. But the specific denotation and connotation varied from telling to telling, and each story built on past stories and looked forward to stories yet to be told. Moreover, the animal-changing idiom was not confined to discussion of priestly powers. Changing into a hare was 'universally believed throughout Ireland'[35] to be a way that a neighbour used fairycraft to steal milk and butter, while more generally 'making a hare' of someone was a metaphor for making a fool of them. In Carleton's story, *The Midnight Mass*, one schoolmaster arguing against another master claims '"if I'd choose to let myself out, I could make a hare of you in no time entirely." "And an ass of yourself," retorted the other.'[36] Stories of were-animals and shape-changing are of course found widely outside Ireland.[37] To use them to argue for specific recognition of the unique powers of priests is both to dismiss the symbolic aspects of such stories in the wider culture and to ignore the idiomatic meanings of everyday language.

Drunken priests were widely reputed to have even greater powers than other priests, but the reasons vary with the tellers. Anthropologist, Lawrence Taylor, based on fieldwork in southwest Donegal in the 1980s, concluded that the people understood that the bishop normally controlled priests' extraordinary power. Drunken priests, however, when punished by the bishop for their behaviour, were released from this *smacht* and so could direct their powers towards extraordinary cures or other miraculous feats.[38] A mid-nineteenth-century evangelical Protestant offered the explanation that the drunken priests merely pretended to cure people as a way to get money to support their boozing.[39] In County Galway round the turn of the twentieth century, a Catholic tenant told his Protestant landlord that the bishops forbade priests to perform cures 'because the whisky they drink to give them courage is very apt to make drunkards of them'.[40] The significance of these cases is that the powers attributed to priests were not those taught by Rome; thus, in so far as orthodox Catholic teaching and devotional practice were extended, in some ways priests suffered a decline in their powers.

The Galway Protestant landlord who recorded her conversation with her Catholic tenant was none other than the writer and folklore collector, Lady Augusta Gregory, née Persse. Some activities she ascribed to the fairies more easily seem to be by secret societies among the poor.[41] This is an example of the strategic use of their 'beliefs' by the less powerful in front of those with power over them. For another example, MacDiarmid and Waters analyse the ambiguities in a story told to Gregory by one of her tenants who came to beg at her house. After she promised to help him, he told her a short tale about a woman who had no food for herself and her children. The woman, the tenant said, went to ask for help from four rich women but returned empty-handed. She then told a man who came to her door what had happened, and he directed her to open a chest that had been empty but which she now found to contain 'every sort of [good] thing'. The man told her, 'From this day you will never be in want, but as to those four women that refused you, before a twelve-month they will come begging to your door.' Not only did this come to pass, but the woman had all she needed from then on, including three daughters in America that helped her. 'For the man who came to tell her that was an angel from God.'[42]

As MacDiarmid and Waters note, the tale combines a possible threat (but which could plausibly be denied by the narrator) veiled under a surface thank-you for Gregory's charity. The thanks is direct and instrumental in that Gregory was interested in folklore and this is what the poor man gave her, but it also is more metaphorical in its praise of charity-givers.[43] All this is combined with a wistful glimpse of a future world-upside-down, where the poor narrator would no longer be forced to beg and the rich would be subject to the same humiliation that the poor begging woman suffered at the hands of the rich women. It takes little imagination to see the poor man's wish to escape his dependence on his landlord. He needed to nourish not only his body but also his sense of being a worthwhile human being. He needed recognition and affirmation as well as food. At the same time, he tells her Ladyship what will get him what he desperately needs right then, a small sum of money, some food and a promise of some fuel for his fireplace. Moreover, while the last sentence assures him — and the audience — that God is on the side of the poor, by having the message delivered by 'an angel from God', the poor man avoids ascribing any credit to priests or the Catholic Church's mediation with God. In front of a Protestant landlord, it was safest not to praise anything Catholic. That God was not on the side of the uncharitable rich is explicit, but left unstated is the position of the charitable rich, like Gregory in that context, in God's eyes.

Though their own predilections may have led Lady Gregory, and her friend and collaborator William Butler Yeats, to emphasise the malign influence of the Catholic clergy,[44] she did report their positive influence too. Clearly, however, the withholding or offering of selective stories or versions of stories by her Ladyship's tenants played a role too in determining what she recorded. Her informants never mentioned to her the infamous Gregory Clause, named for its author, her late husband.[45] Neither do we learn from her that the local people considered her ancestors to have acquired their lands by dispossession of the rightful owners, or that they suppressed holy wells, or that they engaged in proselytism and souperism, the very worst kind of exploitation that gave the poor the choice of satisfying their bodily hunger at the price of their eternal souls. But we find these damning judgments of the Persse and Gregory families in the folklore collected in the same area by insiders or social equals.[46] We can be confident that tenants of other landlords engaged in similar strategic telling of stories in other contexts, for other immediate purposes, but in response to their dependence and poverty.[47] One historian has noted that 'depending on which source is used to assess contemporary opinion, the Trench family was looked upon in east Galway either as patriotic benefactors or reactionary tyrants' in the pre-famine era.[48] (The Trench and Gregory families were connected by intermarriage as well as by their shared status as landlords in the county.) What needs to be emphasised is that the different views were not so much held by different persons, as articulated for different reasons to different audiences and in ways that left different kinds and amounts of evidence now available to researchers.

Selective and political use of stories was not limited to tenant and landlord interaction. A nineteenth-century magistrate reported 'it was a very common trick for people who speak English most fluently when being questioned about matters in which they want to be very guarded in their replies to declare that they "haven't the English only badly", so that one cannot elicit inconvenient truths from them'.[49] Moreover, strategic silence or feigned ignorance was not confined to the poor. When it suited their purposes, other groups too could act similarly. After Bridget Cleary was burned to death in 1890s' Tipperary by relatives who suspected she was a changeling left by the fairies, nobody in the area wanted to talk. 'Though everyone knew the tales, no one admitted knowing anything about fairycraft.'[50] This included publishers, priests, doctors, constables, public officials, and self-avowed nationalists among others. One relevant lesson for researchers is that when we read stories of priests' power we need to be alert to the social context that elicited the descriptions and accounts now available. Who were the intended audience for the account? What was the purpose of the account? What did it set out to achieve?

A second and very important lesson is that researchers need to pay attention to the figurative dimensions of stories, not just their literal meanings. In a critique of the way American history is presented in US school textbooks, James Loewen made a point that has broader application. He quotes from one typical text's description of the religion of the continent's original peoples:

> These Native Americans [in the south-west] believed that nature was filled with spirits. Each form of life, such as plants and animals, had a spirit. Earth and air held spirits too. People were never alone. They shared their lives with the spirits of nature.

While the account tries to show respect, Loewen argues that it reduces the believers to simple-minded caricatures. Their beliefs are presented as childish make-believe. A similarly literal version of Christianity would offend believers:

> These Americans believed that one great male god ruled the world . . . They ate crackers and wine or grape juice, believing that they were eating their [god's] son's body and drinking his blood. If they believed strongly enough, they would live on forever after they died.

Loewen points out that textbooks never describe Christianity this way. The reason is not hard to find: believers would immediately recognise that such literalism fails to convey either the symbolic meaning or the spiritual satisfaction of sharing in the beliefs and practices of a religious community.[51] Rather than reducing their faith to a listing of the bizarre and the irrational, researchers need to pay as much respectful and sympathetic attention to the attitudes, beliefs and behaviours of the underdogs of the world as they do to those of the orthodox elites and the powerfully established. It is too facile merely to list such things as peasants' beliefs in fairies or priests' powers, charms to ward off ill-luck, circuits of holy wells, and other 'superstitions', especially if our knowledge of these derives from outsiders blinded by ignorance, arrogance and hostility. We are indeed fortunate to have Daniel Campbell's insider account of pre-famine Knock and its religious terrain.

Campbell's purpose in recounting several tales about priests was to describe and justify Knock Catholics' faith in their extraordinary powers, a faith he shared, and to describe the role of the priest. In these stories, priests do have extraordinary power but it often or even usually flows along ecclesiastically unorthodox channels. In confronting challenges from many quarters, the priest dramatically constructs the moral boundaries of the community. Whether it is with proselytisers, the fairywoman or believers in fairies, the irregularly married, or revellers at the pattern, the priest is engaged in constant battle. A close look at some of Campbell's stories will show the complex ways in which the priest's role was understood in the religiously contested arena of the time. (It is likely that not all people shared Campbell's views though undoubtedly most did, to some extent.) Consider first the 'irregular marriage' case that Campbell recounts at length:

> I will relate another true story which may be a warning to those who do not believe in the power given to Catholic priests. This happened publicly and was known to hundreds — it was no private concern. A certain man whom I could name I will give as P.C.; his wife died and his sister-in-law kept house for him and his two sons. He got his wife's sister into trouble, which he thought he could make alright by getting married to her. One day Revd P. O'Grady was riding by his house and he went and spoke with him and told him he wanted to get married to his housekeeper, telling the priest more about the affair than I need tell here. But he concealed the relationship. But he did marry them, being his parishioners, for he had that authority at that time from the bishop. Other parishes had to apply to him for certificates of marriage. And the writer of these lines saw him marry parties in his father's house, but about P.C.'s marriage, it was done in his own house before witnesses [and] the priest liberally paid, as well as the bishop — 5/–. So Father Pat rode to his curate's house in Aughamore and related to him what he had done. The curate's name was Father Myles Sheridan. It was he who baptized the writer of these lines. But now for the marriage of P.C. When the P.P. informed the curate who it was that he married, the curate said: 'Oh, Father Pat, did you know the relationship that existed between them? She is his wife's sister.' So Father Pat ordered his horse directly and rode to P.C. as fast as his horse could carry him, and called on him and told him send the woman away immediately, throwing the marriage-money to him, telling him it was no marriage. And he told him if he did not send her away he would be cursed from the altar on the Sunday following at Knock and Aghamore. But he would not send her away, and Father Pat did curse him and her with bell, book and candle, as the old saying is, and I will relate it as my father and mother tell it, for they were both at the chapel of Knock that day.
>
>   When Mass was over Father Pat O'Grady told the congregation not to leave the church, for he said he had a painful duty to perform. But he should be neglecting his duty to his God if he did not do it. So he went into the sacristy and took off his vestments. He returned to the altar, unbuttoned his knee-breeches [and] turned down his stockings so that his bare knees were on the altar-step. Then he rang the big hand-bell, put the candles out in the Holy Water, [and] then he gave P.C. his curse and God's curse. He afterwards turned to the people and told them not to believe there was a God in heaven if that man was alive that day 12 months, if he did not send the woman away. My father and mother were present at Mass that Sunday and there were not many present with a dry

eye. There was a mist in the church at the time and all the congregation
were terror-stricken. Well, it seems he did not send the woman away,
but lived with her. Before the 12 months were at an end and he went a
good way up the country to a fair to buy a horse and put up at an inn for
the night after buying the animal. So before going to bed he went to the
stable to see that the horse was alright, and the saying goes that the
horse kicked him to death, or at least he died that night or [the] next
morning. So I will leave him, but I will give his name to show that it is
no fiction: Patrick Conway, wheelright (sic) and farmer, Coogue, near
Balina Costolo.[52]

The marriage was performed in the man's house and Campbell stresses
that it was in front of witnesses and that the priest was paid and the bishop
too. It is evident that the conflation of paying the clergy and receiving the
sacraments was not confined to the case of confession at station masses.
Marriage, in the public's eye, required the priest, payment and witnesses.
After all, the man would not have asked to be married if this was not the
common understanding. Indeed, it is possible that the cohabitation was a
stratagem to force the priest to consent to the marriage in the interests of
preventing public scandal.[53] The priest's telling the man it was no marriage
was accompanied by his dramatic gesture, in the idiom the people understood, of flinging back the money. Having asserted his own standards for
valid marriage, the priest was not automatically obeyed. Despite the threat of
being cursed from the altar, the man would not send the woman away.
Campbell describes the formal cursing of the man 'with bell, book and
candle' in the church after mass. Befitting a struggle over the definition of
communal standards for what constituted marriage the conflict was publicised in a dramatic way. 'It was no private concern.' The priest selected the
stage most favourable to him, the church after mass, and told the congregation to stay. This public staging not only punished the individual deviant but
also was a 'means of involving the whole congregation in a complete rejec-
tion of both the individual and his crime'.[54] What Campbell recounts is his
parents' reports of an event that 'was known to hundreds', his life as
annotated text.[55] Even such formal cursing on the priest's chosen stage did
not achieve the goal the priest sought. He could tell the congregation to stay
after mass but what of those who were not at mass? The priest sought to
influence them too. Hence, as Campbell shows, the curse the priest gave was
not just his own but 'God's curse' too.

What made this claim credible was not just the collective validation of the
underlying belief in the power of the priest's curse. Campbell relates that the
cursing did have an effect: the priest had played his trump card by telling the
people not to believe there was a god in heaven if the man was alive a year
later. As recalled and recounted as object lesson, within that year the man
was kicked to death by a horse. The death could convince even those not at
mass. In a sense, the priest's resort to such cursing is indicative of the failure

of his more orthodox means of persuasion to achieve their intended goal. To an outsider, being kicked by a horse would be an accident unconnected with curses. A scientist would see the people's drawing a connection between the curse and the death as a logical fallacy, of mistaking temporal sequence for a causal relationship. However, in the battleground of the sacred there are no coincidences and stories are moulded by the logic of beliefs and standards already established. What is left ambiguous is the question of precisely who initiated the man's death. Was it God or was it the priest? Was it God working through the priest or was it the priest invoking God's power? Alternatively, did the man precipitate his own death? In many ways, the hearers could fill in the unstated statement of who the active agent of good was, priest or God. Evil, however, was given a very personal face.

During the formal cursing in church, Campbell tells us there was 'not many present with a dry eye' and 'there was a mist in the church at the time and all the congregation was terror stricken'. The people were not just witnesses but participants in the cosmic drama. A naturalist would explain a mist in meteorological terms with no relationship to the ritual performed but did the congregation interpret it, and Campbell remember it, as a supernatural sign of the priest's power backed up by God's power over the weather? Did the narrators of the story add that detail, a conventionally understood sign within the genre of priest stories, as validation for themselves and others of the truth of the story, and hence of the reality of the priest's power buttressed by God's power? Both rhetorical processes are involved in the social construction of the power of the priest. Moreover, these processes reinforce each other in that the narration of the case at hand, the mist in church, both builds on and strengthens by reiteration the underlying general assumption about priests' powers. At this remove it is impossible to disentangle the various possibilities of how each particular story was constructed and reconstructed in the ongoing processes of telling, remembering, and retelling that is at the heart of social and cultural life. What is clear is that stories like this one are the people's parables. Campbell related this story 'as my father and mother *tell* it' (emphasis added), even though both were dead. These parables were timeless, remembered because they had significance for both listeners and narrators; to determine what was meaningful we need to explicate what is tacitly assumed in the social world to which accounts like Campbell's are our maps. Regardless of the precise methods by which they worked, stories such as this constructed the priest as God's agent. Details such as the mist or being kicked to death by a horse are rhetorically important because they are interpreted by the community of believers as manifestations of the power of God/priest. They are statements of the power of the other world made visible in this one. Moreover, each story is given credence not because of the specific empirical evidence it provides but because it is embedded in a cultural framework and told to an audience that already accepts the more general underlying faith. Each telling and retelling provides corroboration, not new information.

Is this story 'folklore'? Campbell tells us that he heard this story from his parents and so there is reason to consider it as folklore even if its content was not so similar to other stories. However, a neat distinction between 'folklore' and 'fact' exists only in the minds of outsiders with a positivist faith that it is in theory possible to determine what 'really happened'. For Campbell, and for the original audience for the story, this was no mere story. It was factual. Campbell's naming of both the parish priest and the curate would enable locally-informed hearers to determine that this incident took place sometime before 1836. A list of Tuam priests for that year has Fr Patrick Gready as PP and Fr Patrick Heaveney as CC for Knock while Fr Miles Sheridan was PP of Kilmeena, a post he would have received after being a curate. O'Grady was PP of Knock 1822–1852 according to one local historian, while another says he became PP in 1829.[56] Campbell's naming of the priests involved also constructs these 'facts' for the historian.

This case exemplifies Connolly's conclusion from his study of disputes about marriage between priests and people in the pre-famine era. While the population was generally hostile to premarital and extramarital sex and so agreed with church teachings on these issues, the people were much less concerned with the niceties of who was a prohibited marriage partner because of too close affinity or consanguinity, and were more likely to disregard church laws in these matters. It is doubtful that the people generally would ostracise a widower who married the sister of his deceased wife.[57] Instances of elopement, bride-abductions, threatened or actual cohabitation or other tactics to force the clergy and/or parents to accept otherwise canonically impermissible marriages 'cannot be seen as casting off the discipline of the Catholic Church', but as ways to 'bend the rules of that discipline, or at most to step temporarily outside them, as a short-term means to the end of a legitimate marriage'. Since these tactics were generally successful, the priests' influence over the marriages of their congregations was 'at best a limited one'.[58]

If, in enforcing his definition of marriage, the Knock priest was ultimately victorious in this case because of divine intervention, he was able to suppress the apostates and proselytisers in his parish only with the help of factions among his flock.[59] Consideration of this warfare, too, highlights other sources of the priest's power. When Andrew Flatley was discovered secretly teaching Protestant tracts in the school, which Campbell labels the Catholic school as if asserting it made it so, the priest could 'demand' of the teacher, the school's proprietor, to see the books and tracts and summarily arrange to burn them. The schoolmaster had to make public reparation for allowing his school to be used by the proselytisers. 'And so he did . . . [and] was once more restored to the friendship of the priest and the people of Knock.'[60] In Campbell's formulation, the 'people of Knock' are linguistically equated with those who support the priest. The Flatleys and other local converts are constructed as not-Knock people.[61] 'Private' property in the form of books or schoolhouse had no protection; in the area of religious education, the priest's word was local law.

The priests were also protected by higher powers that ensured that those who disrespected them were punished. A man who interrupted mass to berate the priest came to no good end, dying by his own hand.[62] This is an example of a kind of story found widely elsewhere. For example, from Inishowen, in Donegal, we have the story of a man who was criticised by a priest for some bad deed. In reaction, he threw his beads into a lake, 'his first open act of apostasy', and then went insane before dying miserably in his barn, his body being eaten by rats.[63]

Despite the large numbers of stories and reports about the great powers attributed to priests, we cannot reach simple conclusions about what 'the people really believed'. 'Beliefs' are not like software programmes installed in people as if they were computers and which operate in a consistent and similar manner in different computers. Even Campbell, in addition to telling about the power of the priest's curse and showing how the priest was protected by higher powers, provides evidence of the limits of that power. Immediately following the story of Patrick Conway in his memoir, Campbell recalls another man who was similarly cursed for cohabiting with a woman. The priest's curse brought no result and neither did the curse Bishop MacHale pronounced on the couple when he visited the parish for confirmation. However, soon afterward at Mass on Sunday, the curate 'asked the congregation to join with him in saying a few Hail Marys for the intention of separating these parties', and that very night the woman left the man. As Campbell writes, 'Fr James Grogan's prayers had more effect than Archbishop MacHale's or the parish priest's curses'.[64] Just as fairylore was not an inexorable determinant of people's behaviour, neither was their priestlore with its repertoire of stories cataloguing the powers and curses of priests. Some of the most famous fairy men and women were reputed to have power to control or resist priests, at least in some circumstances.[65] Moreover, undoubtedly there was variation in the degree of credibility different people accorded to stories like Campbell's. 'The people' was not a homogenous mass but individuals in various relationships to others, living their lives in situations they did not choose but nevertheless making different choices among the beliefs available to them.

In station- masses, as we have seen, confession and paying the priest were combined as much in Fr O'Grady's book as in Campbell's mind. Looming large in Campbell's memoirs is the priest's salary. No doubt reflecting the concerns of his Knock neighbours, Campbell is acutely sensitive to the priest's income. He gives us precise figures: a family owed the priest 2/2 per year and a curate's salary was 30 pounds per annum,[66] plus oats for his horse that he collected from house to house. He remembers what days had collections at the church and what days were free. He knows that the 'bishop's due' at marriage was five shillings and accurately notes this fact as if it is significant in his story about the priest cursing the adulterer.[67] In the case Campbell describes, the prevention of the scandal of open cohabitation seems to have been Fr O'Grady's reason for marrying the couple initially and as Campbell writes, the priest had 'the power [dele-gated] from the bishop' to act in such a case.

The Strike against the Priests

That many, if not most Knock people were less than enthusiastic about the payments to priests is obvious from a public protest demonstration that Campbell describes to reduce a family's annual contribution. The people may have resented the priest's exactions but they did not feel they could dispense with his services. In a sense, their protest is testimony to their commitment as Catholics. Hence, their two responses of overt collective pressure for reduced fees and the covert griping represented by the half-serious, half-joking comments about bribing the parish clerk to get the station mass to bypass your house. The two responses are quintessential weapons of the weak. The poverty of the people combined with the indispensability of the priest made conflict over payments to him endemic. There were frequent protest movements in various parts of the country, including pre-famine Mayo, to reduce the exactions of the priests[68] and Campbell recounts one such episode that he remembered. What transpired and how Campbell recalls it are both worthy of comment.

> I remember some parties stric[k]ing against the priest's salary, [and they] wanted to reduce him 2d per year and give him 2/– instead of 2/2. I do not know who began it, but I know it was got up at Aughamore, and a procession was formed and it was getting larger as they marched from house to house and extorted a promise from the owner of the house to pay no more that 2/– per year, but they did not interfere with the collection at the church on Easter or Christmas Day. They were not satisfied with the promise above mentioned, for each house had to send one [occupant] with the procession until they went to a certain number of houses — I forget how many. But I, though a boy (which I am sorry to say), had to go for fear's sake, for my father would not go on any account on such an errand. And for fear of [them] doing us an injury, I was advised to go instead of my father. It had the desired effect, and instead of the half-yearly 1/1 it was 1/– for the whole family, not amounting to 1/2d per week.[69]

This episode was part of what has been identified as the 'last major outbreak of agitation on the subject of clerical fees' which took place only in two baronies in east Mayo, including the Knock area, and two adjoining baronies in county Sligo in the winter of 1842–43.[70] Unlike earlier protests that used intimidation, destruction of property, physical violence against persons including priests, and other tactics of secret agrarian societies, this episode relied on peaceful demonstrations and taking of oaths. However, the tactics were alike in being weapons of the weak; the first relied on hiding the identity of perpetrators but the second made everyone a participant and hence made difficult the isolation of individuals for retribution. The organisers did adopt one tactic common in disputes about land, the anonymous threatening letter publicly posted or sent to someone. One such letter was handed to a curate near Kiltimagh about five miles from Knock in January 1843. It listed the maximum fees chargeable by priests for marriages, baptisms, mass for the dead and other services, and it included a series of other demands: 'No legacies, confess at the chapel, no oats for the curates, no potatoes for the clerks. If they employ servants, let them pay them . . .' The letter continued by promising that 'any man refusing to join this paper . . . will be punished,' and ended with a call for action together with a restatement of one of the earlier demands, presumably the one that was most important. 'And don't ye delay until ye serve the parish, and ye must meet at James Egan's Crossroads on Saturday next, to go into the tower, and serve the priest, and let them confess at the chapel . . . No more'.[71] Campbell makes clear that his was a reluctant involvement in the protest demonstration and from different sources we learn that others had been punished for not supporting the demonstration or its goals. Connolly[72] reports the burning of one man's house and another's turf-stack and shots being fired into a second house. However, the emphasis was on open demonstration of popular disapproval rather than threats or intimidation, and that as one contemporary reported, 'the oath regarding priests' fees appears to have been willingly taken and enthusiastically carried from one district to the next'.[73] In this case, as in the cases considered above of tenants when dealing with landlords or other powerful people, individuals could participate in mass demonstrations with the appearance of enthusiasm while harbouring private reservations. Observable behaviour is no sure guide to private feeling when that behaviour is on a public stage.[74]

In Knock, the reduction sought in what a family owed the priest per year was from 2/2 to 2/−, that is from 26 to 24 old pence. Notice that the amount payable was the same for every household. What the protesters wanted was not so much to reduce the priest's total income but to prevent the development of social distinctions and unequal access to the services of the priests that the protesters believed would follow if everyone paid what they could afford. Otherwise why should the protesters be concerned if some families chose to contribute 2/2 or even more? Of course, their tacit assumption was that priests did give more attention to those who paid them more. There is good reason to believe that the assumption was founded on fact. A Baptist scripture-reader who worked in pre-famine Sligo, Roscommon, Leitrim and Mayo, claimed that when a poor Catholic was buried,

> no priest attends; it is sufficient for the priest to gather a handful of clay, and to bless it, and some holy water; the clay is thrown into the grave, and the water sprinkled . . . But if it be a person of ability (wealth) there will be from one to six priests in attendance.[75]

A west Clare priest in the 1830s admitted to similar practices but explained that the priests could not possibly attend all burials.[76] Of course, the question arises as to which ones they did attend. Was a rich farmer as likely as a poor labourer to have no priest present when he was put in the grave? Even a modern priest/historian recognised a double standard at a later period in Achonry. Usually, one priest said low mass at funerals of the poor, while the socially more respectable dead were sent off with Solemn Requiem High Mass requiring at least three and usually four priests for its celebration.[77] It is against such a background that the 1842–43 communal demonstration developed in Knock. The thrust of the protest was a levelling one, consistent with the values articulated even if not always practised in rundale-based communities. Just as all should equally contribute to the priest, so in the protest all households had to contribute a member to the public procession carrying the message throughout the parish.

By fixing everyone's contribution at two shillings, the protesters were trying to control both the priest's exactions and the pretensions of the richer parishioners and preferential treatment they received from the priests. The underlying logic was that the priest was to serve the whole community rather than sell his services to the highest bidders. In this, of course, the protesters were canonically more correct than the priests were. The whole episode affords a textbook example of the underdogs' criticism of the top dogs through invocation of the very values to which their superiors paid lip service.

Campbell makes it clear that his father disagreed with the protest and he himself apologises for his own participation, twice appealing to fear as the reason. Finally, he minimises the yearly payment to the priests before going on to note that Sunday mass was usually 'free'. In the disputes over priestly payments, Campbell's sympathies lay with the priests. It was not they but the protesters who had 'extorted'.

Mass Attendance

Campbell's single paragraph on attending mass at Knock provides by its silences a great deal of evidence about the importance or rather relative lack of importance of going to mass. It describes how people travelled to mass, tells us the time of Sunday mass and finally notes that the 'religious portion of the congregation performed the Stations of the Cross, said the Rosary and taught the Catechism' at the chapel.[78] Campbell gives us no indication of how many people attended mass and he does not include saying mass in his list of the priest's responsibilities. He mentions people 'doing their Easter duty' of yearly confession and communion while discussing station masses in people's houses. The general impression is that people did not attach central importance to regular Sunday mass attendance. Evidently, it was not a distinguishing characteristic of a practising Catholic as popularly under-stood. (An exchange in the Castlebar paper, *The Telegraph or Connacht*

Ranger, in 1830 over an alleged convert made clear that attending holy wells rather than mass was seen as defining who was a Catholic.) There was only one Sunday mass at Knock, even when there was a curate to serve the Aghamore part of the combined parishes.[79] Knock lies in a large swath of the country north and west of a line from Dundalk to Limerick, where the best estimates are that attendance at Sunday mass in 1834 was between 20 per cent and 40 per cent of the Catholic population.[80] *The Parliamentary Gazette of Ireland* in 1844 said the 'Roman Catholic Chapel [of Knock] has an attendance of 1000'.[81] Given that probably over 99 per cent of Knock's population (3,374 in 1841 and more by 1844), were Catholics, this indicates an attendance rate under 30 per cent.[82]

In the diocese of Achonry consisting of parishes nearby in Mayo and adjacent parts of counties Roscommon and Sligo, Sunday mass attendance rates averaged about 30 per cent in 1851, according to priest/historian Liam Swords.[83] But this figure differed significantly from parish to parish, from under 20 per cent to over 50 per cent. Swords cites no sources or evidence to support his claim, but assuming he is accurate the variation was likely mostly due to the popularity of specific priests, since there were no parallel differences between the parishes in socio-economic terms. Ulsterman, William Carleton, noted that 'the people look upon that priest as the best and most learned who can perform the ceremony of the mass in the shortest period of time,'[84] and the same was probably true elsewhere. In addition and contrary to orthodox teaching, masses said by some particular priests were thought more efficacious and hence were more desirable than others were.[85] This attitude persisted: in the late 1870s at St Mary's Augustinian Abbey in Ballyhaunis, Sunday attendance varied dramatically depending on which priest was scheduled to say mass.[86]

Going to Sunday mass in Knock was an occasion to display social standing. 'Well-to-do' farmers would ride on horseback while others attended barefoot or carried shoes and stockings as they walked to mass and put them on as they approached the church.[87] In the chapel itself, there were no seats 'except 4 pews at the expense of the owners'. Even over thirty years later, Campbell remembered the families who occupied these pews[88] and devoted time to describing each set of owners. Consciousness of people's relative social standing was pervasive and intense in Knock as indeed throughout the country.[89] It is noteworthy that in at least two of the four cases the pew-owning families were related to priests. Pat McGreal, who along with his wife and father-in-law owned one pew, was a node in a kinship network of priests. Not only did he have two brothers who were priests but his wife also had two brothers in the priesthood.[90] Travelling to the village of Knock to attend Sunday mass also provided an opportunity to drink in unlicensed shebeen-houses until drunk,[91] leading to 'sore heads and black eyes the next morning' and in this was quite like the pattern to celebrate the parish saint's day. Mass attendance did not imply a heightened ethical conscience or a more developed interior spirituality.

That some among the laity used the gathering at the chapel to say the Rosary, do the Stations of the Cross or teach catechism before or after the mass[92] points to other important points. First, there was a nucleus of committed laity involved in the church-centred Stations of the Cross devotion. Second, there were organised catechism lessons. Thirdly, to the extent that the Stations of the Cross were read and the Rosary prayed in it, the chapel was becoming the focal site for religious expression and experience, even if the priest's role in these activities was limited and certainly different from his canonical role as the celebrant of the mass, the sacramental re-enactment of Christ's bloody sacrifice at Calvary. It seems that, for Campbell, masses celebrated at Knock were important retroactively as it were, because the chapel was the site later on of the apparition of the Virgin Mary and other figures in 1879.[93] He tells us that the names of priests who said masses and their mass-servers was the most important information that he wished he had not forgotten when he was writing after Knock became famous for its apparition. Of course, he had not forgotten the beliefs, stories and practices that were centrally important in 'the interpretive community' of the Knock of his youth.

In Knock, the ratio of priests to laity was extremely low. While in Connaught as a whole in 1834 there was one priest for every 3,675 lay people, a ratio that was 'approaching disaster' in the view of the official Catholic authorities, the ratio was even worse in the archdiocese of Tuam (1:4,199). County Mayo was largely comprised of Killala and a large part of Tuam, two of only three dioceses in the whole country where the ratio was over 4,000:1.[94] The combined parishes of Knock and Aghamore containing about 10,000 persons usually, but apparently not always, had two priests. Even with two, the ratio was more extreme than even the worst diocesan level and when there was but one priest, the situation could only be considered catastrophic from the official pastoral viewpoint. However, such ratios calculated at the parish level should be treated with extreme caution because we simply do not know the catchment area from which people travelled or chose not to travel to attend mass in a given church.

Priests and Holy People

Priests had no monopoly on access to the sacred. Lay people did not have to use the mediation of priests to participate in pilgrimages or penances at local sites. We have already discussed the fairywoman but there were other intermediaries also whose canonical status was more ambiguous. One of the most significant stories Campbell tells is how supernatural power saved Knock from catastrophe. The intervention is ascribed to a 'holy pilgrim'. (I discuss this story in chapter 6.) Campbell also uses the term 'pilgrim' in referring to Mary Morris, a woman who 'was not a native of Knock but got a living among them' (sic).[95] To answer the question he assumed readers would have, Campbell wrote that the Knock people 'respected religious people' such as Morris. We are left to surmise that her religiosity was what made the local people willing to support this outsider. Perhaps she was a beggar; regardless, she was devoutly religious and was accorded special status in that the priest permitted her to enter the sacristy in church, thereby corroborating and contributing to her public persona as a religious person. The priest also shared his Sunday breakfast with her, practising the generosity and charity that expressed the Christian message as understood, and simultaneously embodying and enacting the communal ideology of sharing and concern for the well-being of all. This story presents a counter-image to that of the avaricious priest that Campbell shows us existed in Knock.

Campbell uses the term 'pilgrim' on these two occasions and does not mean a priest. Once the adjective 'holy' is attached and, in Mary Morris' case, 'pilgrim' seems to be equivalent to 'religious person'. In Morris' case, and most likely in the other one too since the pilgrim was a 'traveller', these holy people were from outside Knock, though one of them had made it her home. Other observers of rural Ireland in the nineteenth century noted similar roles for pilgrims. Lady Wilde,[96] for example, refers to a 'sacred fraternity of beggars' whose members, 'being looked on as holy men endowed with strange spiritual gifts . . . are entirely supported by the voluntary gifts of the people, who firmly believe in the efficacy of their prayers and blessings and prognostics of luck'. Among the 'strange spiritual gifts' widely ascribed to such itinerant beggars was that of prophecy, especially of a millenarian kind foretelling the reversal of fortunes when some leader would appear and overthrow the Protestants.[97] The year 1825 especially was widely believed to be the time of deliverance.[98] A nineteenth-century priest/historian of the diocese of Meath recorded numerous cases of holy men, often priests, who were revered and remembered for the sanctity of their lives.[99] Unlike what Wilde and others imply, Campbell's account shows that this was not a role reserved for males. The American woman, Asenath Nicholson, who travelled throughout the country, mainly on foot, just before the Great Famine reading from and handing out bibles, was welcomed with kindness and generosity almost universally among the poor; in many cases it is clear that they regarded her as a saintly pilgrim, even one sent by God.[100]

4

Threats and Balances

I will argue later that the 1879 apparition in Knock was a culturally-mediated response to a community-wide crisis in clerical authority. How similar earlier crises developed and were addressed is important in understanding the 1879 episode, and we are fortunate to have Campbell's evidence from within the local interpretive community. As we have seen, people invoked fairylore in dealing with their individual troubles in their own particular situations. However, when threats arose to the wider community generally, the response was very different as is clear from several cases recounted by Campbell. The threats ranged from a cholera epidemic and more general 'plague and pestilence', including famine fevers, to continuing oppression and feared return of naked repression by the landlord ascendancy, especially the Browne family, and to the insidious onslaught of proselytisers.[1] Such problems threatened everyone and required a very different type of supernatural intervention. Significantly, this tapping of the powers of the other world was the achievement, not of ordinary people or even ordinary priests, but of a 'holy pilgrim' in the case of plague and of Archbishop MacHale in the cases of cholera and the Brownes. I will examine what Campbell tells us about these various cases in turn and show what this and the other evidence available tells us about the pre-famine Knock religious scene.

The Blessed Straws Chain-Prayer

> Now there is a little story I will tell about the cholera and the straw. I remember Pat Egan of Cloonterriff coming to our house in a great hurry and leaving a straw drawn from the thatch of another house, and the family so served was to say three Hail Mary Marys, I think, for the cholera to cease. And the occupier of the house [was to serve] three more houses on the same condition. Some had to travel miles before they could meet a house that was not served. I remember the words Pat Egan used when he left the straw at my father's house. He said: 'Oh John! Make haste! Bishop MacHale is coming down the road with his carriage full of straw.' We were so excited that my father could hardly wait to say the three Hail Marys until he was on his errand serving the

straw as above stated. I do not know how far it travelled that night, nor how it originated or finished, for it is as long [ago] as I can remember.[2]

This whole statement of Campbell's and especially the comment about MacHale's carriage full of straw is exceedingly cryptic; to appreciate its significance we need to place it in several contexts, a challenging proposition since Campbell's description is the only thing we know about the episode in Knock. It is also important to examine what Campbell wrote in light of what researchers know about the arts by which people excluded from power resist domination.[3] Campbell's short paragraph uses a 'restricted linguistic code' where much is left unsaid because it rests on tacit assumptions shared by both speaker (or here, memoir-writer) and audience.[4] Even though Campbell's knowledge of what happened was limited, we can use other sources to tease out the meaning of his story. First, we can locate the event in a specific temporal and spatial context. It is associated with the epidemic of cholera that caused great alarm in 1832, killing over 20,000 people that year in the country.[5] In June of 1832, perplexing reports began to reach the political authorities in Dublin Castle describing people day and night running helter-skelter from house to house throughout the country. The letters recounting these strange doings were written by alarmed persons who saw the runners and in some cases talked to them. Historian Sean Connolly has examined these accounts to open a door on the society and culture of the time.[6] His findings describe the bigger picture within which we can understand what the young Campbell witnessed.

The earliest of the 1832 reports said the runners claimed that the Virgin Mary had appeared on a church altar in Charleville, County Cork, and indicated a way to escape the plague of cholera which was threatened at the time. She gave ashes that she said afforded the only protection and ordered that small packets of these ashes were to be distributed to nearby houses, and the owners of these houses, in turn, were to take ashes from their own chimneys and distribute them to four other houses giving the same instructions they themselves received. In this manner, the number of houses reached increased by geometric progression with the result that the message, though spread only by word of mouth, was heard over most of the island in less than a week. This is impressive evidence of the existence of a consistent world-view shared by at least some classes throughout the whole country.

As the message spread, however, the details changed, as would be expected. The material to be carried varied, with ashes, clay or turf (sometimes lighted), stone, charred wood, and 'blessed straws' being reported. The number of houses to be served was sometimes four, other times five, and still other times seven. The most interesting changes occurred in the explanations the people gave of the start of the whole episode. The earliest reports saying that it was due to the Virgin Mary's direct command were soon followed by others of runner-messengers ascribing it to the initiative of angels, 'the priests', or of specific named priests or bishops, but in Knock and nearly every other place, the ritual activity was explained as a way to ward off cholera. However, there was a very big difference in the case of one bishop mentioned as instigator, James Doyle, Bishop of Kildare and Leighlin. While some reports said that ashes blessed by Bishop Doyle would prevent the spread of cholera, others gave a very different rationale: that, because of Doyle's curse, balls of fire from heaven had destroyed some town or even a whole county and distributing the ashes would save the recipients from such a fate. Later I will address the question of why there was so great a difference between the explanations of the events in Doyle's area and other locations where materials were distributed to ward off cholera.

The 1832 episode can be usefully considered in the context of apocalyptic expectations widespread among the Catholic populace in the 1820s. Prophecies widely circulated predicting the extirpation of Protestants in 1825.[7] Limited evidence from Knock prevents me from making more than a few conjectures. The widespread anticipation of imminent wholesale extermination of Protestants seems to have been reinforced by the influence in 1823 of the German Catholic priest, Prince Alexander Hohenloe, during which many direct miracles were attributed to him. Claims and counterclaims about these both heightened sectarian tensions and increased popular Catholic faith in miraculous delivery from oppression. 'This was also the period when, in many remote villages, night by night, lighted turf was being conveyed in some strange symbolism from cabin to cabin.'[8] Unfortunately, we have no evidence from participants about what that activity meant to them, and know only that 'it certainly had an alarming effect on outside, Protestant witnesses'.[9] The distribution of materials from house to house clearly was not an innovation at the time of the 1832 cholera threat: as a ritual, the practice was available as a cultural resource that persons could activate. Whether it spread in a particular time and place would depend on the responses of some initiator's neighbours and their willingness to continue the chain by 'passing it on'. Are we stretching the available evidence to suggest that the 1832 event in Knock might have recalled the earlier experiences of the Catholic population confronting their Protestant oppressors, either in the form of a millenarian turning of the world, that was anticipated in 1825, or the reality of the ousting of landlord Denis Browne from Parliament in 1826? Was there some symbolism that tied MacHale to both episodes? Was there some significance in his travelling in a carriage, 'coming down the road' in Knock, which was outside his then diocese of Killala, perhaps echoing the enormous impact of his travels round that diocese shortly after his appointment in 1825? (To my knowledge, no other reported instigator of the blessed straws distribution was accorded a carriage or indeed any mode of transport at all.) Despite the prophecies, the world did not end for Protestants in 1825. Without more evidence we can only speculate about what might have changed in Knock. Nationally, beliefs in liberators certainly did not end, as Daniel O'Connell's career and reputation amply demonstrate. The poetry of the itinerant peasant, Anthony Raftery, is filled with apocalyptic themes in the later 1820s, perhaps reflecting the understanding of many people in south-east Mayo where he grew up. Raftery was born in Killeadan, a parish close to Knock. However, he was then living in south Galway, much closer to the scene of O'Connell's epic election victory in Clare in 1828, and neither his poetry nor his politics may be a good indication of what people in his home area were thinking. While Raftery encouraged people to pay the 'Catholic Rent' of a halfpenny a week to support O'Connell's efforts, Campbell makes no reference at all to it or to O'Connell. Neither is there in his memoir any other evidence of any kind of mass politicisation of the kind that O'Connell, through the priests, successfully instigated throughout most of the country.[10] It is significant that around the turn of the twentieth century, in south Galway (Anthony Raftery's stomping ground almost literally, since he lived there travelling from house to house playing music (as he said) to empty pockets), the rural people remembered O'Connell as a Liberator while MacHale seemingly was not remembered at all, even though his cathedral seat of Tuam was in the north of the same county. MacHale is not mentioned in *The Kiltartan History Book* that Lady Gregory compiled based on what her local informants in south Galway told her about the history of the country, but it seems that, in his own dioceses, MacHale came to be remembered like O'Connell was elsewhere.

Several other aspects of the Blessed Straws episode Campbell remembered in Knock are noteworthy here. The first is the involvement of Bishop MacHale. Though he was not yet bishop of the area, in Knock he was cast as the agent of communal salvation and as the instigator of the ritual needed to ensure deliverance from the cholera. Second, as elsewhere, the response was communal as opposed to the particularistic responses typical of fairylore where one's own individual benefit was sought. Here, people distributed straws to benefit the *recipients,* not themselves. At most, they could help themselves only by helping others and after they themselves had been helped. Finally, that a 'popular panic'[11] beginning in County Cork and spreading virtually to the whole island also swept through Knock is proof, if any were needed, that Knock's culture was of a piece with that of the lower orders countrywide.

While the 1832 chain-prayer was not founded on fairylore, the underlying assumptions diverged greatly from orthodox Catholic teaching. The people believe implicitly in direct supernatural intervention in the world; for them, 'natural' and 'supernatural' are not separate and distinct but interpenetrating realms. The easy interchangeability of the Virgin, angels and particular named ecclesiastics such as Bishop Doyle or MacHale as instigators of the events is founded on the fact that they share a status as intermediaries between these worlds.

Supernatural Protection

Campbell recounts another episode of supernatural protection being provided to the whole community through the intervention of another holy man.

> Now I will relate one particular saying which I heard as a child and can never forget it: that was, that no plague or cholera should ever rage on Knock . . . The reason why I will tell as I heard it related many years ago: a holy pilgrim was travelling and met a man who was driving a horse and cart and the pilgrim or holy man asked him for a ride or lift, which he [the man] cheerfully granted . . . The holy pilgrim prayed and prophesied that no plague or pestilence should ever enter Knock. The writer of these lines saw the prophecy partly fulfilled, for he lived at Knock the time cholera was raging on every side of the parish, when hundreds were dying in the surrounding towns and parishes. Still Knock was free from the plague, excepting one solitary case, and that was . . . I think the name was Mrs Follard of Ballyhaunis: she was a native to Knock, sister to Charles and Pat Foard of Knock. The cholera was raging in Ballyhaunis, and to shun the danger Mrs Follard left Ballyhaunis where she lived and came to her brother's house, Pat Foard's of Ballaghhooley, but she was not many hours at Knock when she died of the cholera, but no other person took it, and so the cholera ended without any more victims at Knock. So that was the part of the prophecy fulfilled.[12]

The holy pilgrim, however, was responding to the charitable deed of the very human man who offered him a ride in his cart. Altruism had its reward. It is a fact that compared to neighbouring areas, Knock had a very low mortality rate during the Great Hunger of the 1840s. Regardless of the empirically demonstrable reasons social scientists might adduce for low mortality, for Campbell, characteristically, a supernatural explanation was self-evident and sufficient.[13] He sees divine intervention, triggered by the pilgrim's prayer, as the cause. (I examine social scientific explanations and relevant evidence in chapter 6.) As in the Blessed Straws event, as well as in the whole body of fairy stories, what is assumed here is that the supernatural world is very near to this one, and that there are ways to act in this one to influence the other world and shape interactions between the two.

Threats to the general welfare were not confined to 'natural' events such as diseases. Indeed, the identification of diseases as 'natural' phenomena is not one that Campbell or pre-famine Knock people generally would make. W. H. Maxwell, a visitor to Mayo about 1830 noted that human diseases were ascribed to supernatural causes. For example, sudden faintness and exhaustion was ascribed to what Maxwell called *faragurta*. According to him, 'some assert that it is brought about by treading upon a poisonous plant; others, that it is occasioned by fairy influence; while more affirm that it is produced by passing over the place where a corpse has been laid down'. He smugly points out what was obvious to him: that 'this mystified disorder is, after all, nothing but exhaustion consequent upon hunger and fatigue'.[14]

Had he realised that *faragurta* was a rendition of *féar a' ghorta,* the grass of famine or the hungry grass, he might have had some greater insight into how the people understood their sudden weaknesses. There was an extensive folk medicine comprising modes of prevention, diagnosis and treatment of a whole range of ailments, typically understood very differently from modern medicine.

Supernatural responses were needed to counter threats, whether natural or not. Threats could well emanate from particular persons, as often was the case where fairy belief was involved. Campbell discusses two particular categories of threatening people: first the politically powerful landlords who were Protestant oppressors and, secondly, local people who became Protestants and especially became proselytisers. While they may have been born in Knock and live there still, Campbell constructs these latter as 'not-Knock' people. Again, such generalised threats required a communal response: electoral battle under the direction and inspiration of MacHale in the first case, and a great faction fight to defeat the proselytisers in the second.

MacHale versus the Brownes

In his memoir, Campbell apologises for 'spend[ing] so much of my time over so bad a lot as the Browns or Oranmores, for they were neither good for King or country', and he writes that 'the sooner the families and titles are extinct the better for the country'.[15] His reference is to what was the most politically powerful family in the county of Mayo, the Brownes. Several members sat in parliament. When John Browne replaced his brother James as MP in 1831, and joined their relative Dominick Browne in parliament as the two MPs for Mayo, he claimed that one or more members of his family had represented the county in parliament continuously for over seventy years.[16] Two Brownes represented Mayo in Campbell's time and other family members represented other constituencies. The Brownes were at the apex of an ascendancy system in which political and economic power in the county of Mayo was concentrated in the hands of a small, religiously alien minority.

Campbell remembers one John Browne, MP for Mayo, as Seán na Sagart; and recalled that he had expressed a wish in Parliament to be able to hang priests for saying mass. The generic soubriquet Seán na Sagart (Seán of the Priest) was applied to notorious priest-hunters during the period of the Penal Laws a century earlier. Different individuals were so called in different areas. In Mayo, a man named John Mullowney, a native of Ballintobber parish, was one Seán na Sagart.[17] What Campbell's memory indicates is popular conflation between the different priest-hunters. As perceived, they constituted one unified bloc regardless of whether they were gaoling or even executing priests in the past or expressing anti-Catholic sentiments in the present. The memory of sectarian oppression during the Penal Laws was doubtless refreshed in 1798 and its aftermath.[18]

The most infamous member of the family, Denis Browne (1763–1828), High Sheriff for Mayo and later MP, so distinguished himself for repression, especially after the rebellion and French invasion of 1798, that he was called Donncha a' Rópa (Denis of the Rope), for the number of people he hanged. One source estimated that Browne had 200 men hanged, 200 transported and 100 more pressed into service in the British army overseas or to salt mines on the continent.[19] As a young man in 1786, selectively and judiciously using the law as High Sheriff of the county, he had hanged one George Robert Fitzgerald, a potential political rival;[20] in 1801 he was elected unopposed to the British parliament after he eliminated an opponent in a duel.[21] One admiring observer wrote around 1830 that

> [Denis Browne] did all as religiously in the King's name as ever Musselman in that of the Prophet . . . he imprisoned and transported as he pleased; and the peasantry to this day will tell you that he could hang anybody whom he disliked . . . [He] was absolute in authority; dictator for twenty years, and ruled the county [Mayo] during the period with a rod of iron.[22]

Considering that this was from an admirer of Browne's, one can only begin to imagine what his enemies or his victims felt. At mid-century, William Wilde selected Browne as an exemplar of the bullying landlord, and at the end of the century Douglas Hyde recorded that he was still remembered and detested in Mayo.[23] A 1930s' Mayo local historian wrote

> It is no exaggeration to say that Denis Browne . . . was entrusted with power of life or death, wielded his authority ruthlessly, surrounded himself with a band of satellites who were pliant and willing tools in the execution of his schemes, and even his magistrates, who were of his own creation, were . . . spineless and cowardly.[24]

According to the same writer, Browne's 'chief amusement was hanging and flogging the Irish during the day, and drinking and worse during the night', and so this 'absolute ruler of the county' left his name reprobated.[25] As late as the 1930s, Browne was remembered in Knock as a 'tyrant without mercy who was always called Hangman Browne; he hanged men from the upraised shafts of carts for hunting hares or rabbits on Browne's land.'[26] Among Browne's victims after 1798 were two priests, Fr Manus Sweeney and Fr Andrew (or James) Conroy, PP of Addergoole parish where John MacHale was then a child of about seven. So bloodthirsty was Browne, according to one folk memory, that he hanged Fr Sweeney just as a rider carrying a reprieve for him came within sight of the scaffold.[27] Given Browne's reputation, it would be a surprise if Campbell had nothing to say about him.[28]

Particularly galling in Campbell's youth was the legal requirement that everybody, including the overwhelming majority that was Catholic, had to contribute tithes to the support of the 'established Church', the Church of Ireland, which in the language of the time was referred to as the 'Protestant' church. The popular Catholic feeling of outrage at this injustice is clear from a sarcastic letter to the editor of *The Telegraph, or Connaught Ranger*, 3 March 1831, from 'a Costello Catholic' writing from Ballyhaunis:

> There are four Parishes in this County, viz: Aughamore, Knock, Becan and Annagh, (attached to the Union of Kiltulla in the County of Roscommon,) in which there is only *one Protestant family*, (and they live within four miles of Claremorris), yet, so anxious are the spiritual *author-ities*, to make us *forsake the religion of our forefathers*, that they have sent an *established Soul Saver*,[29] to reside in this little *Popish Town*, with the *inten-tion of Building a Church here*, though we *paid £900 within the last three years*, for building one *at head quarters*, (Ballinlough in the County Roscommon,) where *there are not a dozen Protestants*.

The writer exaggerated the facts, but only a little. According to an official enumeration there were twenty-three Protestants in Knock parish in 1834, a more plausible number. But the precise figures are less important than the fact, blatantly obvious to all, that a huge majority of the people — the same source recorded 3,247 Catholics in Knock — were forced to pay tithes to support a tiny, religiously alien minority, being thus humiliated by the public display of their powerlessness as well as being kept economically impoverished.

The Brownes especially, but also the whole ascendancy class, exploited the people economically and dominated them politically at local as well as national levels. According to the admiring contemporary observer already quoted, the most powerful aristocratic families in Mayo, exercising an 'illegal authority' they had usurped, 'put tenants in the stocks *ad libitum*, and cared no more for the liberty of the subject than they did for the king's writ'.[30] But it was their arrogance that most stayed with Campbell; their presumption that what they wanted would be done affronted the common people's dignity. 'And the Marquis of Sligo, who is another Brown and relation to the two MPs for Mayo, often boasted that he could get his cowherd [elected] an MP for Mayo.' Similar memories are recorded of several other oppressive and politically influential landlords and the uniformity of their formulation again shows how much Campbell shared the commonsense views of the day. According to a local Mayo historian in the 1930s, Denis Browne's boast was that he could return his carthorse to Parliament,[31] while in the adjacent county of Galway, the Marquis of Clanrickard reportedly said he could elect his white horse.[32] Scott argues that the sense of wounded dignity is more universal than economic and political exploitation in the experience of the underdogs of the world[33] and his claim seems vindicated in this case. The remembered boast about electing whomever or whatever pleased them is what Campbell relates; he is silent on any local anti-tithe agitation of a kind that was so widespread in the country in the 1820s and 1830s.

The people's public humiliation in the present was reinforced by their fresh memories of brutal repression following the events of 1798, and the knowledge that the Brownes would be happy to repeat their earlier atrocities. Referring to one of them, Campbell writes,

> John Brown of Westport, [of whom] it was reported that in one of his speeches in the House of Commons — he made but a few — he said that he wished to see the day when he could hang a priest for saying Mass: from that day he was called 'Shawn na Sagart'.[34]

Of another Browne, Campbell writes, 'he would be as dutiful as his father [in repressing and persecuting] if he had the same chance of hanging croppies in middle of the street'. Campbell remembered an election ballad whose language indicates the popular hatred for the Brownes and their ilk. Among other things, they are referred to 'the tithe-eating gentry', 'bloodsucking traitors', 'the cursed Brunswick crew' and Seán na Sagart himself as a 'hireling of State'.[35] ('Brunswick Clubs' were organised by hard-line Protestants to resist the drive for Catholic Emancipation being spearheaded by Daniel O'Connell and his movement. In practice they replaced the Orange Order when it was outlawed in the 1820s.)

The instrument by which God protected his people from the Brownes and the powers behind them was Archbishop John MacHale. Campbell recounts the popular memory that after he became Archbishop of Tuam in 1834, MacHale 'soon shifted the Browns who were always M.P.s for Mayo'.[36] Campbell also 'heard it commonly stated' that the one Browne to remain in Parliament did so only because of his mother's plea to MacHale not to turn him out, as he had the other members of the family. In popular understanding freedom for Catholics would come through overthrowing the power of the Brownes. Where Campbell recalls Archbishop MacHale as the instrument of that revolution, other folk understandings predicted a foreign intervention, specifically from France. Mairtín Ó Cadhain recalled this poem from Connemara:

> O Denis Browne, I would gladly take your hand
> Not to greet you but to grab you
> I'd hang you high with a hempen rope and
> I'd stick my spear in your big belly
> For it's many the good boy you sent abroad
> They'll yet come back and help with them
> In red uniforms and white hats
> And the French drum playing with them[37]

Regardless of the instrument however, Catholics would triumph. After all, Campbell tells us the people said that the devil had taken Denis Browne's soul and body from the graveyard, assured proof that God was on their side.

> [T]he big-bel[l]ied Denis Brown is gone, the hangman, and his remains
> are deposited in the little Protestant church of Claremorris where the
> people say that the Devil came and took his body and [his] soul as well.[38]

As in the Blessed Straws chain-prayer, MacHale was identified and remembered as the people's champion. He was instrumental and effective in instigating communally beneficial behaviour in the realms of both cholera and politics. These were not clearly distinguished spheres or arenas of activity and neither was separable from religion. Religion was not differentiated clearly from the non-religious, and neither was 'nature' clearly distinguished from the supernatural.

Proselytism

Campbell devoted considerable time to describing the conflict in Knock between local Catholics and other local people, backed by outsiders, who sought to convert Catholics to Protestantism. He presents those local people who became Protestant and/or tried to convert others as not really Knock people at all. They are not members of the Knock community as he constructs it even though they were natives of the place, and in fact the main family of converts constituted 'the strongest faction in the parish'.[39] The would-be proselytes were members of the extended Flatley family, again an index of the significance of kinship ties in the society. Campbell's stories about several different Flatleys show how the boundaries of the community were socially constructed. Those who became Protestant did so when they were not honest participants in the community. They either were abroad and thus removed from their true community, or they merely pretended to be Protestants to get jobs, or they recognised the error of their ways and returned to the true faith. Those who persisted in their Protestantism were punished by God, dying young and by suicide. According to Campbell, there was no way a Knock person could in good conscience and without coercion become and remain a Protestant.

The attempted proselytism had begun underhandedly with the surreptitious teaching of Protestant tracts in the local school, but when this was discovered the Flatley faction was defeated in a big faction fight by the Beirne and Corry factions. After the battle, the schoolmaster had to atone for allowing the teaching of Protestantism in his school, however secretively. Because the affront was to the whole community, the penance had to be public:

> He was spoken of publicly and denounced by the priest from the altar.
> He was to be excommunicated unless he made public reparation for the
> scandal given. And so he did. He came bare-headed and bare-footed to
> the church in the presence of the whole congregation to ask forgiveness
> for his offence against the Church. So he was once more restored to the
> friendship of the priest and the people of Knock.[40]

The schoolmaster's offence against the Catholic Church was simultaneously a scandal in the community because that Church had become equated with the community. It is worthy of note that the priest's power to require public penance 'presupposed that the Church's condemnation of the offence . . . was shared by the people before whom the sinner confessed his guilt and displayed his repentance.'[41] A long tradition in sociology shows that communities reinforce commitment to shared values by public punishment of deviance against the shared standards.[42]

Stories of Faith

In chapter 1 I examined the role of fairylore and the place of pilgrimages to local outdoor sites in the religious life of Knock people. I continued with an analysis of the role and power of the priest. In this chapter I have examined the various communal threats to Knock in Campbell's time and how the people responded to them. Had I adopted an orthodox Catholic perspective, I would have focused on compliance with Tridentine regulations and would have concentrated first on rates of mass attendance, *the* mark of a practising Catholic according to Trent, and considered other behaviour as evidence of pastoral failure that permitted superstition to flourish. I could collect descriptions from outsiders and critics, many of whom waxed indignant at the superstitions of the simple-minded, or looked with contempt or amusement at the irrational, the bizarre, and the backward scenes that caught their attention. Too often in the past, social researchers as well as ecclesiastical officials have fallen into this trap.

If, however, instead of starting with an institutional orthodoxy as a benchmark, we put the people and their experiences in living communities centre-stage, we discover a very different reality. Social researchers cannot avoid using some categories for their analyses; I have chosen to use insiders' categories as much as possible. (After all, it was to insiders that the 1879 apparition appeared.) Thus, the relative attention I have devoted to topics such as the fairies, holy wells, priests, the mass, Bishop MacHale, sectarian struggles and others mirrors the relative importance they have in Daniel Campbell's memoir. No source besides Campbell enables us to make this judgment about what was more or less important.

Neither should we limit study to those beliefs and practices that can be interpreted as variations on or violations of orthodox institutional versions of the same. That is, researchers should not restrict themselves to using categories for analysis that derive from the orthodox teachings. The people's religion was not neatly separable from the rest of their non-religious behaviour. Rather, religious beliefs and practices broadly defined to include all I have discussed, permeated all aspects of life. Moreover, in a society where oral stories were centrally important, stories with religious themes, similarly broadly defined, were common and perhaps can be considered as communally validated sermons. Such stories are less well documented than the externally visible pilgrimage sites or fairy forts that outsiders could note, and they were also less likely to attract the negative comments of churchmen. Moreover, people like Douglas Hyde collected the longer stories less easily than shorter prayers and other religious materials. Nevertheless, many such stories are available[43] and among the most useful for illustrative purposes is one called 'The Friars of Urlaur',[44] because we have a long version that we know was orally transmitted, and because Urlaur is an actual place close to Knock. Hyde got the story around the turn of the twentieth century from an old man in the Workhouse in Athlone whom he had asked to collect stories from inmates from all over Connaught.

This is the story. There once was a house of friars beside Loch Urlaur and all was well in the country. But an evil spirit in the shape of a black boar entered the lake. Sometimes the boar sat near the lake and made such a din as to make the friars deaf, and other times it entered the water and created terrible storms that shook the friary. After the abbot was unable to banish the evil spirit, the friars called in the bishop. The bishop divined that the devil had entered the friary and so called on each friar by name; when Friar Lucas was called, he revealed that the bishop had once fed meat to his hound while the poor went hungry. The friar then revealed himself as a hairy being, before running off and joining the boar in the lake. The bishop tells the abbot that he is too blind to be in charge of the friary because he mistook the devil for a friar. But the bishop, too, failed to banish the evil spirits. The bishop then called on the saint of the county, but he was struck ill. With abbot, bishop and saint all being unsuccessful, the friars prepare to leave Urlaur. Then in a dream one night the abbot sees an angel, dressed in white, who tells him to call in Donagh O'Grady, a man the angel tells him who did more good than all the priests and friars in the country. When the abbot tells his dream to the other friars they realise that they all had the same identical dream, which they take as a sign from God, and they determine to call in O'Grady. This man is a selfish, careless, drunken piper who refuses to go to the friary unless he is paid in advance, and once at the friary, refuses to play until he is given lots of whisky. He asks if the angel in the friars' dream was male or female, and on being told it was female he remembers the single unselfish deed he has done in his entire life. He had once given a small coin to a poor woman who was about to prostitute herself. Saved from this fate, the woman led a good life and died a good death. She was the angel who had appeared in the friars' dreams. When O'Grady began to play his pipes at the lakeside, the boar and his assistant charged at him but a white dove flew over and shot lightning down killing them both.

Several things are noteworthy about this story. First is the nearness of the other world and the close interpenetration of the different worlds, heavenly, hellish and earthly. The angel is not just from heaven but is the spirit of a poor local woman. Urlaur is a very real place in a parish close to Knock and it had a very real friary for centuries. Second, the shape-shifting idiom is prominent: the devil takes the form of a boar and Friar Lucas is revealed to have been the hound to which the bishop gave meat. Shape shifting is a language for describing the relationships and interactions between the different worlds. Even the official church could recognise the dove as from heaven. Third, there is the criticism of the bishop who neglected the poor and this sin is the reason he was unable to banish the evil spirits. The moral of the story is that one good deed by a drunken rake outweighs the power of abbot, bishop and saint; no good deed is ever forgotten; conversely, no failure of charity especially by the clergy is ever forgotten and even heaven will speak against a bishop who fails to meet his responsibility. In fact, the world as constituted by this and similar stories is one great chain of giving: in this case, first, from O'Grady to the poor woman, and then reciprocated in the angel's message to the friars. The story restates a central theme we have identified as at the heart of other complexes of ritual belief and action: communal sharing as the cardinal virtue, but a transcending sharing that incorporates the other worlds as well as this one, the dead as well as the living, in a great system of reciprocities.

Communal sharing was taught not only by words in stories of faith such as this one, and by the practices such as distributing straws to help others or the priest's sharing of his Sunday breakfast with Mary Morris, but by the everyday objects the people used. In briefly sketching material conditions in Knock, Campbell wrote that 'a labouring man thought himself well off if he could have a noggin of buttermilk with some potatoes for his dinner'. After explaining that a 'noggin' was a quart-size wooden vessel, he noted that 'every house in the parish took care to be supplied with one for each of their family and one or two over for strangers if they happened to drop in'.[45] It is very likely that many families could not afford a noggin for every member, but the shared ideal in contrast to the reality was not one each but rather one each plus some more for strangers who might drop in. That the ideal of sharing was not the universal practice, however, is clear in another of Campbell's observations. 'Bacon was seldom to be had unless at the table of the well-to-do farmers, and they very sparingly supplied it to the labourer, unless at Christmas and Easter Sunday.'[46]

A System of Checks and Balances

So far, I have described various aspects of the religious life of Knock people in the pre-famine era. Many observers have commented on one or other element in the total picture elsewhere, but they have failed to comprehend how the parts were interrelated. To understand the world from the inside we need to see how all these, as well as elements I have not described, were interconnected. It is obvious that there was a pronounced localism across the various arenas: from fairy forts in nearby fields to local holy wells or other pilgrimage sites, to celebration of the local saint's day to stories such as the Friars of Urlaur. People made contact with other worlds in very specific, tangibly accessible local sites.[47] This nearness of the other world was not just a matter of geography but of interpenetration and interconnection of the various levels. Campbell's mother and aunt went to do a station in the local churchyard not just because it was within walking distance, but also because they knew that miracles happened there, that the sacred intersected the mundane at that time and place. In fact, people might well travel considerable distances to some particularly efficacious sites. The nearness of the otherworld was a constant across 'official' and 'unofficial' Catholic beliefs and practices. People might seek a cure at a local holy well dedicated to some local saint and at the same time leave a rag on the adjacent bush as recognition of the demands of the fairies.[48] Campbell's father, who led the congregation at mass in doing the Stations of the Cross, also participated without a second thought in distributing straws to ward off cholera. But locally sited devotions were complemented by others with a more universal significance such as the mass, various sacraments and orthodox prayers (such as the repeated *Paters* at pilgrimages sites) and the Stations of the Cross.

The heightened localism does not imply uniformity of practice or consensus in belief. Campbell's evidence not only confirms what many more superficial observers, usually outsiders, have described about some elements of pre-famine religion, but also shows that their descriptions are misleading because of their one-sidedness. Campbell shows how widespread beliefs were systematically negated and thus did not predict behaviour. People believed in fairies — except when they did not. Recall the fairy fort in Knock where people grew crops, or the man who asked the fairywoman about his non-existent wife. Priests' curses had extraordinary power — except when they were ineffective. Recall not only the case of PC but the other man cursed by both the priest and the bishop but to no effect. People went on pilgrimage around local holy wells to do penance — except when they did so to avoid the sorcery of the Druids or to protect their cattle from the fairies. At holy wells and patterns, pilgrims might well have bleeding heads from fighting as well as bleeding knees from praying.[49] People might go to mass — or they might not. If they did go, they might also get drunk at the shebeens near the chapel. Priests were greedy — except when they were generous. Recall how the Knock priest, who commingled dues and duties in his book and was the target of a strike, also shared his Sunday breakfast with the poor holy woman. Even after he was paid for marrying the farmer/wheelwright, the priest 'flung the money back at him' after learning of the illicit nature of the 'marriage'.

The other worlds were not only near but there were established ways to act in this one to influence what happened in the other one(s).[50] People used different agents to communicate with the other world (or worlds) and to tap its (or their) powers. As we have seen they consulted the fairywoman in matters of concern to themselves as individuals but communal threats required different kinds of agents, priests or especially Archbishop MacHale.

For some rituals, no intermediary at all was needed, such as doing pilgrimages at the various local holy sites, and in everyday life people followed established patterns for appropriate behaviour. There was a prayer for almost every imaginable situation;[51] people observed a wide variety of rituals and paid attention to a wide variety of omens for good or bad. A final category of people who interacted with the transcendent realm was the 'holy pilgrims' whose involvement was episodic but not random; their contributions came unsought as a reward for local people's laudable behaviour. And a story like 'The Friars of Urlaur' constructed even the most dissolute of locals as capable of being a pilgrim in this sense.

Finally, we need to understand the relationships in people's minds among these various sorts of intermediaries with the otherworld. The total framework of beliefs included a whole series of checks and balances among the constituent elements. Analogous to the American constitutional system, any one power-holder was limited by the powers granted to others and extremism along any dimension was apt to provoke some countervailing power. First, in Knock the priest condemned the fairywoman and she complied, but only to the degree necessary to get what she wanted from the priest. She wanted her children to be baptised and to be herself churched after giving birth: once these were accomplished, she reverted to her usual practice. We have a lot of evidence that similar interactions were found beyond Knock, but the case could be much more complex. Some priests were regarded as having special powers to cure physical ailments, not unlike fairymen or women, and on occasion we have evidence of a fairy-priest.[52] In Knock, local people, ignoring the priest, provided enough of a clientele to keep the fairywoman in business.

If we look at the power of the priest, we find that people believed in his curse but also that they ignored his curses. According to Campbell's memoir, both PC, the farmer/wheelwright, and the other man similarly cursed from the altar ignored the curses even though it is clear, in PC's case at least, that he sought the priest's approval of his marriage. Even when seen as God's agent, the priest was unable to suppress the behaviours that we know he opposed, such as the secular amusements at patterns. Also, of course, people did not always attend mass, and organised a public demonstration against the fees the priest collected. The people could and did appeal to higher powers, Jesus and Mary, to counter the priests' demand for money or to discredit their condemnation of keening at funerals. Even the strongest episcopal cursing could fail, as MacHale's curse failed to separate the cohabiting couple in Knock, or be negated as in the case of Bishop Doyle during the 1832 chain-prayer episode (see chapter 10). And the idiom of priestly power could be used to tell a joke.

The culture included mechanisms to put priests and bishops in their proper places. Those clerics who, in the people's eyes, 'went too far' would be held accountable. In the folklore generally there is recognition that priests who tried to intervene and put a stop to fairy curers were subject to the powers of the fairywomen or fairymen. A common pattern in the stories about these confrontations was that the specialist fairy-curer would cause the priest's horse to stick to the ground and be unable to move. After the priest finally acknowledges his wrongdoing, the fairywoman or man releases the horse and the priest goes away having learned not to interfere with the fairy-healers.[53] Bishops like MacHale could rein in avaricious priests but Biddy Early, probably the most famous wise woman in nineteenth century Ireland, could thwart even MacHale.[54] A story like 'The Friars of Urlaur' pointed to the limited powers of priest, abbot, bishop and saint and recognised those of the everyday poor rake and sinner. A priest who failed to say masses for which he was paid was condemned to purgatory until he did so.[55]

Finally, recognising that the system incorporated checks on the powerful provides new insights into some familiar cases. Despite MacHale's resurrecting a House of Commons guard (see chapter 5), there is no evidence that people ever approached him for a cure not to mention a resurrection. Indeed, one anthropologist wrote that nobody ever approached a bishop for a cure. Yet, that seems to be not quite true. In chapter 2, I noted that the Bishop of Ohio in 1834 recorded in his diary receiving a letter from a woman called Ogier asking for his intervention to raise her newly dead nephew from the grave. If we assume that this woman was Irish, what would her letter mean? I suggest that, at most, it represents the view of someone with an incomplete command of the resources of her culture. If Ogier, on the Ohio-Kentucky border area in the 1830s, was in fact Irish, the likelihood is that she was not living in an intact Irish cultural community. Without the checks and balances implicit in such a culture she might have taken literally what elsewhere would be understood metaphorically or limited in application, and hence have written her request that startled the bishop. Similarly, in the Bridget Cleary case, what one peasant woman told Lady Gregory makes sense: persons who knew only half their own culture burned her to death. They lacked access to those features of the belief system that in the usual case acted as brakes on the literal enactment of the claims made in the fairylore.[56] What those brakes or checks were has to be decided by empirical research in the particular circumstances of each case.

5

The People Make
a Saint

On the night of John MacHale's birth a certain Counsellor Bourke was
on his way home to Carrowkeel, in Addergoole parish, when he saw a
strange star in the sky and thereby knew that a remarkable child had
been born somewhere in the parish. On enquiry he found that a sixth
child had been born to Patrick MacHale and Mary Mulhern, so there-
upon the Counsellor predicted the child's greatness.[1]

John MacHale had been a bishop for nine years already when he became
Archbishop of Tuam, which included Knock, in 1834 and he was to continue in the post until his death in 1881. Even more amazing than his
fifty-six years as a bishop was his reputation. Well over half a century after
his death, one informant told a folklore collector that people in every town
in the diocese still remembered and talked about him, and another in 1942
recalled a storytelling competition in Tuam 'seven years ago' at which con-
testants were required to tell a tale about MacHale.[2]

To explain the occurrence of the Knock apparition it is necessary to grasp
the cultural and religious understanding of the ordinary people who beheld
it and the figure of MacHale was centrally important in their world.

It is important to see Catholicism from below, as it were, for another
reason. Many historians have emphasised how church officials, especially
bishops, viewed events and personalities in nineteenth-century Irish
Catholicism. Thomas McGrath's two books on Bishop Doyle of Kildare and
Leighlin are superb examples of their genre but the genre, per se, looks at
evidence from an 'establishment' perspective.[3] For example, we know from
letters written to the Dublin Castle authorities in 1832 that Doyle was
reported by many people to have cursed whole towns to such effect that
they were destroyed by thunderbolts.[4] In his reading of Doyle's correspondence and other archival material, McGrath found no evidence whatever of
the 1832 episode;[5] consequently, his portrait of Doyle is systematically flat-
tened because such popular views were not articulated in ways that left
evidence in diocesan and other ecclesiastical archives. I will argue that
MacHale's believed involvement in the same 1832 'chain-prayer' was a con-
stitutive element in the power that he wielded for over half a century.

A further reason for studying MacHale's popular image is that in his case specifically we are not likely to ever have a satisfactory biography unless and until his papers and diocesan records are found. They were missing from the archbishop's house after his death in 1881. It is generally assumed that his nephew, Fr Thomas MacHale, took them. Bernard O'Reilly who published a two-volume biography in 1890 in the United States had access to at least some of MacHale's papers but his whole approach is so one-sidedly adulatory that it does not inspire confidence is his objective use of the totality of evidence available to him. Moreover, the records that O'Reilly did have were incomplete. For example, he wrote that MacHale's last confirmation trip was in 1878 but newspapers reported several later trips.[6] Thus, the diocesan records crucial for a thorough study of MacHale are lost; the one writer who had at least partial access was violently biased in favour of MacHale, selective in his use of evidence and tendentious in argumentation. The recent biography by Andrews follows the same partisan approach and we are not surprised to learn that the writer is in fact related to her subject, being a great-grandchild of MacHale's younger half-sister Catherine.[7] If we combine this state of affairs with the enormous amounts of negative material his detractors committed to paper now available in ecclesiastical archives, we understand why a fully fleshed out picture of MacHale, in all its dimensions, is unlikely ever to be produced. With such difficulty in getting conventional evidence, it is even more important to use the available material to fill out the popular image of MacHale.

In the second quarter of the century, MacHale acquired an extraordinary reputation among his followers that his longevity as bishop does little to explain. Of course, priests and bishops were credited with canonically appropriate supernatural powers, such as the celebration of the Eucharist, but popularly priests were credited with powers that were not canonically recognised or sanctioned. There is evidence that people ascribed powers of doing harm to priests. Some scholars argue that Literary Revival figures such as Yeats and Lady Gregory overstressed the malign influences ascribed to priests.[8] They had powers to do good as well as we saw earlier. Moreover, as is clear from Daniel Campbell and many other sources, the priest was defined as a person who could tap and channel the power of God or one through whom God worked.[9] However, not all priests were equally regarded. The 'Apostle of Temperance', Fr Theobald Mathew, was the miracle-working priest with the largest impact in the country in the mid-nineteenth century.[10] The historian of the diocese of Kilmore estimated that there was approximately one 'healing' priest in the diocese in each generation.[11] Some priests were particularly esteemed and renowned and MacHale occupies a unique place among these.[12] It is not an exaggeration to say that for some people he was almost a demi-god. He occupied a virtually unprecedented place in the consciousness of the people, especially of the poorer classes in the two dioceses in which he served.

I have already noted the report of the star announcing his birth. The year was probably 1791. (As part of his mystique, even his birth year is reported differently; see page 157 below.) So great did the fame of that child become that when, as coadjutor Bishop of Killala, in 1828 he dedicated a new church in Dromard parish in County Sligo, his 'more than ordinary powers' so impressed the local people that their descendants related them to a new priest in their parish 126 years later.[13] What were those powers and why did they so impress the people? In his later years, Archbishop MacHale was often at loggerheads with other bishops and with Rome. Anthropologist, Lawrence Taylor, has shown that in nineteenth-century Ireland priests who were disciplined by their bishops, often for drunkenness, were believed to have more supernatural power than other priests did, since their priestly powers were now released from their bishop's *smacht* or control.[14] By analogy, we might argue that an archbishop disciplined by the pope would be even more powerful. It is also undoubtedly true that MacHale was adept at self-promotion, so that one could say that MacHale's reputation in his later years was the product of a half-century of public relations efforts driven by a massive ego. Most historians recognise that for decades MacHale was the most articulate, courageous and adamant 'nationalist' bishop in the country. However, although defiance of Rome perhaps and his strident nationalism likely added to it, neither was the source of MacHale's popularly ascribed power. Long before the conflicts with Rome and even before his long-time rival, Archbishop Cullen of Dublin, joined the hierarchy in 1850, MacHale had the reputation that was to persist not only as long as his long life but for decades after its end.

If we examine the question from the perspective of outside researchers, several factors seem likely to have been important in the production of his popular image. Already by 1828 we have the evidence of Dromard, so MacHale's reputation was established early in his episcopal career. When he was translated from Killala to Tuam in 1834, his fame was already so great that a crowd estimated, and probably exaggerated, at 100,000 watched his crossing of the bridge between the two dioceses.[15] This timing alone suggests several probable contributing causes. That he was appointed coadjutor bishop of Killala in 1825 over the objections of the British government most likely gave him the benefit of any early ignorance or doubt locally about where he stood, and in an ideological battlefield between *Gael* and *Gall*, that was a crucial point.[16] Another likely contributing factor to MacHale's early fame was his first work following his appointment to Killala, a small poor diocese covering north Mayo and extending into County Sligo. Immediately on taking up his position he organised and led what can only be called a diocese-wide travelling revival to celebrate this jubilee year of 1825. He mobilised the priests so that up to fifteen clergymen on horseback would descend on a parish and conduct an intensive ten-day mission before departing for the next parish. 'The ignorant were instructed, the careless were made good, the sinners were converted, the weak were confirmed and strengthened, and the blessings and graces of the jubilee were brought home to each home and to each individual in Killala.'[17] So concentrated an encounter with so many priests with such a focus on evangelism must have impressed many. Like the parish missions so common in the rest of the country in the post-famine era,[18] this can be expected to have effects in stimulating religious practice more acceptable to the ecclesiastical authorities, but an indirect effect would be to enhance the public reputation of MacHale, especially as he himself accompanied the priests into every parish in the diocese throughout this period. Indeed, there is good reason to expect that in Killala the effect would be even greater because of the scale of the revival and its novelty, especially in the remote west.

MacHale was as energetic in the election campaigns of 1826 as he had been in the jubilee of 1825:

> He denounced in unmeasured terms the severities of the penal code, which had affixed the stamp of inferiority on their [Catholic] brows. In the agitation of 1826 his spirit was . . . omnipresent, by night and day, on the altar steps and on the mountain side, on the high-ways and in places of public resort, calling up the memories of the past, denouncing the wrongs of the present, and promising imperishable rewards to those willing to die in their struggle for the faith.[19]

Even if we discount the exaggeration of this later admirer, MacHale had a tremendous impact locally. He was not only willing, but seemed eager, to say bluntly to the powerful what doubtless was on the minds of the poor oppressed Catholics of his diocese. This is what makes a leader 'charismatic', according to James Scott, who makes the point that 'the first public declaration of the hidden transcript . . . has the force of an earthquake' for the underdogs, who experience the release as almost like a resurrection and recapture of their human dignity and self-respect.[20] When in 1826 the Protestant Archbishop Trench of Tuam denounced what he called the 'damnable doctrines of the Catholic Church', MacHale responded with a letter that even an admirer called 'scathingly severe'.[21] MacHale waxed indignant at Trench's lack of charity, intolerance and insolent bigotry. He pointed out that the cathedral in which Trench spoke had once been consecrated in the service of the religion he criticised, and mocked the Protestant side for 'keeping a body of strolling auxiliaries in pay, to prop up the declining cause of the establishment, by pouring their vapid abuse on the Catholic church'. Further, he warned Trench in future not to 'engage in a feast of triumph' over Catholicism 'lest some mysterious hand should draw more fully the character and destiny of your Church on the walls of the Cathedral in Killala'.[22]

Even in his early years as a bishop we also see MacHale's acute sensitivity about how to enhance the people's receptivity to his message. (That he was a native of the diocese no doubt made it easier for him to understand the local scene.) He wrote to a contact in Rome, none other than Paul Cullen, asking for a supply of rosary beads that he could distribute among the laity on his travels. He noted that his supply was exhausted and, very important for our purposes, throughout the letter he indicated that he was in competition with friars for public acceptance. 'I am annoyed by applications to bless St Francis' chord' (sic), he wrote, 'the people imagining that as I have some such powers I can do all'. He asked Cullen to get him the needed authority and permission (faculty) to bless the cords, 'in order that I may have as much power as the Friars'.[23] Since the friars at the time were closer to the people and also commonly associated with various holy objects such as scapulars, MacHale realised that without distributing some similarly tangible blessed objects he would be handicapped in winning the people's hearts. In the next decade, Fr Mathew in his temperance campaign was to recognise a similar utility for 'holy' objects, in his case medals. While MacHale was critical of Mathew, his criticism of the medals centred on Mathew's alleged profiting from their sale rather than the fact of their use. Apparently, throughout his life MacHale continued to distribute rosaries; we have accounts of him doing so on several later occasions.[24] Significantly, these reports come to us from the perspective of the recipients, an indication both of how closely attuned MacHale was to popular attitudes and how greatly the common people appreciated him and the rosaries they sought from him.

Probably the single most important factor in creating MacHale's reputation early on was the unseating of Denis Browne, MP. Given Browne's awful reputation and practice as 'dictator of the county', getting rid of him was experienced as a great liberation. Precisely because Browne was such a Goliath, MacHale was cast as David.[25] The removal of Denis Browne from Parliament in 1826 and MacHale's travelling revival meetings were not neatly separable events, especially in retrospect, and it is probable that each multiplied the effects of the other. Moreover, the effects of all these factors were dependent on MacHale's reading and moulding of the popular understandings. The myriad conflicts in which MacHale was involved in later decades provided opportunities for his image as a sectarian gladiator to be further developed because they provided occasions for the people to interpret him as their David.

And after the defeat of Denis Browne, MacHale was extraordinarily lucky in the rivals he faced in the persons of two successive occupants of the Protestant see of Tuam. Archbishop Power Le Poer Trench (1819–1839) and his successor Bishop Thomas Plunkett (1839–1866) were perhaps the two most polarising Protestant bishops in the whole country in all the nineteenth century. They were champions of the evangelicals who directly targeted Catholics for aggressive proselytism. Charges and counter charges flew about their sponsorship of individuals and organisations allegedly engaged in 'souperism', the practice of giving relief and aid only to those who converted to Protestantism. Trench welcomed into his diocese ministers who had been disciplined or disowned in other dioceses for their extreme evangelical views,[26] while Plunkett, as a landlord, was accused of the mass evictions of tenants who refused to send their children to Protestant schools he set up.[27] We could say that MacHale was the right man to take advantage of a unique combination of circumstances in Mayo in the second half of the 1820s, but that is too static a way of understanding what was not a precisely datable event with one cause but a complex, ongoing and multifaceted process of hero-construction.

Most historians who have commented on MacHale start by describing his personality, as if individual psychology is the key. Explanations of his popularity along the lines I sketched above appeal to most social scientists determined to explain what really happened. However, such approaches still give little insight into what his followers saw in him. If we are to understand popular religious beliefs and attitudes, we must enter 'the interpretive community of believers' and take seriously what they have to say,[28] rather than explaining them in terms of social, economic, political or other factors or relying on outsiders' descriptions. MacHale was a charismatic leader as classically defined by Max Weber. Weber used the term charisma to denote 'a certain quality of an individual personality by virtue of which he is considered extraordinary and treated as endowed with supernatural, superhuman, or at least specifically exceptional powers or qualities'.[29] Among the examples Weber mentioned were 'berserk' soldiers in medieval Byzantium, persons suffering epileptic seizures recognised as shamans in some societies, and even perhaps a sophisticated swindler. The key factor is not a leader's personal psychology but how that person is perceived by others. Different audiences of potential followers may require different proofs that speak to their specific situations. In the backlands of Brazil, for example, there is a tradition of millenarianism in which several successive individuals have been recognised as twentieth-century reincarnations of Jesus. Many claimants appear, but to be accepted they have to be recognised as performing miracles of healing.[30] In nineteenth-century Mayo, MacHale was recognised for very different powers.

To enter the interpretive community that believed in MacHale, I have examined the stories popularly told about him. Half a dozen MacHale stories were collected by the Irish Folklore Commission in the 1930s and 1940s and are now housed in the archives of the National Folklore Collection, at University College Dublin. While their number is not large, these stories cover a wide range of issues and have a very high quality as evidence. Doubtless, the stories that survived were but a small fraction of those told during MacHale's life and those recorded by collectors comprised an even smaller fraction. Given that MacHale was dead for over fifty years when the collectors began their work, we should be surprised not at the paucity of the stories but that any at all were still told. Daniel Campbell's memoir adds several significant stories about MacHale. In addition, MacHale was the subject of numerous popular poems and ballads that I have used as well. Inevitably, many such works were ephemeral but a corpus of surviving material has been collected in an unpublished PhD thesis Antoine Boltúin wrote on MacHale and the Irish language.[31] What John Steinbeck wrote about songs applies also to the stories that are told even if not sung by the relatively less powerful in society:

> Songs are the statements of a people. You can learn more about people by listening to their songs than in any other way, for into their songs go all the hopes and hurts, the angers, fears, the wants and aspirations.[32]

Singing is just one, albeit important, way of telling stories. What Steinbeck said about American workers' songs applies as well to other oppressed groups, including the stories and tales recounted by Campbell that he recalled from his youth in pre-famine Knock and the stories collected by the Irish Folklore Commission. In the 1820s even the Chief Secretary in Dublin Castle recognised that songs 'rather follow than lead the public taste'.[33] The people passed on those stories and songs and constantly re-made them, making them their own as they confronted each issue, whether a new one or an old one in the guise of something new. Finally, I have drawn information about MacHale's popular image from a variety of other contemporary sources.

It may well be that 'sentimental recollections of . . . Archbishop MacHale as a western Napoleon surrounded by a staff of priests, "generals in fact, who were the bravest of the brave", distort rather than illuminate' if we want to understand MacHale the individual, as one historian argued.[34] However, popular stories and songs do enable us to understand the mentality of the people who created and transmitted them. In the case of MacHale, we can catalogue the powers and attributes ascribed to him in the stories and the ways the people explained his powers. Moreover, we can compare informa-tion in the stories with the conventionally documented MacHale and note the concurrences, omissions, selective emphases, and other types of reframing and interpretations we find in the folklore. Disjunctures between the 'popular' and the 'historical' figure tell us about the consciousness of the people who told and retold the stories that have been collected. The distor-tions themselves are extremely illuminating.[35] When examined in association with the 'officially' documented life, MacHale's image tells us more about the people who believed in his supernatural power than it does about the man himself. We need, however, to keep well in mind that con-ventional written evidence is itself necessarily distorted, selective, and from some particular limited perspective and that folklore materials are not a second best source for historical research. As evidence, folklore speaks to different questions and replaces or complements more conventional kinds of evidence about historical figures.

To the people, MacHale was divinely chosen even before he was born. His birth was attended by the strange star whose meaning Counsellor Bourke recognised. He was intended not just for greatness but for the particular position he held for nearly half a century (1834–1881).

> He was appointed the Lord's anointed
> Before his birth in his mother's womb,
> To wear the mitre, as no man was brighter,
> To be Archbishop in the see of Tuam.

And he would be a Moses who would free the people from bondage and overthrow their oppressors, a Saint Patrick who would expound the gospel and tirelessly

> Direct [his] flock all on St Peter's rock
> And keep them safe from those wolves of prey
> Who be in wait against our holy faith.

Here he is identified as the ever-vigilant defender of the downtrodden, as defender of Catholics against the Protestant 'wolves of prey'. Moreover, he would be victorious.[36]

One explicit statement in the folklore on the origin of MacHale's extraordinary power says that he received it from the water of the holy well in his birthplace, Tobbernavine. Usually this place name is understood to refer to the Fianna, the legendary warrior-band of pre-Christian Ireland famed for heroism, wisdom and mighty deeds. Thus, *Tobar na bhFiann*, the well of the Fianna, a well whose powers go back beyond Christianity, gave its nourishing power to the young John MacHale.[37] This story was built on a pervasive belief in the significance of holy wells, which were such a central part of the religious life of the people.[38] However, MacHale, according to the folklore, was not just a beneficiary of an existing well but transcended this routine level of interaction with the sacred. He created his own well, on a new sacred spot, to benefit his home area when he visited it in 1834 on his way to take up his appointment as Archbishop of Tuam.[39]

The emphasis here on MacHale helping the people of his native place is an instance of a recurrent theme in the folklore: MacHale's concern for his own people. He was their particular advocate and they were his particular charges. He represented them. Several divergences between the folklore and some demonstrable facts amply document this.

MacHale's father, Padraig Mór, was a well-off farmer and innkeeper who hired labourers and kept household servants. He purchased flax from his neighbours and sold it in the Linenhall in Castlebar. Certainly, he was not a poor peasant.[40] Yet the folklore tells a very different story and the folk remembered a very different history. According to one version, Padraig Mór owed his prosperity to his son's power. This account tells that when the English were settling in County Belfast (sic), and schooling was forbidden to Catholics, John MacHale's father, here called Haonrai, was evicted from his farm along with hundreds of other families. He was forced to go live on a hillside until his young son John showed the landlord that his agent had wrongly evicted the people and convinced him to restore them all to their rightful places. The landlord was so impressed that he reinstated the father rent free for life and provided him with livestock, seeds to plant and a horse and plough.[41] Typical of folklore, this account telescopes history, including items ranging in time from the plantation of Ulster early in the seventeenth century, to the Penal Laws in the eighteenth, to perhaps the exodus of Catholic refugees from Ulster following the Battle of the Diamond in 1795 and John MacHale's seminary studies early in the nineteenth century.

Even ignoring the dates for a moment, there is no evidence to support one claim of the story, that MacHale had an Ulster origin or heritage. On the contrary, there is lots of evidence that he did not. MacHale was among the most common names in Mayo in the 1855–57 Griffith's Valuation, but it was almost exclusive to that county: of fifty-one babies named MacHale whose births were registered in the whole country in 1890, only one was not born in Mayo.[42] Though his mother had remote Donegal ancestors,[43] very likely the bishop's paternal forebears were resident in Mayo for long generations. In the 1640s there were four families named McKeale in the townland where John MacHale was born a century and a half later.[44] Why then would the stories remember him as of poor origin and as a refugee from Ulster? If this is just a piece of droll exaggeration, as Boltúin claims,[45] how can we explain why this particular piece of nonsense was what was remembered and retold? The key to grasping the significance of the story is to recognise that it associated MacHale with the evicted tenants and the displaced Catholics, and thus it resonated with the people's own nineteenth-century memories and current experiences as people oppressed by landlords and targeted by proselytising Protestants. In Mayo, there was a considerable number of 'Ultachs', Catholics who had been driven by force and threat from the sectarian cockpits of Ulster in the late eighteenth and early nineteenth centuries, for whom this piece of alleged drollery would have particular resonance.[46]

This story also provided a compelling explanation of how the son of a prosperous merchant/farmer could be such as advocate for the poor. The oppressed did not expect to find champions among the better off and when they did, some ideological work was needed to account for what would otherwise be an anomaly. Such ideological reframing is obvious in other stories about MacHale which dispense with any mention whatever of his relatively privileged background and remember him, inaccurately, as 'the son of a cowherd at the butt of Nephin' (as Daniel Campbell did) or 'from the rock of Nephin',[47] Nephin being the desolate mountain near his birthplace. In his travels in Mayo in 1849 Thomas Carlyle heard an 'indescribably vague' account of MacHale's poor origin.[48] As noted, other stories while acknowledging MacHale's father's success ascribe it to the son, exemplifying the youth's ability to help his people. One tells how the young John not only convinced the landlord to reverse the eviction of hundreds but earned special treatment for one of the evicted tenants, MacHale's own father. Such 'mistakes' in the folklore are not errors at all but powerful evidence of taken-for-granted understandings shared by the story-tellers and their audience in the community of believers. Given the landlords' political and economic ascendancy, young John MacHale's success in convincing one of them to restore the evicted tenants in itself was so extraordinary as to be worthy of being related down the generations.

The youth's success in reversing the evictions was just an early example of his power to overturn injustice, the power of Moses to make Pharaoh release God's chosen people that the folk attributed to MacHale. He was credited with the defeat of the politically powerful John Browne in an 1836 election for Parliament, as he had been ten years earlier in ending the Parliamentary career of Denis Browne. A song recalled by Daniel Campbell gives us a vivid version of the World-Upside-Down apocalyptic belief that cast MacHale as the deliverer, the David who destroyed Goliath:

> Says his wife to John Brown, 'You look very blue'
> 'By my soul', said poor John, 'you may say what is true:
> Archbishop MacHale gave me such a hit
> That I never again will in Parliament sit.
> Och, oh, chone, what shall I do?
> A few years ago I heard people say
> That 'Croppies lie down' was the toast of the day;
> But now all is changed in country and town,
> And the cry of the people is 'Brown lie down!'
> Down, down, down!
> Brown lie down.[49]

The reversal of roles is encapsulated in another memory recorded by Daniel Campbell: the mother of another Member of Parliament, Dominick Brown, begging MacHale not to turn him out of Parliament.

It is even possible that there was an apparition of MacHale among some of his followers in the late 1820s or early 1830s perhaps at the time of the Blessed Straws episode (June 1832) or the election that ended Denis Browne's career in Parliament (1826). A long mocking poem concerning Papist superstition and priestly manipulation of the poor for monetary gain that centred on just such an apparition by MacHale, was published in December 1833 in the *Dublin University Magazine*, an organ of evangelical Protestantism. There probably was some now-lost report, written or oral, that the poem parodied, but even if this was not the case, the poem nevertheless quite accurately identified MacHale as the most likely ecclesiastical subject of a miraculous apparition. Speaking about him, it said

> For, behold you, the Bishop was clad like a sprite
> In a blazing array and a wonderful light –
> Some thought it was an angel come down in disguise
> And some thought the Bishop was bound for the skies.[50]

This continues for seventeen verses, each followed by the chorus, 'which nobody can deny, which nobody can deny'.

MacHale's reputation as a defender of Catholic and Irish rights was to grow as the decades passed and he got involved in battle after battle that his people could interpret through their lens of him as their advocate and deliverer. A song transcribed in 1920 but dated to around 1868 asked

> Cia thug buaidh do na Gaedhil, acht ArdEaspog MacAil
> Is dubhairt go fearamhail tabhair a gceart do Ghaedhil?
> (Who gave victory to the Gael but Archbishop MacHale
> And in a manly way said (to) give their rights to the Gael?)

The particular victory celebrated here was the election to parliament of George Henry Moore.[51]

Repeatedly, MacHale confronted the enemies of his people as they saw them. Against Protestants and against the government he was tireless but even against less obvious foes he protected the interests of the common people, the poor tenant farmers and workers who populated his diocese. The people remembered and retold the stories about these confrontations. A collector for the Irish Folklore Commission wrote down one such story in 1937 from an eighty-year old farmer who had heard it twenty years earlier from a seventy-five-year-old.[52] It tells how in a Tuam butcher's shop MacHale questions a poor man about the large amount of mutton he is buying. The man says the meat is for the priests' breakfast following a station mass next day, and that to pay for it the man had sold his only two sheep to the butcher. MacHale asks if the man or his neighbours have potatoes, milk and a few eggs. On learning that they do, MacHale tells the man to prepare a breakfast of potatoes and milk with an egg for each of the two priests who would be at the station. Telling the butcher to return the man's sheep, MacHale writes a letter that he seals in an envelope. He instructs the man to place the envelope on the breakfast table at the station and to return later to report to MacHale how the priests reacted. Next day while the station meal was being readied everybody was watching and the two priests were laughing, mocking the poor fare. Their tune changed when they opened the letter and read what MacHale had written.

We appreciate why this story resonated with people when we remember priests' reputation for avarice. MacHale's stance contrasted with the proverbial greed of priests. His genuine concern for his flock is made manifest. At an explicit level, the story tells how MacHale put greedy, arrogant priests in their proper place and protected the downtrodden and exploited. Additionally, there is a very significant implicit message in the tale. MacHale shows concerned interest in the lives of the people. He questions the poor man's buying of meat not to berate him perhaps for living beyond his means or for putting on airs. MacHale knows immediately that something is amiss in the man's purchase of so much mutton and pays him the courtesy of listening to what he has to say. By thus validating the credibility of one of the poor, he was reinforcing his own credibility in their eyes. We, as readers, and the listeners to the story are left to surmise the precise contents of MacHale's letter but of its gist and effect there is no doubt. Just as MacHale trusted the poor, they trusted him as their protector and advocate to embody their values and to articulate their hopes and wishes.

This story is important also for another reason. It gave ammunition to critics of priestly avarice. It discredited the priests' usual way of behaving by appealing to a higher power, in this case the priests' ecclesiastical superior. By thus sustaining an ideal of an ungreedy priest, the story presents an image of a desirable state that could be used to criticise the status quo. Such appeals to higher powers or to the ideals to which superiors claim adherence are a perennial tactic among the underdogs of the world.[53] Without some such critique of priestly exactions, we would not have had the 'strike' against them in Knock in 1842–43 that Campbell recalled at length.

The British government in 1851 enacted the Ecclesiastical Titles Bill forbidding Catholic bishops to use British place names as part of their official titles. MacHale's response was a letter in the public press which he signed 'John, Archbishop of Tuam', daring the government to prosecute him under the new law.[54] When the government declined, the law became a dead letter and MacHale's stature grew among the oppressed. In 1857 when MacHale appeared before a Select Committee of the House of Commons in London, he used the illegal title. Immediately after he was sworn in this exchange took place:

> What is your Christian name? — John.
> What position do you hold in the Roman-catholic church? — Archbishop of Tuam.
> *Chairman*   You are quite aware, I presume, that that is a title which this Committee cannot recognise; we know you as Archbishop, and are perfectly willing to recognise that as your title, but we cannot recognise you as Archbishop of Tuam? — I beg to explain, for a moment, that I have not obtruded the title upon the Committee; I should not do anything that would appear at all offensive, but, as the question was put to me, I do believe, and I am certain that I am the Archbishop of Tuam; but at the same time, if that should not be my legal identification here, I am quite satisfied with the title of Archbishop M'Hale.[55]

In an account written more than a century later that combines orally transmitted memories with archival evidence, Waldron describes how 'even in the very chambers of the House of Commons itself, he [MacHale] brazenly broke the law by insisting on using his full title'.[56] This instance provides a good example of how what 'officially' occurred was transmuted into something else when refracted through the prism of popular conceptions.[57] Did the episode take place 'in the very chambers of the House of Commons'? Experts on parliamentary procedures and architectural arrangements in Westminster would say not, but such distinctions between, for example, 'the very chamber' and different committee hearing rooms are superfluous niceties, distinctions that made no difference for the people of MacHale's diocese. It mattered less whether MacHale intended to be 'brazen' in flouting the law than this is how his behaviour was perceived. MacHale was always alert to how his behaviour could and would be seen by the people of his diocese and the wider country. With a continuing flair for politically dramatic gestures, MacHale donated signed portraits of himself for a Fenian fundraiser in Chicago; he said mass in Tuam for the Manchester Martyrs; and he refused to discipline priests who criticised Cardinal Cullen.[58] Some historians suggest that MacHale deliberately cultivated his image as a nationalist bishop in reaction to his loss of influence among the Irish bishops and in Rome caused by Rome's support and elevation of Cullen, especially under the papacy of Pius IX. Though such factors probably added to it among Irish people outside his own diocese and especially abroad, MacHale's reputation and dramatic gestures preceded these transitions. In Knock he was remembered locally as the driving force in the Blessed Straws episode of 1832, and on a national stage a decade earlier in his public letters (under the name of Hierophilos), he had adopted a 'tone which was ironic and contemptuous about the vaunted advantages of the British constitution'.[59] In the O'Connell era, MacHale was so visibly involved in controversy and so engaged in passionate polemical writings on social, political and religious questions that by 1845 he was, after Daniel O'Connell, the most popular man in Ireland.[60] In another politically charged gesture, he had gone to Richmond Prison on 3 July 1844 to say mass for O'Connell when the Liberator was imprisoned there.

Politics, especially campaigns to elect members of parliament, provided an arena where MacHale and his mobilised followers confronted their enemies. In the 1826 election, at a national level MacHale was credited with the defeat of Denis Browne[61] and Mayo returned two MPs in favour of Catholic Emancipation, the burning political issue of the day. Daniel Campbell's local perception was different in interesting ways. The national setting is not visible at all and the event is interpreted through the lens of what was locally significant, the defeat of Browne. This was a major reversal for the erstwhile 'dictator' of the county for twenty years.[62]

In subsequent elections, MacHale mobilised Catholic electors, often using priests as marshals bringing electors to the polls and persuading them to vote contrary, in most cases, to the wishes of their landlords. In two parliamentary elections, Mayo in 1857 and Galway in 1872, candidates MacHale supported were successful at the polls but were unseated after objections by losing candidates about undue 'clerical influence' on the electors; these two tumultuous campaigns together with the hearings and investigations that followed them, deserve more attention than historians have given them.[63] In both cases, it is clear beyond any doubt that the final outcomes were seen differently by MacHale's supporters than by the legal and political establishment. A key to understanding 'clerical influence' is to see it in its community context as an instance of a cleric such as MacHale leading the enforcement of a communal morality against would-be deviants. One historian who studied accusations of undue clerical influence at the 1868 general election in Wales concluded that the charges were 'better understood as evidence of a strong tradition of community morality in rural areas [of Ireland as well as Wales]'.[64] The cases in which MacHale was charged certainly support this conclusion.

In 1942, a collector for the Irish Folklore Commission transcribed a story that distils popular attitudes toward MacHale after his confrontations with parliament over issues such as the Ecclesiastical Titles Bill and the 1857 and 1872 elections. A seventy-four-year-old farmer who said he had heard it forty to fifty years earlier from his father, grandfather and other old people of the area told the story.[65] As nearly always, the story has an important sectarian dimension. The incident related is set in some unspecified period 'when the *Easbog gallda* was trying to banish' MacHale and hence Catholicism from the country. *Easbog gallda* means, literally, 'foreign bishop', but in the vernacular of the time it meant the Protestant bishop, an indication of how closely religion and national identity were fused.[66] This sectarian/national/class idiom pervaded all social life, even to distinguishing shoemakers: one who made brogues for the common people was a *gréasaidhe Gaedhealach* while a *gréasaidhe Gallda* made boots for the gentry.[67] After failing to get his way in law in Dublin, the Protestant bishop arranged that the case would be heard in London, in the House of Commons, believing that MacHale would be afraid to go there and hence the Protestant side would win. However, undaunted, MacHale does go. An armed guard blocks the door to the House. On MacHale's approach, his gun and sword drop from the guard's hand, and then, the guard himself drops dead. MacHale proceeds inside, makes his case, and wins justice because nobody dares to speak against him. On his way out, MacHale restores the dead guard to life.

MacHale is remembered here for both his human qualities and his supernatural powers. He had the courage to confront the enemy in the very heart of the establishment and his eloquence and steadfast vehemence brought victory. After all, he *and* Catholicism still survived the attempts by the *Easbog gallda* to banish them. MacHale bearded the lion in his den and overcame the Protestant bishop and the powers behind him. By pointing to a power higher than the law and parliament, the story also indicted the whole legal system that had unseated the 'right' winning candidates that MacHale had backed in 1857 and 1872 and confirmed the people's views that parliament had no legitimacy to begin with. His, and theirs, was a moral victory over the machinery of the state. The power of life, death and resurrection was on the side of MacHale and his people.

Significantly, the phrase I have translated as saying the guard dropped dead is ambiguous, probably deliberately so. After telling that the guard's gun and sword fell 'from him down on the floor in the door', the narrator continues [*agus*] *thit sé héin os a gcíonn,* literally that he himself (the guard) fell on top of them (the weapons). The phrase can be read either literally or figuratively. In English, a comparable statement saying that a man 'fell on his sword' would normally be understood to mean that he had sacrificed himself by his own hand. But this does not preclude a very prosaic statement that the man had just tripped and fallen on his sword without being injured in the least. What would we make of a statement that someone 'fell on his sword and his gun'? The listener is free to construct the meaning by interpreting the various pieces of information the narrator provides. In this story, the whole setting is presented as one of warfare, of perennial conflict between the *Gael* and the *Gall*, though in this instance the battlefield is the House of Commons. While the setting is the parliament, the language of the story is of the courthouse where cases are tried, evidence heard and verdicts given, all in an adversarial mode. The explicit and implicit references to warfare and confrontations suggest a metaphorical rather than a literal reading of *thit sé héin os a gcíonn*. Moreover, there is reason to suspect that the storyteller was aware of the English language metaphorical meaning of falling on swords. He himself told the version we now have at a *feis* in Tuam 'seven years ago,' according to the man who provided it to the folklore collector in 1942, and the provision of a sword to the guard, along with his gun, conveniently sets the stage for him to fall on it. For MacHale to raise him on his way out, the guard had to have fallen. That this 'fall' was more than a momentary slip is clear not only from the time elapsed while the case was tried but also from the language used to describe the raising.

> *Nuair a bhí sé 'goil amach a' doras, thóig sé a lámh os cíonn an ghárda seo, agus d'eirrí' sé 'n'a sheasa agus thóig sé a ghunna agus a chaidhne mar bhí sé í dtosach. Agus bhí íontas ag achuile duine ga ru sa teach ins a' mbealach a d'eiri' gon ghárda, agus ní ru aon nduine acab i n-ánn fhocal amháin a rá ná a labhairt gur imi' an t-Easboc Mac Éil.* [When he (MacHale) was going out the door, he raised his hand over this guard, and he stood up and he took his gun and sword as he was at the start. And everyone in the house was amazed at how the guard got up, and not one of them was able to say or utter one word before Bishop MacHale went away.]
>
> (Here and elsewhere, except for using h instead of a *buailte*, spellings have not been modernised or punctuation changed in Irish-language original materials in the National Folklore Collection archives.)

When I mentioned this story in a group of historians one said immediately that 'it never happened'. We could search the records of proceedings in the House of Commons and find that MacHale in person never attended in the chamber. If we have faith in Hansard, we can even prove this negative. Doubtless, *The Times* would have reported the resurrection of a Commons guard. However, as we have seen, MacHale did indeed appear in a House of Commons Committee Room before a panel investigating charges of clerical intimidation during the 1857 election for Mayo. However that occasion might be interpreted, social scientists recognise that if people define situations as real, their definitions have consequences. In this sense, 'it did happen'. What the story documents is not one specific datable occasion such as his testimony before the Commons committee in 1857, but MacHale's long-term, continuing presence in the daily conversation, the routine thinking and feeling of the common people, most of whom were illiterate. These people did not 'read' MacHale's letter on ecclesiastical titles but they certainly got its message. Just as surely, they got the message of his championing the Catholic cause and people in the timeless conflict with the Protestants/Foreigners.

That the House of Commons story was told and retold enough to be remembered over sixty years after MacHale's death is crucial evidence about the mentality of the people. The story is important for the historian precisely because it was significant for the people of MacHale's time and place. Their consciousness was the prism through which were refracted the specific events that can be documented in Hansard or archives of other written materials. It was through this prism that meaning was constituted by and for the people.[68]

Another law-related story provides further insight into the popular image of MacHale but in this instance, while the issue might be similar, the setting is very local indeed, MacHale's own house. In 1943 the Irish Folklore Commission collected this tale from a seventy–year-old Tuam worker who had heard it years earlier from the *muintir* (community) around Headford:

> I heard my father say there was a small piece of land on Ballygaddy Road in Tuam. The Protestants held it for a time, and then the Archbishop got it, no thanks to the Protestants. The Protestants did not like allowing the land to go to him and they put the law on him with a process. At that time, the process-server in Tuam was a Protestant. He got the process with orders to serve it on the Archbishop. The Protestant got the process but he did not serve it. He put it in his pocket afraid to go to the Archbishop with it because he was a black Protestant. The Protestant process-server died with the Archbishop's process in his pocket. The people laying out his body found the process in his pocket and gave it to the law people. The next man then that got the job of process-server in Tuam was a man they called Seán Ó Maoláin. Ó Maoláin was a Catholic. Ó Maoláin got the process with orders to serve it on Archbishop MacHale. He went up to the bishop's palace and knocked on the door. [After the process-server engaged in conversation with a servant . . .], the bishop came to the door thinking this man has some sort of trouble. 'What's wrong, poor man?' said the Archbishop when he saw Ó Maoláin at the door. 'Tell me your story'. Ó Maoláin put his hand in his pocket and pulled out the process and held it out toward the Archbishop. The Archbishop opened the process. 'What's your name?' 'Seán Ó Maoláin', said the process-server. 'Well, Ó Maoláin,' said the Archbishop, 'the luck of the fern on you. That's you, green in the morning and withered by evening.' That was the curse the Archbishop put on Seán Ó Maoláin. I heard Ó Maoláin never did any good from that day on. The poor man lived only a short time. It was few processes he served after that.[69]

A story such as this did not stand alone. Like the priests who were protected by God's power made manifest against their enemies in Daniel Campbell's stories from Knock, MacHale is protected by a power greater than the law with its process-servers, Protestant or Catholic. This is just one more in a continuing list of stories of how God sustained the priest's power, and all the stories through which the priest was constructed as god's agent validated each other. This story recalled the sectarian oppression Catholics faced but by using the language of green plants withering, a recognised metaphor for the reversal of Protestant domination,[70] like the House of Commons tale discussed above, this one shows how God was on the side of the Catholics. In both, MacHale was the instrument through which God protected his people.

The phrase I have translated as 'the luck of the fern' is sufficiently ambiguous to enable the listener to believe that MacHale, while acting appropriately for an archbishop, nevertheless could curse someone and his curse would be effective in bringing harm. In Irish the phrase is *rath na raithne (ort)*, which literally means 'the luck of the fern (or bracken) (on you)'. Conventionally, however, this was a way of wishing a person good luck, presumably on the analogical basis that ferns or bracken tended to proliferate. Idiomatically, wishing someone the luck of the fern was the equivalent of wishing that they would prosper like ferns. Indeed, one Irish–English dictionary translates the phrase as 'Long may [you] flourish!'[71] As used in this story about MacHale however, the phrase has another meaning that is understood by the audience although perhaps never actually stated by MacHale. Ferns or weeds generally tend to flourish, but any individual weed can be pulled out by the roots and have anything but a prosperous future. By labelling the bishop's comment a 'curse', the story's narrator puts the conventional idiomatic blessing in a new context in which the process-server was identified as a weed that would not prosper thereafter and the audience recognizes MacHale's comment as ironic. Moreover, while readers of the written tale can use the position of the inverted commas to separate MacHale comments from those of the narrator, a person who hears a spoken version has no such definite marker. The narrator and different hearers may understand different authors for the statement about weeds being green in the morning and dry by evening. In other words, the quote might well have been 'closed' a sentence earlier than it is in this written version, and then these words would be the narrator's, not MacHale's. Ambiguity about precisely where to 'close quotes' was a strategic resource, available to be deployed as found suitable to the occasion. By such linguistic means was MacHale constructed as a powerful advocate for the Catholic cause, even if that involved him using words that were not canonically appropriate for a bishop. The words themselves had power because MacHale spoke them. MacHale in putting a curse on Ó Maoláin even when he used the idiom of blessing, stands in sharp contrast to his contemporary bishop in Kildare and Leighlin, James Doyle, whose terrible curses were negated by the people's distribution of ashes.[72]

When an informant in 1943 told a folklore collector 'as I heard the stories about him, MacHale was a living saint', this was no mere figure of speech.[73] A recent historian has used the very same phrase to describe how MacHale was viewed in 1879.[74] Just as the folklore about Daniel O'Connell credits him with the sexual prowess of early Irish secular heroes,[75] stories about MacHale endow him with the virtues, powers and experiences of remembered Irish saints. We have already noted the extraordinary star that attended his birth and the belief that God selected him before he was born to be Archbishop of Tuam. In his youth, he displayed extraordinary ability in restoring his family and hundreds of others to the land from which they had been evicted. He created a holy well near his birthplace. However, it is in a long tale about MacHale's trials and tribulations in his efforts to become a priest that the saintliness attributed to him is most apparent.

According to the standard biographies, when the young John MacHale began his study for the priesthood, accompanied by an older brother he went on horseback across the country from his home in the western county of Mayo to Maynooth College, the national seminary in County Kildare, near Dublin on the east coast. Again, folklore tells a different story. In his youth, his family was evicted and thrown onto a barren hillside, recalling Saint Patrick. MacHale left his family and community in the north of Ireland (the county of *Béal da Lua* which is glossed as Belfast) and trekked alone and on foot until he came to a school in the wilderness[76] in the southern county of Waterford. After a year there, he met the landlord whose agent had evicted his family and the landlord took him to 'Howth College' (sic) — this name is given in English in the story told in Irish — in Dublin where he paid the young seminarian's fees until he became a priest. All this trekking constitutes the *turas*, the pilgrimage/circuit of the island often attributed to early saints. In the wilderness, MacHale endured forty days of near death from cholera.[77] His words themselves had special power as we saw in the story of Ó Maoláin. Finally, MacHale's saintly attributes include prophecy: it was recalled after the 1879 apparition that MacHale had foretold that something great would happen in Knock.[78]

While he had many of the qualities of saints, the people saw MacHale as very much one of them. He spoke their language both literally and metaphorically. At a time when Irish was often the badge of backwardness, he let it be known that he preferred to be addressed in Irish. A man from near his birthplace who wrote a poem praising him at the time of his episcopal golden jubilee in 1875, heard that MacHale agreed to listen to it only if it contained no word of English.[79] 'MacHale was the only prominent man in Irish life who kept faith with the Irish language between the demise of Young Ireland in 1848 and the emergence of the Gaelic League in 1893.'[80] At a time when priests only rarely preached[81] MacHale gave a fine sermon in Irish every Sunday at his Cathedral in Tuam.[82] It is probably no coincidence that all the MacHale stories in the National Folklore Collection holdings are in Irish.

MacHale also sang the songs of the people. One of his favourites was a mock elegy, a satiric prayer for the soul of a particularly rapacious land agent that he sang 'with great animation and spirit'.[83] Some of the words in English translation run as follows:

> Such wailing and loud lamentation
> We've ne'er heard in Erin before,
> For we've lost our best friend in creation
> The kind, tender-hearted Owen Cóir!
> 'The same as he was to the neighbours
> May Jesus be to him today!'[84]

MacHale came to embody the struggle of Catholics against Protestants: he was their protector against 'the wolves of prey who lay in wait against our holy faith'. Any Catholic weapon used in the arena came to be identified with him. Throughout much of Connaught in the middle and later decades of the century the Catholic catechism in use was popularly called 'MacHale's Catechism' although he did not write or perhaps even translate it. Recognising the need to counteract the work of Protestant evangelical societies, MacHale along with several other western bishops decided that an Irish-language catechism would be adopted and used as widely as possible. In the 1830s they commissioned a translation from the English language catechisms already in extensive use in other parts of the country and the translation was made, mainly from Donleavy's catechism, by a Fr Loftus of MacHale's diocese.[85] After the resultant bilingual catechism was published, it was universally referred to for decades as 'MacHale's Catechism' and had a powerful impact.[86] One scholar argued that because it was often the only formal instruction or education the poor of Connaught were likely to receive in Irish, its memorisation 'united Catholics in the understanding of and loyalty to the inherited faith' and 'coloured the local sphere of catechetics with political and nationalistic overtones'. So profound was its influence that 'its Tridentine phrases, sanctioned by tradition as well as institution, resonate[d] in the consciousness',[87] with phrases from the catechism finding their way into popular songs. So completely was the catechism identified with MacHale that it is only recently that scholars realised that he neither wrote nor perhaps even translated it, they had not questioned the pervasive popular references to it as 'MacHale's'. Daniel Campbell was one of the many who unhesitatingly believed MacHale had his own catechism.[88] When Douglas Hyde was collecting the vernacular prayers and poems of the Connacht poor around the turn of the twentieth century, he encountered some suspicion in Mayo, no doubt in part due to the fact that he was the son of a Church of Ireland clergyman. He was able to establish his good faith, in several senses, by answering by rote questions from 'MacHale's Catechism' that the sceptics put to him.[89]

As we have already seen, the figure of MacHale looms large in Daniel Campbell's memoir, the only insider's account we have about pre-famine Knock. From his confirmation by MacHale, to MacHale's catechism, to the archbishop's role in election campaigns and his overthrow of the Brownes, to his involvement in the Blessed Straws episode, even after Campbell's three decades in England MacHale permeates his consciousness like nobody else.

In all their stories MacHale triumphs over the enemies of the people but he does not emerge victorious in every confrontation. Significantly, however, only true Gaels could get the better of him. One story tells how MacHale examines an old man on the catechism when he visits a parish to administer confirmation. Finding the man very ignorant about the faith, MacHale publicly criticises the parish priest for not getting him properly prepared for the sacrament. When in response the priest says the man has only very recently moved to the parish, MacHale asks if that were so and where he had come from. It was true, said the old man, and he had come from Tuam town, MacHale's own parish.[90] The most famous wise woman/fairy healer in the whole country, Biddy Early, also got the better of a bishop who is not named but from the details included the story implied that it could only have been MacHale. Significantly, this story was collected in MacHale's diocese rather than in Biddy's home areas.[91]

Finally, the MacHale image is explicitly used as a benchmark against which to measure other ecclesiastics. The only story in the archives of the National Folklore Collection about John MacEvilly, MacHale's successor as Archbishop of Tuam, is prefaced by the narrator's comment that the people had 'no regard at all for MacEvilly like they had for MacHale'. The story itself was that MacEvilly owned a house that he had rented to one of his own relatives who then failed to pay the rent. Ultimately, the archbishop sought to regain possession of the property. When MacEvilly approached the house to evict him, the tenant threw a stone that passed through the carriage and the archbishop retreated, leaving the tenant in occupation. Here, MacEvilly is cast in the role of everything that MacHale was not. He has violated the expectations of family loyalty in seeking to evict his own relative. As an evicting landlord, MacEvilly personifies evil in the ideological world of rack-rents, famine clearances and evictions. In addition, MacEvilly is a loser. He failed even in his attempted eviction: he lacked the courage and steadfastness that was characteristic of MacHale. Finally, the story says that the stone the tenant threw passed through the archbishop's carriage suggesting that it entered through the open window on one side and exited through the opposite window. At this point, MacEvilly retreated. Why is this detail important? The answer is left to the imagination of the hearer but both interpretations that were available and plausible to the listeners cast MacEvilly in a negative light. He was either superstitious in a decidedly non-episcopal way, or, much more likely, the stone's path indicated divine intervention against the eviction. Heaven was criticising the archbishop, and he knew it. The successive tellers of the story found the detail significant enough to be remembered and related because it corroborated these options to an audience that already assumed them. The stone's trajectory was not irrelevant and neither was it to be explained by the laws of physics and probability.[92] In the 1930s a local historian in Mayo was scathing in his judgments on MacEvilly.[93] In contrast to these, however, MacEvilly was remembered fondly by at least some people in his other diocese of Galway, where he was bishop before he succeeded MacHale as Archbishop of Tuam. In Galway, he was not found wanting as inevitably he was when measured against the incomparable MacHale.[94]

The stories about MacHale were told and remembered by people who did not spell out everything they believed. What the narrators take for granted or leave unsaid is important evidence for us. What we might call 'unstated statements' are implied in all the tales. We are not told what MacHale wrote in the letter that he addressed to the priests at the station mass, but we do not need to know his words to know his meaning and the meaning of the story for the later tellers. The idiomatic blessing that MacHale directed at the process-server Ó Maoláin is transmuted into a curse. The same story, which I deliberately translated as literally as possible, by its mantra-like repetition of the word 'Protestant' — six times in seven short opening sentences — evokes a sense of the ubiquity of sectarian battle in which MacHale led his forces. In the House of Commons story, the narrator says MacHale made his case and nobody dared speak against him, but does not say that MacHale went to London to testify before a committee investigating charges that he and other clerics had unduly influenced a recent election. Also left unsaid (and unremembered) is the official result of the hearing — the candidate MacHale favoured was unseated. Instead the story constructs him as triumphant over the forces of evil embodied in the government, parliament, the law, and the Protestant bishop. Very probably, unstated in this story, there is some implied limit on MacHale's power. For example, there could have been a view that he had the power of life and death only when he used it for the benefit of his whole people, not particular individuals. The folklore collector would not record such a belief precisely because it would be another of the 'unstated statements' that permeate the folklore. Finally, the Blessed Straws story that Daniel Campbell recounted tells us that MacHale was reported to be 'coming down the road with his carriage full of straw' in Knock. Campbell tells us that he did not know how the episode started and mentions no instigator. However, precisely because no cause was made explicit and MacHale was in fact mentioned by the man who brought the straw to Campbell's father, listeners fill in the unstated statement, that MacHale had started the chain-prayer and moreover had a carriage full of straw yet to be distributed.

6

Population and Religious Continuity

There are two reasons to focus attention on Knock's demographic history during the Great Famine of the 1840s. First, the parish had an unusually low population loss, an important contributory factor to the traditionalism of the area at the time of the apparition a generation later. Secondly, different explanations of this positive outcome highlight contrasts between outsider and insider accounts, on the one hand, and between 'rational' explanations based on wider scientific 'laws' and 'humanistic' interpretive understanding of the unique case on the other.

The boundary line between the baronies of Costello and Clanmorris divides the parish of Knock into two parts. The 1879 heavenly visitors appeared in the larger part, in Costello barony. Census figures for the parish as a whole and its two unequal sections tell an important story, because they show that where the apparition occurred was comparatively mildly affected by the Great Famine of the 1840s, something very unusual in the west of Ireland.

TABLE 6.1
POPULATION OF KNOCK PARISH

	1841	1851	1861	1871	1881
Barony of Costello, Parish of Knock (part)	2,755	2,671	2,755	2,732	2,738
Barony of Clanmorris, Parish of Knock (part)	619	500	516	510	503

Source: Census of Ireland 1881

The Costello part of Knock parish saw about a 3 per cent population decline between 1841 and 1851, but by 1861 it held as many people as it did in 1841, and was fairly stable thereafter until after the apparition. The Clanmorris part of the parish lost 19 per cent between 1841 and 1851 and never again approached its pre-famine population. In other words, the area where the 1879 apparition occurred had relative population stability since before the Great Famine. How rare this was becomes obvious when we consider that Mayo was the county most affected by the population decline caused by the famine. Within that whole devastated county, only one rural parish had a population increase (2 per cent) in those years, two other parishes had small decreases (–2 per cent) and Knock parish (at –6 per cent) had the next smallest decrease. As we have seen, this 6 per cent decline was the result of a 19 per cent decrease in the smaller part of the parish, and a modest 3 per cent drop in the larger part. All other rural parishes in the county had declines ranging from 15 to 60 per cent, with the four parishes that adjoined Knock losing between 15 and 21 per cent of their populations.[1]

There is no immediately obvious reason why Knock had such a favourable outcome compared to other nearby parishes. Indeed, there were good reasons to expect the opposite. Writing in June 1846 in the early stages of the famine, the Chairman of the Swinford Union Board of Guardians, G. V. Jackson, named Knock as one of the two most vulnerable in a district comprising nineteen parishes in the Gallen and Costello baronies. 'The population of the parishes of Toomore and Knock must perish ... if employment be longer delayed'.[2] Precisely because of its implicit comparison of Knock with other parishes, we should accord more significance to this statement from a man who had no reason to be less than truthful than we should to descriptions of any one parish.

Three explanations have been suggested for why famine population decline was modest in Knock. Two of these are by outsiders concerned to explain 'what actually happened': first, exceptional landlord behaviour; and, second, in-migration during the famine. The third explanation, supernatural protection from famine fever, is an insider one concerned not just with empirical evidence of what did or did not happen, but also especially with why Knock had the fortunate outcome it did. The two 'external' explanations are not necessarily mutually exclusive but we lack definitive evidence to decide which was the more accurate or indeed if either of them was the key. Moreover, the relationship between the 'outsider' and 'insider' explanations is complex.

The claim that the landlord of the area was unusually benevolent has long been made and there is considerable evidence to support it. The credit is given to Charles Strickland, agent for the absentee landlord Lord Dillon. Strickland was heavily involved in relief work, being chairman of relief committees in both Ballaghaderreen town and the barony of Costello, as well as serving on the Gallen barony committee.[3] His energetic and selfless work in relief was widely recognised at the time. There is some evidence that the most important agency, the Friends Relief Committee, knowing of his concern and tireless energy, sent more than usual supplies for him to distribute.[4] The passing of resolutions of thanks to various public officials was almost ritualistic at the time so we must be careful not to read too much into what might well have been empty gestures. But when two such resolutions were voted for Strickland they contained unusually specific details of what he had done. The Swinford Board of Guardians on 13 October 1846 formally thanked him for not alone his indefatigable zeal and his valuable assistance in carrying into effect the object of the committee, but for his very great and laudable exertions in being the means of procuring a large quantity of the provision for the poor in this, the barony of Costello.[5]

At a meeting on 4 December 1846 the Ballyhaunis Relief Committee also thanked him for 'his invaluable services during the past trying season; and also for his having taken upon himself the whole expense attending the sale of Meal at reduced prices, and having returned several Loans without any deduction whatever'.[6] In July 1847 the *Tyrawly Herald* newspaper selected Strickland as one of only two agents in all of County Mayo for recommendation as 'examples worthy the noblest to imitate' in their relief efforts and recognised that 'hundreds of lives must have been preserved by them, while the condition of thousands had been preserved from the fearful pinchings of starvation'.[7] In July 1849 Strickland wrote to officials administering the Quaker Relief efforts, 'I have not thrown down a house or turned out a tenant from Lord Dillon's estate in all these distressed years. A few have given up their land but are left in their houses.'[8] When a priest attacked him during the famine, for political reasons, the Catholic clergy of Knock and Aghamore came to Strickland's defence in the newspapers. 'They bluntly said he was a good man who had done all he could to assist the local relief committees and to protect the people.'[9]

Later observers too acknowledged Strickland's efforts. Newspaperman, Henry Coulter, writing in the early 1860s on his travels in the west of Ireland, had high praise. According to him, the population of the Dillon estate fell 'only six or seven hundred' from an 1841 figure of nearly 33,000, approximately a 2 per cent decline, while neighbouring estates were 'almost depopulated' in the famine decade.[10] Coulter says that Strickland gave considerable abatements of rents during the famine years and that he provided food at a cheap rate so as to bring it even to the poorest of the tenants.[11] During the Land War in 1880, *The Times* of London sent Finlay Dun as a correspondent to report on land issues in Ireland. Dun organised his dispatches by devoting each one to a particular landlord and his estate and, as luck would have it, one of the landlords he wrote about was Lord Dillon.[12] Dun was critical of most landlords but was full of praise for Dillon and especially for Strickland. From before the famine until the time of writing, the estate was managed by the 'improving' landlord and agent. 'During the famine years of 1847, 1848 and 1849,' noted Dun,

> Thirteen stores were opened on various parts of the estate, and provisions sold at prime cost; the needy were freely helped. In favourable contrast to many other Irish estates there was consequently no serious destitution, no decimating famine fever, no great exodus of the survivors.[13]

As late as the 1970s there was a recollection in the Knock area of the landlord sending food during the crisis, though this tradition also claimed that there was less need for food because the potato crop was less severely affected there than elsewhere.[14] However, even while admitting their efforts, crediting either Strickland or Dillon for the good result cannot be the final answer since it begs the question of why and how they might have helped the Knock area specifically, given that famine mortality was high elsewhere on Dillon's extensive estate.

A possibly complementary explanation is provided by historian Donald Jordan. Building on Cousens' arguments and estimates of famine mortality, Jordan suggests that the east Mayo parishes with low famine population declines, such as Knock, might have experienced in-migration of people who had been evicted from their holdings in the more commercialised area of central Mayo with better land, and these people would have colonised marginal wastelands.[15] In the general case this explanation could be combined with 'the improving landlord/concerned agent' one, because Finley Dun noted that on the Dillon estate in the 1848–50 period much work was done on lowering riverbeds and improving drainage, which would have made more land available for cultivation.[16]

Rather than citing authorities, we can approach Knock's population history in the famine decade by examining the census figures there, in an effort to detect any patterns that might account for the comparative stability. Most of Knock parish, the section in Costello barony, was part of the Swinford Poor Law Union, an administrative district that contained all or the greater part of twelve parishes. Census figures in 1841 and 1851 for these dozen parishes show two very distinct patterns of population decline. Eight parishes had declines ranging from nearly one-fifth to over one-third: Achonry (−18.5 per cent), Aghamore (−20.6 per cent), Bohola (−32.4 per cent), Killasser (−30.3 per cent), Killeadan (−19.6 per cent), Kilmacteige (−36.7 per cent), Meelick (−31.2 per cent) and Toomore (−33.3 per cent). In clear contrast, four parishes (including Knock), had much lower declines or, in one case, a tiny increase. Both Kilbeagh and Kilconduff had 2.3 per cent declines, Kilmovee was essentially unchanged, and Knock had a decrease of 3.0 per cent.

Different reasons seem largely to account for each of these four parishes' divergence from the general pattern of high population loss in the region and throughout the whole county. In the case of Kilconduff, the stability of the aggregate census numbers is misleading because of the Swinford Workhouse. Not in existence in 1841, it contained 942 persons in 1851 largely counterbalancing heavy population loss in the non-inmate population of the parish. Kilbeagh too had a new centre of population in 1851; the settlement then known as Newtown Dillon and later called Charlestown had 119 inhabitants. Without the people in the new town the parish would have seen a decadal decline of 9.3 per cent.

As Jordan suggested, in-migration is a possible contributing factor in a few places but that explanation raises questions about why migration occurred into these, rather than other areas. In the parish of Kilmovee, several townlands saw significant increases in the number of houses, the best but by no means perfect indicator of in-migration in the published census returns. Cloonieran added ten houses to the thirty-four there in 1841, Glentavraun grew from fifty-four to sixty houses, Shammerdoo went from ten to fifteen while Uggool added seven to its thirty-three and Urlaur added eight to its seventy-two. At the same time, the village of Kilkelly increased from twenty-nine to thirty-nine houses. Overall, the number of houses in the parish increased from 1,062 to 1,092 in the decade, a major key to the relatively stable population numbers.

The factors that account for the stable census figures in these three parishes do not, however, apply in Knock. There was no new workhouse or settlement in the parish to boost the population recorded in 1851. An examination of population change at the townland level doesn't support the claim of in-migration. The townland of Cloondace did increase significantly, growing from sixty-nine people in thirteen houses to 126 in twenty-four houses and Cloontarriff grew from forty-five in eight houses to eighty-two in twelve. Two other townlands (Derrada and Rooskey) each went from fifteen to eighteen houses. Overall, however, the relevant part of the parish (the part in Swinford Union because it was in Costello Barony), saw a decrease in houses from 500 to 488. Had there been extensive parish-wide in-migration, we would expect to see a different pattern. Moreover, it is unlikely that Knock would have escaped the famine fevers, an escape which so impressed Daniel Campbell who lived in Knock through much of the famine. It is also likely that some, if not most, of the new dwellings in a few townlands were occupied by people who moved within the parish. That also probably happened in those other townlands and parishes that increased their number of houses. Presumably the majority of the inmates counted in Swinford Workhouse in 1851 had moved there from parishes in the Union. Where did the inhabitants of Newtown Dillon come from? Even in parishes with precipitate population declines we find a few individual townlands that grew. Knockfadda in Killasser parish for example increased from thirteen people in two houses in 1841 to 112 in nineteen houses ten years later, even though the parish declined by 30.3 per cent. In the case of Knock, there is not much evidence of any migration of the kind that is suggested by the data for Kilmovee parish. The available census data do not permit researchers to establish the contribution of migration, either within or between townlands and parishes, to changes in the aggregate population figures in the decade of the famine.

The census evidence presented above as well as the various claims about the actions of the landlord's agent all betray the researchers' usual positivism and concern to uncover 'what really happened', a bias shared by twentieth-century historians such as Jordan, and nineteenth-century reporters such as Coulter and Dun. However, even when they are accurate on their own terms, such 'outsider' explanations necessarily fail to comprehend the meanings insiders might attach to situations. This is not because these researchers were outsiders — Jordan was American and the two reporters British — but because they did not approach their questions with the insider's cultural framework. Even the very questions they asked might not have occurred to insiders who predictably had their own different hierarchies of relevant issues, values and concerns.

Considering that he lived through much of the Great Famine in Knock, we might well have expected Daniel Campbell to have something to say about it. But famine features in his memoir only as the occasion for the miraculous deliverance of Knock. He alludes to hunger only once and then indirectly. Describing how the priest usually shared his breakfast after mass with the poor woman Mary Morris, Campbell remarks that 'we often grudged (sic) her' the food. The concept of a single episode bounded in time that can be called 'The Great Hunger' is not to be found in Campbell. In this, understandably, he is more similar to folk accounts than to positivist views of 'what really happened' that underlie nationalist constructions that became politically important later, as well as more recent academic accounts of the period. As has been pointed out, the term *Gorta Mór* is rarely used in Irish-language recollections and is likely a translation from the English 'Great Famine'. Rather, the common Irish term was *An Drochshaol*, the bad life, a term that could refer to other occasions of hunger or death in other periods or to other times when life was bad.[17] Likewise, the terminology used in the folklore shows that the years of the famine from the mid-1840s to the early 1850s were not experienced or recalled as one undifferentiated stretch of time, as is implied by giving it one label with unique connotation as well as denotation. For example, particular years and seasons were named and recalled differently in different areas. Historian Niall Ó Ciosáin has compiled several examples: 1846 was called *Bliain na Spéire*, the Year of the Sky, in south Galway; in Kerry, the summer of that same year was *Bliain na Tuile* (Year of the Flood); in Clare, the winter of 1846 was *Bliain an Board of Works*.[18]

Campbell used no term at all but rather relates what Knock parish was saved from: 'plague and pestilence', a term that potentially encompasses not only hunger-related famine fevers from any period but also episodes such as the 1832 cholera epidemic. At some earlier time, Campbell recounts, a 'holy pilgrim' had prophesied that 'no plague or pestilence' would come on Knock and this prophecy was fulfilled at a time when 'hundreds were dying all around'. Given that on the evidence of his memoir, Campbell had no concept of 'The Great Hunger' perhaps it is less surprising that we read in vain to get some inkling of his explanation of the death and destruction all around. Did he blame the government, or an angry God, or the fairies? (The first, voiced by Archbishop MacHale, (among others), was to become part of nationalist ideology; the second and third are found in local folk explanations where they had not been affected by later nationalist claims.) Campbell just does not say. And his silence is characteristic of much of the famine memories recorded by folklorists.[19] Like most famine folklore, Campbell's account is determinedly local in focus and concern. Knock was his world and at the risk of exaggeration we could say that everything outside Knock was alien to him.[20] Only in passing does Campbell even mention the main landlord in his area, Lord Dillon, whose extensive holdings in Mayo and Roscommon included all but a few townlands in the parish of Knock. (Campbell lived in Eden, one of these.) Neither does he mention Dillon's agent, Charles Strickland, whose actions contemporaries and later writers frequently credited for low mortality in the area. His focus on other big Mayo landlords, the Protestant and politically dominant Browne family, provided him with an appropriate foil for Archbishop MacHale's triumphs.

Characteristically, for Campbell a supernatural explanation was necessary, plausible and sufficient. In foregrounding *why* Knock was saved and minimising mere mechanisms of the process through which this was accomplished, Campbell's explanatory framework is incommensurate with the positivism of later writers. Moreover, to the limited extent that he gives credit to any human person, it is to the Knock man who embodied the local communal ethos by helping the pilgrim, rather than an outsider such as the landlord's agent. Campbell's view of things at base incorporates other worlds and his description unquestioningly accepts Catholicism as the truth. His narrative serves not as evidence of facts but as the expression of a worldview, and as such it is the very best evidence available on the fabric of religious life of Knock before and during what later generations constructed as 'The (unique) Great Hunger'.

While Campbell gives what we might call a supernatural explanation, he does not present the causal factor as something completely other than human or natural. Neither is the supernatural intervention arbitrary or capricious. Rather, the holy pilgrim who made the prophecy had prayed for that outcome in response to the charity shown to him in Knock where he had been offered a ride in a horse and cart. In other words, the individual's good deed in helping, in this case, someone from outside the community had its rewards in the protection of the whole community. Of course, at one level, this is an ideological statement of communal solidarity, but that cultural emphasis on solidarity was part and parcel of the localistic society based on a rundale land-use system and organised around extended kinship. Campbell's construction of Knock's good fortune, as supernatural recompense for the earlier charity of the man who helped the pilgrim, does not prevent him from filling in the mundane details of how the prophecy was fulfilled. Fever killed but 'one solitary case' in Knock while hundreds were dying in surrounding parishes. Campbell noted that this one victim was a woman, native to the parish, who had been living in Ballyhaunis and returned home to escape the diseases raging in that town but died within hours of her homecoming, presumably before she had infected others. One does not have to endorse Campbell's supernatural explanation to realise that escaping of famine fevers for whatever reason might well have been one key to Knock's relative population stability.[21] Given the absence of evidence for in-migration in Knock in contrast to the parish of Kilmovee, as well as Campbell's comments about

Knock's escaping the ravages of fevers, it is likely that the population was stable not just in numbers but also in the particular individuals who survived. Of course, positivists can feel free to give credit to Charles Strickland.

Whatever the causes, the documented population stability in Knock can be expected to have important effects. Pre-famine cultural patterns would persist there more strongly and for longer than was typical elsewhere. Even if Jordan's hunch is correct— that in-migration contributed to the stability of population size — we would expect above average levels of cultural continuity because the newcomers would be from the poorest strata left homeless elsewhere, people least affected by the devotional revolution and assorted related changes. This is not to deny that there were 'new' patterns — in fact, there were, as I show later — but a 'pre-famine religious' worldview was an important element in the system of cultural assumptions and beliefs that the seers brought with them to the events of 21 August 1879.

Earlier researchers, such as K. H. Connell,[22] argued that the famine generated cultural change by the shock it caused, especially (according to David Miller),[23] through the repeated failure of the staple potato crop which undermined the traditional popular faith in the earlier magic-infused folk Catholicism. I have earlier pointed out several significant problems with Miller's claim[24] and Ó Ciosáin very logically noted that if Miller's assumption — that when a particular religion fails to deal with catastrophe it is abandoned — were in fact the case, then

> No religion, perhaps no system of belief which purported to explain the natural world, would have lasted until the middle of the nineteenth century. Indeed, it could be argued that providing a satisfactory explanation of catastrophe is in fact one of the strengths of a religious or magical view of the world, as opposed to a scientific or material one.[25]

Thus, the fewness of fatalities in Knock might well have served to reinforce beliefs among the survivors that they were especially chosen by divine intervention. Well aware of their good fortune compared to surrounding parishes, the people of Knock might be expected to become more rather than less conservative in the area of religious belief and practice.

Before marshalling and reviewing the evidence available about religion in post-famine Knock up to the time of the apparition, it is necessary to consider the so-called 'devotional revolution' thesis which has dominated historical research on changes in Catholicism in nineteenth-century Ireland. However useful it is as a description of developments at a national level, the thesis is far too constraining if used to explain the particular circumstances of specific local areas such as Knock.

The Devotional Revolution Thesis

Emmet Larkin coined the term 'devotional revolution' in a 1972 article that quickly set the agenda for research. According to him there was a massive transformation in the practice of Catholicism in Ireland in the third quarter of the nineteenth century. From below 40 per cent in the 1830s,[26] Sunday mass attendance rates reached over 90 per cent and probably approached 95 per cent in the 1870s. This change was accompanied by the development of a plethora of new Rome-promoted and endorsed devotions and sodalities, and by a host of other changes. The practice of Catholicism moved from the home or outdoor sites like holy wells, to parish churches where mass and other ceremonies were celebrated with ever more elaborate ritual and ceremony. The parish churches themselves became ever more impressively ornate and set apart from the mundane business of everyday life. For example, the exposition of the Blessed Sacrament in the tabernacle on the altar, rare before the famine, became the norm in the following decades. In addition, priests were increasingly separated from other men by being required to wear distinctive clothing and being banned from other occupations or common pastimes in which earlier generations of priests had engaged. The whole process was facilitated by a great increase in the ratio of clergy to lay people, itself a product of both increasing numbers of clergy and a major decline in population caused by the Great Famine and the massive emigration of later decades. The revolution was brought about by an increasingly united body of bishops under the direction of Archbishop Cullen of Dublin, who gradually disciplined the lower clergy and these in turn, using methods such as parish missions, were progressively able to expand orthodox Catholic practice among ever more of the laity.[27]

Earlier critics have pointed to many problems with the thesis. In what Larkin acknowledged as a 'very persuasive article',[28] I argued that lay people were selective in what they accepted from the church teachings and therefore we have to pay attention to what they attended to and why. 'To understand the degree and nature of the success of preaching from the top, we have to understand the audience at the bottom.'[29] Land hunger among the tenant farmer class led them to adopt the stem family system, and this in turn made them receptive to those teachings that emphasised the unity of the family under one head; the different, complementary but ultimately subordinate role of women in the family and society; the rigid control of sexual expression; and other features of the stem system that became dominant in rural Ireland. These demographic and family changes themselves resulted from the growing commercialisation of Irish agriculture, a process that had begun long before the famine.

What Larkin highlighted as post-famine religious developments were found among the 'strong farmers' decades before the 1840s. When the famine decimated the cottier and labourer classes, these tenant farmers became the numerical majority and increasingly the culturally most powerful stratum in rural Ireland; they and their distinctive brand of Catholicism triumphed together. The discipline manifested in routine mass attendance was one aspect of a growing discipline in family life, in which individuals' aspirations were subordinated to the long-term capacity of the family farm to support those dependent on it, at an acceptable living standard. Later I argued that 'orthodoxy' itself was not unchanging but was being modified all through the period. For completely different reasons, in the mid-nineteenth century the Catholic ecclesiastical authorities in Rome were promoting congenial teachings such as the Doctrine of the Immaculate Conception, promulgated in 1854, and the claim to Papal Infallibility formally adopted in the First Vatican Council in 1870.

> For their own respective reasons, Irish farmers and the papal bureaucracy in Rome each had a vested interest, because of their positions and experiences in the world, in emphasising the authority of the head, the necessity of obedience, and the special asexual nature of the ideal woman. It was the coincidence of the felt needs of the Roman Catholic hierarchy and its most committed Irish members that made the audience especially receptive to official teachings that stressed obedience, familism, and the subordinate but special moral role of mothers as teachers.[30]

The tenant farmer class, however, ignored those teachings of the church that did not resonate with their own experiences or felt needs. Officially the Catholic Church supported early marriage but this was neither taught by the Irish clergy nor followed by the farmers. Fenianism and the Land War provide abundant evidence that the priests could lead the people only in the direction in which they wished to go. A hundred thousand people attended Parnell's funeral despite being forbidden to do so by their priests.[31] Many other examples could be adduced to refute any suggestion that the people were passive recipients of orthodox teaching.

In a widely cited article, Thomas McGrath also took issue with Larkin's timing of the revolution, though for very different reasons.[32] According to him, Larkin failed to recognise that what he uncovered in the third quarter of the nineteenth century was not new, but rather the tail end of a centuries long process through which generations of reforming bishops in Ireland had gradually and cumulatively extended the reach of ecclesiastical discipline and devotional practices that had been mandated by the Council of Trent in the sixteenth century. Building on the work of Sean Connolly, Donal Kerr and others, Nigel Yates argued that much of the internal reform and 'ultramontanisation' Larkin attributed to Cullen had begun in the late eighteenth century and was the achievement of earlier bishops.[33] In effect McGrath and other historians accept Larkin's assumptions about the appropriate standards and by extending his logic to a longer time-frame McGrath compounds Larkin's one-sided emphasis on top-down changes. But we need to question the underlying logic. What is relevant for ecclesiastical officials is not, per se, the only relevant evidence for historians. Why take Trent as the model? Of course, that question does not arise if one assumes that whatever Rome and the ecclesiastical authorities decide *is* the model. Thomas McGrath not only did not understand how Bishop Doyle, an ecclesiastic he wrote two books about, was seen by people who distributed ashes and straws to counter his terrible curses, he did not find any evidence whatever of the extraordinary episode where these poor lay people devised a way of protecting themselves from his episcopal anathemas.[34]

Questions about its timing and causes arise because of more fundamental problems with the conceptualisation of the revolution than have so far been articulated. Like the term 'modernisation' in theories of economic development so popular in the 1950s, in Larkin's usage the 'devotional revolution' is a change that is unilinear and unidirectional, a movement only from less to more modern where the modern is equated with the orthodox, ecclesiastically defined practice of Catholicism. The only possible future is a more 'modern' one whose features already exist in already more modernised areas. Like a train moving along its track, the only variable in the process is its speed; the track and the stations down the line are already in place and the direction is fixed so we need to learn only the power of the engine and the weight it has to haul to explain where it ends up and how long it takes to get there. Hence, in this framework, there is little exploration, not to mention appreciation, of the religious practices and behaviours of the people in the period before the so-called revolution. By taking orthodoxy as defined by the Council of Trent as the measuring rod, historians essentially take an ecclesiastical–pastoral perspective on local religion. Instead of depicting the reality of religious belief and practice as those involved lived it, in effect we get a picture of clerical dissatisfaction with that reality.

This orthodox focus is accentuated by an over-reliance on ecclesiastical sources, such as episcopal edicts or correspondence with Rome where, predictably, clerical perspectives predominate. The effect of this 'establishment perspective' plus the dependence on church archives for surviving evidence is that the earlier practices are defined as deficits. What we get as an artefact of this methodology is what we may call a 'deficit-model' of Catholicism. If before the 'revolution' the only relevant characteristics or features of local practice are its deficits (described in such terms as 'abuses', 'superstitions', 'pastoral failings', etc.), as compared to an officially defined orthodoxy, then the paradigm prejudges the causal mechanisms bringing about changes. It blinds researchers to a range of potentially important variables at the local level. Implicitly, change is conceived as progressive elimination of deficits and, of course, the agents of change then become those who target the identified deficits.[35] This is the unstated assumption at the heart of the devotional revolution thesis. Such an orientation diverts attention from both grassroots factors, such as conflict within families or between farmers and cottier/labourers, and more macro-level but non-ecclesiastical processes such as parliamentary actions or O'Connell's Catholic Emancipation and Repeal movements as potential important causal agents.

More recently Larkin has begun to look at the era before his revolution, but his focus bears out my contention. He devoted his 2005 article 'Before the Devotional Revolution' and a long chapter in his 2006 book largely to calculating the ratio of priests to lay Catholics in the country and changes in this ratio across time and space. In effect he sets out to establish the horse-power of what he sees as the locomotive of change. While he recognises that pre-famine society was *sui generis* he makes little effort to understand its religious life on its own terms. Rather, he documents the paucity of clerical personnel, seeing this as *the* reason why the ecclesiastical centre was unable to extend its discipline. The laity thereby are reduced to mere objects of an ecclesiastical campaign to move them down the line toward orthodoxy.[36] However, improved clergy/lay ratios are an insufficient cause or explanation of the changes that occurred in the way people practised their Catholicism. Moreover, without the continuing willingness of many sons and daughters of the strong farmer class to devote their lives to religion as priests, brothers and nuns, even the drastic fall in the numbers of the poor cottiers and labourers would not have improved the ratio. It is likely that calls to the religious life were heard more loudly when the alternative was life-long celibacy without the social status of priest, brother or nun. While reform of the ecclesiastical administrative machinery and personnel was extremely important, without changes in the wider society, it could not have occurred as it did.[37]

The changes that occurred were not inevitable and the process was not inexorable. Changes were not linked together like the carriages of a train. All roads did not necessarily lead to Rome.[38] At no time was the future of Catholic practice determined and fixed; at any point, things could have gone off in all kinds of directions, for any number of reasons. Both Larkin and McGrath proceed by implicitly or explicitly assuming that Tridentine standards are the relevant ones and largely rely on the evidence of ecclesiastics who assumed the same thing. Teleology is apparent in how they look at some later point in time and proceed to seek earlier seeds for the later existing patterns. A preoccupation with mass attendance rates is one result of this approach to history. David Miller in 1975 was the first to document and seek to explain the proportions of Irish Catholics who were officially (by the government) estimated to have attended mass on one given Sunday in 1834. Miller was right in his intuition that the differences in mass attendance rates pre- and post-famine required an understanding of the earlier period on its own terms. By pointing to the workings of a whole range of popular shared rituals, especially what he called customary magical practices linked to the cycles of the agricultural year, he moved decisively beyond reliance on an ecclesiastical-centred explanatory framework. He argued that the pre-famine customary magical practices became ineffective and were abandoned when the people lost faith in them after the staple potato crop failed repeatedly in the years of the Great Hunger.

While Miller's analysis of the popular magical practices left much to be desired, he was looking in the right direction. Rather than building on his work, however, too many critics have become overly concerned with the mass attendance rates.[39] Miller's documentation of a wide regional range of attendance rates on that one Sunday in 1834, and especially his establishment of low rates (perhaps 20 per cent) in many areas led to suggestions that he ignored the fact that lots of people (including the very young, the sick, nursing mothers and others), were canonically excused from attendance at mass. These criticisms miss the mark for two reasons. First, there is little reason to suspect that different rates of illness, nursing women, numbers of children, etc, account for his well documented systematic differences in mass attendance between regions.[40] Second, and more fundamentally, like Larkin the critics assume without question what has to be demonstrated: that mass attendance was *the* measure of Catholic identity and practice. The available evidence suggests this was not at all the case. Arguing that early nineteenth-century bishops did not appear to be very upset about low mass attendance rates, one early critic of Larkin and Miller suggested their evidence documenting the low rates must be wrong.[41] In response, I pointed out that the apparent contradiction could be resolved if we assumed that mass attendance was less important in the pre-famine era, even in the eyes of the clergy, than it was to become later.[42] Later research has indeed shown this to be the case.

We now know that priests and bishops in the pre-famine era usually took making one's Easter duty, rather than regular Sunday mass attendance, as the touchstone of orthodox Catholic practice. Kerr documents many instances of this and even Larkin has come to recognise this reality.[43] Keenan had already made the same point but it was overlooked in the field of research dominated by Larkin's thesis.[44] According to his biographer in 1882, Archbishop MacHale said daily mass only for about the last sixteen of his over sixty years in the priesthood, and before that, three times weekly, when 'daily Mass had not been so much the custom [for priests] in Ireland, as it is at present'.[45] Lest this evidence be discounted on the grounds that MacHale was a laggard when it came to modernisation, we note that James Warren Doyle of Kildare and Leighlin, by many accounts the most energetic and committed reforming bishop, celebrated mass 'sometimes daily, always two or three times a week'.[46] Castlebar, the biggest town in Mayo, had three priests in 1834 who provided masses on Sundays and on only three weekdays.[47] The most reasonable explanation is that none of these priests said mass on the other weekdays. In other words, the cultural, social and even pastoral significance of the mass, even for priests and bishops, changed over time.

What was true for the clergy was even more the case for lay people. When we look at the meaning of Sunday mass attendance from the inside rather than from the perspective of ecclesiastical orthodoxy, we see much greater diversity than the binary categories of attendance and non-attendance would suggest. In discussions of converts, mass attendance was one but not the most important factor in being acknowledged as a Catholic in Mayo around 1830.[48] We need only think of 1930s' Spain or 1980s' Poland to make the obvious point that attending mass means different things in different contexts. Catholic politicians found it useful to be seen at mass whether in 1930s' Roscommon or among the New York Irish in the 1880s. When the Tuam rock band, the Saw Doctors, sang in the 1990s of going to mass to watch a particular woman walk to and from communion, they were following in a long tradition.[49] But going to mass had other meanings that changed over time. An early nineteenth-century observer noted in Sligo that a young woman first attended mass as a signal that her parents were interested in receiving marriage proposals.[50] What would 1950s' Children of Mary say? For the 1936–37 Schools Folklore Project, a pupil in a Knock school wrote what an old woman neighbour told her about marriages 'long ago', including the established practice of newly married couples positively *not* going to mass the first Sunday after the wedding but attending the following Sunday.[51]

And even 'attendance' itself is not unambiguous. In pre-famine Cork city, a German visitor described people too poor to pay the fee required at the chapel door but who congregated outside and felt they had attended mass when they had heard the bell.[52] In his autobiography, the writer Aidan Higgins described his parents' involvement in mass in 1930s' Kildare. His mother often took flowers from her own garden to decorate the altar. 'It was her way of attending Mass, *in absentia*, on Saturday when nobody was about.' In contrast, says Higgins,

> Dado preferred to arrive late and take his place halfway up the choir-loft stairs with the other malingerers . . . The priest's mumbled Latin was virtually inaudible and the sermon listened to with half an ear . . .
> Thus Dado was both attending and not attending, half present and half absent, both damned and saved.

Going to mass, said Higgins, was a way his father got up an appetite for lunch.[53] The meaning of going to mass is not obvious and if researchers or contemporaries equate 'attendance' with 'devotion' they do so at their peril, because those involved did not equate them.[54] Moreover, charting change over time becomes even more problematic because the connection itself between attendance and devotion underwent change. Using mass attendance rates to gauge devotional change is to measure with an elastic yardstick.

Irish Catholicism never had a fixed future but the same teleological logic that underlies the preoccupation with mass attendance also informs Larkin's own explanation of his revolution. In Irish the use of the terms *Gael* and *Gall* (Irish and foreigner) as synonyms for Catholic and Protestant was long established; this binary was used in pre-famine Knock to construct locals who became Protestants, as not members of the community.[55] Larkin argued that the new orthodox practice of Catholicism gave the Irish a distinct identity that they were in danger of losing with the decline of the Irish language and culture over the preceding centuries. He quotes the Dominican preacher Fr Tom Burke who said in 1872, 'Take an average Irishman — I don't care where you find him — and you will find the very first principle in his mind is I am not an Englishman because I am a catholic.' It would perhaps be unfair to criticise Larkin for his 1972 view were it not for the fact that he has reiterated the same argument much more recently.[56] Even if we grant the coherence of such an idea as an identity crisis, this explanation could account, though only after the fact, for any possible set of religious practices that the Irish might have adopted with the single exception of those practices the Irish believed to be British. It would explain which beliefs and behaviours Irish people would not accept, not the ones they might, and certainly not the ones they did.[57]

A Redemptorist priest who ministered in Britain recounted that 'a priest in Liverpool showed me an entire street in which the Irish lived and where they are too lazy to go to church. And at the same time they believe and maintain that they are the best Catholics in the world. With them, being Irish and Catholic are identical as is English and protestant.'[58] That was right at mid-nineteenth century. Among the Irish of New York City half a century later, 'many of those [Irish] who were in the Church's eyes "bad Catholics" continued to be in their own eyes loyal Catholics, to practice their religion in their own way and to pass it on to their children'.[59] Irish people, even when they spoke English as their vernacular, could have retained an identity as other than British while their Catholicism was anything but canonically orthodox. Even if Fr Burke and the Liverpool priest were both correct and accurate, as well they could be in reporting what they themselves had experienced, it would not explain why the Irish practised Catholicism in the way that they did.

Researchers who have probed the connection more recently between Catholic practice and identity in Ireland have documented a wide range of possibilities. In Dublin, one interviewee said he was Catholic and hoped to remain so but added 'I don't believe in Jesus Christ or anything like that.'[60] In Northern Ireland, a young professional told an interviewer that 'I'm a Catholic, but I don't believe in all that stuff.' She did not believe in God or attend mass but wanted her children to play Gaelic games and learn Irish. She was representative of one of the four types of linkage between identity and practice that the researcher documented in a very small sample of people, only half of whom were 'Catholic'.[61]

Their deficit-model of popular Catholicism blinds researchers to evidence of other features of the earlier period's religious field. For one example, they are likely to overlook the coherence of the system of devotional pilgrimages around local sacred sites such as holy wells.[62] Daniel Gallogly, historian of the Ulster diocese of Kilmore, could write about the Stations of the Cross as primarily a post-famine devotion only by ignoring contrary evidence both in English from lay insiders such as Ulsterman, William Carleton, and in Irish in the form of Archbishop MacHale's comments, circulating manuscript copies of the devotion such as the one printed by Ó Cuív and a Monaghan-published book in Irish containing the devotion that went through at least three editions before 1835.[63] Gallogly did not see the significance of evidence he himself presented.[64] Rafferty and Fenning note that Larkin similarly wrongly saw the rosary as 'new'.[65] When this process is repeated for other devotions the result is that a large number of practices are wrongly seen as new and together they are seen as constituting a coherent syndrome. But if we want to understand the religious life of some people we have to put *them* centre-stage, not how outsiders described them or what ecclesiastical critics focused their negative attention upon. Taking Trent as the measuring rod begs the key questions. Because researchers use establishment terms such as 'superstitions,' 'abuses' and 'pastoral failings' or ecclesiastically relevant distinctions such as mass attendance/non-attendance, their terms — as well as their perspectives and sources — lead them to downplay continuities between the 'old' and the 'new' devotionalism.[66]

If we keep alert for continuity rather than novelty, however, we see that the tenant farmer class was 'practising' long before the famine, providing the church with most of its economic support, its clergy and its most committed members. Much of the basic infrastructure of church buildings was in place before the famine.[67] Convinced by Keenan's evidence, Connolly has revised his earlier view.[68] Many 'new' Roman devotions were already widely followed.[69] Even in terms of worldview there was continuity between old and new. The new devout, churchgoing, orthodox Catholic was already familiar with a supernatural world, whose members could be asked for help and protection and whose intervention in the form of miracles or graces granted was expected and common. The 'new' devotions such as praying for the souls in purgatory or adoring the Blessed Sacrament were in important ways like the 'old' devotions: belief in fairies, local saints' cults, and pilgrimages to holy wells. Both presupposed a 'nearness of the other world' and provided for a close relationship with supernatural beings and a means for interacting with them.[70]

The term 'devotional revolution' implies both the development of a level of devotionalism hitherto lacking,[71] and uniformity in what came to be (in that it approached the orthodox model of practice which is treated ahistorically as fixed, stable and universal). Rather than accept without question the teleology, novelty and uniformity implied by the term, researchers need to question all three. We need in all cases to demand contextual specificity: exactly what features of an assumed coherent syndrome are at stake? Rather than assume that any given devotional practice can be neatly pigeon-holed as either pre- or post-revolution, we need to chart the genealogy of each component of the devotional life extant at any place and period. The search for that chronology is likely to push ever deeper into the past.[72] Rather than assume uniformity, we must be alert for multiplicity in devotional forms. The Italian Marxist theorist, Antonio Gramsci, famously pointed out that there was no one Catholicism and Kerby Miller has recognised the same thing in pre-famine Ireland where, he wrote, Catholicism was 'an unstable mixture of elements, still in the process of coalescence: rural and urban, peasant and bourgeois, and Gaelic and Anglicized outlooks competed for legitimacy'.[73] We must disaggregate the seemingly homogenous and homogenising macro-process of religious change into a variety of disparate processes, moving at different speeds across time and space, with their effects perhaps appearing intermittently as often as linearly. We must allow for a variety of origins and antecedents of what might later appear to be uniformity or similarity, and recognise diverse trajectories from the pasts to the time and place we are investigating.

Researchers too often identify religion as an established institution, neatly identifiable as a church or churches. With such a narrow definition, we pay attention only to official evidence such as frequency of church attendance, institutionally recognised devotional practices, sacraments, etc. We need a broader, more flexible working understanding of religion as a cultural resource and not just an organisation. We need to recognise that symbols can be mobilised in unexpected and uncontrollable ways, often in tension with 'establishment' practices. We need to let our subjects speak for themselves as much as possible so their voices are neither drowned out nor constrained to answer only our questions which may be of minor significance to them. We should be open to the possibility of greater variation from individual to individual than we might assume from the fact that they all self-identify as members of a supposedly monolithic 'Catholic' church. We should approach individual religiosity as eclectic, more of a bricolage constructed from a wide range of culturally available options than would be the case if people merely internalised the teachings of a canonical catechism, the full catechism, and nothing but the catechism. Symbols, language rituals and practices may be used for reasons other than what an institution intended.[74]

It may well turn out in the long term that Larkin's thesis has been so influential in recent decades not only because of what it tells us about the nineteenth century but because, in 1972, it so shockingly confronted the conventional wisdom that saw Irish Catholics as loyal to their faith 'through dungeon fire and sword' in the Penal Law era and risking death to protect their fugitive priests. The evidence that lots of Irish Catholics chose not to go to mass when they were free to do so in the nineteenth century, long after the Penal era, challenged that received understanding. Still operating under the influence of the inherited mind-set, some researchers have sought to advance arguments explaining why so many Irish Catholics *could not*, rather than would not or did not attend mass. Was it due to a shortage of adequate buildings? Miller showed that the existing ones were not fully used, and Larkin has recently come to agree. That the poor lacked adequate clothing to attend mass without shame? As Connolly recognised, 'embarrassments of this kind could of their nature affect only a minority conspicuously more impoverished than their neighbours'. Too few priests? But it was Rome at the behest of Irish bishops that drastically reduced the numbers of friars in Ireland. Priests were restricted to saying one public mass? This was not generally the case, but even if it was (in some places or times), why was it so? Surely, if the institutional church put the mass at the heart of the pastoral responsibilities of priests it could change any laws restricting them to saying only one Sunday mass in public. The evidence has piled up that the Sunday mass obligation was simply being widely ignored.[75] Especially when used to help understand developments in particular local places such as Knock, 'devotional revolution' as a catchy label lumps together disparate elements. Because it imposes a simple unidirectional process of change, it is simplistic as description and empty as explanation. (In this regard, Larkin is not to be blamed for the sins of his too enthusiastic but uncritical acolytes; see the discussion of church choirs in chapter 7, note 85.)

7

Religion in
Pre-Apparition Knock

Significant features in Knock's religious and social life before 1849 were still prominent at the time of the 1879 apparition. Stability in the size of the population and likely also in the actual persons who survived the 1840s famine in Knock would lead us to suspect cultural continuity but it by no means guarantees it. Moreover, it is plausible that the survivors in Knock would have their faith in their 'old' beliefs strengthened precisely because they were very aware just how fortunate they had been compared to the neighbouring parishes. If Daniel Campbell, after over thirty years in England, could 'never forget' how Knock had been preserved, it is probable that the local people in Knock, embedded in their ongoing community of interpretation, would have their faith in miraculous deliverance even more powerfully reinforced.

Ideally, evidence to support or challenge this claim of continuity would be drawn from insiders' accounts like Campbell's but from the later period. In the absence of such sources, I have relied on a variety of other kinds of evidence, which, fortunately, are available. In 1986 a book-length edited 'portrait' of the immediately adjacent parish of Bekan was published;[1] its contributors were largely local people, many of whom drew not only on original written source materials in archives or official publications over the centuries, but also on local memories passed on orally. Especially informative are the stories and memories provided by Michael Higgins. His age is not given but his photograph shows an elderly man and we are told that Higgins was a driver for the parish priest in the 1920s; thus he was probably born in, if not before, the first decade of the twentieth century. Higgins identified 'the time I am talking about [as] from after the Famine to about 1920'.[2]

Bekan and Knock parishes shared a long border without any geographical or other barrier to easy communication and cultural contact between them. Both were rural and overwhelmingly Catholic. In both the land was boggy and poor while the tenant farms were very small. The principal landlord in both was Lord Dillon.[3] In Bekan, as in Knock, temporary migration of young men to England was an important means of earning the rent, though the migration might sometimes be a stage in a young man's life rather than a seasonal event.[4] Finally, in addition to their propinquity and the similarity of economic conditions in Knock and Bekan, we know that marriages were contracted between people in the two parishes. The most important family among the 1879 Knock apparition witnesses, the Beirnes, had two daughters married to Bekan men. The eight-year old seer, Catherine Murray was the daughter of Eliza Beirne and William Murray of Bekan; she was staying at the house of her grandmother in Knock on the day of the apparition and was apparently still living there when *The Nation's* correspondent interviewed her early in 1880.[5] Another apparition witness, Mary Beirne, later married James O'Connell of Bekan.[6] Since marriages were arranged between social equals,[7] this is very strong evidence of the similarity of social life in the two adjoining parishes.

On point after point we find striking similarities between what Campbell described for pre-famine Knock and what Higgins and others remembered or recounted from post-famine Bekan. Supernatural intervention saved both from famine deaths: a 'pious pilgrim's prophecy' in Knock, the prayer of St Béacán, the parish patron, in Bekan.[8] Bekan, like Knock, saw conflict between clergy and lay people.[9] As was true in pre-famine Knock, in post-famine Bekan 'the bishop was held in great reverence and awe and people feared and respected him'.[10] Daniel Campbell described the importance of pattern days in pre-famine Knock; in post-famine Bekan 'everybody turned out on that day, the rich and the poor, the weak as well as the strong, the old and the young'.[11] In Bekan, like Knock, there was a strong belief in the fairies and their involvement in human affairs and a general sense of the nearness of the other world.[12] Public penance was required in Bekan of those guilty of scandalous sin as it was for the schoolteacher in Knock. 'In order to free himself of the guilt, (the poor victim) might have to stand before the altar dressed in a white robe or sheet each Sunday [at mass] for maybe three months or six months according to the penance imposed on them' (sic).[13] Just as Campbell distinguished 'strong' farmers from the rest of the rural population, so too did post-famine Bekan society.[14] Except for the addition of fish — 'herring could be bought for one shilling a dozen', and were then smoked over the turf fire — even the food remembered for post-famine Bekan[15] is strikingly similar to what Campbell described for the earlier period.

In addition to these similarities, Higgins described many patterns of behaviour that we can be confident were also found in Knock even though Campbell did not mention them. Examples include the working of the rundale system, games played at wakes, how the rent was paid, the arrangement of marriages and the adjustments of household members to the marriage of the heir, rituals surrounding death and burial, and the work and importance of blacksmiths. The 1937–38 Schools Folklore Project provides evidence for some of these in post-famine Knock. For one example of an 'older' pattern of religious practice, Higgins tells us that funeral masses were not said in post-famine Bekan, the coffined dead being brought directly from their house to the graveyard, and the same thing is recalled in Knock.[16] The absence of funeral masses is evidence that the official church had not extended its hegemony to the extent of making death a church-centred experience.[17] In both parishes, when a person was near death, they were taken from their bed and laid on the floor to reduce their suffering by has-tening their dying.[18] Particular 'superstitions' found in the pre-famine era were also recalled by Knock informants in the 1930s and in many cases the beliefs were presented as still held.[19] A blessed well near Mannin Lake was still in the 1930s the site of pilgrimage, according to a fifty-three-year-old informant in Eden, Daniel Campbell's native townland.[20]

The evidence of the Bekan parish history and especially the memories of the post-famine period in both parishes, convincingly supports the claim that cultural beliefs and practices found in Campbell's Knock persisted strongly there. We can conclude that in both parishes elements of pre-famine religious culture persisted down to the time of the apparition. This is understandable given that the economic arrangements operated as a mechanism to preserve the old ways.[21] The small farms could not generate enough income to enable the tenants to pay their rents. In most of the country in the nineteenth century permanent emigration of many young unmarried adults became institutionalised as a way to reduce the numbers dependent on the land, increase farm size and facilitate increased commercial farming. Rather than adopt that strategy, however, the people of Knock and similar areas clung to their traditional holdings, even when they had to migrate to earn their rents. Knock lay near the border of the two Poor Law Unions with the highest rates of seasonal migration in all of Ireland in 1880. 'Not surprisingly, those unions that show the highest rate of seasonal migrants were those where subdivision of holdings and early marriages persisted and where post-Famine re-popula-tion was most complete.'[22] Even temporary sojourns in England did not make permanent emigration more desirable. When the temporary migration strategy too ran into difficulties in the 1870s' compelling permanent emigra-tion for more and more, as Jordan noticed, 'it is significant that small farmers were driven to abandon their marriage traditions in order to preserve a share of the small farm economy for the fortunate few who could secure land'.[23] Those children of the small farms not lucky enough to be chosen as heir or to marry an heir had 'to travel' not only to make their own way in the world, but in the expectation that they would send money back to support the 'home' family. They were 'reared for emigration'[24] and there is evidence that families encouraged more education for girls than boys in a kind of 'foreign invest-ment' strategy: emigrant daughters were more likely than sons to reliably remit money from their jobs in America, and extra schooling before departure enhanced their earning potential.[25]

There is additional evidence of cultural traditionalism in Knock right up to the time of the apparition. The mid-summer Bonfire Night tradition per-sisted, even though a Jesuit mission priest characterised it as a celebration of St Aloysius' Day in honour of the parish priest, Fr Cavanagh, whose middle name was Aloysius.[26] St Aloysius' Feast day was 21 June conveniently close to

St John's Night when the summer bonfires traditionally were lit throughout the whole country. But the date alone is not enough to support the Jesuit's claim. Where else do we find evidence that a priest's middle name was significant for the people's devotional life? And if by some odd circumstance some of the people of Knock had developed a devotion to St Aloysius, why would they express their new devotion by lighting bonfires? It strains credulity to believe that acknowledgment of a new saint in the people's pantheon should replicate exactly the mode of a traditional practice merely through coincidence. (This is most likely evidence of 'infrapolitics'.[27] It's likely the people understood the bonfire in one way and explained it in another way congenial to him when the Jesuit asked about it. After all, what was to be gained by admitting superstitious practices to a Jesuit missioner? Perhaps he was willingly misled.) Moreover, if it was in some way in recognition or honour of Fr Cavanagh, why would the practice have continued long after the priest's death? In the 1930s a Knock informant recalled that at least one person from each household should attend the bonfire lit in each village and take home a lighted coal from the fire and use it to bless their fields and animals.[28]

Another indication of conservatism is found in patterns of naming. Traditionally, families gave their children names that were passed along the generations in a definite pattern. In the Beirne family, for example, the names Brian, Dominick and Pat recur generation after generation back at least to pre-famine times and probably much longer. This convention tended to highlight where the holders of the names fit in a family structure extending through the generations and to minimise their unique individual identities. While the repetition of names often thoroughly confused outsiders (as did the two Dominick Beirnes among the 1879 apparition witnesses), insiders could easily distinguish who was who. Far from being abandoned in the post-famine period, the practice was still very visible and the tradition still intact at the time of the apparition. In February 1865 two boys were baptised within three weeks of each other, both named Pat Beirne. On 4 February the son of Thomas Beirne and Anne Feeley was baptised, to be followed on 25 February by the baptism of Pat, son of Pat Beirne and Winnie Murray. If the Pat Beirne reported as a sixteen-year-old seer of the 1879 apparition and identified as a son of Pat Beirne was the second of these children, he was two years old before being baptised.[29] Unfortunately 1865 is the earliest year for which these records are available so we cannot know if another Pat Beirne had been baptised a couple of years earlier. Records of baptisms in Knock and Aughamore in the 1870s show continued use of traditional names by the numerous Beirne families in the area.[30]

One feature of the post-famine culture in both Bekan and Knock of obvious significance for understanding apparitions is that 'visions' were known and recounted not as something that happened in distant times or places but as occurring in the present time to locally identifiable people. Having a vision was an option in the people's cultural tool-kit. How rare or common these were is impossible to say, but I have found evidence for quite a few even though the sources available were not centrally concerned with them. References to 'visions' appear almost in passing in accounts of other topics or the everyday routines of living. Had somebody set out to collect them many more instances could likely have been documented. The visions are diverse in who saw them, what they saw, when they occurred, whether they are recounted as 'facts' or 'reports' (i.e. in the first or third person), and in many other ways, but in spite of this diversity they share the cultural understanding of a 'vision' as some kind of communication or message from some realm other than the mundane everyday one.

As messages from another world, visions had particular and diverse social and rhetorical uses when talked about in this one. Apart from the famous apparition, the vision reports in Knock or Bekan include the following. In Knock in the 1930s an informant recounted that thirty years earlier three men saw the ghosts of two women who had been robbed and killed a few years earlier.[31] From Bekan we learn of 'a young lad who, while ringing the bell for morning mass, mysteriously encountered an old priest who had come back from the grave and sought permission to say Mass'.[32] One local man recalled that 'people have sworn to me that they have seen one of their neighbours who might have been dead for years, and other near-relations of the person verified that they had also seen the person'.[33] Another story told of a Bekan man who witnessed the execution of his friend in Castlebar in 1798. On his trip home,

> night overtook him on the Claremorris–Knock road and he stopped at the little chapel at Barnycarroll. There he was surprised to see the door open and the interior illuminated. He got off his horse and looked in. A strange scene met his eyes. His friend's execution was being re-enacted within the chapel exactly as he had witnessed it earlier that day in Castlebar.[34]

It would be wrong to think that 'visions' were confined to the 'superstitious' poor or people least affected by the devotional revolution. Michael Ronayne was born near Ballyhaunis in 1869, became a priest in 1895 and served in the archdiocese of Tuam for nearly ten years. While a curate in Glenamaddy

> he had a dream, or 'vision' as he cared to describe it, in which he received a call to leave the world — 'to give up all in order to gain all' — and to devote his life to prayer and full time service to God. The scene fixed itself in his mind . . . [He then decided to make a retreat at a monastery.] Thither he went, and reaching the main entrance, there before him, clearly and unmistakeably were the gates of his vision.[35]

Fr Michael Ronayne became a monk.

Much can be made of these visions but two points are most important for my purposes. One is the use of visions as a way to criticise clerical abuses.

The story of the old priest returning from the grave with a request to say mass was found widely. It was believed that priests who took money to say masses but failed to do so would be unable to rest after death until they had made good their debt. Such stories are criticisms of greedy priests and statements of the ultimate fairness of the world. God would punish the avaricious or lazy priests by requiring them to search for opportunities to say mass, and people would get the masses they paid for even if priests were sinful. While these stories castigated sinful priests they also underlined their duty. God condemned a priest who did not meet the obligations of his role to his own purgatory of continuous seeking to find someone to serve his mass. That mass-server was almost always a layperson, a vivid reversal of the usual subservience of the laity to the clergy occasioned by the transgressions of a particular priest. The requirement in such stories that the mass server be a male also underscored the official church requirements for the valid celebration of the mass promulgated at the Council of Trent. Thus such stories, widespread as they were, constituted no simple absence or reversal of orthodoxy. In many ways they served to buttress such official teachings as the centrality of the mass, the existence of purgatory, and the interdependent relationships among the living and the dead in the community of the faithful. They too served to discipline the clergy.[36]

Another significant feature of these vision reports is that while the experiences were usually ascribed to particular individuals, the community collectively in some fashion endorsed them. The recalling of these stories in our sources is evidence of this. Even more direct evidence is provided in the story about people reporting meeting long-dead neighbours. These seers were not considered deluded or fraudulent; rather 'other near-relations of the person verified that they had also seen the person'. This communal validation came from people who did not doubt the credibility of the 'seer' and who shared the belief that seeing the dead was not only possible but that it happened in their time and place. Such validation by conversation is at the heart of social and cultural life.

Researchers using Larkin's terminology agree that the devotional revolution was delayed in the archdiocese of Tuam. In general, the changes associated with the revolution had their roots among the more substantial tenant farmer class and in the towns of the south-east and spread geographically from that heartland. Tuam, on the western seaboard, would be expected to be among the last dioceses to be devotionally revolutionised and indeed in broad stokes this was the case. Describing the late 1870s, Larkin wrote that Rome considered the pastoral condition of the diocese as 'simply nothing less than deplorable'. The list of problems included a shortage of priests, extensive nepotism on the archbishop's part, heavy debts of the diocesan seminary, Protestant missionaries making inroads, proliferation of secret societies, and priests denouncing each other and their parishioners publicly.[37] Other distinguished historians agree. Although he is more careful to distinguish his own conclusion from the claims made by contemporaries, Sean Connolly concluded that 'by the time of his death in 1878, Cullen's program of reform had failed to penetrate the archdiocese of Tuam still governed by the formidable John MacHale.'[38] And Desmond Bowen too agrees with that assessment.[39]

The only sustained analysis of religious life in Knock before the apparition is an undergraduate thesis by Patrick Nold who follows Larkin and other historians of the devotional revolution in writing that it occurred later in the west of the country. He cites a communication from Larkin to the effect that the Knock area was ten to twenty years behind the rest of the country in the arrival of the revolution. He says it was brought to Knock by the waves of pilgrims after the apparition. 'Indeed', claims Nold, 'Knock did not even have the bare essentials for celebrating basic Catholic rituals.'[40]

Before answering whether the devotional revolution was late in Tuam or in Knock, we need to recognise that different changes are conflated in the term. If we look at the provision of church buildings, at the national level researchers have come to recognise that the great era of church building preceded the famine,[41] and the same thing was true in Tuam. In 1825 the diocese had only fifteen slated chapels and about eighty inadequate thatched buildings for 106 congregations, but within a quarter century no less than sixty new chapels and a cathedral had been constructed,[42] including the chapel at Knock with its cornerstone dated 1828. Knock church and another in Aghamore, the other parish served by the parish priest of Knock, were part of 'the spate of church building' that began in the diocese in the 1820s.[43] But the devotional revolution term is also commonly understood to connote behaviours ranging from lay people routinely attending Sunday mass to the discipline of priests or the degree of unity among the bishops as well as changes in various devotions or rituals.

There are good reasons to be cautious in accepting the conclusions by Larkin, Connolly and other historians about the 'deplorable state' of catholic practice in Tuam in the late 1870s and especially in accepting that what might be true for the archdiocese in general was necessarily the case for Knock in particular. A closer look at Knock and its neighbouring town shows a more complex and nuanced situation. Notice that in characterising the deplorable state of things in the archdiocese, Larkin highlights deficiencies in the ecclesiastical personnel system. Priests were too few and ill-disciplined; the training of other priests was threatened by the debts of the diocesan seminary; their promotion patterns were skewed by nepotism; the clergy were ineffective in countering proselytism; the archbishop was infirm in body and probably in mind. Lay practice becomes of concern because of the alleged spread of secret societies. Even if we grant that all these charges were true we cannot say much about the religious life, the beliefs and practices of most of the laity. (Of course, the Larkin thesis presumes that the prime moving force for change is a well-oiled and staffed ecclesiastical administrative machine.) But can we accept the charges?

Larkin wrote that the claim about 'the deplorable state' of the diocese was supported by 'overwhelming' evidence.[44] He cites four letters to Archbishop

Tobias Kirby, the Rector of the Irish College in Rome, who was the de facto agent in Rome of most Irish ecclesiastics. It was through Kirby that most attempts to influence the Roman Curia were channelled, most intrigues and political manoeuvres were orchestrated, and Roman political winds assessed. Because of his pivotal role in the hierarchical structure of the official church, one recent researcher considered Kirby the most important bishop in nineteenth-century Irish Catholicism,[45] a status usually ascribed to Cardinal Cullen. Of the four letters Larkin cites, two were from John MacEvilly and all four were dated between 8 January and 10 February 1878.[46] These were part of a coordinated campaign in a struggle between Archbishop MacHale and MacEvilly, bishop in the neighbouring diocese of Galway, whose goal was to so discredit him in Rome as to either make MacHale resign or force Rome to remove him and to make MacEvilly Archbishop of Tuam. MacEvilly was notified on 6 February 1878 that he had been appointed coadjutor to MacHale.[47] He had in fact been selected in late 1876 but his appointment had been kept secret.[48]

The problem from a researcher's viewpoint is that the evidence in the Kirby papers is systematically biased. It highlights deficiencies in Tuam but not other dioceses and it minimises or omits mention of other causes of the problems so as to discredit MacHale. When succession to a diocese was being deliberated, as was the case in Tuam where MacHale was then in his late eighties, claims of pastoral shortcomings proliferated as suited various parties with a vested interest in the outcome. This was the case, for example, for the archdiocese of Cashel a few years earlier.[49]

Historian Patrick Corish prepared 'a guide to the material of public and political interest' in the Kirby Papers for the period from 1862 to 1883 for which he excluded letters about the business of Rome's Irish College or routine Irish ecclesiastical administrative affairs. Even with this limitation the guide lists no fewer than nine letters from MacEvilly to Kirby in 1879 alone.[50] And most of MacEvilly's messages in 1879 and earlier years were echoed or corroborated by similar letters from Archbishop Cullen until his death in 1878 and later his successor Archbishop MacCabe. In his biography of MacEvilly, Liam Bane has documented the cooperation to the point of collusion between MacEvilly and Cullen in reinforcing and endorsing each other's communications with Kirby.[51] When MacEvilly wrote to Kirby in April 1879 that 'the state of the diocese [Tuam] is simply awful', he sought to discredit in advance any claims to the contrary. He listed his allies as the only bishops whose word on the matter could be taken and warned Kirby not to heed any input from bishops in other nearby dioceses.[52] Another reason the Kirby Papers do not reflect MacHale's version of affairs in his diocese is that years earlier he had antagonised a bishop who was to become a very important and powerful person in Rome, Cardinal Barnabo, Prefect of the Propaganda, the body in Rome responsible for overseeing Irish affairs. Barnabo wrote via MacEvilly to other suffragan bishops in the province of Tuam completely by-passing MacHale who as archbishop would in normal cases be the conduit, and he sought input and advice from MacEvilly's allies in the province while ignoring those bishops allied with MacHale.[53]

Cullen, in contrast, was a protégé of Barnabo and had gained the friendship of the pope for his behaviour during the revolution of 1848 when Cullen took charge of the Propaganda at a time when it seemed that followers of Mazzini would take it over. Larkin documents Cullen's intricately close ties in Rome which looked with favour on him in part because he was an alumnus of the Propaganda.[54] Kirby was not only well connected in Rome but was personally close to Cullen, having served as his vice-rector when Cullen was rector of the Irish College. The close working ties between the two men is clear from the 500 letters from Cullen to Kirby in the 1850s alone. That both Cullen and Kirby had direct access to important and powerful decision makers at the very highest reaches of Rome's ecclesiastical administration is made clear by the numerous letters that Cullen wrote to Kirby in Italian: they were meant for the eyes of the Italians in the Curia.[55] MacHale, recognising Kirby as Cullen's man, wrote little if at all to him. There is not one letter from him in all the years covered by Corish's guide. Thus, relying on the Kirby papers for evidence about religious practice in Tuam is at best one-sided. At times, as we will see, charges levelled by MacEvilly were demonstrably false, at other times greatly exaggerated. Even Corish admits that 'no one could claim that he (MacEvilly) is a detached witness' in reporting on the state of affairs in the Tuam diocese in these years.[56] For example, MacEvilly often claimed Tuam priests had a major drinking problem, for which he blamed MacHale. Yet, other dioceses also faced similar criticisms. Hoppen[57] documents charges of drunken priests and even bishops for the dioceses of Cashel, Kerry and even Dublin in the 1870s and 1880s.

Ó Tuairisc argues that the criticism of priests in politics was as accurate in MacEvilly's own diocese of Galway as in MacHale's Tuam. He also points out that after MacHale's death in 1881 MacEvilly did not in fact take any dramatic steps to deal with abuses he had alleged would take 'generations of archbishops' to undo.[58] No doubt suspecting MacEvilly's bias, Propaganda asked the Archbishop of Armagh to investigate matters, and after a quick visit during which he did get MacHale's side of the story, Dr McGettigan reported early in 1879 that there was 'no ground for anxiety about the state of religion in Tuam'.[59] But to counter the well-coordinated campaign to influence Rome's decisions against him, MacHale had no resources in the Holy City. When it came to ecclesiastical political manoeuvres in Rome, 'Cullen had all the advantages except the standing MacHale had among the Irish people'.[60] The day after the Knock apparition, 22 August 1879, the very day seven priests in the diocese wrote to Propaganda opposing MacEvilly, Cardinal Simeoni wrote to MacHale telling him that the pope was going to send MacEvilly to Tuam to carry out the duties of a coadjutor.[61] One historian wrote of MacHale that 'throughout his episcopate he appeared in Roman eyes to be a stubborn, provincial, quarrelsome and authoritarian individualist'.[62] While this might be debated for the early years of MacHale's work in Killala and Tuam, there is no question that it became ever more the case with the passing of the decades. These very qualities, however, were virtues rather than vices when viewed from the vantage point of the common people, the poor and oppressed of his diocese. (See chapter 5.) Being 'stubborn' and 'provincial' on their behalf endeared him to them, and being 'quarrelsome' was laudable when you joined battle with the right enemies. We need to assess the evidence and significance of MacHale's 'standing among the people' as well as the evidence and significance of his powerlessness in Rome.

Even within the Larkin paradigm, quite apart from MacHale's regime there were many factors that delayed many changes usually subsumed in the term devotional revolution. Tuam was geographically the biggest diocese in the country. In the 1870s, the annual *Irish Catholic Directory* claimed that it had more Catholics than any other diocese except Dublin. A large flock spread over an expansive territory might not have been a significant obstacle if other factors were favourable, but they were not. What Moody wrote of County Mayo was even more the case for the Tuam archdiocese, which also included most of the wilds of Connemara in County Galway. It contained 'in its vast bogs, its gaunt bare mountains, and its lonely peninsulas and islands some of the wildest, most remote, and most barren country in Ireland'.[63] Two of the biggest lakes in the country, Loughs Corrib and Mask, almost cut the diocese in two along a north–south axis, adding circuitous routes to bad roads, long distances and difficult terrain as obstacles to travel. Not only did Tuam have a large population for a diocese but it had perhaps the greatest proportion of desperately poor people, however measured, of any diocese.[64] Additionally, the proportion of Irish speakers was among the highest in the country. Another factor was the targeting of Tuam by Protestant evangelicals. In no other Irish diocese were the Catholic authorities confronted by such a well financed, organised, widespread and long-term systematic effort to win converts to Protestantism from the Catholic population. For those who see religious change as shaped by social and material circumstances rather than individual clerics, as I do, an important factor was the persistence of pre-famine economic arrangements. As late as the 1890s the per capita consumption of potatoes was at pre-famine levels of over one ton per annum in places such as Claremorris.[65]

Other causes, too, could be adduced, such as a low ratio of priests to the laity, but was this due to the weakness of orthodox Catholic practice, as MacHale's critics held, or to the inability of the poverty-stricken population to economically support the ratio of clergy found elsewhere, as his defenders claimed? Arguments can be made on both sides, but politically tainted claims are dubious evidence. In the decades-long controversy and conflict between MacHale on one side and Cullen, MacEvilly and later McCabe on the other, as we have seen the versions of reality painted by MacHale's critics are over-represented in the Roman archives to the point of excluding alternative views.

Constrained in his thinking by the assumptions built into the devotional revolution paradigm, Nold seeks evidence to support his conclusions about how backward Knock was in terms of Catholic practice. Organised pilgrimages after the 1879 apparition frequently brought gifts for Knock church, including sacred vessels and other items used in the liturgy. Reasoning that organisers of these pilgrimages were not likely to donate unneeded items, Nold sees these gifts as evidence that the church at Knock lacked the basic essentials for celebrating the liturgy. However, other interpretations seem more reasonable. Even if the local church already owned one, some large pilgrimages would require the use of several ciboria, for example, the ciborium being the vessel used to hold communion wafers. More generally, sacred vessels received as gifts were likely to be more ornate versions of items already owned. One such gift was a monstrance with gold and inset precious stones. However, the local church already had a plain metal monstrance, used to display the consecrated Host.[66] A Cork pilgrimage presented a 'magnificent' ciborium in 1880.[67] Other gifts were of items not used in normal Catholic ritual; examples are the banners that served to commemorate particular pilgrimages.[68] The evidence of the gifts at the young shrine does not support the conclusion Nold builds on it. Moreover, it is unlikely that money was spent on adding a belfry, installing stained glass windows, buying statues and making other documented improvements to the chapel before the apparition if the essential items for celebrating mass and other liturgical needs were lacking.

The evidence we have on religious practice in pre-apparition Knock is mixed and sometimes indirect and circumstantial, yet it supports a different interpretation from Nold's or what would be suggested by a simple application of the Larkin thesis to the local scene. The best evidence possible about religion in Knock just before the apparition would be insiders' accounts, like Daniel Campbell's memoir for the earlier period. In the absence of such ideal evidence, we have to rely on other materials that were originally intended for other purposes.

The pre-famine pattern of religiosity included fairylore commingled with beliefs in the special power of the priests, local access to the sacred, pilgrimages to local sites such as holy wells, and nearness of other worlds. How much did these persist up to the time of apparition along with more officially endorsed Catholic practice? What new devotions or practices were to be found? We lack anything similar to the Campbell memoir for the post-famine era, and investigations after the 1879 apparition were few to none. In contrast to some apparitions on the European continent, little material was collected that now can be grist to the historian's mill.[69] There was no attempt by the government authorities to investigate the affair or suppress the devotion after the apparition. The official ecclesiastical investigation was superficial at best and no documents from it are to be found in church archives. There was no media coverage at all for months after the initial apparition claim and thereafter the newspapers that reported on it were very supportive and accepting, serving largely to propagate the version of events formulated by the local priests involved with the investigation. Even then, the main national paper, the *Freeman's Journal*, as well as the important local paper, the *Connaught Telegraph*, published relatively little on the Knock events compared to *The Nation* and its cheaper version, the *Weekly News*. Sceptical newspaper reports were few, the one notable exception being by Andrew Dunlop in the (London) *Daily News*. Moreover, after very extensive positive reporting in *The Nation* throughout most of 1880, coverage of Knock dropped abruptly. Another half century was to pass before local promoters began the process that turned Knock into a major pilgrimage shrine. Even if a major effort had then been made to recover the reality of pre-apparition Knock, the passage of so much time inevitably limited what was possible. As it was, what pre-apparition 'history' was written was in service to the promotion of the claim to supernatural intervention.

We need to ask if the devotional revolution paradigm is the most appropriate context for understanding insiders' experiences. Other explanatory frameworks were far more important for Knock people. Even if we accept the Larkin terminology, we should be careful not to force the available evidence into a procrustean bed of a one-dimensional movement in the direction of more orthodox practice. For the diocese as a whole, supposedly so backward in the new devotionalism, Archbishop MacHale's funeral in 1881 featured highly elaborated ceremonial ritual, featuring 'all the spectacular manifestations of ultramontane liturgy'.[70] As we have seen, the allegedly 'new' Stations of the Cross devotion existed in pre-famine Knock. By 1879, in Knock there is clear evidence of 'pre-devotional revolution' elements in Fr Cavanagh's behaviour but also of 'devotionally revolutionised' practise on the part of lay people. In fact, both 'old' and 'new' practices were likely both represented, in strength, in Knock; perhaps one of Knock's distinguishing features was a very intimate association between the different orientations.

Fr Cavanagh's own religiosity combined features of both 'old' and 'new' religious regimes. It is difficult to decide how much his reputation for holiness was an *ex post facto* explanation after the apparition of August 1879. We can safely assume he was responsible for the improvements in the church building and for promoting or at a minimum allowing the church choir before that, and that in that sense he was a moderniser. As parish priest, Cavanagh oversaw many improvements in the parish chapel. He built a belfry and installed stained glass windows in the chapel, and bought statues and other devotional objects. O'Connor mentioned the Stations of the Cross, for example; Fr Cavanagh told one reporter a new set was installed around 1878 to replace earlier ones damaged in a storm, and other improvements were made.[71] Yet in 1879 the chapel still lacked seating except for a few pews, as in pre-famine days. Items for devotional and religious use rather than for creature comfort seem to have been Cavanagh's focus.

The only contemporary pre-apparition documentary evidence we have of Cavanagh's behaviour in Knock is his denunciation of early local organisers of the agitation on the land issue. In late May 1879, he attacked several men by name from the altar.[72] Such public denunciation violated the Statutes of the Council of Thurles, the blueprint for increased ecclesiastical discipline involved in the devotional revolution,[73] but it reflected the thinking of earlier generations of priests that emphasised external behaviour more than interior spirituality, public shame rather than private guilt. A pre-revolution outlook also appears in his almost complete absence of scepticism over what constituted a 'miraculous' cure evident in the lists of cures he compiled and had published after the apparition. Indeed, one reporter with whom he talked concluded that Cavanagh used the terms 'miracle' and 'cure' as synonyms.[74]

His use and distribution of cement from the apparition gable, including by mail, shows his view of miracle was close to the older traditions that held as sacred, for example, clay from particular holy sites (such as some priests' graves, and 'caves' at specific holy wells such as Ardmore), rather than to a devotionally revolutionised spirituality. He told the *Daily Telegraph* reporter of being called to give the last rites to a young man who was 'apparently near death, but conscious'. After ministering to him, said Cavanagh, 'I called for a glass of water, and sprinkled on it a few particles of the mortar from the gable wall of the chapel, and bade him drink. He did so; at once, he began to recover, and is now well.'[75] The priest attributed the recovery to the mortar rather than to natural factors or to the canonically appropriate sacrament, Extreme Unction, which he administered to the man. Similarly, he bottled the pooled rainwater at the church gable the morning after the apparition and distributed it to the faithful.[76] He records in his diary as a miracle that his housekeeper Mary McLoughlin was cured of stiff knees by the water.[77] He also later admitted/claimed to have seen lights and other supernatural sights.[78]

But there were other sides to Fr Cavanagh's religiosity. After the altar denunciation precipitated a protest demonstration against him, by one account he began to say a special set of 100 masses for the souls in purgatory.[79] Nold may be right when he sees this story as possibly apocryphal since the earliest source for it is the Nun of Kenmare who moved to Knock over two years after the apparition,[80] but we do know from other sources of Cavanagh's devotion to the souls in purgatory[81] and one apparition witness in a position to know repeated the story throughout her life.[82] Assuming the story is true, it would indicate Cavanagh perhaps having a view of the priest's role as that of one who offers sacrifice and makes atonement for the community. But our evidence is too scant to offer more than this speculation about Cavanagh's acceptance of a mass-centred understanding of his priestly role. We have much stronger evidence to the contrary.

According to Canon Ulick Bourke, who sat along with Cavanagh on the commission investigating the Knock apparition, Fr Cavanagh liked mixing with the gentry and sought their recognition and approval.[83] He was also a man of strong beliefs. Even though (in the eyes of critics) he was credulous to the point of naivety about miraculous cures (in the eyes of believers, Cavanagh was a man of the utmost faith), he was not easily swayed when he had formed an opinion. He brooked no criticism or defiance from his own flock whether they were, as he alleged, Fenians and revolutionaries before the apparition, or from the Nun of Kenmare or her supporters in the parish afterward.

Lacking anything like Campbell's memoir for the post-famine period in Knock, and with a dearth of material like that generated in Lourdes, Marpingen, and elsewhere on the continent, I have used the evidence from the adjacent parish of Bekan, which we already reviewed. Because Bekan had a much higher death rate during the Great Hunger we would expect less continuity than in Knock, so the evidence of substantial continuity there makes it even more likely that pre-famine beliefs and practices persisted quite strongly in Knock. The 1930s Schools Folklore Project also offers supportive evidence from Knock. The behaviour of the early pilgrims at the apparition site, to be discussed later, also provides evidence of their 'pre-devotional-revolutionised' orientation, as does the survival in Knock of the mid-summer bonfire tradition. On the other hand, there is evidence of the 'new' piety and church-centred religiosity. We should regard this not as contradicting but as complementing what the Famine demographics and the Bekan evidence would lead us to expect or what researchers in the devotional revolution tradition would predict.

For the Schools Folklore project undertaken by the Irish Folklore Commission in 1937–38, a teacher in Rooskey National School in Knock parish recalled earlier schools in the area. One was started in the townland of Kincon in 1867. This was not a state-supported national school since Archbishop MacHale was opposed to accepting funds from the government for schools. In most dioceses, while the government paid the national teachers' salaries, the school manager was the priest and he had the power to hire and fire teachers. Instead, the teachers in the school at Kincon were paid by the parents of their pupils and consequently they were very poor and dependent. The school was held in a private farmhouse. Another similar school in the parish was held in a cow-barn and because of the shortage of space, pupils in these two schools attended in two shifts, day and night. The teaching in these schools was through English. The Kincon school had two teachers, a man named Waldron and a woman named Garvey. In addition to running the school, these two

> also taught Catechism in Irish every Sunday after mass in the church [at Knock] — and the chapel used to be full to the door every Sunday of people, young and old, learning about God and the sacraments.[84]

Catechism taught in chapel had to be in Irish because the older people were monolingual Gaelic speakers, but the demand that the young be taught in school through English represents their parents' appreciation that English was the language of progress. The packed church for these catechism lessons is evidence of a popular demand for them and the presence of the elderly shows that these people had not earlier learned their catechism. Here is evidence of interest in church-centred orthodoxy. It is well to keep in mind, however, that the catechism was taught in the church on Sundays in pre-famine times also, as Campbell tells us but he does not mention the chapel being crowded for the occasion.

The school at Kincon started in 1867, the very year that Fr Cavanagh became parish priest in Knock. Whether he initiated the catechism teaching after mass cannot be ascertained but he obviously permitted and very likely actively supported it. It may be the case that Sunday catechism lessons had continued without interruption from the pre-famine days; but it is also possible that lessons were provided when suitable or willing teachers became available as with the two new teachers in Kincon, or when there was demand for instruction. We have no evidence about how long the arrangement persisted. We also do not know the teachers' precise motives. Were they paid and thus using the catechism lessons to supplement their meagre earnings as teachers? Or were they religiously devout individuals driven by some new missionary zeal? Perhaps their chapel teaching served to advertise their availability as teachers while simultaneously offering assurances of their religious bona fides. What is clear is that because they were not national teachers they were not directly dependent on Fr Cavanagh for their positions as teachers. A decade later, several national teachers are identifiable as important leaders of religious life in the parish but these were all directly answerable to Fr Cavanagh in his role of school manager.

In her superb study of how convent life developed in nineteenth-century Ireland and how nuns contributed to changes in devotional practice, Mary Magray wrote that 'singing became an increasingly important part of the new piety'.[85] In Knock church, there was a well-regarded choir several years before the apparition. Giving advance notice of a day of special devotion and plenary indulgence at the renovated St Mary's Augustinian Abbey in Ballyhaunis in 1876, the *Connaught Telegraph* wrote that 'an excellent choir' was expected to be present. (This comment itself is evidence of the rarity of choirs and hence their newsworthiness.) In reports after the ceremony, we learn that this choir was from Knock.[86] This was not the first time the choir sang in Ballyhaunis. At a Corpus Christi procession there the preceding June, a newspaper reported that 'the choir from Knock, under the direction of Miss Anderson, delighted all who had the pleasure of hearing them, with the excellent way in which they discoursed the sacred music on the occasion'.[87] It would have been very unusual for a rural choir to be featured at ceremonies in a bigger town. The reverse is what we would expect: 'a choir was got in for the occasion [of church dedications] usually from one of the towns'. In the diocese of Kilmore a choir from the town of Cavan sang when a new church was dedicated in Belturbet in 1868, and in 1888 at a similar occasion in Crosserlough choirs from Cavan and Cootehill was present.[88] At a January 1881 meeting, a Dublin priest leading an attempt to promote liturgical music identified some obstacles in the way including 'the apparent apathy of ordinary non-Dublin clergy to the concept of music reform' and the fact that the number and quality of choirs left a lot to be desired. Another speaker, Bishop Gillooly of Elphin, a diocese close to Knock, said that 'even when the parish clergy were interested in music, they found it almost impossible to get singers to form choirs'. A journal published by the reformers commented a few months later that, even where they existed, choirs were founded on the basis that members were doing a personal favour to the priest, their rehearsals were mere social occasions and, not unrelatedly, their musical standards were low.[89] Against this backdrop, the existence of the Knock choir obviously reflects at least to some extent Fr Cavanagh's support. The choir was labelled 'excellent' and praised by a perhaps musically-undiscriminating newspaper reporter, but the fact of its being invited more than once to perform in Ballyhaunis testifies to its standing relative to other choirs in the area. On the dimension of singing as part of the liturgy, Cavanagh's promotion of the choir places him in the first ranks of the 'devotional revolutionaries' among the clergy of his region.[90]

Fr Cavanagh was a good friend of Fr James Anderson, the Augustinian prior who had spearheaded the rebuilding of St Mary's and likely the invitation to the Knock choir was extended through him, but the invitation also recognised the quality of the choir's music and singing. This is even more significant when we realise that Fr Anderson was a great promoter of music and had purchased instruments and organised a choir after he arrived in Ballyhaunis in 1874; his choir made its debut on Christmas Day that year. When he founded a temperance society, it had its own brass band.[91] Apparently by 1876 the Knock choir outshone the one in Ballyhaunis if indeed the latter was still even functioning. Unfortunately our sources say nothing about the size of the Knock choir and do not identify its members except for its director, Miss Anderson, the principal of the girls' national school at Knock.[92] Since Fr Cavanagh, as manager of the school could hire and fire teachers and principals, it is likely that Cavanagh's and Miss Anderson's religious outlooks and attitudes were mutually congenial and compatible. We are not surprised to find that she was one of the seers of what was taken to be the second major apparition in Knock, early in January of 1880.[93] We do not know how long the Knock choir was in existence, but it may well have been started around the time of the building of the new seventy feet tall belfry, which was constructed with an opening to the church interior to serve as a choir loft.[94] At the very least this design indicates that a choir was being contemplated if not yet in existence in 1872 when the belfry was built; almost certainly the choir was functioning by the time a harmonium was added in 1875.[95]

As school principal, Miss Anderson answered to its manager, Fr Cavanagh, to whom she owed her position. She was not the only religiously involved layperson that Cavanagh hired as teachers in the schools of his parish. Her assistant was a Miss Kennedy who also saw a vision. Another devoutly religious person was Honoria Gaffney, a teacher at the Rooskey National School, who contemplated becoming a nun. For some years she prayed about the decision, with advice from several priests.[96] She eventually entered the convent, joining Sr Mary Francis Clare (Margaret Anna Cusack), when that famous woman, the Nun of Kenmare, attempted to found a new order at Knock in 1882–3, and became her greatest supporter and indispensable advisor. Gaffney was one of four women who left Knock for England with Cusack in 1883, and she later accompanied her to America. When Cusack later left the convent in the United States, Gaffney, known in religion as Sr and, later, Mother Evangelista, took over as head of the order and shepherded it into success when an early demise seemed likely.[97] Other teachers too seem to have been more than usually devout and energetic, though the evidence is from the immediate post-apparition period. A Mr and Mrs Henry Taafe were also teachers, and the woman was among the miracle cures at Knock.[98] In 1880 teachers in the various schools in the parish prepared their students for a major procession at the apparition church in Knock. When a newspaper report mentioned only Miss Anderson, Martin J. Flanagan, another teacher in the parish, felt strongly enough to write to the editor pointing out that the other teachers also deserved recognition.[99] Flanagan had already published a poem in honour of Our Lady of Knock as well as poems celebrating Christmas and advising young women not to emigrate.[100] If just one teacher in Knock was unusually religious or involved in church activities we would look to her or his own situation and experience for an explanation. But when several are involved as in Knock, we have to ask what they had in common. They all were hired and retained by Fr Cavanagh in his capacity as school manager. They tell us the types of people he sought as teachers for the children of the parish. They were religiously devout, involved in church activities and energetic people. They provide a significant clue to Cavanagh's own values.

As for the mass itself in Knock by the time of the 1879 apparition, we lack attendance figures. While only one mass on Sunday was offered in pre-famine days (Campbell memoir), in January 1880 there were Sunday masses at 9.00 a.m. and 12.00 noon as well as mass on weekdays.[101] Evidently, Fr Cavanagh said daily mass at least for a few months before the apparition, a change from the norm for priests in 1834. We cannot be sure when the second mass was first said on Sunday. Possibly it was a post-apparition attempt to provide for the pilgrims who were thronging to the shrine at the beginning of 1880. It is very likely that the crowd of people who filled the chapel on Sundays for catechism classes after 1867 also attended mass. But what was the chapel's capacity and how did that figure compare to the population in the area it served? Using the dimensions of the building as given by reporters and allowing five square feet per person, I estimate that it had a capacity of about 450,[102] while a visitor in February 1880 (when Knock was full of pilgrims) estimated that 600 could squeeze in.[103] Thus even assuming a packed chapel at each, two Sunday masses in the months before the pilgrim crowds started would not accommodate the Catholics of Knock parish. (The 1881 census recorded 3,241 people in the parish probably 3,200 of whom were Catholic; certainly 2,000 could not be canonically excused from attending mass.) We cannot assume that the 'service-area' of any given chapel coincided with parish boundaries, but it is more likely than not that the Knock Catholics who did not attend mass in their parish church, did not go to any other church either.

One historian simply asserts that mass 'was attended by virtually every person in a locality' in 1879 Mayo.[104] Perhaps this was indeed so, but the writer provides no evidence on the point and I know of no evidence either way; it seems that he could make the claim only by assuming what needed to be proven, that the devotional revolution train had arrived at the station. Until we can determine the meaning of their mass attendance, trying to count the congregation provides less useful evidence than first appears. Whatever the nature of their devotion to the mass immediately before the 1879 apparition, it did not prevent Fr Cavanagh's entire congregation from (according to one account) walking out of the chapel one Sunday to join a demonstration against him. (See pp. 151, 154 below.)

Much of the devotional revolution literature suggests that the changes in Catholic practice generally spread from urban to rural areas, so it is important to see whether 'new' devotions might have come to Knock from the towns. One nearby small town was Claremorris. Evidence on the state of orthodox religious practice there is sparse. If we are to accept Bishop MacEvilly's claims, it was worse than deplorable. Twice he wrote to Kirby that the parish priest there from 1875 to 1878 had never said mass and that eventually he abandoned his parish.[105] As usual we have to take MacEvilly's criticism with a large dose of scepticism. The priest in question was Fr Richard MacHale, a relative of the Archbishop. MacEvilly's animus toward Archbishop MacHale was extended to anybody associated with him and any ammunition was used if it might further embarrass MacHale in Rome. Newspaper reports of various events in Claremorris town and parish show Fr MacHale actively engaged in what we would expect of him as a priest, such as saying funeral masses,[106] and holding meetings, fundraising, buying a building to be used as a convent and organising various efforts to bring the Sisters of Mercy to the town.[107] Ó Tuairisc found that Claremorris parish records of marriages, baptisms and other events all indicate that Fr Richard MacHale was an involved priest in his parish. He cites letters to Fr MacHale from others as well as several newspaper obituaries of the priest to the same effect.[108] MacEvilly's repeated claim that he never said mass is just wrong. Of course we have already noted the motivation behind such charges. MacEvilly also claimed that Fr MacHale abandoned his parish; what he failed to point out was that the priest was fatally sick when he left. A newspaper report of his death states, 'For some years past he suffered from occasional attacks of chest disease. Declining in health and acting under medical advice he went to reside [near Dublin] where he died.'[109] He died on 16 September 1878. The latest evidence I have found shows him at work in his parish just a few months earlier. MacEvilly later claimed that the priest, who was only thirty-nine, died from too much drink and because he refused to take care of himself. This might be true but we certainly cannot believe it just because MacEvilly claimed it.[110] Even if MacEvilly was correct in all his charges against Fr Richard MacHale, we should keep in mind that Claremorris usually had two curates as well as the parish priest.

There is some reason to expect that orthodox religious practice likely received a boost in Claremorris in the years immediately before the Knock apparition. The Sisters of Mercy had opened a convent in the town at the beginning of 1877, and started primary schools which quickly filled with pupils; there were over 300 by August that year, which must have been the majority of children in the area. (Patrick Hill, the young witness to the 1879 apparition, lived in Claremorris so it is very likely he attended the nuns' school there. Estimates of his age range from eleven to fourteen.) Like nuns elsewhere, we can expect those in Claremorris promoted the more orthodox religiosity.[111]

On 8 September 1877 the *Connaught Telegraph* reported on a confirmation trip Archbishop MacHale made that week to Ballyhaunis. Much of the report describes how, on his arrival, the townspeople welcomed MacHale, showing their 'deep-rooted regard and abiding affection' for 'their illustrious archbishop' and 'venerated visitor' with bonfires, triumphal arches and banners, and a parade with a band playing patriotic airs. The following day over 700 people received the sacrament, some of them outside the chapel. A first glance would suggest this large number most likely included many adults, an indication that they had not been confirmed earlier. Another possibility is that the 1877 report was wrong or at least overstated the numbers. MacEvilly and other critics of MacHale claimed the reports in the press were painting a misleading picture of MacHale's health and energy. But even if the papers exaggerated MacHale's vigour it does not follow that they exaggerated the numbers he confirmed. Indeed, MacEvilly confirmed even more, 750, in Ballyhaunis less than three years later.[112] MacHale's open-air administration of the sacrament in 1877 indicates the parish lacked an adequate building. At the time, fundraising efforts were underway to enlarge the chapel. When MacEvilly administered confirmation in the town in 1880 he expressed his 'most unqualified satisfaction at [the children's] thorough and accurate knowledge of the Christian doctrine'.[113] Perhaps what had changed most from 1877 to 1880 was not the lay practice but MacEvilly's perspective: no longer seeking the position of Archbishop by denigrating everything about MacHale, he was now the shepherd of the flock in Ballyhaunis.

There is no clear pattern to suggest that any changes in Catholic Knock came there from nearby towns; Knock was sending its choir to events in

Ballyhaunis three years before the apparition but we might expect a boost to orthodox participation in Claremorris in the year before 1879. The available evidence on religion in Knock before the apparition shows considerable continuity with the pre-famine picture. If we adopt the language of a 'devotional revolution' we see an intricate mixture of 'old' and 'new', but we are forced to recognise that the 'new' was often not so new after all (such as in the Stations of the Cross) and the 'old' was not past but of continuing significance (such as the priest's use of mortar or the continuing use of a blessed well as late as the 1930s). What needs to be revised is the understanding of religious change as a clergy-directed, unilinear and one-dimensional process of increasing the orthodox practice of Catholicism. At every step we see syncretism rather than substitution or replacement of elements in the people's religious life.

8

Authority Structures
Shaken

In this chapter I describe the social situation in Knock just at the time the apparition occurred and how it had developed as a result of various changes in the post-famine period. After setting the wider scene I move in for a closer look at local circumstances. As much as possible I look at these from the inside, using the cultural lenses through which insiders interpreted them and made them meaningful. Because, as I will argue, problematic relationships with superiors is one key issue in the apparition, I pay particular attention to challenges to the authority of both the landlord and the clergy in Knock and to the confused family authority situation in the case of the Beirnes, the main family among the apparition witnesses.

Like so many other places where apparitions occurred, Knock in the summer of 1879 was characterised not so much by abject poverty, but by multiple and ramifying social changes that upset hitherto established and shared understandings and patterns of expectation in most areas of social life.[1] In Durkheimian terminology, Knock was in a state of extreme anomie. How one should behave toward others or what to expect from them or for oneself had been relatively clear to all, but suddenly that was no longer the case. In particular, questions concerning proper authority relationships were raised but no sure answers were forthcoming. These changes, especially when exacerbated by the imminent threat of famine, meant that there were profound disruptions in most of the most fundamental bases of social cohesion including the economy, the organised religious field, and family life. The tempo of these changes was also speeding up, and their cascading nature meant that the various disruptions were not just added one to another, but were patterned in such a way as to reinforce and multiply the effects of each one taken separately. Consideration of the changes, their causes and patterns shows why the Knock area and especially the witnesses to the apparition were among those likely to be most deeply affected.

Commercialisation and Cultural Change

In many parts of the west of Ireland, after the catastrophic population losses of the 1840s' famine, society returned to relative stability for several decades and emigration was less than elsewhere in the country. Historian David Doyle summarises what many others have described:

> The social system was traditional . . . People lived in clusters of cottages (*clachans*), farmed on the strip system, shared farm tasks (*meitheal*), and observed fairly rigorous social and familial discipline. From the 18th century, income was supplemented from commercial cereal growing, cattle production, and linen weaving: rents rose gradually, population more rapidly, but the social fabric largely held firm. Even during and after the Famine years few from these regions migrated to America, though seasonal work in England was not uncommon.[2]

There is considerable truth in this provided we keep in mind that the reality on the ground was never as idyllic as painted with the brush of scholarly nostalgia. Moreover, far from being timeless, the 'traditional ways' were often relatively recent innovations. The rundale system, for example, was not a legacy from some dim and misty Celtic past, but a relatively recent development, in response to population growth and other social pressures.[3] By the 1870s, however, this 'post-famine adjustment' was no longer working satisfactorily for the people of the region. Multiple factors, directly or indirectly associated with increased commercialisation, provoked a crisis and ultimately a 'collapse of traditional culture and attitudes':

> The *clachans* broke down. Farm families decided to make ends meet by policies of going it alone to meet rising rents. The region was networked by stone walls, litigation, demoralisation of the landless and anti-land-lord agitation . . . National schools and railroads and metropolitan newspapers began to strip away the mental machinery of the past, and replace it with a weary and cynical acquiescence in the monetarised world which seemed now everywhere. Thus, at the same time there spread a realization of how impossible the past poverty and frugality was, viewed with eyes that could read letters from Boston or Manchester. Tenacious family affections, deep religious convictions, gave way with the greatest reluctance to the dissolvents of a new world.[4]

One key item in this list is 'farm families decided to make ends meet by policies of going it alone to meet rising rents'. What was involved here was a drastic redefinition of both 'family' and 'farm'. The change was often instigated by landlords' effort to change tenure practices rather than deliberately chosen by tenants themselves. In the rundale system, a group of extended kin — often many siblings and cousins and their respective households — persisted through generations, usually along with some other similar kin-organised groups, while working the rented land that they shared. Shared descent and frequent intermarriages tied the individual members closely to the whole group. Individual loyalty was tied up in this kinship grouping (which often became the nucleus of a 'faction' that competed and fought with rival factions). Each co-tenant worked plots of land that were intermingled with those of other co-tenants, and which were also periodically redistributed so that a given person or nuclear family permanently held no identifiably delimited piece of ground independent of other tenants. Consequently, there could be no identification through the generations of a particular stem family with its unique holding. When rundale was abolished, individual farms were carved out and fenced off one from another. As Doyle put it, 'the region was networked with stone walls' (or their equivalent in other types of boundary fences between farms). Each of these tenant holdings was then passed down within the stem family, in the usual case from father to inheriting son. In contrast to the situation under rundale, other sons had no access to land. Children were 'reared for emigration' in the hope they would send money home to help pay rents, shop debts, and more passages overseas.[5] More distant familial relationships were weakened and the power of the father in the nuclear family was reinforced because of his control of land and the selection of the heir. 'Keeping the name on the land' became the by-word for maintaining the particular fields identified as 'the family farm', rather than the scattered and commingled plots that were part of the communal land resources under rundale.[6]

On his estate, landlord Lord Dillon and his agent Charles Strickland had long promoted the replacement of rundale by individual farms. The transition involved extensive negotiations and demarcation of separate farms and was a time-consuming one for the agent but it was a world-altering one for the tenants requiring recalibration of relationships within the nuclear family and also in the extended kinship network and wider community generally. For the area immediately surrounding the site of the apparition in Knock, that change had taken place by 1859.[7] Inherited attitudes would not change overnight, and by 1879 in Knock we can be confident that cultural orientations associated with the new system had not completely replaced the older patterns, with consequent confusion and uncertainty about how to respond in new circumstances.[8]

Historians have examined the evidence for changing family structures in the different regions in post-famine Ireland. The spreading adoption of the stem system with its one heir, impartible inheritance of farms, and arranged marriages and dowries can be charted in many demographic indices. Marriages were at later ages and more people remained unmarried where and when the stem system spread. Various studies show that in the 1870s and 1880s, the west began to converge with patterns already established decades earlier in the rest of the country,[9] another index of the end of the west's period of post-famine return to stability. County Mayo was to the forefront in the speed of the collapse as measurable in many demographic variables. The marriage rate for single women fell more rapidly after 1871 in County Mayo than in any other county.[10] The proportion of adults never marrying increased dramatically in the county after 1871.[11] The proportion of women aged 20–24 who were married, easily calculated from census data, is a convenient proxy for a host of other variables more difficult to measure, such as the proportion of women who would ever marry as well as average ages at marriage, which indicate how widely the stem system was in operation. What Cousens noted decades ago has not been changed in its outline by more sophisticated studies:

> [In Ireland as a whole,] far fewer women were married in the age-group 20–24 in 1881 than had been the case ten years earlier, and the decline was most emphatic in the West. In Leinster the proportion fell by 1 or 2 per cent, for example, in Louth from 18.9 per cent to 17.6 per cent, in Wexford from 14.8 per cent to 12.5 per cent, and in Wickow from 13.4 per cent to 12.9 per cent. In Ulster changes were on much the same scale. In Connaught, however, the smallest loss, from 29.0 per cent to 23.2 per cent, was in Galway, and the largest, from 29.5 per cent to 20.9 per cent, was in Mayo.[12]

Kerry had a similar large drop in this figure indicating how rapidly the western seaboard counties were converging in their demographic patterns with the rest of the country. This shows how quickly the people of these areas lost confidence in the viability or even desirability of the way of life that had sustained them for decades if not longer.

Another measure of rapid cultural disintegration in western Ireland is the shift from Irish to English as the everyday language. Gaelic speaking often protected patterns of life at the local level that remained impenetrable to supra-local social movements. For the pre-famine period, Daniel Campbell emphasised that Michael Flatley 'got' his Protestantism in England as if that were sufficient to discredit it. Campbell does not refer to any national movement in Knock before the 1840s' famine. Even when he was concerned with Catholic oppression, he never refers to anything that we can associate with Daniel O'Connell's movements for Emancipation or Repeal. Given Campbell's focus on religion, we might expect some recognition of Fr Mathew's temperance crusades but we find none. Using as memory devices the stories he heard as a young man in Knock, Campbell interprets even the nationally significant elections that ended the parliamentary careers of Denis Browne and John Browne through the prism of local realities, the triumph of Bishop MacHale. However, the protective linguistic shield collapsed fast in places like south-east Mayo. 'The end came suddenly. The contraction of Irish speaking areas was swift and the period of bilingualism probably brief. And this coincided with the west's catching up in its experience of population decline.'[13]

Around Knock, the language change was most dramatic in the declining numbers of monolingual Irish speakers. While the 1851 census recorded 58.7 per cent of the population of Clanmorris barony and 49.3 per cent of Costello Barony as Irish speakers, these figures were still over 43 per cent in both baronies in 1891. This suggests considerable continuity but in fact the suggestion is misleading, since the 1891 proportion is exaggerated because of the large scale emigration of younger people more likely to not speak Irish. A more accurate indicator of the abrupt transition is that very few people spoke only Irish at the later date. Monolingual Irish speakers declined in absolute numbers from 5,309 to 113 between 1851 and 1891 in Costello and from 1,181 to just 71 in Clanmorris.[14] The shift in language was fuelled by the growing recognition by parents that English was needed to secure a future for their children, an implicit if not always explicit recognition that their inherited way of life was untenable, that their society was falling apart. A 1930s' pupil in Coogue national school in Knock parish, recounted neighbours' stories of three 'old thatched schools' before the national schools arrived. These three, at Larganboy, Aghtaboy and 'here' had teachers who were paid by parents, but the language of instruction was English. When other similar schools were started elsewhere in the parish of Knock around the 1860s, such as at Kincon in 1867 and at 'Cluanlaogh' around the same time, the language of instruction was likewise English even though the Sunday catechism lessons in the chapel in the very same years had been in Irish for the benefit of monolingual older people.[15] Schoolteachers and parents in Knock considered Irish as not 'stylish' and punished pupils if they used it.[16]

Later, English was the language of practically all speeches at land agitation meetings, even where the audience held thousands of native Irish-speakers, a fact that astonished one very interested Irish-American, the Fenian John Devoy.[17] On one occasion, however, when Land League leader Davitt resorted to giving his speech in Irish to befuddle a government note-taker at a demonstration meeting, he was followed by a priest speaking Irish so that 'every one of his auditors understood him', and by a tenant-farmer 'who failed in the English, then delivered in Irish a most impassioned speech on the wrongs of his class, and a fierce invective against persons who encouraged the landlords in rack-renting by coveting their neighbours' land'.[18] It would appear that the tenants at that meeting at least were more comfortable with Irish than with English. Doyle claimed that people in Knock in 1879 commanded both languages fluently but that 'Irish would have been the domestic and village language, English the language of the school, of intercourse with travellers, and of business with the nearby towns',[19] but even if that were so it was far from being a stable situation. Doyle was concerned to emphasise that the apparition witnesses gave precise testimony in English and so asserted their competence in that tongue. More likely, different individuals and groups in the village and the parish had different levels of competence in each language; the available evidence points to greater use of Irish than Doyle suggests. A visitor to Knock very early in February 1880 noted that the priest 'gives out notices to the congregation and exhorts them in Irish — he speaks to them in English too: but they seem to love the old tongue'.[20] Language fluency divided the people of Knock along generational and class lines and likely along gender lines.

Differences between people of different ages operated to hinder the transmission of traditional cultural attitudes and understandings. Among the

1879 apparition witnesses we find both Bridget Trench, a woman in her mid seventies, who could give her testimony only in Irish, and several children whose schooling very likely was exclusively in English. We do not have information on the fluency in English of the other adults though for most it was likely their second language. Among the children-seers is Patrick Hill, who gave the most detailed description of the apparition scene of all the witnesses. It is probably no coincidence that many of the descriptive details of orthodox iconography that he gave were to be found in contemporary representations in pictures and statues being circulated through the schools.[21] He told a reporter that the altar and the lamb in the apparition appeared 'as represented in Catholic pictures'.[22] There is a high probability that Hill was a pupil at the new school in Claremorris run by the Sisters of Mercy, where he would certainly have been exposed to modern religious prints, but even other schools had such material objects.[23] The same visitor who described Fr Cavanagh's speaking in Irish in chapel also mentioned visiting a house of a local family where 'we were accommodated with the finest milk and butter, fresh eggs, and such bread as I have seldom seen equalled, as white as a hound's tooth, and as free from girt (sic) as possible'. Recall that this was at a time of famine in the area,[24] so this family was clearly better off than most. Unlike the visitor, we are not surprised to learn that the people of that house 'spoke English with a distinctness of accentuation and fluency that made [him] wonder', but at the same time 'they did not neglect their native Celtic for which they have an undying love'.[25] In contrast, Thomas Sexton, *The Nation's* correspondent, was unable to understand the Irish he heard in another cottage in the village. Perhaps his lack of Irish is one reason that Sexton did not interview some of the original adult witnesses, despite his repeated visits to the village where several of them lived. As late as 1904 a school inspector in Knock noted that 'many of the pupils know Irish fairly colloquially', even though they were not taught the language in school.[26]

Another set of changes disrupted established patterns of male/female relationships, and again these were more intense in Mayo than elsewhere and, likely, more intense again in the Knock area than even in other parts of Mayo. Population stayed level or returned to pre-famine sizes and other cultural patterns persisted in places like Knock, largely because tenants could earn their rents by working as agricultural labourers in England.[27] Except in a few areas such as Achill, these seasonal migrants were almost all males.[28] Mayo alone sent almost half of all harvest workers to England:[29] on the Dillon estate about three quarters of the tenants migrated annually to England.[30] In the Knock area, very likely most men migrated.[31] In England and in their travels, these people used more English and we would expect them more than females to be bilingually fluent. However, as the prospects dimmed of having a satisfactory life in Ireland, young women and/or their families became even more committed to schooling as a way to prepare for life abroad. In counties like Mayo, girls quickly caught up in literacy rates with their brothers. In 1841 less than one tenth of Mayo's young women aged 15–24 could read and write compared to a quarter of the young men, but the gender gap closed in the succeeding decades. By 1881, 58.5 per cent of Mayo females in this age cohort were literate compared to 62.7 per cent of the males.[32] In the next decades the parishes around Knock were to experience a substantially higher emigration of women than of men.[33]

We know that women's emigration specifically was on the minds of people in Fr Cavanagh's parish, because Martin J. Flanagan, a teacher in Aghamore, published a poem called 'Are You Going To America, Mary?' in December 1878.[34] After cataloguing the attractions of America — to Flanagan these were the various geographic landmarks and landscapes: he does not mention anything of social freedom or economic opportunity — Flanagan continues

> No — leave not the old land, Mary
> O, leave not the dear lov'd Isle
> Where the freshening seas breathe a gentle breeze,
> And the green fields softly smile;
> Where the hills and the beauteous valleys
> Are by matchless verdure blest,
> And the blooming girls are far brighter pearls
> Than the pride of the distant West.

Emigration is not opportunity, and America is a 'land of scorching sun and basking snakes'. As Kerby Miller has shown, for most Irish emigration was constructed as exile.[35] Poetry like this can be condemned as maudlin sentimentality, but it is evidence of the apprehension overtaking even the 'respectable' people in places like Knock, and their sense of powerlessness to change their 'doom'. Flanagan never asks whether the 'lov'd Isle' would provide a fulfilling life for the women he urged to stay at home. Would the green fields feed bullocks? Could the verdure blest sustain satisfying lives, with husbands and children, for all the Marys?

Underlying the various changes in family life, access to land, demographic patterns, and language use was the deepening penetration of commercialisation in more areas of people's lives.[36] While money to pay the rent was required in the pre-famine era, more cash was seen as necessary in the post-famine years to finance ever more consumer items from abroad.[37] Connacht had twenty-six shopkeepers per 10,000 people in 1841 but this number had greatly increased to forty-four by 1881; in Mayo, the increase was even more dramatic, from eleven to forty-one.[38] One contemporary noted that 'the general rise in the scale of comfort . . . is simply enormous'.[39] In Mayo, the number of banks operating rose from three in 1855 to nineteen in 1878,[40] indicative of increased cash savings available to be deposited. Archaeological evidence shows that even labourers and cottiers in rural north Roscommon before the 1840s' famine owned imported items such as pottery teacups and pipes, evidence that they consumed tea and tobacco.[41] There is no comparable evidence for Knock, but based on Daniel Campbell's memoir, it would appear that Knock was much less integrated into a wider market for such items. He tells us that tea was very rarely drunk. He mentions local non-alcoholic and alcoholic drinks both, and felt the need to describe the locally made 'noggin' wooden drinking vessels.

Campbell tells us in contrast that tobacco, which of course was imported, was widely used. Demand for and consumption of externally produced 'non-essential' items indicates dissatisfaction with local alternatives and acceptance of the implied claim that the 'imports' are preferable to them. The 'new' has greater prestige. It is a step in the acceptance by 'modernising' insiders of the implication that their own traditional bases for marking status are no longer credible, and in their acceptance of the external criteria to measure their claims to status. The use of foreign consumer goods in places like Knock is evidence of the 'symbolic violence'[42] by which the local is subordinated to the more 'modern' even in the eyes of the locals. By 1879, the cottage of the main Beirne family presented considerable evidence of such an orientation. It had two doors in front at a time when most cottages including Fr Cavanagh's had only one.[43] *The Nation*'s correspondent described the home as 'comfortable and neat in appearance. The "dresser" . . . stood laden with its rows of plates and dishes. The furniture . . . was suitably substantial'.[44] The dresser was an item of furniture used not only to store but to display the plates and dishes, in the process displaying the family's status by making their consumption conspicuous. It was a recognised status symbol in nineteenth-century rural Irish houses.[45] The photographer from Limerick who praised the bread he ate in Knock as 'white as a hound's tooth' had internalised the 'modern' message that white flour was superior to whole grain for bread-making, and that consequently shop-bought white flour was preferable to locally ground grain. He also assumed that this was significant information to publish for the readers of his account.[46] Presumably, the local Knock family (not the Beirnes) where he ate this bread also measured status, including its own relative standing, with the same yardstick. Status distinctions based on food use, even when they make no nutritional sense, still operate to produce and sustain more elaborate inequalities in how people judge themselves and others. Of course, the distinctions were not just symbolic; in a place where many were hungry, having food at all was quite obviously of material importance. But having the 'right' kind of food sustained not only physical health but feelings of social and cultural superiority.

In Daniel Campbell's time, Knock was very much a locally focused place. Despite the onslaughts of proselytisers and the need to migrate to earn their rents, people's loyalties were centred on and their identities were constituted in local arenas. Campbell's constant practice of identifying individuals by placing them in their kin networks is one index of this. Even for insiders, however, there is evidence that Knock became less central than it once had been. There was a long-term decline *in the eyes of insiders* in the centrality and importance of the local village or parish vis-à-vis other places, especially Claremorris.[47] Campbell mentioned three young men who walked five or six miles from near Claremorris to finish their education in Knock because

Claremorris at the time had no schoolmaster as good as the one in Knock. But Knock was to become less important as a node or focus for local activities. This decline was to become more pronounced when the nearby towns of Claremorris and Ballyhaunis were connected to the railway system in the 1860s. With the coming of the railroads, 'the Dublin–Newport mail coach ceased to run on the highway a mile south of the village: and from then on Knock came to be regarded as a remoter, inaccessible spot'.[48] At the time of the 1879 apparition, the 'village' of Knock[49] had only less than a dozen houses. 'Six straggling little thatched cottages,' said Cork pilgrims in 1880.[50] Yet that village could boast a police barracks, separate boys' and girls' primary schools, and a post office, all emblematic of new intrusive institutions. And it held an imposing church building visible for miles around, a reminder of how much more important it once had been in the local hierarchy of places.

The Land War

In this situation of cultural fragility, pressures that might otherwise have had little effect could prove catastrophic. Events in the late 1870s would have a devastating impact because the system was already tottering.[51] Triggered by a combination of successive weather-related bad harvests, plummeting prices for agricultural products caused by imports from the US and elsewhere, and a 'New Departure' leading to cooperation between agrarian radicals, political revolutionaries and the Irish Party in the House of Commons, what is called the 'Land War' struck at the very heart of the legally established property system. For centuries most land in Ireland had been owned by landlords but worked by tenants who paid rent. In the late nineteenth century, this structure was challenged and eventually virtually destroyed. Under the pressure of agitation, continuing massive demonstration meetings with speeches extensively reported in newspapers, boycotts, passive resistance of all kinds and widespread threatened and more rarely actual violence by tenants, the government passed a series of laws that effectively turned the workers of the soil from rent-paying tenants to owner-occupiers of their farms. This fundamental revolution in the basic economic arrangements predictably profoundly affected practically every social relationship in the society:

> Making all due allowance for differences of scale and scope, the land war
> of 1879–1882 is to Irish history rather as the revolution of 1789 is to
> French history.[52]

It amounted to what its key leader, Michael Davitt, characterised as 'the fall of feudalism in Ireland'.[53]

One of the distinguishing tactics of the Land War was the holding of regular public demonstrations of a size unseen in Ireland since O'Connell's 'monster meetings' of the 1820s and 1840s during the campaigns first for

Catholic Emancipation and later for Repeal of the Union with Britain. The first mass public meeting to demand redress of tenant grievances was held at Irishtown, in south-east Mayo, on 20 April 1879. The Knock apparition on 21 August 1879 was less than a dozen miles away, and Knock was within what historians have identified as the core area for the start of the war.[54]

Their closeness in time and place suggests more than a coincidental connection between the Land War, and especially its beginning and early stages in south-east Mayo, and the apparition at Knock. Historians of the Land War, however, have virtually ignored the apparition. Clark, concentrating on understanding the Land League as a social movement, mentions the apparition only in passing in a footnote that recognises it competed with the land agitation for attention in the papers.[55] Bew, focusing on the divergent class interests of different participants in the movement, doesn't even mention Knock.[56] Moody's biography of Michael Davitt, probably the most important Land League leader, similarly ignores the apparition, as does Jordan in his book on land and popular politics in Mayo.[57] One historian who did investigate it became a believer in the supernatural explanation of the apparition.[58] Except for a dissertation by John White,[59] very few analysts have examined the connection between the Land League agitation and the apparition and these only in passing. In a study of nutrition, Crawford suggested the apparition might be due to hallucinations induced by the disease of pellagra to which persons dependent on a diet of Indian meal were supposedly susceptible.[60] Donnelly has effectively discredited this explanation.[61] The pellagra was supposed to have been caused by dietary deficiencies from which the seers were not likely to have suffered (because they were not then reliant on Indian meal that was later distributed as famine relief) and which none of the many reporters mentioned in their accounts of the seers. Moreover, if pellagra and hallucinations were involved, why was Knock the particular site where people saw apparitions? In any case, the apparition occurred before there was any famine, although famine was very clearly threatened at the time, and appeared later. Sociologist Michael Carroll claims there was an 'extraordinary increase in rents' after crop failures in 1877 and 1878, and that 'mass evictions' took place when tenants were unable to pay these high rents.[62] Unfortunately there is no evidence for increased rents in those years, and no evidence for increased evictions before the 1879 apparition. In a review of Bew's book on the Land League, Gilley called for recognising the Knock episode as a people's religious response to oppression and suffering.[63] Finally, in a polemical study of how the image of the Virgin Mary has been used by world wide conservative and reactionary forces in society and in the Catholic Church, Perry and Echeverria wrote that the Knock apparition and the Land League were publicised side by side in *The Nation* from February through October 1880, thereby suggesting that in some way the apparition was promoted to help the Land League cause.[64] In contrast, others have suggested that the publicity given to Knock in *The Nation* was a way to counter the Land

League by effectively marginalising another paper, the *Connaught Telegraph*, at the time virtually the mouthpiece of the movement, published and edited by an important leader of the agitation, James Daly.

Nobody seems to have noticed that there probably was a direct economic incentive for *The Nation*'s coverage. There was some business arrangement before the apparition between the newspaper and a Dublin businessman called J. J. Lalor. Regular notices in the paper before the apparition, at least since 1876, advised its subscribers to send their money orders or cheques, made payable to Lalor, at the address of the paper. Such an arrangement allowed both parties to the agreement to know how much money Lalor, whose place of business was at a different Dublin address, was receiving for *The Nation* subscriptions. Lalor was a seller of political souvenirs and religious artefacts and was later to advertise heavily various Knock medals and other devotional items.[65] When *The Nation*'s proprietor, T. D. Sullivan, published his 'Special Correspondent's' reports on Knock as a short book in the spring of 1880, he included an advertisement for Lalor offering a 'Medal of the Knock Apparition' available in prices ranging from sixpence to three shillings and sixpence (for a 'richly gilt' medal in a 'neatly finished case, lined with blue satin and plush', and with postage paid.)[66] The book also included illustrations credited to the Limerick photographer, T. O'Connor, whose business sold prints of the Knock scene. Promotion of the Knock cult was very obviously to Lalor's and O'Connor's economic benefit. In addition, Knock coverage was likely to increase the paper's own circulation. Canon Ulick Bourke, a priest on the Investigation Commission and on good terms with Sullivan, estimated that the paper's circulation increased from 70,000 to 80,000 during the six months of extensive coverage of Knock.[67]

Believers in the supernatural provenance of the apparition frequently claim that the Virgin came to Ireland, to a poor village at a desperate time, to console the suffering people and to reward them for loyalty to the true faith through centuries of persecution.[68] In the 1930s an extensive and successful campaign was launched to extend devotion and pilgrimage to the shrine at Knock. Promoters including especially local judge and prolific writer, William Coyne [Liam Ua Cadhain], said that the apparition gave down-trodden farm tenants the courage to challenge the power of the exploiting landlords, leading eventually to the overthrow of the landlord system.[69] There are two main objections to this interpretation, purely on the basis of empirical and historical evidence. The first Land War meeting, at Irishtown, took place in April 1879 and the Knock apparition the following August, so to claim that the apparition led in some way to the Land War and/or Land League is at the very least to put the cart before the horse. Second, there is no contemporary evidence to suggest that the August event led to any increased Land War activity. A sociologist who wrote a PhD dissertation on Land League ideology and who intensively studied speeches at Land League meetings — they were extensively reported in the local and national press — wrote that:

> In my analysis of land meeting speeches I have found no references to
> the Knock apparition, no linkage between the Virgin's appearance and
> the land movement. Though I have not been specifically looking for
> such references, I would have noticed them as they would be highly
> symbolic.[70]

There were important linkages between the apparition and the land movement, but the particular connection I posit will show why Land League
organisers did not regard the apparition as inspirational.

Landlords and Tenants

The tenant movement and popular agitation presented unprecedented problems for the government as well as for Irish nationalist politicians, whether
Home Rulers or Fenians, and led to leadership struggles and splits in the
various parties.[71] But it was ordinary people, and not government ministers
or political activists of whatever stripe, who reported the heavenly visitors.
To appreciate how the Land War affected people in general and people like
the Knock witnesses in particular, it is necessary to describe how the tenure
system under attack had actually worked in their particular lives. It is
against that reality that they would have defined and experienced their
hopes and fears.

In his important sociological study of the War, Samuel Clark pointed out
the importance of 'non-contractual' elements in the relationships that, up to
that transition, existed between tenants and landlords or their agents. In
theory, a tenant owed a definite amount of rent for a specific defined area of
land over a defined period. In other words, the particular farm, the amount
of rent and the length of the rental period were all known and agreed at the
outset of the contract. In practice, things were never so calculable. Each
piece of land was unique, and if 'improvements' were made in the course of
the rent period, how were they to be defined? How would they be factored
into the contract? Moreover, nature in the form of each season's weather or
even crop failure due to 'new' diseases as happened in the Great Hunger was
unpredictable. Comprehensive and precise agreements were difficult if not
impossible to negotiate or maintain. In such circumstances, over the course
of years or even generations, particular understandings had emerged
between landlords and individual or groups of tenants that were nowhere
codified in law and often were not written down.[72]

Rather than being simply an economic transaction in a capitalist system
where two parties with equal power and information negotiated a contract
to pay a rent for a given farm, the relationship was almost feudal in nature.
'On some properties marriages cannot be consummated without the
sanction of the landlord or his agent', declared one critic in 1879.[73] 'Feudal'
was no mere derogatory label to be wielded as a weapon to mould public
opinion in the political arena; rather it is an accurate label for some features

of the tenure system as it then operated in practice. Slater and McDonough catalogue contemporary descriptions of a wide range of feudal style impositions in the nineteenth century. These included the persistence of 'non-monetary dues' such as mandatory contributions of eggs, poultry, and other goods and the provision of services such as labour on the landlord's land and crops, either unpaid or paid at below market rates. Moreover,

> tenants were subjected to a variety of estate rules which went well beyond the usual contractual obligations of lessees. These rules included obtaining permission from the landlord to marry, forbidding the exercise of overnight hospitality, encouraging the attendance of children at Protestant schools, fines for setting snares and traps, and maintaining the secrecy of landlord/tenant dealings.[74]

The authors could have added the expectation that tenants would vote as their landlords desired. 'This social control over the tenantry is not in essence a mere contractual relationship, but must be maintained by extra-economic coercion and the personal domination of the landlord over the tenant.'[75]

Landlords as well as their critics characterised the system as feudal[76] but it is still necessary to qualify the statement in several ways. First landlord–tenant relationships were far from uniform from one estate to another. Considering only the level of rents, Jordan noted in Mayo 'great discrepancies . . . from estate to estate and from farm to farm within a single estate'.[77] In fact, landlords' and agents' relationships with tenants were highly particularistic. Some 'privileges' that one landlord recognised might be denied by another while tenants elsewhere might see them as 'rights'. 'Non-contractual privileges' included permitting tenants to 'sell' their interests in a holding, undisturbed occupancy if rents were paid, and relatively moderate rents.[78] Nearly every issue of the *Connaught Telegraph* in the summer of 1879 carried stories indicating not only how landlords were being challenged but also how highly variable and individualistically worked out were their relationships with tenants.

A second qualifying consideration is that legal theory and actual practice bore little relation to each other. Proprietors had vast legal powers to end a tenancy but rarely used those powers. 'The tenants had an ineradicable belief in their right to continuous occupancy so long as they paid their rents and landlords generally took the line of least resistance.'[79] Rents were generally moderate and tenure secure as long as rents were paid, and evictions were rare.[80] This pattern, however, just tended to reinforce the importance of particularistic relationships.

Thirdly, there is good reason to believe that the 'understandings' between landlords and tenants were not mutually shared. Fundamentally, the two sides had different interpretations of what was involved in their 'contract'. The public transcript did not square with the hidden transcripts of either party.[81] Even when they showed deference to their landlord or cheered for his agent, not far beneath the surface was a popular conviction that 'the people' (vaguely defined) had an inalienable right to the land they and their ancestors had worked. The other side of this coin was the claim that the landlords owed their position to conquest in earlier centuries and political oppression and economic exploitation in the present where they constituted an English garrison keeping the country in bondage.[82] Tenants could also hold a wide variety of other beliefs about the legitimacy of landlords; there is no reason to expect that their expressed attitudes were very consistent.[83] Historian K. T. Hoppen recognised that 'both "paternalism" and "deference" could be endlessly manipulated by all concerned'.[84]

While, like the peasants of the Ethiopian proverb, the smallholders of Mayo and elsewhere found it wise to 'bow low and silently fart when the great lord passed by', their exaggerated displays of deference actually masked their sense of powerlessness. As Hoppen also recognised, even consciously sophis- ticated evasions were humiliating nonetheless.[85] Landlords did not usually directly personally coerce tenants. Rather, their power was exercised more indirectly (for example through their input to the machinery of the state and its workings) and more subtly (through the effects of tenants' powerlessness on their ideas of what was possible for them to achieve).[86] Tenants' depend- ency was manifested and reproduced through gestures of subordination and deference, such as doffing their hats to the landlords. On many estates events, such as the return of the landlord after living or travelling abroad, were marked by 'loyalty demonstrations' involving such practices as tenants unhitching the horses from the lord's carriage and pulling the carriage them- selves, along with 'welcoming committees, laudatory speeches and congratulatory addresses, illuminations, triumphal arches, torchlight proces- sions, fireworks, bands and music, and commemorative verse'.[87] Newspapers before the Land War routinely carried accounts of such happenings. On one such occasion in 1878, for example, tenants from Lord Clanmorris' Mayo estate sent a delegation, including the parish priest, to one of his other estates in County Galway, to participate in ceremonies to mark his wedding, a journey requiring several days of travel. The tenants collected money to buy a gift of plate and a silver necklace worth 100 guineas for the bride. At the same time this landlord was having difficulty collecting his rent.[88]

However, the dissonance between tenants' public utterances and private feelings became intense when the whole system came under overt challenge, as it did in the Land War.[89] Within a year the very paper that reported the loyalty demonstration at length was roundly condemning this same indi- vidual landlord.[90] What was any particular tenant to do? There was no clear path ahead. In keeping with one politically useful view — that landlords got their lands first through conquest in earlier centuries — the Land League was to articulate forcefully the rights of tenants as an historic claim.[91] However, even though evictions between the Great Famine and the Land War were in fact rare, the very possibility that landlords could resort to them, and actually did so in a handful of notorious cases, served to remind tenants of their vulnerability. Against cliometricians who argued that beatings in the American slave system were rare and that the vast majority of slaves were never beaten, Herbert Gutman pointed out that the public whipping of one slave had a terrorising demonstration effect on thousands more. Every slave was profoundly affected, not just those bloodied by the whip.[92] The same was true of those tenants who were not evicted in the post-famine decades in Ireland: statistics on their number can never penetrate the meaning of an eviction for those not involved. Precisely because the famine reinforced throughout the society the recognition that 'land was life', almost literally, the threat of losing one's farm bore even greater weight.

The progressive elimination of rundale was also a progressive undercutting of obligations toward extended kin; those facing eviction could less and less count on the 'obligatory hospitality' of relatives. Paradoxically, the reduction in the numbers of farm families did not enhance the security of the survivors, because more and more acres were required to support a family at an acceptable standard of living. As economic trends increasingly favoured livestock over tillage farming, more and more families at the bottom of the pyramid were forced out of agriculture, bringing those above them at every level ever closer to the bottom. And at the time of the 1879 apparition, 'many Mayo smallholders were faced with the prospect of being unable to make their rent payment, and were candidates for eviction'.[93]

Clark recognised that, generally, 'the transfer of ownership of an estate . . . presented tenants with the danger that the non-contractual privileges they had enjoyed in the past would not be respected by the new owner'. Because in the usual case so much of the tenants' relationships involved idiosyncratic unwritten understandings, negotiated over time with landlords or usually agents, *any* changes dictated by law or forced by public protests introduced new uncertainties for tenants.[94] Even new formal rules threatened to undermine personalistic relations between patrons and clients. The wholesale confronting of the whole system of landlordism, represented by the widespread agitation and demonstrations, could only have added to such anxiety among tenants unless their victory was guaranteed, which was certainly not the case in the summer of 1879.

There is very good reason to believe that in Knock, on the Dillon estate, the alarm and anxiety generated for tenants by the land agitation would be even greater than on other estates in Mayo (the birthplace of the Land War), or elsewhere. This is the case primarily because the landlord and his agent were both 'good'. Though he was an absentee living in England, Lord Viscount Dillon was reputed a good landlord. More especially, his agent, Charles Strickland, had a very long history of concerned involvement in the lives of the people. His relief efforts during the famine of the 1840s were recognised at the time and remembered much later. His good work was recognised in the famine years by Quaker relief officials, local Boards of Guardians and relief committees, Knock priests, and Mayo newspapers and it was attested by later newspapermen, such as Coulter in 1862 and Dun in

1880. (See chapter 6.) Almost unique among agents, Strickland escorted electors to the polls to vote contrary to the 'strict orders' of their landlord in an 1852 parliamentary election.[95]

In the midst of the Land War, *The Times* of London sent a correspondent to Ireland to report on the background to the agitation. This journalist, Finley Dun, chose to organise his dispatches from Ireland by examining selected landlords' estates, including Dillon's.[96] Dun was no apologist for landlordism and criticised other landlords' greed, inaction, short-sightedness and incompetence. His depiction of the Dillon estate, however, was very different. There, he wrote, 'the tenants have practically fixity of tenure; all improvements have belonged to the improver . . . [and] rents are low; many have remained unchanged for thirty years'.[97] Moreover, Dillon had brought about many 'improvements'. He had consolidated holdings in a manner that 'the keen little farmers, most jealous regarding their interests and rights' 'unanimously' saw as fair and just; built roads, fences and even a railway; improved drainage; distributed food during the Great Famine, etc.[98]

According to Dun, Dillon's agent, Charles Strickland, was deeply involved in the people's lives in ways that went well beyond the usual agent's work. He was their 'guide and counsellor . . . their mentor in agricultural matters, and their arbiter in their settlements and personal disputes, which are [were] constantly brought to him for his adjudication'.[99] Memories from near Loughglynn, where Strickland lived, recalled him intervening in a quarrel between neighbours over trespassing geese but also that he stressed the importance of education and helped support numerous schools.[100] Moreover, as agent, Strickland had kept a record of every tenant, 'his history and his family, and of every important transaction submitted for consideration or settlement'.[101] This record-keeping included having surveyors make detailed maps of each tenant's holdings, either when rundale was replaced by separate holdings for each tenant, or when Dillon acquired the property.[102]

Memories from Knock in the 1930s confirm Dillon's positive local reputation. For the Schools' Folklore Project, pupils in schools throughout the parish recorded testimony to this effect. From Rooskey school we learn that Dillon was much better than landlords elsewhere; he was not greedy for money and thus rents were not nearly as high as elsewhere. From the boys' school in Knock we are told that Strickland 'settled all disputes about land between tenants'. At the girls' school a pupil recorded that unlike landlords generally who were merciless and frightful, Dillon was a

> very good landlord and ruled well and he was the best landlord in Mayo. He was a very charitable landlord. Sometimes when any of his tenants were not able to pay their rents every year he would let them off and give them full receipt.[103]

Note the reference to Dillon as one who 'ruled well'. This is not the language of free-market contract relationships; neither is the reference to Dillon as a 'very charitable landlord', in contrast to others who were merciless and frightful.

In the early months of the land agitation, numerous demands were made on landlords to reduce rents. In a two-sentence item, the *Connaught Telegraph* on 31 May 1879 said Strickland had 'flatly refused' abatements, but in its next issue the paper highlighted a 'CORRECTION'.

> We are informed, on reliable authority, that Mr Strickland told them [the tenants' delegation] to reduce to writing their demands and that he would submit it to their landlord (Lord Dillon), and that he would feel pleasure if his lordship reduced their rent 50 per cent. A cold or blunt refusal would not be in keeping with Mr Strickland's previous acts towards the tenantry.

Coming as it does from the newspaper that at the time was virtually the mouthpiece of the tenants' movement, this statement speaks volumes for the popular reputation of Strickland. Strickland and his wife were deeply involved (and had been for decades) in charity work and public improvements of all sorts. For example, she provided First Communion dresses to poor girls in her Loughglynn neighbourhood and then, after the mass, provided breakfast for all the children of Loughglynn schools.[104] She donated a 'very pretty Maltese Cross and Earrings' as a prize for a fundraising bazaar for the Mercy Convent in Claremorris.[105] In 1878, Viscount Dillon 'per C. Strickland' gave five pounds toward the cost of a new stained glass window in Ballyhaunis Friary,[106] a window of which we will hear more later on. We even encounter Strickland in accounts of cures at Knock shrine after the apparition. When a young girl injured her eye with a table fork, Strickland arranged for her to go to a special hospital in Dublin but before she went there her eye was cured at Knock.[107] Dillon was by far the biggest of seventy-six Mayo landlords who granted rent abatements in the Land War and his 30 per cent reduction was also way above average.[108] It became the standard by which tenants on other estates measured the rent reductions they hoped their own landlords would grant.[109]

When in October 1879 word was received that Lord Dillon had reduced rents by 30 per cent, the *Connaught Telegraph* noted that this was equal to a 50 per cent–60 per cent reduction by other landlords since Dillon had not increased rents in Mayo for over sixty years, due 'in great measure to the great interest his agent (Mr Charles Strickland) evinced toward his tenants'.[110] Bonfires on hillsides for miles around greeted news of the abatement and in Ballyhaunis town there was a great street celebration featuring music by the local temperance band, free drinks provided by a tavern, and many 'hearty cheers' and prayers for the Stricklands.[111] At a Land League meeting later that month, in Fr Cavanagh's parish, Lord Dillon was cheered.[112] The apparent paradox of tenants cheering for a landlord at a Land League meeting says a lot about the conflicting feelings to which Dillon's tenants in Knock were subject. The anxiety and apprehension generated by the general anti-landlord agitation would, paradoxically, have been more threatening to the Dillon tenants, precisely because Strickland had been so immersed in their lives and their 'non-contractual privileges' were so extensive compared to tenants on other estates. Any disruption of the landlord–tenant ties would be more worrying for Knock area tenants than those on other estates because they had more to lose.

There was yet another reason for the tenants to fear for their relationships with Strickland and the landlord. Viscount Dillon died in 1879 and was suc-ceeded in the title by his brother.[113] This could also provoke unease but we lack evidence of how tenants viewed the transition. I have found no evi-dence that Dillon's death was even noticed locally. The landlord was an absentee living in England; far more important and salient as a subject of their daily considerations and conversations was his resident agent. It was for Strickland that the street revellers in Ballyhaunis offered cheers and prayers when they heard their landlord had reduced rents. But Strickland had been an agent for over forty years, since before the famine.[114] The tenants obviously were aware that the aging man could not continue in his position for long. And who then would respect or even know of unwritten understandings? What would a new agent know or make of tenants' under-standings or agreements they had worked out with Strickland, who had paid in 'time and trouble', using 'tact and judgment to balance rival claims' to create more stability and predictability for his tenants?[115] Any change was likely to be for the worse. What Samuel Clark wrote about the sale of any estate would be even more true in this case, 'tenants could hardly be expected to view (it) with anything but alarm'.[116] It is no coincidence that the Knock apparition, in August 1879, occurred at the time of the greatest anxiety about Dillon's actions on rent, between the demands for abatement, in late May, and the news of the 30 per cent reduction received in early October. But this was but one of the many anomie-producing social pres-sures that affected the Knock area in the summer of 1879.

The Land War also tended to undermine the traditional landlord–tenant relationship in other ways. Many landlords granted rent abatements on com-passionate grounds but still did not escape being targeted in the wholesale denunciation of the landlord system by land agitators. This in turn prompted some landlords to determine to enforce their legal rights, including evicting tenants for non-payment of rents, a departure from usual practice up to then.[117] Catholic landlords such as Walter Bourke were par-ticularly assailed for not siding with the distressed tenants.[118] Having been known as a 'good' landlord was no longer sufficient in the eyes of the tenants.[119] As a result, 'the landlords as a class felt themselves victims of a monstrous conspiracy, by which their property rights, their social status, and their loyalty to the union were all brutally and unjustly attacked'.[120] Landlords or agents such as Strickland who prided themselves on their just paternalism, found that the deference traditionally given them by their tenants was suddenly gone. 'The old familiar world they had known seemed to be breaking up before their eyes in a welter of class hatred, intimidation, and violence, instigated and organized by the Land League.'[121]

More directly, tenants' inability and unwillingness to pay their rents struck an economic blow at landlord living standards. George Moore, who owned a 12,000-acre Mayo estate with a nominal income of £3,596 per annum, spent his days in Paris mixing with painters and writers such as Manet, Degas and Zola. This life came to an abrupt end in August 1879 when he received a letter from his Mayo agent telling him that 'the tenants were refusing to pay rents and that he was afraid to risk his life by serving eviction orders to collect them'. The 'traumatic shock' of this news sent Moore into a panic.[122] Similar traumatically changed circumstances on other estates inevitably strained expectations on everybody's part. A police officer who served in Mayo at the time recalled that 'it was only then [in the Land War] that the landlords began to feel that their position was not as secure as they had believed'.[123]

Moore, for one example on the landlord side, was forced to support himself by his writing. He was to publish autobiographical and slightly-disguised 'naturalist' accounts of the whole society then in turmoil. In his childhood he had seen the peasants as alien and frightening but the agitation forced him to recognise the hardships they suffered. While he prided himself on his family's feudal paternalism he recognised that 'if we (landlords) thought bullocks would pay us better we ridded our lands of [tenants] . . . and I remember how they used to go away by train from Claremorris in great batches bawling like animals'.[124] This led him to feel ambivalent, if not ashamed of landlordism, which alienated him from his relatives and others of his own class. He was equally ambivalent in his attitudes toward small farmers, priests, Land League leaders, and others. But he recognised the stark reality that things had changed fundamentally and forever. 'Never has the world seen, not even in France in time of revolution, such a reversal of fortune as that threatened in Ireland', where 'the tenant farmers will dictate their terms to the landlords and those of [this] already enfeebled class, whom the assassin scare will gradually starve to death or exile'.[125] Moore had been considered a benevolent landlord; his father was George Henry Moore, whose election to parliament in 1868 was celebrated as the triumph of Archbishop MacHale over the enemies of the people.[126] Moreover, though many biographers consider he was in practice an atheist ever since his teens, George Moore had been raised a Catholic and so that identity was fixed indelibly in the minds of the people.[127] Being a good Catholic landlord afforded no protection to Moore or others like him. But what was in the hearts and thoughts of the tenants, without workable cultural blueprints for how to behave in the new order?

The new circumstances provoked quite distinct unease in others also in the early summer of 1879. The 'New Departure' was an arrangement worked out between leaders of the agrarian agitation, some revolutionary nationalists ready to use force to achieve Irish independence, and some nationalist politicians in the Irish Party to coordinate their strategies. This framework was agreed in the late 1870s and was in existence before the crisis of 1879 hit. The heart of the matter was that agrarian radicals like Michael Davitt, who were determined to attack the whole system of land-lordism at its root, were abetted by nationalists in and out of parliament who saw this as a step in severing the link to Britain and establishing Irish political independence.[128] At a meeting in Claremorris in March 1879, an agreement to cooperate on this step was reached between Davitt and local Fenian leaders in Mayo,[129] many of whom were key leaders of the land agitation. Landlords understandably were appalled, and so were their allies, initially including almost all the Catholic clergy. Socially conservative, priests generally accepted landlords and indeed saw them as playing essential roles in society. It was probably to the political and social revolutionary thrust that the Knock priest Fr Cavanagh was reacting when he denounced local leaders of the land agitation in early summer of 1879.[130]

Fr Cavanagh and his Parishioners

Conflict between Catholic priests and their parishioners, a potent generator of anomie, was more intense in Knock than almost anywhere else. The early land demonstration meetings at Irishtown, Westport and elsewhere were held 'in the teeth of clerical opposition'. The frequently retold story that the first target of the agitation was a priest-landlord (acting as agent for his recently deceased brother, nephew or uncle) is, in fact, untrue;[131] nevertheless, clerical–lay relationships were severely stressed.[132] One of the earliest and most outspoken clerical critics of the new agitation and its organisers was Archdeacon Bartholomew Cavanagh, the Parish Priest of Knock. He denounced it from the pulpit. We have several different reports of Fr Cavanagh's words and actions, largely because they provoked a huge demonstration against him that was in turn reported in the press and was the subject of a 'confidential' intelligence report prepared for the Irish Chief Secretary in Dublin. In addition, a memory of the protest demonstration passed down in the family of one of the apparition seers was recorded a century later. Each account highlighted issues and evidence relevant to the teller and was constructed with particular audiences in mind. What 'really happened' can be seen only through the various perspectives through which people then or later viewed it.

The *Connaught Telegraph*, the mouthpiece of the land agitation and edited by its important leader, James Daly, focused on issues central to its concerns. Under the headline, 'Monster Indignation Meeting at Knock', the paper reported that a crowd of between 20,000 and 30,000 people including 'fully fifteen thousand men [who] marched into Knock' on 1 June, 1879, came to enter a 'solemn and emphatic protest against the language used by the Venerable Archdeacon Cavanagh from the altar of the Parish Church on the previous Sunday'.[133] The article described what led up to the meeting and what the various speakers said at the demonstration. Tenant farmers in the area had been attempting to get landlords to reduce the rents because of the depression and were organising meetings to make their demands. 'On this head, Archdeacon Cavanagh, it is said, for the purpose of shielding certain landlords who were not inclined to accede to the just and reasonable demands of their tenants endeavoured to suppress the meetings.' Moreover, Cavanagh had claimed that one local organiser, Mr J. O'Kane, was 'engaged with others in preparing the country for a revolution'. Hearing such malicious and 'gross misrepresentations from a quarter they least expected', the people determined to hold the demonstration meeting to condemn Fr Cavanagh.

As reported by Daly's newspaper, the meeting was chaired by a local respectable tenant-farmer named Tobias Merrick, who regretted the need for such a demonstration. Merrick said they were accustomed to having their motives and actions maligned by their enemies but not by the priests from whom they expected protection and support. He hoped the priests and people would never be disunited, but if they were it would not be the people's fault. If the people were united and faithful, they could make their country 'great, glorious and free'. He would be sorry to say anything disrespectful to a priest but would say 'don't stand between the people and their rights: if you do, you must be prepared to accept the consequences'. 'We are neither infidels nor assassins', he continued, and assertions to this effect were 'wicked, false and malicious and calculated to engender feelings of bitterness and hostility'. He hoped that this would be the last time they would need such a meeting to respond to such 'wilful and malicious misrepresentations as they had heard lately'. The meeting then unanimously passed two resolutions. The first, proposed by J. W. Nally, condemned 'any line of action that would be calculated to alter the cherished relations that have ever, through weal and woe, existed between the Irish peasant and his pastor'. The second, proposed by a Mr Jones and seconded by O'Kane, was that while recognising how their enemies constantly sought to impugn their motives and blacken their names that 'it is with pain, if not indignation, we have heard these misrepresentations coming from a quarter where we should expect to find defence in our helplessness and excuse for our exasperation at crushing wrongs instead of unmeasured and unjust denunciation'. Finally, 'Mr O'Kane, being a particular favourite in this part of the country, was accorded an ovation on leaving the field'.

Not only was the demonstration directed at Cavanagh but the newspaper's report clearly articulated the case against him, and implicitly against any other priest, including Archbishop MacHale, who might take a similar position against the developing land agitation or those organising it. Again and again the report insinuated that Cavanagh had lied wilfully and maliciously and suggested he did so to protect some landlords. People expected the priests to act differently. If there was to be a rift between priests and the people it would be because priests like Cavanagh had abandoned their historic calling to protect the people. The message was that Cavanagh was not acting in a proper priestly fashion. From the perspective of the land agitation's leaders, the meeting and the newspaper account of it was designed to put hostile clerics like Cavanagh on the defensive.

The *Connaught Telegraph* report is not the only account we have of the events on 1 June 1879 in Knock. The demonstration was also the subject of a 'confidential' report for the Chief Secretary in Dublin Castle, which shows just how seriously police took the episode. The report apparently was prepared in Claremorris with input from the Kiltimagh constabulary and was dated 3 June, two days after the event. In contrast to the journalist, the police writer, Sub-Inspector 2nd Class J. C. Carter, focused on the political/nationalist aspects of the meeting and the military-style behaviour of the demonstrators:

> All the men, about 300 who *marched* to Knock, on that day assembled at a place called Barny-Carrol and proceeded thence in fours.
>
> They were profusely decorated with green sashes, rosettes, ribbons and laurel branches and leaves. They were commanded by [and here the document identifies four men]. All these men addressed the people assembled on the occasion who numbered about 1500.

The gist of the speeches is given, as well as the responses from the crowd. Finally, the report stated that a resolution was passed that his tenants should stand together against a local landlord named Nolan Farrell.

The report identified the four 'suspects' who 'had command' at the meeting as J. W. Nally, John O'Kane, P. J. Gordon and a man named Sheridan from nearby Bohold[134] (sic) but who was introduced at the meeting as 'W. Jones from Dublin'. Sheridan spoke first, saying Fr Cavanagh had tried to label them blackguards, ('cries down with him — cut off his supplies'). He had referred to one man by name, saying he was 'actually drawing money and importing arms', to which the crowd responded with 'Shame' and nine cheers for O'Kane. Their motive was 'the common benefit of our Country, that, by banding themselves together against the tyrant Landlords'. Sheridan continued by noting the police presence and referring to them as 'setters', 'in allusion to the formation of a barrack at Knock'.

O'Kane spoke next, saying that if wanting freedom for his country made a man a Fenian, then they were all Fenians. Did Fr Cavanagh wish to be reconciled to British rule? England was as hostile as ever. Who had made a desert of the country? 'The fair fields of Ireland are converted into bullock pastures.' If they stayed united, they could work out the freedom of their country, and they would embrace their opportunity when it came. O'Kane too spoke of police, calling them 'ruffians'. No police station was required at Knock. 'They should resist the invaders and drive them into the Atlantic.' Gordon directed the people to pay no rent without getting an abatement. If the landlords resisted, they'd make the tenants not pay.

The police report noted, finally, that a resolution proposed by Sheridan was passed, that the tenants of Nolan Farrell should 'hold out' against 'this tyrant landlord who would crowd the workhouses of their saxon enemies and their Gaols'.[135]

A journalist in the 1970s heard yet another account of the demonstration, this one passed down orally in the family of one of the apparition seers:

> A crowd of those Whiteboys or Ribbonmen, or some of them, came along into Knock on horseback with bugles blowing. The whole congregation left the church and attended a meeting at the crossroads . . . Later, Patrick Walsh apologised to Archdeacon Cavanagh for hearing him denounced at this meeting which he attended.[136]

This story is an exaggeration, if not fiction, but nevertheless it conveys a meaningful message. The congregation leaving the mass is not mentioned in the *Connaught Telegraph* account or in the police report especially where we would expect to see such a dramatic episode recorded. Moreover, members of the protesting crowd probably began to converge on the meeting after mass in their various home parishes and likely would have arrived in Knock after the Sunday mass there was concluded. Typical of orally transmitted memories of other episodes, this memory tells us more about the later time of telling than about the supposed events. Like the story of Archbishop MacHale at the House of Commons for example, this one is meaningful to those who already accept the underlying theme that it corroborates. It should be considered as part of a corpus of stories about Fr Cavanagh that helped constitute the portrait of him painted later by Knock shrine promoters such as Judge William Coyne. Coyne's 1953 biography of him is replete with hagiographical stories about Cavanagh and the evil forces arrayed against him and how his holiness enabled the evildoers to repent and mend their ways. This story's denouement, an apology to Cavanagh is just an explicit statement of this theme. To those who already see Cavanagh, as saintly, or who wish to present him as such, this story provides confirmation by corroboration of what they already believe.[137]

Neither Daly's *Connaught Telegraph* nor the confidential police report provides much detail on what probably triggered Fr Cavanagh's denunciation of O'Kane. By one account, originally from either Donegal or Derry, O'Kane had been a student for the priesthood at Maynooth, but had been expelled after arms were found in his room at the college.[138] He had moved to Claremorris where he was deeply involved in Fenian organising. Earlier in May that year, O'Kane and another Fenian, P. J. Gordon also of Claremorris, had convened a meeting of about two hundred people outside the town to discuss getting parts of big, mainly grazier farms for the small farmers.[139] Such a thing if it were to come about would not just undermine landlordism but shake the rural class structure at every level.

Besides their common failure to give an adequate context for Cavanagh's actions, the two contemporary ostensibly factual descriptions of the 1 June demonstration — the police and newspaper reports — disagree on a great many aspects of the story, including the size of the crowd, who addressed it and what they said, reactions and comments from the audience, the identities of the leaders, and what resolutions were passed. Despite these differences, it is clear from both accounts, which would have been prepared independently of each other, that Fr Cavanagh was vehemently attacked by several speakers who insinuated that he was shielding some landlords or was supportive of British rule.[140] Moreover, the crowd loudly cheered O'Kane, the man Cavanagh had singled out for harshest public criticism, and voices in the crowd had called for cutting off Cavanagh's 'supplies'. (This term probably refers to stopping contributions to the priest, not to boycotting him, but it was ambiguous enough to be interpreted to mean the latter. In my youth I heard 'supplies' used as a collective noun to refer to shop-bought goods, especially those regularly purchased such as tea and sugar.) While the police, very understandably, were concerned with the attitudes expressed toward them, Daly's account says nothing along these lines, probably because he was most concerned with putting pressure on priests like Cavanagh to support the tenants or at least not to oppose their 'just and reasonable demands'. Castigating the police would merely confuse his central message. Daly also ignores the denunciation of grazier activity probably because at that moment he wanted to keep all tenants, graziers and non-graziers alike, as united as possible in opposition to landlords.

The police, in contrast, are more concerned with the political/nationalist than the agrarian dimension of the conflict. They concentrate on documenting evidence of Fenian sentiment at the meeting, such as the equating of support for landlords with support for British rule. They record how landlords are construed as a garrison of a foreign power and how police are labelled ruffians and setters. (The derogatory label of setter meant that the police used any means at their disposal, including bribed or blackmailed informants, perjured testimony, or other nefarious methods to punish or silence persons innocent of crimes. Persons who cooperated with them were 'felon-setters', or traitors.) In contrast to the police who use the language of criminal investigation and are alert to the use of aliases by 'suspects', Daly is at pains to present the demonstrators as 'respectable' people who were not violent, but rather orderly, determined, united and 'reasonable'. Rather than being anti-clerical, the people were hurt by what they considered to be unwarranted attacks by priests like Fr Cavanagh. Daly had no interest in giving the legal authorities ammunition to prosecute any speaker at the meeting, so it is understandable that he would use such a transparently fictitious name as Mr Jones for one of them. Was the first speaker a local respectable tenant farmer named Tobias Merrick, Sheridan from Bohola or Mr Jones from Dublin? If the police were right that the first speaker was Sheridan, though using the name Jones, why does Daly give the name Merrick? Was this a further step in hiding legally admissible evidence about the speaker's identity from the authorities with the obvious alias of Jones used to divert attention from a more subtle hood-winking? One wonders how many of the demonstrators in the crowd or readers of the newspaper knew perfectly well the real identities of the speakers. Local hearers surely could tell a Mayo accent from a Dublin one. Here a complex, multi-level game is being played by underdogs to frustrate the powerful, even when everyone knows some subterfuge is afoot.[141]

The Knock demonstration of 1 June dramatically shows how the authority of the priests and the landlords was intertwined. Challenges by the underdogs in one of these authority relationships could not be confined to it alone but reverberated to implicate the other as well. Tenant challenges to landlord power or lay challenges to priests' traditional prerogatives necessarily tended to reinforce each other and so their effects were compounded. Once begun, such questioning would become an escalating challenge to ever more figures of authority with effects cascading through more and more areas of social life. Clearly, some of the speakers fundamentally rejected the established political system and challenged as alien to the nation most, if not all, landlords as well as those priests who defended that arrangement. The British government, landlords, and the police were all rhetorically subsumed in the category of 'invaders' who should be driven into the Atlantic. The effects on those initiating and making each successive challenge can be seen in their growing confidence to attempt ever more, to demand ever more, even beyond what they had earlier hoped for, thought possible or perhaps even imagined. While most early land meetings demanded rent reductions, later ones called increasingly for abolishing landlordism as a system. But even from the first days of the Land War, political revolution was being suggested. Towns around Irishtown were placarded with signs of 'Down with Invaders, Down with Tyrants'.[142] The escalation of confidence, along with articulation of new demands and increased action to achieve them is at the heart of social movements such as the early land war.[143] But each successive demand made by movement leaders also more profoundly disorients those in the society unsettled by the challenges or threatened by the changes sought. While the land agitation's leaders were pushing their demands and dramatically increasing their demonstration activities in the summer of 1879, we can well expect to find many others, and not just those in authority, who were increasingly discomforted and disoriented.[144]

The challenge to Fr Cavanagh in Knock in June was not the end of the questioning. For those who would support him because he was a priest, a further significant twist of the spiral of challenge to their taken-for-granted world was but weeks away. Other priests were seen to be very publicly joining the very agitation and leaders that Cavanagh had condemned. If Cavanagh, as a priest, was to be defended, how could other priests, as priests, not be condemned? The entire situation forced people to reconsider their usually hitherto unarticulated assumptions about priests and their roles. The 'magnificent' demonstration meeting held in Claremorris on Sunday, 13 June provides one example that cannot have failed to attract attention in Knock. The crowd of 20,000 included contingents of 'horse and foot' from all the surrounding areas.[145] The *Connaught Telegraph*[146] listed no fewer than eleven priests on the platform, along with a large number of lay leaders including all those mentioned at Knock (except Jones and Merrick, which fuels suspicion that the latter was 'invented' by Daly, as Jones was by those running the Knock meeting): O'Kane, Nally, Gordon and Sheridan.

In the report on the demonstration we read that 'a large contingent arrived from Ballyhaunis, headed by the Very Revd Fr Anderson, OSA, and accompanied by the temperance band'. Claremorris and Ballyhaunis were the two towns closest to Knock; in travelling to the demonstration Fr Anderson and his band could well have passed through Knock parish. The shortest route between the two towns ran south of Knock through Bekan, but we have evidence that others going from one town to the other went through Knock. Ten days after the August apparition, P. J. Gordon from Claremorris attended mass in Knock most likely while on his way to the demonstration arranged for later that day in Ballyhaunis. Perhaps some of the Ballyhaunis people going to Claremorris similarly used Knock. Even if he did not cross their parish or pass by their chapel on his way to Claremorris, we can be sure that people in Knock were well aware of Fr Anderson and his activities. He was a friend of Fr Cavanagh and, moreover, the Knock choir had performed at least twice in his church in Ballyhaunis. Yet, he spoke at the Claremorris meeting and even proposed one of the resolutions. Moreover, his band was one of two at the meeting that 'delighted the people with national airs during the day'. (It may be to the passing of the band near the Knock church that the oral memory of the 1 June anti-Cavanagh demonstration referred when it recalled 'bugles blowing', even though none of the contemporary accounts mentions music. If the memory actually conflates the 1 June Knock meeting and the 13 July Claremorris meeting, it is plausible that people may have left mass in Knock to follow the demonstrators to Claremorris. Some members of the Ballyhaunis delegation might well have deliberately travelled via Knock to encourage the locals to join them.) Where did all this leave Fr Cavanagh, even in the eyes of those most committed to defence of the priests or most obedient to their authority? Where did it leave his would-be supporters? A vivid indication of how rapidly things were changing in this topsy-turvy world of landlords, agents, priests and people is that six weeks before the Claremorris demonstration, on the very Sunday of the 'monster indignation meeting' in Knock, Fr Anderson had accompanied the Ballyhaunis Total Abstinence League on their annual outing, visiting among other places Loughglynn 'where the picturesque demesne ha[d] been left open to them by its worthy owner, Charles Strickland, Esq.'[147]

Archbishop MacHale's Reputation

Turmoil over clerical authority in Knock was not restricted to the confrontations with Fr Cavanagh. The esteemed archbishop, John MacHale, too was to become the centre of a firestorm of controversy. As chapter 5 documented, MacHale had come to occupy an unprecedented status in the eyes of many people as their steadfast protector and courageous advocate, endowed with powers that were, if not divine, well above those canonically recognised as archepiscopal. In later years MacHale continued to enjoy an extraordinary reputation. He remained enormously popular among ordinary people for the decades after the 1830s when the 'Blessed Straws' event occurred and his reported approach to Knock in his coach. While the myriad changes during his episcopacy

Archbishop John MacHale

such as the Great Famine, spreading commercialism, and the language shift obviously had impacts, MacHale's image as their champion not only survived but was strengthened among a significant segment of the population. Even those who disagreed could not ignore the fact of his popularity. For a variety of reasons, most of which were beyond his influence, MacHale became so much *the* nationalist bishop that his reputation extended beyond his own diocese and he was revered wherever Irish people lived. Explanations of MacHale's appeal beyond the local area, therefore, have to be placed in the context of the wider question of the development of nationalism.[148] But it is to the local scene rather than the international arena that we must look to understand MacHale's significance in places like Knock. According to Michael Davitt, MacHale was 'probably the strongest personality in Ireland' in 1879; a modern historian's assessment is that he was 'perhaps the most beloved and respected public figure in Connacht' at the time.[149]

In the early stages of the land agitation, its leaders faced clerical resistance and denunciation. Shortly thereafter, the question of who would direct the movement, specifically what role the priests would play, escalated dramatically. Canon Ulick Bourke, MacHale's nephew, proposed a meeting at Claremorris, the first priest to call for such a meeting. But James Daly immediately attacked his motives in the pages of the *Connaught Telegraph*, alleging Bourke was attempting to co-opt the agitation and channel it in directions supportive of the exclusively Catholic ecclesiastical status quo. Throughout the summer, Bourke was denounced as the pawn of his uncle.[150] One land meeting did take place without any priests present and the *Connaught Telegraph* claimed they had been forbidden to attend by Fr Thomas MacHale, who was allegedly running the diocese for his uncle.[151]

In July, MacHale supporters invited him to attend a meeting they proposed near Ballyhaunis. Whether their intent was primarily to support the tenants' demands or to provide clerical leadership and direction, i.e. whose interests would be paramount, the tenants' or the priests', is unclear. Davitt later recalled that the meeting was 'in rivalry with the new movement' and that its organisers ignored the existing lay leaders.[152] MacHale's response to the invitation was not only crystal clear, but it was so directly at odds with what his reputation for decades would lead many people to expect, that it must have seemed incredible to them. Indeed we have evidence that many among the common people refused to believe that John MacHale actually authored the letter that was published in the widely circulated *Freeman's Journal* under his name. MacHale wrote that the priests had always stood by the people and warned against any attempt to 'dissever' such a sacred relationship. He questioned the leadership of 'a few unknown strolling men' and warned that when these men had gotten what they wanted from the agitation, they would abandon the tenants.[153] In other words, he accused the agitation's leaders of merely using the local people to climb to power and that once successful they would have no concern for or loyalty to the very people who had been the means of their rise.[154] In the summer of 1879, the question of the role of the clergy in the land movement was centre stage, but the final act was not yet known or even written.

Michael Davitt was taken aback by MacHale's attack, but neither he nor the other leaders of the movement believed they could challenge him directly and publicly. Nevertheless, they recognised that the success of their movement depended on neutralising the opposition of priests. If particular clerics remained hostile, at least their influence had to be minimised or they were to be effectively sidelined. Other priests were to be welcomed into the movement. The June demonstration against Fr Cavanagh and another one in his parish in October that year are examples of meetings called to confront or contain hostile clerics.

Davitt replied to MacHale's public letter by pointing out that he was no unknown outsider. Although he had spent much of his life in England, he had been born in poverty to a small tenant family in Mayo, but his family had been evicted and forced to emigrate. Davitt had lost an arm when it was crushed by machinery in a Lancashire factory where he worked as a child. He had served long years in prison for his Fenian activities, and was now out on ticket-of-leave. He had been welcomed home by bonfires in Mayo when he visited before 1879. Far from being a cynical career-building step, as MacHale intimated, Davitt pointed out that if his activities on behalf of the poor tenants were to lead him anywhere it was most likely back to picking oakum in prison when the government revoked his leave. But words without actions would not win, and the land movement leaders determined to act. In September, they staged a 'peaceful mass occupation' of Tuam, MacHale's cathedral city, after deliberately not consulting him, other local priests, or the town council in advance. Reports of the event say over 5,000 men, 200–300 of them on horseback, were in attendance. No priests were on the platform although one Jesuit was reported in attendance.[155] At the meeting itself, condemnations of MacHale or of other priests were restrained. Of course, the holding of numerous earlier demonstration meetings all through the summer is itself evidence of the systematic way in which lay people had ignored the strictures of hostile clerics including MacHale. Now, backed by thousands of the laity, the leaders were flaunting their power in his own back yard, but given his reputation it is understandable that their criticism of him was indirect and muted. The Tuam invasion itself rather than anything said there was the message.

While Daly lambasted Fr Bourke in the pages of the *Connaught Telegraph* and questioning of Fr Cavanagh's role escalated, the archbishop's role too was made problematic. MacHale's letter's meaning was crystal clear, but given his reputation we are not surprised that people refused to believe what it said. MacHale's denunciation was conveniently ascribed to his nephew, Fr Thomas MacHale, who supposedly was manipulating the archbishop in his frail old age and senility.[156] Alternatively, MacHale was supposed to have been misled by priests in the Westport deanery who were angry about not being consulted about a land meeting in Westport; a voice in the crowd there suggested he had gotten into bad company,[157] and so his warning, based on misinformation as it was, could safely be ignored. Some journalists and newspapers also found it convenient not to take MacHale at his word.[158]

There were new as well as continuing sources of MacHale's positive popular reputation in the late 1870s. New factors became important as MacHale grew older. There is some evidence that the hero-making was consciously promoted by some of his admirers. While some biographers say MacHale was born in 1789, the more compelling evidence is that 1791 is correct. Most writers[159] give 6 March 1791 as MacHale's date of birth, based on a document produced when he began his seminary studies in Maynooth in 1807 and which relied on information he himself provided. However, other authorities say he was born two years earlier.[160] All these alternative accounts can be traced back to two biographies of him, one in English and one in Irish, penned shortly after his death by Canon Ulick Bourke, his nephew. Bourke's reasoning is that family memories recalled MacHale as a boy serving mass for the priest in his home parish of Addergoole, Fr Conroy (or Conry) who had been executed in 1798 by the infamous Denis Browne. According to Bourke, MacHale had to be more than seven years old at the time, and hence born before 1791.[161] Bourke accepted that the young MacHale did indeed serve at Fr Conroy's mass. The claim, however, is most likely an effort to associate MacHale in the popular imagination with the martyred priest. MacHale was also remembered later as dispatching messages for Fr Conroy despite his own tender years, as the priest called upon local people to join the French invaders.[162] The information MacHale himself provided in 1807 is far more reliable as evidence of his year of birth.

By the time of Bourke's biographies, Fr Conroy's execution was over eighty years in the past, but its memory was kept fresh and was soon to be commemorated anew both in songs and in memorial statues or crosses.[163] In Canon Bourke's books and in numerous popular accounts, MacHale's long life was seen to virtually parallel the travails of his country and people. In this incarnation, he came to embody the suffering people.[164] Indeed in some folklore, as we saw, his life extended from the early seventeenth-century when he was evicted along with his family at the time of the Plantation of Ulster. That Bourke was consciously extending MacHale's life rather than merely echoing popular accounts seems likely. While he wrote that MacHale was older than seven in 1798, and so born in 1789 rather than 1791, he did not similarly add two years to MacHale's age at other milestones of his career. To have him ordained at twenty-six rather than twenty-four, for example, would have detracted from the image of precocious development that permeates Bourke's account of his uncle's early life, about how he was appointed a seminary professor before he was even ordained, how he became a bishop before ever being a pastor, how he was one of the youngest archbishops. The 'error' in Bourke's report of MacHale's age, is the result of the same hero-making process and social construction of his biography that is evidenced by the story of the star marking his birth.

As MacHale grew older his critics claimed he was merely an automaton in the power of a clerical clique or faction.[165] Whether that was 'really' the case is less important than how the various writers or publics regarded him. As we have noted, there was widespread refusal to accept his condemnation of the land agitation's leaders. In the immediately preceding years, public displays of deference and reverence continued to accompany his confirmation visits. Even outside his own diocese MacHale was feted. When he passed through Ballinasloe in Clonfert diocese the people gave him an engraved address praising his patriotism and his literary work.[166]

Two months before the Knock apparition one newspaper reported that in Castlebar MacHale confirmed over 870 persons in a little over two hours 'to the great admiration of all present'.[167] The administration of the sacrament normally required the bishop to 'lay hands' on each person confirmed. If MacHale actually did this it can only have been momentarily; recipients must have somehow approached him and then moved under his hands. If the newspaper is accurate,[168] in less than nine seconds another person received the sacrament from his hands. Rather than as assembly-line efficiency, I suggest that many people probably saw this as evidence of MacHale fulfilling his role to the utmost of his strength. Even as he confirmed them, he confirmed *for* them his position and practice as their shepherd. I cannot prove this suggestion, but the response from the Catholic world to the later years of Pope John Paul II's life, and to his attempts to speak throughout his last illnesses, shows just how emotionally potent can be such visible demonstration of an already well-loved leader's devoted service to the very end. MacHale's faithfulness to the last of his physical ability would be highly visible in the Knock area. Bernard O'Reilly, who had access to the now-lost diocesan records, reported that MacHale's final confirmation trip was to Aghamore and Knock on 22 and 23 July 1878 and two other nearby parishes the following two days. In Knock, he confirmed 180.[169] However, newspapers reported a later confirmation visit by MacHale to the adjacent parish of Bekan in early summer of 1879.[170] Thus, even without any conflict over the land agitation or any other issue MacHale would be very much on the minds and consciousness of people in Knock in the year before the 1879 apparition.

But MacHale's authority was the centre of controversy for many additional reasons, ranging from politics to his relationships with his priests, with other bishops and even with the pope. All of these lines of authority were made problematic to a degree unimaginable just a short time earlier. As noted in chapter 7, other bishops were harshly criticising MacHale in the late 1870s. This was nothing new. In the 1830s and 1840s MacHale was a leader in the hierarchy on many issues and especially among those opposing 'Godless education', first in the national schools and later in the Queens Colleges, set up and funded by the government. But after the 1840s' famine, his position among the bishops was to change but not his position in the hearts of his faithful people. The hierarchy changed while MacHale did not. The change can be associated with the key figure of Paul Cullen. After three decades of seminary education, training and experience in Rome, Cullen was appointed Archbishop of Armagh in 1850. Two years later he was translated to the Archdiocese of Dublin, Ireland's most populous and most important see. Cullen was extremely well connected in Rome all the way up to the pope himself, and he was armed with the power of an Apostolic Legate to enhance the discipline of the Irish church.

Cullen led the movement to more thoroughly mould the Irish church along 'official' Roman lines. Although MacHale initially supported Cullen's appointment, it was predictable that the two would clash as they did repeatedly and vehemently throughout most of the third quarter of the century. Their struggle sometimes has been portrayed as just a clash of personalities but to understand its significance we must see the two archbishops as representative of two conflicting tendencies within Irish Catholicism of the time. If Cullen represented the ultramontane view, emphasising the centrality of Rome and the papacy and calling for uniformity in official practice, MacHale among other key differences, stressed the authority of each bishop within his own diocese. To oversimplify, MacHale's authority derived from his articulation of popular feeling, while Cullen's depended on his formal title and Roman connections. Charismatic in Weber's sense of the term,[171] MacHale's leadership faced the classic problem inherent in such a personal authority, that of sustaining continuity and an orderly transition to a successor. Cullen could be smoothly replaced by another Archbishop of Dublin but that was not possible in Tuam, given the personal charismatic appeal of MacHale the man.

Already a bishop for twenty-five years when Cullen returned from Rome, MacHale had an established reputation as an outspoken critic of the Protestant dominated government of the United Kingdom, to which he voiced the popular feeling of probably most Irish Catholics of being a nation held in subjugation by force. In church government, he stressed the authority of each bishop within his own diocese. Already in the 1860s, the nationalist journalist, politician and historian, A.M. Sullivan (and a great partisan of MacHale), could write that in the 1850s,

> An open war raged between sections of the clergy and the people who ranged themselves under the banners of Dr MacHale and Dr Cullen respectively.[172]

The two clashed on issue after issue, on matters of church politics and policies and on matters secular. The deteriorating relationship between the two men developed its own momentum, becoming both cause and effect:

> As the two became more rivals than partners in the leadership of the Irish Catholic hierarchy, their suspicions of each other's policies grew. As their political views diverged on how to achieve the best for their flocks, personal hostility between them increased. The result was that as MacHale grew closer to the nationalist politicians, Cullen grew more hostile to them.[173]

Cardinal Cullen died in 1878 not long after his good friend Pope Pius IX. As long as they both lived, Cullen was able to engineer the promotion to episcopal rank of men who shared his philosophy to the various dioceses as they became vacant. The result was that MacHale was progressively isolated within the ranks of the Irish bishops. As ever more dioceses in the country were led by bishops in the Cullen mould, not only was MacHale increasingly set apart, but church discipline and devotional practice in his diocese were increasingly singled out for dishonourable mention by hostile clerics and others. His isolation was vividly illustrated in 1875 when MacHale reached the milestone of fifty years as a bishop, something no Irishman had done, at least since the Reformation. Significant celebrations could be expected, and a major event did occur but it was as significant for those who did not attend as for those who did. While the lay people of his diocese celebrated with bonfires until it appeared the whole country was aflame, Bishop MacEvilly in the neighbouring diocese of Galway acknowledged the occasion by scheduling a mandatory spiritual retreat for his priests for the very days of the jubilee celebrations in Tuam. The jubilee was virtually boycotted by the other members of the hierarchy, with only Bishop Nulty of Meath attending.[174]

Rome grew increasingly unhappy, not only with MacHale the man, but with the state of the church under his jurisdiction. All the time, MacHale grew older and more fixed in his ways. Larkin described the 'extraordinary problem' MacHale presented to Rome as comprised of two factors. The diocese was in a deplorable pastoral state, but MacHale's nationalist reputation and popularity made it impossible to remove him in his old age without outraging Irish people around the world.[175]

It is important to recognise that the 'deplorable state' was the perception in Rome. How accurate it was is a separate question, which I addressed in the previous chapter. In the year and a half before the Knock apparition of August 1879, the authorities in Rome were seeking to fashion some solution to the problem they saw. One of the last acts of Pope Pius IX was to impose on MacHale, over his strenuous objections, as coadjutor (that is an assistant with the right of succession), Bishop John MacEvilly of the neighbouring diocese of Galway.[176] MacEvilly was not just any bishop; for decades he was one of Cullen's most loyal supporters and one whom MacHale most bitterly detested.[177] MacHale studiously ignored MacEvilly. In response, 'Propaganda [the Roman department responsible] with the sanction of His Holiness wrote to Dr MacHale to give up all powers to Dr MacEvilly immediately, adding that if he did not do so, his Holiness will give them himself after 30 days from the date of the letter'.[178] MacHale, however, was not yet vanquished. He threatened to resign if forced to accept MacEvilly and then to publish his own account of the whole proceedings, in effect threatening to instigate the outrage among nationalists that Rome wanted to avoid. Rome blinked, and MacHale stayed in office with MacEvilly in the anomalous position of carrying much of the work load in the diocese without any recognition from the aged archbishop.

As documented earlier, MacHale had earned a reputation as an advocate of the people and a courageous critic of the government. He was a stout defender of his own claims to authority. Cullen's position as Apostolic Legate reduced not only the powers of individual bishops within their dioceses but reduced that of the hierarchy as a body, unless Cullen agreed. Before Cullen, when the bishops met, they tended to decide questions by majority vote, a practice that favoured the more strong-willed and assertive, like MacHale. With Cullen as Apostolic Legate, however, nothing the Irish bishops agreed on, even if near-unanimously, carried much weight unless and until it was approved in Rome, where Cullen's voice was clearly heard and his counsel followed.

MacHale was not a man to tolerate challenges even from other religious and certainly not from lay people. For example, he opposed as inopportune the declaration of the pope's infallibility at the First Vatican Council in 1870. Around the same time he resisted moves by most of the Irish bishops that led to a papal condemnation of Fenianism.[179] He defied the Roman authorities, including the pope, in refusing to discipline the 'Fenian priest', Fr Patrick Lavelle.[180] Within his own diocese, he prevented the Redemptorists, an order of priests specialised in giving parish missions, from giving such missions for twenty years before 1877.[181] He considered the 'Apostle of

Temperance', Fr Mathew, 'a vagabond friar' and absolved those who had taken his life-long pledge against alcohol from keeping it.[182] He simply refused to allow the Sisters of Mercy in his diocese to attend a conference of their order called to discuss the nuns' relationships with episcopal authority.[183] On some occasions when Cullen and his allies were attempting to get the hierarchy to agree on some issue and it looked like MacHale would be in a minority, he simply did not attend meetings called with the hope of forging a consensus. Archbishop MacHale did not compromise. Even his own nephew admitted that as MacHale aged, his 'unwillingness to cooperate . . . became a settled state of mental conviction'.[184] Given this history, it would not have been surprising to an outsider that he reacted so vehemently to what he interpreted as a lay challenge to priests' and his own prerogatives, and condemned the organisers of the land agitation. It is not surprising that he wrote public letters condemning the movement's leaders and castigating them as a 'few strolling men'. The public nature and trenchant language of the letters impugning others' motives were character-istic of the man. What is significant is the reaction. The Land League agitation was the first mass movement in the rural west started by lay people without priests being involved; it was to continue despite vehement opposi-tion from the clergy. When they could no longer stop or control it, many priests were to get aboard the land-demonstration bandwagon largely in the hope that they could influence its direction.

By 1879, MacHale had also lost the confidence of his priests. As he grew older it was understandable that individual priests would begin to look to their standing in the administration of his successor, and would have less reason to support MacHale. His loss of influence with his own priests is man-ifest in their vote for MacEvilly as coadjutor archbishop.[185] In 1874 MacHale's candidate for parliament was opposed by most of his priests. Many had addi-tional reasons to withdraw their support. Some blamed his interference in the electoral process for the debacle that resulted when candidates he supported were unseated after complaints of undue clerical influence on voters. After 1857, landlords held Mayo seats in parliament for decades.[186] People like P. J. Gordon who supported other candidates felt MacHale's interference, even if well-intentioned, had prevented the election of more nationalist politicians. Gordon in 1874 had led a 'mob' that attacked the rival mob of the 'the priests' candidate'.[187] James Daly in the *Connaught Telegraph* was to insinuate that Canon Bourke, MacHale's nephew, had tried to bribe one candidate to with-draw.[188] Yet if MacHale was not 'Fenian' enough for advanced nationalists like Gordon, he was 'too Fenian' in the eyes of most clerics.

Fr James Anderson, who led his temperance band from Ballyhaunis to Claremorris in July 1879, was in the diocese probably only because of MacHale. Anderson was among the best known 'Fenian priests' of the 1860s, second only to Fr Patrick Lavelle according to Cardinal Cullen. As an Augustinian, he moved from monastery to monastery of his order, but was repeatedly silenced by local bishops for his unacceptably advanced nationalist political activities and ideas. He had already been suspended by the bishops in Waterford, Cork and Galway before 1874 when he came as prior to St Mary's Augustinian Priory in Ballyhaunis, where MacHale permitted him to exercise all the faculties of the priesthood, as Anderson curtly informed the Bishop of Galway. Probably no other bishop in the country would have given him faculties.[189]

We may debate the significance for the laity of ecclesiastical high politics and of relationships among the various levels of clergymen. What is clearer is that the challenges to both Fr Cavanagh and Archbishop MacHale over the land agitation were not simply matters of lay questioning or resisting authority. Precisely because he was so identified as 'a living saint' and had been for so long and so courageously involved in protecting the common people, MacHale's about face (for those who believed his letters) must have seemed a betrayal of the greatest magnitude. Because of the ideology of the 'priest and people together', Fr Cavanagh's criticism would be read the same way. A sense of betrayal is palpable in the report of the anti-Cavanagh demonstration in Knock on 1 June: the people were indignant at attacks from quarters where they had every right and reason to expect support and protection.[190] James Daly summed up their feelings in the title of his newspaper report: 'Monster Indignation Meeting at Knock'. A recent researcher has identified 'moral outrage' as a central emotion in revolutionary movements.[191] Outrage at the clergy may well have accelerated the commitment of some early demonstrators in the Land War. Because so much was expected from priests, especially 'nationalist' ones like Canon Bourke, their defence of landlord interests 'caused pain and anger, and undoubtedly added to an already anxious situation'.[192]

Famine Imminent

'It was repeatedly stated and widely believed in Ireland during 1879 that a catastrophe comparable with the great famine was impending', and in few places was the dread as great as in Mayo, the county that had suffered most in the earlier calamity.[193] 'Remember '47' read one banner at a Mayo land meeting in July.[194] Historians have weighed the evidence for the apprehension. Mainly because of unfavourable weather for several successive years all the main crops suffered heavy losses, not just the potato as in the 1840s. Hence all classes of farmers were threatened and not just the poorest who were dependent on the potato for subsistence. Rain fell on two of every three days from March to September 1879 and the year's harvest was the worst since the famine. The potato yield, for example, was only 1.3 tons per acre in 1879 compared to 4.7 tons in 1876 and an average of 3.3 tons for 1871–1876[195] before the bad harvests of 1877 and 1878. Because so much deferred hope was riding on it, following two other years of poor crops, the failure of the harvest of 1879 must have had a devastating effect on people's sense of security. Famine stared them in the face. *Aimsir an Drochshaoil*,[196] the time of poor living, had returned. It is no coincidence that the reported apparition occurred 'during the very same week that incessant rain made people admit that the 1879 harvest was to be a failure'.[197]

Tenant farmers large and small as well as cottiers and landless labourers were directly threatened. 'Three years of agricultural losses depleted the savings of the strong farmer and exhausted the credit of the weak.'[198] Shopkeepers and moneylenders, who had extended credit to their customers for several years, found themselves being forced toward bankruptcy. A *Freeman's Journal* reporter claimed on 1 September that migrants returning from England with their earnings faced a race between the shopkeeper and the landlord to see which of them could first get their hands on some cash. The whole of society seemed at risk.

But there were new factors mitigating the chances of famine compared to the 1840s. Nationally, the population had been much reduced by the earlier famine and emigration; Indian meal was widely available for import and it could be more easily distributed by an extended railway system; that all classes were involved 'created conditions favourable to a nation-wide movement of self-assertion'[199] that was facilitated by the growth in literacy and the spread of newspapers. All these factors provoked an immense outpouring of both government action and private charity from around the world, especially the much enlarged Irish diaspora, and led to relief efforts that averted massive starvation. But it was not until the abundant potato harvest nationally in 1880 — though yields in Mayo and Galway were 35 per cent below the national average — that the fear of another great famine was removed.[200] Late August 1879 was thus when the threat was starkest. While the dread threat had materialised, there was as of yet no evidence of the massive relief efforts that were to be mounted later and which did stave off catastrophe.[201]

The weather was not the only factor contributing to the dismal situation. General economic depression in the United Kingdom and increased imports of American foodstuffs, especially beef, reduced demand for Irish cattle and grain and prices fell substantially. Statistics can be piled up documenting the lower yields and reduced prices for practically every crop or animal produced on Irish land in the late 1870s. Market demand for young cattle, for example, practically ceased.[202] While the depression was nationwide, 'the distress was most severe in Connacht and worst of all in Mayo'.[203] Places like Knock, where most families depended on harvest work in England to earn the rent, were further affected by the reduced earnings of the migrants. Connacht alone was estimated to have lost a quarter of a million pounds in expected wages for seasonal work in England in 1879.[204] The labourers generally expected to make in a few weeks on the English harvests twice their annual income in Ireland.[205] The reduced earnings would also have become apparent in Ireland just at the time when the prospects for the harvest at home were being confirmed as dismal. On 1 September 1879, William O'Brien of the *Freeman's Journal* reported from Ballyhaunis that he had learned at the post office there, that local men who had gone for harvest work in England were remitting less than one-third the amount they had in 1878. Some could not even pay their fare home.[206]

The Seers' Social Situation

Of fifteen witnesses who gave depositions to the commission set up to investigate reports of the August 1879 apparition, up to nine were connected by kin ties. Five of them lived in one household. These five were the three siblings, Mary, Margaret (Maggie) and Dominick Beirne, Jr, all single and in their late teens or twenties, their widowed mother Margaret, and their niece Catherine Murray. Also giving witness testimony was a cousin of these siblings, another Dominick Beirne (designated as Senior to distinguish him from Dominick Jr), Dominick Sr's six-year-old nephew, John Curry, who lived with him, and their neighbour, sixteen-year-old Pat Beirne who very likely was also a relative. Another Beirne cousin, Pat Hill, who was anywhere from eleven to fourteen, was also among the witnesses giving depositions. Because of the centrality of this extended kin group among the witnesses, and because the investigating panel of priests accorded them signal importance, it is appropriate to examine their place in local society. The evidence we have shows that in terms of their experience of anomie-producing pressures, the Beirnes were again extreme even when compared to other Knock people.

Because of their closeness to Fr Cavanagh, of which we have ample evidence, it makes sense to believe that the Beirnes would be more affected than most by the massive demonstration against him. Mary Beirne believed that the apparition was vouchsafed to Knock because of Fr Cavanagh's holiness; it must have been painful for her to see him defied, insulted, threatened and perhaps even abandoned by his congregation. Her widowed mother reportedly had three uncles in the priesthood,[207] a circumstance likely to make the family supportive of the clergy for reasons both of faith and of family loyalty. At the time of the apparition, some members of the family had just returned from a trip to the seaside near Westport; speculation has it that they were visiting a relative who was a priest there. We also know that the Beirnes were the church sacristans, whose duties apparently involved opening and locking the church building each morning and evening (although they may have gotten this job simply because they lived close to the church). In Daniel Campbell's time decades earlier, for his Sunday breakfast (which he ate in the church after mass), the priest had cake and punch brought from one nearby Beirne household.

In the pre-famine sectarian struggles in Knock that Campbell also detailed, the priest was able to subdue the proselytising Flatley faction only with help of the Corry and Beirne factions. The Beirnes were thus long allies of the priests. At the time of the 1879 apparition, it is likely that relations between the Beirnes and at least some of their neighbours would be strained by their defence of Fr Cavanagh. The huge public demonstration against the priest would also likely have placed Cavanagh's housekeeper, the apparition witness Mary McLoughlin, in an awkward position with at least some people in the community. She was not a native of Knock and apparently had no kin ties there[208] so when she sought friendship, it is understandable that she turned to the Beirne household where she could count on an attitude supportive of priests generally and of her employer in particular. There is reason to suspect that other witnesses also would be more likely than most to be close to the priest. One was Judy Campbell, whose mother was Daniel Campbell's aunt: Daniel's clerical sympathies are clear in his memoir and he also makes clear that his own father opposed the 'strike' against the priest in 1842–43, so it is likely that other family members were similarly sympathetic toward the priests. Also, when a storm in about 1878 damaged the Campbell home, we are told that Fr Cavanagh permitted the family to live in the chapel sacristy until neighbours rebuilt the house.[209] Finally, the man who testified he saw a light at the chapel gable from a distance on the night of the apparition is also likely to have been a clerical supporter. Three of Patrick Walsh's sons were priests.[210]

Considering their centrality to the whole story, we know almost nothing about the Beirnes except what we can deduce from general patterns.[211] The main Beirne household was in the throes of a generational transition, a time when the various underlying fault lines in any family could well cause a tumultuous upheaval on the surface. Lines of authority were ambiguous because of the death of the household head. The sixty-eight-year-old Mrs Margaret Beirne is almost universally referred to in the sources as 'the widow Beirne', one indication of the importance of familial and marital statuses in the construction of identity in the local society. There were many other 'Mrs Beirnes' in the parish but still there were other possible ways to distinguish each individual one, such as by the traditional way of listing her line of ancestors back as far as necessary to specify the particular individual of concern. The stem family system was one in which the father had great power because of his control of land. The importance attached to 'keeping the name on the land', through inheritance by one male heir, was a response to the need to control land in a society where the people had learned that, almost literally, land was life. The farm was identified with the father and through him with the family down through the generations. In *The Nation's* version of the apparition witnesses' testimony, Dominick Beirne, Jr., the son of this widow, a young man who appeared to *The Nation's* correspondent, Thomas Sexton, to be twenty-two or twenty-three, says that he saw the apparition when he came 'from *my father's house*'.[212] Even after death, the father still was the owner of the family home![213] Dominick's sister, Mary, referred to the same dwelling both as 'my house' and 'my mother's house'.[214] Another witness referred to it as the 'widow Beirne's house'. The investigating commissioners did not make a verbatim transcript of the seers' testimony (another version has Dominick saying he was coming from 'our house').[215] Even if the words were not Dominick's, the fact that some note-taker, transcriber, summariser, rewriter, or popu- lariser of the testimony wrote 'my father's house' indicates just how strong was this cultural identification of father and family-house.

Even in the best of circumstances generational change whereby an inher- iting son, for whom a marriage was arranged, replaced an aging father was a traumatic transition.[216] Because it shaped the life prospects of everyone involved and moved questions of authority in the family to centre-stage, the convulsion shook the relationships among the family members.[217] Even when the cultural template provided fairly clear guidelines, as when the father was clearly in control, the transition was likely to be experienced as difficult by those involved. Where the father was already dead, and there was therefore uncertainty as to who was in charge, we can expect even greater trauma. In the case of the main Beirne family at the time of the apparition, the oldest son, Bryan, was away in England, one of hundreds of migrant harvest workers from the Knock area, but he was returning home soon thereafter to get married.[218] At the time of the apparition, then, who was the 'head' of the household? Who had authority? Was it the oldest son (away in England), the widowed mother, the dead father (as the younger son's published testimony hints), or perhaps someone else, such as the twenty-six to twenty-nine-year- old unmarried daughter Mary (whom many considered the main seer)? Could it have been Dominick, Jr, and the only adult male in residence? Or was he an 'adult'? Age was no definite marker of adulthood. Another Beirne cousin, Patrick Hill, who was perhaps thirteen, referred to twenty-four-year- old John Durkan, as a 'servant boy', and males if they were unmarried could still be 'boys' at forty.[219] There was no simple answer. And the absence of def- inite cultural guidelines generated uncertainty and ambiguity.

Moreover, Bryan's impending marriage created uncertainties for all, whether they anticipated it with dread and resignation or perhaps joy and hope. He would now be regarded by the outside world as the household head but how did that affect the others? What were the apprehensions of the 'widow Beirne', for example, awaiting the arrival of a daughter-in-law, a 'stranger'[220] into her household? In nearby Bekan it was recalled that there was sure to be 'plenty of dissention' in such cases:

> The old queen never seemed to see eye to eye with the new one, and any little change that the young one made was soundly criticised by the old one, so much so that there were many trips to the [police] barracks to complain, and often to the law courts.[221]

How would the two sisters, Mary and Margaret (Maggie), live with the new woman in their home, their brother's wife? How would the younger son, Dominick, react to the realisation or confirmation that he was definitely never going to inherit the family land and hence had minimal chances of ever mar- rying? What would the change do for 'brotherly love'? Is it mere coincidence that the two Beirne siblings who did not succeed in the inheritance competition and marriage market, Dominick and Maggie, were also the two who lost out in the health stakes, both dying of tuberculosis within half a dozen years?

The cousin of the main Beirne family of seers, another seer also called Dominick Beirne (Dominick Sr in most accounts of the apparition), was a cattle dealer, which likely made his place in the community far from fixed and secure. Over the preceding centuries and especially in the post-famine decades, commercial cattle and sheep grazing had spread throughout the country with different regions concentrating on different parts of the cattle trade. Specialised graziers (as well as the typical smallholders who grew crops but also owned a cow or two that had a calf each year) in western counties such as Mayo produced 'store' cattle, buying young calves from their neighbours or occasionally from the dairying regions of the south, and later selling them on to graziers in 'finishing' or 'fattening' areas farther east, in north Leinster. Where raising and dealing in livestock, as opposed to crop-growing, was the main business of the farm, many more acres but fewer workers were required.

In the 1860s, newspaperman Coulter described the grazier economy developing in the west, and it had extended considerably in the following decades before the apparition.[222] The number of cattle in Connacht rose by 82 per cent between 1847 and 1876.[223] However, for many reasons graziers did not fit well into traditional communities. In Mayo, more than a few were foreigners, and were detested for their foreign faith as well as their economic practice. But all graziers were suspect. Many people resented locals who became graziers as upstarts and derided them as 'shoneens' whose acquisitiveness violated traditional notions of sharing. Others condemned them as bulwarks of the landlord system because of their demand for land to rent. Many saw them as monopolising access to land that others needed for subsistence. Anti-landlord feeling often spilled over into anti-grazier sentiment.[224] We have no evidence of the extent of Dominick Beirne, Sr's, cattle-dealing or whether like most of his class he rented land besides his 'home farm' to graze the cattle he bought and sold, but as a dealer he was undoubtedly affected by the crisis of 1879 in at least two ways. If, as seems almost certain, he held store cattle, when the market collapsed for them he stood to take a financial beating. At the bellwether May 1879 fair in Balla, graziers reportedly sold their cattle at a loss in fear of not selling them at all, and prices continued to fall throughout the summer, so that by September prices were reported to be the 'most disheartening since the Famine years'.[225] More generally, the anti-landlord agitation would inevitably put in question his role as one whose use of land to graze cattle prevented people from using that land for survival. Dominick should not be seen as just another poor tenant in a Manichean world of evil landlords and good peasants, as too many writers simplistically construct Knock at the time of the apparition. The clothing visible in the drawing of him in Sexton's book, based on O'Connor's photograph, is not shabby. At the demonstration against Fr Cavanagh in Knock on 1 June 1879, among the complaints made by the speakers was that 'the fair fields of Ireland are converted into bullock pastures'.[226] Clerical condemnation of graziers became common after the 1879 crisis. In a 1907 speech, the then parish priest of Knock was to condemn the practice of graziers as 'a most deadly danger to the welfare of the country'.[227]

Dominick Beirne Sr

Reporters after the apparition described the cottage of the main Beirne family as 'comfortable' with 'substantial furniture' which would lead us to suspect they were better off than most of their neighbours.[228] Apparently they could afford at least occasional trips to the seashore near Westport, perhaps visiting a relative who was a priest there. This travel would have been in part by train and in part by pony and trap, the one requiring money and the other a means of transportation beyond the reach of most households. Yet one son from this household was a temporary harvest labourer in England at the very time of the apparition. Perhaps the family had lost status, compared to its earlier standing in the community. That even the 'better off' had to go to England to earn the rent shows how poor the whole area was. Yet there is evidence that, economically as well as in their ties to priests, the Beirnes were far from the typical peasant smallholder household and, moreover, that they had been atypical for decades. Daniel Campbell tells us that the Beirne family owned the 'second public house' in Knock. Because of Campbell's confusion about the identity of the 'widow Beirne' we cannot be sure whether he was referring to the forebears of Mary Beirne or of her cousin Dominick, Sr (if indeed these were different individuals at that point).

Intriguing evidence is available in the records of Griffith's Valuation of properties in 1856. In Drum, the townland in which the apparition church was located, several Beirnes are listed as tenants of Thomas Nowlan. Bryan Beirne held over twenty-three acres, an above-average sized farm for the area, especially where no co-tenants were listed. Dominick Beirne and Henry Burke are listed as co-tenants of a farm of nearly fifty-seven acres. They are also each recorded separately as having 'Land, House, and Office' where 'office' typically meant some sort of farm shed. The size of their joint holding suggests these men might well have been in the grazier business.[229]

Finally in Drum, Dominick Beirne and Henry Burke together were listed as landlords of a separate property having only a 'house'. It is impossible to say how they came to own this property, something very rare for tenants at the time (at least in government records; probably most sub-tenancies were 'off the books'). The two men owned this premises and given the other evidence available — in the Revised Valuation Lists — it seems that they rented it to a sub-tenant (Martin Walsh). The property was listed as having no area (sic) and having a rateable valuation of five shillings. This possibly meant that the property was less than one perch (30.25 square yards), the smallest unit of area used in these records, but if so, this would be little space even for a shebeen. Most likely, the 'zero area' recorded indicates not the size of the building but the fact that the 'landlords' did not own the land and thus the rateable valuation refers only to the building on it that they did own. While it is clear that Beirne and Bourke had at least this one subtenant, what other relationship they had with him is unknown. If they were in the grazier business, perhaps he was a herd or cattle-driver. Perhaps he worked on their farm when they needed labour, as was the common practice earlier for cottiers throughout the country.

It is almost certain that these two co-tenants/co-landlords were also relatives: that Henry Burke was this Dominick Beirne's brother-in-law.[230] If I am right in this, the 'widow Beirne' who saw the apparition in 1879 was sister of one and wife of the other of these two men. Her husband Dominick's family had at least earlier belonged to what researchers elsewhere have called the 'shopocracy'[231] that was to be so crucial in the commercial and religious change of rural and small-town Ireland in the nineteenth century, and her father had held about eighty acres. She herself reportedly had three uncles in the priesthood, which also suggests 'respectable' standing.[232] It is possible that they had fallen in the world by the time of the apparition, but the involvement of Dominick Beirne, Sr, in the grazier business suggests that at least some branch of the family maintained their status. The erstwhile co-tenants later divided their joint holding; an 1859 Dillon estate map[233] shows them renting separate properties each about half their original holding but still above average size, with Dominick Beirne holding over twenty-six acres valued at £7.5 and Burke holding nearly thirty acres with a valuation of £7.25.[234] Despite any downward mobility they might have experienced, their economic and social 'successes' very likely set these Beirnes apart from other Beirnes in the area. Many Knock townlands recorded multiple Beirne households as tenants or often co-tenants with much smaller holdings than the Drum Beirnes living near the chapel.

At the time of the August 1879 apparition, then, most of the country was in economic depression and in much of the west famine was imminently threatened. The 'post-famine adjustment', centred on seasonal emigration for harvest work in England, was no longer a viable rent-earning strategy for areas such as Knock where it had been established for generations. The anxiety and uncertainty was intensified in Knock by challenges to the basic structures of authority in social life. The Land War was more disruptive on the Dillon estate because the tenants there had more than most to lose, given that their landlord was 'good' and his agent was so extensively involved in all aspects of their lives. The conflict between priests and laity triggered by the land agitation was more prolonged and intense in Knock than almost anywhere else; Fr Cavanagh's denunciations provoked a 'monster indignation meeting' against him. The challenge to priestly authority was compounded because of the simultaneous questioning of the role of the hitherto esteemed Archbishop MacHale and by the recognition that other priests were actively supporting what Fr Cavanagh was condemning. Finally, even within Knock, for the core group of apparition witnesses, the Beirne family, issues of problematic authority structures were multiplied and made even more salient because of their household and family dynamics at the time, their relationship with the clergy, and their economic status.

9

The Social Construction
of the Apparition

On the evening of the 21st of August, 1879, the vigil of the octave day of the Feast of Our Lady's Assumption, the parish church of Knock, Co. Mayo, was the scene of a singular and a beautiful spectacle. At about half past seven that evening, and in daylight, an apparition of Our Blessed Lady, wearing a large brilliant crown and clothed in white garments was distinctly seen by some fifteen persons at the south gable wall of the church. Our Lady is described as having her hands raised as if in prayer and her eyes turned toward heaven. On her right hand was St Joseph, his head inclined towards her, and on her left was St John the Evangelist, attired as a bishop, his left hand holding a Book and his right hand raised as if in preaching. To the Left of St John was an altar on which stood a cross and a Lamb, about 8 weeks old around which the wings of angels hovered. The gable wall where this manifestation was seen was covered with a cloud of light and the vision lasted for fully two hours. During all the time rain fell heavily, yet the figures and the spot where they stood were quite dry.[1]

This account of *the* Knock apparition is representative of literally hundreds of others to be found in the devotional literature on Knock and Marian apparitions. While to believers it describes the episode at the church gable that August evening, it does this in a manner that will be convincing only to those who already believe the story. It is a credible account because it provides corroboration for what is already 'known', not because of the new evidence it presents. I argue that the image we now have presented as 'the apparition' is the result of a process of reality-construction, initially orally and later in print. In this chapter I seek to explain as much as possible how that process worked.

Social scientists are in no position to answer whether or not supernatural personages really appear in this world; what is beyond doubt is that at different times and places people have claimed to have encountered the supernatural in unusually 'real' ways and that these claims are given more or less credence at different times and places.[2] Almost all accounts of the Knock apparition are by people for whom the apparitions were miraculous manifestations of supernatural power and they were and still are accepted by people who share their faith.

Following news of the 21 August 1879 episode other supernatural sights and apparitions were reported by others at Knock, especially after the turn of the year 1880, and then widely elsewhere in Ireland and even in Wales.[3] One reporter in Knock early in 1880 found that 'everyone [he] met was full of what he had heard respecting the wonderful sights beheld at various times within the past six months on the gable of the now famous church'.[4] At midnight between 5 and 6 January 1880, patrolling policemen heard prayer from people outside Knock church who 'had assembled there in hope of seeing the apparition'.[5] It had earlier been arranged that the church bell would be rung by anyone who saw an apparition to quickly inform all those within hearing. A local teacher who saw a supernatural light at the church late at night admitted she had gone there 'in hopes of seeing something'. Another man wrote that along with a companion he left Claremorris around 10.00 p.m. to walk to Knock where they arrived after midnight, because 'our desire was to see the Apparition', which they did at 3.30 a.m.[6] People flocked to Knock and large numbers of miraculous cures of bodily ailments were reported through the application of cement or mortar from the apparition gable. The publicised apparitions and miracles brought crowds of pilgrims for some years in the early 1880s.[7] Clearly, after the August episode and the reports of cures, both local people and visitors were not only alert to the possibility of more supernatural events but were openly expecting something miraculous. This atmosphere of expectancy largely accounts for the later visions and apparitions, though each would be shaped by the local circumstances.

The greater challenge is to explain the occurrence of the 'first' apparition in August. That is the question that I address in this book. ('The Knock Apparition' as promoted by later believers consists of the 21 August episode and rarely mentions any subsequent visions.) In this chapter I seek to understand more precisely the nature of that 21 August 1879 apparition. Of course, no social scientists were at the gable and neither can we be privy to the inevitable conversations, gossip and discussions immediately afterward about whatever transpired there. We have to rely on later reports of what happened. Thus, by necessity we have to start by examining the stories recounted in the published versions of the witnesses' testimonies, and by seeking to understand how the people who wrote these accounts constructed them. Like the stories about priestly powers remembered by Daniel Campbell or the folklore about Archbishop MacHale, the accounts of the Knock apparition tell us about the believers and promoters more than about the stories' ostensible subject-matter. It will become clear as we examine the published evidence that the investigating priests sought to promote belief in the apparition and devotion at Knock, rather than to evaluate the credibility of those claiming to have seen heavenly personages or to investigate inconsistencies or gaps in their testimony.

I argue that whatever the original seers perceived, their experience was recast in the process of reframing 'the apparition'. In particular, I argue that in several identifiable ways the reality of the apparition was transformed. First, the 'St John the Evangelist' figure was earlier perceived as a 'bishop'. Second, whether anyone initially perceived the altar/lamb/cross complex of elements featured in the published versions is debatable. It is plausible that these orthodox Eucharistic symbols were added later, perhaps suggested by priests on the investigating commission. Other changes follow a pattern that enhances the credibility of the claim to the supernatural nature of the apparition.

The description of the apparition scene quoted above is the end product of a process with many identifiable steps. The generally accepted view is that a commission of three priests was established by Archbishop MacHale to investigate the first apparition claims; that this commission took testimony from over a dozen witnesses on 8 October 1879 in the sacristy of the Knock church, and later reported that the testimony taken as a whole was trust-worthy and satisfactory; that the witnesses' depositions were published in two main sources early in 1880; and, finally, that the description quoted above is an accurate summary of that witness-testimony. Thus the belief is that many persons witnessed the apparition, that they gave truthful testi-mony to the investigating priests, that the priests accurately recorded what they were told; and, finally, that this testimony was published in the sources now available. But the evidence for each link in this chain is often inconclu-sive, inconsistent, ambiguous, at times implausible, or contradicted by other evidence with equal or better claims to credibility. Even devout believers in the supernatural nature of the apparition recognise that the investigation 'lacked adequate care, continuity and persistence'.[8] Yet, that does not shake their faith in the truth of the story.

The Investigating Commission

That an investigating commission heard testimony from witnesses in Knock church for one day only, 8 October 1879, six weeks after the reports of the apparitions is not questioned, but practically everything else about it is. Who set up the commission? Who were its members and how many were there? What was its task or who decided this question? How did it do its work? To whom, if anybody, did it report? And what did it report? What relationship do the available published versions of the seers' testimony bear to what witnesses might have told the commission? Answers to these and numerous other basic questions are unclear or unavailable.

The archdiocese of Tuam at that time was in a most peculiar state of eccle-siastical governance. The aged Archbishop John MacHale had finally been defeated in a long struggle with Rome over who would succeed him and when. John MacEvilly had earlier been appointed coadjutor, an assistant with the right to succeed on MacHale's death. MacHale had strenuously opposed MacEvilly, even defying the pope in the process. Finally, with the support and approval of Rome, MacEvilly took up residence in Tuam around 1 September 1879, ten days after the apparition and before the sitting of the commission. The archdiocese was thus in the anomalous position of having two archbishops but no effective diocesan administration. The two, rather than cooperating, by all accounts never spoke to each other. To which of them did priests report or owe allegiance? What canon law might say was one thing but what individual priests might decide was another. MacEvilly complained that he was carrying much of the pastoral load in the diocese without any cooperation, revenue or even recognition from MacHale. MacHale was physically and perhaps mentally weakened by age, and his published letters were widely attributed to his nephew. He had earlier lost the confidence of many of his priests. In the 1876 election to select three names to recommend to Rome for appointment as coadjutor and next arch-bishop, the priests had voted sixteen to twelve for MacEvilly over MacHale's nephew Fr Thomas MacHale (with sixteen votes spread among five others), whom many believed was already in charge of day-to-day administration of the diocese, despite MacHale's making it very clear in advance (indeed in a letter published in the widest circulating newspaper in the country, the *Freeman's Journal*), that he could never accept MacEvilly. The bitterness between the two men was long-standing and apparent to all.

When MacHale was honoured in 1875 on his Golden Jubilee as bishop, MacEvilly, then a bishop in an adjoining diocese had acknowledged the occasion by scheduling a mandatory spiritual retreat for his priests for the very days of the celebration. Thus when he moved to Tuam ten days after the apparition, MacEvilly probably lacked legitimacy in the eyes of many lay people and among a significant minority of the clergy.[9] A story about him collected by the Irish Folklore Commission over a half a century later begins by stating that the people had no regard for him at all compared to MacHale (see chapter 5 above). Vilifying his character, seven parish priests in the diocese had already written to Rome asking that he not be made coadjutor.[10] At the same time Archbishop MacHale, even if mentally competent, had been sidelined when Rome sent in MacEvilly armed with a mandate to exercise all the powers of archbishop. Fr Thomas MacHale, his uncle's vicar-general, by most accounts was disliked by many of the priests and in any case his powers, delegated from his uncle, were canonically indefensible given MacEvilly's mandate. Yet he was his uncle's factotum and was in residence at the archbishop's palace with control over diocesan records. Given the episcopal stalemate and consequent ineffective administration, it is perhaps no surprise that the apparition claims were poorly investigated by the ecclesiastical authorities and that documentation of the investigation and record keeping left a lot to be desired. Neither the civil authorities nor any other outside agency investigated the episode.

All the early accounts say that MacHale appointed the commission, but later writers in the 1920s and 1930s claim MacEvilly did. Monsignor E. A. D'Alton, a respected Tuam priest, who wrote a well-informed two-volume history of the diocese, and who was to be a member of a second commission of enquiry in the 1930s wrote that MacEvilly set up the original commission.[11] Mrs Helena Concannon, an enthusiast for the revived devotion and shrine at

Knock and well connected in clerical circles likewise identified MacEvilly.[12] However, since MacEvilly later wrote[13] that MacHale appointed the commission members we can be relatively confident that the early reports to this effect are indeed correct. But confusion over such a basic point of information is emblematic of the lack of adequate care being taken in the documentation of most aspects of the investigation.

Every early published source that touches on the issue states that the commission was comprised of three parish priests, Archdeacon Bartholomew Cavanagh of Knock as chairman, Canon James Waldron of Ballyhaunis, and Canon Ulick Bourke of Claremorris.[14] Yet, Fr Edward Murphy, a Jesuit priest who was in the area shortly after the commission sat, but before any testimony was published, wrote at the time that MacHale had appointed four priests to the commission.[15] Was he wrong on this point? He seemed to be well informed about what the witnesses reported seeing (according to the later published accounts). Or was he right on this point, and this fourth priest either did not participate or chose not to be associated with the publications of (different) accounts when they appeared later in 1880? Later, at least two and perhaps three other priests were involved in investigating claimed miraculous cures at the young shrine, but we do not know how this came to be. Did these additional priests sit on a separately established commission that also included Cavanagh, Bourke and Waldron? Perhaps these priests were appointed to the original commission at the outset but for some reason did not take part in deposing the witnesses. One report of a parishioner seeing supernatural lights on 8 November 1879 says that five priests on the commission were dining with Fr Cavanagh at the time.[16] Or were they later added to the original commission either by appointment by one or other of the feuding archbishops or by cooption? How and by whom was the mandate of that commission defined? Perhaps the mystery fourth original member began to participate.

It is not clear to whom the commission reported or how or when. MacPhilpin tells us that the commission reported that the evidence (about the original apparition) taken as a whole was satisfactory and trustworthy.[17] Sexton says that Fr Cavanagh informed 'the archbishop' that the commission had fulfilled its assigned task and that he did this before starting his diary of miracle cures at the end of October 1879.[18] By 'archbishop' both Sexton and MacPhilpin would almost certainly have meant MacHale rather than MacEvilly, but it is not impossible that the commission reported to both archbishops. Nold suspects that the commission's report might have been merely an oral one.[19] The fact that a written document has never been found does not, however, mean that one was not submitted. One reporter later speculated that any records were either accidentally lost or perhaps deliberately destroyed.[20] However, official records of all kinds were missing from the archbishop's palace after MacHale died in 1881. In a 12 January 1880 letter, the Jesuit, Fr Murphy, wrote that 'after a searching inquiry and full deliberation, they [the four ecclesiastics on the commission] have all given their written declaration that they can see no reason to doubt the reality of the Apparition,' which suggests at least some preliminary report in written form. However, whatever report was made evidently did not include the original witness depositions since a few of these surfaced over a century later in Washington, D C.[21]

Fr Murphy also records that the panel of priests met for 'deliberation', presumably after but possibly also before they heard the witness testimony. (Unaware of the Jesuit priest's letter, Walsh[22] reached the same conclusion on the basis of internal evidence in the published testimony.) What took place during this 'deliberation' is of crucial importance. The publication within a few months of two different versions of the witnesses' depositions, one of which can be directly traced to Fr Cavanagh and the other equally directly to Canon Bourke, however, shows at a minimum that the commission members did not reach consensus on one definitive description or narrative of the apparition. The published versions of the depositions were neither authenticated nor printed by either MacHale or MacEvilly or any official ecclesiastical body or official. (The archdiocese itself has no records whatever of the commission.) That two accounts clearly linked to the two priests were in fact published without approval from either archbishop shows that the MacHale–MacEvilly stand-off created room for the diocesan priests on the commission to follow their own counsel.

In another letter to *Ave Maria* nearly a year and a half later, the same well-informed Jesuit said that the commission had 'sat frequently and received testimony as to the apparitions and miracles. The result of their deliberations is not yet announced, nor is it thought their enquiries have yet ended.'[23] In addition to Frs Cavanagh, Bourke and Waldron, this letter lists three more priest members, Fr James Ronayne, PP Ballinmote (*recte* Ballinrobe), Fr Peter Gerathy, PP Bekan, and Fr Patrick O'Brien, PP Athenry. Without citing a source, Walsh claimed Archbishop MacEvilly appointed a commission in 1882 to investigate cases of cures,[24] but some such investigation was underway long before 1882. Canon Bourke told a reporter around the first anniversary of the apparition that the commission was meeting monthly on cures,[25] and others reported around the same time that the commission refused to render a judgment on the claims of miracles.[26] The published list of miracle cures is long, mainly in *The Nation* down to October 1880, but it is Fr Cavanagh and not any commission that compiled it. He was credulous and unsceptical to an extraordinary degree and moreover he published the claimed cures before the commission had concluded its work. There is only a hint that the commission ever reached any conclusions or made any report on its investigations and most researchers assume it never made one.[27] The hint comes in a statement made to the Second Commission of Inquiry in the late 1930s by an elderly priest who had earlier served in Knock parish. He recalled seeing a report — whether a copy or an original he did not know — in the priest's house in Knock when he came there. He remembered that the report was about the investigation of claimed miracle cures, but not the apparition, and the gist of it was that the commission found no evidence of miraculous cures. The priest said he left the report in a desk in the priest's house when he left Knock, but it seems not to have survived.[28]

The Witnesses

The early published sources name fourteen persons who witnessed the event at the church gable and a fifteenth who testified he saw a bright light at the church from his farm half a mile away.[29] As we have seen, ties of kinship connected up to nine of the fourteen, and five of the nine lived in the same house. Many considered Mary Beirne the chief witness. A single woman, she was living with her brother Dominick and her sister Margaret (Maggie) along with their niece eight-year-old Catherine Murray and the three siblings' widowed mother, also called Margaret Beirne, who was reported to be sixty-eight. All five testified as seers. The Beirne siblings were between their late teens and late twenties but their precise ages are unclear. The earliest publication of evidence says Mary was twenty-six when the apparition occurred, but in 1932 she said she was twenty-eight at the time and in 1936 she claimed she was twenty-nine. One reporter in 1880 estimated Dominick was twenty-two or twenty-three, but whoever registered his death in January 1885 said he was twenty-four, which would make him only eighteen in 1879.[30] His sister Maggie was a little older than Dominick.

Other witnesses included another Dominick Beirne, aged about thirty-five, a cousin of the three siblings, his six-year-old nephew John Curry who lived with him, and their neighbour Patrick Beirne who was also likely a relative. Patrick is usually reported to have been sixteen. Another Beirne cousin, Patrick Hill, gave the most detailed description of the apparition. He was baptised in 1868 so a modern reporter, assuming baptism soon after birth, wrote he was eleven in 1879 but two journalists early in 1880 said he was thirteen and another that he was fourteen.[31]

Besides the Beirnes and their relatives, depositions were recorded from six others. Mary McLoughlin was in her forties and was Fr Cavanagh's live-in housekeeper. Bridget Trench was a widow in her mid-seventies; apparently she was the only witness who had to give her testimony in Irish. We are told that a priest translated her account into English as she spoke. Two other local women, Judith Campbell and Mrs Hugh Flatley also gave depositions, as did a man named John Durkan, aged about twenty-four. Finally, a farmer named Patrick Walsh stated he noticed a bright light at the church gable from a distance of over half a mile. His age was reported both as fifty-five and sixty-five.

Sources for the Testimony

The commission's report (if any) to either archbishop is unavailable, but versions of the seers' testimonies were initially published mainly in two separate sources early in 1880. Practically all subsequent writers have relied on these for accounts of the apparition. These two sources also give us the above list of witnesses. I refer to them as the MacPhilpin book and the Sexton work, respectively.

John MacPhilpin was perfectly situated and connected to be well informed about the commission's work. He lived in Tuam, the diocesan seat and home to the archbishop. He was owner and editor of the *Tuam News*, which published on 9 January 1880 the first newspaper report of the apparition the previous August. This newspaper had been founded by commission member, Canon Ulick Bourke, who was also MacPhilpin's uncle. Until 1878, when he became Parish Priest of Claremorris, Bourke had lived in Tuam where he was a professor in and later president of St Jarlath's College, the diocesan minor seminary. Uncle and nephew collaborated closely on the paper before the uncle turned over ownership to MacPhilpin. It was known as the canon's own newspaper and he was believed to be directly involved in formulating its editorial content.[32] So closely involved in its workings was he that he had a special Gaelic font cast for his regular contributions in the Irish language.[33] In addition, MacPhilpin's brother, Peter, was a priest serving in the diocese. Given these ties, some have argued persuasively that the *Tuam News* can be regarded as a quasi-official organ of the archdiocese.[34] Living where he was and with such clerical and family ties, MacPhilpin was superbly situated to benefit from the nepotism for which the archbishop became infamous in his later years, and to reflect the sentiment on Knock of at least one important segment of the clergy. It is clear that he would not have published anything over the objections of Archbishop MacHale or the commission, and very likely he received a copy of any commission report from Canon Bourke or even from MacHale's office.[35] He writes that 'the official testimony of those who witnessed the first apparition is here given, in order to give the reader the best reliable and authentic evidence', and adds that the commission had reported that 'the testimony of all [witnesses], taken as a whole, is trustworthy and satisfactory'.[36] These statements show him to be knowledgeable about not only the commissioners' work, but about their conclusions and judgments.

MacPhilpin's book is not just a report of what the witnesses said but a sustained and detailed argument for the truth of the claims of a supernatural apparition and the occurrence of miracles. The book is divided into eight chapters with chapter V, 'What the Witnesses Say' being a record of what the seers told the commission. This was preceded in the book by lengthy descriptions of the event as if it were proven beyond doubt to be supernatural and by a chapter refuting, in advance, any possible objections. The author shows himself to be familiar with accounts of miraculous appearances of supernatural figures in both the Old and New Testaments and in the early days of Christianity. Moreover, later chapters show him to be knowledgeable about more recent apparitions in France (Lourdes and La Salette), Germany (Marpingen) and Poland. MacPhilpin's final chapter is called 'Miracles' and, after a short defence of the idea of miracles, is largely devoted to a list of miraculous cures that Archdeacon Cavanagh had compiled.

As Tuam priest and Knock devotee Fr Michael Walsh noted much later, MacPhilpin displayed knowledge unusual for a layman.[37] His mode of argumentation and presentation of evidence is also decidedly clerical in cast. He very likely benefited from the help or at least the guidance and oversight of his uncle, the canon, and perhaps his brother, the priest, and he obviously had the cooperation of Fr Cavanagh. MacPhilpin's access to the commission members and their work, his family and work ties to important clerics, and the organisation of the book's argument all show him to have what we can call a 'clerical' view of the Knock apparition.

After 9 January 1880 when MacPhilpin's newspaper published the first article about the apparition and while he wrote his book — he dated the preface 25 March 1880 — others reported on Knock. Local newspaper coverage grew, the Dublin-published *The Nation* started sustained extended reporting, and even London papers carried reports. A *Daily Telegraph* correspondent in the area to report on the Land War was received, introduced to some witnesses and generally helped by both Canon Bourke and Archdeacon Cavanagh. MacPhilpin found his report 'A Mayo Lourdes', published on 1 March, sufficiently to his liking that he included it in his book. All in all, rather than being a neutral reporting of witnesses' testimony and its strengths and weaknesses, the book is carefully constructed as an endorsement of the claim to supernatural provenance as the only possible explanation of the events.

What was to become the most extensive national coverage began in mid-January when *The Nation* republished stories from local papers in its issues of 17 and 24 January 1880. *The Nation*, and its cheaper sister version the *Weekly News*, was to become what one priest admirer called 'The Gazette of Our Lady of Knock'.[38] Not content with reprinting local articles, it sent a 'Special Correspondent' to report on the events. This writer's lengthy reports were published in eight weekly issues from 31 January through 20 March 1880. Helped in his work by both Canon Bourke and Archdeacon Cavanagh, the correspondent interviewed for himself several of the witnesses, and he published these accounts in his early reports.

The 7 February 1880 article noted that Archdeacon Cavanagh 'had in his possession at this moment the formal depositions of over a dozen persons regarding both the visions and the cures'. The next week the correspondent wrote that Cavanagh 'informed me that he had in his hands the depositions of sixteen persons, with reference to the visions at the church'. Finally, in the issue of 21 February, the correspondent reports that on 13 February Fr Cavanagh gave him a diary of miraculous cures the priest had been keeping. For the reporter, it was 'the most wonderful record, I certainly say, that has ever come under my observation'. The correspondent also received — presumably from Archdeacon Cavanagh although he doesn't explicitly say so — 'a full and perfect copy of the text of the depositions'. On 21 February *The Nation* printed the testimonies of Mary McLaughlin, Mary Beirne and Dominick Beirne, Jr and the following week, that of Margaret Beirne, Brigid Trench, Catherine Murray, Judy Campbell, Margaret Beirne and Dominick Beirne, Sr. The coverage in the issues of 6, 13 and 20 March largely reprints Archdeacon Cavanagh's Diary of Cures. *The Nation's* coverage, extensive and positive, continued down to October 1880.

Practically all writers assume that *The Nation's* 'special correspondent' was none other than the newspaper's proprietor himself, T. D. Sullivan. In fact he was Thomas Sexton, Sullivan's colleague in journalism and politics who was later to be elected to parliament, to serve on the executive of the Land League, and to be Lord Mayor of Dublin. Sexton is identified by Andrew Dunlop,[39] a contemporary journalist, who says he was told by Sexton himself, and in any case was in a position to know since the two men reported from Knock at the same time. Another well-informed observer, who was in school and served as an altar boy in Knock in the years immediately after the apparition, also wrote that Sexton was *The Nation's* correspondent.[40] Sexton's reports, incorporating his own interviews with some of the most important seers, the 'text of the depositions' of nearly all the others, and the opening parts of Fr Cavanagh's Diary of Cures, were published in what I call the Sexton book. This work also included illustrations derived from photographs of the interior of Knock church and of Mary Beirne and Dominick Beirne Sr, credited to Limerick photographer T. O'Connor, and drawings of the apparition scene and exterior church gable attributed to a nun at the Mercy convent in Claremorris. Finally the book carried an advertisement for Knock devotional items from J. J. Lalor, a Dublin dealer in religious artefacts. The book's publisher was T. D. Sullivan but the place on the title page usually filled by the author's name is blank. We now know that the 'special correspondent' who wrote it was Thomas Sexton. The short work appeared in April 1880.[41]

The Sexton book also has solid claims to be taken seriously as a source of evidence. Even though written by Sexton, rather than T. D. Sullivan as widely assumed later, we may accept that Sullivan (who commissioned and published the reports not only in the paper but also in book form), shared his views. Sullivan was on excellent terms with Archbishop MacHale. At the celebration of the latter's fifty years as a bishop in 1875, Sullivan's brother — fellow journalist and close co-worker in clericalist/nationalist politics, A. M. Sullivan — was the main speaker.[42] For the occasion T.D. Sullivan composed a poem honouring the archbishop, which was included a few years later in Canon Bourke's biography of MacHale.[43] When MacHale acknowledged an invitation to address a meeting in Ballyhaunis called by his supporters in the early days of the demonstrations against clerical condemnation of the Land War leaders, he suggested they invite A. M. Sullivan.[44] Sexton and Sullivan's good relationship with and considerate treatment of the clergy generally, may be seen in Sexton's admission that he knew about the events at Knock for several months before the paper reported them and that he exercised journalistic restraint, because of 'the desire of the clergy that no widespread publicity should be given to the reported occurrences'.[45] Apart from the Sullivan brothers' compatible politics and personal ties with Archbishop MacHale, Sexton was on excellent terms with at least two of the three priests generally claimed to have comprised the commission. He was introduced to various witnesses, accompanied in his travels and generally helped enormously by Canon Ulick Bourke. No doubt such facilitation of the correspondent's work furthered the canon's belief that the apparition should be publicised, but the cooperation also built on a long association between the paper and Bourke. The canon was an Irish language enthusiast and *The Nation* had recognised his work in that area and furthered it by publishing, over the course of many years, weekly short lessons of his on the language and helping him publish them also in Irish–American papers.[46]

Sexton was also received by the chairman of the commission, Archdeacon Cavanagh, who provided him 'with a full and perfect copy of the text of the depositions made before the tribunal of clergymen appointed by his grace the Archbishop of Tuam to investigate the facts regarding the apparition last August',[47] which he published without any indication of alteration. If *The Nation* edited or altered the seers' testimony from the version that Fr Cavanagh gave to Sexton then the priest could have indicated this, but he did not. He even published a letter endorsing the accuracy of press accounts and told Sexton they were 'substantially correct'.[48] He continued a close working relationship with the paper for months. The paper later published long extracts from Fr Cavanagh's continuing diary of miraculous cures at the young shrine, and generally gave Knock extensive favourable coverage throughout almost all of 1880. This suggests that Fr Cavanagh originated any 'changes' or (less likely) endorsed ones *The Nation* made. However, 'changes' may not be the best term here. Since the seers' testimony was obviously never transcribed verbatim but at best summarised and paraphrased by the commission, Fr Cavanagh, as commission chair, could be seen to be producing a 'better' paraphrasing or summary than the version published by MacPhilpin. In other words, the process of formulating the reality of the apparition did not end when the witnesses gave their testimony but continued in the work of the commission members and, possibly, also in the work of the journalists and book writers, MacPhilpin and Sexton.

The MacPhilpin and Sexton works were both 'clerical' in their orientation, and the clergy according to Sexton had discouraged earlier newspaper coverage. Thus the first reports generally publicised in the media were the ones endorsed and promoted by Fr Cavanagh and/or Canon Bourke. Moreover, these reports gave no hint about how the seers interpreted (as opposed to described) the episode. The burden of proof was thereby shifted from those who would claim a supernatural miracle to those who might question or deny it, while all the evidence provided was framed to support the claim. Very quickly the apparition was reported as fact rather than claim. When one promoter wrote that 'the authenticity, both of the apparitions and of the cures effected at the Shrine of Knock has been established beyond all doubt', he was merely stating succinctly the common view among devotees.[49]

If one book claims to present the 'official testimony . . . the best reliable and authentic evidence'[50] and another book prints a 'full and perfect copy of the text of the depositions',[51] how can we account for differences between their versions of the same original witness statements? Most writers have simply ignored divergences between the two; the few who have acknowledged differences have downplayed their significance.[52] While the differences may be of little significance for believers, for historians they provide important evidence about how 'the apparition' was constructed and its image propagated. The explanation of the differences requires consideration of the processes of framing and reframing in the ongoing social construction of the reality of the apparition.

In addition to the two principal works, I use several other early sources, most of which I have not seen cited elsewhere, to fill out my explanation. The Marian Library at the University of Dayton has a copy of an anonymous undated pamphlet called *Full Report of the Visitation of the Blessed Virgin, St Joseph, St John in Knock Chapel, Co. Mayo*.[53] Comprising seven hurriedly written and badly printed pages, it was published by Nugent and Co., 6 High Street, Dublin. The opening paragraphs were printed in the *Mayo Examiner* of 17 January 1880[54] and other parts appear to have been drawn from newspaper articles from January or early February 1880.

On 12 January 1880, Fr Edward Murphy, SJ, wrote to Fr Daniel Hudson, CSC, the editor of the American Marian weekly *Ave Maria*, giving an account of the apparition which he said he 'heard from the very persons who saw it and at the place where it occurred' and specifically naming Mary Beirne 'from whom among others I heard the whole account'. In another letter three days later, he gave further information which he had 'just received from good authority'. Ascribed only to 'a well-known missionary priest of the Archdiocese of Tuam', the letters were published together on 7 February 1880.[55] A week earlier, *Ave Maria* had reprinted the first *Tuam News* article on Knock, a copy of which it had received from Canon Bourke. It is clear that Murphy's second letter followed the *Tuam News* article (unless both were based on some now-unknown common source, unlikely but possible).

The Limerick photographer, T. O'Connor, visited Knock very early in February 1880 with an eye to making pictures for sale in his business.[56] Clearly eager to promote devotion to the emerging shrine, he published a short book on his visit in which he reprinted the seers' testimony as given by MacPhilpin.[57] On his visit he had carried a letter of introduction to Fr Cavanagh and was concerned to get information from the seers. What he heard from Mary Beirne and Dominick Beirne, Sr, provides interesting evidence.

Well over a century after disappearing a few of the original 8 October 1879 witness depositions surfaced. In late 1881, over two years after the first apparition, a famous nun, Margaret Anna Cusack (in religion Sr Mary

Francis Clare and widely known as 'The Nun of Kenmare'), moved to Knock probably with the intention of setting up a convent there. She probably had been invited by Fr Cavanagh, perhaps hoping to capitalise on her fame and enlist her well-known talents as a writer to help promote the Knock devotion. While she did publish a book on Knock pressing for ecclesiastical recognition of the apparition,[58] in her two years at Knock Cusack alienated both Cavanagh and Archbishop MacEvilly. When she left in 1883 she took with her the written statements of at least some of the apparition witnesses to the investigating commission as well as other materials that she probably had received from Cavanagh and which would be useful in publicising the Knock story. Cusack went on to found the Sisters of St Joseph of Peace, and even though her role as its foundress was later downplayed within that order, many documents she took from Knock were preserved in its archives in Washington, DC. I had already examined these records when historian John White announced that he had found them.[59]

Other better known sources on the original apparition include some journalists' interviews with witnesses or what some witnesses said at later investigations. Much of the positive early newspaper reporting has been collected by Tom Neary[60] and the most important sceptical coverage was in the London-published *Daily News*. An 'expert' and professor of science at the national seminary at Maynooth, the Revd Dr Francis Lennon, who was brought in to give his views about the original 21 August apparition claims, wrote a lengthy letter summarising his views on a number of possible natural explanations of the episode and commenting on the worth of the evidence provided by some witnesses. A copy of this letter is in the archives of the archdiocese of Tuam and it has been widely but selectively quoted in the devotional literature.

Individuals, small groups and organised pilgrimages thronged to Knock after newspaper publicity started in early 1880, but by autumn that year reporters were writing about declining numbers and the railway was ending the special trains and rates it had provided earlier to capitalise on the pilgrim trade.[61] Fewer and fewer came in subsequent years until a revival half a century later again turned Knock into a major shrine.[62] By the 1930s, lay and clerical promoters were earnestly pressing the case of Knock. In this atmosphere, the few surviving witnesses were sought out, Mary Beirne being by far the most important. Now Mrs O'Connell, she gave depositions or interviews in 1932, 1935 and January 1936, arranged by persons hoping for official ecclesiastical recognition of the apparition and promoting the revival of devotion at the shrine. A 'Second Commission of Inquiry' was established later in 1936, which arranged for yet another deposition by Mrs O'Connell in August of that year, just weeks before she died. Pat Beirne similarly gave depositions in 1932 and again twice in 1936. The only other surviving witness, John Curry, by then living in a New York City home for the aged, was examined there in 1937 at the request of the commission. These later witness statements too are useful as evidence.

Developing the Picture

Even unquestioning believers such as Walsh accept that the published 'depositions' in Sexton and MacPhilpin must have gone through many stages of development and elaboration.[63] The secretary to the Second Commission of Enquiry that sat in the 1930s recorded that 'it appeared to the judges that all the old depositions attributed to the witnesses must have been cast into form by someone'.[64] The discovery of the manuscript copies of three witness statements enables us to learn more about the process of social construction of the apparition, i.e. the process through which the image later promoted of 'the apparition' was constituted. These manuscript versions are dated 8 October 1879 (the day the commission heard testimony), and at first glance, they are signed by the three witnesses. What ostensibly is the 'signature' of Judy Campbell, however, is in the hand of whoever penned all three statements. In content, these manuscript versions are identical to those printed by MacPhilpin. Though we do not have the evidence to prove it, presumably the other depositions in MacPhilpin's book are similarly unaltered from what was produced on 8 October or following deliberation later. Some significant differences were introduced, however, most likely by Fr Cavanagh, into the accounts published in *The Nation* and then in Sexton's book. But how were the original 8 October accounts produced? The historian who has most searchingly examined the question argues that

> Even in their manuscript form, the depositions are clerically composed documents. The original documents and the subtle changes that take place between the collection of the seers' statements and the publication of those statements over time illustrate the contextual needs of the investigating priests through whose minds these stories were filtered. The stories were made to fit the clerical desire to have those documents state that what the people saw were the *very persons* of Mary, Joseph, and John rather than their statues [that] the seers described.[65]

The evidence supports this claim, though I would add that the clerical 'desire' stemmed from the priests' beliefs and the conclusions they had reached.

It is relatively easy to show changes introduced in the Fr Cavanagh versions reported in *The Nation* and then printed in Sexton's book. Although the evidence is less clear we can detect similar pressures toward a clerical view even in the 8 October versions, whether in manuscript or later published by MacPhilpin. In his 'survey of facts and evidence', even a believer in the supernatural nature of the apparition such as Fr Michael Walsh, recognised that 'we do not know the processes of reasoning by which [the commissioners] arrived at their conclusion', but that they 'formulated a statement embodying the evidence of each witness'.[66] While we might expect that consideration of the witnesses' evidence would have preceded the reaching of a conclusion, evidence suggests that in many ways the 'conclusion' shaped the formulation of the witness statements.

Consider first one example of differences between the two books. In MacPhilpin's version of Mary McLoughlin's testimony we read:

> I saw a wonderful number of strange figures or appearances at the gable, one like the B.V. Mary, and one like St Joseph, another a bishop.

Sexton's version of the same testimony however runs as follows:

> I saw a vision in which there appeared to be three figures — one that of the Blessed Virgin Mary, one of St Joseph, and the other to be, as I thought, the likeness of St John the Evangelist.[67]

The recasting of this one sentence incorporates several kinds of transformation we can identify during the process of formulating the accounts published as 'the depositions'. First, the 'bishop' is reframed as 'St John the Evangelist'. Second, rather than seeing 'a number of strange figures or appearances', McLoughlin now reportedly saw 'a vision in which there appeared to be three figures'. Third, despite these changes, the reworking, the ongoing process of interpretation, is presented as McLoughlin's own: note the use of the first person, 'as I thought', in her reported account in Sexton. Her reported statement is recast as grammatically direct speech. It is important to keep in mind that these two are presented as authentic versions of the same original testimony. The differences between the two versions of Mary McLoughlin's testimony should be understood, I argue, as the result of a process of ongoing interpretation whereby the reality of the apparition and its contents was socially constructed. Both Archdeacon Cavanagh and Sexton were firm believers in the apparition; arguably, for either one to substitute 'St John the Evangelist' for the 'bishop' in McLoughlin's testimony would constitute not changing the evidence, but arranging it and presenting it in a way more easily believed and accepted by others as well as themselves in light of 'conclusions' they had already reached. Of course, we cannot rule out the possibility that Cavanagh consciously lied about what some witnesses claimed. We need not, however, conclude that in changing the testimony he engaged in deliberate dishonesty. In Knock after the apparition story first surfaced, we would expect it to be amplified by touches, embellishments and emendations in the normal processes of oral transmission.[68] By all accounts Fr Cavanagh was an enthusiastic believer and promoter and, of course, he would hear the stories going round. Did he add or suggest his own touches? Available evidence suggests that he did; however he likely was not being dishonest in his own mind. After all, Cavanagh was aware that MacPhilpin was publishing the 'original' depositions in his book and so would be unlikely to provide evidence that in his own mind contradicted these; what he provided to Sexton was in his mind consistent. Had he felt he had significantly altered the testimony, I submit, he would not have given critics ammunition for their charges.

This instance of reframing (defining the bishop figure as St John), I suggest was neither designed to deceive — to believers, it was not deceptive — nor was it unique. In fact, it was but one in a series of elaborations through which the reality we now have presented as 'the apparition' was constructed. Both MacPhilpin's and Sexton's published versions, whether or not they were true to McLoughlin's actual words (at least one and very likely both are untrue), were also framings, and if we could now recover her own words, they too would be a framing, an interpretation. By the time the commission heard their testimony, six weeks after the apparition, the seers' own interpretations and accounts had doubtlessly gone through various stages of formulation, articulation, refinement and selective development. In fact, if we accept the reported witness-testimony as accurate, this process can be seen to operate not only from the initial events but even before them, for many of the witnesses reportedly were called to the church gable to view what those already present interpreted as an appearance of the Virgin.[69] According to some published accounts, while they were at the gable the various seers talked and shared their opinions and interpretations, thereby reinforcing in each other the reality of the event.

The fact that five of the seers were living in the same Beirne household, up to four others were relatives of this family, and another (McLoughlin) was a good friend of Mary Beirne's, doubtless facilitated this process of conversational reality construction but, in any case, in the course of the six weeks before they gave their testimony (and the subsequent months before Sexton and other reporters interviewed them), we would expect that the process would have resulted in considerable stability of the picture they constructed and hence remembered. The reality-construction, the ongoing process of sense-making and interpretation did not end with the seers and their testimony, but was continued by the commissioners and the authors of the two books that are our sources for what the witnesses said. (This process is still ongoing as will be obvious to anyone who compares early visual depictions of the apparition scene with more recent ones.)

Because we have access neither to the original formulations of the seers nor to the commission's original report (if any), we are forced to look through third or later generation sources, as it were, to decipher what the seers saw, through what MacPhilpin and Sexton wrote that the commissioners recorded the witnesses as saying they saw. If we consider that one seer spoke only Irish and that for the others Irish was likely their first language, and there was a further translation (to English) involved, either by the commission (in Bridget Trench's case) or the seers, then we have a fourth generation source. Additionally, of course the questions asked by the commissioners framed the responses. In a 1950s' book called *The Knock Apparition: A Survey of Facts and Evidence,* Walsh recognised that

> the questioner or questioners were fully aware of possible natural expla-
> nations of the occurrence: the details sought and given are not just

> haphazard. They supply information that is necessary for determining
> the nature of the apparition, and such as would be sought by an enlight-
> ened critic.[70]

Walsh was a priest in the archdiocese and his book was published with the
Imprimatur of the Archbishop of Tuam. But he failed to see the implication
of what he recognised in the witness statements. Rather than describing
what they perceived or experienced and giving their depositions as free from
suggestion as possible, emphasising what they saw fit, the witnesses were
responding to particular lines of questioning shaped by the priests' own particular concerns. Berman too assumes the witnesses addressed the priests'
concerns rather than described their experiences as neutrally as possible. He
argues that the most plausible explanation of the episode is that the witnesses saw a projection of slides of statues made by a magic lantern; he
suggests that the priests elicited details in the testimony to refute this explanation in advance. Thus witnesses were reported as saying they saw the
figures before as well as after dark. Berman implies either that the printed
depositions are inaccurate (that they distort what the witnesses did say) or
that what the witnesses did say to the investigating commission was
designed to tell the priests what everybody knew the priests wanted to
hear.[71] (I discuss Berman's claim below.)

Clearly the depositions are not verbatim. There must have been extensive
questioning of witnesses to elicit the information in some depositions. There
must have been extensive formulating of statements. By their own admission,
in one case the commission members provided the words in one witness'
statement and in many cases the form of words must have been supplied by
the priests. Moreover, the MacPhilpin versions, even before being recast in
the Sexton work, 'show traces of the literary embellishments of an editor'.[72]
Thus if we keep in mind that the priests led the questioning and to some
unknowable but perhaps considerable extent provided the language that now
frames the responses, it is clear that the published depositions are several
more generations removed from 'first person accounts'.

Judging from the examples available among other promoters, the questioning of the seers was anything but searching or critical. To say the
inquirers employed leading questions would be an understatement. Sexton's
first statements to three different witnesses he saw separately are as follows:
'How came you to see the vision?', 'I understand, Miss Beirne, I said, that
you saw an extraordinary appearance here at the chapel of Knock', and 'Did
you witness the apparition of the 21st of August?'[73]

It is widely accepted that the commission of priests questioned each
witness alone. MacPhilpin hints this was the case.[74] Canon Bourke told
Archbishop Lynch of Toronto a few years later that fifteen witnesses were
'interrogated apart from each other'.[75] If this is true, then the published
depositions raise doubts about other aspects of the collection and recording
of evidence. The younger Dominick Beirne's deposition includes his

description of how his sister Mary called on him to go to the church gable to see the image to be seen there. It continues: 'I said, "what image?" and then she told me, as she has already described it for your reverence in her testimony.'[76] In Sexton, the wording 'already described' is changed to 'just now described'.[77] Either Dominick had heard his sister give her deposition or the commission members put these words into his mouth. If this was the commission's paraphrase rather than Dominick's words, then it seems that his testimony was reported (deliberately or otherwise) in a way that would not just reduce the chances of recording inconsistency or contradiction between witnesses but preclude its very possibility. This was not an isolated case. On the evidence of the published witness statements, the commissioners either a) interviewed witnesses in each other's hearing or b) someone put words in witnesses' mouths, and did so while making it appear this (commissioners'?) language was that of the witnesses by using the first person in the grammar of the published testimony. I submit that b) is the more likely case by far. We have seen this process already in Fr Cavanagh's reworking of Mary McLoughlin's testimony as written down (presumably on 8 October but perhaps after 'deliberation' later), but casting it into the first person. Here we see another example in an original 8 October deposition. A further example is provided in the testimony of the widowed Mrs Beirne.

While witnesses were most likely examined alone, most writers assume the commission as a body examined them. Some hints survive to raise questions about even this, however. The younger Dominick Beirne's deposition has him saying that his sister told him of the scene at the gable 'just as she has described it for your Reverence',[78] suggesting that only one commissioner was present. The statement of schoolboy, Patrick Hill, has the notation 'Witness Present: U. J. Canon Bourke'.[79] Most of the depositions have no similar statements about who witnessed them. One bears the notation 'witnessed, as the others, by the priests present', but if we do not know which or how many priests were present, we do not know that all the witnesses were examined by the full commission. Even Judge William Coyne, Knock's greatest champion in the revival decade of the 1930s, recognised that the witnesses gave their testimony 'in the presence of one or other of these [three] officially appointed commissioners'.[80] Canon Bourke alone witnessing Patrick Hill's deposition is significant for what it suggests about how the boy's testimony might have been influenced by the priest. Hill lived in Claremorris, just a short distance from Fr Bourke, who was the parish priest there. On several occasions Bourke sent for Hill, an impressive witness and easily available nearby, to give his account to visiting reporters, including ones from the *Daily Telegraph* and *The Nation*. Walsh sees this pattern as evidence of the boy's trustworthiness as a witness[81] but we cannot rule out the possible influence of the recognition and positive attention he was receiving on what Hill had to say. If Canon Bourke alone took the boy's formal deposition, as his being recorded as witness suggests, we should not be surprised if Hill consciously or unconsciously added a little by way of embroidery.[82]

Some witnesses examined were simply characterised as supporting what others said. Patrick Beirne's published deposition begins in the first person but then abruptly the reader is told, 'Young Beirne then told what he had seen regarding the Vision, just as it has been described already by several persons who were present.'[83] Here it would appear that the commission supplied the label 'Vision' to characterise the episode. In the paraphrase-cum-characterisation in Sexton, Patrick is recorded as having seen 'the figures as just described, distinctly and clearly' and as having 'given testimony just in accordance with the other witnesses'.[84] This pattern of asserting agreement rather than recording witnesses' words reaches its extreme in the case of John Durkan, whose deposition is reduced to one sentence in MacPhilpin: 'His testimony is the same as that given by each of the Beirnes',[85] and not mentioned at all by Sexton. Sexton presents the witness statements in a different sequence than MacPhilpin, so we do not know the order in which the witnesses gave their testimony and consequently we cannot decide how many Beirnes had already testified when whatever John Durkan said was reduced to that one sentence. Moreover, this formulation assumes that 'each of the Beirnes' said the same thing, which is not the case. The 'Beirne version' is already privileged in the way the testimony is recorded.

Social relationships among the various seers and their social standing likely influenced the giving and the recording of depositions. In giving greater weight to the Beirnes the commission was merely reproducing the hierarchy of credibility among the witnesses, a hierarchy that replicated the social distinctions made in the local community. John Durkan, whose statement was so easily minimised, was a person of low socio-economic status. He was about twenty-four years old, yet Patrick Hill, aged anywhere from eleven to fourteen, referred to him as a 'servant boy'. Little was remembered later of Durkan but that he was a 'man of the roads' or cattle driver.[86] On the day of the apparition he had been working in the bog with Dominick Beirne Sr, the cattle dealer. It may be that poor Durkan was occasionally employed by Beirne to drive cattle to and from the various fairs, as were men in his position while their employers travelled more comfortably on horseback, by pony and trap or even by train. In the dire circumstances of economic depression and threatened famine, Durkan could hardly be considered free from pressure to know his place and agree with his social betters. He was not generally accorded much respect in society; none of the reporters who visited and promoted Knock, such as Sexton, interviewed him; and the commission merely continued that pattern by treating him as a person whose opinions did not count for much except as corroboration of what the more credible folk had said.

If Durkan was the only such case of questionable independence among the witnesses we might ignore it, but there were others. Fr Lennon, the Maynooth expert on apparitions who visited Knock, claimed that the old woman seer, Bridget Trench, was 'dependent on the charity of neighbours' and was inclined to give less weight to her testimony on that account.[87] She could hardly have been immune to what these neighbours might desire. Mary McLoughlin is yet another instance of compromised autonomy. She was Fr Cavanagh's housekeeper but she was even more dependent on him than were most housekeepers on the priests who employed them. She was not a local woman and apparently had no extended family nearby. It was speculated later that she might have been a famine orphan that Fr Cavanagh had 'rescued' from some workhouse, perhaps in Westport where he served before becoming parish priest of Knock in 1867. Moreover she was illiterate — she put her X on her deposition — and so was ill-prepared to get other jobs to support herself. She had very good reasons to keep her employer happy. When her deposition was printed she reportedly claimed it was 'a mistake of the newspaper' that recorded her as seeing a cross.[88] Her economic dependence on Fr Cavanagh and her illiteracy meant, however, that she was in no position to know or question how he might have recast her deposition. In any case, between 21 August and 8 October, we can be sure that his housekeeper learned what it was that Fr Cavanagh believed about the claims of an apparition. Her's is one of the very first miracle cures that Cavanagh recorded in his diary; her sore knees had been cured by application of water he collected at the church gable the morning after the apparition.[89] The controversial 'Nun of Kenmare', Margaret Anna Cusack, claimed a few years later that McLoughlin was bringing discredit to Knock (by her drinking), and criticised Fr Cavanagh for not sending her away despite Cusack's offer to finance her emigration to the US.[90] 'She had some kind of hold over him', claimed Cusack, but probably not as much influence as he had over her.

Some have argued that it was advantageous to have three local parish priests on the commission in that they already knew the local seers and their reputations for truthfulness, and so could quickly assess their reliability as witnesses.[91] On the other hand, by 8 October when the depositions were taken, all the local priests almost certainly had formed some opinions about the apparition claims.[92] Fr Cavanagh was neither hesitant in forming a judgment nor reticent in sharing it. By one report, the very morning after the apparition claim he collected in bottles the rainwater that had pooled around the base of the apparition gable.[93] The fact that Cavanagh was a fervent believer as well as the employer of one important witness made him a particularly unfortunate choice to chair the commission, but it also ensured an energetic promotion of the apparition later in the media. If the priests knew their parishioners well, it is equally if not more true that their parishioners knew their priests well. While Fr Cavanagh's parishioners might well criticise his words and actions in matters of politics, as many of them had done with great ostentation, they were not likely to openly challenge his claims or suggestions about heavenly matters. Indeed, far from being anti-clerical, their criticisms were designed to get him to act properly as a priest. Being subordinate in the arena of religion, his parishioners had every reason to bow low and agree because Fr Cavanagh was not a man to brook opposition or questioning. He had made that clear earlier that year when he denounced the land agitation organisers from the altar.

Based on the available depositions, the seers unanimously reported seeing three figures, two of which — the Virgin Mary and St Joseph — they had no difficulty in identifying. This was not surprising since statues of the two were common (though much more so in the case of the Virgin), but it does indicate that the witnesses did have mental pictures of these person-ages derived from figures they had seen. The third figure is conventionally identified as St John the Evangelist, but, as already discussed, there is evi-dence the seers originally perceived and reported him (or it?) as a bishop. The first interviewed witness to see anything unusual was Mary McLoughlin, the priest's housekeeper. According to her testimony as pub-lished in MacPhilpin's book, she was walking from the priest's house past the church on her way to visit the Beirne household when she saw 'a number of strange figures or appearances at the gable; one like the Blessed Virgin Mary, and one like St Joseph; another a bishop'.[94] After visiting the Beirnes for half an hour she returned, accompanied by Mary Beirne and saw not only these figures but also an altar 'to the left of the bishop'.[95] In the published versions, it was Mary Beirne who identified this personage as St John the Evangelist. But in her deposition, one of three to survive in manuscript form, Mary's sister Maggie claims to have made the identifica-tion.[96] Following the published versions only we are told that Mary Beirne said she was 'not in any way sure what saint or character the figure repre-sented' but she had at one time seen a statue of that saint (in a church at Lecanvey forty miles away) 'very much resembling the figure which stood now before me'.[97] However, she added that 'the statue which I had formerly seen had no mitre on its head, while the figure which I now beheld had one'.[98] Mary Beirne named the figure as St John the Evangelist and 'then all the others present said the same — said what I stated'.[99] Other witnesses emphasised the mitre, the distinguishing hat of a bishop, even though they called the figure 'St John'. Dominick Beirne, Jr referred to 'St John, as my sister called the bishop';[100] Dominick Beirne, Sr said 'there was a mitre on St John's head, nearly like to that which a bishop wears',[101] and Patrick Hill said 'St John was dressed like a bishop preaching'.[102] Judith Campbell, Bridget Trench, Patrick Beirne and Mrs Margaret Beirne likewise heard others label the figure 'St John'.[103]

Though she was the first to call him St John the Evangelist there is good reason to believe Mary Beirne's earlier perception was of a bishop. She herself indicated that she was not at all sure who it was but that it wore a mitre and St John's statue did not. Decades later, when she was eighty-six years old Mary Beirne, now Mrs O'Connell, was re-interviewed. She had forgotten some details of the figure but she did remember him 'clothed in a cloak falling down in folds like a bishop's'.[104] One very early newspaper account of the apparition described the figure of St John wearing 'on his head a mitre which the people described as being like that worn by the Archbishop', which suggests that the identification of the figure as not just a bishop but the present archbishop was made by the public.[105] Another paper wrote that 'St John, having a mitre on his head . . . held his right hand raised, and in the act of blessing, the index and middle fingers being extended after the manner adopted by bishops'.[106] When Sexton interviewed some of the witnesses in January 1880 they similarly reported the figure: Patrick Hill referred to 'the figure of a bishop, which the people said was St John'.[107] Mary Beirne said the third figure, 'St John . . . He appeared wearing a mitre and a long robe'.[108] Hill told the correspondent for the *Daily Telegraph* that St John was 'dressed like a bishop'.[109]

We cannot now distinguish the various steps through which the St John the Evangelist identification was made. White suggests that the seers' failure to call the bishop St Patrick, whose statues did have a mitre, 'bears testimony to a strong association in the mind of at least one seer that this figure dressed as a bishop was named John'.[110] One possibility is that Mary (or Maggie) Beirne, having framed the episode at the gable as a supernatural event, found at some point that a living personage, such as John MacHale, was not acceptable as a participant in an apparition. This is but a specific example of how one's preconceptions structure perceptions. Both perception and memory are structured by people's social context and cultural heritage.[111] Another possibility has less to do with culture shaping perception than with social power shaping what people can say openly. Perhaps the seers were quite sure they saw a bishop but could not openly say so to the assembled priests because the Virgin's appearance would be read as criticism of MacHale. (I elaborate on this view in chapter 10.) A third possibility is that the St John identification was suggested not by anyone at the church gable that evening, but by the commission or more likely its chairman, Fr Cavanagh, before the commission ever officially deposed witnesses. Historian John White makes such a claim.[112] Besides using evidence in the published depositions as I have to argue that the earlier perception was of a bishop, White challenges the presented explanation of how the figure was identified as St John the Evangelist.

In the iconographic tradition St John was never represented as a bishop and statues of him did not have a mitre. Neither was he represented with a crozier, the other conventional way in the language of statuary to tell that the subject was a bishop. Even Mary Beirne admitted that the Lecanvey statue did not have a mitre while the bishop figure she saw did. Consequently, argues White, Mary Beirne could make a connection between the statue and a bishop only if somebody told her the statue was a bishop. That somebody, he suggests, was Fr Cavanagh. If the commission members seriously considered a Lecanvey statue to be the key to (either of) the Beirne sisters' identification of the figure, we would expect them to at least find out if such a statue even existed. Statues of St John were rare and if one so significant for the Knock story was in the Lecanvey church, White suggests, we would

expect to find some evidence of popular devotion at that site after the apparition, but we find none. The failure of the priests to document the existence of
a Lecanvey statue and the absence of popular devotion led White to doubt its
existence. No such statue has ever been documented in Lecanvey.

In addition White plausibly suggests that for most people in Knock the
word 'bishop' meant John MacHale. MacHale's extraordinary popular reputation was long established; he himself had been archbishop an incredible
forty-five years. MacHale would have been the only bishop almost all the witnesses had ever seen. White suggests that someone did use a statue as a
model in reframing the 'bishop' as 'St John', but not one at Lecanvey church.
Four years earlier in 1875 a larger-than-life statue of MacHale was unveiled in
Tuam during celebrations marking his golden jubilee as a bishop. People in
Knock would have been well aware of the ceremonies and have heard about
the new statue. White suggests that 'the identity of the figure dressed as a
bishop as "John" could have been securely fixed in the minds of several of
the seers' before they left the church gable the night of the apparition. It may
be [White continues more speculatively],

> that upon hearing of the vision and the identity of the three statues,
> Archdeacon Cavanagh, who believed that the Virgin and St Joseph might
> have been capable of appearing at Knock, recognized the impossibility
> of John MacHale hovering a foot or so above the grass in their company.
> Perhaps Cavanagh affixed the appellation 'saint' to the figure of the
> bishop, transferred the location of the statue from Tuam to Lecanvey,
> made handy by the recent return of at least one seer from that location,
> and the statue of John of Tuam was quickly and permanently trans-
> formed into St John the Evangelist.[113]

Clearly, 'the bishop' somehow became 'St John the Evangelist'. Who initiated the reframing and precisely what social-psychological and linguistic
steps were involved in the redefinition cannot definitively be established.
Enough evidence is available to question the conventional published
accounts. While a Lecanvey statue is an unlikely model for St John, I am not
convinced that the MacHale statue in Tuam was a model either. While it
explicitly represented MacHale and showed him with one arm raised either
in blessing or in preaching, like the claimed Lecanvey one, the Tuam statue
lacked both a mitre and a book which nearly all the apparition seers who
reported it said the bishop figure had in the apparition. Evidently there was
so much discussion or speculation (among the seers as well as others), about
who might have seen a statue and where that one witness apparently 'forgot'
or got confused about the story. Judith Campbell testified she had seen a St
John statue at Knock[114] but all the sources agree there was no such statue
and never had been. (Perhaps this is evidence of Campbell's inability to
identify which figures particular statues represented.)

Fr Michael Walsh, the Knock devotee who wrote a book about the evidence, defended the original published identification. Asserting that the

statue in Lecanvey had a book in the left hand and the fingers of the right hand were raised, he wrote that

> it was 'this coincidence of figure and pose' that made Mary Beirne surmise that the third figure was that of St John. That surmise seems reasonable, and the resemblance between the statue and the figure could be accepted as intended by God for revealing the identity of the third figure.[115]

This short passage has characteristic features of belief systems founded on faith and that are self-sustaining. First, Walsh, writing in the 1950s at the 'peak of Marianism' in Ireland,[116] gives no evidence or cites any source for a statue at Lecanvey, never mind for his assertion of what was in its hands. In other words, he assumes in advance what a careful investigation would establish, that Mary Beirne's reported testimony is credible on this point. Second, if the statue did exist it did not have a mitre, which every witness who reported the 'bishop' figure said he wore. Third, the appeal to what God might have intended, of course, makes sense only to those who accept the supernatural nature of the episode and could 'explain' anything that might have been reported.

The step of redefining the bishop figure as St John the Evangelist is implausibly ascribed to the witnesses, claims White,[117] because the locals would certainly be able to identify this saint. St John the Evangelist, one of the few persons at the foot of the Cross when Jesus died at Calvary, was conventionally included in depictions of the crucifixion. White points out that there was a small image of the Calvary scene directly over the altar in Knock church. In fact there were perhaps two representations of the scene above the altar. The illustration of the interior of the Knock church published in Sexton's book and in one New York edition of MacPhilpin, based on a photograph by T. O'Connor, shows one Holy Rood scene immediately above the centre of the altar and another similar scene much higher up in the gable but still directly over the altar.[118] Both representations, one a painting and the other a stained glass window,[119] were small in size but their number and placement would have made them conspicuous. Thus, had a figure appeared arrayed like the figure in this familiar scene, White argues, the seers would have directly identified St John the Evangelist. This line of argument is plausible but unproven and in the nature of the case can never be more than suggestive. In 'small' depictions of the Calvary scene, how distinct would one figure at the foot of the cross be? None is even visible in the Sexton illustration.

Even some early promoter seems to have come to recognise the implausibility of the offered explanation. In a manuscript draft restatement of Mary Beirne's testimony, dated 1 July 1880, the derivation of the St John identification is omitted. The draft is one of three reformulations of witness statements made that day. They appear to be in Cavanagh's hand, and are unpublished. Unlike three other manuscripts apparently of the 'original' 8 October 1879 depositions in the same archive document box, these are not signed by the witnesses. While the handwriting is generally hurried the writer doodled on one page. The reformulated versions are generally shorter than the published originals and include nothing at odds with them. The one notable change is the dropping of Mary Beirne's claimed explanation of how she used the Lecanvey statue to identify the bishop as St John.[120]

Several considerations, then, challenge the conventional presentation of the figure. The earliest depositions we have, even by those who accept the label of St John, including the few manuscript ones, identify a 'bishop'. Second, we have seen how someone, almost certainly Fr Cavanagh, recast Mary McLoughlin's testimony on this point. However, even some early promoter, perhaps Fr Cavanagh himself (my guess based on the handwriting), came to recognise the low credibility of the explanation and dropped it from a draft restatement of Mary Beirne's testimony. Third, the explanation offered of how the bishop was identified as John the Evangelist is implausible, both because the statue said to have inspired it could not have done so and, perhaps, because the seers would have been easily able to identify a representation of this saint.

Putting all the various alternative suggestions together we can identify likely steps in the framing of the ambiguous figure as follows: (i) Some seers at the gable perceive a bishop figure. (This is the version represented by Mary McLoughlin's deposition in manuscript and in MacPhilpin.) (ii) Because of the popular equation of 'bishop' and 'John MacHale' someone attaches the label John or St John to the figure. Alternatively, these steps could have been reversed, i.e. the seers perceive MacHale whom they call 'the bishop'. Given MacHale's place in the popular imagination, I find it implausible to suggest that he crossed the mind of none of the witnesses who reported the 'bishop'. (iii) Fr Cavanagh suggests that 'John' or 'St John' is 'St John the Evangelist'. One or other of the Beirne sisters agrees with and perhaps corroborates this, and is or becomes convinced. Because of their view of Fr Cavanagh as holy and as the very reason the Virgin Mary came to Knock, they would be open to his suggestion.[121] (iv) Other seers, especially those conversing with the Beirne sisters, consciously call the figure St John the Evangelist because of Mary's or Maggie's suggestion sometime between 21 August and 8 October. All this takes place before any official testimony is taken. (v) By 8 October, when depositions are taken, one or other of the Beirne sisters makes the identification and others say they call the figure the Evangelist even though they perceived it as a bishop. Even if not by these precise steps, the 'reality' of the St John the Evangelist figure was constructed by some such linguistic and social process.

As noted, in the recasting of McLoughlin's testimony, not only does the bishop become St John but the whole episode becomes a 'vision'. A similar reworking is evident elsewhere in the Sexton versions compared to MacPhilpin, and it is likely that a similar reframing process was already underway even before the MacPhilpin accounts were constructed. It appears that someone, very likely the commission or some of its priest members during their 'deliberation', formulated or reworked statements, making the apparition more real. The witnesses too in their ongoing conversations, most likely influenced by the input of Fr Cavanagh if not other priests and 'experts', could have come to 'realise' or make real for themselves a memory of a vision. (Patrick Hill was a likely candidate to play a key role in such definitional work. He lived in Claremorris close to Canon Bourke's house and probably attended the new schools in the town operated by the Sisters of Mercy, one of whose members was then, or soon thereafter, to make an illustration of the apparition scene. He told Sexton that the figures appeared as illustrated in Catholic pictures; doubtless he would have seen such pictures at school.) Where witnesses said they saw 'statues' or 'figures' or 'appearances', later versions or characterisations have them seeing 'visions' or even the personages the statues represented.[122] This was one rhetorical technique through which the reality of 'the apparition' was constituted. Ethnographic observation at more recent apparition sites provides evidence of many such linguistic devices.[123] An anthropologist who observed large crowds of pilgrims, expectant seekers and witness-groups during an extended episode of apparitions of the Virgin and other supernatural beings in the Italian town of Oliveto Citra, found that one key linguistic technique through which the facticity of apparitions was constituted for believers, was the transition in their conversation from claim to fact, from saying, for example, 'they say that the Virgin appeared' to 'the Virgin appeared'. Dropping the 'they say' qualification made perfect sense for believers.[124] For believers in the supernatural origin of the Knock visitors, it made similar sense to move linguistically along the line from recording witnesses seeing 'statues' to them having a 'vision' and finally seeing an 'apparition' and heavenly personages themselves.

How the various 'proofs' of a supernatural apparition tended to reinforce each other can be seen in one statement Mary Beirne made years later, about whether the 'figures' were heavenly visitors. William Coyne interviewed her for his 1935 book on Knock. She remembered Archbishop Murphy of Tasmania visiting Knock in thanksgiving for having been cured by use of cement from the apparition gable. Murphy told a group at the gable

> to pray with great confidence that it was not the 'statue' but Our Lady herself that had come there and that he himself was cured [of blindness] through her intercession.[125]

The reality of the apparition was sustained for this witness both by her certainty that mortar from the church gable had cured the Australian archbishop, and by her trust in him as a priest who said the Virgin herself had visited. These grounds for belief reinforced each other. The Knock evidence provides a textbook example of memory being informed by the conclusions that are later established. John Curry, in 1937, said he could not remember whether the lamb was on the altar on under St Joseph's arm,[126] but his 1879 testimony does not mention a lamb anywhere.

The process of reinterpretation of what is perceived, and hence remembered, in light of later 'conclusions' accounts, I submit, for the differences in the accounts of the seers' testimony given by MacPhilpin and Sexton. It explains how the bishop became St John the Evangelist.

What Was Added

Besides the redefinition of the bishop figure, 'the apparition' as publicised by its promoters incorporates a different type of transformation of testimony. There is circumstantial but suggestive evidence that the altar/lamb/cross component of the ensemble was added later than the three personages that all the seers reported, or the 'Three Visitors' as witness John Curry called them in 1937. It may appear implausible to suggest that something was added to an apparition scene; sceptics deny the possibility of the whole episode and see everything reported as 'added' in some way (such as by misperception, delusion or fraud) and believers have faith in the supernatural origin of the whole. Yet, I argue that not all elements in 'the apparition' are equally well evidenced. We do not and cannot now know what the early oral reports of the apparition were. This is one reason to carefully weigh the written reports. But the early media representations were in pictures as well as in words. Since the words were edited and accounts formulated to produce a coherent narrative (though as we have seen the gaps and seams still show) we cannot know precisely what was added, altered or deleted at what stage. It might be understandable that promoters would include details mentioned by some witnesses even if not by all of them. However, examination of some early published visual representations shows that promoters were quite willing to add details not found in the available published or unpublished testimony of *any* witness. An illustration attributed to a

Claremorris nun and published on the front page of the *Weekly News* on 7 February 1880, and then printed in Sexton's book,[127] clearly depicts the Sacred Heart on the front of the altar in the apparition scene, despite the fact that *no* seer reported this and that there are doubts about how many witnesses reported even seeing an altar. The same is true of a similar illustration in one New York edition of MacPhilpin's book.[128]

Apparition Scene

Emmet Larkin reproduced yet another picture of the apparition scene in his 1972 article.[129] On that print this text is printed:

THE APPARITION AT KNOCK Co MAYO
As seen on Augt 21st 1879 (EVE OF THE OCTAVE OF THE
ASSUMPTION
THIS VIEW WAS TAKEN ON THE SPOT BY W. COLLINS
AND SUBMITTED TO, AND APPROVED BY THE SEVERAL PERSONS WHO
SAW THE ABOVE

This print too shows the Sacred Heart that no witness mentioned on the front of the altar, but still claims to have been 'approved by the several persons who saw the above'. Does this include those witnesses who *denied* they saw any altar? Or the large number who make no mention of an altar? Clearly, promoters were willing to go beyond what witness testimony would support. Moreover, it is very likely that the various illustrators built upon each other's work. Perhaps all of them independently added what 'made sense' to them (and this image made sense because devotion to the Sacred Heart was being widely promoted at the time and thus there was a market for scenes depicting it); the alternative explanation that three illustrators independently made the same error is implausible. An additional detail introduced in one is reproduced in the others without reference to whether any witness reported it. Over time, the total scene depicted grows by accretion of ever more details, but such details as fit the scene into a picture 'expected' by the literate promoters and derived from the established orthodox expectations.[130]

Non-orthodox details reported by witnesses are dropped as in the case of the older Dominick Beirne's report of the tiers of saints he saw on the altar. Of course, that several early visual illustrators of the Knock apparition scene added details does not prove that the commission priests did the same. However, no doubt Fr Cavanagh and Canon Bourke knew what the Claremorris nun was including in her drawing of the scene. Moreover, these illustrations were published in the very same newspapers and books that the priests/promoters used to disseminate their apparition claims. The rhetorical strategies that constitute the 'fact' rather than the 'claim' of an apparition are obvious in prints such as these. What does the statement that 'this view was taken on the spot' mean on a print depicting an apparition? Does it suggest, none too subtly, that the heavenly visitors had a material existence as tangible as the church gable and as easily photographed?[131] In fact, the 'apparition scene' as 'taken on the spot by W. Collins' was taken directly from the nun's drawing with some onlookers added in the foreground.

I suggest that other details in 'the apparition' as reported are added. One witness, Pat Beirne, is said to have given the date of the episode as 'the evening before the Octave day' in the Dublin edition of MacPhilpin (p. 39) and on 'the eve of the octave of the Assumption' in one New York edition (p. 55).[132] While this way of identifying when the apparition occurred is not at all central to what believers see in it, it illustrates how the event was embedded within an orthodox ecclesiastical worldview. The Assumption of the Blessed Virgin was indeed celebrated (15 August was its feast day for the official church), but we have no evidence that lay people saw anything significant about the octave of that day and certainly not in the eve or vigil of the octave.[133] Vigils and octaves of feast days is clerical terminology used here to relate in time the 21 August episode to the Feast of the Assumption, and thereby suggest some connection between them. The terminology could have come from the witness as the printed deposition claims, but I suggest it would have done so only if suggested at some earlier point by someone of clerical mindset. Alternatively, this language could have been supplied by the commission members during their 'deliberation'. It is but a small non-central piece of evidence supportive of the claim that the depositions are clerically composed documents. I suggest later that a different calendar of the sacred was more significant for the local people, including the seers.

Promoters added details not reported by any witnesses, such as the Sacred Heart on the front of the altar. Other non-central details are likely altered. It is plausible to suggest that other elements were added, most likely through a process of clerical suggestion rather than dictation that the seers followed.

Because the evidence for the altar, cross and lamb is quite different in quality from that for the three figures of the Virgin, St Joseph and the bishop/St John, I believe this complex could well have been suggested later. In the nature of the case, evidence to definitively prove or disprove my suggestion is not now and is unlikely ever to become available. All those whose depositions are available reported the three figures and none of them ever hesitated later about them (despite the questioned identity of the bishop). In contrast, only some of the witnesses reported the altar/lamb/cross complex. One of two bishops in nearby dioceses who visited Knock even before the witness statements were taken (and who spoke with five witnesses, met with Fr Cavanagh and said mass in the church), mentioned the three personages but did not include the altar/lamb/cross in his description of the apparition in his diary.[134] The very first mention of the apparition to appear in print, a short note in *Ave Maria* of 6 December 1879, in which the editor says Fr Murphy SJ had written him about the apparition of the Virgin Mary, St Joseph and St John at Knock, does not mention any altar, lamb or cross. At least one witness explicitly denied seeing an altar. Some of those recorded as reporting the altar later denied they saw it, or could give no account of it, or omitted any mention of it from later depositions. Moreover, if I am right about the inspiration for the 'three figures' in the scene, which I present later, then the altar/cross/lamb complex would have followed a different trajectory from the original idea to its realisation in the depositions of some, but not all, witnesses and in 'the apparition' as constructed and publicised later.

The 'three visitors' were mentioned by all the witnesses at the gable except for John Curry who was only about six years old and could say little beyond that he saw the figures and the light. In contrast, more than half the witnesses did not mention the altar, lamb or cross. A few witnesses explicitly denied they saw some of these elements. Patrick Beirne, the younger Dominick Beirne, Mrs Hugh Flatley, Bridget Trench, as well as the children Catherine Murray and John Curry all failed to mention any of these elements. Both the older Dominick Beirne and his cousin Margaret Beirne (Maggie, the daughter) mentioned the altar but not a lamb or cross. (Maggie's statement that she did not see a lamb or cross is contained in MacPhilpin (p. 40) but crossed out in the recently found manuscript original. Presumably, whoever later erased the sentence was engaged in further constructing the apparition scene.) Margaret's mother, also Margaret (the widow) Beirne, mentioned the altar and the lamb but explicitly denied seeing a cross. Mary Beirne said 'I saw no cross'. The fact that seers denied seeing these elements shows that they were aware of suggestions of their presence.

Perhaps as significant as the many witnesses, whose depositions do not include these Eucharistic symbols, is that some of the witnesses, whose depositions did include them, seem to be far from being as certain as they were of the 'three visitors'. Mary McLoughlin allegedly said the newspaper was wrong when it claimed she saw a cross. This was reported by a journalist sceptical of the idea of supernatural apparitions and published on 2 March 1880 in the *Daily News*, which had introduced a series of articles with a confident assertion that the 'Lourdes delusion was exposed and refuted' (27 February). Such a source could be easily discredited and ignored. But that could hardly be done in the case of Mary Beirne. While her 8 October deposition in MacPhilpin does refer to an altar and lamb, what she said or did not say later is significant. A few months later, at the end of January, in her interview with Thomas Sexton she reportedly did mention an altar, cross and lamb, but only in passing. Her comment is but half a sentence in a long interview during which 'she was anxious to clear up every point that seemed to [the reporter] to suggest examination'.[135] When she spoke with T. O'Connor on the second or third of February 1880 she 'readily entered into a full account of the Apparition, when I informed her of the nature of my visit, and presented my credentials . . . [but] was able to give no information whatever about an altar',[136] even though she did make a short reference to the altar, cross and lamb like she had to Sexton.

O'Connor was an avid believer; he came to Knock with a letter of introduction to Fr Cavanagh and with an eye to promoting the developing cult there, and he spoke at length with Mary Beirne. Given the newspaper publicity given to the apparition since the start of 1880 we would certainly expect an important witness to remember what it was she saw or testified the previous October to seeing six weeks earlier. Evidently the three heavenly visitors were of more significance to her than were the Eucharistic symbols.

Much later in her life, various people sought Mary out in furtherance of their project of promoting the cause of the apparition. Now Mrs O'Connell, she gave evidence directly or indirectly on several occasions. In a careful statement she made in 1932 before four priests about what she saw that August evening in 1879 she says nothing about an altar, lamb or cross but is clear about the three figures.[137] In or before 1935 she spoke with William Coyne, who was then writing his book on Knock, but he does not mention an altar, cross or lamb in his account of what she said.[138] An energetic promoter of the apparition, it is unlikely that Coyne would have omitted such significant information if indeed he had gotten it directly from the person many considered the most important seer and one of the few still alive. One of the four priests to whom she gave her 1932 statement, then Knock parish priest Canon Greally, along with a Commissioner for Oaths had Mrs O'Connell make another statement in January 1936 and we are told that here she did mention the altar, lamb and cross.[139]

She was interviewed yet again, this time by the so-called Second Commission in August 1936 when she was confined to bed and expected to die shortly. (She did in fact die within a few weeks.) The commission recorded that she 'confirmed' her deposition of 1879. But this was read to her just before she was asked about it.[140] In that set of circumstances, it is fair to question whether her sickbed confirmation was independent of what her 1879 'deposition' included. Even after hearing what Sexton, p. 13, recorded her as having said nearly sixty years earlier, she still doubted one element of the scene, saying, 'I won't swear to what it said about the cross.'[141] The commission did not question her about her 1932 statement that did not mention any of the three elements or (apparently) about omitting these in her conversation with Coyne.[142] It did ask her about her earlier 1936 statement before the Commissioner for Oaths and Fr Greally, where she reportedly mentioned all three elements, but even here she was reluctant to verify what it claimed: 'I don't remember that I said anything about the . . . cross.'[143] It is notable that the commission asked her about her earlier statements that included the altar/cross/lamb complex but not those that did not. Evidently these elements, richly symbolic as they were of the orthodox mass-centred Catholic teaching, were more important to the priests on the Second Commission than they seemed to be for this witness.

Like Mary O'Connell, so also John Curry, the six-year-old boy who had little to say at the 1879 investigation, had his memory refreshed when he was re-examined in New York where he then lived in 1937. Asked if he had read witnesses' depositions on the apparition, he admitted, 'just before I came into this hearing I was given a book and the only part of it I read was the statements by Patrick Hill and Catherine Murray.'[144] Hill had given the most detailed account of all the witnesses, incorporating many features of orthodox iconography that he admitted he had seen in pictures. Understandably, given his age in 1879 and how he 'read all about the apparition in the old country when [he] was a boy going to school' and had his 'memory' so recently refreshed, Curry gave a much more elaborate description of the scene at the gable than he did in 1879. One does not have to be a sceptic to suspect that what Curry recounted more nearly reflects suggestions that he had accepted as his own rather than independently recalled memories. There is no reason to suspect he was lying; no doubt he believed what he said. But his words serve as evidence of his faith, not as evidence of what transpired at the church gable that August evening in 1879.

It may be objected that different individuals would normally give differing descriptions of an event they had witnessed such as an incident in a football game, for example, or a car crash.[145] Eyewitness reports of action-filled scenes and fast-moving developments do differ significantly, as social psychologists have shown. The apparition at Knock was very different in that by all claims the scene was stationary for hours. Judging from the available testimony, the figures were life-size but none of them moved or spoke and none of the elements in the total picture changed position. Moreover nearly all the witnesses are reported as having paid rapt attention to what was before their eyes, and many to have seen what they reported 'clearly' and 'distinctly.' Something else must account for the differences in the number of witness depositions reporting the 'three figures' and the altar/cross/lamb complex.

The Producers of the Picture

I made the point earlier that people in Knock at the time of the apparition, and especially the Beirne family, were experiencing crises of authority in many crucial aspects of life. The strains on hierarchical relationships were by no means confined to the original witnesses, or to the laity. Because of the essential role of the priests on the Commission of Inquiry in producing the picture of the apparition that has been transmitted over the years, it is necessary to inquire into their social situations, as well as the seers'. As soon as we do this, we recognise that for Frs Cavanagh and Bourke, two of the commission's members and indispensable sources for the two early published versions of the seers' evidence, the summer and autumn of 1879 was a period of intense conflict and confrontation over priestly authority, which could only serve to make these men re-evaluate their roles as priests. From below both had their authority as priests directly challenged by lay people and, looking upward, both also inevitably were forced to reconsider their relationship with the ecclesiastical authority of their bishop and civil political authorities. Not only were authority structures under attack but the seers were especially susceptible to the various threats, and the two priests themselves who formulated the seers' accounts into the versions publicised as 'the apparition' virtually embodied the intersecting challenges to lines of authority.

As we have seen, Fr Cavanagh's condemnation of the Land League agitation was met by a major demonstration by his parishioners. At the time of the apparition, Cavanagh had just completed a special programme of saying 100 masses for the intentions of the souls in Purgatory. His defenders say he was able to do this long-planned project because his parishioners, facing hard times, could not afford the usual offerings for masses to be said for their own intentions.[146] Others see it as evidence of his particular religious bent.[147] However, the timing is significant. Assuming no break in the saying of the 100 masses, Cavanagh would have started them about mid-May 1879, around the time of his altar attack on land agitation and its local organisers, but before the monster indignation meeting on the first of June. Why would Fr Cavanagh begin his 100 masses when he did, rather than earlier if the project was not his response to the land agitation? It probably was not his parishioners' ability but their willingness to contribute money for masses that was so suddenly impacted. After all, a voice in the crowd at the 1 June meeting had called for cutting off Fr Cavanagh's 'supplies.' It is possible that Fr Cavanagh clung even more closely to one model of the priesthood available to him, that of the priest as a man set apart, to offer sacrifice on behalf of his flock, to pray for them, to do penance and make amends for their evil doings; that he saw his calling as that of a good man separated from the evil world.[148]

Cavanagh's friendship with landlords and his harsh condemnation of the agitators, while they made him enemies among his parishioners, probably did little to win him friends among other clergy, especially since priests increasingly joined the movement after the summer of 1879.[149] Cavanagh was also subject to the strains common to all the priests during the struggle between Archbishop MacHale and Bishop MacEvilly which I describe below.

Canon Bourke, in the summer and autumn of 1879, was a man being pulled in many contradictory directions.[150] Some of the pressures were new while others had been building up for many years. First, the eclipse of Archbishop MacHale in ecclesiastical politics meant that his nephew's career in the church hierarchy was likely at an end. He had wanted to be a bishop but the influence of Cullenite clerics like Bishop MacEvilly had torpedoed his appointment to the diocese of Clonfert in the early 1870s.[151] A man of undoubted ability and learning who had published many books, in Irish and English, on varied topics religious and otherwise, who had been president of a diocesan seminary — such a man in normal circumstances could aspire to some position higher than Parish Priest of Claremorris.[152] Canon Bourke had to reconcile himself not only to lowered aspirations but to the prospect and then the reality of being subject to the new archbishop, his old nemesis, John MacEvilly. From being among those priests with the best access to their old bishop, Bourke was likely to be one of those on the worst terms with his unwelcome new one.

The land agitation and how to respond to it was another major source of conflicting pressures for Canon Bourke as it was for other priests. He cannot be classified simply as an early supporter of the Land League.[153] The clergy had been presented with a serious dilemma. When they took part in the agitation, they faced opposition to their authority from lay organisers. When they did not, they only strengthened lay control over the movement.[154] Since the clergy in most cases regarded the lay leaders as 'godless nobodies' (as Bishop MacEvilly put it),[155] cooperation with them was distasteful but still came to be seen as more palatable than the alternative: losing authority and standing by amid scenes of increasing disorder. For the first time, the clergy were faced with a mass protest movement that was not under their direction or control. The 'godless nobodies' were indeed showing they were somebodies, and denying they were godless. Even if they agreed with the goals of the land movement — and it was difficult to decide if they did, since the goals were constantly being redefined — most priests would have condemned the methods.

Canon Bourke had his own crops and fences damaged in retaliation for initially opposing the land movement.[156] White suggests that much of the popular resentment of Archbishop MacHale's denunciation of the agitation's leaders was deflected onto Bourke, his nephew and a safer target.[157] Nevertheless, Bourke was the first Mayo clergyman to propose a land meeting in his parish when he called for one in Claremorris. But his motives for doing so were publicly questioned in June and July by *Connaught Telegraph* editor, James Daly, who accused him of acting as the pawn of his uncle to undermine the new movement's independence.[158] The meeting he proposed did occur, but at it Bourke was further pilloried. As Jordan puts it, 'as if to purposely humiliate the embattled priest, Claremorris was full of Fenians from all over Connacht, who used the land meeting as a cover to convene a land meeting of their own.'[159] When Canon Bourke tried to get the meeting to consider resolutions on specifically Catholic matters, the other speakers adamantly refused. Though he was in the chair the meeting was not under his control.[160]

In Bourke's case, all the various cross pressures buffeting the priests generally were exacerbated both by his family ties to Archbishop MacHale, as we have seen, and by his gentry origin and kinship ties to local landlords.[161] Caught between landlords and tenants, between his uncle the Archbishop's condemnation of the land movement's lay leaders and the popular following they commanded, between his duties as a priest and the demands of his Catholic landlord cousins, by the summer and fall of 1879 Canon Bourke's situation contained all the elements of a combustible mixture that was to ignite later in one of the most dramatic episodes involving priests in all the Land War. When in 1881 his cousin Walter Bourke, a very unpopular local landlord, attempted to attend mass at Barnacarroll, he came carrying a gun. (Being Catholic did not protect landlords; in June 1882 Walter was shot dead in County Galway.) Fr Bourke's parishioners demanded that he require his cousin to leave the gun outside and when that did not seem likely to occur, they demanded that the landlord himself be put out. The Canon unsuccessfully tried to have Walter hear mass from the sacristy but refused to order him to leave, whereupon the congregation walked out, carrying Canon Bourke in his mass vestments along with them and leaving the landlord and his servants alone in the church. After Walter went home, the Canon was permitted to re-enter the church, and said mass.[162] Their actions say louder than any words that the lay people there valued the mass but were adamant in requiring the priest to serve the community rather than serve a landlord, even if he was a cousin and a Catholic. His parishioners defined the community to exclude the landlord, and defined the priest's role as serving the community thus defined. The people so valued the priest in his sacramental role that they forced him to join them on their terms. It was a recapitulation of what had happened on a bigger Mayo stage in 1879.

If Fr Cavanagh's initial response to the pressures of being criticised by the laity was to re-emphasise his priestly role, in Canon Bourke's case he came to support a moderated Land League.[163] Although he rarely attended meetings, he was a member of the fifty-four-man executive committee of the National Land League founded in October 1879. A few years later he published an open letter to the prime minister pleading the cause of evicted tenants.[164]

The Aghamore Meeting

Fr Cavanagh's authority was threatened even more strongly and immediately. Movement leaders directly confronted him by calling a demonstration meeting at Aghamore in his parish for Sunday, 26 October 1879. In announcing the meeting, they claimed the location was chosen to give people 'of the whole extent of the county [Mayo] bordering on Sligo and Roscommon' their first opportunity to demonstrate their support for the League, but there is little doubt that Cavanagh's earlier vehement opposition was in their minds. In fact, there already had been meetings in Claremorris and Ballyhaunis. If another meeting was desirable in the east of the county, other small towns such as Swinford or Charlestown would be more accessible than rural Aghamore but, of course, these were not in Fr Cavanagh's parish. In a thinly veiled allusion to his earlier attempt to silence the agitators, but without mentioning Fr Cavanagh's name, the *Connaught Telegraph* noted that 'there are even here amongst us men, who because of the positions they hold, cannot openly express their feelings on a public platform or otherwise, but let it suffice for such to know that we doubt not their heartfelt sympathy with us'. The paper put priests like Cavanagh on the defensive by writing that 'no conscientious man, of whatever type or profession he might be' nor 'any man of sentiment or pure moral feeling' could fail to condemn the injustice and absurdity of the existing land system and hence the legality and even necessity of agitating to change it.[165]

The Aghamore meeting was one in a series of demonstrations called to confront hostile clergymen or persuade hesitant ones to join their movement. At its start, the agitation had been opposed by most priests from Archbishop MacHale on down. Throughout the summer of 1879 most land demonstrations did not include priests. According to the movement leader, Michael Davitt, the organisers of the rallies believed they needed a showdown with the archbishop before a union with the priests was possible.[166] To show they would not be intimidated by clerical hostility, they organised a huge rally for Tuam, the diocesan seat where MacHale lived, for 21 September. This 'peaceful, mass invasion' of the town was planned deliberately without consulting MacHale, the priests or the town councillors. At the meeting, the leaders' speeches were comparatively mild, 'the speakers carefully avoiding mention of the primary reason for the meeting'.[167] The meeting was the message.

On the two following Sundays, rallies were held that one historian considered fetes to welcome the priests into the movement.[168] In Castlebar on 28 September, the parish priest spoke in favour of the movement from the altar at early mass; afterwards 10–15,000 people paraded past his house 'cheering lustily'.[169] But the clerical reaction was different the following Sunday. A demonstration rally scheduled for Ballinrobe was moved to a neighbouring parish to facilitate clerical involvement after the Ballinrobe priest remained hostile. At the new site, several priests did in fact speak in favour of the land movement.

With famine looming after the disastrous harvest and after the demonstrations in Tuam and elsewhere more priests joined the movement, but they usually tried to moderate dissent and direct it into peaceful channels. On the day before the Aghamore demonstration at a meeting in Killala, in north Mayo (the seat of Bishop Hugh Conway of Killala), Conway sent a letter praising the meeting's resolutions for 'properly omit[ting] all references to the irrative question of the relations between landlords and tenants',[170] but Davitt used the occasion to attack landlordism with 'unbridled vigour'.[171] The clergy were not to be allowed to set the agenda or the tone of the meetings.

It is unlikely that the organisers sought Fr Cavanagh's permission, but nevertheless he was in the chair at the Aghamore meeting.[172] Three other priests were on the platform but they were considerably outnumbered by lay leaders of the agitation, including Michael Davitt, James Daly, J. J. Louden, P. J. Gordon, J. W. Nally and several others, including John O'Kane, one named target of Fr Cavanagh's condemnation from the altar earlier that year. Things had changed dramatically since early summer.

Given the location of the meeting the presence of virtually all the key leaders of the movement indicates the importance they placed on confronting Fr Cavanagh. Presumably he was targeted as a stubborn and outspoken critic of the agitation. However, the leaders were likely less than fully satisfied with the turnout. The movement's mouthpiece, the *Connaught Telegraph*, prone to exaggerate the size of such demonstrations, reported vaguely that 'thousands' were present. Doubtless, the heavy rain all day kept some people from attending. We have no way of knowing how many of Fr Cavanagh's parishioners stayed away because of the weather, because in sympathy with him they opposed the agitation, or because they were satisfied with the recently announced 30 per cent reduction in rents on the Dillon estate. In any case, the rain could provide a convenient excuse for those reluctant to participate for other reasons. While the agitation's leaders had reason to be less than enthusiastic about the size of the crowd, they did in fact achieve a significant victory when they succeeded in forcing the reluctant or perhaps hostile Fr Cavanagh to assume the chair at the meeting.

Fr Cavanagh had more reason than the organisers to be unhappy with the demonstration. He spoke first and acted as chair but this does not indicate clerical control of the meeting. The other two priests who spoke, both canons, were interrupted by the crowd and criticised by lay speakers. Cavanagh's awkward position is reflected in the comments he made and the crowd's response. In opening the meeting, he 'trusted no person would

VERY REV. BARTHOLOMEW A. CAVANAGH, PARISH PRIEST OF
KNOCK, AND ARCHDEACON OF THE DIOCESE OF TUAM

make use of any insulting or offensive language calculated to wound the feelings of any section of the community', a pious hope at a demonstration organised by men committed to the destruction of landlordism. Cavanagh recognised that tenants could not pay their rents (due less than a week later on 1 November) because of three successive harvest failures, but the solution was for landlords to 'treat their tenants with kindness and consideration', and he pointed to the example of the landlord Viscount Dillon who had recently granted a 30 per cent rent reduction. This statement is evidence both of Cavanagh's belief in individual charity and of the gulf between his views and those that were becoming dominant in the land movement. He had no criticism of the tenure system itself. In contrast, later speakers at the meeting reiterated calls for peasant proprietorship: that the tenants, the tillers of the soil, should become owners of their farms. Finally, Fr Cavanagh urged petitions to the Lord Lieutenant seeking relief. When another priest later reiterated this call, a voice from the crowd shouted 'no begging or praying', drawing applause. In contrast to Fr Cavanagh's deferential attitude toward landlords, the crowd cheered a heckler who interrupted another priest with the comment, 'If we had a few good cannons, we would soon blow the landlords away.'[173]

It is notable also that the priests on the platform did not present a united front of an agreed and fixed position. In contrast to Fr Cavanagh, Canon Waldron, PP of Ballyhaunis, endorsed the idea of peasant proprietorship. However, he did so only reluctantly, under pressure from hecklers and interjected cross-examination by lay leaders on the platform, especially James Daly, and with reservations about its feasibility. Waldron had been on the platform at the early land meeting in Claremorris on 13 July;[174] Land League leaders probably felt he was more sympathetic to their movement than was Cavanagh. At a meeting at Gurteen, County Sligo, the following Sunday, Daly got involved in a loud and prolonged argument with another priest on the platform over that priest's attitude towards peasant proprietorship.[175] Whatever the reason, at the Aghamore meeting Cavanagh was not subjected to the type of cross-questioning and interruption Daly directed at Canon Waldron or the Gurteen priest the following week. Perhaps his parishioners in the crowd found it easier to heckle outside priests.

Given his evident distaste for the movement, Cavanagh's chairing a Land League meeting in his own parish indicates his probably-reluctant acceptance of a view that was becoming widespread among the clergy: that with or without the priests the land meetings would go ahead and that to maintain at least some influence with the people the priests had to attend meetings called without reference to their wishes.[176] At the meeting, Fr Cavanagh attempted to direct the agitation into moderating channels such as petitions to the Lord Lieutenant and to focus attention on an individual good landlord and away from the evil and injustice of the institution of landlordism. Despite his emphasis on individual charity rather than revolution, conspicuously absent from Fr Cavanagh's remarks was any hint of apology for his earlier denunciation of the agitation. The report on the meeting does not indicate that Cavanagh had anything to say to John O'Kane whom he had publicly vilified just a few months before. But surely neither the people nor Fr Cavanagh could fail to appreciate the altered circumstances. In effect, the priest had been manipulated or even intimidated by the growing massive demonstrations into accepting, however unwillingly, a movement that he had denounced from the altar and, in his own parish, he was a mere figurehead chair of a meeting whose platform was dominated by the leaders whose motives he had impugned.

Fr Cavanagh's relationship with the progressing land agitation and with those of his parishioners who might support it, can be usefully illuminated by contrasting the Aghamore meeting with another land meeting three weeks later. According to the *Connaught Telegraph,* 20,000 people attended that meeting at Kiltimagh. Even allowing for the paper's tendency to exaggerate crowd sizes, it is obvious that very many more people attended than at Aghamore. In addition, and in contrast to Aghamore, there were three brass bands, immense processions, and decorative arches bearing banners, one of which read 'The Priests and People Forever'. The only priest present was the local parish priest, a Land League supporter, who was 'laudably and repeatedly cheered' and who thanked the organisers for the honour of being asked to chair the meeting.[177] That the Kiltimagh parish priest supported the land demonstrations, that he was enthusiastically cheered and the crowd was several times bigger than at Aghamore were probably not mere coincidences. Bad weather, the Dillon rent abatement and/or Aghamore's relative inaccessibility could account in part for the relatively small Aghamore attendance, but surely Fr Cavanagh's opposition or reluctant acquiescence must also have been a factor in depressing turnout.

The Knock apparition had occurred two months before the Aghamore demonstration, and the one-day collection of the seers' testimony had been held in Knock church just eighteen days earlier. Locals including one important seer, Mary Beirne, were later reported as believing that Fr Cavanagh's holiness was the reason the Virgin had come to Knock.[178] Assuming she held that view shortly after the apparition (her recorded testimony is silent on the point), it is likely that others also came to that conclusion. Thus Cavanagh's reputation for inspiring the heavenly visitation could be a factor in explaining why some of his parishioners would be loath to publicly oppose him at the Aghamore meeting. On the other hand the Virgin's appearance could be interpreted, as it traditionally was, as a reproach to priests who failed to properly fulfil their priestly role. We have no way of knowing how widely these views were shared; very likely they coexisted uneasily with Cavanagh's reputation as an opponent of the land movement. In all probability, his parishioners were divided into pro- and anti-Cavanagh factions, both before and after the apparition. His appearance on the Land League platform at Aghamore can be read as an attempt on his part not to lose all influence over some of his flock.

But that did not lead to the conclusion that his parishioners would listen to his condemnations. What Cavanagh would see as proper authority[179] was very visibly undermined a few weeks later, with the active involvement of large numbers of his flock. In the last months of 1879 the land agitation's leaders were encouraging tenants to resist paying their rents while some landlords were resorting to evictions. Scenes of massive opposition to evictions were to become the latest battleground in the Land War. At Balla, on 22 November, an attempted eviction of a small farmer named Anthony Dempsey became the site of a 'military style confrontation' between some 8,000 demonstrators and 100 armed police. The police, placed at a tactical disadvantage by an encircling movement, withdrew, leaving the demonstrators in possession of the hill on which Dempsey's cottage stood.[180] The resident magistrate described the assembled crowd, most of them armed with sticks, as 'much more determined and earnest than on any former occasion, and much more under the control of the persons directing their movements'.[181] While one politician present recalled that Charles Stewart Parnell marshalled the crowd, the local magistrates realised that the demonstrators were directed by local Fenians under P. W. Nally, rather than Parnell. Local landowning interests recognised the threat such meetings posed to established order and quickly petitioned the government to stop them.[182] Those resisting the eviction had been organised in semi-military style with each parish contingent given an assignment for the battle. Fr Cavanagh's parishioners had central roles. 'The Aghamore contingent surrounded the [Dempsey] house while the Knock men occupied the only available cover' for the police. The Crown forces were left surrounded by overwhelming numbers and 'humiliatingly dependent on the demonstration's leaders for permission to withdraw'.[183]

The Aghamore meeting provides significant evidence of Fr Cavanagh's attitudes and orientation. We have already noted his emphasis on individual landlord kindness and consideration and his failure to criticise the tenure system. Despite the presence of most of the leaders of the land agitation and before a crowd that heckled and interrupted other priests, in his speech Fr Cavanagh did not back down or change his position. Opponents might call this stubborn self-righteousness while supporters could read it as evidence of principled courage. However we characterise him, it is clear that Cavanagh was a man of strong convictions who was willing to state them forcefully even when a negative response was predictable. Challenges to his authority were likely to elicit strong responses.

The three priests on the platform at Aghamore were the same men who reportedly comprised the ecclesiastical commission that took testimony from the Knock apparition seers: Fr Cavanagh, who chaired the commission, and Canons Burke and Waldron. Two separate versions of the seers' testimony were to be published early in 1880. What seems clear is that the one-day investigation on 8 October 1879 did not result in one definitive, final and agreed version of the seers' accounts, and that the process of describing and characterising the event continued as one or more commission members rewrote or reformulated the seers' testimony, thereby taking further steps in the process of socially constructing the reality of the apparition as it was to be popularised. The Aghamore meeting in late October and the Dempsey eviction confrontation in November give us vivid evidence of the pressures to which these three priests and especially Fr Cavanagh were subjected between the taking of depositions and the publication of the testimony. It is little to be wondered at that they would be alert and responsive to any hint of a supernatural endorsement of their unique priestly authority, such as the appearance of Eucharistic and Christocentric symbols like the altar, lamb and cross in the apparition.

The Magic Lantern Thesis

A century after the apparition, philosophy professor David Berman presented most cogently a 'naturalist' thesis that had long been hinted at or suspected, that the whole thing was caused by the witnesses seeing images of statues projected on the gable by a magic lantern, a known technology at the time. He sees many features of the publicised apparition as most plausibly explained in this fashion. The figures were life-size but did not move or speak, they were enveloped in light that grew brighter as darkness descended, they looked like statues but seemed to recede into nothingness when anyone tried to touch them, and they hovered a foot or so above the grass at the outside gable of the chapel. In another article, after learning about the protest meeting against Fr Cavanagh earlier in 1879, Berman suggested the priest had a motive to engage in deliberate deception and likely colluded with somebody unknown to actually project the images on the gable. This dovetailed with another hoary suggestion, that a Knock policeman had projected the images thereby deliberately or inadvertently presenting what the seers reported as a visit of heavenly beings.[184]

Early popularisers were obviously aware of this allegation and took steps to refute or discredit it in advance. They emphasised that no 'perch' was available from which somebody could project the pictures. Onlookers would have immediately noticed rays of projected light and seen their own shadows if the light was from behind them, and that was the only possible way for such a projection. MacPhilpin added that the scene was observed both in daylight and after the sun had gone down. Moreover, 'no lens and no electric light known to scientists at the present day can cast fully defined likenesses the size of a man on four hundred square feet of surface for some hours in the light of day and the darkness of night'. Finally, the photographer from Limerick donned the mantle of expert to refute the charge. 'Being, as I am, a practical operator in the art of projecting images by means of lime-light and other brilliant and artificial lights; having frequently exhibited such in public halls, I unhesitatingly assert that the conditions necessary to produce images such as have been seen are entirely absent'.[185]

We might find committed promoters less than convincing on this point. But the sceptical Maynooth professor and scientist, Fr Francis Lennon, who was very open to natural explanations, some short time after the apparition carried out experiments to test its feasibility and was able to his own satisfaction rule out a magic lantern as a proximate cause of what the witnesses reported at the gable.[186]

These early promoters' failure to completely discredit or to disprove the theory to Berman's satisfaction, and even Fr Lennon's experiments, can not be taken as evidence that the magic lantern claim is either correct or incorrect.[187] While the theory is superficially plausible, it suffers some serious flaws. Berman admits, and properly so for a natural scientist, that for him any 'supernatural' explanation is a non-starter, and hence even an unlikely series of natural events is quite sensibly preferred as an explanation over an impossibility. But what needs to be kept separate is the adequacy of explanation for insiders (whether believers or sceptics) and for outsiders (whether rational natural scientists, journalists or others concerned only with what 'actually happened'), be they atheists, agnostics, or believers. Berman's logic is that an event must have a cause that is natural even if the people involved give a supernatural explanation. But this is a false dichotomy: the people involved, merely by talking and behaving as if their explanation is correct, may constitute the reality that requires explanation. Some language is 'performative' and not merely descriptive reporting.[188] For example, when a judge in some modern criminal court formally pronounces a defendant 'guilty' she is not merely reporting the fact but creating or constituting it. From that moment the tried person is treated as 'guilty' in the eyes of the law, regardless of whether he or she feels any psychological guilt at all or has even been framed for the crime charged. In the usual case, the 'guilty' criminal is punished in legally prescribed ways. The taken-for-granted nature of most routine interaction in the workings of social institutions is highlighted, however, when the different parties to interaction struggle to impose their definitions of what happens. Were or are the people locked up in Long Kesh or Guantanamo 'criminals', 'freedom fighters', 'illegal detainees', 'enemy combatants', 'threats to national security', or some other category? Were they 'guilty'? We need to recognise stories about appearances of the Virgin as performative rather than, or as well as (for some) descriptive reports. In much of social life it is simply impossible for either insiders or onlookers to neatly separate performative language from descriptive report. I can report that I am writing this on Thursday, 6 December, 2006, but that report is meaningful only because I am part of a larger community that constitutes this calendrical reality by acting as if it were true, as if 'Thursday' and '2006' exist in nature rather than by collective agreement. Thursday, 6 December 2006 is literally non-sense to people with other calendars. I could signal my recognition of the socially constructed nature of this date by writing 'they say/claim/accept this is 6 December 2006' every time I mention the date and then proceed to specify who 'they' are, followed by an explanation of the Arabic numbering system and why the name of the twelfth month derives from the Latin word for ten. But this attempt at precision would raise more questions and actually result in the opposite, in pedantry. Disputes about the 'reality' of apparitions are disputes about how much they are reports and how much performances; if we insist these are mutually exclusive categories we will fail to comprehend the meaning of such episodes for those involved and consequently fail to explain the beliefs and behaviour of millions if not billions of people in the world. Behavioural scientists can do better.[189]

Besides Berman's condescension toward the deluded peasants, there are two more mundane objections to his thesis. First, there was no 'perch' from which a light could be shone on the gable without attracting the notice of bystanders. Berman attempts to deal with this objection by noting the schoolhouse in the church grounds from which he suggests light could have been cast obliquely on the gable. However, if light was so projected the beam and whatever opening or structure it emanated from would have been just as visible as if projected from directly in front, even if it did not cast the onlookers' shadows on the wall. Early reporters/promoters wrote moreover that there was no available place in the school building, such as a window opening in the direction of the church gable, from which a projection could have been made.[190] Later various suggestions were made that the projection was made by a policeman, perhaps without the knowledge of other policemen. But the police barracks was about 400 yards away so the problem of the availability of a site for projecting the light remains.

Another difficulty in the magic lantern theory is that the reported apparition included such an incongruous grouping of figures/statues and symbols that the possibility of a slide showing just such a set is remote. Additionally, a magic lantern theory cannot account for the different kinds of testimony provided for the various elements in the scene, especially the 'three visitors' and the altar/cross/lamb sets of figures. Of course, whatever the initial stimulus for a perception of heavenly visitors, subsequent discussion and negotiation over the 'reality' of the claims could result in various elaborations. If Fr Cavanagh conspired with others to concoct the appearance of the figures we would certainly not expect a Virgin appearance that could be read as anti-clerical even if others saw it as supportive. If the embattled priest would have liked an explicit endorsement from the Virgin, having her say some words such as 'this is my beloved priest' was impossible if the means available were just pictures of statues, but surely a less ambiguous endorsement could be conveyed visually.

10

Our Lady and the Clergy

Many devotional writers place the Knock apparition in its social setting. However, the context they use is one they themselves construct or assume, such as an asserted centuries-long national faithfulness to the true religion of Catholicism, or of recent local evictions (for which no evidence is provided), and not the context that was meaningful to the local participants in Knock in August 1879. It is *that* context I delineated in chapter 8; chapter 9 examined how 'the apparition' was socially constructed; and in this chapter I show how the context and the process of social construction were linked to each other. I follow the approach I used earlier to explain the devotional revolution. My basic assumption is that all people have a variety of understandings and beliefs available in their culture, and the ones they take most seriously and follow most closely are those that are made most real for them in their everyday experiences in their social situations. People pick and choose among the options available to them, and the ones they select are those validated by their own experiences and their interactions with others. Thus, farm families under the stem system needed to ensure family unity while subordinating every individual member's desires to the ability of the family land to support over the long term those dependent on it. Therefore, they stressed the authority of the male head, the evils of sex except in marriage, and the importance of family unity.[1]

To use the same framework in developing an explanation of the Knock apparition I explored the cultural understandings available to the people who beheld the apparition, and I concentrated on those experiences that would make some of their understandings more salient. To understand the social situations through insiders' eyes, I followed anthropologist Clifford Geertz's call for what he terms 'thick description' that enables an outsider to interpret the meaning of action. Accepting Max Weber's formulation that humans are suspended in webs of meaning they themselves have spun, Geertz drew relevant lessons for social scientists seeking to explain unfamiliar cultures. Such research is not like an experimental laboratory science, where other researchers can double-check any claims, but neither is it based on the arbitrary claims of individual scholars. Rather, research must begin with thick description of actions from the perspectives of insiders and proceed to interpretation. 'Cultural analysis is (or should be) guessing at meanings, assessing the guesses, and drawing explanatory conclusions from the better guesses.' While following that strategy, I became acutely aware of what Geertz pointed out, that

> cultural analysis is intrinsically incomplete. And, worse than that, the more deeply it goes the less complete it is. It is a strange science whose most telling assertions are its most tremulously based, in which to get somewhere with the matter at hand is to intensify the suspicion, both your own and that of others, that you are not quite getting it right.

By necessity, any ethnographic assertion is 'essentially contestable'. Nevertheless, again as Geertz put it, 'it is not necessary to know everything in order to understand something'.[2]

Another theorist whose insights I drew on is James C. Scott. While studying the politics of a village in Malaya, Scott noticed that individuals he spoke with said different or contradictory things at different times. He came to realise that the key was, who else was hearing what they were saying. Scott's informants were not just answering his questions but often simultaneously feeding disinformation to others in the village. Scott recognised this as one tactic used by the local underdogs to resist being dominated by more powerful people in their world. He went on to study the weapons of the weak more generally and identified as part of subordinate group life everywhere a

> politics of disguise and anonymity that takes place in public view but is designed to have a double meaning or to shield the identity of the actors.[3]

One crucial attribute of accounts given by underdogs in the presence of power is their deniability. Frequently, stories are deliberately told to be amenable to more than one interpretation. For a simple example, Br'er Rabbit stories told by American blacks could be presented as mere animal tales to whites, but understood by other blacks as celebrations of how the weak use their wiles continually to get the better of more powerful adversaries. Geertz realised that cultural analysis carried the danger of losing touch with 'the hard surfaces of life, with the political, economic, and stratification realities within which men everywhere are contained'.[4] In effect, Scott forces us to recognise that thick description requires us to understand things not just through insiders' eyes but from the perspectives of multiple insiders situated differently in structures of power, inequality, domination and resistance.

From the beginning of newspaper coverage Knock was publicised as an 'Irish Lourdes' or 'A Mayo Lourdes'. This is evidence of how widely Lourdes was known and how it framed the telling of the Knock story by its promoters.[5] Our Lady of Lourdes was one of the most common motifs in the procession in Dublin marking the centenary of O'Connell's birth in 1875, and newspapers in the later 1870s often mentioned the French shrine, reflecting and creating public interest in it.[6] For example, *The Nation* of 6 September 1879 reprinted a report on 'A Pilgrimage to Lourdes' from the *Standard*. The first Irish group pilgrimage officially recorded in Lourdes was in 1876,[7] and Irish couples were among those married there early in 1877,[8] but Lourdes was known even earlier. Lourdes medals were being advertised in the *Irish Catholic Directory* within a few years of the visions of 1858,[9] and knowledge of the French apparition was widespread in convents since the early 1860s.[10] The so-called (French) National Pilgrimage to Lourdes was the subject of a long report in *The Nation* of 8 July 1876. The *Irish Ecclesiastical Record,* directed toward a clerical readership, had already in May 1870 published a very positive review of what it called the first English-language book promoting the cause of the miracle at Lourdes.[11]

In Mayo and in the immediate local Knock area, the Lourdes story was also being spread before the 1879 apparition. A Mr Bull donated a 'handsome statue of Our Lady of Lourdes' as a prize in a fundraising raffle for Claremorris convent.[12] The *Connaught Telegraph* reported on 15 July 1876 that the bishop of the adjacent diocese of Clonfert had given a banner to Lourdes, the 'first votive offering from Ireland'. A few months later the same paper reprinted a *Freeman's Journal* report on an Irish group's visit to Lourdes, including an eyewitness account of a 150,000-strong pilgrimage.[13] More immediately, there was a statue of Our Lady of Lourdes in Knock chapel prior to the apparition.[14] The statue had been acquired after October 1878, a gift from one of Fr Cavanagh's clerical friends, Fr James Anderson, the Prior of the Augustinians in Ballyhaunis.[15]

Even if Lourdes was 'in the air', as it was, we still need to understand the 'receptor cells', as William Christian put it. The local receptors, however, were attuned to many messages other than the Lourdes one. In fact, Lourdes is very far from being the key to what transpired at Knock. Labelling it an Irish Lourdes is not adequate as an explanation of the time, place, or content of the Knock apparition. If Lourdes was a direct stimulus for apparitions in Ireland we might have expected a response earlier, perhaps during the waves of public enthusiastic support for Catholic France in its war with Protestant Prussia in the early 1870s,[16] or on other occasions such as parish missions, or to other kinds of seers such as Children of Mary, both factors having been suggested as preparing the ground for Knock.[17] Besides being two decades later, there were crucial differences between Knock and Lourdes. The French apparition was to one seer only, though she was observed by hundreds and ultimately thousands having many visions over several months. There were over a dozen seers of the first apparition in Knock and they had no ecstasy or other altered states of consciousness as Bernadette Soubirous had at Lourdes. Very importantly also, in Knock, unlike Lourdes the seers reported other personages and elements besides the Virgin.

If we ascribe Knock to the example or influence of Lourdes we face another difficulty. As perhaps Knock's greatest twentieth-century promoter very logically pointed out, 'it would be a most curious thing' if, of all the people in Ireland, only those in Knock were so influenced by descriptions of Lourdes and other apparitions 'as to think they, too, saw visions'.[18] The Lourdes apparition would have suggested the possibility of heavenly visitors, but that possibility was already recognised in the traditional culture. Lourdes was well known to early writers about Knock, such as Sexton and especially MacPhilpin, and to at least some early pilgrims; travelling by train for his second visit in early February 1880, Sexton met a pilgrim going to Knock who had already visited Lourdes.[19] But the fact that promoters and some pilgrims knew about Lourdes doesn't prove that the local seers also did — although at least some of them almost certainly had heard about it — or that if they did, that this explains the apparition. It does not. We need to explain why the apparition occurred in Knock rather than elsewhere, why in August 1879, to whom it appeared, and why it included what it did. Moreover, if the Knock apparition was triggered by an incoming wave of modern Marianism, we need to account for the failure of Knock to develop a continuing cult. The modern shrine and pilgrimage date from a revival half a century later.

While Lourdes and other manifestations of 'modern' Marianism from outside did have some influence which I describe later, I argue that the Knock apparition the seers experienced was rooted in the traditional local religiosity of the time and place. It was a Knock solution to a Knock problem. The problem was a crisis in authority structures, especially of the clergy's authority but exacerbated by all those other challenges to authority systems that I described in chapter 8. In forging their response, the local people used the resources of the local religious culture, drawing on the beliefs and understandings available to them that had been validated by their own experiences of shaken authority. That it was locally rooted is clear from several aspects of the whole episode. First, the apparition includes many central features that we can document in the pre-existing local religious culture. Second, after the apparition, the local responses were informed by the traditional religious beliefs and understandings. Thirdly, the telling of the story incorporated several rhetorical techniques characteristic of the orally informed popular faith that was still vibrant in Knock in the summer of 1879. The Lourdes precedent had much more influence on the promoters than on the seers. 'The Knock apparition' as publicised in the mass media, shorn of its immediate local context of confrontations over clerical behaviour and authority, consisted of the original as moulded by the requirements and mental furniture of the investigating priests and popularising journalists who worked hand in hand with these same priests, especially Fr Cavanagh.

Frs Cavanagh and Bourke and their associated journalist/promoters portrayed Knock as an Irish Lourdes, as if the Virgin had finally visited Ireland as she had come to France, Germany and Poland in recent years. A 'Hymn to Our Lady of Knock' composed by the Sisters of Mercy in Claremorris, explicitly claimed this was the first time the Virgin came to Ireland.[20] Margaret Anna Cusack (the Nun of Kenmare), a few years later in Knock similarly wrote that Mary had not come earlier, but her claim was part of Cusack's attempt to claim credit for having coaxed the Virgin to visit Ireland, part of her 'religious megalomania'.[21] To the best of my knowledge nobody writing in the aftermath of the August event at Knock ever referred to appearances of the Virgin in Ireland before that time. Nobody, for example, recalled the Virgin's appearance on the altar of the church in Charleville, County Cork, where she was reported to have given ashes, which began the 'blessed straws' distribution throughout the country in 1832. Neither did anybody write about other kinds of Virgin appearances. As we saw in chapter 7, various types of visions were experienced and reported in Knock and nearby areas long before the famous apparition. In this there is no reason to suspect that the area was anything other than typical.[22] Visions specifically of the Virgin were also found. Of course these were a subset of all visions and so were rarer. But in the traditional religious culture, stories about the Blessed Virgin appearing in the here and now world were especially important because they were statements about the proper behaviour of priests. The stories often underlined the awesome importance of the role of the priest and criticised individual priests for failing to carry out their responsibility properly. Others implied that priests were not indispensable.

Some examples will show how, taken collectively, stories of the Virgin's appearance in different circumstances were commentaries on the proper role and behaviour of priests. One story, from nineteenth-century Mayo, told of a man being very seriously injured in an explosion during road building; his companions know he cannot live long but the nearest priest is fourteen miles away:

> 'Don't be uneasy,' said the poor, wounded man, 'I shall not die until I am anointed, for the Blessed Virgin Mary is standing here at my right hand. I see her with my eyes. Go for the young priest in Tully who has the mare.'[23]

Even with the Virgin at his side here, the man wants to receive the last rites administered by a priest. One of the other men speeds across bog and mountain to notify him, and the priest pushes his horse to the verge of collapse in riding furiously to be on time. What stronger statement can we imagine of the priest's being indispensable in his sacramental role? This tacit understanding underpins the actions of everyone mentioned, the injured man, the other workers and the priest. Sure enough, the priest arrives to anoint the man just before he breathes his last. That this faith was held in the present and not just in some remote past is clear from the setting of the incident in the very modern enterprise of road-building using dynamite.

But the Virgin could also visit the dying to reproach priests. Indeed such stories were much more common than the priest-affirming type, understandably so since if they were doing their duty properly priests did not need the Virgin's involvement. (Except for another heavenly intervention in Mayo after the famous apparition of 1879, the pro-priest one above is the only one I know that is simply and unambiguously affirmative of the priest's behaviour as well as of his prescribed role.) One such story tells of some priest being slow to visit a dying person who had led a wayward life. Often a dying man is identified as a poet, the traditional vehicle through which criticisms were made of the clergy.[24] When belatedly the priest does go he finds that the Virgin has already come to the man's deathbed. Again, while this story criticises some particular priest it similarly underlines the importance of priestly ministering to the dying. A priest who omits or delays such duty commits so great a sin that the dying person merits a special visit from the Mother of God. Such stories are the antithesis of anti-clerical; rather they remind not just lay people but priests themselves of their awful responsibility in preparing the dying for eternity. At the same time, these stories suggest that even when a priest fails to act properly the people can rely on heavenly intervention.

Folklore scholar, Anne O'Connor, has examined the abundant Irish material about the deaths of children, especially the cases of unbaptised children and/or infanticide. One widely recorded set of stories is very useful for elucidating how people understood the relationship between the Virgin's appearances and the behaviour of priests. A representative story tells of a woman who had eleven illegitimate children. When she becomes pregnant with a twelfth, the Parish Priest condemns her from the altar and orders everyone to have nothing to do with her. Still shunned when the time comes for her baby to be born, the woman retires to an isolated hut on a lonely mountain. There at night her moaning in labour attracts the attention of a passing boy who, however, cannot see her. Not knowing her identity, the boy asks what she needs and she calls on him to fetch the priest. The boy promises to try but says that the darkness will make it difficult to find the way. On his journey, the boy finds his steps lit by eleven fluttering lights that move in front of him and lead him to the priest's house. There, however, the priest realises whom it is who seeks his services and refuses to go. Overhearing the Parish Priest's adamant refusal, the curate determines to attend the woman and leaves with the boy despite the Parish Priest's threat to lock the door against him on his return. The curate finds the way lit by the eleven lights and also a twelfth one that is small and flickers on and off. On asking, he learns this is the soul of the woman's newborn child. It is weak because it requires baptism, which the curate administers. In some versions of the story, the Blessed Virgin appears and serves as sponsor of the child, whose light now flutters as strongly as all the others. When the curate returns home, the door is opened to him despite the Parish Priest having bolted it shut, and the older priest thereby realises his sin. The appearance of the Virgin simultaneously endorses the curate's proper priestly ministry even toward a repeated sinner, and discredits the older priest's dictation of right behaviour and his altar denunciation of the woman. Spiritual intimidation especially by withholding of the sacraments was unacceptable to the Virgin.[25] Of course, stories like this as well as the ones about ministering to the dying underlined the importance of the orthodox sacraments of baptism and extreme unction.

Appearances by the Virgin in explicit or implicit criticism usually of some individual priest and his particular failure as understood by the people have been documented in other contexts also. There are for example a large number of stories about conflicts between the priest and the 'healer', often a wise woman or a fairy healer. In some of these too the Virgin visits to reproach priests who go too far in their opposition to the work of the healer, an opposition often shown to be based on ignorance of the healer's true behaviour.[26] Unlike the cases where the Virgin appears because the priest failed to do his proper duty, it is noteworthy that these stories criticise those priests who 'go too far' in opposing fairy-healers. As a body of stories, Virgin appearances not only commented on the priest's dutifully carrying out the responsibilities of his calling but also described limits priests should properly observe, thereby defining what those responsibilities were. The repertoire of stories was one of the checks and balances in the system of relationships between clergy and laity described earlier. By means of stories such as these, the priest's proper role was defined by the people at the bottom as well as by the official hierarchy all the way to Rome and the Council of Trent.

Typical of folklore, different versions of stories of the Virgin's appearances were found that resolved the contradictions and assigned blame for wrongdoing differently. Rather than being found in one fixed, established and immutable form, alternative versions were available or could readily be improvised to be deployed as suited various parties in any particular situation or dispute.[27] Stories about the death of a poet called Cathal Buí Mac Giolla Gunna, a notorious drunkard and womaniser, span the spectrum. Some say the Virgin visited him when the priest was loath to do so. Other versions say that when the priest came, when first called, a very modest woman was quietly caring for the dying man. On enquiring later, the priest found that local women refused to attend Cathal because of his bad reputation and so the priest — or at least the people — concluded that the demure woman was the Virgin herself come to succour the poor sinner in his desolation.[28] Virgin appearance was a language for talking about clerical roles and responsibilities. What particular individuals could or did say with that language, of course, varied from case to case; heavenly visitors could endorse or more often criticise the priests or specific priests' behaviour.

There were also stories of the Virgin appearing that had no explicit reference to the clergy at all. For one example, Tim Robinson recently described a holy well, Tobar Mhuire (Mary's well), at Roisín na Mainiach on the coast of Connemara:

> The legend of its origin is still [in the 1980s] remembered locally. A woman whose family was sick with fever saw a beautiful woman there, whom it is supposed was the Virgin Mary. A well of milk appeared on the spot, which nourished the family until they recovered, whereupon it became a well of freshwater.

A plaque under a statue of the Virgin there says it was erected in 1944.[29] At another Tobar Mhuire, Robinson heard a story from a local woman:

> Her mother had visited the well once when a child in the house was ill. But 'the worm that lives in the well' was dead, and when she came home she found that the child had died. Nevertheless, it was obviously felt as a consolation and an honour that the family had been granted this sign.[30]

Apparition stories like these are testament to the people's faith in a direct, clerically-unmediated access to the sacred.

The apparition at Knock on 21 August 1879 was a message about the proper behaviour of clergymen. I make this claim in light of the cultural meaning of Virgin appearances and because the apparition included a figure clearly identified as a bishop along with the Virgin. Given the evidence presented earlier of the unusually low famine mortality and the related cultural conservatism in Knock, as well as the recognition locally of various other kinds of visions, we can be confident that the Virgin appearance as commentary on the clergy idiom was indeed understood.[31] Moreover, at least one seer used that idiom, though not in her published depositions of evidence given to the commission of investigation, and the idiom was understood in Knock in the second half of the twentieth century.

As a statement of the rightful submission of the clergy to the Mother of God, it is highly significant that the Knock Virgin appeared as a figure of authority. Not only was she at the centre of the scene but also she wore a brilliant crown and the other figures were bowing or deferring to her. She was also more central than the altar, cross and lamb set of symbols. She did not come as a Madonna or as subservient to males; she was not like the pre-pubescent girl that Bernadette Soubirous saw at Lourdes. Our Lady of Knock was not the submissive woman whose image was to dominate in Irish Marianism in the following century and which was particularly compatible with the sexually-restrictive, authoritarian patriarchal family structure that dominated rural Ireland.[32] And she wore no blue, unlike many of her appearances in France where this was the colour of the monarchy.

The Knock apparition was a communication about proper clerical behaviour,[33] but what was the message? At a very general level (which virtually all could endorse), it was that the clergy rightfully were subordinate to the higher authority of the Virgin. This implies that Mary was on the side of the people regardless of what priests might or might not do, in effect weakening clerical power generally by setting limits to its exercise. Beyond that, I suggest that the symbolism of the apparition was polyvalent. This is another way of saying that the message was ambiguous on many levels and for many reasons. First, for reasons that James Scott elucidated, in the nature of the case, statements about authority made by the weak in the presence of the strong, such as by the Knock seers before the panel of priests, are inherently ambiguous.[34] They are often designed to be read in different ways. An instructive example is available in the report of the Aghamore land demonstration in the very same month, October 1879, when the witness depositions were taken. According to a newspaper report of the meeting, someone in the crowd shouted, 'If we had a few good cannons, we'd soon blow the landlords away', drawing applause from the audience.[35] Was the shouter calling for violence toward the landlords? Or was he calling on the priests to act properly, to be 'good canons', a very plausible reading given that two of the three priests present were indeed canons whose speeches were not being received well by the crowd. Moreover, younger priests were more supportive of the land movement than the older ones, usually parish priests or even more senior canons.[36] At the Aghamore meeting the two canon speakers were reticent and reluctant to endorse the agitation. Since he was addressing them, was the heckler castigating these canons, or was he encouraging them? We know from other sources that priests felt they had to participate in such meetings to prevent the movement from becoming violent. Did Canons Bourke and Waldron on the platform get the message that if the 'canons' did not do their job, the demonstrators might resort to 'cannons'?

Land League leaders called meetings such as that at Aghamore to confront hostile priests and 'encourage' hesitant ones to join the movement. When the newspaper reporter wrote 'cannons' he was, of course, choosing not to use 'canons' but we can be sure he did not ask the heckler how to spell the word he had shouted out. In addition, the crowd provided the coverage of anonymity to the shouter, ensuring that no one person could be identified as harbouring or voicing subversion. Even if he were identified either by one of the priests or perhaps the police (who could be suspected to be in attendance, perhaps undercover), he could easily deny any wrongdoing by claiming to be just telling a joke. Those who applauded could always claim to be expressing their appreciation for the wit involved, and anybody who objected to the comment could be derided for lacking a sense of humour. A serious message is being conveyed, nonetheless, but in a manner that preserves a protective shield of deniability for all the underdogs involved and provides a seemingly innocuous alternative reading of the statement. The point is not that we in the twenty-first century cannot now decipher the meaning of this shout at the Aghamore demonstration in 1879. Rather, the very persons 'in charge' of the meeting then and there could never determine precisely what it meant. (Fr Cavanagh was in the chair at this meeting.) The comment was (designed to be) open to multiple readings. When relatively less powerful people's statements refer to the Blessed Virgin, this problem is compounded because the Virgin throughout history has been a 'polyvalent figure who appears in many guises'.[37] There is no one right interpretation. For additional reasons too, it was virtually impossible for outsiders, then or especially later, to read one simple message into the Knock episode. The evidence we have about the apparition has been filtered through the accounts in such sources as MacPhilpin and Sexton.

Another reason the message is ambiguous is that in an oral-centred communicative context such as Knock at the time, stories did not come with the explicit endorsement of an unquestioned authority that provided one definitive or canonical reading (in contrast to, for example, the 'one right answer' to a catechism question). The people themselves explicitly recognised this. *Tá seacht gcaoi le sceál a inseacht agus dhá gabháil déag ar amhrán* (there are seven ways to tell a story and twelve versions of a song), was how the idea was recorded in south Galway.[38] Thus, as a recent scholar wrote, 'it is a hopelessly futile task . . . to attempt to ascertain the totality of the meaning of any "text" of oral narrative tradition encountered in written form'.[39] When we recognise that people are more than culturally pre-programmed automatons we realise that individuals can creatively use the same idiom to say very different things.[40]

I suggest the apparition could be and was read either as endorsing or reproaching the behaviour of particular clerics, or both. Fundamentally, it set an agenda by raising questions and requiring deliberation about the proper roles and duties of the clergymen. By 'the bishop', as reported in the apparition scene, whom would seers and local hearers have understood — MacHale or MacEvilly? The great likelihood is that MacHale would be understood. His enormous and saintly reputation was likely revivified locally when he visited for confirmation in Knock in 1878, but at the time of the apparition he was the focus of contention because of his public letters criticising the land agitation leaders. These engaged two powerful and immediately salient concerns, people's relationships with neighbours and their access to land, generating intense anxiety. MacEvilly in contrast was not to take up residence in the diocese until about ten days after the apparition. One reading is that the apparition in which a bishop is prominently featured but less centrally than the Virgin Mary, subordinated even MacHale to the higher authority of the Virgin herself. This was, in new visual language the age-old reproach of clergymen who failed to behave appropriately as men of God and shepherds of their flocks. The bishop appeared in a supernatural tableau — thus being accorded above human qualities — but less central than and visually subordinated to the Virgin. And the mode of criticism, appealing to a higher authority, was also traditional. Given that earlier the people had made MacHale a saint (chapter 5) as well as his official ecclesiastical position in which he defied even the pope, perhaps the only way to 'go over his head' to a higher authority was to a heavenly one. In the two preceding months MacHale's public letters had appeared attacking the land agitation leaders as designing or strolling men, seemingly completely changing his position established over more than half a century of defending the people. Earlier MacHale had put avaricious priests in their proper place by his letter at the station mass, and had put the powers of the government and parliament in their proper place subordinate to God when he resurrected the Commons guard, but now he himself was put in his proper place subordinate to the Virgin Mary.[41]

However, if MacHale condemned the land agitation leaders, many refused to believe he authored the letters published under his name. Thus, despite MacHale's criticisms, the land movement maintained its momentum in the months after the apparition, even including a 'peaceful mass invasion' of MacHale's cathedral city of Tuam. Even then the movement's leaders hesitated to verbally attack the living saint that was John MacHale. Even less could most ordinary people openly criticise him. One historian argues that much of the antipathy toward MacHale was deflected on to his nephew, Canon Bourke.[42] Above I have given a reading of the apparition as criticism of MacHale, but the very same apparition could be read as MacHale supporting the people. The bishop appeared with an arm raised in a manner often described as 'preaching' or 'teaching'. However, as Warner pointed out, his right hand was raised in the traditional and canonically appropriate gesture of blessing, with the first two fingers straight up and the thumb folded across the others.[43] Could he not be seen as giving his blessing to what the people were doing? Indeed, the *Tuam News* early on characterised the gesture as 'blessing', Dominick Beirne told Sexton that the bishop was 'blessing', and the Nun of Kenmare said the bishop was 'blessing Erin'.[44] Importantly, both of these apparently very different readings undercut clerical opposition to the agitation: either the bishop was blessing what the people were doing or the Virgin was castigating him for his opposition. And if MacHale was 'blessing' the agitation, where did that leave Fr Cavanagh's opposition? The key significance of the apparition for the Land War was that it served to neutralise clerical opposition to the tenants' movement. It provided validation for what was already happening on the ground — the people's massive refusal to heed clerical condemnations — but it did so without attacking the authority claims of priests in the religious realm.

One of the leaders whom MacHale specifically targeted in his first public letter was Charles Stewart Parnell, the nationalist MP who had accepted an invitation to address an early land demonstration in Westport in June. Parnell was to become closely identified with the movement and to gain enormous popularity; later he was to make an American tour during which he raised money for famine relief in the west. Speaking to a crowd in Castlebar in April 1880 after returning from this tour, Parnell said he and others had advised people to send their contributions to Bishops McCormack and Conway, naming two bishops in the province, because, he said, 'we knew they were true-hearted men above all others', at which point, 'A voice — [interrupted] Three Cheers for Archbishop MacHale (great cheering).' Parnell's pointed omission of MacHale and insinuation that he was not as 'true-hearted' did not sit well with the crowd, and when he continued with a mention of O'Connor-Power, the local 'advanced nationalist' MP elected despite opposition from most priests (but not MacHale), Parnell was again interrupted by applause and cheers for MacHale.[45] Even while they followed men MacHale criticised and engaged in actions he condemned, many people did not or could not bring themselves to criticise him. Instead, they developed rationalisations that excused him from responsibility for his words. Rarely has a 'leader', or more precisely his image, been more controlled by some followers' wishes.

Recognising stories of appearances of the Virgin Mary as a way of talking about the proper behaviour of ecclesiastics, enables us to understand many features of the witness testimony as published. Again, Scott's insights into the dynamics of relationships between superiors and underdogs are instructive. As he says, in front of top-dogs

> in the short run, it is in the interest of the subordinate to produce a more or less credible performance, speaking the lines and making gestures he knows are expected of him.

The result is that the public transcript is usually systematically skewed toward how things are presented by the dominant.[46] The first interpretation above that the Queen of Heaven herself was criticising the bishop is not only plausible but is among the readings that would be obvious to people in Knock. However, like wise peasants bowing before the great lord in the Ethiopian proverb, or like the anonymous heckler at the Aghamore demonstration, individual lay people cannot openly voice this criticism to their clerical superiors. If asked directly by some reporter they would certainly deny it, and later researchers cannot expect to find straightforward descriptions of what is involved. Persons involved could hint at it and then deny what they hinted at or even that they had hinted about anything of the sort.

As recounted at length earlier, according to their published testimony nearly all the witnesses at the gable in Knock reported a 'bishop', but then nearly all said the figure was St John the Evangelist mainly, they said, because that was what someone else said.[47] Following the links in their published testimony backward to find the originator of the identification leads us to Mary Beirne, but she says that she was not at all sure who the figure was.[48] Everyone preserves a degree of deniability if they should be accused of criticising either MacHale[49] or the clergy, and such deniability was of course most important when they had to testify before a commission of priests. According to *The Nation*, 26 June 1880 and Sexton's book (but not the Dublin edition of MacPhilpin's book), at Fr Cavanagh's request the commission's three members were 'assisted' by six other priests.[50] This was certainly no setting in which to voice a message from heaven criticising some priest or bishop for abuse of his role, especially given, as we are told (though not very convincingly), that each witness was examined alone.[51]

Given his reputation, I find it implausible to suggest that none of the many seers who reported a bishop ever considered that it could be MacHale.[52] Even if the seers did not explicitly tell them, however, the priests could hardly have been unaware of how the Virgin's appearances were traditionally understood. This would help explain why they sought initially to restrict media reports of the episode. Sexton admitted he knew of the apparition claim for months before he printed anything, 'because of the desire of the clergy that no extensive coverage be given' to the episode.[53] When that strategy of minimising the damage to clerical reputations proved ineffective, a few months later the priests involved launched their mass media promotional blitz with both Fr Cavanagh and Canon Bourke working hand in hand with Sexton, MacPhilpin and other promoters to disseminate their inevitably clerical versions of what had occurred. In their construction of the apparition, no hint of questioning of priests is given,[54] just as there is no mention by the promoters of the criticisms levelled at Fr Cavanagh at the 'monster indignation meeting' in Knock just a few months earlier.[55] There is evidence that the priests were consciously countering what they claimed was mischaracterisation of the apparition. Despite surviving evidence to the contrary, MacPhilpin claimed that it was only when his newspaper covered them (in early January 1880) that the people began to ascribe credibility to the events that up to that point had been 'incorrectly narrated'.[56] We can certainly understand why the priest-promoters would (claim to) see a heavenly criticism of clergy or an apparition recounted as such as 'incorrectly narrated'.

If Fr Cavanagh read the Virgin appearance as divine disparagement of how some clerics were performing their role, this would help account for what is otherwise difficult to explain. The early publicists and promoters of Knock completely ignored the anti-Cavanagh demonstration in his parish a few months before the apparition and readers of their accounts would have no reason to suspect he was an object of local indignation. Except for local people around Knock who knew directly or by word of mouth, then, those who read the accounts did not have even the barest information needed to suspect the interpretation I propose.

Decades later some Cavanagh partisans did indirectly acknowledge the reality of conflict but only to further their argument. According to one of them, over seventy years later, Cavanagh's enemies in the land movement were so depraved that at a secret meeting they determined that a suitable punishment for him would be to subject him to a series of increasing threats and finally, if he persisted in criticising the agitation, to cut off his ears. Before they could carry out their plans, however, the Virgin appeared, the sinners recognised the monstrous nature of their intentions and their plans fell through.[57] The most interesting aspect of this story is not that the defenders of Fr Cavanagh and promoters of the apparition enlist the Virgin on their side, but that even if a plan to physically maim the priest was discussed — not at all impossible given Cavanagh's very public and strong

denunciation — his critics could well read the apparition as divine intervention on their side of the dispute rather than on his side. Was there any
need to cut off the ears of a man who had been criticised by the Virgin
herself, especially as he seemed to have learned his lesson? Fr Cavanagh's
behaviour in the months after the demonstration and after the apparition
show that he moved much more toward the view advocated by those he
denounced than they did toward his. He dramatically changed how he acted
toward the land agitation. In May 1879 he had criticised it from the altar,
but the 1 June protest 'put an end to such comments [as Fr Cavanagh's] in
the Knock area'.[58] By October he was in the chair at a demonstration
meeting in his parish, sharing the stage with the very persons he had
denounced. In mid-February 1880, at a large and enthusiastic land demonstration in a field adjacent to the apparition church, Fr Cavanagh had agreed
to be in the chair but was unable to attend because of 'the unexpected visit
of some noble lady to the shrine'. Another man who was called upon to
chair the meeting regretted the 'unavoidable absence of their dear pastor,
(loud cheers for Fr Cavanagh); though he was not with them in person, he
was with them in spirit'.[59]

This meeting passed resolutions calling for the abolition of landlordism, a
system the speakers condemned as founded on confiscation and as the cause
of all their miseries. This was a far more radical programme than that being
proposed in the early summer of 1879. Yet during those eight months of
increasing radicalism, in land demonstrations in his own parish, Fr Cavanagh
went from being denounced to being loudly cheered. The same writer who
recounted the alleged plan to cut off Fr Cavanagh's ears, also wrote that 'as
the full story of [his] life and times is unfolded there will be no difficulty in
overcoming any fixed unfavourable prejudices' about him.[60] We can well
imagine why there might have been 'fixed unfavourable prejudices' about Fr
Cavanagh still in the area seventy years later, even if promoters of his cause
acknowledge them only indirectly, and give no indication of the basis for
them. Fr Cavanagh could not have been unaware of one possible reading of
the apparition as criticism of himself and this may well have been a factor in
his about-face when it came to dealing with the land demonstrators.

Putting the Bishop in his Place

The Knock apparition was a way for some to respond to a bishop who had
'gone too far' in criticism of a popular movement, and also for other people
to respond to mounting criticism of the clergy. That people at the bottom
could use the resources of their traditional religious culture to 'put a bishop
in his place' is clear from another instance where this occurred.[61] In chapter
4, I described the 'Blessed Straws' event of June 1832 and MacHale's role in
it, when he was reported in Knock to be 'coming down the road with his
carriage full of straw', and constructed as the instigator of the ritual that
saved people from the cholera epidemic. But another bishop was

understood to have played a very different role in the same episode, and the people in his area responded to his going too far in criticism. Using the tools in their cultural tool-kit, they creatively devised a way to shield themselves from his wrath.

The earliest reports saying that the distribution of some material was due to the Virgin Mary's direct command were soon followed by others of runner-messengers ascribing it to the initiative of angels, 'the priests', or of specific named priests or bishops. One of those most frequently mentioned was James Doyle, Bishop of Kildare and Leighlin. While some reports said that the ashes blessed by Bishop Doyle would prevent the spread of cholera, others gave a very different rationale: that, because of Doyle's curse, balls of fire from heaven had destroyed some town or even a whole county, but that distributing the ashes would save the recipients from such a fate.[62]

We begin to appreciate the significance of this story about Doyle when we consider it in a bottom-up view, in contrast to a top-down perspective on the Blessed Straws episode and examining how the two interrelated. Doyle, Bishop of Kildare and Leighlin, JKL, was one of the most famous bishops of the day. But in many areas, including Dunlavin, County Wicklow, 'messengers reported that "in consequence of a curse pronounced by Doctor Doyle a ball of fire had fell from heaven in the Queen's County and had completely destroyed it"[63] (similar incineration of other places was reported elsewhere). Distributing the requisite materials would, however, save the recipients, just like the blessed straws would save people in Knock from cholera. Although reported by unsympathetic, often uncomprehending observers, what we have here is evidence of a popular belief in Doyle's extraordinary and extra-canonical powers. (Extraordinary powers were ascribed to MacHale also.) Why would people ascribe such destructive powers to Doyle? Why would they give such a different rationale for the whole episode than found in Knock and widely elsewhere, that distributing some materials would ward off cholera? The popular response to Bishop Doyle in 1832 provides a comparison case for the response in Knock in 1879 after Archbishop MacHale had denounced the local land agitation leaders. The two cases have much to teach us about people's faith.

Historian Thomas McGrath is without question the foremost authority on Doyle, having published two books on him and authored the 2004 *Dictionary of National Biography* entry on him. McGrath relied on diocesan records, bishops' correspondence and other types of contemporary written evidence now available in print or in archives. In this immense quantity of material, he found no evidence whatsoever of the Blessed Straws episode and no evidence of the extraordinary way Doyle was regarded by the runners whose accounts ended up in the letters to the civil authorities in Dublin Castle.[64] However, McGrath's books do provide us with detailed information about what the bishop was writing, preaching and doing in the period surrounding the whole event, and this information supplies the key to the popular response.

Doyle is well known to historians for his public letters in the 1820s on constitutional and political issues, but these were of little relevance to the poor of his diocese, among whom secret agrarian societies were believed to be common. Two groups whose agitation perturbed both the civil and the religious authorities were called the Blackfeet and the Whitefeet. As early as 1821, Doyle in describing his efforts to maintain the confidence of the government and magistrates and to keep the peace, wrote that he was 'obliged to be present everywhere, to stimulate the clergy, to encourage the virtuous portion of the people and terrify the wretched'.[65] It was how he set out to 'terrify the wretched' or to 'terrify into better habits the evildoers' as he phrased it in May 1832,[66] that provides the key to comprehending how he was viewed in the Blessed Straws episode.

The agrarian disturbances escalated in the preceding months. One crucial event occurred on 25 November 1831 when police fired on a crowd of would-be rescuers of a party of alleged Whitefeet being taken to jail under military escort. Five people were killed and several others wounded. In response Doyle ordered, 'that those wounded in the affray be denied the spiritual attendance of the priests and that those killed be denied Christian burial'.[67] However, even this stricture including the burial of the dead in unconsecrated ground[68] failed to end the illegal associations and in April 1832 Doyle again vehemently denounced the ongoing agitation. According to one clergyman of the time, his preaching 'spread through the country with an electrical effect'.[69] Attributing all their actions to the devil, Doyle imposed very severe pre-conditions on the Whitefeet before they could return to the Catholic fold. In front of their former companions they had to publicly renounce their involvement even if that risked their very lives, and they had to make full reparation for all the damage they had done even, if necessary, at the expense of all their possessions. Moreover, they had to do public penance in the chapel for a year. Only then were priests even permitted to hear their confession. These stern requirements were promulgated just at the time that confessionals were already more crowded because of the cholera panic, according to one of Doyle's parish priests, and when the time allotted to 'do one's Easter duty' of going to confession and receiving communion was running out.[70]

It is against this backdrop that the runners' stories about Bishop Doyle make sense. They construct him as extraordinarily powerful; his bringing down balls of fire from heaven on the counties and villages of the wicked was the literal enactment of his recent anathemas. However, the stories also show how the people could counteract that power. By distributing ashes or straws, they could negate his curses and escape his wrath. (This marks one limit on the power of a priest's curse.) As individuals, they might be powerless against the bishop's power, but in cooperation with others, collectively they provided each other opportunities to enact the ritual behaviour that would protect all from even the strongest episcopal cursing. In the case of MacHale, by 1879 he had long been a living saint but now it was necessary to appeal to a higher authority to discredit his public condemnation of the land agitation. In both cases, the people had put the bishops in their place by inventive use of the cultural resources available to them.

The Debate on the Role of the Clergy

The August 1879 apparition was one outcome of the crisis in clerical authority precipitated by the Land War, and which manifested itself in many other ways, such as the confrontations with Fr Cavanagh in the demonstration meetings on 1 June and 26 October 1879. But these challenges to the priests were nothing new in the area. They were of a piece with the criticism of avaricious priests that manifested itself in the proverbs we noted earlier, in stories such as 'The Friars of Urlaur', and very overtly in the 'strike' against the priests that convulsed the area around Knock in 1842–43, the last place in Ireland where such a massive public protest against priestly exactions was noted.[71] Against the bishops' attempts to suppress keening, a Mayo woman pointed out that the Virgin herself had asked women to keen for her Son.[72] Criticisms of 'unpriestly' priests were common in the area even before the Land War, and in nearby areas they had recently been made immediately salient by the way the priests dealt with Fenians.[73] James Daly, the owner and editor of the *Connaught Telegraph*, and arguably the single most important individual in the early Land War, had already confronted the parish priest of Balla on these grounds. The whole spectrum of behaviours appropriate or otherwise for a priest was held up for consideration in a newspaper contretemps between Daly and Fr E. Gibbons, the Balla priest.[74] We probably will never have 'the facts' of the case but for my purposes here, these are less important than the allegations and the standards implicitly assumed by the parties to the affair. The background to the dispute was that Daly had contributed money toward building a church in Balla but Fr Gibbons claimed Daly had not kept a promise to pay more later. Daly refused to make his promised second contribution to protest against how Fr Gibbons dealt with one 'poor Curry'.

Henry Curry was a teacher who, for some reason probably related to his Fenian sympathies, was in straitened circumstances.[75] Apparently Gibbons claimed to have 'helped' Curry financially, a claim that drew Daly's wrathful denunciation. First, if Gibbons had shown charity to Curry, by bragging about it he had acted, not like Christ, but like the Pharisee in the Biblical account, and had humiliated Curry in his poverty. Second, Daly claimed as fact that Curry, as a teacher in a school under Gibbons' management, had his salary payable through the priest, and so any money the priest gave him was not charity but a loan whose security was assured. Gibbons could always recover the money by withholding it from Curry's pay. Thus not only had Gibbons boasted publicly about his charity, but he was not even charitable to begin with. He was being doubly hypocritical. (Of course, Daly is here also deploying the familiar arguments against the avarice of priests.)

Daly was outraged especially by what happened before and after Curry died in August 1876. Because of his Fenianism, he was denied the last rites and was buried without any priest in attendance. Gibbons refused to officiate at the graveside even though, according to Daly, he had earlier promised to attend. The mourning group tried to get Gibbons' curate to read the burial service but he too refused, having been so ordered by Gibbons. Apparently Daly then said some words at the graveside, which Fr Gibbons later alleged amounted to Daly usurping the priests' prerogative. Daly denied that in speaking at the grave he assumed what he explicitly acknowledged was a role only for priests, part of their proper role as religious leaders. His words did not and could not replace a priest's blessing. Curry's Fenianism was no Christian reason for Gibbons to deny him the benefits of a church-blessed burial. When priests acted like Gibbons did, they were not priest-like in their behaviour.

Daly's criticism here of Fr Gibbons' treatment of Curry follows the same script as do the stories about how the Virgin came to sponsor the newborn child baptised by the curate after the parish priest refused to attend the sinful woman. What the orthodox ecclesiastical authorities might lay out as proper for a priest in particular circumstances (for example, in dealing with Fenians unrepentant on their deathbeds), could be undercut by an alternative definition of the proper priestly role of bringing God's sacraments even to the greatest of sinners.[76] (A different version of Fr Gibbons' treatment of Curry says that the priest visited the dying man and found him unwilling to renounce his Fenianism and hence denied him absolution for the sins involved in this. Moreover, this version says that while Curry had earlier been a national teacher, he later ran his own pay school.[77] The 'evidence' for these assertions is largely drawn from local memories recorded in the 1937–8 Schools Folklore Project; we should view them as claims that may or may not have been true. Criticisms of priests can be expected to have become more muted by then, and in any case would be less likely to be submitted to or by school teachers whose jobs depended on the school manager, the local priest.[78])

Daly was no anti-clerical but deeply committed to what he accepted was the proper role for priests.[79] He demanded that priests live up to the responsibilities of their calling but confine themselves to religion, and he was able and prepared to appeal to higher authorities, such as Jesus in the Bible, to criticise priests like Gibbons. Daly's *Connaught Telegraph* report of the 1 June 1879 'indignation meeting' is a trenchant statement of his position that priests properly defended the poor and weak against their oppressors, and in Mayo that meant opposing the landlords and supporting the tenants' 'reasonable' demands. This, he rhetorically established, had been the priests' actual practice in earlier generations and centuries, and Cavanagh was inexplicably abandoning such an historic tradition of 'the priest and the people together'. Rather than accept charges of anti-clericalism, Daly appealed to local history and flung the accusations back with a rhetorical flourish, going so far as to insinuate that Fr Gibbons' ancestors of not many generations earlier included 'lackeys of priest hunters and their descendants'. He was not about to let Gibbons define who or what was a proper priest, as later he was not to let Fr Cavanagh's altar denunciation of O'Kane go unanswered.

It would be wrong to characterise Cavanagh's critics or the leaders of the land agitation in general as anti-clerical. What they opposed was the priests' non-religious political support of, or acceptance of, the landlord system. Daly had made that case explicitly in his report on the first mass demonstration against Fr Cavanagh on 1 June. In September when the land movement leaders were trying to spread the agitation beyond Mayo, the very issue of the *Connaught Telegraph* (27 September) that reported on the 'peaceful mass invasion' of Tuam, printed a letter to the editor that very succinctly made their case. 'Oh! You priests of Roscommon', the writer asked, 'what are you doing? You who are constituted the guardians of the poor, the widow and the orphan, why don't you call meetings and denounce those tyrannous landlords, agents and bailiffs?'

Cavanagh's reputed holiness even after the apparition did not silence his critics. On the platform at the second meeting within six months to confront him in his own parish, at Aghamore in October, was none other than P. J. Gordon whose daughter, Delia, had been miraculously cured at Knock. The eleven-year-old Delia had suffered from persistent and painful earache. Ten days after the apparition the girl and her mother were at mass in Knock when her ear grew so painful that the mother took Delia outside to the apparition gable. Using a shawl pin to dislodge a small piece of mortar from the wall, the mother applied it to the girl's ear, whereupon the ache went away.[80] In Fr Cavanagh's diary of cures, Delia's is the very first cure recorded, ten days after the apparition; that is, before the Aghamore meeting. A miraculous cure of his own daughter did not keep Gordon off the platform at what was in effect an anti-Cavanagh demonstration of Land League strength.[81] He strongly opposed the role the priests had played in parliamentary politics. In 1874 he had led a crowd which defeated the rival mob organised by a faction of Catholic clergy in support of the Catholic landlord MPs and helped elect the IRB/Fenian supported Home Ruler, John O'Connor Power, to parliament.[82]

Though he opposed Cavanagh, Gordon was no anti-clerical. A bootmaker by trade, in all probability he was the 'Mr Gordon' who donated 'an excellent pair of kid boots' to a fundraising bazaar for the new convent of Mercy in Claremorris just weeks before the 1 June 'indignation meeting'.[83] Earlier, he had contributed one pound a year for at least three years to a fund to purchase a convent building to bring the Sisters of Mercy to Claremorris and had given money toward building a new church.[84] His monetary support of church and convent building did not mean he implicitly followed the priests or MacHale in matters of politics. Like Daly, Gordon wanted to get priests to confine themselves to their proper religious role.

Gordon was an important activist. While he advertised himself as a 'Home Rule Bootmaker'[85] he was a dominant IRB/Fenian figure in

Claremorris and may have been the Centre in Mayo. He helped organise the first Irishtown meeting that is usually taken as the start of the Land War and, Maume suggests, as an individual Fenian, though not officially representing the IRB, he worked out an agreement with Davitt to become the land movement's organiser for Connaught. The police suspected he was behind several agrarian murders but lacked firm evidence against him. He was first on a list they compiled of persons to be arrested if and when internment was introduced. He was arrested in March 1881 and convicted of incitement, serving a year in prison. He served two more short sentences later in the 1880s for encouraging tenants to resist eviction.[86] All this did not mean he was anti-clerical. Some have pointed out that Gordon benefited economically from the Knock apparition, in that he rented out cars to pilgrims for the trip to Knock from the railway station at Claremorris,[87] but not only Gordon himself but his wife and daughter were present in the Knock churchyard when Sexton visited in January 1880.[88] Another local man with a similar Fenian/land activist/prisoner career was P. J. Sheridan; after Sheridan escaped to Paris he returned in disguise, briefly visiting among other places the young Knock shrine.[89]

The Ballyhaunis Connection

Any social scientific account of the August 1879 apparition must provide answers to several fundamental questions, the available evidence must support it, and it should suggest new insights into hitherto unrecognised dimensions.[90] Basic questions about the apparition include: When? Where? What? to Whom? and, hence, Why? The Ballyhaunis connection helps provide more specific answers to some of these questions.

In chapter 7, I documented the singing of the Knock choir under the direction of the school principal, Miss Anderson, in the town of Ballyhaunis. The choir was not Miss Anderson's only contact with the renovated Augustinian monastery in the town. She is listed among the donors toward the cost of its new stained-glass window depicting Our Lady of Consolation, contributing seven shillings and six pence.[91] Another Knock woman, Mrs Kelly of Churchfield House contributed thirteen shillings and six pence to the same cause, and she, too, was reported to have seen supernatural lights in the months after the August 1879 apparition.[92] Mrs Kelly's husband, Edmond C. Kelly, was a landlord's agent and a gentleman farmer in his own right and had once been chairman of the Ballyhaunis (Horse) Race Committee.[93] He, too, contributed money for the renovation of the church[94] and for its stained glass window.[95] The involvement of these people with the Ballyhaunis renovation and the existence of the church choir in Knock, points to an important link between Knock and Ballyhaunis sustained by involved church members. Together with the schoolteachers, the Kellys typified the type of people we would expect to find in the vanguard of respectable church-centred Catholicism. Mrs Kelly, like Miss Anderson, was likely close to Fr Cavanagh. A few years later, the Nun of Kenmare claimed Cavanagh's friendship with the Kellys was the reason he refused to do anything when she complained about their behaviour toward her.[96] The Knock-Ballyhaunis connection was strengthened in 1878 when the Scottish firm that installed a new stained-glass window in St Mary's moved directly to a similar task at Knock church.[97] Evidently, the planning for the two windows had been coordinated, further evidence of the close connections that existed between the two churches.

Consideration of both the timing and the form of the Knock apparition buttresses this suggestion of a close relationship between at least some people in Knock, including some August 1879 apparition witnesses and the Augustinian church in Ballyhaunis. First, the late August timing is very significant. Almost precisely two years before the famous apparition, the *Connaught Telegraph* of 25 August 1877 reported that for the Feast of St Augustine at the Augustinian Priory in Ballyhaunis:

> It has been customary since time immemorial that thousands assemble, some who come long distances on a pilgrimage to celebrate the festival with penitence and devotion.

The paper reported the following week that 'vast numbers assembled' for the 'usual religious ceremony'.[98] The size of the gathering may be gauged from a report from the preceding year which refers to 'throngs' of pilgrims from neighbouring counties, mentions masses starting at 6.00 a.m. and lists eight priests involved at the 11.00 a.m. High Mass.[99] This elaborate religious celebration in the last week of August took place each year at least up to 1878 when the *Connaught Telegraph* reported that the Feast was celebrated with 'unusual success'.[100] As the paper reported, the day was 'kept a holiday of prayer and devotion in the Ballyhaunis district'.[101] It was at this event that the Knock choir performed in 1876. It is hardly mere coincidence that the Knock apparition took place in late August 1879; it is very plausible that at least some of the witnesses were attuned to the sacred nature of the timeframe. Significant religious experiences could be expected during that period. I suggest the date was locally sacred because of the annual Ballyhaunis pilgrimage on those days, not because of its setting in the orthodox calendar.

This does not negate the possibility that others found the dates significant for other reasons. Indeed, in accounts of the apparition published later by promoters, its date was given as 'the eve of the Octave of the Assumption'. In the general case there is no suggestion that anybody, including the clergy, saw anything significant about most feast day octaves or the eves of those days. The feast day of the Assumption was celebrated on 15 August but few would even know what its octave was, i.e. either the eight days afterward (counting the 15th), or just the eighth day after (the 22nd), not to mention the eve of that day. However, in the late 1870s the days immediately after the 15th were seen as pregnant with meaning by some particular Lourdes devotees. These were the Paris-based Assumptionist Order and especially its founder and leader, Père Emmanuel d'Alzon who highlighted connections he noticed between his order, Lourdes miracles and the Feast of the Assumption that gave his order its name. He was hoping to get a declaration of the Dogma of the Assumption from the official church (which did happen, but not until 1950) and thought the miracles were a sign for *his* order specifically. In September 1877 he wrote:

> I ask myself why so many miracles in the octave of the Assumption, on a pilgrimage directed by the Assumptionists, why among the cures at Lourdes there is a Petite-Soeur de l'Assomption and, at Nimes, an Oblate of the Assumption. Could it be that the Holy Virgin is beginning to set out the first markers for a definition of the dogma of the Assumption?[102]

This private letter was very unlikely to have been known in Knock but obviously promoters did indeed know of the significance attached to the 'octave of the Assumption'. A possible conduit for information about Assumptionist thinking on the continent is Fr Anderson, who travelled to Rome in 1878 and presumably passed though France where he could have been alerted to Marianist thinking. He had given a statue of Our Lady of Lourdes to Knock church, and it is possible that he also conveyed some sense of the importance of the Assumption octave timeframe directly, or indirectly through Fr Cavanagh, to some of the seers at the gable on 21 August. We have no evidence that this occurred but if it did, it could have reinforced the sacredness of the days of the Ballyhaunis pilgrimage. There were also other possible channels of influence from outside. Without giving his evidence, historian John White says that in the late 1870s the American published *Ave Maria* magazine was widely read by Irish clerics, including Fr Cavanagh.[103] By the time they came to publishing their work in 1880 it is obvious that Knock promoters were attuned to Marianist developments abroad. One symbol of the monarchy in France, the 'Sacred Heart of Jesus' — that no seer reported at Knock but which nonetheless appeared in at least three different prints of the gable scene — had been included in an apparition of the Virgin at Pellevoisin in 1876.[104] Despite Knock's promotion as a Marian apparition, devotion to the Sacred Heart of Jesus was prominent among pilgrims there in 1880.[105]

The close connection between Knock and Ballyhaunis was very likely enhanced by the friendship of the two priests. Fr Cavanagh and Fr Anderson each had special devotion to the Virgin, and they coordinated the installation of stained glass windows in their respective churches. Fr Anderson's new stained glass window showing Our Lady of Consolation was installed in March 1878, and another window immediately afterward in Knock. There is a 50/50 chance that the Knock window depicted the Immaculate Conception since that was one of two windows in the transepts of the chapel at the time of the apparition. (The other was of the Sacred Heart.)[106]

The Ballyhaunis pilgrimage would have brought people to the renovated St Mary's Abbey where in 1878 or even 1879 the new stained glass window might well have helped suggest the display of representations of various figures that was to appear at Knock. The window was impressively large, approximately six feet wide by sixteen feet high. It occupied a focal point in the renovated church directly above the altar and dominated one gable of the building.[107]

The Window in St Mary's

It is clear that some witnesses at Knock had images in their minds of what various heavenly personages would look like. Pat Hill told a reporter that what he saw at the gable was like what he had seen in Catholic pictures. Most often, however, the images in the witnesses' minds are assumed to have been drawn from statues they had seen.[108] What was important at Knock, however, was not just the presence of (statues or figures of) different personages but their relationship to one another, that is, how they were positioned or juxtaposed vis-à-vis each other. It could well be that the perception of the relative positions of the 'three visitors' at Knock was suggested by the Ballyhaunis window scene. The window was crowded with images but several of the most important closely resemble figures reported at Knock. Central in both was the Virgin Mary. Pride of place in the centre of the Ballyhaunis window went to Our Lady of Consolation and on her right was a mitred figure posed in a way that was to be recalled at the Knock scene where St Joseph was reported as turning and bowing toward the Virgin. Lower down in the window there are figures of another mitred figure and another with an open book. It would seem that these two are conflated and combined in the third figure at Knock, the one conventionally identified as St John but first reported by witnesses as a bishop holding a book.

I am suggesting not that the Knock witnesses consciously copied the Ballyhaunis arrangement but that some aspects of the window very plausibly contributed to the perceptions of some seers at Knock. Both the window and the reported Knock gable scene were two-dimensional visual displays of unmoving religious personages. They had a similar juxtaposition of some of the central figures. Mary at Knock was standing while the Ballyhaunis Virgin was a Madonna with the Child Jesus. But what was similar in both was the centrality accorded the Virgin and the subordinate positions accorded to other figures included. Looking at the Ballyhaunis window Knock seers would have seen a mitred figure beside the Virgin and recognised it as 'a bishop' without knowing him as St Augustine or perhaps St Patrick, which could have contributed greatly to the 'bishop' figure that eventually was identified as St John in the published depositions. A mitred figure would be easily recognised as a bishop but Knock lay people who saw the Ballyhaunis window and the figure next to the Virgin were unlikely to be familiar with the special position of St Augustine in the history of the Augustinian order and hence unlikely to recognise him.

The window in Ballyhaunis would be familiar in Knock for several reasons. Knock people were connected to the church there (as evidenced by their contributions both for the window and the renovation of the church) and the Knock choir had sung there on two occasions of which we know and perhaps others of which we don't. Moreover, people from Knock very likely participated in the annual end of August pilgrimage to the Abbey that brought pilgrims from several counties.[109] Finally, the Scottish firm[110] that installed the window in St Mary's in 1878 moved on directly to install another stained glass window in the chapel at Knock, which would inevitably have made the windows a topic of local conversation.

People in Knock could hardly be unaware of it, but that does not mean they knew or could decipher all the elements and symbols incorporated into the Ballyhaunis window. Fr John O'Connor, a modern Augustinian and one of the last priests resident at St Mary's, described the window as follows:

> In the upper tracery of the east window we see Alpha and Omega capitals, and angels bearing a Sacred Heart and various emblems of our Saviour's passion; in the next tier we find at top two angels bearing sacred vessels, with a large M symbol in the centre over the Blessed Virgin's head; we see Our Lady of Consolation (patroness of the Augustinians) with St Augustine on one side and St Monica on the other; in the lower tier we find St Patrick in the central panel, with St Nicholas of Tolentine on one side and St Francis of Assisi on the other. The Augustinian crest and Latin motto, 'Tolle Lege! Tolle Lege!'(Take and Read! Take and Read!), associated with the conversion of St Augustine, is given; with the Latin 'Mater Consolationis ora pro nobis' (Mother of Consolation, pray for us); 'Sancte Augustine Sancta Monica ora' (SS Augustine and Monica, pray); 'Sancte Nicholae Tolentine, Sancte Patriti ora, Sancte Francisce' (SS Nicholas, Patrick, Francis pray).[111]

Despite its long list of saints depicted, Fr O'Connor's description is not at all detailed for the enlightened. The relative positions accorded the various figures, details of the attire, pose or other aspects of the figures and inclusion of numerous other symbols incorporated further layers of conventional meanings for those able to decipher the iconography. The prior who had the new window installed felt it important to add to the *Connaught Telegraph's* report of the previous week and amplify the reporter's description of the window. For one example, rather than simply quoting the Augustinian motto, Fr Anderson pointed out that in the window this was 'on the Book of the Gospels on which are placed the heart of St Augustine, out of which issue a blaze of fire and pierced with an arrow; the mitre, the Episcopal crown, the crozier, and the tincture of the

Order, and under the column in a scroll' are the words of the Motto.[112] Ordinary lay people could hardly be expected to recognise all these symbols and figures, especially since many of them were small. How many educated people for that matter could recognise Greek capitals or read Latin? What would be immediately obvious however, was that the Virgin was given pride of place in the centre of the scene, another figure was bowing toward her, and other figures had a mitre (hence was a bishop) and a book. It is likely no coincidence that these figures appeared in Knock. Mary Beirne said the bishop figure she saw had a mitre but 'not a high mitre, but a short-set kind of one'.[113] Two figures depicted in the window in St Mary's wore low mitres. Moreover, the published testimony of Dominick Beirne, Sr, the cattle dealer, includes some details that are rarely accorded much attention in accounts of the apparition but which could have been conflated with the image of the Ballyhaunis window. Dominick described some non-orthodox features on or near the altar that were not depicted in the various prints and illustrations. Did the crowded Ballyhaunis window with its numerous saints and symbols have anything to do with what he reported at Knock, 'figures representing saints and angels traced or carved on the lower part of the altar?'[114] Dominick told a reporter that 'on the altar there appeared to be, in rows of three, statuettes of angels or saints (He could not define which)'.[115] Given the links between Knock and the Ballyhaunis church, the profusion of figures in tiers represented in the new stained glass window there and the location of that window immediately over the altar,[116] it is plausible to suggest some connection in Dominick's perception between an altar and a scene crowded with rows of saints or other sacred beings.

It might seem that the Ballyhaunis connection contradicts my argument that the apparition was locally rooted, a Knock solution to a Knock problem. However, just because ideas are available does not mean that people simply accept them uncritically. Rather, if they adopt them, they adapt them. They can appropriate them and use them for their own purposes. The Knock seers were both selective and inventive. They might well have read the Ballyhaunis window as showing the clergy, including bishops, as subordinate to the Virgin rather than as depicting the history and calling of the Augustinian order as presumably its designers intended and which Fr O'Connor's description highlights. The seers selected and creatively synthesised understandings from their cultural tool-kit to make a different statement in the apparition. Their Virgin wore a crown.

Other Influences

The Ballyhaunis window suggests a model for the 'three visitors' at the Knock church gable, but not for the altar/lamb/cross set of symbols which, as I have argued based on the published witness testimony, had a different origin. At first glance these 'Eucharistic' symbols highlight the mass as the

ritual commemoration and re-enactment of Christ's sacrifice at Calvary. I
have argued that these elements were of more significance to the investigating priests than to the original witnesses. (This was obviously and
understandably the case in the Second Commission of Inquiry.) However,
there was also a very plausible 'popular' visual model for the
altar/lamb/cross set of symbols. A medal distributed by the 'Apostle of
Temperance,' Fr Theobald Mathew, shows precisely this set of figures. The
medal depicts a shield with a horizontal line representing an altar. Below
the line on the front of the altar are the letters IHS and above it, on the altar,
is a lamb. The altar is topped by a cross around
which angels hover.[117] In his temperance
campaigns of the late 1830s and 1840s
Fr Mathew distributed enormous
numbers of these medals, so it is
probable that they were known
to ordinary Knock people.[118]
Moreover, the medals were
likely to have an even larger
impact because they them-
selves were endowed with
curative powers. 'Rubbing
with one of these [medals] at
once relieved rheumatic pains',
and they had other medicinal uses
also. 'I have seen ophthalmia treated
by hanging two of these medals over a
girl's eyes', noted an 1890s' observer.[119]

The Temperance Medal

Other considerations also help explain why locals were likely to be
especially attuned to the possibility of supernatural intervention around
the very days of the apparition. In his exile in Britain Daniel Campbell
could 'never forget' the prophecy he had heard in his youth, that 'no
plague or pestilence would ever rage in Knock', and everyone had seen or
heard how Knock had been preserved through the Great Hunger of the
1840s. The people of Knock remembered their deliverance then. Now,
however, the anxiously awaited harvest of 1879 was confirmed to be disastrous: *An Drochshaol* (the bad times) had returned. Surely the locals
remembered the prophecy as well as the exile did, and may well have
anticipated or looked for another supernatural deliverance of Knock. It
was against this background that less than two weeks before the apparition
one Land League supporter recalled the Blessed Straws episode of 1832
(in a letter in *Connaught Telegraph*, 9 August 1879) and hoped that Knock
people would not rely only on supernatural help but would help themselves by supporting the land agitation.

Famine was not the only threat to the community. The crisis in clerical
authority was a community crisis precisely because the community had

come to be defined as comprising those people who had 'the friendship of the priest' as Daniel Campbell had formulated it. Just as the various communal crises in Campbell's days before the Great Famine required the tapping of supernatural powers, so also would this latter-day crisis, but MacHale was no longer a reliable instrument to do that tapping, compounding the newest communal crisis.

A further contributory factor to the timing may[120] be related to Fr Cavanagh specifically. He reportedly began a special series of 100 masses and, according to Mary Beirne, had finished them just before the apparition. Assuming no break in the series, 100 daily masses begun in late May after the start of the conflict with land agitators would indeed have been completed about the time of the apparition. What better way for Mary Beirne to be reassured in the rightful authority of Fr Cavanagh, despite the criticisms of him and continuing questioning of the proper role of priests. Here was a heavenly sign affirming and validating the embattled priest. The pre-famine salvation of Knock was due to the charitable deed of a local man and the prayer of a 'holy pilgrim'; was Cavanagh, in Mary Beirne's eyes, a latter day 'holy pilgrim' playing the same providential role as the earlier one? It is clear that she was familiar with the use of Virgin appearances to comment on how some priest met the responsibilities of his role. I argue nearly, if not all, the people in the area would have known this idiom. It is very likely that she was induced to see the apparition as endorsing Fr Cavanagh, despite the silence of the heavenly visitors, precisely because others could and did read the very opposite meaning into the episode.

The seers, like all people in Knock and indeed in Mayo and surrounding counties, were also immersed in the currents of apprehension about landlord authority generated by the land movement. With the rent coming due on 1 November, by August it was clear that many, if not most, tenants would be unable to make payment and would be candidates for eviction. A request for rent reductions had been made to Lord Dillon in early summer but no reply had yet been received. No wonder that in late August there was great anxiety about the landlord's authority; how extreme the anxiety was can be gauged by the reaction when it was allayed to some extent: there were celebratory bonfires for miles around and a great street celebration in Ballyhaunis when word was received in October that Dillon had granted a 30 per cent rent abatement.

The apparition occurred in Knock because there the crisis of authority was most acute, and locals were able to creatively use the traditional cultural tools provided them, including adapting new elements to make an old statement. Knock was the epicentre of all the various currents undermining authority (of priest, landlord, and bishop), which intersected and multiplied each other, exacerbating the psychological disorientation and cultural dislocation. Moreover, the local legacy of confronting priests (most obvious in the 1842–43 strike) was revivified just a few months earlier in the 1 June anti-Fr Cavanagh indignation meeting. We would expect the traditional idiom of Virgin appearances to criticise clergy to have persisted in Knock precisely because of the survival of the traditional culture in the post-famine decades. Finally, the seers' access to models in the Ballyhaunis window may well have contributed to the idea of a visual display of the heavenly visitors, but such a source was neither a necessary nor a sufficient cause for the August apparition.

The most important seers were members of the extended Beirne family.[121] I say this both because Mary Beirne was among the very first to see and name an apparition and because the family was so recognised by the investigating panel of priests. The Beirnes were not just subject to all the anxieties common to other Knock residents, but in their cases all were multiplied because of the family's close ties to priests and perhaps especially to Fr Cavanagh, and they were compounded by their family- and household-life-cycle stage that was making lines of authority problematic.

The two key priests, Frs Cavanagh and Bourke, were embodiments of questioned authority and controversy. The other known member of the investigating commission, Canon James Waldron of Ballyhaunis, apparently had little to do with promoting the story later.[122] Very likely his authority had not been strongly challenged as Fr Bourke's and Fr Cavanagh's had. There is no evidence that he was directly and personally confronted, as were the other two priests.[123] Seers, other locals and the priest-promoters were all caught up in the questioning of authority figures and structures. And the apparition spoke to the concerns of each of these.

The timing and location of the apparition is explained by the conjuncture of several factors. First imminently-expected famine, a prophecy of how Knock would be kept safe, and the locally sacred timeframe all very likely heightened hopes if not expectations of divine involvement. More importantly, the events of the Land War provoked a clerical authority crisis most profound in Knock because of the simultaneous overt challenges to both the priest and the archbishop. The threat of imminent famine was not confined to Knock, but the prophecy that no plague or pestilence would ever rage in the parish was likely believed or remembered only in Knock. It is worth noting the localism of the prophecy: it was Knock, the local community, that would be kept safe, not the county or diocese or country. The days of devotion and penitence in late August brought pilgrims to Ballyhaunis from many other parishes in addition to Knock. Doubtless, there were other priests with strong devotion to Mary, such as Fr Anderson.[124] The factor that distinguished Knock from nearby parishes was the sustained, direct and intense confrontation between Fr Cavanagh and the people. Though some have suggested it, the Lourdes precedent or other 'modern' Marian influences cannot explain the initial Knock apparition or especially the presence in it of the bishop figure.

The original apparition involved many essential elements that we can easily document in the pre-existing religious culture. Among these is a shared understanding of visions as vehicles for communication from one world to another. The apparition epitomises one widely found weapon used by the weak, that of appealing to an even higher authority figure to reproach the unacceptable behaviour of someone in authority. In the Irish Catholic context, this meant having the Blessed Virgin appear in criticism of the failure of clergymen to perform their rightful duties. In the Bekan report of a boy encountering a priest returning from the grave and asking to say mass, we have evidence of a roughly contemporaneous use of another local vision to criticise deviant priests. These were understandings available in the local culture that set limits to the power of priests. Even Mary Beirne's later claim that Fr Cavanagh's holiness was the reason for the Virgin's visit is of a piece with traditional views of individual priests having special powers beyond those recognised by the orthodox teaching of the official hierarchy. As a commentary on the roles and responsibility of clerics, the message was probably of most importance to those closest to the clergy and hence most disturbed by criticism of them. As we have seen, the Knock seers, or at least most of them as best we can judge given the available evidence, most likely fell in that category, and others (Durkan, Trench and McLoughlin) were in no position to disagree.

Local Reaction

Further evidence that the apparition followed a traditional script is that the local reaction to the early reports followed age-old understandings of Virgin appearances as providing access to grace without the mediation of the clergy.[125] The very first recorded cure, that of the schoolgirl Delia Gordon, happened when her mother took Delia out of mass and put mortar from the apparition gable on her ear. (A stronger symbolic statement could hardly be made than the 'old' religion was better than the new mass-centred one.) The people around Knock saw in the new site a place for direct access to the transcendent. In attempts to get possession of miracle-working material, locals stripped the mortar and cement first from the apparition gable and then from other surfaces in and around the church, quickly creating holes in the walls big enough almost for a man to go through, to such an extent that the building was in danger of collapse. Fr Cavanagh arranged to cover the apparition gable with planking up to a considerable height, 'or else', as he told a reporter, 'the wall would have rapidly disappeared'.[126] Journalists soon reported people on ladders using sticks, umbrellas and even a sword to pry mortar loose from above the planking, which reportedly was eventually extended to much greater heights.[127]

These local people and early pilgrims were following traditional ideas about the holiness of materials. Earth from the graves of some priests was seen as sacred; special curative qualities were ascribed also to clay from 'caves' at some holy wells or other sites such as St Patrick's grave in Downpatrick.[128] This ancient tradition was still alive and new holy sites were being created in the post-famine era. Donnelly points to the cults that devel-

Getting Mortar at the Gable

oped around the graves of two priests, and the tradition continues perhaps to the present.[129] In the grounds of Knock chapel in 1880 people were reported praying at the grave of Fr Henry Bourke, a grand-uncle of the widow Beirne, and a Knock parish priest dead for sixty years.[130] In addition to trying by all means to get their hands on some of the precious mortar from the gable, in Knock after the apparition, people dug clay from near the church or even its floor,[131] and a reporter noticed a man and a woman 'near fighting' over rainwater from its roof.[132]

Sometime in the later spring or summer of 1880 Fr Cavanagh stopped permitting people to stay overnight in the chapel because of the 'removal by pilgrims of portions of the wall at the side of the altar'.[133] After the original cement was all gone, one report said there was no demand for the new cement used in repair,[134] while others noted that a substantial iron railing was erected in front of the gable 'to save the new plaster from the fate which befell the old'.[135] Fr Cavanagh put up a notice to the effect that clay from the spot was just as powerful as the mortar.[136] At best this was a temporary stratagem. The digging of clay from around the foundation threatened to undermine the whole wall like dislodging the original mortar had quickly picked it apart.[137] Perhaps that was why a railing was needed. And of course, the supply of clay too was limited and would predictably be exhausted (unless an acceptable way of replenishing it was devised, as was the case at Ardmore, but that took many years or even generations).

It would be wrong to suggest that everyone unhesitatingly believed in the efficacy of such materials. Just as there was some popular scepticism about fairylore or priests' powers, often clothed in the protective garb of humour, we find jocular ambivalence about the mortar. In a 17 April 1880 letter from

Abbeyfeale, County Limerick to 'Batt', which somehow found its way into the Kirby papers in the Irish College in Rome, Patrick Collins regaled his correspondent with stories of the impact of Knock.

> Many persons from different corners of the island have died of indigestion from having imprudently indulged in an article of diet hitherto not appreciated in this benighted land viz Knock mortar . . . [While] Messrs O Callaghan and Coffee — stone-braker(sic) and pedlar respectively may now be seen skipping like French dancing masters through Abbeyfeale, [others were not as positively influenced] . . . Patrick O Plover Collins was sent [to Knock] to try to cure him of telling lies, but though no pains were spared, he being very frequently subjected to applications of holy water and mortar, it was all to no purpose . . . Mrs Johnny Broder for certain reasons best known to herself procured a supply at some expense and thought to induce her beloved Lord and Master J.B. to try its virtues, but it was 'no go', he would not have it and up to the present time I have not heard that her very laudable efforts have been successful.[138]

One notable aspect of the situation is not that the local lay people followed these animistic beliefs but that Fr Cavanagh fully endorsed and encouraged them, and used these materials himself, in contrast to, for example, the priest in Marpingen, Germany where a series of Virgin apparitions was reported in the later 1870s.[139] Cavanagh's diary of miracles included the cure of his housekeeper, Mary McLoughlin, by rainwater he had collected from beneath the apparition gable. He had a sign erected near the gable reading, 'It is important that miraculous cures wrought here would be made known to the parish priest', which doubtless did not discourage the miracles. Rather than seeing himself as mediator between the people and God through the mass and the sacraments, Cavanagh apparently saw his role as secretary/note-taker documenting the people's direct access to the other world and its powers, unmediated by the church and its orthodox priesthood and sacraments. This, of course, was very different from the Tridentine ideal being promulgated in the devotional revolution.

The local people and early pilgrims also followed the available cultural blueprint for devotion and pilgrimage at holy wells, making multiple clockwise circuits outside the chapel while praying, often on their knees. Such 'rounding rituals' were at the heart of traditional holy well devotions.[140]

Many pilgrims initially came seeking some personal favour or cure. Pilgrims who felt cured and no longer needed help walking often left walking sticks or crutches, that were eventually hung in rows covering part of the gable. Similar behaviour has been documented at other sites both before and long after Knock. In 1837 a visitor noted that pilgrims at a holy well in Donegal left crutches when they were cured[141] and at another holy well in Donegal, in 1961 an old man remembered

> there were a whole lot of miracles going on. Anybody doing the station
> there will see the crutches that have been left by people that got cured
> after doing the station.[142]

Even a reporter on the Knock cures in 1880 added that 'such cures are by no
means rare in Ireland; I have myself known of many such cures, the result of
visits to "holy wells"', and added that 'these marvels excite but little attention
in the way of surprise'.[143] In 1980, a doctor reported he had seen such
crutches 'many times' including at wells in Kildare, Clare and Limerick, and
the practice was so common at a well in Cork that it was popularly called
Tobar Ursa, i.e. the well of the crutch.[144]

Another indication of the traditional nature of the episode is that the
telling of the story of the apparition incorporates rhetorical techniques
characteristic of the orally informed popular faith that was still vibrant in
Knock at the time of the apparition. The story as printed incorporated
several features that are easily understood as characteristics of oral stories.
It was emphasised that during the apparition the church gable remained
dry despite the pouring rain that drenched the witnesses and every other
place around. This was a rhetorical technique, recognised within the traditional genre, through which the supernatural origin of some event was
attested. Daniel Campbell's account of the priest cursing an adulterer noted
that 'there was a mist in the church at the time'. In 'The Friars of Urlaur'
story, both the howling gales on land and the storms on the lake are similar
instances used toward a similar rhetorical goal. This figurative language did
not have to refer only to meteorological phenomena: in the story about
Bishop MacEvilly and his attempt to evict a tenant, the same role is played
by the detail that the tenant threw a stone that 'passed through' the bishop's
carriage. Like a black hat in old Hollywood westerns, these were established signs easily understood by those who understood the language of the
traditional orally-transmitted stories about other worlds. Indeed, part of the
'proof' of the otherworldly nature of an experience or happening is the validation provided by the abnormal and otherwise inexplicable events in the
mundane natural world.

A second rhetorical strategy involves what, following anthropologist Mary
Douglas, we can call 'communal complicity' or 'collective collusion', a specific form of what I have called 'validation by conversation'.[145] Patrick Walsh
was reported as testifying to the investigating panel that he saw a bright light
at the church gable from his farm half a mile away, and did not learn until
next morning of the apparition taking place at that exact time. When Daniel
Campbell suggested infanticide in the pre-famine era he noted that it was
ascribed to fairy abduction. Perhaps the child was smothered by the mother
but Campbell wrote that others would testify that they heard the child
crying as it was being carried away by the fairies. These witnesses did not
question (or choose to openly question) either the reality of fairy abduction
or the credibility of a mother who thus explained her child's death.[146]

Another instance is found in the stories people in Bekan told of meeting their dead relatives and having others assert that they too had encountered the same people as alive as ever.[147]

Patrick Walsh had no doubt about either the credibility of those who reported the vision at the gable or of the possibility of an apparition. In this as in the other instances, the communally shared assumptions about the believability (implying both good faith and good judgment) of the claimants and the possibility of the event reinforced each other. Had Patrick Walsh judged heavenly visitors to be impossible he might well have questioned either the good faith or the good judgment of the gable witnesses. As far as we know, given the skimpy way in which the testimony was printed, he did neither. I suggest that later claims, in the twentieth century, that many seers were not examined by the panel of priests are further evidence of this process. Such rhetorical techniques of authentication are important in how reality is socially and linguistically constructed, especially in more orally-informed cultural contexts. The use of this technique is just another piece of evidence about the nature of the socio-cultural communicative context within which 'the Knock apparition' made sense.

A third technique commonly found in orally-transmitted stories, such as those recounted by Daniel Campbell or the ones told about MacHale, involves using direct speech attributed to persons featured in the stories. Campbell, for one example, quotes verbatim from a conversation that, even on his own terms, he could not possibly have heard, one between two priests in private. Such techniques make stories more memorable, quite obviously of importance in a societal context dependent on memory for transmitting not only information but understanding and the lessons leading to wisdom. Many of the changes made in the witness testimony between the MacPhilpin versions and those published in the Sexton work involve switches back and forth between direct and indirect reported speech on the part of the witnesses. These changes show that Fr Cavanagh especially, and perhaps other priests on the commission of inquiry as well as journalists such as MacPhilpin and Sexton, were caught between the demands of the orally-based culture that informed the original witnesses' perceptions and reports and the requirements for rigorous investigation and documentation being demanded by the literate people they sought to influence through the mass media. We should not be surprised at what to modern ears sound like inconsistencies and contradictions. Folklore is characterised by multiplicity. Speaking of the central group among the Knock seers, the Beirnes, the distinguished historian of devotion to Mary, Marina Warner wrote that

> The fabric of the evidence the family itself gave [to the investigating panel of priests] is full of holes that can no longer be mended . . . Why did both Margaret Beirne and Mary Beirne think they should each lock the church at different times that night when they were together in the

same house? Why, when most of the family lived in one house, were three separate journeys made by three different members of it to tell others, and almost all at the same time? (Mary fetched Dominick, at 8pm; Catherine Murray, a niece, fetched Margaret 'at around 8 pm'; Margaret fetched their mother, widow Beirne, at about 8.15.) The only conclusion is that in 1879 the examiners, or the reporters, or both, were distracted; our knowledge of the Knock apparitions is thin indeed.[148]

Another possibility is that these 'holes' were built-in, so to speak, normal attributes of the way stories were used in the local interpretive community. According to her published testimony, Mary McLoughlin left the apparition still in progress and went to tell the priest about it. What happened when she reached his house is confused, to say the least. Trying to reconcile the different accounts printed later and ascribed to McLoughlin (at the Commission of Inquiry), and to Fr Cavanagh and to other seers by journalists who interviewed them, White points out that

> The inconsistencies in the statements of the priest and the seers concerning the priest in the night in question are nearly too many to unravel. Each improbability that is exposed and addressed only serves to expose another in its wake, and on and on it goes. If the stories were to be combined, they would produce a jumble of contradiction.[149]

A similar jumble would result if we compiled all the available statements about what the witnesses did or did not say at the gable. Apparently, however, the various claims did not seem incoherent to the seers or Fr Cavanagh, strong evidence of how immersed they were in a social context that emphasised oral communication. As is clear for example in the way Daniel Campbell recorded his memories of pre-famine Knock, stories contained dense details of persons, places and events that served to aid remembrance and had other rhetorical uses. But whether these details were 'factual' was not always relevant in the story-telling context. When Campbell recalled 'a mist in the church' while the priest pronounced a curse on an adulterous couple we should not read it as a weather report. What he was true to was not the precise details of the specific case but the conventional narrative form within which different elements had a recognised rhetorical significance. A gale outside or a strange star would have served just as well as the mist, and be equally 'true'. A similar faithfulness to a form, rather than the specific case at hand, is well documented in the case of the *caoineadh*. The conventional praise of the dead person in the *caoineadh* often included details at odds with the person's life, and stock formulations could be repeated through numerous specific cases. The most famous one of all, *The Lament for Art O'Leary*, incorporated almost verbatim long sections from a *caoineadh* for another man who died many decades earlier. The keeners were true not so much to the particular dead person being mourned but to the tradition that required he be spoken of in a manner known to the performers and expected, even demanded by the audience.[150] (Hence we should not be surprised if the Knock seers were responsive to what they perceived at their audience's expectations.) For those who do not or did not (want to) understand the oral communicative framework such 'jumbled' statements may seem 'thin' as evidence, or be condemned as 'rambling,' 'incoherent', or *ráiméis* (nonsense).[151] What is significant, however, is that the 'thin' evidence was still credible for millions. The published accounts of what happened at the gable of Knock Church provided corroboration for what people already believed, not proof of anything that they did not already accept.

Fr Cavanagh's ideas about miracle cures owed everything to a traditional, orally transmitted one that equated cure with miracle when the outcome was effected by some sacred material, like the mortar from the apparition gable. But such a view would carry no weight with 'modern' thinkers either in medical science or in the wider official church. Investigation of miraculous cures within a rational framework was beyond him. In the commission's work on the question of cures, we find a letter to Fr Cavanagh from an expert he consulted about a question that apparently shattered the bounds of his thinking. A sick pilgrim had gone to Knock in search of a cure and returned home uncured. If that person was cured later, could the case be counted as a (Knock) miracle?[152] But Cavanagh shared the local people's (and probably most early pilgrims') beliefs in the nature of miracle cures. When the sceptical journalist, Andrew Dunlop, asked about the condition of a woman whose cure had been publicised in the newspapers a few weeks earlier, Cavanagh told him that the woman had died. ('She's dead since . . .') While Dunlop trumpeted that admission as evidence undermining the claims of supernatural involvement in the Knock events, the death did not seem to disconcert the priest very much.[153] Among the dozens of surviving letters from grateful pilgrims that told Cavanagh of miraculous recoveries or asked for cement from the apparition gable, is one edged in mourning black. It is from a Tipperary mother who had brought her very sick daughter to Knock. Even though the letter told of the girl's death soon after their return home, the mother gave thanks for the miraculous cure her daughter experienced in Knock, and asked the priest to send some cement for her ailing husband.[154] Quite obviously, the rational journalist and this believing mother had very different assumptions about what was a miracle; equally obviously, Fr Cavanagh's worldview was closer to that of the pious mother than to the sceptical reporter's.

Failure

Understanding the 'first' apparition on August 1879 as a culturally conditioned response to a crisis in clerical authority enables us to more fully explain the failure of the young shrine, after a few busy years, to become a centre of pilgrimage. Different reasons account for the failure on the local and national or international stages. In Knock, there was a failure to provide what would be required to develop as a continuing pilgrimage site, especially sufficient accommodations for pilgrims and a direct railway connection.[155] While sufficient to curtail long-distance pilgrimage, these factors are but symptoms of a more fundamental cause. Had there been a persistent and widespread need felt in the wider Irish society, some person or group very likely would have emerged to successfully champion resources for pilgrims in Knock. The railway had indeed shown itself willing to respond to the demand with special fares and trains for pilgrims. But no successful champions appeared in the Irish lay or clerical community for nearly half a century.

While no archbishop of Tuam endorsed it for the next half century this alone does not explain the failure of the shrine and cult to develop. Many apparitions have attracted huge followings without the approval of local bishops. Since the Second Vatican Council numerous apparitions have attracted supporters almost always without episcopal approbation. In some cases apparitions have triumphed despite the express disapproval and opposition of the local bishop, the case of Medjugorje in the 1980s being a good example. While Bishop Pavao Zanic was hostile and dismissive, his influence was either negated or his views simply ignored. Medjugorje was championed by others both inside and outside the official ecclesiastical bureaucracy, especially by local Franciscan priests and another Yugoslavian archbishop, who had their own reasons for promoting the devotion and pilgrimage. But such apparition entrepreneurs could be successful only because there were responsive people, willing and perhaps even waiting to follow someone who would proclaim the continued relevance of the Virgin Mary and her involvement in the world. In the Medjugorje case, the followers numbered in the tens of millions. (Many traditionalist Catholics felt the Virgin had been downgraded by the Second Vatican Council.)[156] What is significant by contrast in the Knock case was the absence of a successful champion, testimony to its failure to speak to a continuing issue. Despite Fr Cavanagh's energetic promotion and Canon Bourke's media savvy, and the involvement of nationalist journalists like Sexton, Sullivan and MacPhilpin in the early years, and a large potential following in the Irish diaspora, it was not until a half century later that devotion and pilgrimage was revived at Knock. Then the key lay promoters were not locals but a middle-class couple transplanted from Dublin who were enthralled with Lourdes and almost abjectly deferential to clerics, and the key issue was not clerical authority but global battle against communism and 'modern' threats to sexual purity.[157]

A crisis, almost by definition, does not last indefinitely. In Knock the crisis of clerical authority dissipated when many priests, including Fr Cavanagh, moved to support the tenants, and when MacEvilly took over uncontested administration of the diocese on MacHale's death in 1881.

There was no guarantee that Fr Cavanagh would come to support the land agitators. He could have continued his opposition, or stayed silent, or acted as some other priests did. In January 1880, for example, Fr P. Sheridan attempted to break up a meeting to organise a branch of the Land League at Mayo Abbey in his parish. He called on those present to leave, saying he would not allow any man to interfere with his parish, but the people in attendance responded by cheering for Parnell and Davitt, cheers they repeated later outside the priest's house.[158]

The lack of a direct train connection and absence of accommodations for pilgrims cannot account for the decline in numbers of pilgrims from the immediate vicinity. Locally, a major reason for the failure of the shrine to thrive is that the response to the miracle-working material was essentially self-limiting because the supply of cement/mortar and clay was finite: it would and did run out. Why return for a second or later visit when the miracle working substance was no longer available there?

In the case of Lourdes, willing and able champions of national pilgrimage were available in the wider French society. Huge pilgrimages, as the defining feature of the Lourdes devotion, emerged only after the events of 1870–71. The national humiliation of quick defeat for France in the war with Prussia was followed by the Paris Commune, an uprising in which working-class artisans seized power, massacred priests and executed the Archbishop of Paris. The Prussians released thousands of prisoners of war to the command of a French general to help suppress the Commune, which the defeated army did at the cost of 25,000 lives. Interpreting these traumatic events as divine chastisement of France, for many reasons priests like the Assumptionists and others were motivated to organise and promote pilgrimage to Lourdes, as part of a national atonement for what they saw as their country's abandonment and betrayal of the church and especially of the pope, and millions of their countrymen listened to their message.[159] The First National Pilgrimage to Lourdes was in 1873. No comparable set of influences operated in Ireland. The clergy and most of the laity were proud of the country's loyalty to the true faith of Catholicism and the pope. Rather than withdrawing troops from Italy as France did to fight Prussia, Ireland had sent volunteers to defend the pope, whose earlier flights from Rome were equated with the experience of fugitive priests during the Penal Laws in Ireland.[160] There was in Ireland no significant rationalist view of the universe that in both France and Spain provoked the media promotion of what earlier might have been 'rather local circumscribed miracles' and led to the development of long-distance pilgrimage by train.[161] In other words, in Ireland there was no widespread persisting need felt to which the Knock apparition meaningfully spoke as Lourdes spoke to devout Catholics in France, and elsewhere where secularism was making headway. While Knock languished, the farmers in the Irish stem family system felt clearly the need for family unity under the authority of the family head, and control of sexuality as well as of land, for as long as the stem system prevailed, which in most areas of the country was for generations and in many areas for well over a century. This system made the people receptive to a model of Mary that was submissive, chaste and silent.

11

Conclusion

Once when a band of !Kung Bushmen had performed their rain rituals, a small cloud appeared on the horizon, grew and darkened. Then rain fell. But the anthropologists who asked if the Bushmen reckoned the rite had produced the rain were laughed out of court. How naïve can we get about the beliefs of others?[1]

We make a mistake if we assume that others take their professed religious beliefs only literally. If we laugh with derision at people who claim to have seen fairies or heavenly beings it is not because they are stupid but because we are closed-minded. The Ohio bishop who noted getting a letter from a woman requesting his help in restoring her nephew to life finished his sentence with an exclamation mark. We can speculate whether that expressed his incredulity or his exasperation, but at every mass he would have professed the Apostles or Nicene Creed with its list of fundamental canonical beliefs, including faith in the 'Resurrection of the Dead'! Neither priests nor peasants necessarily understand their religious stories literally.

The Knock apparition story must first be seen in the context of other stories of faith I have examined in this work. Whether they were about fairies, or about the powers of priests, or about Archbishop MacHale resurrecting a House of Commons guard, or about the *bean feasa/Cailleach*, the stories were told in particular contexts to particular audiences who were capable of interpreting them in complex ways. Though told as if they were straightforward descriptions, such stories had an important didactic role; they were not neutral reports but stories with a message. When the community accepted that other worlds were close at hand, what might in outsiders' eyes be seen as 'natural' or 'obvious' could easily be set within a meaning structure that related the different worlds, and used in narratives that were dramatically engaging and memorable for people who relied on orally transmitted wisdom. Well after the apparition in Knock, a local teacher in Aghamore recognised the persistence of this way of thinking. With his keen interest in history, John J. Jordan saw in the landscape archaeological evidence of ancient pathways across bogs in the area and one narrow road in particular connecting two churches. Some time after World War II, however, he wrote,

No old Carrowneden [a local townland] man would admit that it was a road. Here would be his explanation of it: 'The people of this district misbehaved themselves in some way, and St Patrick up in Heaven was so angry with them that St Crónain's church left its site, and tore a way for itself in the ground, and never stopped 'til it landed where the graveyard now is in Aghamore. The people heard the mighty noise, and next morning, their church was gone. The track it made remains in places to this day.' It would be useless to point out to him that the foundation of the church is still there at Carrowneden, and that the church ruins at Aghamore village are much bigger than Kilcronain. He heard it from his grandfather, and that is the last word.[2]

Notice that the communal validation of this story was buttressed by evidence of the noise the church made as it abandoned its old site.

It has been suggested that episodes like the burning of Bridget Cleary occurred when people confused the literal and metaphorical meanings of traditional cultural elements such as belief in fairy changelings. Cleary's husband did not know half his culture (See page 69 above). The Ohio woman who wrote to the bishop asking him to raise her dead nephew very likely was unfamiliar with all the understandings available in the depths of popular Irish Catholic culture. There is something similar at work in episodes like Knock. I do not have the evidence to evaluate it but I want to point to a suggestive possibility that perhaps can be evaluated by ethnographic studies at other apparition sites. In his study of stories about the wise-woman healer, Gearóid Ó Crualaoich noted that 'in the way that these traditional oral narratives operated in the communities where they were given renewed expression and transmission, there was an ambiguous "operational" belief in their truth. They themselves were told as if they were true.'[3] But as we have seen, insiders were perfectly capable of holding a range of attitudes towards the literal truth of such narratives, including accepting a stance of persistent uncertainty. As we noted, the sceptic was always to be found. Stories often played on the differences between the literal and metaphorical meanings of what was said, for example, MacHale's comment to the process-server, *'rath na raithne ort'*, or the narrator's statement about the Commons Guard, *'thit sé héin os a gcíonn'* (pp. 83–6 above).

In Knock and nearby Bekan various types of visions are documented after as well as before the famous apparition. Stories about such visions would usually be understood within the local interpretive community in some non-literal sense or at least be amenable to a range of interpretations ranging from the literal to various types of figurative or metaphorical ones. In 1937 an eighty-three-year-old Knock man told the Second Commission of Inquiry into the apparition that 'some believed it and others were in a way they couldn't be sure',[4] capturing the variations in belief in the literal truth of the story and the acceptance of uncertainty. Perhaps in Knock in 1879, when others (especially their social betters) were attuned to the possibilities of bodily visits by heavenly beings, this figurative language was interpreted literally. Here we would have a version or rather a reversal of the usual condescension of the elites toward the backward peasants but with the added complication of the endorsement by apparition entrepreneurs of the (alleged) simple faith of the poor. Especially if it suited the underdogs to go along with what those social betters would suggest, as is the case of the Knock lay seers vis-à-vis Fr Cavanagh, we could have a mechanism for the generation of literal apparition stories. It is clear that the Knock case does not fit what anthropologist, Michael Allen, claimed was a common pattern of children's imaginative worlds giving rise to such stories when what one or more children imagine is corroborated by other people with credibility in the local community and in the wider societal context and culture.[5]

Some specific aspects or features of the apparition can plausibly be seen as connected in some way to the social context but since evidence to definitively prove or disprove these implied linkages or even to describe them adequately cannot be provided, my discussion of them will be brief. It is tempting to suggest that the appearance of the vision on the outside gable of a chapel symbolised the movement of Catholic practice from the outdoor sites of earlier days to the more modern church-centred ritual. The apparition was neither in the church nor away from it and the story included elements redolent of natural settings (such as the rain) as well as the sacred building itself. But this interpretation would have to be taken on faith (in the devotional revolution paradigm), and not based on evidence of local perceptions. For the early local pilgrims, the building was important largely as a deposit of miracle-working material, and their devotion was outside, centred on the apparition gable and usually included circuits of the building as if it were a holy well or other outdoor site. The building was sacred not because there the priest offered mass or there the consecrated Host was kept, as in the Tridentine discipline, but because the Virgin visited there, bypassing the clergy and imbuing the mortar with miraculous power. For sceptics who suggested that the whole affair was the result of the seers witnessing slides of statues projected by a magic lantern, the building merely presented a convenient surface onto which some prankster or conspirator projected the images.

Other writers have suggested that the silence of the apparition figures made sense in that they could choose neither Irish nor English and communicate with all the seers. Any language they might have used would predictably have left some people unhappy.[6] However, that the children among the seers were being schooled through the medium of the English language does not mean that they could not speak or understand Irish. As late as 1904, a school inspector in Knock noted that the pupils spoke Irish passably well even though they were taught through English.[7] All the seers in Knock would have understood Irish. Given MacHale's well known championing of the Irish language, I suggest that had the Virgin communicated in Gaelic, her words would have undercut the message communicated in symbols that denounced him. Her Gaelic would also fly in the face of the Catholic authorities' pushing of English nationwide. Silence in Knock was significant for institutional politics rather than cross-generational understanding.[8]

Given that the months of largest crowds of pilgrims at Knock from January 1880 to the first anniversary in August was also a time of most desperate hunger locally,[9] and also given later promoters' claims that the heavenly beings came to comfort a people in dire distress, we might expect to see some connection between the hunger and Knock devotion. Yet there is little evidence of any concerted appeal being made to the Blessed Virgin or any type of group resort to Knock in dealing with the famine. I have found no suggestion that people went there to seek supernatural help in getting food, though the absence of such evidence does not prove that this did not occur. The early promoters were keen to downplay the difficulties of travel to Knock and alluding to food shortage was far from their agenda. Indeed one went out of his way to emphasise the fine food he ate in Knock.[10] One insider reference in Knock to famine at the time was in the acknowledgement of hunger among his hearers by a speaker at a land demonstration in a field adjacent to the apparition church in mid-February 1880.[11] Hungry people in the area however did take other kinds of direct collective action. On January 31, the *Daily News* reported

> About 3 o'clock this evening large bodies of excited peasantry came thronging into Claremorris. When about 600 had collected they proceeded in procession to the Relief-Committee-rooms, and demanded relief as their families were starving. They also demanded the expulsion of two or three members of the committee. Receiving a promise of both demands being complied with, they left and paraded several streets.

The same London newspaper on 16 February reported that a crowd of 4,000 peasants determined to have 'blood or bread' was with difficulty dissuaded from again marching into Claremorris, while police guarded depots in the area. Their actions suggest that the people, rather than seeing prayer or pilgrimage at Knock as the way to address their problems saw demonstration marches to Claremorris as appropriate and perhaps efficacious. This is what we would expect from people who saw the Virgin appearances as criticism of those clerics who counselled resignation and restraint. The huge crowds that attended land meetings or other events in the Land War during this period suggest the same thing.

Near the end of the nineteenth century, William Butler Yeats wrote:

> All over Ireland there are prophecies of the coming rout of the enemies of Ireland, in a certain Valley of the Black Pig, and these prophecies are, no doubt, as they were in the Fenian days, a political force.[12]

The prophecy varied in details but there are reasons to ask if it had particular relevance in Mayo and especially for some of the Knock seers. The war

would be between true religion and heresy, which in the popular understanding was between Catholicism and Protestantism. The Valley of the
Black Pig was usually understood to be a ditch marking the boundary of
Ulster. Importantly, one version of the prophecy foretold that 'only those
who have escaped across the Shannon into Connaught will be saved'.[13]
From the late eighteenth century several waves of Catholic refugees from
sectarian violence in Ulster settled in Mayo, where their descendants could
later be distinguished by their surnames. Several names of Ulster origin
figure in the Knock story, including among the seers. Daniel Campbell tells
us his grandfather and father came from Armagh and his grandmother from
Fermanagh. The witness Judy Campbell, or more likely her father, was
Daniel's cousin. Another Ulster name among the seers was Curry. In the sectarian struggle that Daniel Campbell recalled in Knock decades earlier, the
proselytising Flatleys were defeated by the combined Beirne and Corry, or
Curry, factions.

Not only did the Beirnes and Currys cooperate in supporting the priest in
the pre-famine conflict, but their families likely were closely connected later,
including by inter-marriage. The young witness John Curry, baptised in
January 1874, was the son of Martin Curry and Mary Ann Beirne. He was
living with another witness, his mother's brother Dominick Beirne, Sr, at the
time of the apparition. The sixteen-year old seer, Patrick Beirne, later married
Rose Curry.[14] Two others seers may also have had Northern connections. It
was speculated later that John Durkan, whose testimony was reduced to a
single sentence, was perhaps 'from the North'.[15] Finally, two early promoters
named the priest's housekeeper, whose name is elsewhere given as Mary
McLoughlin, 'M'Laughlin', the way the name was usually spelled in counties
Derry and Donegal.[16] Apparently neither Durkan nor McLoughlin/M'Laughlin
had kin ties in the Knock area, and little was remembered of them there afterwards.[17] The seers with Northern names, however, were far from the most
central ones. Much more important were the Beirnes, and far more important
for them was their own family and household dynamics at the time, even if
they were closely tied to the Currys originally from Ulster. Despite the plausible relevance of this specific prophecy for at least some seers I have no
evidence that the apparition in Knock was interpreted locally in this way.
That could at least in part be a result of the very careful 'clerical' way in which
it was promoted in the newspapers.

Some, perhaps many, pilgrims did see the apparition as vindicating
Catholicism over Protestantism. The Tipperary mother who wrote to Fr
Cavanagh relating the miracle her daughter experienced in Knock, though
the girl died soon after their return home, emphasised that two Protestant
neighbours were impressed by the miracle. There was some sense of
Catholic triumph in overcoming the powers of ascendancy Protestants, but
this was not especially linked to the apparition. Locally, this reversal of
fortune was most visible in the symbolism of the Sisters of Mercy coming to
Claremorris and opening schools at the beginning of 1877; the building

purchased for their use as a convent had once been the home of none other than the infamous Denis 'The Hangman' Browne. Possibly one reason that Land League leaders did not mention the apparition in any speech that has survived is that they were intent on building a non-sectarian tenant movement. In Claremorris in July 1879 and at various other meetings they resisted priests' attempts to adopt resolutions on purely Catholic issues. Trumpeting an appearance of such a Catholic icon as the Blessed Virgin would have undercut their non-sectarian thrust. The Land War targeted Catholic as well as Protestant landlords, and in the Knock area one of the most unpopular was Walter Bourke. It was at Walter's house that two bishops of adjacent dioceses stayed overnight when they visited Knock early in October 1879. Walter was shot dead in County Galway in 1882, and it appears the assassination was at least in part planned in the local area.[18]

I have argued that the apparition was in response to a crisis in clerical authority, a crisis in which Knock was at the epicentre. Threats to constituted authority in realms ranging from the challenges to the landlords to the family situation of the Beirnes exacerbated and compounded this crisis. The salience of family authority was heightened for the Beirnes but it was present for almost all families in the time and place where the stem family system was in the process of being moulded from the ashes of rundale.[19] As the land tenure system was dramatically shifted toward a system of impartible inheritance by one heir to each family farm, most young men were denied access to land and thereby condemned to lifelong singlehood or emigration. These constituted a growing 'pool of potential activists'[20] who could be recruited by agitators when emigration was blocked by the American slump of 1873–79 and mobilised by the Land League when the sources of their cash income, especially migratory farm work in Britain, dried up in 1879.[21] There is evidence that the Fenian movement used the land meetings in 1879 Mayo to recruit such young men to their ranks.[22]

Important both for the Land War and the Knock apparition is that compared to their counterparts elsewhere in rural Ireland, farmers' sons in places like Knock differed in at least two significant ways. First, their common necessity of seasonally migrating to England is evidence of lesser weight of their father's power since any land he could bequeath was still inadequate to support a family. Moreover, as a contemporary noted, 'having lived the gipsy life during the summer [in England], sleeping in barns and outhouses, and far from their chapels, they no longer feel for [their priest] the reverent awe with which they knelt to him in childhood'.[23] Second, they were at most a few decades past rundale and had some recollection of the access to land that all sons then enjoyed. Thus the power of neither father nor priest was on as secure a foundation as in most other areas of the country. Such a background created a generation less submissive to authority figures and especially attuned to questions of their legitimacy. It is more than a coincidence that such a revolutionary movement as the Land War had its origin in the very same area. Many of the factors that other researchers have identified as important causes were found earlier elsewhere. Samuel Clark, for example, highlighted the development of a class of town-based activists whose economic interests were intimately intertwined with the wellbeing of the rural tenant farmers and who formed common cause with them in challenging the landlords. But such a town-based stratum had developed earlier in other parts of the country without leading to anything similar to the Land War. How many young men like Dominick Beirne, Jr., were induced to challenge the political and economic status quo either as Fenians or in the Land War? How many looked to heavenly signs to validate the authorities they accepted but others found problematic?

One group among whom we might expect Knock to find special resonance was the Irish abroad. After all, these would likely see an 'Irish' apparition as opposed to a local Knock one as relevant for them. Indeed MacPhilpin quoted a correspondent 'from the south of London' that, given that she appeared in other countries, 'it was only congruous that our Blessed Lady should manifest her presence in some remarkable way to her devout and devoted people in Ireland'. MacPhilpin ascribed the 'Irish Lourdes' label to this exile.[24] The solidarity of Irish-Americans was challenged in the early 1880s by a long list of issues, highlighting their need for some unifying focus which Knock promised to provide.[25] The great potential following for Knock is indirectly indicated by the many publications directed toward Irish Americans. Two different New York City publishers early on brought out editions of MacPhilpin's 1880 book, and the Nun of Kenmare devoted a whole chapter in her 1882 book to connecting the Knock Virgin to St Patrick, the Irish national saint.[26] (She does not explain why the 'bishop' figure in the vision was not seen as St Patrick whose statues did have a mitre, but rather publicised as St John the Evangelist. Of course this version was publicised two years earlier, long before Cusack moved to Knock.)

Cusack's book and one of the New York editions of MacPhilpin were brought out again by P. J. Kenedy in a single volume in 1904. Of three archbishops who patronised Knock in the early years, two were from Australia and one from Canada, all part of the Irish diaspora. Fr Edward Murphy, SJ promoted Knock as a focus for 'the sea divided Gael'.[27] So intent was Archbishop John Lynch of Toronto on getting a 'national' shrine for Ireland that he was in the country at the very time of the Knock apparition seeking to promote Lough Derg as such a shrine. Not surprisingly, Lynch was a strong promoter of Knock. In August 1882 he visited the area and wrote advocating the case to other Canadian bishops and arranged to have his letter published in the *Freeman's Journal* in Dublin. He also sent one of his priests to Knock with a banner.[28] Paradoxically, Lynch's support was likely counterproductive in getting bishops in Ireland to look favourably on the apparition. Archbishop MacEvilly saw him as a friend and admirer of the dead MacHale, and anything or anybody associated with MacHale was suspect in his eyes, and so Lynch's advocacy of Knock fell on the deaf ears of MacEvilly.[29]

The continued yearning of Irish-Americans for a shrine of their own is indicated by an episode half a century later. After the stock market collapsed in October 1929 news spread that miracles were happening at the grave of Fr Patrick Power in a cemetery outside Boston. Power had died sixty years earlier shortly after he was ordained, but now clay from his grave was generating cures like the mortar from Knock. Multitudes of pilgrims, mostly Irish-Americans, thronged to the scene; estimates range from 400,000 to 1,500,000 in just the month of November 1929.[30] Their loss of the Irish language in the diaspora apparently did not turn these people to only the orthodox practice of Catholicism.

Knock and the Devotional Revolution Thesis

Some researchers have suggested that the Knock apparition was related to the devotional revolution but they have not articulated very precisely the connections they imply. Larkin's influential 1972 article in the *American Historical Review* was accompanied by an illustration of the apparition scene.[31] Hoppen referred to Knock as a totally new centre of devotion of the most modern kind.[32] Donnelly described many devotional changes that he held facilitated the spread of Marian devotion at the shrine after the apparition but he did not seek to explain the occurrence of the initial apparition itself.[33] Patrick Nold claimed that 'the Devotional Revolution allowed Knock to prosper, but Knock did not originate out of the Devotional Revolution',[34] while John White argued almost the direct opposite. 'The Knock apparitions, the pilgrimage, and belief that Knock cement had miraculous powers to heal did not happen in spite of the Devotional Revolution; they happened because of that revolution', and at the same time the failure of the shrine afterwards was also due to the success of that very same revolution.[35] Sean Connolly suggested that the apparition could be seen as 'reflecting a hunger among sections of the laity for a certainty and immediacy that was being left behind by recent changes in official religious culture . . . the devotional revolution,' but immediately indicated his dissatisfaction with this view, preferring instead to see in Knock evidence of long-term persistent belief in direct supernatural irruptions, manifested also in the Blessed Straws episode in the 1830s and later apparitions in the 1980s. He does not explain why the irruptions were so punctuated.[36] A major reason for the imprecision and disagreement among researchers is a failure to disaggregate what is meant by the term.[37] None of these researchers suggest answers to such fundamental questions as 'why Knock rather than someplace else?' and 'why 1879?' We need especially to ask if the devotional revolution paradigm is the most appropriate context for understanding insiders' experiences. These various researchers all use Larkin's terminology when other explanatory frameworks were far more important for Knock people.

The Knock apparition points to serious limitations at the heart of the devotional revolution paradigm. First, and contrary to analyses that credit a progressively more united episcopal body for the changes identified as the revolution, the case of the Land War highlights the effects of grassroots pressures for changes. It would be difficult to imagine a more divided hierarchy on any issue. Early on, most bishops held aloof or were hostile toward the tenants' movement but over time some of them changed their stances. By October 1879, five bishops were known to be supportive of the agitation, five sympathetic, nine were neutral and nine opposed.[38] In Tuam, while MacHale and MacEvilly were both hostile, they detested each other and never even spoke to each other. The supportive bishops included those in Achonry and Clonfert, two adjacent dioceses to Tuam.[39] Rather than implementing an agreed policy of the hierarchy, clearly individual bishops were reacting in diverse ways to pressures from below. Ideas about the inexorable advance of the devotional revolution are simply inadequate to capture the complexity of what was happening.[40]

Before and during the Land War locals steeped in the traditional local religion deployed a thoroughgoing critique of priestly misbehaviour, which they had articulated by drawing on very traditional attitudes, standards, and arguments. The significance of James Daly and others like him for understanding religious change especially in places like the post-famine west of Ireland is that the improved discipline of the priests was imposed not just 'from above' by better seminary training and episcopal control (as in the devotional revolution paradigm) but also 'from below'. Lay activists like Daly were economically independent and educated enough to challenge the priests on their proper behaviour, while at the same time being intimately familiar with both the economic plight of the poor and their traditional religious worldview that included a critique of priests' avarice or other failure to meet their responsibilities. Daly had been educated by the Christian Brothers but that did not cut him off from the common people; rather, he had a 'masterly command' of the details of the land system in practice, so much so that neither hostile landlords nor government commissions even challenged most of the evidence he provided about exorbitant rents, and were able to shake it in only a handful of cases.[41] And as a journalist and newspaper proprietor Daly had a vehicle through which to address the increasingly literate lay public. But his criticism of priestly misbehaviour was built on the traditional understanding of the priest's role and responsibility. In Knock as elsewhere, Catholic clerics had a responsibility to support and guide the people, especially in confrontations with oppressive government or exploiting landlords or even local Catholics who presumed they deserved preferential treatment. It was because he so visibly had done this for so long that MacHale was regarded as saintly. It was because the priests in Knock and elsewhere failed to meet this responsibility that the 'strike' against them occurred in 1842–43 that Daniel Campbell recalled. Just a few months before the Knock apparition, a 'monster indignation meeting' had been held in Knock to protest Fr Cavanagh's violation of the expectations of 'priests and people together'. We also need to recognise that popular understandings of *cumhacht an tsagairt*, the priest's power, were built not primarily on the Tridentine model of priest as celebrant of the Eucharist but on the popular local view of priest as magician, as recorded for example by Daniel Campbell.

The Knock evidence also undermines the claim that orthodox Catholicism appealed to Irish people who were suffering an identity crisis with the decline of the Irish language. Officially-endorsed Catholicism became in this view the functional equivalent of the lost language. The equation of Catholic with Irish and Protestant with foreign was already made long before the language change. The use of the terms *Gael* and *Gall* to refer in the Gaelic language to the two groups was widespread, and was found in pre-famine Knock (as Daniel Campbell's memoir shows) as well as in much of the folklore from the region in general. Thus MacHale had been seen as confronting and overcoming the *Easbog Gallda*. Catholicism, per se, might well be a component of Irishness for many, but this is equally true pre- and post-devotional revolution.

While it undercuts central features of the devotional revolution paradigm, the evidence in this book also forces reconsideration of some aspects of other approaches and of my own earlier work. Even later when it appeared that the Catholic Church held a 'moral monopoly' in Ireland[42] James Scott's work on domination and resistance reminds us not to take surface appearances at face value. Delay has provided lots of supportive evidence from letters that lay people wrote to bishops in the post-famine decades.[43]

In earlier articles I argued that people were selective in what teachings they accepted from the orthodox menu. But the menu metaphor is too limited: 'take it' or 'leave it' were not the only options for any particular item. There always were different religious understandings available including traditional local ones that were not endorsed or promoted, but perhaps permitted or tolerated by the church authorities, and elements from a range of understandings could be combined and intermingled. We thus need to address not only what people selected from the options available to them, but how they adapted it while doing so. In their syncretism people could make very creative use of the tools at hand. The 1832 'Blessed Straws' chain-prayer episode provides perhaps the clearest evidence for this process. In most of the country, straws, turf or other material was distributed to ward off cholera. Whatever the local explanation and rationale given at the start of the episode, it is clear that the ritual was put to different uses in different places and we can explain these different uses by reference to the concerns of the people in those specific places. In Knock, the cholera-fighting interpretation was enacted in a manner that constructed Bishop MacHale as the author of the community-saving ritual, but in Bishop Doyle's diocese the same tools were put to a very different use, to counter his anathemas and protect the community from the strongest episcopal cursing. A respectable Catholic merchant in Kilkenny saw the affair as evidence of the credulity of his poor co-religionists which would make them a laughingstock among Protestants. Still others said that Protestant ministers had started the whole episode to have revenge for the non-collection of tithes, while some Protestants saw the distribution as subversion, a possible prelude to Catholic attacks on the Protestant population.[44] Beyond just picking and choosing among cultural items available, people pick them for their own particular purposes and they are quite capable of creatively putting the tools available to diverse uses. One key reason they adopt new ways is that they can adapt them. Though it was implied in studies that I cited, I failed to clearly emphasise this important point in my earlier work.

I have argued that the apparition scene at Knock was likely influenced by some seers' recall (probably unconscious in my view) of the scene depicted in the new stained glass window in Ballyhaunis. However, in drawing from that inspiration the seers endowed the Virgin with a crown that she did not wear in the original, incontrovertibly constituting her as a figure of authority. A similar creativity and openness to new forms through reworking the old can be found in most areas of ritual. In Knock and else-where, station-masses continue in the twenty-first century.[45] Even the most 'traditional' or 'local' manifestation of what the official church might regard as superstitions could reappear in new guises. The traditional story, 'The Friars of Urlaur' that Douglas Hyde collected around the turn of the twen-tieth century was later turned into a one-act play called 'The Piper of Tavran' by Bernard Duffy, first performed at the Abbey Theatre on 5 November 1921. In the twenty-first century Hyde's version of the story was rewritten as a play for a local Mayo pattern by John Caulfield, apparently stimulated by a 2002 reprint of the story in the local newspaper.[46] Of course the journey from folklore to stage play to tourist attraction/business venture changed the meaning of the story, but in each reworking there is still recognisable continuity.

Neither the Larkin thesis nor my own work pays much attention to Catholicism elsewhere, never mind to other religious traditions. The term devotional revolution wrongly suggests that the myriad changes it described were necessarily closely connected. Seeing the changes as Romanisation of the Irish church is too simple. 'Rome' is taken as a given while the metaphor of increasing scale imposes too simplistic a social determinism; it lumps together disparate social transformations, and imposes too neat an evolu-tionary bias on what did occur or what was brought about.[47] The issue becomes central when we ask how apparitions were regarded by the official church. But what precisely was 'the official church'? It is well recognised that Rome's sympathy for apparitions waxed and waned over the centuries and between the reigns of different popes.[48]

When we see evidence of the influence say of Lourdes in Ireland, should that be interpreted as 'modernisation' or 'Romanisation'? Certainly there was diffusion from the continent but what came through these channels was not necessarily orthodox. Certainly, Rome did not require acceptance of the authenticity of Bernadette's visions. What diffused was often quite different from the original, transformed by the recipients at every step.

Bernadette's experience in Lourdes, when validated by credible people within the local community and interpreted within a centuries-long tradition of such visions, led to a conviction that a chapel/shrine should be constructed in honour of the Virgin. Locals in Lourdes early on competed with each other to so honour Mary, the local quarrymen, for example, donating their labour.[49] But on a bigger stage, because of the polarisation of French society along monarchist/republican lines, Lourdes became one focus in the nationwide political struggle.

In Knock, while its promoters and publicists were much influenced by the Lourdes case, both the local arena and the larger national context were very different. Locally, rather than build a new church, as we have seen, early pilgrims threatened to dismantle the existing one in their scrambling to get miracle-working cement and mortar. When the Nun of Kenmare tried to build a convent in Knock in 1882–83, one major difficulty she ran into was that her general contractor found it very difficult to hire workers because of the exorbitant rent they would have to pay for accommodation in the area.[50] Presumably these differences reflected different local understandings of the significance of the Virgin's visits, but beyond the local, even clerical promoters of Marianism did not send a consistent message. The articles appearing at the time in the important weekly, *Ave Maria*, contained many built-in contradictions, some of which were the result of resistance from the readership and some the unintended consequences of applying ideas to new circumstances, evidence that 'elites can be factionalised and even the "centre" of an authoritative institution can be a space for ideological interpretation, negotiation, and variation'.[51] If this was the case for one explicitly Marianist devotional publication with the same priest editor over these years, what greater range of interpretation and emphasis was to be found in the totality of 'official' offerings? '[Orthodox religion] did not enforce a uniform metanarrative to which regional folk [religious] narratives were subjugated, but instead provided a kind of porous metanarrative, which facilitated a patchwork of variegated micronarratives'.[52] We need to pay more attention to these micronarratives which means researchers need to concentrate more on local studies.

Like the devotional revolution thesis on the history of Catholicism, too much history of secular developments in Ireland has been written 'from the centre'. Even people in the central Land League headquarters in Dublin failed to understand things from the perspectives of local tenants in the poor west. Gerard Moran argued that this failure was a major reason James Daly became disillusioned with the Land League and withdrew his support.[53] How figures such as Daniel O'Connell and Archbishop MacHale were seen locally was often quite different from their national reputation. By investigating local understandings in religion, politics, agitation or other areas, we are also penetrating to the reasons why supra-local movements or institutions had the impacts they did. The study of religion would benefit from a focus on different local areas in Ireland similar to the study, for example, of diverse local realities in the later revolutionary era in the years just before and after 1916.[54]

In France in the nineteenth century demand in the wider society led to the promotion by the mass media of numbers of visions, including Lourdes, that earlier might have been 'rather circumscribed local miracles' and to long distance pilgrimages fed by railways. Something similar happened later in Spain where religious devotion as in France challenged a rationalist view of the universe. As William Christian noted, these were not medieval reactions to the modern world but part and parcel of modernity.[55] Knock too was to enjoy media publicity, commercialisation and, early on, crowds of pilgrims coming by railway. It is true that there was a failure to provide amenities for pilgrims in Knock, especially accommodations. But there was also no sustained and compelling demand for what Knock had to offer, given that in the wider Irish society few rationalists were to be found, and there was nothing similar to the trauma for France of humiliating defeat in the war with Prussia in 1870–71. Neither was there any attempt by the government to suppress the devotion, unlike the contemporary case of Marpingen in Germany.[56] In the metaphor I used earlier, the Knock apparition and the Lourdes apparition were both locally rooted, but the ground in which Lourdes was planted was much more congenial to continued spreading in France than late nineteenth-century Ireland was for Knock.

In this work I have attempted to understand the local community and culture in Knock from the inside, to discover the meaning of the apparition story the seers told. These people were steeped in a local Catholicism that I delineated as clearly as possible. However, the publicised accounts of the apparition were passed through many filters before they became what they were later, the only sources for what was 'known', accepted and remembered, about the episode.

While precipitated by a crisis in clerical authority, the apparition was publicised in a very different fashion. The most important journalist-promoter, Thomas Sexton, working hand-in-hand with Fr Cavanagh, did not even understand Irish, never mind begin to penetrate the local religious understandings expressed in that language. The other key journalist-promoter, John MacPhilpin, similarly cooperating with Canon Bourke, also did not explore the traditional local understandings transmitted through the Irish language.[57] The local priests, Frs Cavanagh and Bourke, successfully monopolised presentation of the apparition case in the wider media. Practically all the early reporters relied on the cooperation of these priests and interviewed persons they selected. Even the sceptical Andrew Dunlop wrote about what he saw and what Fr Cavanagh told him. The priests set the agenda, a very important dimension of power.[58] What was left out of the press reports, and which even sceptical reporters such as Dunlop were incapable of discovering given their ignorance of the language, was the traditional idiom of Virgin appearances as commentary on the role of priests. What the promoters certainly were aware of, but nevertheless did not mention, were the overt challenges to the priests around the time of the apparition. They did not mention, for example, the demonstration against Fr Cavanagh in June, or the damaging of Fr Bourke's crops and fences or the way he had been vilified in the pages of the Connaught Telegraph in June and July. 'Respectable' Catholics in the rest of the country very likely also were reluctant to be reminded of such 'superstitions' on the part of their co-religionists, just as the 'respectable' people in Tipperary denied any knowledge of fairylore in the aftermath of the burning of Bridget Cleary a decade and a half later.

Knock was modern in that it used modern technology. Early pilgrims (though likely only a small minority of them) came by train, and the apparition was reported in newspapers, commercialised, and photographed. What was most distinctly modern in the Irish sense, however, was the alliance between the priests and politicians such a Sexton, and journalists such as MacPhilpin, in presenting the case to the wider public.

Notes and References

ABBREVIATIONS

ACSJP   Archives of the Congregation of St Joseph of Peace
ARCAT   Archives of the Roman Catholic Archdiocese of Toronto
CM   Campbell Memoir
CT   *Connaught Telegraph*
NFC   National Folklore Collection, followed by Volume and Page Number
NFCS   National Folklore Collection, Schools, followed by Volume and Page Number
UNDA   University of Notre Dame Archives

1 PREFACE

1   Ruth Harris, *Lourdes: Body and Spirit in the Secular Age* (New York: Viking, 1999); David Blackbourn, *Marpingen: Apparitions of the Virgin Mary in Bismarckian Germany* (Oxford: Clarendon Press, 1993); Cheryl Porte, *Pontmain, Prophecy and Protest: A Cultural-Historical Study of a Nineteenth-Century Vision* (New York: Peter Lang, 2005).

2   Emmet Larkin, 'The Devotional Revolution in Ireland, 1850–1875', *American Historical Review* 77 (1972), pp. 625–52; David Miller, 'Irish Catholicism and the Great Famine', *Journal of Social History*, 9 (1975), pp. 81–98.

3   Eugene Hynes, 'The Great Hunger and Irish Catholicism', *Societas*, 8 (1978), pp. 137–155.

4   Eugene Hynes, 'Nineteenth-Century Irish Catholicism, Farmers' Ideology, and National Religion: Explorations in Cultural Explanation', in *Sociological Studies in Roman Catholicism: Historical and Contemporary Perspectives*, ed. Roger O'Toole (Lewiston, NY: Edwin Mellen Press, 1989), pp. 45–70.

5   Clifford Geertz, *The Interpretation of Cultures: Selected Essays* (New York: Basic, 1973).

6   James C. Scott, *Domination and the Arts of Resistance: Hidden Transcripts* (New Haven: Yale University Press, 1990).

7   Erving Goffman, *Frame Analysis: An Essay on the Organization of Experience* (New York: Harper and Row, 1974), p. 1.

8   Marvin Harris, 'Cultural Materialism is Alive and Well and Won't Go Away Until Something Better Comes Along', in *Assessing Cultural Anthropology*, ed. R. Borofsky (New York: McGraw-Hill, 1994), pp. 71–2.

9   Paolo Apolito, *The Internet and the Madonna: Religious Visionary Experiences on the Web*, trans. by Antony Shugaar (Chicago: University of Chicago Press, 2005), pp. 20–1.

1 WHAT DANIEL CAMPBELL REMEMBERED

1   Daniel Campbell, *Untitled Memoir*. The original memoir no longer exists but its contents are known through a typescript made at a later date by Fr John Baptist Byrne. In a short note to the typescript Fr Byrne said he received the loan of the original work from Campbell's grandson to copy. Both Fr Byrne and the grandson, a man named

Brennan, were members of the Passionist Order in Mount Argus, Dublin. Initially unaware of each other's interest, Dr Nollaig Ó Muraíle of the School of Irish at the National University of Ireland, Galway, and I had independently planned to publish the work. As a result of our discussions, it is likely we will do so together, along with a scholarly apparatus (including a discussion of the provenance of the memoir), and an explanation of why we are confident that the Fr Byrne typescript is accurate and complete. Copies of the Byrne typescript are in the National Library, Dublin, *Typescript copy of a manuscript history of the parish of Knock, Co, Mayo; transcribed by Revd John Baptist Byrne 1900?* (sic), Manuscripts Collection, ms 31,718, and in Knock Museum. Ó Muraíle has added paragraph numbers to the work and in this book I cite these rather than page numbers. Hereafter, references to this work will take the form CM (for Campbell Memoir) followed by the paragraph number.

2   In those rare cases when we do get access to what some poor people said, we often find that their statements were intended to influence or even mislead those in authority or power and therefore were shaped by their positions as supplicants. James Scally, for example, examined various petitions from tenants to the Crown authorities in the celebrated case of Ballykilcline townland in Roscommon and Ruth-Ann Harris studied petitions from women to their landlord or his agent on the Shirley estate in Monaghan. Such petitions were also shaped by the demands of those who wrote them as intermediaries: the Ballykilcline tenants were not their own scribes. Robert J. Scally, *The End of Hidden Ireland: Rebellion, Famine, and Emigration* (New York: Oxford University Press, 1995); Ruth-Ann M. Harris, 'Negotiating Patriarchy: Irish Women and the Landlord', in *Reclaiming Gender: Transgressive Identities in Modern Ireland,* eds Marilyn Cohen and Nancy J. Curtin (New York: St Martin's Press, 1999), pp. 207–25. We have hundreds of another kind of written statement from the poor, threatening letters sent to persons or posted in some public place, but these are scattered widely in time and space and often are very short, and more importantly, not only are they anonymous but the writers went to some lengths to disguise their identity. Stephen Gibbons, *Captain Rock, Night Errant: the Threatening Letters of Pre-Famine Ireland* (Dublin: Four Courts Press, 2004). Nevertheless, when such letters exist in sufficient numbers on a given episode, they can provide evidence of popular belief; see for example, James S. Donnelly Jr, 'Captain Rock: Ideology and Organization in the Irish Agrarian Rebellion of 1821–24', *Éire/Ireland,* 42, 3/4 (Winter 2007), 60–103, on the Rockite movement. Direct first person accounts tend to come from the educated who wrote letters or memoirs. Even a volume devoted to the local history of the Great Famine in North Connacht and called *In Their Own Words* consists, not of the words of the starving poor, but of documents produced by others: various reports by relief officials, petitioning pleas by priests, resolutions of Poor Law Guardians, local constabulary reports, and accounts by resident magistrates and other local government functionaries that describe the suffering second-hand.

3   Even if he was baptised in 1825 we cannot assume he was born that year.

4   CM 21 and conclusion.

5   Kerby Miller, *Emigrants and Exiles: Ireland and the Irish Exodus to North America* (New York: Oxford University Press, 1985), p. 71.

6   CM 42.

7   CM 21.

8   CM 7.

9   Richard White, *Remembering Ahanagran: Storytelling in a Family's Past* (New York: Hill and Wang, 1998), p. 50.

10   CM 24.

11   CM 23.

12   CM 44, 45.

13   Guy Beiner, *Remembering the Year of the French: Irish Folk History and Social Memory* (Madison: University of Wisconsin Press, 2007), p. xi; Cormac Ó Gráda, *Black '47 and*

Beyond: The Great Irish Famine in History, Economy, and Memory (Princeton: Princeton University Press, 1999), pp. 194, 222. Ó Gráda had written the same thing in Irish five years earlier, *An Drochshaol: Béaloideas agus Amhráin* (Dublin: Coiscéim, 1994), p. iii. See also Stiofán Ó Cadhla, *The Holy Well Tradition: The Pattern of St Declan, Ardmore, County Waterford, 1820–2000* (Dublin: Four Courts Press, 2004), p. 13, for historians' 'shameful neglect' of folklore sources.

14 Chris Morash, 'Literature, Memory, Atrocity', in *'Fearful Realities': New Perspectives on the Famine,* eds Chris Morash and Richard Hayes (Dublin: Irish Academic Press, 1996), p. 113.

15 Tim P. O'Neill, 'Famine Evictions', in *Famine, Land and Culture in Ireland,* ed. Carla King (Dublin: University College Dublin Press, 2000), pp. 29–70.

16 See, for example, Pádraig G. Ó Laighin, *Bánú Phartraí agus Thuar Mhic Éadaigh* (Dublin: Coiscéim, 1997).

17 Robert Scally, *End of Hidden: Rebellion, Famine and Emigration,* pp. 111–12.

18 An instructive example is provided by Richard White's examination of a Petition for Citizenship filed in the US by an Irish immigrant named Jack Walsh in January 1933. White found much of the information Walsh gave on the form was wrong. He was off by three years for the year his wife was born. He failed to list one of their children and gave a wrong birth date for another. Arguably, Walsh did not know or remember the precise dates or ages but surely he was capable of counting his children. Walsh apparently knew these details were irrelevant for purposes of his seeking citizenship and gave little thought to them. He did, however, give one exact piece of information: 1 December 1927, as the date he entered the United States. But that precise date was not only wrong, its very precision was calculated to mislead the authorities. Walsh had actually entered the US illegally years earlier, but later travelled to Canada and on that date made a documented re-entrance to the US with an eye toward citizenship. The information Walsh gave on the Petition for Citizenship was designed to conceal that truth which, if revealed, would have kept him from becoming a citizen. White, *Ahanagran,* p. 139.

19 White, *Ahanagran,* p. 139.

20 Elizabeth Tonkin, *Narrating Our Pasts: The Social Construction of Oral History* (New York: Cambridge University Press, 1992), p. 115.

21 Some of Campbell's stories contain details that are factually implausible or even demonstrably inaccurate but nevertheless they convey meaning whose significance we can grasp. What some might see as the 'errors' he makes, rather than being grounds for dismissing his evidence as unreliable, become crucial clues themselves. Eugene Hynes, 'Making Sense of "Mistakes" in Oral Sources', in *Orality and Modern Irish Culture,* eds Nessa Cronin, John Crossan, Louis de Paor and John Eastlake (Camridge: Cambridge Scholars Press, forthcoming). At one point, for example, Campbell refers to Archbishop John MacHale as the son of a cowherd, but this is factually wrong. Far from being very poor, MacHale's family kept servants. Yet he was remembered not only by Campbell but also by others as coming from humble origins (see chapter 5). There is abundant evidence MacHale was seen as a protector and advocate for the poor and a fighter for their cause. In a world where he did battle with the powerful, MacHale was conceived as a David confronting Goliath. This cognitive framework structured the details of the stories told about him and remembered by people such as Campbell. To add to the drama of the David slaying Goliath analogy, MacHale had to be made smaller than life, which is precisely what Campbell does. While he is thus factually inaccurate about MacHale's early biographical details, Campbell, even when he least realises it, provides very significant evidence about the worldview of the people amongst whom he grew up.

22 Robert Darnton, *The Great Cat Massacre and Other Episodes in French Cultural History* (New York: Random House, 1985), pp. 78, 99.

23 See Ó Gráda, *Black '47,* pp. 28, 239–40.

24 CM 23, 19, 26.

25 CM 26.

26 Basil Bernstein, *Class, Codes and Control, Vol 1* (London: Paladin, 1971).
27 See p. 47 for another example. Many sociologists since Maurice Halbwachs wrote his classic, *Les cadres sociaux de la mémoire* (Paris: Alcan, 1925), have made a similar point on the importance of 'interpretive communities', and the idea has become influential in many disciplines. For one example, Stanley Fish explicitly building on the work of sociologist Harvey Sacks has applied the idea in the area of conventional literary understanding. Stanley Fish, *Is There a Text in This Class? The Authority of Interpretive Communities* (Cambridge: Harvard University Press, 1980).
28 White, *Ahanagran*, p. 171.
29 Peig Sayers, *An Old Woman's Reflections: The Life of a Blasket Island Storyteller* (Oxford: Oxford University Press, 1962), p. 34.
30 Angela Bourke, *The Burning of Bridget Cleary: A True Story* (New York: Viking, 1999), p. 68.
31 Lewis Hinchman and Sandra Hinchman, *Memory, Identity, Community: The Idea of Narrative in the Human Sciences* (Albany: State University of New York Press, 1997), p. xxiv.
32 Bourke, *Burning*, p. 33.
33 See Ó Gráda, *An Drochshaol*, p. 7.
34 Catherine Bell, *Ritual: Perspectives and Dimensions* (New York: Oxford University Press, 1997), p. 202.
35 CM 8.
36 *Béaloideas*, 1942, XII, p. 207.
37 Diarmuid Ó Giolláin, *Locating Irish Folklore: Tradition, Modernity, Identity* (Cork: Cork University Press, 2000), pp. 140–1. Moreover, it was not only field collectors whose selections were guided by their presuppositions. The directions they received as to what might be worth collecting also could be shot through with bias. For example, the Schools Folklore project in 1937–38 resulted in nearly 400 pages of material from five schools in Knock parish but makes no mention whatever of the local pre-famine sectarian struggle that Campbell recounted at length. Conceivably the later powerful populist Catholicism constructed a tradition that filtered out memories of willing conversions to Protestantism. For one revealing case study see Nancy Jacobs, 'The Great Bophuthatswana Donkey Massacre: Discourse on the Ass and the Politics of Class and Grass', *American Historical Review*, 106, 2 (April 2001), 485–507. That the sectarian struggle in pre-famine Knock was forgotten locally is thus conceivable, but still unlikely; local historian Nollaig Ó Muraíle of Knock assures me that it is still remembered in the new millennium. Moreover, souperism was remembered in an east Galway rural community in the 1980s and in Roscommon as late as this century. John S. Flynn, *Ballymacward: The Story of an East Galway Parish* (Privately published, 1991), p. 178; Patrick Vesey, '"I Flatter Myself We Have Strangled the Evil In the Bud"', in *Hanging Crimes: When Ireland Used the Gallows,* ed. Frank Sweeney (Cork: Mercier Press, 2005), p. 25. A more likely explanation for the gap is that the pupils/ collectors were led to concentrate on other named topics, such as beliefs about cures, local foods and how they were prepared, and other non-controversial issues. Cormac Ó Gráda makes a similar point about another special collection of folklore, that of 1945–46 about the Great Famine: the responses were very much in tune with the directions given, *An Drochshaol*, p. 1. Teachers in the schools also shaped the folklore recorded, Pádraig Ó Baoill, *Glórtha Ár Sinsear: Béaloideas Oirdheisceart na Gaillimhe* (Dublin: Coiscéim, 2005), p. xix.
38 Marjorie Howes, 'William Carleton's Literary Religion', in *Evangelicals and Catholics in Nineteenth-Century Ireland,* ed. James H. Murphy (Dublin: Four Courts Press, 2005), pp. 107–22; Irene Whelan, *The Bible War in Ireland: The 'Second Reformation' and the Polarization of Protestant-Catholic Relations, 1800–1840* (Madison: The University of Wisconsin Press, 2005), pp. 211–2.
39 For example, one story about Archbishop MacHale conflates events stretching from the Plantation of Ulster in the early seventeenth century when MacHale was reportedly a

youth, to his attendance at Maynooth College, which was founded in 1795, to his becoming a priest in the early nineteenth century. In the 1930s a pupil in a Knock school wrote that the Danes had built castles locally about 'three hundred years ago' and even a teacher wrote about 'an eighteenth century man who was a fenian'.

40 Ó Gráda, *An Drochshaol,* pp. iv–v; Ó Gráda, *Black '47 and Beyond,* pp. 194–223, quoted at page 196.

2 LOCAL WORLDS

1 The absence of trees was evidence not only of poor soil but of poor people. Trees were status symbols. 'Only the gentry could afford to have woods or tree-lined avenues'. Angèle Smith, 'Landscape Representation: Place and Identity in Nineteenth-Century Ordnance Survey Maps of Ireland', in *Landscape, Memory and History: Anthropological Perspectives,* eds Pamela Stewart and Andrew Strathern (London: Pluto, 2003), p. 76.
2 By the mid-1820s, migrants from Lord Dillon's holdings who worked in London's bricklaying trade were sending home over one thousand pounds annually. D. Fitzpatrick, '"A peculiar tramping people": the Irish in Britain, 1801–70', in *A New History of Ireland, Vol. 5: Ireland Under the Union 1, 1801–1877,* ed. W. E. Vaughan (Oxford: Clarendon Press, 1989), p. 656. Most of Knock parish was included in Dillon's large estate. The numerous seasonal agricultural migrants probably carried back home several times that much cash when they returned. The Dillon estate had also made arrangements that enabled migrants to transmit their earnings directly to Ireland through an agent, before leaving England for home so as to not risk losing the cash on the return trip, which was a constant threat. The agent deducted the tenant's rent before turning over the balance back in Ireland. Historians disagree on whether the service was otherwise free to the workers. Ruth-Ann Harris, *The Nearest Place That Wasn't Ireland,* Ames: University of Iowa Press, 1994), n. 211, pp. 182, 230; Anne O'Dowd, *Spalpeens and Tattie Hokers: History and Folklore of The Irish Migratory Agricultural Worker in Ireland and Britain* (Dublin: Irish Academic Press, 1991), p. 262.
3 Eugene Hynes, 'The Great Hunger and Irish Catholicism', *Societas,* 8 (1978), pp. 137–55; and 'Family and Religious Change in a Peripheral Capitalist Society: Mid-Nineteenth-Century Ireland', in *The Religion and Family Connection: Social Science Perspectives,* ed. Darwin Thomas (Provo, Utah: Brigham Young University Religious Studies Center, 1988), pp. 161–74.
4 Sean Connolly, *Priests and People in Pre-Famine Ireland* (Dublin: Gill and MacMillan, 1982), pp. 100–108; W. H. Maxwell, *Wild Sports of the West* (New York: Frederick Stokes Company, [1832], 1915), chapter xxxiii.
5 Dermot MacManus, *The Middle Kingdom: The Faerie World of Ireland* (1959; reprint, Gerrard's Cross, UK: Colin Smythe, 1973).
6 CM 30–3.
7 NFCS 108, pp.177–8.
8 Diarmuid Ó Giolláin, *Locating Irish Folklore: Tradition, Modernity, Identity* (Cork: Cork University Press, 2000), p. 67.
9 Angela Bourke, *The Burning of Bridget Cleary: A True Story* (New York: Viking, 1999).
10 Kai Erikson, *Wayward Puritans: A Study in the Sociology of Deviance* (New York: Wiley, 1966). In his introduction to the 2004 classic edition of this work, Erikson reviews many other studies of how deviance marks out the moral boundaries of communities.
11 When we approach fairylore as an abstract from a social context rather than a text, we expect that the corpus of fairy belief will change as social circumstances change. Vejvoda compared the ways women are understood in two classic collections of fairy-tales from the same area of south-west Munster, those by Thomas Crofton Croker in the pre-famine era, and by Jeremiah Curtin in the 1890s. The positions of women in the two sets of stories are very different, reflective of the changed social circumstances of women in the post-famine society where Curtin collected his tales. Kathleen Veyvoda, 'Too Much Knowledge of the Other World: Women and Nineteenth-Century

Irish Folktales', *Victorian Literature and Culture,* 32 (2004), pp. 41–61. As a language, fairylore was available for commenting on perennial or newly salient issues in the lives of community members. In the 1930s an old illiterate Connemara man was perfectly capable of using the idiom of fairylore to comment on the experiences of younger Connemara men confronting the options available to them in England as stigmatised speakers of a marginalised language. Angela Bourke, 'Legless in London: Pádraic Ó Conaire and Éamon A. Búrc', *Eire/Ireland,* 38 (Fall/Winter, 2003), pp. 54–67.

12   While he calls her a 'fairywoman', what Campbell describes here is a 'bean feasa' or 'wise woman'. There were different kinds of wise women: some travelled with the fairies, others were recognised as herbal healers, and still others made prophetic diagnoses. Many combined these abilities as the Knock 'fairywoman' did. Gearóid Ó Crualaoich, 'Reading the *Bean Feasa*', *Folklore,* 37, 3 (2005), pp. 37–50. Campbell's terminology was widely used.

13   CM 24.

14   William Wilde, *Irish Popular Superstitions* (Totowa, New Jersey: Rowman and Littlefield, 1973 [1852]), pp. 57–8.

15   For numerous examples of such 'orthas', see Douglas Hyde, *Religious Songs of Connaught,* especially Volume 11, pp. 267ff.

16   Richard P. Jenkins, 'Witches and Fairies: Supernatural Aggression and Deviance among the Irish Peasantry', *Ulster Folklife,* 23 (1977), pp. 33–56, reprinted in *The Good People: New Fairylore Essays,* ed. Peter Narvaez (New York: Garland Publishing, 1991), pp. 302–35.

17   James C. Scott, *Domination and the Arts of Resistance: Hidden Transcripts* (New Haven: Yale University Press, 1990).

18   Angela Bourke, 'The Virtual Reality of Irish Fairy Legend', *Eire/Ireland,* 31 (1996), p. 13.

19   MacManus, *The Middle Kingdom,* p. 100.

20   Kerby Miller, *Emigrants and Exiles: Ireland and the Irish Exodus to North America* (New York: Oxford University Press, 1985), p. 74.

21   The much debated theory is most often attributed to anthropologist George M. Foster, 'Peasant Society and the Image of Limited Good', *American Anthropologist,* 67 (April 1965). For one application, see Eugen Weber on fairytales in France, 'Fairies and Hard Facts: The Reality of Folktales', *Journal of the History of Ideas,* XLII (1981), pp. 93–113.

22   Lady Wilde, *Ancient Legends of Ireland* (New York: Sperling Publishing Company, 1991), p. 32.

23   It is easy to see some connection between fairylore and contemporary social arrangements, especially rundale, but a detailed exploration of the link is beyond the scope of this work and in any case is not possible given the limited amount of research that has been carried out on rundale. See Michael Turner, 'Rural Economies in Post-Famine Ireland, c. 1850–1914' in *A Historical Geography of Ireland,* ed. B. J. Graham and L. J. Proudfoot (New York: Academic Press, 1993), p. 311; Tom Yager, 'What Was Rundale and Where Did It Come From?', *Béaloideas,* 70 (2002), pp. 153–86.

24   On rundale generally, see Yager, 'Rundale'; James Anderson, 'Rundale, Rural Economy and Agrarian Revolution: Tirhugh 1715–1855', in *Donegal History and Society: Interdisciplinary Essays on the History of an Irish County,* ed. William Nolan, Liam Ronayne and Mairead Dunleavy (Dublin: Geography Publications, 1995), pp. 447–69.

25   Quoted in Henry Coulter, *The West of Ireland: Its Existing Condition and Prospects* (Dublin: Hodges and Smith, 1862), p. 199.

26   Rosa Meehan, *The Story of Mayo* (Castlebar: Mayo County Council, 2003), p. 43.

27   As described by many others, for example, Martina O'Donnell, 'Settlement and Society in the Barony of East Inishowen, c.1850', in *Donegal History and Society,* p. 540.

28   Coulter, *The West of Ireland,* p. 200.

29   Quoted in Lawrence Taylor, *Occasions of Faith: An Anthropology of Irish Catholics* (Dublin: Lilliput Press, 1985), p. 63.

30 Robert J. Scally, *The End of Hidden Ireland: Rebellion, Famine, and Emigration* (New York: Oxford University Press, 1995), p. 35. Also see Anderson, 'Rundale', p. 448; Taylor, *Occasions of Faith*, pp. 62–3.

31 NFC 1231, pp. 215–36. The story is printed and translated in Séamus Ó Catháin and Patrick O'Flanagan, *The Living Landscape: Kilgannon, Erris, County Mayo* (Dublin: Comhairle Bhéaloideasa Éireann, 1975), pp. 188–203. My quotations are from their translation. At one point in the story Ó Catháin and O'Flanagan translate the fairy leader as saying to Micheál that 'we will give you food . . . but we will not give it to you'. The original Irish uses two different verbs for 'give' here, and both can be translated as 'give', but they differ in connotation. I prefer to translate the phrase as 'we will bring food to you . . . but will not give it to you'. The sentence is not self-contradictory. In the context of the story, 'we will bring food to you' can be understood as a metaphorical statement of how they will enable Micheál to satisfy his hunger by participating as a member of the exchange network that is the townland community.

32 Yager, 'Rundale', p. 174.

33 Anthropologists of poor communities in rich countries as well as of hunter-gatherer societies point out that reliance on networks and sharing is a survival strategy. While these networks allow everyone to survive as long as anyone in the group has resources to share, the reciprocal sharing expected in return virtually guarantees that nobody will escape from dependence on the network. Among numerous examples, see Carol Stack, *All Our Kin: Strategies for Survival in a Black Community* (New York: Harper and Row, 1974) on a black community in an American city. In a classic article anthropologist Richard Lee describes the different understandings insiders and he, as an outsider, had on one occasion of food-sharing among a group of !Kung San in the Kalahari desert. Lee was coming to the end of his stay living with and studying this hunter-gatherer group where equality and sharing were highly emphasised. To thank them for their friendship and cooperation, Lee presented the group with a cow he had arranged to purchase in a nearby agricultural village; he expected they would enjoy the good time and good eating that the cow-meat would provide. It took him a long time to understand why the group was neither grateful to him nor complimentary of the meat: his gift was too big and his departure too soon for the San to be able to reciprocate. They resented being placed in the position of not being able to meet their newly-multiplied obligations to their guest. To recognise Lee as superior in generosity would simultaneously require the San to recognise themselves as less-worthy, transgressing the value they ascribed to sharing and equality in their society. They cut Lee down to proper size by denigrating the cow and claiming Lee was a fool for having paid so much for it. Richard B. Lee, 'Eating Christmas in the Kalahari', *Natural History*, 78, 10 (December 1969), 1–3.

34 On 'models of reality' and 'models for reality', see Clifford Geertz, *The Interpretation of Cultures: Selected Essays* (New York: Basic, 1973), pp. 93–4.

35 CM 32.

36 Given that Campbell assumed that it was the mother who carried out infanticide and old women who reported hearing the child's cry, the episode can be read as collusion among women to shield themselves from accusations of murder.

37 Anthropologist Mary Douglas has used two formulations to convey what is involved: a form of 'community-wide complicity' based on 'mutually supportive collusion', that are suggestive provided we avoid the connotations of illegality, deliberation or wrongness sometimes carried by 'complicity' and 'collusion'. Mary Douglas, 'Introduction to the Second Edition', in her *Purity and Danger* (New York: Routledge, 2002), pp. xii–xiii. The shared beliefs could and often did lead to communal recognition of physical evidence of fairy abductions. For one example see Ó Catháin and O'Flanagan, *The Living Landscape*, pp. 119–20.

38 NFCS 108, p. 186. For a picture of such a group of children in County Sligo around 1900, see Seán Sexton, ed., *Ireland in Old Photographs* (New York: Little Brown, 1994), p. 87.

39 For one Mayo case, see CT, 7 October 1877; Michelle McGoff-McCann, *Melancholy Madness: A Coroner's Casebook* (Cork: Mercier Press, 2003), pp. 70–108.

40   Maxwell, *Wild Sports,* pp. 36–7.
41   Lady Augusta Gregory, *Visions and Beliefs in the West of Ireland, with Two Essays and Notes by W. B. Yeats* (London: Putnam, 1920; Reprinted London: Colin Smythe Ltd., 1970), p. 81.
42   ibid., pp. 93–5.
43   Sean Connolly, *Priests and People in Pre-Famine Ireland,* Second edition (Dublin: Gill and MacMillan, 2001), p. 112.
44   CM 31, 33.
45   Bourke, 'Irish Fairy Legend', p. 13.
46   Richard P. Jenkins, 'Witches and Fairies: Supernatural Aggression and Deviance among the Irish Peasantry', in *The Good People: New Fairylore Essays,* ed. Peter Narvaez (New York: Garland Publishing, 1991), p. 328.
47   CM 25.
48   CM 32.
49   CM 24, 32.
50   Gearóid Ó Crualaoich, *The Book of the Cailleach: Stories of the Wise-Woman Healer* (Cork: Cork University Press, 2003), p. 22, emphasis in original.
51   Even central tenets of major religious traditions are interpreted differently. See, for example, William H. Sewell, Jr, 'The Concept(s) of Culture', in *Beyond the Cultural Turn: New Directions in the Study of Society and Culture,* eds Victoria Bonnell and Lynn Hunt (Berkeley: University of California Press, 1999), p. 53, on the Christian concept of the Trinity.
52   Patricia Lysaght, 'Fairylore from the Midlands of Ireland', in *The Good People: New Fairylore Essays,* ed. Peter Narvaez (New York: Garland Publishing, 1991), p. 39.
53   William Butler Yeats, *The Book of Fairy and Fairylore: Folk Tales of Ireland* (London: Octopus Publishing Group, 1994 [Reprint of originally separate volumes *Fairy and Folk Tales of the Irish Peasantry* (1888) and *Irish Fairy Tales* (1891)], p. 6.
54   But see Timothy C. Correll, 'Believers, Skeptics, and Charlatans: Evidential Rhetoric, the Fairies, and Faith Healers in Irish Oral Narrative and Belief', *Folklore,* 116 (April 2005), pp. 1–18, for a recent important contribution on this very issue.
55   Gregory, *Visions and Beliefs,* pp. 203–4.
56   Michael P. Carroll, *Irish Pilgrimage: Holy Wells and Popular Catholic Devotion* (Baltimore: Johns Hopkins University Press, 1999).
57   For example, Peter Harbison, *Pilgrimage in Ireland: The Monuments and the People* (London: Barrie and Jenkins, 1991), p. 229; Stiofán Ó Cadhla, *The Holy Well Tradition: The Pattern of St Declan, Ardmore, County Waterford, 1820–2000* (Dublin: Four Courts Press, 2004), p. 11, sees this number as a 'conservative estimate'.
58   Antoine Boltúin, *MacHeil agus an Ghaeilge: A Shaothar agus a Dhearcadh* (PhD Thesis, Department of Modern Irish, University College Galway, 1992), pp. 356, 363.
59   J. F. Quinn, *History of Mayo,* Vol. 1 (Ballina: Brendan Quinn, 1993), p. 29. On p. 48 of the same work, Quinn quotes the same source to the effect that the pilgrim did seven rather than eleven circuits at the various steps.
60   Carroll, *Irish Pilgrimage*; see, for example, Ó Cadhla, *Holy Well,* p. 27.
61   See Archbishop Kelley's 1825 statement quoted in Connolly, *Priests and People,* p. 131; F. Westlander, *A Memoir of William Moore, Late Scripture Reader in the Province of Connaught* (London: J Nisbet and Co., 1843), p. 176.
62   Carroll, *Irish Pilgrimage*; Ó Cadhla, *Holy Well.*
63   Among many writers, see Patrick Logan, *The Holy Wells of Ireland* (Gerrard's Cross: Colin Smythe, 1980); Connolly, *Priests and People,* pp. 135–8.
64   See Ó Cadhla, *Holy Well,* especially pp. 9–13, for insightful comments on such descriptions.
65   Philip Dixon Hardy, *The Holy Wells of Ireland* (Dublin 1836), p. 101, as quoted in Harbison, *Pilgrimage in Ireland,* p. 231; Diarmuid Ó Giolláin, 'Revisiting the Holy Well', *Eire/Ireland* 40, 1–2 (Spring/Summer 2005), pp. 23–4, and Logan, *The Holy Wells,* p. 114.

66 Harbison, *Pilgrimage*, 139–40, p. 174.

67 See Jack Mulveen, 'Tóchar Phádraic: Mayo's Penitential and Sculptured Highway', *Journal of the Galway Archaeological and Historical Society,* 51 (1998), pp. 167–81.

68 Etienne Rynne, 'The Round Tower, "Evil Eye" and Holy Well at Balla, Co. Mayo', in *Dublin and Beyond the Pale: Studies in Honour of Patrick Healy*, ed. Conleth Manning (Bray: Wordwell, 1998), p. 182.

69 CM 8.

70 Appeal to one's relatives or neighbours was a common rhetorical device in legitimising narratives of cures by traditional wise-women healers, Ó Crualaoich, *Book of the Cailleach*, pp. 96–7.

71 Seán Ó Súilleabháin, *Irish Wake Amusements* (Cork: Mercier Press, 1967), pp. 146–58.

72 Liam Swords, *A Hidden Church: The Diocese of Achonry, 1689–1818* (Dublin: Columba Press, 1999), p. 258.

73 CM 33.

74 *Béaloideas* 1942, Vol. XII, p. 205, also in Angela Bourke, 'More in Anger Than in Sorrow: Irish Women's Lament Poetry', in *Feminist Messages: Coding in Women's Folk Culture*, ed. Joan N. Radner (Urbana: University of Illinois Press, 1993), p. 166.

75 Lawrence M. Geary, 'Prince Hohenloe, Signor Pastorini and Miraculous Healing in Early Nineteenth-Century Ireland', in *Medicine, Disease and the State in Ireland, 1650–1940*, eds Greta Jones and Elizabeth Malcolm (Cork: Cork University Press, 1999), pp. 40–58.

76 Irene Whelan, *The Bible War in Ireland: The "Second Reformation" and the Polarization of Protestant-Catholic Relations, 1800–1840* (Madison: The University of Wisconsin Press, 2005), p. 193–203; Connolly, *Priests and People*, p.126.

77 Thomas McGrath, *Politics, Interdenominational Relations and Education in the Public Ministry of Bishop James Doyle of Kildare and Leighlin, 1786–1834* (Dublin: Four Courts, 1999), p. 115; Whelan, *Bible War*, p. 194.

78 It was not only in competition with the official church that memories such as Campbell's registered a local miracle. In stories about wise women healers, Ó Crualaoich shows that loss of speech can be seen as a code for a range of psychosomatic disorders for which there was no known cure, but for which the stories provided means of coping, *Book of the Cailleach*, pp. 75–7, 201–4.

79 Connolly, *Priests and People*, p. 135.

80 See ibid., pp. 135–18, and Carroll, *Irish Pilgrimage*, for analyses of the changing clerical attitudes towards patterns in the pre-famine period.

81 CM 37.

82 Emmet Larkin, 'The Rise and Fall of Stations in Ireland, 1750–1850', in *Chocs et ruptures en historie religieuse: fin XVIIIe–XIXe siecles*, ed. Michel Lagree (Rennes: Presses Universitaires de Renne, 1998), pp. 19–32; Larkin, *The Pastoral Role of the Roman Catholic Church in Pre-Famine Ireland, 1750–1850* (Dublin: Four Courts Press, 2006), pp. 189–258.

83 *Irish Pilgrimage*, pp. 158–64.

84 Stephen Gibbons, *Captain Rock, Night Errant: the Threatening Letters of Pre-Famine Ireland* (Dublin: Four Courts Press, 2004), p. 259; John C. MacTernan, *Olde Sligo: Aspects of Town and County Over 750 Years* (Sligo: Avena Publications, 1995), p. 302.

85 Priest-historian Liam Swords, *Hidden Church*, pp. 244–7, gives an account of station-masses in the adjoining diocese of Achonry that is much more sympathetic to priests' perspectives.

86 CM 37.

87 Swords, *Hidden Church*, p. 237.

88 Connolly, *Priests and People*, p. 244.

89 Miller, *Emigrants and Exiles*, p. 82; Douglas Hyde, *Religious Songs of Connacht* (nd), Vol. 1, p. 168. While this proverb is recorded from Mayo, it was by no means confined to that county. It is widely attributed to the Munster poet Eoghan Rua Ó Súilleabháin; Daithi Ó h-Ógáin, *The Hero in Irish Folk Poetry* (Dublin: Gill and MacMillan, 1985), p. 244. Catholic Archbishop Kelley of Tuam in 1825 included

payments to priests in a list of popular complaints; Connolly, *Priests and People*,
p. 16. Also, see James Berry, *Tales from the West of Ireland* (Dublin: Dolmen, 1966),
pp. 67–8, 81–2, where a nineteenth-century Mayo writer recounts stories of two
priests who were renowned precisely because they were exceptions to the rule and
were not greedy. In addition, one of the remembered virtues of Archbishop MacHale
that set him apart was his generosity and his punishment of greedy priests.

90 CM 36.
91 CM 47.
92 CM 2, 21. To a person immersed in a culture of literacy this seems a self-contradic-
    tion because literacy implies the ability to read more than one story. Learning to
    'read' one particular piece of material is more characteristic of an oral culture, the
    one Campbell was living in. However, we should be wary of assuming that literacy
    was only possible in English. Niall Ó Ciosáin has pointed out that probably more
    people read Irish in the first half of the nineteenth century than ever before. 'Gaelic
    Culture and Language Shift', in *Nineteenth-century Ireland: A Guide to Recent Research*,
    eds Laurence Geary and Margaret Kelleher (Dublin: University College Dublin Press,
    2005), p. 138.
93 Joan Hoff, and Marian Yeates, *The Cooper's Wife Is Missing: The Trials of Bridget Cleary*
    (Oxford: Basic Books, 2000), p. 22.
94 Joseph Prost, C.Ss.R., *A Redemptorist Missionary in Ireland, 1851–1854: Memoirs of
    Joseph Prost, C.Ss.R.* Translated and edited by Emmet Larkin and Herman
    Freudenberger (Cork: Cork University Press, 1998), p. 93.
95 ibid., p. 92.
96 ibid., p. 93.
97 Connolly, *Priests and People*, p. 98, and Oliver P. Rafferty, 'Carleton's Ecclesiastical
    Context: The Ulster Catholic Experience', *Bullaun* 4, 2 (Winter 1999/2000), p. 109,
    are among the many who agree.
98 Hoff and Yeates, *Cooper's Wife*, p. 22.
99 Daniel Gallogly, *The Diocese of Kilmore, 1800–1950* (Cavan: Breiffne Historical Society,
    1999), pp. 63, 70; for Larkin's review see *Catholic Historical Review*, 86, 3 (2000), p.
    515. When I brought Campbell's memoir to the attention of a very distinguished his-
    torian of Catholicism in nineteenth-century Ireland, so convinced was he that the
    statement about the Stations of the Cross could not be accurate that he dismissed the
    whole memoir as of little evidentiary value.
100 Boltúin, *MacHeil*, p. 343; Brian Ó Cuív, 'An Irish Tract on the Stations of the Cross',
    Celtica, 11 (1956), pp. 1–29; James Hardiman, *The History of the County and the Town of
    Galway From the Earliest Period to the Present Time* (Galway, [1820] 1832), p. 276, as cited
    in Ó Cuív, 'Irish Tract', p. 29.
101 'Irish Tract'.
102 Ó Cuív, 'Irish Tract', n. 9, p. 19, and n. 21, p. 21.
103 ibid., p. 2, n. 2.
104 Malachy McKenna, 'A Textual History of *The Spiritual Rose*', *Clogher Record*, 14 (1991),
    pp. 52–73; Malachy McKenna, ed., *The Spiritual Rose* (Dublin: Institute for Advanced
    Studies, 2001); Boltúin, *MacHeil*, p. 365.
105 Pp.87–116 in the 1800 edition.
106 Hyde, *Religious Songs*, Vol. 1, p. 285.
107 CM 9, emphasis added.
108 Based on two other manuscript versions of the Way of the Cross from County
    Waterford dated to the late eighteenth and early nineteenth centuries and an English-
    language Cork one from the 1730s, Boltúin, *MacHeil*, pp. 340–1, thinks it possible
    that there was not one 'Irish' version but rather separate Munster and Connacht ver-
    nacular versions of the devotion. Carleton's description of the devotion in pre-famine
    Tyrone differs from what Campbell described in Knock.
109 See Boltúin, *MacHeil*, p. 342.
110 See Hyde, *Religious Songs*, Vol. 2, p. 283ff.

111 Boltúin, *MacHeil*, pp. 356, 363.

112 ibid., p. 363. MacHale had brought the Stations of the Cross from Italy around 1838. Padraig Ó Tuairisc, *Árd-Dheoise Thuama agus Cartlann Choláiste Na nGael sa Roimh san 19ú Aois Déag* (MA Thesis in History, University College, Galway, 2000), p. 590. Citing another source, Boltúin, *MacHeil*, pp. 363, 374, says that MacHale purchased Stations of the Cross on the continent in 1861 at a cost of nearly £200. If these were for the Cathedral, they were replacements for the ones purchased in 1838 and mentioned by Prost in 1854.

113 See Boltúin, *MacHeil*, p. 471. The published work lists MacHale as the translator.

114 Carleton, *Works*, Vol. I, p. 726, first emphasis added.

115 Carleton, *Works*, Vol. II, p. 367; see also page 361.

116 Quoted in Boltúin, *MacHeil*, p. 342.

117 A recent historian of the order claims the last friar left around 1870 but the well informed John MacPhilpin wrote in 1880 that mass was celebrated there until thirty-five years earlier so perhaps the monastery did not survive the 1840s famine. Stephen Josten, 'Ballinsmale Carmelite Abbey, 1288–1870' (1985), accessed 28 February 2005 at http://carmelites.ie/Ireland/ballinsmale.htm. John MacPhilpin, *The Apparitions and Miracles at Knock. Also, The Official Depositions of the Eye-Witnesses* (Dublin: Gill and Son, 1880), p. 17.

118 Hugh Fenning OP, *The Undoing of the Friars of Ireland* (Louvain: Publications Universitaires de Louvain, 1972).

119 Liam Swords, *A Dominant Church: The Diocese of Achonry 1881–1960* (Dublin: Columba Press, 2004), p. 396.

120 Ó Tuairisc, *Árd-Dheoise Thuama*, p. 37.

121 Prost, *Redemptorist Missionary*, p. 82.

122 Hyde, *Religious Songs*, Vol. 1, p x–xiii; see also Nollaig Ó Gadhra, 'Gaeltacht Mhaigh Eo', in *Mayo: Aspects of its Heritage,* ed. Bernard O'Hara (Galway: Regional Technical College, 1986), p. 131.

123 Hyde, *Religious Songs*, Vol. 1, p. vii.

124 J.J. Jennings, *The Big Rock* (Privately published, 1989), p. 85.

125 Swords, *Dominant Church*, p. 396. In an obvious typographical error, Swords gave the year as 1818.

3 THE ROLE AND THE POWER OF THE PRIEST

1 For example, Oliver P. Rafferty, 'Carleton's Ecclesiastical Context: The Ulster Catholic Experience', *Bullaun,* 4, 2 (Winter 1999/2000), p. 109.

2 CM 35.

3 CM 25.

4 Perhaps surprisingly, Campbell does not mention that attending the dying and administering the last rites were among the most central of the priest's tasks, backed up by the people's expectations. Most accounts see these as the priest's most crucial roles. I initially assumed that by 'death' in this sentence Campbell meant these tasks as well as funerals, and I suspect most readers would assume the same. However, we cannot blithely make such an assumption. In a very detailed insider's description of the events surrounding death and burial in Inishowen in Donegal in the middle of the nineteenth century, the priest is first referred to when he meets the funeral party as the coffin is being carried to the graveyard for the burial. There is no mention of sick calls or the last rites. It would seem that death was not a church centred experience, an indication of the limited reach of the official church's teaching. Hugh Dorian, *The Outer Edge of Ulster: A Memoir of Social Life in Nineteenth-Century Donegal*, eds Breandán Mac Suibhne and David Dickson (Dublin: Lilliput Press, 2000), pp. 309–20; Lawrence Taylor, 'Bás i n-Éireann: Cultural Constructions of Death in Ireland', *Anthropological Quarterly,* 62 (October 1989), pp. 696–712. It was recalled both from post-famine Knock and nearby Bekan that there were no funeral masses.

5   CM 37.

6   CM 26.

7   Joseph D'Arcy Sirr, *A Memorial of the Honourable and Most Reverend Power le Poer Trench, Late Archbishop of Tuam* (Dublin: William Curry, Jun., and Co., 1845), p. 532; see page 526 also.

8   W. H. Maxwell, *Wild Sports of the West* (New York: Frederick Stokes Company, 1915 [1832]), p. 95.

9   Carleton inserted a footnote in one of his stories to the effect that he had 'no hesitation in asserting that the bulk of the uneducated peasantry really believe that the priests have this power [to turn Protestants into asses]'. William Carleton, *The Works of William Carleton*, 2 vols (Freeport, New York: Books for Libraries Press, 1970 [1881]), Vol. 2, p. 744. In his novel, *The Black Mare*, Liam O'Flaherty has the superstitious people of Connemara believing that the priest could change a person into a goat. In other works he paints priests as spiritual tyrants concerned mainly with their worldly well-being. In contrast to the anti-clerical tradition that includes O'Flaherty, there is another tradition that lauds the *soggart aroon* and his close relationship with his people. Gearóid Denvir sensibly argues that both traditions are one-dimensional caricatures. *Litríocht agus Pobal* (Indreabhán: Cló Iar-Chonnachta, 1997), pp. 193–5.

10 Liam Kennedy, 'Profane Images in the Irish Popular Consciousness', *Oral History*, 7 (1979), p. 43.

11 James C. Scott, *Domination and the Arts of Resistance: Hidden Transcripts* (New Haven: Yale University Press, 1990).

12 Recognition of such stratagems is a recurrent theme throughout Carleton's *Traits and Stories of the Irish Peasantry*, for example in *Works*, Vol. II, pp. 1077, 1109–11.

13 Scott, *Domination*.

14 Asenath Nicholson, *The Bible in Ireland* (New York: John Day, 1927), p. 265.

15 Kerby Miller, *Emigrants and Exiles: Ireland and the Irish Exodus to North America* (New York: Oxford University Press, 1985), p. 94.

16 Bernard H. Becker, *Disturbed Ireland: Being Letters Written During the Winter of 1880–81* (London: MacMillan, 1881), p. 98.

17 Pádraig Ó Héalaí, 'Moral Values in Irish Religious Tales', *Béaloideas* pp. 42–44 (1974–1976), pp. 192–3.

18 George Rooper, *A Month in Mayo: Comprising Characteristic Sketches (Sporting and Social) of Irish Life* (London: Hardwicke, 1876), pp. 34, 39.

19 The poet Raftery refers to Protestants as *lucht feóla oidhche chéasta* (the meat on Good Friday people) and says that those who do not fast on Friday will not see heaven. Douglas Hyde, *Songs Ascribed to Raftery* (Shannon: Irish Academic Press, 1973 [1903]), p. 193; also see pp. 114, 120, and. Douglas Hyde, *The Religious Songs of Connacht*, 2 vols (Dublin: Gill and Son, nd), Vol. 1, p. 11. In a story collected by Hyde, meat that was secretly put into a priest's bag to manufacture damaging evidence against him was miraculously turned to fish on Friday. Dubhglas De h-Íde (An Craoibhín Aoibhinn) [Douglas Hyde], *An Sgealuidhe Gaedhealach (Sgeálta as Connachta)* (Dublin: Institiút Béaloideasa Éireann, 1933), pp. 1–8. Friday abstinence was one of the most common moral themes in stories collected by the Irish Folklore Commission. Ó Héalaí, 'Moral Values', p. 209. The anthropologist, Mary Douglas, has explained the symbolic significance of the Friday abstinence for those whom others patronised as 'Bog Irish', poor Irish Catholic communities in twentieth-century Britain. Douglas, *Natural Symbols: Explorations in Cosmology* (London: Barrie and Rockliff, 1970), pp. 37–53.

20 Albert Memmi, *The Colonizer and the Colonized* (Boston: Beacon Press, 1967), pp. 79–89.

21 For example, Charlotte Elizabeth Tonna, *Irish Recollections,* ed. Patrick Maume (Dublin: University College Dublin Press, 2004 [1841]), p. 54.

22 Liam Kennedy, 'Profane Images', p. 42, citing the Countess of Fingall, *Seventy Years Young* (London: 1936), p. 206.

23 Sr Mary Agnes McCann (Contributor), 'Documents. Bishop Purcell's Journal, 1833–36', *The Catholic Historical Review*, 5 (1919), p. 243.

24 Mrs. [Matilda] Houston, *Twenty Years in the Wild West, or Life in Connaught* (London, John Murray, 1879), p. 160.

25 ibid., pp. 34, 78–9.

26 ibid., pp. 29, 138–9.

27 K. Theodore Hoppen, *Elections, Politics, and Society in Ireland, 1832–1885* (Oxford, Clarendon Press, 1984), p. 212.

28 Quoted in Emmet Larkin, *The Roman Catholic Church and the Home Rule Movement in Ireland, 1870–1874* (Dublin: Gill and MacMillan, 1990), p. 132.

29 Terence McGrath, [pseudonym for Sir Henry A. Blake], *Pictures From Ireland,* 6th edition (London: Kegan Paul and Trench and Co, 1888), p. 4.

30 Quoted in Pádraig Ó Héalaí, 'Cumhacht an tSagairt sa Béaloideas', *Leachtaí Cholm Cille,* 8 (1977), p. 123.

31 The English sportsman in 1870s' Mayo reported the reverse: a drunken man was unimpressed by a priest's threat but took it seriously once he was sober. Rooper, *Month in Mayo,* pp. 57–58.

32 Michael J. Murphy, *Now You're Talking* (Belfast: Blackstaff Press, 1975), pp. 11–2, 160.

33 Patricia Ewick and Susan Silbey, 'Narrating Social Structure: Stories of Resistance to Legal Authority', *American Journal of Sociology,* 108 (May 2003), pp. 1328–72.

34 One priest in Wexford in 1824 who apparently believed he could perform an exorcism on a young child but whose treatment killed her, while onlookers did not intervene, was charged with murder and found guilty but insane. Connolly, *Priests and People in Pre-Famine Ireland,* p. 117.

35 William Wilde, *Irish Popular Superstitions* (Totowa, New Jersey: Rowman and Littlefield, 1973 [1852]), pp. 56–7.

36 Carleton, *Works,* Vol. II, p. 871; see also p. 1091. See Joan Hoff and Marian Yeates, *The Cooper's Wife Is Missing: The Trials of Bridget Cleary* (Oxford: Basic Books, 2000), p. 189, who cite W. B. Yeats, ed, *Irish Fairy and Folk Tales* (1993 reprint), pp. 221–222.

37 Priests in folklore had power to raise people from the dead, Ó h-Héalaí, 'Cumhacht', pp. 114–5. We will see that Archbishop MacHale was credited with resurrecting a House of Commons guard.

38 Lawrence Taylor, *Occasions of Faith: An Anthropology of Irish Catholics* (Dublin: Lilliput, 1995), pp. 115–66.

39 Sirr, *A Memorial of . . . Trench,* p. 532.

40 Lady Augusta Gregory, *Visions and Beliefs in the West of Ireland, with Two Essays and Notes by W. B. Yeats* (Putnam 1920; Reprinted London: Colin Smythe, 1970), p. 44.

41 Selina Guinness, 'Visions and Beliefs in the West of Ireland: Irish Folklore and British Anthropology, 1898–1920', *Irish Studies Review* 6, 1 (1998), p. 42.

42 Lucy MacDiarmid, and Maureen Waters, 'Introduction', in their edited volume, *Lady Gregory: Selected Writings* (New York: Penguin, 1995), pp. xxiii–xxvi.

43 Beggars had a whole repertoire of such stories about the virtue of almsgiving: see Hyde, *Religious Songs,* Vol. 1, pp. 289–309.

44 Guinness, 'Visions and Beliefs'; for Gregory's reports of priests curing people see her *Visions and Beliefs in the West of Ireland* (Gerrard's Cross: Colin Smythe, 1970 [1920]), pp. 295–301.

45 I owe this observation to Professor James Donnelly. The clause was perhaps the most detested of all in the law. It required anyone seeking admission to the workhouse to give up any land they held over a quarter of an acre, a guarantee that if they did not die in the workhouse they could look forward only to destitution afterward. The clause was blamed for numberless deaths in the Famine and it continued to stink in the nostrils of rural people long after Lady Gregory's life. James S. Donnelly, Jr, *The Great Irish Potato Famine* (Stroud, UK: Sutton Publishing, 2001), pp. 110–12.

46 Pádraig Ó Baoill, *Glórtha Ár Sinsear: Béaloideas Oirdheisceart na Gaillimhe* (Dublin: Coiscéim, 2005), pp. 5, 62.

47 For a similar case with the added ingredient of the priest's attitude see Mary Carbery, *Mary Carbery's West Cork Journal 1898–1901, or From the Back of Beyond*, ed. Jeremy Sandford (Dublin: Lilliput Press, 1998), pp. 30–1.

48 Irene Whelan, *The Bible War in Ireland: The 'Second Reformation' and the Polarization of Protestant-Catholic Relations, 1800–1840* (Madison: The University of Wisconsin Press, 2005), p. 238.

49 Quoted in Miller, *Emigrants and Exiles*, p. 74.

50 Hoff and Yeates, *The Cooper's Wife*, p. 157.

51 James Loewen, *Lies My Teacher Told Me* (New York: Simon and Schuster, 1995), pp. 114–15.

52 CM 26–7.

53 Connolly, *Priests and People*, p. 212.

54 ibid., p. 181.

55 Richard White, *Remembering Ahanagran: Storytelling in a Family's Past* (New York: Hill and Wang, 1998), p. 170.

56 www.from-ireland.net/diocs/archtuam.html accessed 13 February 2003; John Gallagher, *A Look into Our Past: Our Irish Heritage* (Knock: Knock Shrine Society, 1990), p. 134; John P. Jordan, 'Notes on the Parish of Aghamore', Retrieved 22 March 2005 from http://www.aghamoregaa.com/society/historical.htm. Campbell says O'Grady was PP when he was baptised in 1825. The cornerstone of the church in Knock, dated 1828, named O'Grady as parish priest.

57 Later in the century while it was still illegal, a prominent local politician in the region did this without damaging his electoral popularity. Íde Ní Liatháin, *The Life and Career of P. A. McHugh, A North Connacht Politician, 1859–1909* (Dublin: Irish Academic Press, 1999), p. 11.

58 Connolly, *Priests and People*, pp. 212–3.

59 CM 14, 15.

60 CM 21.

61 Eugene Hynes, 'The Construction of Insiders as Outsiders: Catholic Accounts of Protestant Converts in Pre-famine Western Ireland', *Cultural and Social History*, 6 (2009), forthcoming.

62 CM16.

63 Dorian, *Outer Edge*, p. 76.

64 CM 28.

65 Pádraig Ó Héalaí, 'Priest Versus Healer: The Legend of the Priest's Stricken Horse', *Béaloideas,* 62/63 (1994–5), pp. 171–88; Gearóid Ó Crualaoich, *The Book of the Cailleach: Stories of the Wise-Woman Healer* (Cork: Cork University Press, 2003), p. 182.

66 CM 37.

67 CM 26. The 'bishop's due' was a fee payable to the bishop in cases where his dispensation was required to permit marriages that normally would be forbidden, or to permit marriages without the customary 'reading of banns'.

68 Connolly, *Priests and People*, pp. 243–52; Miller, *Emigrants and Exiles*, p. 82; on Mayo, see Donald Jordan, Jr, *Land and Popular Politics in Ireland; County Mayo From the Plantation to the Land War* (Cambridge: Cambridge University Press, 1994), pp. 89–94.

69 CM 38.

70 Connolly, *Priests and People,* p. 250.

71 The letter is reprinted in Stephen Gibbons, *Captain Rock, Night Errant: the Threatening Letters of Pre-Famine Ireland* (Dublin: Four Courts Press, 2004), p. 259. Possibly, 'tower' in the last sentence should read 'town', but fine penmanship most likely was not a high priority of the author's or of the police officer who copied the letter to submit to the authorities.

72 *Priests and People*, pp. 251–2.

73 Violence was used against such a travelling crowd of demonstrators in County Sligo. John C. MacTernan, 'The Rout of the Penny Boys' in his *Olde Sligo: Aspects of Town and County Over 750 Years* (Sligo: Avena Publications, 1995), pp. 300–5.

74   Scott, *Domination*.
75   F. Westlander, *A Memoir of William Moore, Late Scripture Reader in the Province of Connaught* (London: J. Nisbet and Co., 1843), p. 149.
76   Ignatius Murphy, *Before the Famine Struck: Life in West Clare 1834–1845* (Dublin: Irish Academic Press, 1996), p. 52.
77   Liam Swords, *A Dominant Church: The Diocese of Achonry 1881–1960* (Dublin: Columba Press, 2004), p. 407.
78   CM 34.
79   Patrick Corish has suggested that priests in Connaught probably were permitted to say only one public Sunday mass but the available evidence, though sparse, suggests the case was more complicated. Corish, *The Irish Catholic Experience: A Historical Survey* (Dublin: Gill and MacMillan, 1985), p. 186. Even if there was a formal rule to such effect, bishops could grant exemptions. In Ulster, where there was such a rule, in Kilmore diocese most priests said two Sunday masses. Ulsterman William Carleton, *Works*, Vol. II, p. 865, claimed that priests could say three masses on Christmas Day and two all other days. By Corish's count, in 1834, ninety-nine Tuam priests provided 108 Sunday masses, so some said at least two, pp. 186–7. Orders of priests complained that bishops would not permit their members to say two Sunday masses while allowing their own diocesan priests to do so. Hugh Fenning, OP, *The Undoing of the Friars of Ireland* (Louvain: Publications Universitaires de Louvain, 1972), p. 48. In Clarenbridge in Galway diocese in the 1820s the local landlord family of Redingtons offered to finance a chaplain for the newly arrived Patrician Brothers on the condition that he also be their own private family chaplain. The bishop, however, concerned that the local parish priest would no longer be required as chaplain, refused to allow the newly arrived priest to say two masses in private on Sundays, one for the Brothers and one for the Redingtons. Presumably, up to that time, the parish priest had been saying a Sunday mass in public as well as the private Sunday mass for the Redington household. The landlord family appealed to the archbishop of Tuam who took their side in a letter to Rome. The matter went no further because the bishop died suddenly. Joseph Murphy, *The Redingtons of Clarenbridge: Leading Catholic Landlords of the 19th Century* (Privately published, 1999), p. 24. Clearly, the local bishop could allow priests to say two Sunday masses, even two private masses, even if there was a general rule to the contrary. Even if there was a rule against saying two masses in the same church, as perhaps was the case in parts of the Cashel province (Corish, p. 186), a parish priest and his curate could each say mass in the churches in Knock and Aghamore that fell under the jurisdiction of the Knock pastor, providing the laity with two opportunities to hear mass in the nearest church. There is some ambiguous evidence on the issue in an 1834 official government report on attendance at church services, including mass. The parish of Kiltullagh close to Knock had two priests in 1834, who were recorded as providing mass at the chapel at Garraulahan every Sunday, at Cloonfad chapel 'on each alternate Sunday', and also 'at a private house in this parish, at which a considerable number attend[ed]'. *First Report of the Commissioners of Public Instruction, Ireland* (London: Printed by William Clowes and Sons for His Majesty's Stationery Office, 1835), p. 43d. Unfortunately, the report does not tell us how frequently mass was said at the private house. If we assume that this mass alternated with the mass at Cloonfad, the evidence would perhaps support Corish's hunch. Mass was said in private houses in several other nearby parishes, especially in the Ballyhaunis area where it was said in one house in Bekan parish and two in the parish of Annagh. All these areas are close to the eastern border of the Tuam archdiocese where chapels were much more accessible than in the remote west. At Cong, there were two Sunday masses in the chapel and mass was also provided 'at Curranamona in a private house (in the open air in fine weather), for the convenience of remote parishioners' (ibid., p. 37d). But remoteness is hardly the key to explaining the provision of mass in private houses in the Ballyhaunis area. While 500 attended the mass in Curranamona and 800 attended mass in a private house in Maam, both

remote sites in Connemara (ibid., pp. 37d, 43d), we are not given attendance figures for the private houses around Ballyhaunis. David Miller in his 1975 article on mass attendance showed that the available churches were not used as much as possible. Perhaps one reason was that many people were reluctant to attend and that the priests reached out by saying masses in private houses closer to home for some of them in lieu of the mass in the church. That might have been the case in Kiltullagh. On the other hand, if the private house mass was a regular Sunday event, then the two priests in the parish said three masses every second Sunday. The available evidence does not permit us to determine which of these two scenarios was more accurate.

80 David Miller, 'Mass Attendance in Ireland in 1834', in *Piety and Power in Ireland, 1760–1960: Essays in Honour of Emmet Larkin,* eds Stewart J. Brown and David W. Miller (Belfast: Institute for Irish Studies, Queen's University, 2000), pp. 172–3.

81 *Parliamentary Gazette of Ireland,* 1844, p. 573.

82 This makes no allowance for the number of people canonically excused from attending. On the other hand, given the capacity of the chapel, the 1,000 figure, if accurate, must have involved two masses rather than the one that Campbell recorded.

83 Liam Swords, *A Hidden Church: The Diocese of Achonry, 1689–1818* (Dublin: Columba Press, 1999), p. 224.

84 Carleton, *Works,* Vol. II, p. 748.

85 For an earlier example, see Swords, *Hidden Church*, p. 221.

86 Ballyhaunis Housebook/Anderson Papers, Irish Augustinian Archives, Dublin.

87 CM 34.

88 CM 39–42.

89 Connolly, *Priests and People*, pp. 30–1.

90 The former two served in Tuam archdiocese (p. 39).

91 CM 4.

92 CM 2, 34.

93 CM 2.

94 Corish, *Irish Catholic Experience*, p. 184; Connolly, *Priests and People*, p. 60.

95 CM 48.

96 Lady Wilde, *Ancient Legends of Ireland* (New York: Sperling Publishing Company, 1991), p. 114.

97 See Carlton, *Works*, Vol. I, p. 960; Vol. II, p. 726.

98 James S. Donnelly, Jr, 'Pastorini and Captain Rock: Millenarianism and Sectarianism in the Rockite Movement in East Munster, 1821–4', in *Irish Peasants: Violence and Popular Unrest 1780–1914,* eds Samuel Clark and James S. Donnelly (Madison: University of Wisconsin Press, 1983), pp. 102–139; Corish, *Irish Catholic Experience*, p. 180.

99 Alfred P. Smith, *Faith, Famine and Fatherland in the Nineteenth-Century Irish Midlands: Perceptions of a Priest and Historian Anthony Cogan 1826–1872* (Dublin: Four Courts Press, 1992), pp. 146, 28.

100 Nicholson, *The Bible in Ireland*, pp. 180, 211 and passim.

4 THREATS AND BALANCES

1 CM 10–23.

2 CM 23.

3 James C. Scott, *Domination and the Arts of Resistance: Hidden Transcripts* (New Haven: Yale University Press, 1990).

4 Basil Bernstein, *Class, Codes and Control*, Vol. 1 (London: Paladin, 1971).

5 Joseph Robins, *The Miasma: Epidemic and Panic in Nineteenth Century Ireland* (Dublin: Institute for Public Administration, 1995), p. 108. See also Neil Buttimer, 'Pláig Fhollasach, Pláig Choimhtheach: "Obvious Plague, Strange Plague"', *Journal of the Cork Historical and Archaeological Society,* 102 (1997), pp. 41–68.

6 Sean Connolly, 'The "Blessed Turf": Cholera and Popular Panic in Ireland, June 1832', *Irish Historical Studies*, xxiii, no. 91 (1983), pp. 214–32.

7 James S. Donnelly, Jr, 'Pastorini and Captain Rock: Millenarianism and Sectarianism in the Rockite Movement in East Munster, 1821–4', in *Irish Peasants: Violence and Popular Unrest 1780–1914*, eds Samuel Clark and James S. Donnelly (Madison: University of Wisconsin Press, 1983), pp. 102–139.

8 Gibbons, *Captain Rock*, p. 35.

9 ibid., p. 35.

10 Fergus O'Ferrall, *Catholic Emancipation: Daniel O'Connell and the Birth of Irish Democracy, 1820–30* (Dublin: Gill and MacMillan, 1985).

11 Connolly, 'Blessed Turf'.

12 CM 22.

13 In Bekan, a parish adjoining Knock, popular memory attributed a claimed low famine death rate to supernatural intervention, in this case to the intercession of its patron, St Béacán. Nollaig Ó Muraíle, 'A Glimpse of Bekan During the Great Famine', in *Béacán/Bekan: Portrait of an East Mayo Parish*, eds Fr Michael Comer and Nollaig Ó Muraíle (Privately published, 1986). However, census figures, in contrast to Knock, show high population loss in Bekan in the famine decade. We need to remind ourselves that claims or accounts such as Campbell's are evidence of what was believed, not (necessarily) of what happened. See also Cormac Ó Gráda, *An Drochshaol: Béaloideas agus Amhrain* (Dublin: Coiscéim, 1994), pp. 27–34.

14 W. H. Maxwell, *Wild Sports of the West* (New York: Frederick Stokes Company [1832] 1915), pp. 218–9.

15 CM 46.

16 *Telegraph, or Connacht Ranger*, 4 May 1831. The claim was true: for a listing of County Mayo MPs in the Irish Parliament see Edith M. Johnston-Liik, *History of the Irish Parliament 1692–1800: Commons, Constituencies and Statutes*, 6 Vols (Belfast: Ulster Historical Foundation, 2002), Vol. II, p. 295. For the London parliament after 1800: Brian Walker, *Parliamentary Election Results in Ireland, 1801–1922* (Dublin: Royal Irish Academy, 1978).

17 Bernard O'Hara, ed., *Mayo: Aspects of its Heritage* (Galway: Regional Technical College, 1986), p. 243.

18 Guy Beiner, *Remembering the Year of the French: Irish Folk History and Social Memory* (Madison: University of Wisconsin Press, 2007).

19 http://homepages.ie/~fagann/1798/songs7.htm, accessed 26 January 2005.

20 J. F. Quinn, *History of Mayo*, Vol. 1 (Ballina: Brendan Quinn, 1993), pp. 14–24. Fitzgerald was convicted of abetting the abduction of a young woman by a man who hoped to force her family to agree to her marrying him (the abductor).

21 Johston-Liik, *Irish Parliament 1692–1800*, Vol. II, p. 283.

22 Maxwell, *Wild Sports*, pp. 377, 80.

23 William Wilde, *Irish Popular Superstitions* (Totowa, New Jersey: Rowman and Littlefield, 1973 [1852]), p. 24; Douglas Hyde, *Abhráin atá Leagtha ar an Reachtuire: Songs Ascribed to Raftery* (Shannon: Irish Academic Press [1903] 1973), p. 193.

24 Quinn, *History of Mayo*, Vol. 1, p. 17.

25 ibid., p. 39.

26 NFCS 208, pp. 128–9.

27 Padraig Ó Móráin, *An tAthair Mánus Mac Suibhne, Sagart ó Mhaigh Eo in Éirí Amach 1798/ Fr Manus Sweeney, A Mayo Priest in the Rebellion of 1798*, ed. and trans. Sheila Mulloy (Westport: Westport Historical Society, 1999), p. 10.

28 Very probably it is more evidence of strategic storytelling that Lady Gregory heard from the people that Denis Browne had repented of his sins: her own as well as her husband's ancestors had occupied in Galway a position in the ascendancy not unlike that of the Brownes in Mayo: James Pethica and James C. Roy, 'Introduction', in Henry Stratford Persse, *'To the Land of the Free from this Island of Slaves': Henry Stratford Persse's Letters from Galway to America, 1821–1832*, eds James L. Pethica and James C. Roy (Cork: Cork University Press, 1998), pp. 3–5; Lady Gregory, *Kiltartan History Book*; Peter Somerville-Large, *The Irish Country House: A Social History* (London: Sinclair-Stevenson, 1995), pp. 250, 256.

29 This was likely the Reverend de Vere Conys who was appointed curate in the Ballyhaunis area in 1831. According to an evangelical Protestant source, Conys was very successful in preaching to the people, but after being threatened with death, he left Ballyhaunis in 1832 and went to evangelise the Irish of St Giles in London. Joseph D'Arcy Sirr, *A Memorial of the Honourable and Most Reverend Power le Poer Trench, Late Archbishop of Tuam* (Dublin: William Curry, Jun, and Co, 1845), pp. 568–9. He later became Professor of Irish at Trinity College, Dublin.

30 Maxwell, *Wild Sports*, p. 375.

31 Quinn, *History of Mayo,* p. 58.

32 Such a representative might have proved a pleasant alternative, according to a recent historian! Marian McDonagh, 'An Early Victorian Scrapbook', in *The District of Loughrea, Vol. 1: History 1791–1918*, eds Joseph Forde, Christina Cassidy, Paul Manzor and David Ryan (Loughrea: Loughrea History Project, 2003), p. 146.

33 Scott, *Domination*, pp. 111–5.

34 CM 43.

35 CM 45.

36 CM 43.

37 Mairtín Ó Cadhain, *Tone Inné agus Inniú* (Dublin: Coiscéim 1999), p. 30, my translation. Though he did not think the earlier nineteenth-century poet composed it, Douglas Hyde included a version of this poem in his *Songs Ascribed to Raftery*, pp. 193–9.

38 CM 46.

39 CM 15; I have examined the episode in 'The Construction of Insiders as Outsiders: Catholic Accounts of Protestant Converts in Pre-famine Western Ireland', *Cultural and Social History*, 6 (2009), forthcoming.

40 CM 21.

41 Connolly, *Priests and People*, p. 133.

42 For example, Kai Erikson, *Wayward Puritans: A Study in the Sociology of Deviance* (New York: Wiley, 1966). Erikson reviews this tradition in his 2004 'Introduction to the Classic Edition' of this work.

43 Pádraig Ó Héalaí, 'Moral Values in Irish Religious Tales', *Béaloideas,* 42–44 (1974–1976), pp. 176–212.

44 Douglas Hyde, *Religious Songs of Connacht*, 2 vols (Dublin: Gill and Son, no date), Vol. 1, pp. 329–351. Stories with similar themes were given 'a local habitation and a name' in numerous areas, but we have less reliable or complete versions of most of them. For example, 'The Legend of the Black Hound', explaining how the parish of Kilconduff in east Mayo got its name, was reprinted in *The Connaught Telegraph* from *The Lamp*, but it may well have been written or edited to fit the demands of that Catholic devotional magazine.

45 CM 29.

46 ibid., p. 29.

47 This pronounced localism manifested itself in other ways that perplexed and outraged the ecclesiastical authorities. Some priests, presumably when they came from the local area (and especially from some powerful faction in the community) to begin with or came over time to embody local community ideals could be seen as local holy men, rather than as sacred because of their ordination by the universal Catholic ecclesiastical authority. In many cases, extended families helped a young man to become a priest and then expected that he would be assigned to their parish. Thus we see instances of parishes refusing to accept parish priests appointed by the bishop, or even pitched battles between different factions in a parish over where their dead pastor would be buried. When Fr Paul MacGreal, whose family owned a pew in Knock church, died during the famine while parish priest of Turlough, the people of the two half-parishes under his jurisdiction, Turlough and Keelogues, engaged in a faction fight over where he would be buried. J. F. Quinn, *History of Mayo*, Vol. II (Ballina: Brendan Quinn, 1993), p. 50.

48 Connolly, *Priests and People*, pp. 104–11.

49 Stiofán Ó Cadhla, *The Holy Well Tradition: The Pattern of St Declan, Ardmore, County Waterford, 1820–2000* (Dublin: Four Courts Press, 2004), pp. 14–31.
50 An important question, but one beyond the scope of this work, is to what extent people believed in one as opposed to a plurality of 'other worlds' and in the latter case, how the various worlds were interconnected. Like everything else, people actively chose when, how and where to believe what about transcendent realms. Of course, what they chose was shaped by their own experiences and their interaction and conversation with others.
51 For numerous examples of such 'orthas' see Hyde, *Religious Songs*.
52 Connolly, *Priests and People*, p. 112.
53 Pádraig Ó Héalaí, 'Priest Versus Healer: The Legend of the Priest's Stricken Horse', *Béaloideas*, 62/63 (1965).
54 Dermot MacManus, *The Middle Kingdom: The Faerie World of Ireland* (Gerrard's Cross: Colin Smythe, 1973), p. 164. MacHale is not named in this story about Biddy Early but he has to have been the bishop involved. Early's area of operation was her native north Clare and the adjacent part of south Galway. The bishop 'from the north of the county' can only have been MacHale whose cathedral seat was in Tuam in the northern part of county Galway. The story is not mentioned in the popular studies of Early by Meda Ryan, *Biddy Early* (Dublin: Mercier Press, 1978) and Edmund Lenihan, *In Search of Biddy Early* (Cork: Mercier Press, 1987). It is significant that the story was told in MacHale's diocese rather than the area of Early's practice. Of course, Biddy existed in the narrative tradition rather than in flesh and blood: Gearóid Ó Crualaoich, *The Book of the Cailleach: Stories of the Wise-Woman Healer* (Cork: Cork University Press, 2003), p. 96.
55 Patricia Lysaght, '"Is there Anyone Here to Serve My Mass?": the Legend of "the Dead Priest's Midnight Mass" in Ireland', *Arv* 47 (1991), 193–208.
56 Lady Gregory, *Visions and Beliefs in the West of Ireland* (Gerrard's Cross: Colin Smythe, 1970 [1920]), pp. 360–1.

5 THE PEOPLE MAKE A SAINT

1 Edward MacHale, 'Aguisín 1: John MacHale 1791–1881', in *Leon an Iarthair: Aistí ar Shean Mac Héil*, ed. Áine Ní Cheannain (Dublin: An Clóchomhar, 1983), p. 88.
2 NFC 795, p. 361; NFC 867, p. 251.
3 Thomas McGrath, Politics, *Interdenominational Relations and Education in the Public Ministry of Bishop James Doyle of Kildare and Leighlin, 1786–1834* (Dublin: Four Courts Press, 1999) and *Religion, Renewal and Reform in the Pastoral Ministry of Bishop James Doyle of Kildare and Leighlin, 1786–1834* (Dublin: Four Courts Press, 1999).
4 Sean Connolly, 'The "Blessed Turf": Cholera and Popular Panic in Ireland, June 1832', *Irish Historical Studies,* xxiii, no. 91 (1983), pp. 214–32.
5 Personal communication.
6 Bernard O'Reilly, *John MacHale, Archbishop of Tuam: His Life, Times and Correspondence,* 2 Vols. (New York and Cincinnati: Fustet, 1890), Vol. 2, p. 656; CT, 24 and 31 May 1879; *The Nation*, 23 August 1879.
7 Hilary Andrews, *The Lion of the West: A Biography of John MacHale* (Dublin: Veritas, 2001), Acknowledgments and p. 67.
8 For example, Selina Guinness, 'Visions and Beliefs in the West of Ireland: Irish Folklore and British Anthropology, 1898–1920', *Irish Studies Review* 6, 1 (1998), pp. 37–46.
9 Pádraig Ó Héalaí, 'Cumhacht an tSagairt sa Béaloideas', *Leachtaí Cholm Cille,* 8 (1977), pp. 109–31.
10 John F. Quinn, *Fr Mathew's Crusade: Temperance in Nineteenth-Century Ireland and Irish America* (Amherst: University of Massachusetts Press, 2002); Paul A. Townend, *Fr Mathew, Temperance and Irish Identity* (Dublin: Irish Academic Press, 2002).
11 Daniel Gallogly, *The Diocese of Kilmore, 1800–1950* (Cavan: Breiffne Historical Society, 1999), pp. 348–9.

12   Antoine Boltúin, *MacHeil agus an Ghaeilge: A Shaothar agus a Dhearcadh* (PhD Thesis, University College Galway, 1992), pp. 447–8.

13   E. MacHale, 'Aguisín 1', p. 88.

14   Lawrence Taylor, *Occasions of Faith: An Anthropology of Irish Catholics* (Dublin: Lilliput, 1995), pp. 145–66; Sean Connolly, *Priests and People in Pre-Famine Ireland* (Dublin: Gill and MacMillan, 1982), pp. 205–6, 218.

15   Oliver J. Burke, *The History of the Catholic Archbishops of Tuam, from the Foundation of the See to the Death of the Most Rev. John MacHale D.D. A. D. 1881* (Dublin: Hodges, Figgis and Co, 1882), p. 255.

16   Nationally, MacHale's public letters as Hierophilus in the early 1820s left no doubt at all, which is why the political authorities opposed his elevation to bishop. The government similarly opposed his promotion to archbishop in 1834: Donal Kerr, 'The Catholic Church in the Age of O'Connell', in *Christianity in Ireland: Revisiting the Story*, eds Brendan Bradshaw and Daire Keogh (Dublin: Columba Press, 2002), p. 177.

17   E. A. D'Alton, *History of the Archdiocese of Tuam*, 2 vols. (Dublin: Phoenix Publishing Co., 1928), Vol. 1, p. 378.

18   Emmet Larkin, 'The Parish Mission Movement, 1850–1880', in *Christianity in Ireland: Revisiting the Story*, eds Brendan Bradshaw and Daire Keogh (Dublin: The Columba Press, 2002), pp. 195–204; James H. Murphy, 'The Role of the Vincentian Parish Missions in the "Irish Counter-Reformation" in the Mid-Nineteenth Century', *Irish Historical Studies*, 24 (1984), pp. 152–71.

19   Burke, *Catholic Archbishops of Tuam*, pp. 243–4.

20   James C. Scott, *Domination and the Arts of Resistance: Hidden Transcripts* (New Haven: Yale University Press, 1990), pp. 202–27.

21   D'Alton, *History of the Archdiocese*, Vol. 1, p. 378.

22   MacHale, *Letters*, pp. 214–25.

23   Irish College, Rome, Archives, C 82, MacHale to Cullen, 10 April 1833, in Padraig Ó Tuairisc, *Ábhar a Bhaineann le Árd-Dheoise Thuama sa 19ú Aois i gCartlann Choláiste Na nGael sa Roimh, curtha in eagar, Maille le Réamhra agus Notaí* (MA Thesis in History, University College, Galway, 1982), pp. 85–6.

24   Boltúin, *MacHeil*, p. 442.

25   Critics of MacHale might like to extend the biblical analogy and claim that like the Biblical David, MacHale eventually became drunk on his own power. See Dean Ludwig and Clinton Longnecker, 'The Bathsheba Syndrome: The Ethical Failure of Successful Leaders', *Journal of Business Ethics*, 12 (1993), pp. 265–73.

26   Dean Acheson, *A History of the Church of Ireland, 1691–1996* (Dublin: Columba, 1997), p. 157.

27   Pádraig G. Ó Laighin, *Bánú Phartraí agus Thuar Mhic Éadaigh* (Dublin: Coiscéim, 1997); Gerard Moran, *The Mayo Evictions of 1860: Patrick Lavelle and the 'War' in Partry* (Westport: Westport Historical Society, 1986).

28   Richard K. Emmerson, 'The Secret', *American Historical Review*, 104, 5 (December 1999), pp. 1603–14.

29   Max Weber, *Economy and Society: An Outline of Interpretive Sociology*, eds Guenther Roth and Claus Wittich (New York: Bedminster Press, 1968), p. 75.

30   Patricia Pessar, *From Fanatics to Folk: Brazilian Millenarianism and Popular Culture* (Durham, NC: Duke University Press, 2004), chapter 2.

31   Boltúin, *MacHeil*, especially pp. 437–58.

32   John Steinbeck, 'Preface', in John Greenway, *American Folksongs of Protest* (University Of Pennsylvania Press, 1953), p. vii; Steinbeck, 'Foreword' in *Hard Hitting Songs for Hard-Hit People*, eds Alan Lomax, Woody Guthrie and Pete Seeger (New York: Oak Publications, 1967), p. 8.

33   Quoted in Fergus O'Ferrall, *Catholic Emancipation: Daniel O'Connell and the Birth of Irish Democracy, 1820–30* (Dublin: Gill and MacMillan, 1985), p. 73.

34   K. Theodore Hoppen, *Elections, Politics, and Society in Ireland, 1832–1885* (Oxford: Clarendon Press, 1984), p. 248, citing NFC 1198, pp. 318ff.

35 Hynes, Eugene, 'Making Sense of "Mistakes" in Oral Sources', in *Anáil an Bhéil Bheo: Orality and Modern Irish Culture*, eds Nessa Cronin, Seán Crossan and John Eastlake (Cambridge: Cambridge Scholars Press, 2009).

36 'A New Song in Praise of Bishop M'Hale', an undated ballad sheet reproduced in Boltúin, *MacHeil*, p. 517. The song was printed and 'sold wholesale by Alex Mayne,' a Belfast printer who commenced business in 1852, an indication of how widespread was MacHale's appeal.

37 Anderson, *Lion*, p. 40; E. MacHale, *Aguisín* 1, p. 88.

38 Taylor, *Occasions of Faith*, pp. 35–76; Michael Carroll, *Irish Pilgrimage: Holy Wells and Popular Catholic Devotion* (Baltimore: The Johns Hopkins University Press, 1999).

39 E. MacHale, *Aguisín* 1, p. 88.

40 O'Reilly, *MacHale*, Vol. 1, pp. 8–9; D'Alton, *History of the Archdiocese*, Vol. 1, p. 368.

41 NFC 712, pp. 149–70; this is a version of the story that William Carleton published as 'The Poor Scholar'.

42 Nollaig Ó Muraíle, 'Bekan Families, 1856 (Griffith's Valuation)' in *Béacán/Bekan: Portrait of an East Mayo Parish*, eds Fr Michael Comer and Nollaig Ó Muraíle (Privately published by Comer, 1986), pp. 182–93; Brian Smith, *A Guide to Your Mayo Ancestors* (Dublin: Flyleaf Press, 1997), p. 67.

43 Ulick J. Bourke, *Life and Times of the Most Rev. John MacHale, Archbishop of Tuam and Metropolitan* (Dublin: Gill and Son, 1882), pp. 18–9.

44 Patrick Corish, *The Irish Catholic Experience: A Historical Survey* (Dublin: Gill and MacMillan, 1985), p. 185.

45 Boltúin, *MacHeil*, p. 450.

46 Patrick Hogan, 'The Migration of Ulster Catholics to Connaught, 1795–96,' *Seánchas Árd Mhacha*, 9, 2 (1978–79), pp. 286–301; Patrick Tohall, 'The Diamond Fight of 1795 and the Resultant Expulsions', *Seánchas Árd Mhacha*, 3, 1 (1950), pp. 17–50. In her study of Brazilian millenarianism, *From Fanatics to Folk*, anthropologist Patricia Pessar noted that those leaders recognized as living saints all had unknown kinship ties. Nobody, including their closest followers, knew where they had come from. In a society structured by ties of kinship and patronage, their freedom from particularistic attachments permitted them to be seen as universal in their service. Perhaps giving MacHale geographically remote origins had the same effect in Mayo.

47 Poem in Boltúin, *MacHeil*, p. 517.

48 Thomas Carlyle, *Reminiscences of My Irish Journey in 1849* (London: Sampson Low, Marston, Searle and Rivington, 1882), p. 259.

49 In a by-election for Mayo held on 6 May 1836, Robert Dillon Browne got 599 votes and John Browne 305. MacHale wrote to Cullen, 'The poor Catholics returned a talented and honest Catholic to represent them' (27 May 1836). Some years earlier two correspondents of MacHale's predecessor as Archbishop, Oliver Kelley, indicated what was at stake. One wrote, 'Mr John Browne M.P. has made lately a speech in Parliament on which occasion he spoke very incautiously and disrespectfully of the Catholic Clergy of this Country, and whatever friends he had before are now hostile to him in consequence of his unwise and uncalled for speech. I assure your Grace it has made repealers of persons who hitherto were indifferent to the measure.' (Martin Browne to Oliver Kelley, 1 April 1834), Kelley's niece noted that 'The people are quite incensed against John Browne. He made a speech in the House of Commons that gave great offence. It is the general opinion that he will never get up from the county again.' (Eleanor Donoghue to Oliver Kelley, 5 March 1834. The letters are to be found in Ó Tuairisc, *Árd-Dheoise Thuama*, pp. 120–1, 125, and 153. Ó Tuairisc gives the Irish College, Rome, Archives references as NC 6.1 for the letters.) One historian has described the winner of the by-election, Robert Dillon Browne who came from a minor branch of the family, as 'MacHale's chief political henchman in Mayo'.

50 'The Tale of the Tub: or the Strange Thing that Happened to Bishop M'Hale', *The Dublin University Magazine*, 11 (December 1833), pp. 601–2; also in Boltúin, *MacHeil*, pp. 507–8.

51 Boltúin, *MacHeil*, p. 496.

52 NFC 349, pp. 309–12.

53 Scott, *Domination*; Patricia Ewick and Susan Silbey, 'Narrating Social Structure: Stories of Resistance to Legal Authority', *American Journal of Sociology*, 108 (May 2003), pp. 1328–72.

54 Bourke, *Life and Times of MacHale*, p.163.

55 *Mayo Election, Minutes of Evidence taken before the Select Committee on the Mayo Election Petition, with the Proceedings of the Committee and Index* (British Parliamentary Papers, House of Commons, 182, Session 2, 15 July 1857), p. 163.

56 Rev Jarlath Waldron, 'The 1857 Mayo Election', in *Mayo: Aspects of its Heritage,* ed. Bernard O'Hara (Galway: Regional Technical College, 1986), p. 103.

57 The popular memory not only distorted but also was quite selective in what it remembered or overlooked. Nobody mentions that MacHale's rival, Archbishop Cullen, similarly publicly used the illegal title. Steven Knowlton, *Popular Politics and the Irish Catholic Church: The Rise and Fall of the Independent Irish Party, 1850–1859* (New York: Garland, 1991), p, 167. Neither have his popular admirers then or later pointed out that during the Famine in 1846 MacHale urged his flock to observe the Lenten fast. He also apologised for not providing an Irish copy of his Lenten Pastoral, which was just as well according to a recent historian, since the people were thus spared his diatribe in which he blamed the government's proposed 'godless Colleges' and anyone who supported them for the famine visitation. Brendan Ó Cathaoir, *Famine Diary* (Dublin: Irish Academic Press, 1999), pp. 34–5. The fact that MacHale produced an English but not an Irish version of the Pastoral shows that he was addressing a wider national audience rather than the people of his own diocese where Irish was the dominant tongue.

58 Ó Tuairisc, *Árd-Dheoise Thuama*, pp. 30–31.

59 Emmet Larkin, 'John MacHale', *Oxford Dictionary of National Biography* (2004), p. 1.

60 ibid., p. 3.

61 Fergus O'Ferrall, *Catholic Emancipation: Daniel O'Connell and the Birth of Irish Democracy, 1820–30* (Dublin: Gill and MacMillan, 1985), p. 133.

62 See W. H. Maxwell, *Wild Sports of the West* (New York: Frederick Stokes Company, 1915 [1832]), p. 380. While perhaps the premier historian of the Emancipation movement, Fergus O'Ferrall simply states that MacHale was credited with the defeat of Denis Browne, but the situation was not as simple as he implies. The implication is that Browne was opposed to Catholic emancipation and was defeated by sympathetic forces under MacHale's inspiration or direction. However, Browne, who had sat earlier as MP for Mayo, was a sitting MP for Kilkenny since 1820 and apparently sought to be elected for one of the two seats in Mayo which in practice were virtually Browne family seats. However, he actually withdrew from the contest before the election and there was no poll, two other Brownes being returned unopposed. But Denis was a supporter of Emancipation. Before a Lords' Committee shortly before the election he said, 'I do declare to your Lordships that I am of the opinion that there never will be peace or security in Ireland — that it never will be a safe ally or possession of this country until all disabilities on account of religious belief are done away — all civil disabilities' (quoted in John Solan, *Religion and Society in the Ecclesiastical Province of Tuam Before the Famine* (MA thesis, University College, Galway, 1989), p. 254). Keeping a man of such views out of parliament can hardly be taken as evidence of success in promoting the Catholic cause. By the 1820s, Browne had mellowed considerably from his earlier days, but even early in his career, Browne 'combined a firm opposition to radicalism with strong sympathies in favour of Catholic political rights'. It would appear then that it was Browne's reputation for repression in the past rather than his current views that was crucial in creating the perception that his withdrawal from the electoral contest was a victory for the Catholic cause. Patrick M. Hogan, 'From Reaction to Reform: The Mellowing of a Connacht Squire, The Right Hon. Denis Browne, MP (1763–1822)', *Journal of the Galway Archaeological and History Society*, 57 (2005), pp. 29–37; L. M. Cullen, 'The Politics of Clerical

Radicalism in the 1790s', in *Protestant, Catholic, Dissenter: The Clergy and 1798,* ed. Liam Swords (Dublin: Columba Press, 1997), p. 298.

63   There is a semi-popular account of the 1857 election and an article on the 1872 Galway one, but otherwise these elections appear only as part of studies with other focal concerns. Waldron, 'The 1857 Mayo Election', and Michael Liffey, 'The 1872 By-Election', in *The District of Loughrea, Vol. 1: History 1791–1918,* eds Joseph Forde, Christina Cassidy, Paul Manzor and David Ryan (Loughrea: Loughrea History Project, 2003), pp. 326–48.

64   Matthew Cragoe, 'Conscience or Coercion?: Clerical Influence at the General election of 1868 in Wales', *Past and Present,* No. 149 (1995), p. 167.

65   NFC 867, pp. 251–57.

66   See the poem by Art MacCumhaigh in which the Catholic Church, speaking in Irish, debates the Protestant church, called the *Teampall Gallda,* speaking in English. *Verse in English from Eighteenth-Century Ireland,* ed. Andrew Carpenter (Cork: Cork University Press, 1998). Kerby Miller, *Emigrants and Exiles: Ireland and the Irish Exodus to North America* (New York: Oxford University Press, 1985), pp. 94–5; Liam Swords, *A Hidden Church: The Diocese of Achonry, 1689–1818* (Dublin: Columba Press, 1999), p. 137.

67   Douglas Hyde, *Abhráin atá Leagtha ar an Reachtuire: Songs Ascribed to Raftery* (Shannon: Irish Academic Press [1903] 1973), p. x of the 'Notes'.

68   What the use of *Easbog Gallda* in this story indicates is that all the various institutions of the 'ascendancy' — church, government, parliament, and others — were perceived as one unified bloc. Despite this hegemony, MacHale triumphed. It is worth noting that unlike the Mayo 1857 election case when MacHale went to London to testify, the Galway election inquiry was in Galway and headed by the infamous Judge William Keogh. It is understandable that such a hearing could be conflated both with a court case and a parliamentary debate since all were understood as machinations of the powerful. The reference to the *Easbog Gallda* in disputes about elections is understandable, especially after the 1872 election hearing in which Judge Keogh awarded the seat to a member of the same family as Archbishop Power Le Poer Trench of Tuam. The ultra-Tory, Captain the Hon. William Trench, was seated despite receiving only 658 votes compared to 2,538 for his opponent, the Home Ruler Captain John Nolan. To discredit him in the run-up to the election, Nolan's supporters had publicised Trench's family connections. Marie-Louise Legg, *Newspapers and Nationalism: The Irish Provincial Press 1850–1892* (Dublin: Four Courts Press, 1999), pp. 83–4. For how some high churchmen saw Keogh's decision see Emmet Larkin, *The Roman Catholic Church and the Home Rule Movement in Ireland, 1870–1874* (Dublin: Gill and MacMillan, 1990), pp. 122–34.

In an important sense, despite everything I have written above, perhaps the whole episode 'never happened' even in the sense of the narrator's claims that it did. The story was collected from a man who said he told it at a storytelling competition where he won a monetary prize for the best story. With prize-money as well as reputation as storyteller on the line, what better set of circumstances could we imagine to encourage some inventive exaggeration, some strategic reworking or more likely addition to an existing story? Perhaps the man pulled the wool over the eyes of the judges, and then continued the charade when approached by the Irish Folklore Commission collector. And if he were still alive, perhaps he would be smiling at pulling the leg of a professor and those who might read this book. Precisely because we know it from the storytelling competition rather than a more naturalistic setting, we have to be alert to the greater potential for strategic creativity in this than in the other MacHale stories. I would argue, however, that even deliberately and consciously invented stories are shaped both by the narrator as that person is moulded by the culture, and by the audience's expectations. After all, the story had to sound convincing to the judges and the other competitors at the feis. An implausible story would have won no prize. Moreover, even if the narrator invented the story and concocted a provenance for it by claiming falsely that he had heard it from his father and grandfather decades earlier, he did not invent it out of whole cloth. In this worst case scenario for my use of it as evidence of popular understandings, the story would document the man's wish or fantasy as these were shaped by his life situation and experience and given articulate shape in his community of believers. Anthropologists have convincingly shown how such fantasies reflect cultural preoccupations. See for example the separate articles by M. Rosaldo, Solomon, and Levy in *Culture Theory: Essays on Mind, Self, and Emotion,* eds Richard Schweder and Robert LeVine (New York: Cambridge University Press, 1984). Supportive findings have been detailed in studies of groups as diverse as weapons scientists and head-hunters: Hugh Gusterson, *Nuclear Rites: A Weapons Laboratory at the End of the Cold War* (Berkeley: University of California Press, 1996), and Renato Rosaldo, *Ilongot Headhunting, 1883–1974: A Study in Society and History* (Stanford: Stanford University Press, 1980). For a sociological argument on how culture shapes what people will imagine see Kai Erikson, *Everything in its Path: The Destruction of Community in the Buffalo Creek Flood* (New York: Simon and Schuster, 1978), p. 81.

69   NFC 869, pp. 576–8.
70   Whelan, *The Bible War*, p. 147.
71   *Foclóir Gaeilge-Béarla*, ed. by Niall Ó Dónail (Dublin: An Gúm, 1977), p. 983, under 'raithneacht'.
72   See pages 228–31 below.
73   NFC 867, pp. 251–7.
74   John J. White, *The Knock Apparitions and Pilgrimage: Popular Piety and the Irish Land War* (PhD Dissertation in History, Boston College, 1999), p. 47.
75   Gearóid Ó Tuathaigh, 'The Folk-Hero and Tradition', in *The World of Daniel O'Connell,* ed. Donal McCartney (Cork: Mercier Press, 1980), pp. 30–42; Diarmuid Ó Muirithe, 'O'Connell in Irish Folk Tradition', in *Daniel O'Connell: Portrait of a Radical,* eds Kevin B. Nowlan and Maurice R. O'Connell (Belfast: Appletree Press 1984), pp. 509–546; Ríonach Ui Ógáin, *Immortal Dan: Daniel O'Connell in Irish Folklore* (Dublin: Geography Publications, 1995).
76   'San uaigneas', literally 'in the loneliness'. As Angela Bourke reminded me, 'loneliness' today carries a psychological connotation quite different from nineteenth-century rural Mayo where a 'lonely place' was one bereft of human habitation.
77   NFC712, pp. 149–70.
78   Sr Mary Frances Clare [M. F. Cusack], *Three Visits to Knock, with the Medical Certificates of Cures and Authentic Accounts of Different Apparitions* (New York: P. J. Kennedy, [1882] 1904), p. 3; 'Luach', 'St Patrick in Mayo', *Knock Shrine Annual*, 1961, pp. 28–32 [reprinted from the *Knock Shrine Annual,* 1940].
79   Liam Pleimann, 'Seán Mac Haeil, Árd-Easbog Thuama', *An Cnoch agus an Chearnóg* (July/August, 1927), p. 3, reproduced in Boltúin, *MacHeil*, p.497; See ibid., p. 442, for many other similar references.
80   Larkin, 'John MacHale (1791–1881)', p. 6.
81   Liam Swords, *A Dominant Church: The Diocese of Achonry 1881–1960* (Dublin: Columba Press, 2004), p. 394.
82   Boltúin, *MacHeil*, p. 443.
83   P. W. Joyce, *Irish Music and Song* (Dublin: Gill, 1903), p. 4.
84   Brian O'Rourke, 'Mayo in Gaelic Folksong', in *Mayo: Aspects of Its Heritage* (Galway: Regional Technical College, 1986), p. 196.
85   Michael Tynan, *Catholic Instruction in Ireland 1720–1985* (Dublin: Four Courts Press, 1985), pp. 85–6. Boltúin, *MacHeil,* pp. 128–30, questions Tynan on this point and argues that Loftus and MacHale collaborated on the translation.
86   Tynan, *Catholic Instruction*, pp. 85–92.
87   William J. Mahon, editor and translator, *Doctor Kirwan's Irish Catechism by Thomas Hughes* (Cambridge, MA: Pangur Publications, 1991), pp. xxvi–xxvii.
88   For others in the folklore accounts, see Boltúin, *MacHeil*, p. 163, note 17.
89   Dubhglas De h-Íde (An Craoibhín), [Douglas Hyde], *An Sgealuidhe Gaedhealach (Sgeálta as Connachta)* (Dublin: Institiút Béaloideasa Éireann, 1933), p. xiv.
90   Boltúin, *MacHeil,* p. 451.

91 Dermot MacManus, *The Middle Kingdom: The Faerie World of Ireland* (Gerrard's Cross, UK: Colin Smythe, 1973), p. 164.
92 Also see Boltúin, *MacHeil*, p. 450.
93 J. F. Quinn, *History of Mayo*, Vol. 1 (Ballina: Brendan Quinn, 1993), pp. 392–406.
94 Tomás Laighléis, *Seánchas Thomáis Laighléis*, ed. by Tomás de Bhaldraithe (Dublin: An Clóchomhar, 1977), pp. 38–9.

6 POPULATION AND RELIGIOUS CONTINUITY

 1 James S. Donnelly, Jr, *The Great Irish Potato Famine* (Stroud: Sutton Publishing, 2001), chapter 7, summarises many historians' work on famine mortality; they agree that Mayo was the hardest hit county. See also T. W. Moody, *Davitt and Irish Revolution 1846–82* (Oxford: Clarendon Press, 1982) pp. 3–4; Cormac Ó Gráda, *Black '47 and Beyond: The Great Irish Famine in History, Economy, and Memory*. (Princeton: Princeton University Press, 1999) p. 69; Joel Mokyr, *Why Ireland Starved: a Quantitative and Analytical History of the Irish Economy, 1800–1850* (Boston: 1983), pp. 266–67; Liam Kennedy, Paul S. Ell, E. M. Crawford and L. A. Clarkson, *Mapping the Great Irish Famine* (Dublin: Four Courts Press, 1999), p. 38, Figure 5.
 2 G. V. Jackson to the Undersecretary, 25 June 1846, Distress Papers DP 2661, quoted in Liam Swords, *In Their Own Words: The Famine in North Connacht 1845–1849* (Dublin: The Columba Press, 1999), p. 40.
 3 ibid., p. 421.
 4 Desmond Bowen, *Souperism: Myth or Reality?* (Cork: Mercier, 1970), p. 229.
 5 Swords, *Own Words*, p. 88. Even though the Barony of Costello suffered horrendously during the famine, population decline 1841–51 was even greater in all seven adjoining baronies. Liam Kennedy, Paul S. Ell, E. M. Crawford and L. A. Clarkson, *Mapping the Great Irish Famine* (Dublin: Four Courts Press, 1999), Map 5.
 6 See Ivor Hamrock, ed., *The Famine in Mayo, 1845–1850: A Portrait from Contemporary Sources* (Castlebar: Mayo County Council, 1998), p. 40.
 7 ibid., p. 28.
 8 Charles Strickland to Quaker officials, Society of Friends Famine Papers 2/506/23, 12 July 1849, quoted in Swords, *In Their Own Words*, p. 386.
 9 Bowen, *Souperism*, p. 229.
10 To evaluate this claim we would need to catalogue the townlands included in full in Dillon's estate and make some allowance for townlands he owned in part. I do not have the information needed to do that. I suspect that Coulter's claim of only a 2 per cent drop is as exaggerated as the parallel claim that neighbouring estates were depopulated. If my hunch is correct, what we have here is evidence of Dillon and Strickland's popular reputation more than of their behaviour during the Famine. Coulter wrote nothing to suggest he checked the census figures.
11 Henry Coulter, *The West of Ireland: Its Existing Condition and Prospects* (Dublin: Hodges and Smith, 1862), p. 364.
12 Dun Finley, *Landlords and Tenants in Ireland* (London: Longman, Green and Co., 1881), pp. 210–07.
13 Dun, *Landlords*, p. 203.
14 Catherine Rynne, *Knock, 1879–1979* (Dublin: Veritas, 1979), pp. 6–7.
15 Jordan, *Land*, p. 123. Mokyr, *Why Ireland Starved*, pp. 263–74 and Donnelly, *The Great Irish Potato Famine*, p. 169, have criticised Cousens' estimates of famine mortality but Jordan's hypothesis stands or falls independently of their accuracy.
16 The evidence of the Ordinance Survey maps and later oral memories shows that this type of settlement did sometimes take place during the famine period in the part of Roscommon county adjoining Mayo. Mary Cawley, 'Aspects of Continuity and Change in Nineteenth-Century Rural Settlement Patterns: Findings From County Roscommon' *Studia Hibernica*, 22–23 (1982/1983), pp. 106–27.
17 Niall Ó Ciosáin, 'Famine Memory and Popular Representation of Scarcity', in *Memory*

and Commemoration in Irish History, eds Ian McBride and D. G. Boyce (Cambridge University Press, 2001), p. 117; Séamus Ó Catháin and Patrick O'Flanagan, *The Living Landscape: Kilgannon, Erris, County Mayo* (Dublin: Comhairle Bhéaloideasa Éireann, 1975), pp. 2–3, had made the same point earlier and specifically in the Mayo context.

18 Ó Ciosáin, 'Famine Memory', p. 117.

19 See Cormac Ó Gráda, *An Drochshaol: Béaloideas agus Amhrain* (Dublin: Coiscéim, 1994), p. v.

20 Living near Birmingham as he was when he wrote his memoir, Campbell was quite conscious of the parochial vision of the people and times he recalled from his earlier life: tongue-in-cheek he wrote that the highest point in Knock was the highest point in Ireland.

21 The fact that the lone victim died so quickly after returning from the town strongly suggests that the disease was cholera and since that disease in the years of the Great Famine seems not to have reached the west until March 1849 [see Joseph Robins, *The Miasma: Epidemic and Panic in Nineteenth Century Ireland* (Dublin: Institute for Public Administration, 1995), pp. 109, 139] after Campbell had left Knock, his story is about the 1832 epidemic. Significantly, however, he does not distinguish one 'bad time' from another — he was likely thinking of '*An Drochshaol*' — and applies the same explanatory framework to both. The vagueness of his formulation, 'plague and pestilence', is indicative of the imprecision of his thinking about temporally distinct episodes. In other words, he deployed what was culturally available to him, a supernatural explanation of *an drochshaol*. This is a good example of the apparent paradox of a memory of an event being in existence prior to that event that has been identified in folk history. Beiner, *Remembering the Year of the French*, pp. 317–8.

22 K. H. Connell, *Irish Peasant Society: Four Historical Essays* (Oxford: Clarendon Press, 1966), p. 167.

23 David Miller, 'Irish Catholicism and the Great Famine', *Journal of Social History*, 9 (1975), pp. 81–98.

24 Eugene Hynes, 'The Great Hunger and Irish Catholicism', *Societas* 8 (1978), pp. 138–9.

25 Ó Ciosáin, 'Famine Memory', p. 113.

26 Miller, 'Irish Catholicism'.

27 Emmet Larkin, 'The Devotional Revolution in Ireland, 1850–1875', *American Historical Review*, 77 (1972), pp. 625–52.

28 Larkin, *The Historical Dimensions of Irish Catholicism* (Washington: Catholic University of America Press, 1984), p. 6.

29 Hynes, 'Great Hunger'; Hynes, 'Nineteenth-Century Irish Catholicism, Farmers' Ideology, and National Religion: Explorations in Cultural Explanation', in *Sociological Studies in Roman Catholicism: Historical and Contemporary Perspectives,* ed. Roger O'Toole (Lewiston, New York: Edwin Mellen Press, 1989), p. 46.

30 Hynes, 'Nineteenth-Century Irish Catholicism', pp. 55–6, quoted at p. 56.

31 Hynes, 'Great Hunger', p. 148; 'Nineteenth-Century Irish Catholicism', pp. 57–63.

32 Thomas McGrath, 'The Tridentine Evolution of Modern Irish Catholicism, 1563–1962: A Re-Examination of the "Devotional Revolution" Thesis', *Recusant History*, 20 (1991), pp. 512–23.

33 Nigel Yates, *The Religious Condition of Ireland 1770–1850* (Oxford: Oxford University Press, 2006), p. 313.

34 Personal communication from Thomas McGrath, 12 May 1997.

35 Larkin sees the revolution as a project of the episcopacy and especially of Archbishop of Dublin (Cardinal after 1866) Paul Cullen who, armed with the powers of an Apostolic Legate, moulded the bishops into a unified body that effectively extended clerical discipline, and through the priests turned the Irish followers of Rome into practicing Catholics. It is well to note, however, that Cullen's funeral in 1878 was a 'muted affair' with only about one third as many people attending as had been present for the 1877 funeral, also in Dublin, of John O'Mahony, a Fenian who had died in America. Clare Murphy, 'Varieties of Crowd Activity from Fenianism to the

Land War, 1867–79', in *Crowds in Ireland, c. 1720–1929*, eds Peter Jupp and Eoin Magennis (New York: St Martin's Press, 2000), p. 182.

36 Emmet Larkin, *The Pastoral Role of the Roman Catholic Church in Pre-Famine Ireland, 1750–1850* (Dublin: Four Courts Press, 2006), pp. 9–60; Larkin, 'Before the Devotional Revolution', in *Evangelicals and Catholics in Nineteenth-Century Ireland,* ed. James H. Murphy (Dublin: Four Courts Press, 2005), pp. 15–37. Cara Delay, 'The Devotional Revolution on the Local Level: Parish Life in Post Famine Ireland', *US Catholic Historian,* 22 (Summer 2004), pp. 41–60, documents this problem with many examples.

37 K. Theodore Hoppen, *Elections, Politics, and Society in Ireland, 1832–1885* (Oxford: Clarendon Press, 1984), chapter 4.

38 Larkin's monographs as opposed to his devotional revolution article collectively comprise a superb examination of the evolution of the hierarchy as a body in the nineteenth century. Where he errs, in my view, is in assuming that the whole ecclesiastical structure was tightly coherent, that what Rome decided, the hierarchy then implemented transmitting Roman ways and discipline down via the priests to the lay people at the bottom. This is why he writes as if all the myriad changes in Catholicism formed a coherent syndrome, and why he writes from the perspective of the ecclesiastical authorities. Other researchers emphasise how bishops or priests were caught between top-down expectations and resistance from below. See, for examples, Paul Connell, *The Diocese of Meath Under Bishop John Cantwell 1830–1866* (Dublin: Four Courts Press, 2004) on an individual bishop, and Cara Delay, 'Confidantes or Competitors? Women, Priests, and Conflict in Post-Famine Ireland', *Eire/Ireland*, 40, 1/2 (Spring-Summer 2005), pp. 106–25, on priests.

39 For several such critics' comments, see John F. Quinn, *Fr Mathew's Crusade: Temperance in Nineteenth-Century Ireland and Irish America* (Amherst: University of Massachusetts Press, 2002), pp. 26–7.

40 David Miller, 'Mass Attendance in Ireland in 1834', in *Piety and Power in Ireland, 1760–1960: Essays in Honour of Emmet Larkin,* eds Stewart J. Brown and David W. Miller (Belfast: Institute for Irish Studies, Queen's University, 2000), pp. 158–79.

41 Desmond Keenan, *The Catholic Church in Nineteenth-Century Ireland: A Sociological Study* (Dublin: Gill and MacMillan, 1983), pp. 97–9.

42 Hynes, 'Nineteenth-Century Irish Catholicism', p. 54.

43 Donal Kerr, 'The Catholic Church in the Age of O'Connell', in *Christianity in Ireland: Revisiting the Story,* eds Brendan Bradshaw and Daire Keogh (Dublin: Columba Press, 2002), pp. 167 ff; Larkin, *Pastoral Role*, pp. 184–5; see also Thomas McGrath, *Religious Renewal and Reform in the Pastoral Ministry of Bishop James Doyle of Kildare and Leighlin, 1786–1834* (Dublin: Four Courts, 1999), pp. 156–7.

44 Keenan, *The Catholic Church,* pp. 99, 104.

45 Ulick J. Bourke, *Life and Times of the Most Rev. John MacHale, Archbishop of Tuam and Metropolitan* (Dublin: Gill and Son, 1882), p. 195.

46 McGrath, *Religious Renewal,* p. 90.

47 *First Report of the Commissioners of Public Instruction, Ireland* (London: Printed by William Clowes and Sons for His Majesty's Stationery Office, 1835), pp. 36d–37d.

48 Eugene Hynes, 'The Social Construction of Insiders as Outsiders'.

49 The Saw Doctors, 'Useta Love Her', on their album *If This Is Rock and Roll I Want My Old Job Back* (1990); this was Ireland's best selling song of all time, according to ickmusic.com/index.phe/category/irish accessed 14 August 2007. James Berry, *Tales from the West of Ireland* (Dublin: The Dolmen Press, 1966), p. 164.

50 Shaw Mason, cited in Swords, *Hidden Church,* pp. 224–5.

51 NFCS, Vol. 108, p. 182.

52 Patrick Corish, *The Irish Catholic Experience: A Historical Survey* (Dublin: Gill and MacMillan, 1985), p. 169.

53 Aidan Higgins, *Donkey's Years: Memories of Life as Story Told* (London: Secker and Warburg, 1995), pp. 129–9.

54 See John McGahern, *That They May Face the Rising Sun* (London: Faber and Faber, 2001), p. 2.

55   Hynes, 'Constructing Insiders as Outsiders'.

56   Emmet Larkin, 'Cardinal Paul Cullen', in *Varieties of Ultramontanism*, ed. Jeffrey von Arx, SJ (Washington, DC: The Catholic University of America, 1998), pp. 61–84.

57   Hynes, 'Great Hunger', p. 139.

58   Joseph Prost, C.Ss.R., *A Redemptorist Missionary in Ireland, 1851–1854: Memoirs of Joseph Prost, C.Ss.R.*, trans. and eds, Emmet Larkin and Herman Freudenberger (Cork: Cork University Press, 1998), p. 23.

59   Hugh McLeod, 'Popular Catholicism in Irish New York, c1900', in *The Churches, Ireland and the Irish*, eds W. J. Shields and Diana Woods (Published for the Ecclesiastical History Society by Basil Blackwell, 1989), p. 355.

60   Bernadette Flanagan, *The Spirit of the City: Voices from Dublin's Liberties* (Dublin: Veritas, 1999), p. 122.

61   Claire Mitchell, *Religion, Identity and Politics in Northern Ireland: The Limits of Belonging* (Aldershot: Ashgate, 2005).

62   Michael Carroll, *Irish Pilgrimage: Holy Wells and Popular Catholic Devotion* (Baltimore: Johns Hopkins University Press, 1999).

63   Malachy McKenna, 'A Textual History of *The Spiritual Rose*', *Clogher Record* 14 (1991), pp. 52–73; Malachy McKenna, ed., *The Spiritual Rose* (Dublin: Institute for Advanced Studies, 2001).

64   Daniel Gallogly, *The Diocese of Kilmore, 1800–1950* (Cavan: Breiffne Historical Society, 1999), p. 70.

65   Oliver Rafferty, book review, *Journal of Ecclesiastical History*, 49/3 (1998), p. 582; Hugh Fenning, OP, 'A Time of Reform: From the "Penal Laws" to the Birth of Modern Nationalism, 1691–1800', in *Christianity in Ireland: Revisiting the Story*, eds Brendan Bradshaw and Daire Keogh (Dublin: Columba Press, 2002), p. 142.

66   'Studies of Catholicism elsewhere as well as . . . social scientific theories of culture and ideology provide us with overwhelming evidence of the complex interaction of the local and the orthodox, of interpenetration of the little traditions and the great, of culture continuity in the face of seemingly overwhelming change, and of the active rather than the passive stance of ordinary people in constructing their own cultural and religious understandings.' Hynes, 'Nineteenth-Century Irish Catholicism', p. 53. The 'new' regime is then assumed to exclude the older patterns of religious behaviour and practice. For example, we know that bishops and the hierarchy as a body came to condemn the holding of house-station masses, but we cannot assume that their directions led to the disappearance of the practice. Whether they did or not is an empirical question to be decided on a case by case basis and not assumed to have the same answer everywhere. I know from direct personal experience that station masses continued in at least my home area until the end of the twentieth century and, depending on how we define them, still continue. They still are held in the parish of Knock.

67   Keenan, *The Catholic Church*, chapter 8.

68   Sean Connolly, *Priests and People in Pre-Famine Ireland*, 2nd edition (Dublin: Four Courts Press, 2001), pp. 20, 107–8.

69   Donal A. Kerr, *Peel, Priests, and Politics: Sir Robert Peel's Administration and the Roman Catholic Church in Ireland, 1841–1846* (Oxford: Clarendon Press, 1982), chapter 2.

70   The last part of this paragraph is taken from Hynes, 'Nineteenth Century Irish Catholicism', p. 53. Ann Taves, *The Household of Faith: Roman Catholic Devotions in Mid-Nineteenth-Century America* (South Bend: Notre Dame University Press, 1981), pp. 62, 47.

71   The evidence available shows that the people were very devout before Larkin's revolution. Near the turn of the twentieth century in Mayo Douglas Hyde found numerous versions of orally transmitted prayers for almost every imaginable occasion. A Jesuit priest who published another collection wrote that 'the first thing to be said of such prayers is that they make a sacrament of every moment and every act of a person's life . . . they unite heaven and earth, God and the human, Christ and the sinner'. Diarmuid Ó Laoighre, SJ, *Ár bPaidreacha Dúchais* (Dublin, 1975), Preface [my translation].

72 See Hugh Fenning, OP, 'A Time of Reform: From the "Penal Laws" to the Birth of Modern Nationalism, 1691–1800', in *Christianity in Ireland: Revisiting the Story*, ed. by Brendan Bradshaw and Daire Keogh (Dublin: Columba Press, 2002), p. 142.

73 Kerby Miller, *Emigrants and Exiles: Ireland and the Irish Exodus to North America* (New York: Oxford University Press, 1985), p. 235.

74 Although some of my terminology in this paragraph is taken from Meredith McGuire, 'Linking Theory and Methodology For the Study of Latino Religiosity in the United States', in *An Enduring Flame: Studies on Latino Popular Religiosity*, eds Anthony M. Stevens-Arroya and Ana Maria Diaz-Stevens (New York: Bildner Centre, 2004), pp. 199ff, I made many of these points earlier at greater length and with illustrative examples from nineteenth-century Ireland. My argument derives from both general sociological theories and from studies of Catholicism elsewhere. See Hynes, 'Nineteenth Century Irish Catholicism', for more extensive discussion and documentation.

75 Miller, 'Irish Catholicism'; Connolly, *Priests and People*, 2nd ed., pp. 103–4; Larkin, *Pastoral Role*, pp. 184, 278; Fenning, *Undoing of the Friars*.

7 RELIGION IN Pre-Apparition Knock

1 Fr Michael Comer and Nollaig Ó Muraíle, eds, *Béacán/Bekan: Portrait of an East Mayo Parish* (Privately published by Comer, 1986).

2 Michael Higgins, 'In Bekan Long Ago', in *Béacán/Bekan: Portrait of an East Mayo Parish*, eds Fr Michael Comer and Nollaig Ó Muraíle (Privately published, 1986), pp. 93, 203, 102.

3 Nollaig Ó Muraíle, 'Landlord and Tenant', in *Béacán/Bekan: Portrait of an East Mayo Parish*, eds Fr Michael Comer and Nollaig Ó Muraíle (Privately published, 1986), pp. 149–51; Catherine Rynne, *Knock, 1879–1979* (Dublin: Veritas, 1979), p. 7.

4 Higgins, 'Bekan Long Ago', p. 98.

5 Rynne, *Knock,* p. 37–8.

6 Rynne, *Knock,* p. 21.

7 Higgins, 'Bekan Long Ago', pp. 98–9.

8 The local memory was of 'the prayer of St Béacán as a result of which nobody died of hunger in the parish during the Famine'. Fr Ciaran Waldron, 'Memories of Willie Kelly', in *Béacán/Bekan: Portrait of an East Mayo Parish*, eds Fr Michael Comer and Nollaig Ó Muraíle (Privately published, 1986), p. 167. The censuses show that the population of Bekan declined from 5,589 in 1841 to 4,724 in 1851, but a local historian claimed that 'a good portion of this decline can undoubtedly be attributed to emigration'. Nollaig Ó Muraíle, 'A Glimpse of Bekan during the Great Famine' in Fr Michael Comer and Nollaig Ó Muraíle, eds *Béacán/Bekan*, p. 147. Asserting this, however, does not make it so. This case highlights the difficulty in judging how population decline might have affected cultural continuity. Making two simplifying assumptions: 1. that fatalities would be concentrated amongst the poorest and conversely, in the poorest areas of the country like Mayo, emigration would be more common among the better off, and 2. that the poorest strata were most conservative culturally and the better off more influenced by 'new' ideas and practices, then population decline caused by excess deaths would accelerate cultural change (see Eugene Hynes, 'The Great Hunger and Irish Catholicism', *Societas*, 8 (1978), 137–155, for this idea developed to explain the devotional revolution); conversely, population decline caused by emigration would strengthen the more conservative elements in the socio-cultural system. This might have happened in the Bekan area.

9 ibid., p. 106.

10 ibid., p. 95.

11 ibid., p. 96.

12 ibid., pp. 101–4.

13 ibid., p. 95.

14 ibid., pp. 93, 96–97.

15 ibid., p. 97.
16 ibid., p. 101; NFCS 108, p. 200.
17 Lawrence Taylor, '*Bás i n-Éireann*: Cultural Constructions of Death in Ireland', *Anthropological Quarterly,* 62 (October 1989), pp. 696–712.
18 Higgins, 'Bekan Long Ago', p. 99, for Bekan, and NFCS 108, p. 32, for Knock.
19 For example, NFCS 108, pp. 162–3.
20 ibid., pp. 348–9.
21 Donald Jordan, Jr, *Land and Popular Politics in Ireland: County Mayo from the Plantation to the Land War* (Cambridge: Cambridge University Press, 1994), p. 139ff.
22 ibid. p. 141.
23 ibid. p. 130.
24 David Fitzpatrick, 'Ireland since 1870', in *The Oxford Illustrated History of Ireland,* ed. Roy F. Foster (Oxford: Oxford University Press, 1989), p. 215.
25 David Fitzpatrick, '"A Share of the Honeycomb": Education, Emigration and Irishwomen', *Continuity and Change* 1, 2 (1986), pp. 217–234; Fitzpatrick, 'The Modernisation of the Irish Female', in *Rural Ireland 1600–1900: Modernisation and Change,* eds Patrick O'Flanagan, Paul Ferguson and Kevin Whelan (Cork: Cork University Press, 1987), pp. 162–80.
26 Edward Murphy, SJ, to Daniel Hudson, CSC, no date, 1882, UNDA [CHUD] x–2–I; *Ave Maria,* 12 August 1882.
27 James C. Scott, *Domination and the Arts of Resistance: Hidden Transcripts* (New Haven: Yale University Press, 1990).
28 NFCS 108, pp. 172–3.
29 Uncertainty about people's ages, including their own, was not confined to those like Daniel Campbell born before the famine. The 1879 seer Mary Beirne was reported in 1880 to be twenty-six at the time of the apparition, but in 1932 she claimed she was twenty-eight and in 1936 she said she was twenty-nine. Rynne, *Knock,* p. 18, says Mary recognised her true age when she became eligible for the Old Age Pension that people aged seventy or more could collect after 1909. The prospect of a pension likely encouraged some people to 'realise' they were older than they had thought. Widespread vagueness about ages, even of the apparition witnesses, is actually evidence of traditionalism at the time.
30 I consulted these records on-line, as posted by genealogists, accessed 2 June 2004 at http://archiver.rootsweb.com/th/read/IRL-MAYO-KNOCK/2002. The records are combined for Knock and Aghamore, the two parishes under the jurisdiction of the parish priest of Knock. The Aghamore records are more complete, starting earlier, in 1865, and continuing beyond the early 1870s when the Knock series has a gap until after the apparition.
31 NFCS 108, pp. 403–5.
32 Waldron, 'Memories of Willie Kelly', p. 168.
33 Higgins, 'Bekan Long Ago', p. 101.
34 Michael Kelly, 'The Bekan Area in the Year of the French', in *Béacán/Bekan: Portrait of an East Mayo Parish,* eds Fr Michael Comer and Nollaig Ó Muraíle (Privately published by Comer, 1986), p. 147; Richard Hayes, *The Last Invasion of Ireland: When Connacht Rose* (Dublin: Gill and Son, 1937), p. 312.
35 T. P. Flanagan, 'Fr Jarlath Ronayne', in *Béacán/Bekan: Portrait of an East Mayo Parish,* eds Fr Michael Comer and Nollaig Ó Muraíle (Privately published, 1986), p. 165.
36 Patricia Lysaght, '"Is there Anyone Here to Serve My Mass?" the Legend of the "the Dead Priest's Midnight Mass" in Ireland', *Arv,* 47 (1991), pp. 193–208.
37 Emmet Larkin, *The Roman Catholic Church and The Creation of the Modern Irish State, 1878–1886* (Philadelphia: American Philosophical Society, 1975), p. 13.
38 Sean Connolly, *Priests and People in Pre-Famine Ireland* (Dublin: Gill and MacMillan, 1982), p. 72.
39 Desmond Bowen, *Paul Cullen and the Shaping of Modern Irish Catholicism* (Dublin: Gill and MacMillan, 1983), pp. 232, 292.

40   Patrick Nold, *The Knock Phenomenon: Popular Piety and Politics in the 'Modern' Ireland* (Undergraduate Thesis, University of Michigan, 1993), pp. 23, 26, n. 60.
41   Connolly, *Priests and People,* 2nd ed. (Dublin: Four Courts, 2001), p. 108.
42   K. Theodore Hoppen, *Elections, Politics, and Society in Ireland, 1832–1885* (Oxford: Clarendon Press, 1984), p. 205; J. Coombes, 'Catholic Churches in the Nineteenth Century: Some Newspaper Sources', *Journal of the Cork Historical and Archaeological Society,* lxxxi (1975), p. 2; *Irish Catholic Directory,* 1843, p. 317, as cited in Emmet Larkin, *The Pastoral Role of the Roman Catholic Church in Pre-Famine Ireland, 1750–1850* (Dublin: Four Courts Press, 2006), p. 177.
43   Kieran Waldron, 'The Churches of the Archdiocese of Tuam', *Cathair na Mart,* 18 (1998), p. 163.
44   Larkin, *Catholic Church . . . 1878–1886,* p. 13, n. 7.
45   Jacinta Prunty, *Margaret Aylward, 1810–1889: Lady of Charity, Sr of Faith* (Dublin: Four Courts, 1999), p. 15.
46   Larkin, *Catholic Church . . . 1878–1886,* p. 13.
47   Transcripts of the four letters in question, K/78/13, 19, 20 and 22, are to be found in Padraig Ó Tuairisc, *Ábhar a Bhaineann le Árd-Dheoise Thuama sa 19ú Aois i gCartlann Choláiste Na nGael sa Roimh, curtha in eagar, maille le Réamhra agus Notaí* (MA Thesis in History, University College, Galway, 1982), pp. 502–8. The two from MacEvilly are synopsised by Patrick J. Corish, 'Irish College, Rome: Kirby Papers', *Archivium Hibernicum,* 30 (1972), p. 81.
48   Ó Tuairisc, *Ard-Dheoise Thuama,* pp. 50–1.
49   In that case, Cardinal Cullen wrote Kirby that 'the state of the diocese is not good. Many ignore the decrees of Thurles', at a time when he was supporting a candidate, Thomas Croke, who had gotten not one vote from the priests of Cashel to become archbishop of that diocese. MacEvilly, Cullen's ally, had two days earlier informed Kirby that 'the state of discipline in Cashel was somewhat relaxed'. Corish, 'Kirby Papers' p. 78, Cullen to Kirby, 6 April, 1875; ibid., p. 77.
50   Patrick J. Corish, 'Kirby Papers', pp. 84, 85, 86, 87, 88, 90.
51   Liam Bane, *The Bishop in Politics: The Life and Career of John MacEvilly* (Westport: Westport Historical Society, 1993), pp. 56–7; Also see Emmet Larkin, *The Roman Catholic Church and the Home Rule Movement in Ireland, 1870–1874* (Dublin: Gill and MacMillan, 1990), pp. 56–7.
52   Larkin, *Catholic Church . . . 1878–1886,* p. 13.
53   Larkin, *Catholic Church . . . 1870–1874,* pp. 57–8.
54   Emmet Larkin, 'Cardinal Paul Cullen', in *Varieties of Ultramontanism,* ed. Jeffrey von Arx, SJ (Washington, DC: The Catholic University of America, 1998), pp. 61–84.
55   Larkin, *Catholic Church . . . 1870–1874,* p.70.
56   Corish, 'Kirby Papers', p. 30.
57   Hoppen, *Elections,* p. 209ff.
58   O Tuairisc, *Ard-Dheoise Thuama,* p. 34.
59   O Tuairisc, *Ard-Dheoise Thuama,* p. 52; O'Reilly, *John MacHale,* Vol. 2, pp. 621–2.
60   Ó Tuairisc, *Ard-Dheoise Thuama,* p. 22, my translation.
61   O'Reilly, *John MacHale,* Vol. 2, p. 624, Ó Tuairisc, *Ard-Dheoise Thuama,* p. 52.
62   Desmond Bowen, *The Protestant Crusade in Ireland, 1800–1870: A Study of Protestant-Catholic Relations Between the Act of Union and Disestablishment* (Montreal: McGill-Queens University Press, 1978), p. 15.
63   T. W. Moody, *Davitt and Irish Revolution 1846–82* (Oxford: Clarendon Press, 1982), p. 2.
64   A large part of the archdiocese lay in Mayo, the county with the highest percentage of its houses classified as Fourth Class, the worst possible level, in both 1841 and 1861. Liam Kennedy, Paul S. Ell, E. M. Crawford and L. A. Clarkson, *Mapping the Great Irish Famine* (Dublin: Four Courts Press, 1999), p. 79, Figure 18. It had the lowest average valuation of agricultural holdings and an 'egregiously uneven' distribution of farms, with the vast majority of tenants crowded onto very small farms of inferior quality. See Moody, *Davitt,* p. 2, or almost any historian of rural life in nineteenth-century Ireland.

These various comparative figures would only be worsened when the Connemara part of the archdiocese was considered.

65 Cormac O Gráda, 'Seasonal Migration and Post-Famine Adjustment in the West of Ireland', *Studia Hibernica*, 13 (1971), p. 74.

66 Both monstrances were later held in the Knock Museum and are pictured in one of its guides. Tom Neary, *'Auld Acquaintance': A Guide to Knock Folk Museum*, 2nd ed. (Knock, 1980), unpaginated.

67 ibid.

68 John White, *The Knock Apparitions and Pilgrimage: Popular Piety and the Irish Land War* (PhD Dissertation in History, Boston College 1999), pp. 267–8.

69 In the case of Lourdes, conflicts between ecclesiastical supporters and opponents of the apparition claims, as well as the varied interests of different civil authority figures, along with a divided press and republican/royalist political conflict throughout the French state, all led to detailed investigations, arguments and considerations from many diverse perspectives. Ruth Harris, *Lourdes: Body and Spirit in the Secular Age* (New York: Viking, 1999). The apparition of the Virgin in Marpingen in Bismarck's Germany became a focal point in church/state conflict, an important battleground in the *Kulturkampf*, leading to undercover police investigations, numerous civil trials, depositions, interrogations, claims and counterclaims, all contributing to a mountain of evidence. Three eight-year-old girls who claimed to have seen the Virgin were interrogated no fewer than fourteen times by various state officials and subjected to two comprehensive medical examinations, and thousands of pages of records resulted from the questioning of numerous other local people. David Blackbourn, *Marpingen: Apparitions of the Virgin Mary in Bismarckian Germany* (Oxford: Clarendon, 1993), p. 136 and *passim*.

70 Hoppen, *Elections*, p. 210. When it came to episcopal vestments, MacHale from the beginning wore the most elaborate and ornate. At his consecration in 1836, his vestments were of 'beautiful long rich white satin, overlaid with gold, in a pattern of chaste and splendid execution . . . a variety of diamonds'. B. W. Noel, *Notes of a Short Tour Through the Midland Counties of Ireland*, p. 175–6, as quoted in Hoppen, *Elections*, p. 202, n. 1.

71 The bell installed is dated 1874, Tom Neary and Seán Egan, eds, *Knock Parish Church 1828–2006* (no publisher given), p. 15; O'C[onnor], T., *A Visit to Knock* (Limerick: T. O'Connor, 1880), p. 12; [Thomas Sexton], *The Illustrated Record of the Apparitions at Knock: The Depositions of the Witnesses, Lists of the Alleged Miraculous Cures . . . (reprinted from the 'Weekly News')* (Dublin: T. D. Sullivan, [1880]), p. 27.

72 CT, 31 May 1879.

73 Denunciations from the altar were also forbidden by the Tuam archdiocesan synod in 1858.

74 *Daily News*, 27 February 1880.

75 John MacPhilpin, *The Apparitions and Miracles at Knock. Also, The Official Depositions of the Eye-Witnesses* (Dublin: Gill and Son, 1880), p. 59.

76 O'C[onnor], *Visit*, p. 20.

77 Sexton, *The Illustrated Record*, p. 29.

78 Knock Museum has a copy of a print called *2nd Apparition at Knock, Co. Mayo, as seen by the Venerable Archdeacon Cavanagh PP & Others on Friday Jany 2nd 1880* (Dublin, W. Collins, March 17, 1880).

79 See Fr Michael Walsh, *The Apparition at Knock: A Survey of Facts and Evidence* (Tuam: St Jarlath's College, 1955; second edition, 1959), p. 51; in the 1930s Mary Beirne told this to a promoter. Liam Ua Cadhain, *Knock Shrine* (Galway: O'Gorman Printing House, 1935), p. 54. The earliest report we have is from 1882, Sr Mary Francis Clare [Cusack], *Three Visits to Knock . . .* (New York: P. J. Kenedy, 1904 [1880].

80 Nold, *The Knock Phenomenon*, p. 24.

81 [Cusack[, *Three Visits*, p. 55; Donnelly, 'Marian Shrine', p. 14.

82 Ua Cadhain, *Knock Shrine*, p. 54.

83 ACSJP 3A 260, p, 51b, Canon Bourke to Monsignor Tobias Kirby, 25 January 1884.
84 NFCS 108, pp. 102–4, quoted at p. 103; my translation.
85 Mary P. Magray, *The Transforming Power of the Nuns: Women, Religion, and Cultural Change in Ireland, 1750–1900* (New York: Oxford University Press, 1998), p. 90. Other researchers also noted the importance of music as a marker of the devotional revolution (Hoppen, *Elections*, pp. 203–4). Recognising that the history of choirs was not necessarily a simple spread of the practice from more to less modern areas and that they very likely in most areas had more complex genealogies, we should note that William Carleton mentioned church choirs on at least two occasions for the pre-famine era but in neither were they singing in church. In 'The Emigrants of Ahadarra', a 'rustic choir, whom the parish clerk had organised and in a great measure taught himself, approached the body [of a recently dead woman] and sang a hymn over it, after which the preparations for its removal [from the house to the graveyard] began to be made.' In 'The Party Fight and Funeral', a funeral cortege on its way to the graveyard was met by 'a dozen singing-boys, belonging to a chapel choir, which the priest who was fond of music had sometime before formed. They fell in, two by two, and commenced singing the *Requiem* or Latin hymn for the dead': William Carleton, *The Works of William Carleton*, 2 Volumes (Freeport New York: Books for Libraries Press, 1970 reprint of 1881 edition), Vol. I, p. 559 and Vol. II, p. 793. How widespread were such choirs and how long in existence? Was singing mostly associated with death rituals? A County Monaghan parish had rules, written down in 1832, that specified that 'no person in either choir . . . shall go to wakes out of their own town, under pretence of singing': Nigel Yates, *The Religious Condition of Ireland 1770–1850* (Oxford: Oxford University Press, 2006), p. 177. What was the significance of the choirs' gender composition? Is it possible that priests sometimes promoted (male?) choirs to sing at funerals rather than in church, perhaps in some sort of relationship with the practice of keening? Were priests providing an alternative? Or were the people demanding or improvising a substitute for the declining *caoineadh*? Was the promotion of choirs at funerals a (conscious?) step to make death a more church centred experience? Such questions have to be answered by empirical research and not by definitional fiat.
86 CT, 26 August 1876.
87 CT, 24 June 1876; also see CT, 3 June 1876.
88 Daniel Gallogly, *The Diocese of Kilmore, 1800–1950* (Cavan: Breiffne Historical Society, 1999), pp. 386, 147.
89 Information in this paragraph from Kieran Anthony Daly, *Catholic Church Music in Ireland, 1878–1903* (Dublin: Four Courts Press, 1995), pp. 54–7.
90 An obituary of Cavanagh noted that 'he got a Dublin lady to form a choir in both vocal and instrumental music' in the mid-1870s. 'A Loss to Catholicity: The Late Archdeacon B. A. Cavanagh, PP, V. F., Knock, Ballyhaunis, Co. Mayo', *The Lamp*, L1V, No. 315 (1898?), p. 19. It is thus unlikely that Miss Anderson, who was from Castlebar, started the choir.
91 Catherine Mary Dwyer, 'James Augustine Anderson, O.S.A.', *Seánchus Árd Mhacha*, 7 (1974), pp. 240–1.
92 Given that Anderson was not a common name, one is led to ask if she was related to the Ballyhaunis priest. While I have no evidence that the two were related, I cannot prove that they were not. Miss Anderson was from Castlebar while Fr Anderson was born in Drogheda in 1837.
93 Sexton, *Illustrated History*, p. 16.
94 O'C[onnor], *Visit*, p. 12.
95 For these dates, see Ua Cadhain, *Archdeacon Cavanagh*, pp. 48–9.
96 Fr Cavanagh very likely was better informed about nuns' lives than most priests. He had been confessor to a convent of nuns in Westport for seventeen years before becoming parish priest of Knock. On Gaffney, see 'A Brief History of the Order of Sisters of St. Joseph of Peace, Written by Mother Evangelista', 'The Bishop's Questions and Pages of Answers [By Mother Evangelista]', and 'A Brief History of the Institute of Saint Joseph's Sisters of Peace', in ACSJP, 7A 1 10 and ACSJP 7A 5 10, in File Drawer C2.

97   ibid.
98   White, *Apparitions,* p. 236.
99   CT, 4 September 1880.
100 CT, 6 March 1880, 21 and 28 December 1878.
101 O'C[onnor], *Visit,* p.16.
102 Sexton, *Illustrated History,* p. 6, MacPhilpin, *The Apparitions,* p. 11, and O'C[onnor], *Visit,* p. 12, all estimate some dimensions of the cross-shaped church. See the floor plan of the building printed in Sexton, p. 6, and MacPhilpin p. 12; I assume the plan accurately represents the relative lengths of all the dimensions. Larkin, *Pastoral Role,* chapter III, uses the five square feet figure in estimating the capacity of chapels in the prefamine era.
103 O'C[onnor], *Visit,* p. 12.
104 White, *Apparitions,* p. 206 n. 36.
105 On 2 September and 20 October 1879, see Ó Tuairisc, *Ard-Dheoise Thuama,* p. 525.
106 See CT, 13 July 1878 for one example.
107 The efforts were successful. The first nuns arrived around 1 January 1877 and by the following August they were teaching nearly 300 boys and girls in the schools they set up. In November that year, three women entered the religious life at that convent at a ceremony attended by 11 priests, including Fr Richard MacHale. CT, 30 December 1876, 4 August 1877, and 24 November 1877.
108 *Ard-Dheoise Thuama,* p. 525, n. 60.
109 CT, 21 September 1878.
110 Ó Tuairisc, *Ard-Dheoise Thuama,* p. 590, also marshals evidence to refute another of MacEvilly's charges: that MacHale had done nothing to maintain or improve the furnishings of the cathedral in Tuam.
111 CT, 30 December 1876 and 4 August 1877; Magray, *Nuns.*
112 CT, 8 May 1880.
113 CT, 8 May 1880.

8   Authority Structures Shaken

1   David Blackburn, *Marpingen: Apparitions of the Virgin Mary in Bismarckian Germany* (Oxford: Clarendon Press, 1993), chapter 2.
2   David N. Doyle, 'Knock 1879: Message to a Deprived People', *Doctrine and Life,* 30, 2 (February 1980), p. 73. Doyle was here relying mainly on Eric Almquist, *Mayo and Beyond: Land, Domestic Industry and Rural Transformation in the West of Ireland* (Boston University, PhD thesis, 1977). The indispensable study is Donald Jordan, Jr, *Land and Popular Politics in Ireland: County Mayo From the Plantation to the Land War* (Cambridge: Cambridge University Press, 1994).
3   Tom Yager, 'What Was Rundale and Where Did It Come From?' *Béaloideas,* 70 (2002), pp. 153–86.
4   Doyle, 'Knock 1879', pp. 73–4.
5   David Fitzpatrick, 'Ireland Since 1870', in *The Oxford Illustrated History of Ireland,* ed. Roy F. Foster (Oxford: Oxford University Press, 1989), pp. 215–6.
6   For a superb evocation of the emotional ties between farm and family in this part of Mayo and how they were sustained, see John Healy's account of the fields that constituted his mother's family's farm, *Nineteen Acres* (Galway: Kenny's, 1978). In his study of devotion to Our Lady of Mount Carmel among Italian immigrants in New York City, Robert Orsi used the term *domus* to refer to the complex entity that incorporated both the family members and the physical homes in which they lived. Orsi, *the Madonna of 115th Street: Faith and Community in Spanish Harlem, 1880–1950* (New Haven: Yale University Press, 2nd edition 2002). Originally developed by Emmanuel LeRoy Ladurie, in *Montaillou: the Promised Land of Error* (New York: Braziller, 1978) the concept of *domus* is particularly appropriate in the Irish stem family case.
7   A map showing the lay-out of the farms near the church was made that year. Over 160 such large scale maps have survived from various areas of Dillon's estate, dating from

at least the 1830s to the 1860s. Though some of the maps were made at the time the property was acquired by Dillon, it seems likely that many were made when the landlord's agent took advantage of the expiration of leases by different groups of co-tenants to divide the farms.

8 The breaking of hitherto unproblematic ties between a tightly-knit community and its physical setting predictably has profound psychological effects but it is usually difficult to trace these effects to their causes. Those involved may not consciously recognise any links and researchers have difficulty finding relevant evidence. However, occasionally a catastrophic alteration of the geographic setting provides vivid evidence. Peter Munch studied what happened to the people of Tristan da Cunha, a small island in the middle of the south Atlantic, when a volcanic eruption forced their evacuation, mostly to England. Munch's title for his book, *Crisis in Utopia*, captures the people's sense of disorientation even when living together in exile and makes understandable their ultimate decision to return to their threatened island home. Another case where destructive reshaping of their physical surroundings undermined people's psychic security was the flooding of an Appalachian coal mining valley when a dam broke releasing millions of gallons of floodwater that carried away 'everything in its path'. Kai Ericson's study shows how the 'everything' was much more than the drowned victims and washed-away landmarks, but included survivors' sense of who they were, when it became impossible to sustain their hitherto unquestioned identities as community members that were anchored by their participation in shared life-activities with others in familiar physical spaces and places. Erickson documented what later has been called 'Post Traumatic Stress Syndrome'. People feel 'out of place' when 'their' place is transformed. It is little exaggeration to claim that people torn from a culture of rundale would experience similar disorientation. Peter Munch, *Crisis in Utopia: The Ordeal of Tristan da Cunha* (New York: Crowell, 1971); Kai Erikson, *Everything in its Path: The Destruction of Community in the Buffalo Creek Flood* (New York: Simon and Schuster, 1978).

9 For example, Rita M. Rhodes, *Women and the Family in Post-Famine Ireland: Status and Opportunity in a Patriarchal Society* (New York: Garland Publishing, 1992), pp. 68–76.

10 Brendan Walsh, 'Marriage Rates and Population Pressure: Ireland 1871 and 1911', *Economic History Review*, second series, 23 (1970), pp. 148–62.

11 Jordan, *Land*, pp. 126–7.

12 S. H. Cousens, 'The Regional Variations in Population Changes in Ireland, 1861–1881', *Economic History Review*, 2nd series, 17 (1964), p. 320.

13 K. Theodore Hoppen, *Ireland since 1800: Conflict and Conformity* (London: Longman, 1989), p. 226.

14 Nollaig Ó Gadhra, 'Gaeltacht Mhaigh Eo', in *Mayo: Aspects of its Heritage,* ed. Bernard O'Hara (Galway: Regional Technical College, 1986), pp. 129.

15 NFCS 108, pp. 103–4.

16 NFCS 108, p. 25.

17 T. W. Moody, *Davitt and Irish Revolution 1846–82* (Oxford: Clarendon Press, 1982), p. 312.

18 D. B. Cashman, *The Life of Michael Davitt, with a History of the Rise and Development of the Irish National Land League* (Boston: Murphy and McCarthy, 1881), pp. 187–8; Moody, *Davitt*, p. 348.

19 Doyle, 'Knock 1879', p. 75.

20 T. O'C[onnor], *A Visit to Knock* (Limerick: T. O'Connor 1880), p. 16.

21 Lisa Godson, 'Catholicism and Material Culture in Ireland 1840–1880', *Circa,* 103 (Spring 2003), p. 44.

22 [Thomas Sexton], *The Illustrated Record of the Apparitions at Knock: The Depositions of the Witnesses, Lists of the Alleged Miraculous Cures . . . (Reprinted from the 'Weekly News')* (Dublin: T. D. Sullivan, [1880]), p. 5.

23 M. F. Cusack, *Life Inside the Church of Rome* (New York, 1890), pp. 214–18, cited by White, *Apparitions*, pp. 103–4.

24 One important relief agency, the Mansion House Committee, in the spring of 1880 estimated 2,500 of the approximately 3,200 people in the parish were receiving emergency relief. It summarised the position of the parish as 'terrible destitution; people half-starved' in Knock, while in Aghamore, 'people actually starving'. *Proceedings of the Mansion House Committee for Relief of Distress in Ireland During the Months of January and February* (Dublin: Mansion House, March 1880), p. 34.

25 O'C[onnor], *A Visit*, p. 17.

26 Sexton, *Illustrated Record*, p. 27. My thanks to Grace Mulqueen for sending me copies of the School Inspectors' Reports.

27 Cormac Ó Gráda, 'Seasonal Migration and Post-Famine Adjustment in the West of Ireland', *Studia Hibernica*, 13 (1971).

28 Sr Mary Frances Clare [M. F. Cusack], *Three Visits to Knock, with the Medical Certificates of Cures and Authentic Accounts of Different Apparitions* (New York: P. J. Kennedy, [1882] 1904), p. 45; M. F. Cusack, *The Story of My Life* (London: Hodder and Staughton, 1891), p. 293; J. W. Boyle, 'A Marginal Figure: The Irish Rural Labourer', in *Irish Peasants: Violence and Political Unrest, 1790–1914*, eds Samuel Clarke and James S. Donnelly, Jr (Madison: University of Wisconsin Press, 1983), p. 320; Jordan, *Land*, p. 141; James Redpath, *Talks About Ireland* (New York: P. J. Kenedy, 1881), p. 86; Gerard Moran, '"A Passage to Britain": Seasonal Migration and Social Change in the West of Ireland, 1870–1890', *Saothar*, 13 (1988), pp. 22–31. For the Achill exception to the general pattern see Deirdre Quinn, 'Mayo Women and the Politics of the Land in the Latter Half of the Nineteenth Century, Part 1', *Cathair na Mart: Journal of the Westport Historical Society*, 16 (1997), p. 94; and Alexander I. Shand, *Letters from the West of Ireland, 1884* (Edinburgh: Blackwood, 1885), p. 110.

29 Moody, *Davitt*, p. 3.

30 Finley Dun, *Landlords and Tenants in Ireland* (London: Longman, Green and Co., 1881), p. 204; Moody, *Davitt*, p. 304.

31 Jordan, *Land*, pp. 141–142.

32 David Fitzpatrick, 'The Modernisation of the Irish Female', in *Rural Ireland 1600–1900: Modernisation and Change*, eds Patrick O'Flanagan, Paul Ferguson and Kevin Whelan (Cork: Cork University Press, 1987), p.163. Fitzpatrick compares Mayo to the rest of the country on many measures of modernisation of female behaviour in post-famine Ireland. David Fitzpatrick, '"A Share of the Honeycomb": Education, Emigration and Irishwomen', *Continuity and Change*, 1, 2 (1986), pp. 217–34.

33 Jordan, *Land*, p. 127.

34 CT, 28 December 1878.

35 Kerby Miller, *Emigrants and Exiles: Ireland and the Irish Exodus to North America* (New York: Oxford University Press, 1985).

36 Rhodes, *Women*, pp. 39–83; Samuel Clark, *Social Origins of the Irish Land War* (Princeton: Princeton University Press, 1979); Joseph Lee, *The Modernisation of Irish Society 1848–1918* (Dublin: Gill and MacMillan, 1973).

37 Clark, *Social Origins*, pp. 107–52, 230–1; Jordan, *Land*, p. 160ff.

38 Clark, *Social Origins*, p. 127; Jordan, *Land*, p. 166.

39 Quoted in Lee, *Modernisation*, p. 70.

40 Jordan, *Land*, p. 164.

41 Charles Orser, 'Symbolic Violence, Resistance and the Vectors of Improvement in Early Nineteenth-Century Ireland', *World Archaeology*, 37 (2005), pp. 392–407.

42 Pierre Bourdieu, *Outline of a Theory of Practice* (New York: Cambridge University Press, 1977), p. 191.

43 Compare the photographs in Tom Neary, *I Saw Our Lady* (Mayo: Custodians of Knock Shrine, 1977), p. 20, and on the cover of Liam Ua Cadhain, *Venerable Archdeacon Cavanagh, Pastor of Knock Shrine, 1867–1897* (Boyle, Co. Roscommon: Trustees of Knock Shrine, 1953). A clearer but later photograph of the still-unchanged Beirne cottage may be seen in James Robertson, *The Holy Ground: Mary's Knock* (Knock: Custodians of Knock Shrine, 1975), p. 20.

44 Sexton, *The Illustrated Record*, p. 12.

45 See K. Theodore Hoppen, *Elections, Politics, and Society in Ireland, 1832–1885* (Oxford: Clarendon Press, 1984), p. 89.

46 O'C[onnor], *Visit*, p. 17.

47 *The Parliamentary Gazetteer of Ireland*, 1844, had a different take. Of Claremorris, it wrote 'its influence, as a seat of trade, of sessions, of a constabulary force, and of church, chapel and schools, amounts to that of a practical metropolis of the east of Mayo.'.

48 Mary Purcell, 'Our Lady of Silence, Knock 1879', in *A Woman Clothed With the Sun*, ed. John Delaney (Garden City: Hanover House, 1960), p. 132, also Liam Ua Cadhain, *Knock Shrine* (Galway: O'Gorman, 1935), p. 22.

49 'Knock' was the name for both a parish with clear, legally defined boundaries and a 'village' where some rural roads intersected near the middle of that parish. However, there was no townland called Knock and there was no legal or administrative delimitation of the 'village', so that the number of houses it contained depended on how far along the various roads any given commentator decided to count the scattered dwellings.

50 Catherine Rynne, *Knock, 1879–1979* (Dublin: Veritas, 1979), p. 138; M. F. Cusack, *The Story of My Life* (London: Hodder and Staughton, 1891), p. 291, said one house and the rest hovels.

51 Gerard Moran, *The Mayo Evictions of 1860: Patrick Lavelle and the 'War' in Partry* (Westport: 1986), p. 125.

52 R. V. Comerford, *The Fenians in Context* (Dublin: Wolfhound Press, 1985), p. xxx.

53 Michael Davitt, *The Fall of Feudalism in Ireland: or The Story of the Land League Revolution* (London: Harper and Brothers, 1904).

54 Jordan, *Land*, pp. 199–229.

55 Clark, *Social Origins*, p. 282, n. 69.

56 Paul Bew, *Land and the National Question in Ireland, 1858–82* (Dublin: Gill and MacMillan, 1978) Recognising his omission, Bew later wrote a short account that unfortunately is unduly dependent on later devotional works, especially Coyne's 1953 hagiographical life of Fr Cavanagh for evidence, and largely focused on P. J. Gordon whom he mischaracterises as a 'bitter anticlerical'. Paul Bew, 'A Vision to the Dispossessed? Popular Piety and Revolutionary Politics in the Irish Land War', in *Religion and Rebellion*, eds Judith Devlin and Ronan Fanning (Dublin: University College Dublin Press, 1996), p. 151, n. 7.

57 Moody, *Davitt*; Jordan, *Land.*

58 Doyle, 'Knock 1879'.

59 John J. White, *The Knock Apparitions and Pilgrimage: Popular Piety and the Irish Land War* (PhD Dissertation, Boston College, 1999).

60 E. M. Crawford, 'Indian Meal and Pellagra in Nineteenth-Century Ireland', in *Irish Population, Economy and Society: Essays in Honour of the Late K. H. Connell*, eds J. M. Goldstrom and L. A. Clarkson (Oxford: Clarendon Press, 1981), p. 131, n. 38.

61 James S. Donnelly, Jr, 'The Marian Shrine at Knock: The First Decade', *Eire/Ireland*, 28, 2 (1993), pp. 56–7.

62 Michael P. Carroll, *The Cult of The Virgin Mary: Psychological Origins* (Princeton: Princeton University Press, 1986), p. 210. Carroll cites a devotional work by Mary Purcell who says eighteen families were evicted, but Purcell gives no source for this and seems to rely on a statement by Archbishop John Lynch of Toronto who visited the area and in a well-publicised letter did describe recent evictions. But that was three years later, when evictions had increased dramatically. The eighteen evictions Lynch referred to were likely those of 1882 on the Walter Bourke estate for which we have lots of other documentation. Lynch to Dr Walsh, Bishop of London, Ontario, 13 June 1882, Archives of the Roman Catholic Archdiocese of Toronto, LAGO3.11. Lynch's letter is widely reprinted in the devotional literature.

63 Sheridan Gilley, 'The Background to Knock', *The Tablet*, 18 September 1979.

64 Nicholas Perry and Loreto Echeverria, *Under The Heel of Mary* (New York: Routledge, 1988), 136–7.

65 Donnelly, 'The Marian Shrine', p. 73, n. 69.

66 Sexton, *Illustrated History*, p. 35.

67 Donnelly, 'The Marian Shrine', p. 71; Laicus Peregrinus, 'Knock and the Nun of Kenmare,' in unidentified newspaper *circa* 1920, cutting in ACSJP, 3A, 289.

68 See almost any issue of the *Knock Shrine Annual* published yearly since 1939.

69 See Ua Cadhain, *Knock Shrine*, 1935. The government Minister for Education at the time, Thomas Derrig, made the same point in a well publicised public lecture arranged by Knock's promoters. F. P. Carey, *Knock and its Shrine* (Dublin: Office of the 'Irish Messenger', 1946), p. 23.

70 Anne Kane, Personal communication; see also Anne Kane, 'Theorizing Meaning Construction in Social Movements: Symbolic Structures and Interpretation during the Land War, 1879–1882', *Sociological Theory*, 15 (1997), pp. 249–76.

71 Lee, *Modernisation*, p. 72.

72 Clark, *Social Origins*, p. 164 ff; Terence Dooley, 'Landlords and the Land Question, 1879–1909', in *Famine, Land and Culture in Ireland*, ed. Carla King (Dublin: University College Dublin Press, 2000), p. 120.

73 John O'Connor Power, 'The Irish Land Agitation', *The Nineteenth Century*, Vol. VI, Number XXXIV (December 1879), p. 960.

74 Eamonn Slater, and Terrence McDonough, 'Bulwark of Landlordism and Capitalism: The Dynamics of Feudalism in Nineteenth Century Ireland', *Research in Political Economy*, 14 (1994), p. 74.

75 ibid., p. 74.

76 See Peter Somerville-Large, *The Irish Country House: a Social History* (London, Sinclair-Stevenson, 1995), pp. 253–64, for many examples.

77 Jordan, *Land*, p. 148.

78 Clark, *Social Origins*, pp. 166–71; Moody, *Davitt*, p. 31; K. Theodore Hoppen, *Elections, Politics, and Society in Ireland, 1832–1885* (Oxford: Clarendon Press, 1984), pp. 113–4. For other examples, in the *Connaught Telegraph* in 1879, see the series of letters signed 'Semper Idem', 'The Gracchi', 'Mr Snee', and the letter from 'Rory' in the 12 July 1879 issue.

79 Moody, *Davitt*, p. 300.

80 W. E. Vaughan, *Landlords and Tenants in Mid-Victorian Ireland* (Oxford: Clarendon, 1994).

81 James Scott, *Domination and the Arts of Resistance: Hidden Transcripts* (New Haven: Yale Univesity Press, 1990).

82 See John William Knott, 'Land, Kinship and Identity: The Cultural Roots of Agrarian Agitation in Eighteenth- and Nineteenth-Century Ireland', *Journal of Peasant Studies*, 12 (1884), pp. 93–108. See also Tim P. O'Neill, 'Famine Evictions', in *Famine, Land and Culture in Ireland*, ed. Carla King (Dublin: University College Dublin Press, 2000), p. 58, and the sources he cites.

83 See Moody, *Davitt*, p. 35.

84 Hoppen, *Elections*, p. 136.

85 ibid., p. 159.

86 For empirical descriptions and theoretical explanation for similar cases elsewhere see Steven Lukes, *Power: A Radical View* (London: MacMillan, 1974) and especially John Gaventa, *Power and Powerlessness: Quiescence and Rebellion in an Appalachian Valley* (Urbana: University of Illinois Press, 1980).

87 Laurence M. Geary, 'Anticipating Memory: Landlordism, Agrarianism and Deference in Late-Nineteenth-Century Ireland', in *History and the Public Sphere: Essays in Honour of John A. Murphy*, eds Tom Dunne and Laurence M. Geary (Cork: Cork University Press, 2005), p. 131; Somerville-Large, *The Irish Country House*, pp. 290–1.

88 See CT, 4 May and 2 July 1878; Clark, *Social Origins*, p. 159; Dun, *Landlords*, p. 213.

89 Another historian has argued that because of low rents that enabled the strong farmers to reap the benefits of post-famine prosperity and their own mounting debts 'the writing was on the wall for many of the landlord class' even before the Land War. Here

was another contributor to the general weakening of the whole social structure. Roy F.
Foster, 'Ascendancy and Union', in *The Oxford Illustrated History of Ireland*, ed. Roy
Foster (New York: Oxford University Press, 1989), p. 211.
90 See Jordan, *Land*, pp. 152–4.
91 See James Redpath, *Talks About Ireland* (New York: Kenedy, 1881). Lee, *Modernisation*,
p. 96, correctly points out that this claim 'reflected not a timeless voice from the grave
but of astute propagandists from the platform'.
92 Herbert G. Gutman, *Slavery and the Numbers Game: A Critique of Time on The Cross*
(Urbana, University of Illinois Press, 1975).
93 White, *The Knock Apparitions*, p. 19.
94 Clark, *Social Origins*, pp.164–72.
95 K. T. Hoppen, 'Landlords, Society and Electoral Politics in mid-nineteenth-century
Ireland', *Past and Present*, 75 (1977), p. 90.
96 Dun, *Landlords*, chapter 17.
97 ibid., pp. 205, 206.
98 ibid., pp. 201–7.
99 ibid., p. 201.
100 Vera McDermott, *The Woodlands of Loughglynn* (Privately published, 1998), p. 10ff.
101 Dun, *Landlords*.
102 These maps are now in the National Library in Dublin.
103 NFCS 108, pp. 124, 274, 190.
104 CT, 23 June 1877.
105 CT, 31 May 1879.
106 CT, 6 July 1878.
107 *The Nation*, 28 February 1880.
108 Jordan, *Land*, p. 207.
109 See the letter from 'Correspondent' on the 'Shragh Estate', CT, 22 November 1879.
110 Strickland was by no means universally popular. When a local man named Edward
Duffy became a Fenian organiser in the early 1860s, Strickland, according to one
account, responded by firing two of his sisters who were teachers in a school of which
he (Strickland) was manager. He also allegedly intervened with the Board of National
Education to deny a pension to a third Duffy sister when failing eyesight forced her to
give up a teaching position she had held for eleven years. Duffy's biographer calls
Strickland a 'tyrant', but even his evidence points to a more complex and nuanced
relationship with tenants: Pádraig Ó Laighin, *Eadbhard Ó Dufaigh 1840–1868* (Dublin:
Coiscéim, 1994), pp. 6, 107–8. Strickland had many years earlier provided a cabin for
the Duffys' widowed mother and her then-young children. This, together with his
management of schools in Bekan, Kilvine, and other nearby parishes [Fr Michael
Comer, 'Schools in Bekan Parish', in *Béacán/Bekan: Portrait of an East Mayo Parish*, eds
Fr Michael Comer and Nollaig O Muraíle (Privately published by Comer, 1986), pp.
86–7], and the other activities we know he was involved in, including founding the
town named after him, Charlestown, during the height of the Great Hunger suggests
that Strickland might better be called a paternalist and his attitude one of *noblesse
oblige*; that, in return for his willing exertions on behalf of tenants he expected them to
be deferential and grateful. When this deference was not forthcoming, he was not
reluctant to retaliate against family members of those who crossed him. The charac-
terisation of Strickland as a tyrant is more a product of the invention of tradition, in
this case a 1994 biography of a Fenian, than of the best contemporary evidence. The
Duffy sisters helped their brother in his Fenian organising but it is not clear that they
did so before being fired or that Strickland knew of their involvement. It is not even
clear that it was Strickland who fired them, as Ó Laighin wrote. Another historian,
citing *The Irish World*, May 1914, lists the case as an example of the clergy retaliating
against relatives of Fenians: Brian Griffin, 'Social Aspects of Fenianism in Connacht
and Leinster, 1858–1870', *Eire/Ireland*, 21 (Spring 1986), p. 24. Neither historian
cited sources from the 1860s to support their different claims that Strickland and

priests dismissed the Duffy sisters. Local memories much later did lay responsibility at Strickland's door but claimed he 'had no option' but to terminate the employment of the sisters, an interesting instance of ideological work: McDermott, *Woodlands of Loughglynn*, p. 27. The woman who recorded this, a Loughglynn native who emigrated to England after World War II, generally gives glowing accounts of Strickland, especially of his behaviour during the famine and his support of schools in the subsequent decades. There is little reason, however, to believe that most priests' and Strickland's attitudes toward Fenianism would differ. Both would have looked down on Fenians' failure to show adequate deference to their social betters. Griffin points out that the parish priest of Ballaghaderreen, near Strickland's home in Loughglynn, was specifically singled out, in a letter published in the *Irish People*, 21 January, 1865, for his snobbery and condescending attitudes toward the lower orders after the priest poked fun at a 'common tailor' from Boyle.

Strickland's 'benevolence' does not imply altruism on his part. Given that most farms were very small, and that the ill-drained soil was often useless for most cultivated crops, even large farms could not generate much in the way of rent. Keeping as many tenants as possible on the land, therefore, was one way to maximise income by maximising the numbers of tenants who would earn the rents by harvest work in England. Moreover, the *Telegraph's* statement that rents had not been raised for sixty years is questionable. On the Dillon Estate in two Poor Law Unions, including the one containing Knock, the rental increased from £5,000 to £25,000 from the 1840s to 1887. Gerard Moran, '"A Passage to Britain": Seasonal Migration and Social Change in the West of Ireland, 1870–1890', *Saothar*, 13 (1988), p. 31, n. 24. Dillon increased his holdings in these years but likely not by 500 per cent. In 1879, Daly may well have known about increased rents but chose instead to exaggerate Dillon's abatement perhaps to put pressure on other landlords. In other words, the claim may not be so much factual as tactical. We certainly should not accept it uncritically.

111 CT, 18 October 1879.
112 CT, 1 November 1879.
113 Gerald Dillon, 'The Dillon Peerages', *The Irish Genealogist*, 3 (1958), p. 89.
114 Dun, *Landlords*, p. 201.
115 ibid., p. 202.
116 Clark, *Social Origins*, p. 173.
117 Moody, *Davitt*, p. 333.
118 White, *The Knock Apparitions*, p. 67.
119 Jordan, *Land*, p. 237.
120 Moody, *Davitt*, p. 333.
121 ibid., p. 333.
122 Malcolm Brown, *George Moore: A Reconsideration* (Seattle: University of Washington Press, 1995), p. 15; Carla King, 'Introduction', in *George Moore, Parnell and His Island* (Dublin: University College Dublin Press, 2003), pp. ix, x.
123 Thomas Fennell, *The Royal Irish Constabulary: A History and Personal Memoir* (Dublin: University College Dublin Press, 2003), p. 118.
124 Quoted in Somerville-Large, *The Irish Country House*, p. 293.
125 George Moore, *Parnell and his Island,* ed. Carla King (Dublin: University College Dublin Press, 2004), pp. 34–5.
126 David Barr, 'George Henry Moore and his Tenants, 1840–1870', *Cathair Na Mart: Journal of the Westport Historical Society*, 8 (1988), pp. 66–79; Anderson, *Lion of the West*, pp. 135–6 (See page 80 above.). An ancestor of the family, John Moore, had been proclaimed President of the Republic of Connaught at the time of the French invasion of 1798. Such Catholic and 'nationalist' pedigrees did not save the Moore mansion from being deliberately burned in January 1923, probably because locals hoped to acquire some of the Moore demesne land. Guy Beiner, *Remembering the Year of the French: Irish Folk History and Social Memory* (Madison: University of Wisconsin Press, 2007), p. 181.

127 King, 'Introduction'; Brown, *George Moore,* pp. 17–18.
128 Moody, *Davitt,* chapter VI; Bew, *Land and the National Question,* p. 73.
129 Patrick Maume, 'Rebel on the Run: T. J. Quinn and the IRB/Land League Diaspora in America', in Patrick Maume and Marguerite Quintelli-Neary, *19th-Century Irish and Irish-Americans on the Western Frontier* (Working Papers in Irish Studies, 00–1 Nova Southeastern University, 2000).
130 White, *The Knock Apparitions,* pp. 27–8.
131 Moody, *Davitt,* pp. 292–5.
132 Davitt, *Fall,* pp. 151–2; Moody, *Davitt,* pp. 296, 337–8; Clark, *Social Origins,* p. 281–90; Bew, *Land and the National Question,* pp. 68–9; Jordan, *Land,* chapter 6; see White, *The Knock Apparitions,* chapter 2, on what he calls 'the myth of solidarity of priests and people'.
133 CT, 7 June 1879; this article along with the police report on the meeting is available in the Irish National Archives in Dublin, Registered Papers 9632/79.
134 The misspelling of Bohola is one clue that the police-inspector who wrote the report was not well informed about the local scene. That the subject was not then living in Bohola suggests a deeper ignorance even on the part of the local police on whose information, presumably, Sub-Inspector Carter relied. While the family was originally from Bohola, 'Sheridan had formerly been Master of Swinford Workhouse but now kept a cheap hotel in Tubbercurry, Co. Sligo; his wife and mother ran the business while he travelled the province as IRB organiser': Maume, 'Rebel on the Run', pp. 1–2.
135 David Berman, 'The Knock Apparition: Some New Evidence', *The New Humanist,* 102, 4 (December 1987), p. 8, has printed almost all of the police report.
136 Rynne, *Knock,* p. 83.
137 A different oral memory recorded in 1929 says Fr Cavanagh gave his blessing to the 'Pikemen of Aghamore' as they were on their way to the Claremorris meeting. Rynne, *Knock,* pp. 84, 182. On the surface, these two stories make apparently contradictory factual claims: his congregation walked out of mass to attend a demonstration against him, but Fr Cavanagh gave his blessing to parishioners going to such a meeting. The surface 'facts' are less important than the common message in both stories, that Cavanagh was on the side of the people in confronting landlords. The first story implies that his critics came to see this and so apologised to Cavanagh, the second never acknowledges any opposition and hence any need for an apology. The two stories are also a good illustration of the surface 'contradictory' nature of folklore, even when it carries a consistent message at a deeper level. The story that Fr Cavanagh blessed the 'Pikemen' is anachronistic in that pikes were associated with 1798 rather than the Land War, but is an attempt to identify Cavanagh as a 'patriot-priest'. Of course, this view of Fr Cavanagh is a later reconstruction, and is wildly at odds with what we know from the contemporary evidence of what transpired in Knock in early summer of 1879, before the apparition. This 'patriot-priest' model was the standard used in 1879 Knock to criticise Cavanagh, and lay leaders and followers drew on it to criticise unsupportive priests throughout the Land War. The model was to remain important in the new Irish state in the 1920s and later. One side of a 1798 monument unveiled in Castlebar in 1953 showed a pikeman receiving a priest's blessing while the other side showed the Virgin Mary: Beiner, *Remembering the Year of the French* p. 270.
138 Pádraig Ó Baoighill, *Nally As Mayo* (Dublin: Coiscéim, 1998), pp. 117–8.
139 ibid., p. 142.
140 The crowd probably knew that Fr Cavanagh's brother Thomas, a veterinary surgeon, held a commission to buy horses for the British army and attended all the big horse fairs in the country. Liam Ua Cadhain, *Venerable Archdeacon Cavanagh, Pastor of Knock Shrine, 1867–1897* (Boyle, Co. Roscommon: Trustees of Knock Shrine, 1953), p. 25.
141 On underdogs' tactical name-switching in such situations, see Scott, *Domination,* p. 32.

142　Terry Golway, *Irish Rebel: John Devoy and America's Fight for Irish Freedom* (New York: St Martin's Press, 1999), p. 119.

143　For use of this 'dialectic of conscientization' framework to explain the rise and fall of a political challenge in one small Kansas town in the 1980s, see Eugene Hynes, 'Elite Control and Citizen Mobilization in a Small Midwestern Town', *Critical Sociology*, 17 (Spring 1990), pp. 81–98.

144　Michael Davitt recalled a man who could not even grasp the thought of abolishing landlordism. He asked to whom would the tenants then pay the rent?

145　Clare Murphy, 'Varieties of Crowd Activity from Fenianism to the Land War, 1867–79', in *Crowds in Ireland, c. 1720–1929*, eds Peter Jupp and Eoin Magennis (New York: St Martin's Press, 2000), p. 183.

146　CT, 19 July 1879.

147　CT, 24 May 1879.

148　During and after the Great Hunger of the 1840s MacHale had denounced government inaction with Swiftian eloquence and indignation; later, as constructions of the event as genocide spread in the Irish Diaspora, MacHale's stance resonated with nationalists. One very important early populariser of the Knock apparition story was John MacPhilpin whose book early in 1880 presented the seers' testimony embedded in a sustained argument for the supernatural origin of the vision. When the book was published in the US, on the title page MacPhilpin was wrongly identified as 'Nephew to the Archbishop of Tuam' presumably because the author and/or the New York publisher felt that the association with MacHale's name would add to the book's sales. (It is worth noting that the publisher did not need to spell out who the 'Archbishop of Tuam' was. MacPhilpin actually was a nephew of Canon Ulick Bourke who in turn was MacHale's nephew.) A different New York publisher likewise highlighted the MacHale link on the cover of his book by noting that the testimony it printed was collected by a commission set up by MacHale. Near the end of his life, when ecclesiastics in Rome and Dublin, along with MacHale's rival and unwelcome coadjutor Archbishop MacEvilly, were actively campaigning to force his removal or resignation, the Archbishop of Dublin was astute enough to realise that deposing him would be a disaster for the Catholic Church in Ireland and wherever Irish people lived abroad. Archbishop McCabe paid him the backhanded compliment that 'in the English speaking world, his name is known but his infirmities are not'. James Joyce has a character in the story 'Grace' in *Dubliners* remark that 'I once saw John MacHale . . . and I'll never forget it as long as I live'. Even a staunch Protestant writing for a readership in Britain could take for granted that her readers would know exactly whom she meant by 'John of Tuam', 'regarding whom I had of course heard much': McCabe to Kirby, K/80/139, 13 March 1880, in Padraig Ó Tuairisc, *Ábhar a Bhaineann le Árd-Dheoise Thuama sa 19ú Aois i gCartlann Choláiste Na nGael sa Roimh, curtha in eagar, Maille le Réamhra agus Notaí* (MA Thesis in History, University College, Galway, 1982), p. 561; Joyce, *Dubliners* (New York: Viking, 1967), pp. 169–70; Mrs [Matilda] Houston, *Twenty Years in the Wild West, or Life in Connaught* (London: John Murray, 1879), p. 198.

149　Davitt, *Fall*, p. 152; Moody, *Davitt*, p. 303.

150　CT, 28 June, 5 and 12 July.

151　CT, 14 June 1879. Like the strategic silences so often found among the underdogs in front of power, this may well be a case of strategic deafness. It suited Daly's project not to direct his wrath at the saintly archbishop.

152　Davitt, *Fall*, p. 159; Moody, *Davitt*, p. 314.

153　*The Nation*, 12 July 1879.

154　CT, 12 July 1879. As it turned out, many researchers argue, this is precisely what happened in the later years of the Land League. James Daly was only one of many who came to believe the League abandoned the small western tenants. But all this was in the future. Paul Bew, *Land and the National Question in Ireland, 1858–82* (Dublin: Gill and MacMillan, 1978); Gerard Moran, 'James Daly and the Rise and

Fall of the Land League in the West of Ireland, 1879–1882', *Irish Historical Studies,* xxix (1994), pp. 186–207.

155 CT, 27 September 1879; Davitt, *Fall,* p. 159; Jordan, *Land,* p. 242; Moody, *Davitt,* p. 314.

156 Ó Tuairisc, *Árd-Dheoise Thuama,* pp. 32ff. Refusal to take MacHale's letter at face value continues even among some recent historians. Bernard O'Hara, *Davitt* (Castlebar: Mayo County Council, 2006), p. 46, claims 'it is now generally believed' that Fr Thomas MacHale wrote the letter. Davitt described the letter as a 'bolt from the blue' (Moody, *Davitt,* p. 357), but surely the lay-led challenge to the landlords and the government must have been a similar bolt to MacHale. Daniel McGettigan, Archbishop of Armagh, who investigated the situation in Tuam at the request of the Roman authorities, wrote in February that MacHale was 'quite able to fulfil all his episcopal functions': Bernard O'Reilly, *John MacHale, Archbishop of Tuam: His Life, Times and Correspondence,* 2 Vols. (New York and Cincinnati: Fustet, 1890), Vol. II, p. 624, or Andrews, *Lion of the West,* p. 328. Larkin, *The Roman Catholic Church and the Creation of the Modern Irish State,* p. 20, plausibly suggests that the archbishop intended by the letter to show Rome that he was still in control of his diocese but even without that consideration, Clark, *Social Origins,* p. 284, and White, *The Knock Apparitions,* p. 43, correctly note that MacHale's letter was only being consistent with the views he had expressed over decades, that priests and landlords they supported were the natural leaders of the Catholic laity. It may be because the public defied him earlier that MacHale reiterated his condemnation. In another public letter the preceding month he had lashed out against meetings 'organised by a few designing men' and 'convened in a mysterious and disorderly manner'. The public nature of these two letters and their trenchant language questioning other people's motives were characteristic of the archbishop. He had first come to national prominence nearly sixty years earlier as the author of public letters scathingly scornful of the government, and ever since had rarely let an opportunity pass without publicly attacking somebody. MacHale administered confirmation in Castlebar, Bekan and other places earlier that summer and in August he unveiled a statue in Dublin, at which event he gave a coherent speech (O'Reilly, *MacHale,* Vol. 2, p. 652, and Andrews, *Lion,* pp. 334–5), so it is difficult to sustain an argument that he was mentally incompetent in July. The very week of the apparition he administered confirmation in Cliften where, *The Nation* of 23 August 1879 reported, 'he appeared in excellent health'. Nobody has produced any positive evidence that the nephew wrote the letters condemning the land agitation leaders.

157 CT, 14 June 1879.

158 White, *The Knock Apparitions,* pp. 45–9. It suited the agendas of many to pretend that MacHale was not opposed. It says much about his reputation that neither Fenians, James Daly, radicals like Davitt nor Rome could say publicly and directly what they thought of him.

159 Oliver J. Burke, *The History of the Catholic Archbishops of Tuam, from The Foundation of the See to the Death of the Most Rev. John MacHale D.D. A. D. 1881* (Dublin: Hodges, Figgis and Co, 1882), p. 240; John Lyons, 'John MacHale, Archbishop of Tuam', *Journal of the Westport Historical Society,* IV (1984), p. 39; Emmet Larkin, 'John MacHale', *Oxford Dictionary of National Biography,* 2004; Edward MacHale, 'Aguisín 1: John MacHale 1791–1881', in *Leon an Iarthair: Aisti ar Shean Mac Héil,* ed. Áine Ní Cheannain (Dublin: An Clóchomhar, 1983), p. 88; Antoine Boltúin, *MacHeil agus an Ghaeilge: A Shaothar agus a Dhearcadh* (PhD Thesis, Department of Modern Irish, University College Galway, 1992), p. 8.

160 For example, O Tuairisc, *Ard-Dheoise Thuama,* p. 7.

161 D'Alton accepts that MacHale served mass for Fr Conroy, but does not add years to his age. E. A. D'Alton, *History of the Archdiocese of Tuam* (Dublin: Phoenix Publishing Co., 1928), Vol. 2, pp. 368–9.

162 Beiner, *Remembering the Year of the French,* p. 217. An American Cardinal with Mayo roots later reported that MacHale told him that Fr Conroy had advised the local

people against joining the French. Cardinal James Gibbons, 'Archbishop MacHale – An Appreciation', *Tuam Herald,* 15 July 1916, reprinted in *Glimpses of Tuam Since the Famine,* ed. John A. Claffey (Tuam: Old Tuam Society, 1997), pp. 122–3.

163   'The Priest of Addergoole', in *Local Songs, Poems and Ballads from the Shadow of Nephin,* ed. Tony Donohue (Ballina, no date), pp. 9–10; the ballad originated in one composed by William Rooney which won a prize in 1898 for the best poem on 1798. Also see Sheila Mulroy, 'The Clergy and the Connacht Rebellion', in *Protestant, Catholic and Dissenter: The Clergy and 1798,* ed. Liam Swords (Dublin: Columba Press, 1997), pp. 267–8; Beiner, *Remembering the Year of the French,* pp. 217–8, 262–3.

164   'Dr MacHale witnessed three rebellions; four famines; nine land agitations; the struggle for Emancipation (from 1823–29); the struggle for primary education from 1812 to 1830, and that struggle continued (from 1830 to 1881) for pure Catholic education; and for University Education (from 1845 to 1881). He led the stand-up fight between religion on the one side and godlessness protected by the state on the other. He shared in the tithe war, and fought a hundred fights from 1812 to 1881, with the hydra of proselytism. He opposed the poor laws which tend to punish poverty as if it were a crime, to lay a burden of taxation on honest men, without making the paupers useful citizens or contented. In the great repeal campaign, he was second in command, next to O'Connell. He joined Isaac Butt in the national demand for Home Rule. To gain land rights for the oppressed peasantry, and political freedom for the clergy, he directed and blessed the New-Ireland triumvirate, Frederick Lucas, George Henry Moore, and Charles Gavan Duffy (1851)': Ulick J. Bourke, *Life and Times of the Most Rev. John MacHale, Archbishop of Tuam and Metropolitan* (Dublin: Gill and Son, 1882), pp. 200–1. Bourke has a similar catalogue of how MacHale lived so much of the history of the Catholic Church both in Rome and in Ireland. He was the longest serving bishop in the whole church; he was a contemporary of seven popes and of eight Primates serving as Archbishop of Armagh; he had presided at a Provincial council, and participated at two National Councils as well as at the Vatican Council.

165   MacEvilly to Kirby, 20 July 1879 and 21 July 1880, Kirby Papers K/79/285 and K/80/343, in Ó Tuairisc, *Árd-Dheoise Thuama,* pp. 520 and 568, respectively. Echoing MacEvilly, McCabe charged this, but MacEvilly's lying about other aspects of the scene undercuts his credibility.

166   *The Nation,* 2 September 1876.

167   CT, 31 May 1879.

168   The confirmations were in Castlebar on the last Sunday in May. The paper reported that MacHale confirmed 560 more on Thursday at Carnacon, before returning to Tuam on Friday in preparation for more confirmation trips the following week. The newspaper writer emphasised that MacHale looked 'as hale, hearty, and active in mind and body as he was twenty years ago' and 'not the least fatigued by his week's labours'. CT, 31 May 1879.

169   O'Reilly, *John MacHale,* Vol. II, p. 656.

170   CT, 24 May 1879.

171   Max Weber, *Economy and Society: An Outline of Interpretive Sociology,* eds Guenther Roth and Claus Wittich (New York: Bedminster Press, 1968), pp. 241–5.

172   Quoted in Bourke, *Life and Times,* p. 108.

173   Steven Knowlton, *Popular Politics and the Irish Catholic Church: The Rise and Fall of the Independent Irish Party, 1850–1859* (New York: Garland, 1991), p. 69. Once the reputations of figures such as MacHale or Cullen were established in the public mind, their partisans used 'evidence' selectively to reinforce their preconceptions, further confirming the images of their respective champions and their nemeses. Imagine, for example, what MacHale's defenders might make of it if Cullen, during the famine, had urged his flock to observe the Lenten fast? MacHale did just that: Brendan O Cathaoir, *Famine Diary* (Dublin: Irish Academic Press, 1999), p. 34. And MacHale partisans ignored the fact that Cullen had also publicly flouted the law by using his illegal title in reaction to the infamous 1851 Ecclesiastical Titles Act: Knowlton, *Popular Politics,* p. 76. Through such ongoing processes the images were reproduced and transmitted down the decades.

174 Accounts of the Jubilee are to be found in *Freeman's Journal*, 10 June 1875; O'Reilly, *John MacHale*, Vol. 2, pp. 570–97; Andrews, *Lion of the West*, p. 325. The reference to the countryside ablaze is in a poem composed for the occasion by a man near his birthplace and published in 1927 in *An Stoc agus an Chearnóg*, a periodical from University College, Galway. The poet had carried fuel for a bonfire to the summit of Nephin Mountain: Boltúin, *MacHeil*, p. 497.

175 Larkin, *The Roman Catholic Church and the Creation of the Modern Irish State*, p. 13.

176 ibid., p. 12.

177 Liam Bane, *The Bishop in Politics: The Life and Career of John MacEvilly* (Westport: Westport Historical Society, 1993), chapter 2.

178 Larkin, *The Roman Catholic Church and The Creation of the Modern Irish State*, p. 12, quoting a letter from Cardinal Cullen to another bishop, 8 June 1878.

179 Comerford, *The Fenians*, pp. 181–2.

180 Gerard Moran, *A Radical Priest in Mayo: The Rise and Fall of an Irish Nationalist, 1825–1882* (Dublin: Four Courts Press, 1994).

181 John Sharp, *Reapers of the Harvest: The Redemptorists in Britain and Ireland, 1843–1898* (Dublin: Veritas, 1989), p. 200.

182 John F. Quinn, 'The "Vagabond Friar": Fr Mathew's Difficulties With the Irish Bishops, 1840–1856', *The Catholic Historical Review*, 78 (October 1992), pp. 542–56; Paul A. Townend, *Fr Mathew, Temperance and Irish Identity* (Dublin: Irish Academic Press, 2002), p. 172ff.

183 Mary P. Magray, *The Transforming Power of the Nuns: Women, Religion, and Cultural Change in Ireland, 1750–1900* (New York: Oxford University Press, 1998), pp. 363–4.

184 Bourke, *Life and Times*, p. 141.

185 On 17 August 1876 the priests met to postulate a coadjutor. MacEvilly received 16 votes, Dr Thomas MacHale twelve votes and sixteen votes were spread among five others, including nine for Thomas Carr, a Maynooth Professor who was very likely in the Cullen-MacEvilly camp and later succeeded MacEvilly as Bishop of Galway (Diary of Bishop Francis J. McCormack, McCormack Papers, 1871–78, Box 24, No. 26, Galway Diocesan Archives). I thank Professor Jim Donnelly for this reference. As usual, MacHale made his views known publicly, in a letter in the *Freeman's Journal* of the previous day and in an address to the assembled priests.

186 See Jordan, *Land*, p. 177.

187 Maume, 'Rebel on the Run', p. 1.

188 White, *The Knock Apparitions*, pp. 50–2; CT, 28 June 1879.

189 'Antiquarian', 'Fr Anderson's Scrap-Books: Famous Augustinian Patriot', Series of 14 articles and reprints in *Connaught Telegraph*, dated 23 April 1938 and weekly thereafter except for 18 June until 30 July 1938.

190 Daniel Campbell had concluded his account of the failed proselytism attempt in pre-famine Knock by noting that the schoolteacher made a public display of his penance at the church and 'was restored to the friendship of the priest and the people of Knock', implicitly defining the Knock community as those who have the priest's friendship.

191 John-Pierre Reed, 'Emotions in Context: Revolutionary Accelerators, Hope, Moral Outrage, and Other Emotions in the Making of Nicaragua's Revolution', *Theory and Society*, 33 (2004), pp. 653–703.

192 White, *The Knock Apparitions*, pp. 68–9 and chapter 1 generally.

193 Moody, *Davitt*, p. 330; Jordan, *Land*, p. 246.

194 *The Nation*, 2 August 1879.

195 Clark, *Social Origins*, p. 226.

196 Séamus Ó Catháin and Patrick O'Flanagan, *The Living Landscape: Kilgannon, Erris, County Mayo* (Dublin: Comhairle Bhéaloideasa Éireann, 1975), p. 2.

197 White *The Knock Apparitions*, p. 6.

198 Moody, *Davitt*, p. 329.

199 Moody, *Davitt*, p. 330.

200 Moody, *Davitt*, pp. 330–1; Lee, *Modernisation*, p. 79.

201 Gerard Moran, 'Famine and the Land War: Relief and Distress in Mayo, 1879–1981', *Cathair na Mart,* 5 (1981), pp. 111–27.

202 Bew, *Land,* p. 57.

203 Moody, *Davitt,* p. 329.

204 Moody, *Davitt,* p. 329; Bew, *Land and the National Question,* p. 57; Clark, *Social Origins,* p. 228.

205 Bew, *Land and the National Question,* p. 57. In June of 1878 two men were killed and a third seriously injured at Ballyhaunis railway station in a rush of harvestmen to get on an overcrowded special train. CT, 15 June 1878. In a trial that resulted from the incident witnesses testified that the regular train was already overfilled, and the special train provided was so packed that men were not only sitting on the seats but standing on them, sitting on their backs and laying beneath them. Only about a third of those waiting at Ballyhaunis could get on the train, even though one man testified he had tried to get in to at least eight carriages. At a later station, 'cattle trucks' were attached to the train to carry men. The jury found the company negligent in not antic-ipating the need for more seats and not controlling the rush at the station. They awarded £300 to the widow of one man killed, but the judge stayed the judgment until the company could lodge an appeal. (An account of the trial is available in CT, 22 March 1879.) The very trains that eased travelling to England also promoted the grazier business. The 'cattle trucks' that carried the harvest labourers on the special train were normally used to transport store cattle from the west to the fattening areas of north Leinster. The arrival of the railroad — in Ballyhaunis by 1861 — was one physical manifestation of the penetration of commercial ties and 'modern' ideas into the area. An advertisement for a 226–Irish-acre 'Grazing Farm to be Let' specified that 'The Farm is most conveniently situated, being close to the M. G. W. Railway Station, at Ballyhaunis'.(CT, 4 May 1878) The Midland Great Western Railway advertised in advance the stations from which livestock could be sent by rail. In just the month of October in 1876, for example, looking at just Mayo and adjoining counties, livestock could be railed from Athenry (on the 13th, 16th, 20th and 21st), Dromod,(14th), Carrick-on-Shannon (15th and 21st), Ballina (16th and 17th), Ballymote (16th,28th,and 30th), Castlebar (18th), Claremorris (23rd), Ballinasloe (25th), and Boyle (25th). These dates were coordinated with the days of fairs in the vicinity of the various stations. See Lee, *Modernisation,* for the impact of the railways.

206 Gerard Moran, '"A Passage to Britain": Seasonal Migration and Social Change in the West of Ireland, 1870–1890', *Saothar,* 13 (1988), p. 28.

207 Sr Mary Frances Clare, [M. F. Cusack] *Three Visits to Knock, with the Medical Certificates of Cures and Authentic Accounts of Different Apparitions* (New York: P. J. Kennedy, [1882] 1904), p. 48.

208 Rynne, *Knock,* p. 48.

209 ibid., p. 85.

210 ibid., p. 53.

211 Warner, 'What the Virgin of Knock Means to Women', *Magill* (September 1979), pp. 30–9.

212 *The Nation,* reprinted in Rynne, *Knock,* p. 168 emphasis added.

213 On men 'exercising power beyond the grave' in this family system see David Fitzpatrick, 'The Modernisation of the Irish Female', in *Rural Ireland 1600–1900: Modernisation and Change,* eds Patrick O'Flanagan, Paul Ferguson and Kevin Whelan (Cork: Cork University Press, 1987), p. 173. Rynne claims Dominick was 18 but if his mother was 68 as reported, Dominick was likely to be closer to the upper than to the lower end of this range of estimates of his age.

214 John MacPhilpin, *The Apparitions and Miracles at Knock. Also, The Official Depositions of the Eye-Witnesses* (Dublin: Gill and Son, 1880), p. 36.

215 MacPhilpin, *The Apparitions,* p. 40.

216 For a classic ethnographic description from the 1930s, see Conrad Arensberg and Solan T. Kimball, *Family and Community in Ireland,* 3rd edition with a new

introduction by Anne Byrne, Ricca Edmondson and Tony Varley (Ennis: CLASP, 2001).

217   Fitzpatrick, 'Modernisation of the Irish', p. 163.

218   Cusack, *Three Visits,* p. 61; Rynne, *Knock*, p. 33. A visitor in Knock in February 1880 noted that Mary Beirne had two brothers living in her house which indicates that Bryan had returned: O'C[onnor], *A Visit*, p.18. Sometime in the 1970s journalist Catherine Rynne interviewed a son of this Bryan; the son was ninety so was born sometime in the 1880s. Rynne, *Knock,* p.33.

219   Higgins,' In Bekan Long Ago', p. 98.

220   According to one scholar, the archives of the National Folklore Collection 'constantly' refer to the incoming daughter-in-law as 'the stranger'. Rhodes, *Women*, p. 122.

221   Higgins, 'In Bekan Long Ago', p. 99.

222   Henry Coulter, *The West of Ireland: Its Existing Condition and Prospects* (Dublin: Hodges and Smith, 1862), p. 355; Jordan, *Land*, p. 99–100.

223   Clark, *Social Origins,* p. 111.

224   Clark, *Social Origins*, p. 301. The best study on graziers is David S. Jones, *Graziers, Land Reform, and Political Conflict in Ireland* (Washington DC: The Catholic University of America Press, 1995) and Jones, 'The Cleavage Between Graziers and Peasants in the Land Struggle, 1890–1910', in *Irish Peasants and Political Unrest 1780–1914,* eds Samuel Clark and James S. Donnelly, Jr (Madison: University of Wisconsin Press, 1983), pp. 373–417. See also Fergus Campbell, *Land and Revolution in the West of Ireland, 1891–1921* (New York: Oxford University Press, 2005) pp. 19–20.

225   CT, 3 May, 14 June and 27 September 1879; Jordan, *Land*, p. 202.

226   See the police report printed in Berman, 'The Knock Apparition', p. 8.

227   Jones, *Graziers,* p. 236.

228   Compare the photographs in Neary, *I Saw,* p. 20, and on the cover of Liam Ua Cadhain, *Archdeacon Cavanagh*. A much clearer but later photograph of the Beirne (still-unchanged) cottage can be seen in James Robertson, *The Holy Ground: Mary's Knock* (Knock: Custodians of Knock Shrine, 1975), p. 20.

229   There is very clear evidence of the penetration of grazier activity in the adjoining townland of Churchfield where Thomas O'Grady held almost three hundred acres along with a 'herd's house' and 'offices'. At the time of the 1879 apparition, this property was held by Edmond Kelley whose wife figures in our story later.

230   This is my best guess. Daniel Campbell had written that the widow Beirne was the daughter of Toby Bourke. He also called her Bridget when her name was Margaret. By the time Campbell wrote he had been gone from Knock for over three decades and did not have up-to-date information about the various seers reported in the newspapers. What this 'error' indicates is the importance of kinship as a tool for thinking and recalling for Campbell, reflecting its centrality as an organising principle in the Knock he knew. However, a Dillon Estate map from 1859 shows the farms of Dominick Beirne and Henry Burke side by side, both adjacent to Knock church. Though I cannot prove it, it is very likely that this Beirne farm remained in the family's hands from 1859 to the time of the apparition when the family's cottage was close to the church. Local historian John Carty, former TD and now Senator, informed me that Mrs Margaret Beirne was indeed daughter of Toby Bourke and that her sister Bridget married another man also named Beirne. I suspect but cannot prove that this latter couple were the parents of the 1879 seer usually called Dominick Beirne, Senior. If this is the case, the two seers called Dominick Beirne were first cousins because their mothers were sisters, not as we might surmise because their fathers were related, though this may also have been the case. According to John Carty, Toby Burke divided his farm between his son Henry and two daughters Margaret and Bridget, and these daughters each married a man called Beirne. Thus before this subdivision Toby's farm had been about eighty acres, a very substantial farm for that time and place.

231 Jim MacLaughlin, 'The Politics of Nation-Building in Post-Famine Donegal', in *Donegal History and Society: Interdisciplinary Essays on the History of an Irish County*, eds William Nolan, Liam Ronayne and Mairead Dunlevy (Dublin: Geography Publications, 1995), p. 585.

232 Cusack, *Three Visits*, p. 48. One of these, Fr Henry Bourke who died around 1820 as Parish Priest of Knock, was actually her father's uncle.

233 Presumably the map was made when Dillon acquired the property from Nowlan. The Dillon maps are now in the National Library.

234 These valuations of between five and six shillings per acre indicate that the land was of poor quality. The extensive bogs and mountains of West Mayo had lower valuations per acre, but the adjacent parishes just west of Knock all had much better land as indicated by average valuations. See Jordan, *Land*, p. 133.

9 THE SOCIAL CONSTRUCTION OF THE APPARITION

1 Liam Ua Cadhain, *Venerable Archdeacon Cavanagh, Pastor of Knock Shrine, 1867–1897* (Boyle, Co. Roscommon: Trustees of Knock Shrine, 1953), pp. 79–80, quoted with permission of the Knock Shrine Society. Ua Cadhain took this almost verbatim from a print of the scene by G. P. Warren in 1880, where however the time is given as eight o'clock rather than seven thirty.

2 William Christian, *Moving Crucifixes in Modern Spain* (Princeton: Princeton University Press, 1992); Barbara Corrado Pope, 'Immaculate and Powerful: The Marian Revival in the Nineteenth Century', in *Immaculate and Powerful: The Female in Sacred Image and Social Reality*, eds Clarissa W. Atkinson, Constance H. Buchanan and Margaret R. Miles (Boston: Beacon Press, 1984), pp. 173–200; Thomas Kselman, *Miracles and Prophecies in Nineteenth Century France* (New Brunswick: Rutgers University Press, 1983).

3 James S. Donnelly, Jr, 'The Marian Shrine at Knock: The First Decade', *Eire/Ireland*, 28, 2 (1993), pp. 54–99.

4 [Thomas Sexton], *The Illustrated Record of the Apparitions at Knock: The Depositions of the Witnesses, Lists of the Alleged Miraculous Cure . . . (reprinted from the 'Weekly News')* (Dublin: T. D. Sullivan, [1880]), p. 12.

5 John MacPhilpin, *The Apparitions and Miracles at Knock. Also, The Official Depositions of the Eye-Witnesses* (Dublin: Gill and Son, 1880), p. 50.

6 MacPhilpin, *The Apparitions*, p. 51.

7 Donnelly, 'The Marian Shrine'.

8 Catherine Rynne, *Knock, 1879–1979* (Dublin: Veritas, 1979), pp. 6, 18.

9 A year later it was still newsworthy that MacEvilly's 'spiritual sway was acknowledged' when he visited the Aran Islands for confirmation. CT, 21 August 1880.

10 Irish College, Rome, Archives, Kirby Papers, N.K. B.4., in Padraig Ó Tuairisc, *Ábhar a Bhaineann le Árd-Dheoise Thuama sa 19ú Aois i gCartlann Choláiste Na nGael sa Roimh, curtha in eagar, Maille le Réamhra agus Notaí* (MA Thesis in History, University College, Galway, 1982), pp. 519–20. The letter was dated 22 August 1879, just one day after the Knock apparition. It was enclosed in a letter from Clonfert priests dated 19 July 1879 that criticised both their own bishop Patrick Duggan and MacEvilly for giving public scandal by their criticisms of MacHale even among lay people.

11 E. A. D'Alton, *History of the Archdiocese of Tuam*, 2 vols. (Dublin: Phoenix Publishing Co., 1928), Vol. II, pp. 224, 235.

12 Mrs Thomas Concannon, *The Queen of Ireland: An Historical Account of Ireland's Devotion to the Blessed Virgin* (Dublin: Gill and Son, 1938), p. 338. Similarly, a two-page leaflet published 'cum permissu Superiorum' in 1935 and available from Canon John Greally, PP of Knock, cites MacPhilpin as saying that the commission was set up by 'His Grace, The Archbishop of Tuam (late Dr. MacEvilly)', without indicating that the three words in parentheses were not in MacPhilpin. This leaflet is among the records of the Second Commission in the Archdiocese of Tuam archives. Ecclesiastical

politics may well have led 1930s' promoters to downplay MacHale's involvement.

13 Ó Tuairisc, *Ard-Dheoise Thuama,* p. 566. MacEvilly to Kirby, 14 June 1880, Kirby Papers, K/80/294.

14 Sexton, *The Illustrated Record,* p. 21; MacPhilpin, *The Apparitions,* p. 29; T O'C[onnor], *A Visit to Knock* (Limerick: T. O'Connor, 1880), p. 30; *The Tablet,* 13 September 1880. Even if MacHale officially appointed them the question remains of who, in fact, selected the members. MacHale's independence and mental competence at the time has been questioned. Were the commissioners self-selected volunteers? Were they selected as MacHale loyalists? Bourke was his nephew, and MacHale had recently given Cavanagh the purely honorific title of Archdeacon rarely held by more than one priest in a diocese. Either possibility does little to inspire confidence in the objectivity of their work. Perhaps geography and rank were the key factors; the members were senior priests either in Knock itself or nearby parishes.

15 He wrote this in November to Fr Daniel Hudson, the editor of the University of Notre Dame-published Marian magazine *Ave Maria* (see *Ave Maria* 6 December 1879) and again in his 12 January 1880 letter which appeared on 7 February.

16 Sr Mary Frances Clare [M. F. Cusack], *Three Visits to Knock, with the Medical Certificates of Cures and Authentic Accounts of Different Apparitions* (New York: P. J. Kennedy, [1882] 1904), pp. 68–9. (She lists Frs Cavanagh, Waldron, Bourke, Ronayne and O'Brien.)

17 MacPhilpin, *The Apparitions,* p. 15.

18 Sexton, *The Illustrated Record,* p. 29.

19 Patrick Nold, *The Knock Phenomenon: Popular Piety and Politics in the 'Modern' Ireland* (Undergraduate Thesis, University of Michigan, 1993), p. 31.

20 Rynne, *Knock,* p. 104.

21 John White, 'The Cusack Papers: New Evidence on the Knock Apparition', *History/Ireland,* iv, 4 (1999), pp. 39–44.

22 Fr Michael Walsh, *The Apparition at Knock: A Survey of Facts and Evidence* (Tuam: St Jarlath's College, 1955, Second edition, 1959), p. 36.

23 Fr Edward Murphy, SJ to Daniel Hudson, CSC, 26 June 1881, published in *Ave Maria,* 30 July 1881.

24 Walsh, *Apparition,* p. 87.

25 *The Irish Times,* 24 August 1880. Direct evidence of the investigations is available in ACSJP, Series 1A, 245.

26 Catherine Rynne, *Knock, 1879–1979* (Dublin: Veritas, 1979), pp. 103–5.

27 For example, Walsh, *Apparition,* p, 87.

28 Rynne, *Knock,* p. 104.

29 Some twentieth century commentators and even one of the visionaries later claimed that some witnesses were not examined by the commission. Walsh, *The Apparition,* p. 39–40; John J. White, *The Knock Apparitions and Pilgrimage: Popular Piety and the Irish Land War* (Unpublished PhD Dissertation in History, Boston College, 1999), p. 85. Such claims are likely to tell us more about the circumstances of the later claims-making than about 21 August 1879. One of the two bishops in neighbouring dioceses who visited Knock and spoke to Fr Cavanagh a week before the commission sat noted in his diary that the apparition was seen by thirteen witnesses. Fr Murphy reported fourteen witnesses in his 12 January letter. The published testimony is from fourteen at the gable and one at a distance. There is no evidence in the published work of the commission that they ignored any witness, and the fact that it included the one sentence summary of the testimony of a six-year-old would indicate that anybody with even very little to add to the story was heard. It has been suggested that perhaps some witnesses to the apparition on 21 August were unavailable by the time the commission sat six weeks later because they might have been in England working on the harvest. Seasonal migration for the English harvest was a well-established pattern in the Knock area, but the great majority would have left earlier, long before the August episode. Moreover, it was primarily men who migrated while most if not all of the supposed uninterviewed visionaries were women, including all three named by Mary Beirne. (See sources cited in chapter 8 note 28.)

Bishop James Fergus claimed that 'the whole village saw [the apparition] and the commission only interviewed a selection'. He made this statement in the late 1970s to Catherine Rynne, a journalist and a firm believer in the Knock apparition, who was then writing a book on the history of Knock 1879–1979 (Rynne, *Knock*, p. 39). As a young priest in the late 1930s, Fergus was the secretary to the so-called Second Commission. By then, however, Knock was becoming recognised; the Archbishop of Tuam had first openly visited Knock in 1929, and in the mid-1930s local promoters were achieving considerable success, the very existence of the Second Commission being evidence of this. In an accepting atmosphere it is not surprising to find many claims made that one's family members or others had been among the original visionaries. Such reflected glory and invented family tradition is, I suggest, at least as plausible as the claim that the commission, headed as it was by the Archdeacon Cavanagh, a true believer and hard working promoter of Knock in 1879 and the following years, overlooked corroborating testimony. Against the suggestion that the whole village saw it, we must place the memories of a man who was born in the village in 1898 and who claimed that nothing was heard about the apparition while he was growing up, and Mary Beirne's son, born in 1886, and who left home around 1901, who said the same thing (Rynne, *Knock*, pp. 39, 23). Given the inadequacy of the investigation the suggestion that supportive evidence was not collected serves to buttress the beliefs of the committed. Had anybody claimed at the time to being a witness to the event but not interviewed, it is likely that the many journalists who promoted Knock energetically throughout most of 1880 would have presented their stories.

Of course to claim that the commission didn't interview everybody *could* serve to weaken one's faith in what evidence the commission did produce. Perhaps the commissioners interviewed witnesses using as a criterion for selection some principle they either didn't recognise or didn't acknowledge and if this were so, perhaps any 'excluded' testimony would conflict with rather than corroborate that given by those interviewed. Another logical possibility is that some witnesses were interviewed but their evidence was discounted for one reason or another. Perhaps the priests felt they added nothing to the story; perhaps what they had to say did not fit the conclusions the priests reached and promoted. Sexton omitted the witness John Durkan mentioned almost in passing by MacPhilpin. My best guess however is that the supposed 'uninterviewed witnesses' never existed in fact; rather, claims that they did are evidence of communal complicity in the story, especially later during the flowering of Marianism in the revival period.

Some writers invoke other witnesses. Gilley mentions that 'the witnesses to aspects of the apparition were not all uneducated labourers but included a schoolteacher and two subconstables from the recently opened barracks of the Royal Irish Constabulary': Sheridan Gilley, 'Catholicism in Ireland', in *The Decline of Christendom in Western Europe, 1750–2000*, eds Hugh McLeod and Werber Ustorf (Cambridge, Cambridge University Press, 2003), p. 106. But he is being a little disingenuous. These persons reported their visions months after the 'first' apparition that was the subject of the archbishop's commission of inquiry. As far as we know, their reports were never investigated by any ecclesiastical body. Similar reports about seeing supernatural lights and figures were made by Fr Cavanagh himself, so if his commission undertook any investigation he would not just be a judge of evidence and an employer of a seer (as he already was), but a witness himself. What he might have told himself could hardly be regarded as convincing evidence. Modern promoters of Knock almost never mention the various visions reported by a variety of people, elsewhere as well as in Knock, after 'the Apparition' of 21 August 1879, though Rynne, *Knock*, pp. 12, 123, and Walsh, *The Apparition*, pp. 99–107, mention them as 'false visions'. What may be as significant as the 'respectable' standing of later local visionaries in Knock is their jobs. The police were harshly criticised by those who had demonstrated against Fr Cavanagh, and the teacher too, Miss Anderson, the choir director and school principal, was likely to be a Cavanagh supporter in the divided parish community. Did any of his outspoken critics see heavenly visitors? The daughter of P.J. Gordon the Fenian and land agitation leader was miraculously cured by cement from the apparition gable, but visions and cures were different experiences of the sacred.

It may be that the vision reports in January 1880 from such respectable people as policemen and schoolteachers did serve to convince the priests to actively promote the story. White says these people added credibility to the poor people's earlier story. However, the principal witness family of Beirnes were not stereotypical 'poor peasants' or 'simple villagers' (White, *The Knock Apparitions*), p. 84, and several reporters did indeed point to their 'respectable standing'. Sexton, *The Illustrated Record*, p. 29, and O'C[onnor], *A Visit*, p. 25, report that Fr Cavanagh interpreted these later visions as a sign from God that a shrine and cult should be developed at Knock. White, *The Knock Apparitions*, pp. 82–3, suggests that the priests went to press when the story of the apparition was broken by the American magazine, *Ave Maria*. MacPhilpin says he was publishing the story to counter 'incorrectly narrated' versions of the event that were spreading. These are not mutually exclusive reasons, though only the last one would account for why the priests initially opposed publicity for the apparition. It is also the only one we have directly from a promoter himself.

30 Rynne, Knock, p. 36.
31 Rynne, *Knock*, p. 40; Sexton, *The Illustrated Record*, p. 30; MacPhilpin, *The Apparitions,* p. 55.
32 Rynne, *Knock*, p. 59; White, *The Knock Apparitions*, p. 51.
33 Rynne, *Knock*, p. 59.
34 White, *The Knock Apparitions*, 50; Walsh, *The Apparition*, p. 17.
35 See Walsh, *The Apparition*, pp. 16–17.
36 MacPhilpin, *The Apparitions*, Preface and p. 15.
37 Two editions appeared in New York City. P. J. Kenedy, Excelsior Publishing House, 5 Barclay Street, New York, published an edition, copyright 1880, with the title *The Apparitions and Miracles at Knock. Also, The Official Depositions of the Eye-Witnesses. Prepared and Edited by John MacPhilpin, Nephew of the Archbishop of Tuam.* An edition with the same title and publisher appeared in 1904 along with Sr Mary Francis Clare [Margaret Anna Cusack], *Three Visits to Knock.* The two books are paginated separately but bound together in one volume, the spine of which reads *Apparitions and Miracles of Knock* and the front cover, *All That Is Known of Knock.* A different edition was published in New York by Thos Kelly, 17 Barclay Street. No author is listed and slightly different titles are given on the cover and the title page. The cover reads: *Tuam Edition. The Apparitions and Miracles at Knock. Full Official Testimony of the Eye Witnesses.* The title page is: *Apparitions and Miracles at Knock. The Official Depositions of the Eye Witnesses before the Commission Appointed by His Grace, The Most Rev. John McHale, Archbishop of Tuam. List of Cures from the Diary of the parish priest, Ven. Archdeacon Cavanagh.* This work seems to be later than the Kenedy edition since it includes a larger number of cases from Fr Cavanagh's continuing diary of miracle cures. No publication year is printed but 1880 is handwritten under the publisher's name in one copy I have seen.
38 Donnelly, 'The Marian Shrine', p. 70.
39 Andrew Dunlop, *Fifty Years of Irish Journalism* (Dublin: Hanna and Neale, 1911), p. 241.
40 Laicus Peregrinus, 'Knock and the Nun of Kenmare', article from unidentified newspaper, undated but circa 1920, ACSJP, Series 3A, 289.
41 Donnelly, *The Marian Shrine*, p, 69.
42 Bernard O'Reilly, *John MacHale, Archbishop of Tuam: His Life, Times and Correspondence,* 2 Vols. (New York and Cincinnati: Fustet, 1890), Vol. 2, pp. 574–6; Donnelly, 'The Marian Shrine', p. 68.
43 Ulick J. Bourke, *Life and Times of the Most Rev. John MacHale, Archbishop of Tuam and Metropolitan* (Dublin: Gill and Son, 1882), pp. 189–90.
44 MacHale's public letter in the *Freemans Journal*, 7 July 1879; see Donnelly, 'The Marian Shrine', p. 68, on the Sullivans' nationalism/Catholicism and clericalism.
45 *The Nation*, 31 January 1880.

46 Marie-Louise Legg, *Newspapers and Nationalism: The Irish Provincial Press 1850–1892* (Dublin: Four Courts, 1999), p. 96; Rynne, *Knock*, p. 59.

47 *The Nation*, 21 February 1880.

48 *Weekly News*, 12 February 1880; Sexton, *The Illustrated Record*, p. 20.

49 A. M. Sullivan's book *The Story of Ireland* was a big seller in America and went through countless editions and updates brought out by numerous publishers. One such edition published in Boston in 1885 by Murphy and McCarthy reported on Knock, pp. 644–9. P. D. Nunan wrote the relevant chapter, largely paraphrasing O'Connor's account, quoted at p. 649.

50 MacPhilpin, *The Apparitions*, p. 6.

51 *The Nation*, 13 February 1880; Sexton, *Illustrated History*, p. 20.

52 Walsh, *The Apparition*, p. 73.

53 Vertical File item 18,988. I have provided a photocopy to Knock Museum.

54 As reprinted in *The Nation* on 24 January 1880.

55 Volume 16, pp. 113–4. Based in Galway City, Fr Murphy travelled around Ireland giving missions.

56 He later advertised prints of the apparition scene and surroundings. *The Nation*, 13 March 1880.

57 O'C[onnor], *A Visit*.

58 Sr Mary Frances Clare, [M. F. Cusack] *Three Visits to Knock, with the Medical Certificates of Cures and Authentic Accounts of Different Apparitions* (New York: P. J. Kennedy, [1882] 1904).

59 John White, 'The Cusack Papers: New Evidence on the Knock Apparition', *History/Ireland*, iv, 4 (1996), pp. 39–44 and Eugene Hynes, 'A Chalice in a Bog, Or Fools' Gold?', my response in the next issue of the same journal.

60 Tom Neary, *I Saw Our Lady* (Knock: Custodians of Knock Shrine, 1977).

61 *Daily News*, 11 October 1880.

62 James S. Donnelly, Jr, 'The Peak of Marianism in Ireland, 1930–60', in *Piety and Power in Ireland 1760–1960: Essays in Honour of Emmet Larkin*, eds Stewart J. Brown and David W. Miller (Note Dame: Notre Dame University Press, 2000), pp. 252–83.

63 Walsh, *The Apparition*, p. 41.

64 Fr [James] Fergus, 'Notes Taken During the Process', Tuam Archdiocesan Archives, Box 109, Archbishop Gilmartin Papers, BA/9–1/8.

65 White, *The Knock Apparitions*, p. 8.

66 Walsh, *The Apparition*, pp. 40–1.

67 MacPhilpin, *The Apparition*, p. 34; Sexton, *The Illustrated Record*, p. 21.

68 Blackbourn appositely refers to 'an apparition narrative being constructed through a process of suggestion and accretion', including suggestions or questions from onlookers or interested third parties, *Marpingen*, p. 132. Paolo Apolito, *Apparitions of the Madonna at Oliveto Citra: Local Visions and Cosmic Drama*, translated by William Christian (University Park: Pennsylvania State University Press, 1998) is an extended ethnography of the process in operation. A Mexican-American family in Phoenix, many of whose members have had apparitions of Mary since the 1980s, audio-taped their discussions as they attempted to make sense of their initial experiences, in the process moving their apparitions from 'subjective to objective reality': Kristy Nabhan-Warren, *The Virgin of El Barrio* (New York: New York University Press, 2005), pp. 52–81, quoted at p. 77. Anthropologist Michael Allen describes the process in 1980s' Ireland, especially in the case of the visions at Inchigeeela in Cork. Allen, *Ritual, Power and Gender: Explorations in the Ethnography of Vanuatu, Nepal and Ireland* (New Delhi: Manohar, 2000), pp. 299–367.

69 Michael P. Carroll, *The Cult of the Virgin Mary: Psychological Origins* (Princeton: Princeton University Press, 1986), pp. 206–7.

70 Walsh, *The Apparition*, p. 18.

71 David Berman, 'Papal Visit Resurrects Ireland's Knock Legend', *The Freethinker*, 99 (1977), pp. 145–7,160; Berman, 'The Knock Apparition: Some New Evidence', *The New Humanist*, 102, 4 (December 1987), pp. 8–10.

72 Walsh, *The Apparition*, p. 16.
73 *The Illustrated Record,* pp. 12, 14, 4.
74 *The Apparitions*, p. 18.
75 See Rynne, *Knock*, pp. 66–7; Walsh, *The Apparition,* p. 15.
76 MacPhilpin, *The Apparitions*, p. 40.
77 *The Illustrated Record,* p. 22.
78 MacPhilpin, *The Apparitions,* p. 40.
79 MacPhilpin, *The Apparitions*, p. 34.
80 Liam Ua Cadhain, *Knock Shrine* (Galway: O'Gorman, 1935), p. 47.
81 Walsh, *The Apparition*, pp. 58–62.
82 Hill was baptised in 1868 and based on her assumption that baptisms were within a few days of birth, Rynne says he was eleven in 1879. However, early in 1880 two different reporters wrote that Hill was thirteen and a third that he was 'about fourteen' MacPhilpin, *The Apparitions* pp. 29, 55; Tom Neary, *I Saw Our Lady* (Published by the Custodians of Knock Shrine, Mayo, Ireland, 1977), p 27). Whether this was their estimates or based on what he told them cannot be determined. He would not be the only youngster to exaggerate his age, especially in circumstances like Hill's. Moreover, he might well have been less than certain about exactly how old he was. His willingness to please his questioners and affirm their suggestions is evident in his interview with Sexton, *The Nation's* reporter and avid Knock promoter:

> What were you talking about when you were there [at the gable]?
> About nothing only what we saw.
> Did you say your prayers?
> Oh, yes, sir: all the people went on their knees and were saying the Rosary and their prayers.

Sexton, *The Illustrated Record*, p. 5; *Weekly News,* 14 February 1880; Neary, *I Saw,* p. 28.
83 MacPhilpin, *The Apparitions,* p. 39.
84 Sexton, *The Illustrated Record,* p. 23.
85 MacPhilpin, *The Apparitions* p. 46.
86 Rynne, *Knock*, p. 56.
87 A copy of Lennon's letter is in Tuam Archdiocesan archives, Archbishop Gilmartin Papers, Box 108, BA/9–i/5.
88 *Daily News*, 2 March 1880.
89 Sexton, *The Illustrated Record,* p. 29.
90 M. F. Cusack, *The Story of My Life* (London: Hodder and Stoughton, 1891), p. 270.
91 For example, Walsh, *The Apparition,* p. 40.
92 White, *The Knock Apparitions*, p. 87.
93 O'C[onnor], *A Visit*, p. 20.
94 MacPhilpin, *The Apparitions,* p. 34; Rynne, *Knock*, p. 45.
95 MacPhilpin, *The Apparitions*, p. 35; Rynne, *Knock,* pp. 45–6.
96 ACSJP, Series 1A, 240; See White, *The Knock Apparitions*, p. 91.
97 MacPhilpin, *The Apparitions*, p. 37; Rynne, *Knock*, pp. 20–1.
98 MacPhilpin, *The Apparitions*, p. 37; Rynne, *Knock*, p. 20.
99 MacPhilpin, *The Apparitions*, p. 37; Rynne, *Knock*, p. 21.
100 MacPhilpin, *The Apparitions,* p. 40; Rynne, *Knock*, p. 37.
101 Rynne, *Knock*, p. 40.
102 Rynne, *Knock*, p. 42.
103 MacPhilpin, *The Apparitions*, pp. 44, 42, 39, 45; Rynne, *Knock*, pp. 51, 55, 27, 34.
104 Rynne, *Knock*, p. 24.
105 *Mayo Examiner*, 17 January 17, reprinted in *The Nation,* 24 January1880; *Full Report of the Visitation of the Blessed Virgin, St Joseph, St John in Knock Chapel, Co. Mayo* (Dublin: Nugent and Co., [1880?]), p. 3.
106 *Tuam News*, 9 January, reprinted in *The Nation,* 17 January 1880, p. 7.
107 *The Nation,* 31 January 1880.

108 *The Nation*, 14 February 1880.

109 In MacPhilpin, *The Apparitions,* p. 55.

110 White, *The Knock Apparitions,* p. 108.

111 'A Jewish visionary will see visions of the seven heavens because his religious imagination is stocked with these particular symbols. Buddhists see various images of Buddhas
and *bodhisattvas;* Christians visualize the Virgin Mary.', Karen Armstrong, *A History of
God: The 4000–Year Quest of Judaism, Christianity and Islam* (New York: Gramercy,
1993), p. 214. The English historian Christopher Hill wrote 'When I walk in the
country . . . if I see something white where I am expecting to see a signpost, a signpost
it becomes; whereas in fact it turns out to be a piece of paper. If I were expecting to see
a ghost, it would no doubt have become a ghost. So I can understand how in the seventeenth century old men and women (or indeed the greater number of short-sighted
people there must have been) saw armies fighting in the sky, and other portents, at
times when they were conditioned to expect them.' *England's Turning Point: Essays on
Seventeenth-Century English History* (London: Bookmarks, 1998), pp. 197–8. For a
broader case, see Darren Oldridge, *Strange Histories: The Trial of the Pig, the Walking
Dead, and other Matters of Fact from the Medieval and Renaissance Worlds* (London:
Routledge, 2005). I know of no evidence that would suggest that Mary or Maggie
Beirne would consider it impossible for a living person to appear in an apparition, but
such a view might well have been held by priests such as Fr Cavanagh or others
familiar with continental apparitions.

112 White, *The Knock Apparitions,* p. 107ff.

113 White, *The Knock Apparitions,* p.115.

114 MacPhilpin, *The Apparitions,* p. 44.

115 Walsh, *The Apparition,* pp. 78–9. Others have dealt with the issue differently. Rynne,
for example, assumes the statue existed but has then to explain how it came to be
there and why it was not to be found later. She admits that statues of St John the
Evangelist were rare and that there was no particular devotion to him in the
Lecanvey area. 'It can only be assumed', she writes, 'that the parish priest of Westport
had the statue installed because of a special attachment of his own', and furthermore,
that all trace of the statue vanished when the Lecanvey church was replaced by a new
one in 1891 (Rynne, *Knock,* p. 11). Not only has no such statue been documented in
Lecanvey, if White is right as I believe he is on this point, no statue ever of St John
had a mitre.

116 Donnelly, 'Peak of Marianism'.

117 White, *The Knock Apparitions,* p. 108ff.

118 Sexton, *The Illustrated Record,* p. 25; The Dublin edition of MacPhilpin does not carry
that illustration.

119 O'Connor refers to a 'stained-glass window above [the altar], inserted in the partition
that separates the sacristy from the church', *A Visit,* p. 12. Sexton describes it as a 'very
small stained glass window representing the crucifixion of our Lord', *The Illustrated
Record,* pp. 20, 27, and Fr Cavanagh, too, reportedly referred to it as a Crucifixion
scene, Sr Mary Francis Clare, *The Life of the Blessed Virgin Mary, Mother of God* (Dublin:
Gill and Son, 1880), p. 714.

120 Source: ACSJP Series 1A p. 240.

121 Walsh, *The Apparition,* p. 49; Liam Ua Cadhain, *Knock Shrine* (Galway: O'Gorman
Printing House, 1935), p. 54.

122 White, *The Knock Apparitions.*

123 Philip H. Davis and Jacqueline Boles, 'Pilgrim Work: Symbolization and Crowd
Interaction When the Virgin Appeared in Georgia', *Journal of Contemporary
Ethnography,* 32, 4 (August 2003), pp. 371–402.

124 Paolo Apolito, *Apparitions of the Madonna at Oliveto Citra: Local Visions and Cosmic
Drama,* translated by William Christian (University Park: Pennsylvania State
University Press, 1998).

125 Ua Cadhain, *Knock Shrine,* p. 54.

126 Rynne, *Knock*, pp. 31–2.

127 Sexton, *The Illustrated Record*, p. 17. This book was already at proof stage when I learned from Paul Carpenter that the Claremorris nun was Sister M. Patricia Bodkin.

128 On the cover and also between pages 48 and 49 in the Kelly edition. The detail on page 198 is from this illustration.

129 Emmet Larkin, 'The Devotional Revolution in Ireland, 1850–1875', *American Historical Review,* 77 (1972), p. 643.

130 A ballad about the apparition added the instruments of the Passion to the altar, lamb and cross in the scene. *A New Song on the Wonderful Apparitions, of the Blessed Virgin, St Joseph, and St John, in Knock Chapel County Mayo* (Dublin: Nugent and Co., no date).

131 Several social scientists have investigated how the photographing of supernatural personages or signs contributes to constructing the reality of apparitions. See Jessy Pagliaroli, 'Kodak Catholicism: Miraculous Photography and its Significance at a Post-Conciliar Marian Apparition Site in Canada', *Historical Studies* 70 (Annual 2004), pp. 71–98, for a review of various studies. Also see Daniel Wojcik, '"Polaroids From Heaven": Photography, Folk Religion, and the Miraculous Image Tradition at a Marian Apparition Site', *Journal of American Folklore,* 109 (Spring 1996), pp. 129–48, for a case study of one American site. For a superb historically-sensitive analytical overview that highlights the unintended consequences of such photography see Paolo Apolito, *The Madonna and the Internet: Religious Visionary Experience on the Web* (Chicago: University of Chicago Press, 2005), pp. 101–20.

132 Also see Sexton, *The Illustrated Record*, p. 23.

133 Sociologist Michael Carroll, *Cult of the Virgin Mary*, pp. 205–10, does see the date as significant. He argues that the apparition was an 'illusion' which he defines as a misperception of something that was actually there, which he posits was some sort of (otherwise unexplained) globe of light, and that Mary Beirne interpreted this ambiguous stimulus as the Virgin Mary and the other personages in the apparition. Other seers followed Mary Beirne's suggestion. Carroll then considers why the Virgin was reported as she was, hovering a foot or two above the ground. He claims that 'there is one iconographic situation in which Mary regularly appears a few feet off the ground, and this is in traditional depictions of the Assumption of Mary into heaven in bodily form', p. 208. Carroll suggests that Dominick Beirne would be attuned to the Assumption feast because in his role as sacristan he would 'have been very much involved in setting up the church for the various devotions that took place during the octave of the Assumption', ibid., p. 209. And because Mary Beirne sometimes substituted for her brother, she too could have been similarly involved. But Carroll's evidence is deeply flawed. First, there is no evidence that 'various devotions took place during the octave of the Assumption' in Knock, so any speculation about what, if anything, her brother might have done to set up the church for them is unconvincing about Mary Beirne's experience. As far as we know, his job as sacristan involved only opening and locking the church each morning and night. Second, despite Carroll's claim, depictions of the Assumption did not regularly show the Virgin a few feet off the ground. A quick internet search failed to find any representation like Carroll described. In contrast, in depictions of her Assumption the Virgin is very commonly painted in the sky attended by angels, and the perspective is one in which the viewer gazes heavenward. Famous paintings of the scene by Bartolome Murillo (c.1640), Titian (1516–18), Correggio (1526–30), Carracci (1590 and 1600–01) and numerous others all follow that pattern. This historic pattern continues to the present as can be seen for example by examining the offerings of sellers of Catholic devotional art, such as at catholiccompany.com/product_detail. Some depictions of the Assumption do show persons on the ground, usually clustered around the Virgin's open grave, and Carroll cites two such paintings to support his claim. But these still show Our Lady in the sky, and in one of them a large cloud is beneath her feet. Carroll further claims that 'it has become iconographic convention to include St John the Evangelist in portrayals of Mary's Assumption', ibid., p. 208. I have not

found it so. Moreover, in depictions of the Assumption the Virgin is usually shown without a crown, the attribute every seer at Knock focused on.

134 Diary of Bishop Francis J. McCormack, 1878–1888, McCormack Papers, Box 26, Number 1, Galway Diocesan Archives. Entry for 2 October 1879. I owe this reference to the generosity of Professor Jim Donnelly. McCormack, then Bishop of Achonry, was accompanied by Bishop Hugh Conway of Killala.
135 Sexton, *The Illustrated Record,* p. 14.
136 *A Visit,* 18, 21.
137 Walsh, *The Apparition,* pp. 48–49, quotes the statement in full.
138 Ua Cadhain, *Knock Shrine,* pp. 53–55.
139 Walsh, *The Apparition,* p. 50.
140 Walsh, *The Apparition,* p. 50.
141 Walsh, *The Apparition,* p. 51.
142 Walsh, *The Apparition,* p. 51.
143 Walsh, *The Apparition,* p. 51.
144 Quoted in Walsh, *The Apparition,* p. 57.
145 See Walsh, *The Apparition,* p. 73.
146 Cusack, *Three Visits,* p. 77.
147 Donnelly, 'The Marian Shrine', p. 60.
148 Aidan Nichols, OP, *Holy Order: The Apostolic Ministry from the New Testament to the Second Vatican Council* (Dublin: Veritas, 1990), pp. 111–2.
149 Donald Jordan, Jr, *Land and Popular Politics in Ireland: County Mayo From the Plantation to the Land War* (Cambridge: Cambridge University Press, 1994), pp. 234–7; Samuel Clark, *Social Origins of the Irish Land War* (Princeton: Princeton University Press, 1979), pp. 286–90.
150 White, *The Knock Apparitions,* pp. 49–54.
151 Emmet Larkin, *The Roman Catholic Church and the Home Rule Movement in Ireland, 1870–1874* (Dublin: Gill and MacMillan, 1990), pp. 56–7.
152 Proinsias Ó Maolmhuaidh, *Uilleog De Búrca: Athair na hAthbheochana* (Dublin: Foilseáchain Naisiúnta Teoranta,1981); Helena Concannan, 'Canon Ulick J. Bourke (1829–1887)', *Irish Ecclesiastical Record* (May 1950), pp. 405–17; Donnelly, 'The Marian Shrine', p. 70.
153 Donnelly, 'The Marian Shrine', p. 67 n. 39.
154 Clark, *Social Origins,* pp. 285–6.
155 Clark, *Social Origins,* p. 286.
156 Jordan, *Land,* p. 238.
157 White, *The Knock Apparitions,* pp. 49, 52.
158 CT, 28 June, 5 and 12 July 1879.
159 Jordan, *Land,* p. 239.
160 This account of the meeting is based on Jordan, *Land,* pp. 237–41.
161 Ó Maolmhuaidh, *Uilleog De Búrca,* pp. 15–16, 150–1; White, *The Knock Apparitions,* pp. 56–7.
162 CT, 4 June 1881; White, *The Knock Apparitions,* pp. 60–1.
163 Peasant proprietorship was relegated to second place in its list of objectives, reduced rents being first: Jordan, *Land,* pp. 248–50.
164 Ulick Bourke, *A Plea for the Evicted Tenants of Mayo* (Dublin: Browne and Nolan, 1883).
165 CT, 18 October 1879.
166 Davitt, 1904; Jordan, *Land,* p. 242.
167 Jordan, *Land,* p. 242.
168 Jordan, *Land,* pp. 242–3; See also Clark, *Social Origins,* pp. 286–90.
169 Jordan 1994, *Land,* p. 242; CT, 4 October 1879.
170 CT, 1 November 1879.
171 Jordan, *Land,* p. 248.
172 CT, 1 November 1879.
173 CT, 1 November 1879.

174 CT, 19 July 1879.
175 CT, 22 November 1879.
176 See Bishop MacEvilly's statement to this effect quoted in Clark, *Social Origins*, p. 286.
177 CT, 22 November 1879.
178 Mary Francis Cusack, *The Nun of Kenmare: An Autobiography* (Boston: Ticknor, 1889), p. 284.
179 After all he reportedly preached that Mary came to teach us to be submissive to God's will Ua Cadhain, *Archdeacon Cavanagh*, p. 78.
180 T. W. Moody, *Davitt and Irish Revolution 1846–82* (Oxford: Clarendon Press, 1982), p. 349.
181 Quoted in Jordan, *Land*, p. 251.
182 Clark, *Social Origins*, p. 311.
183 Maume, 'Rebel on the Run', p. 2, citing a letter from an old Fenian 'Irishtown-Claremorris', *Mayo News*, 30 March 1929.
184 David Berman, 'Papal Visit Resurrects Ireland's Knock Legend', *The Freethinker*, 99 (1979), pp. 145–7, 160, and Berman, 'The Knock Apparition: Some New Evidence', *The New Humanist*, 102, 4 (December 1987), pp. 8–10. For earlier claims about the policeman see Berman's second article and James S. Donnelly, Jr, 'The Marian Shrine at Knock: The First Decade', *Eire/Ireland*, 28, 2 (1993), pp. 54–99.
185 Sexton, *Illustrated Record*, pp.6–7; MacPhilpin, *The Apparition*, pp. 25–6, O'C[onnor], *Visit*, pp. 27–8.
186 Rynne, *Knock*, p. 65.
187 Bishop Michael Browne of Galway (1937–1976) suspected that it was true. He consulted experts in the early 1950s about the possibility of the apparition being caused by a magic lantern hoax and was told that it was impossible, yet he still refused to authorise any Diocesan Pilgrimages from his diocese to Knock, or even to allow groups from the diocese, such as the Legion of Mary, to identify themselves by diocesan affiliation. I thank Professor Jim Donnelly for this information which is based on documents he consulted in Bishop Browne's papers in the Galway Diocesan Archives.
188 For an introductory explanation of 'performative language' see Allan G. Johnson, *The Forest and the Trees: Sociology as Life, Practice and, Promise* (Philadelphia: Temple University Press, 1997), pp. 166–72. Various philosophical and sociological traditions contribute to the concept including importantly J. L. Austin, *How To Do Things With Words* (Cambridge: Harvard University Press, 1962).
189 Another Dublin academic fell into the same trap of treating natural and supernatural as mutually exclusive explanatory frameworks. Reacting to how Soviet bloc intellectuals condescendingly dismissed stories of Virgin apparitions in Poland, historian David Doyle read about the Knock case. Not finding a 'natural' explanation, and finding the published witness testimony compelling, he came to believe that the Virgin had come to Knock: David N. Doyle, 'Knock 1879: Message to a Deprived People', *Doctrine and Life*, 30, 2 (February 1980), 69–79. When Daniel Campbell recalled the supernatural protection afforded Knock during an epidemic of cholera he was quite able to specify the mundane 'natural' means by which this was accomplished. A Maynooth professor and believer in Lourdes who reviewed a book that highlighted Bernadette's psychological predisposition as key, could see in this God's plan to prepare her for the visit of the Virgin. S. O'Riordan, CSsR, 'Book Review': *Irish Ecclesiastical Record*, 89, Series 5 (1958), pp. 141–7.
190 The *Daily Telegraph* reporter looked inside the building not only for any window or opening toward the chapel but for evidence that one had existed earlier: MacPhilpin, *The Apparitions*, p. 61.

10 OUR LADY AND THE CLERGY

1 Priests, professors, politicians and playwrights as well as peasants pick and choose among the available options, adopting those made credible by their own experience and situations. Larkin's ideas on the Devotional Revolution added to the pool of ideas

available from which different groups could select, adopt and perhaps adapt. The paradigm highlights the centrality of Rome and the importance of a united hierarchy working through the priests to spread orthodox devotion and practice. Such an emphasis resonates with two different groups. First, anti-Catholics, who see Rome and especially the pope as the antichrist, see in the revolution another success of the enemy in spreading its tentacles. An article posted on Ian Paisley's website in 2005, for example, accepts Larkin's account of the growing influence of Rome. Clive Gillis, 'Rome Harnesses Folk Superstition to Revolutionise the Religion of Ireland', posted 12 April 2005 on www.ianpaisley.org/article, accessed 12 November 2005.

On the other hand, one is struck by the number of Catholic priests who have written religious history within Larkin's framework. Daniel Gallogly, James H. Murphy, Ignatius Murphy, Liam Swords, and Patrick Corish, who criticised David Miller's estimates of 1834 mass attendance rates as too low, all are or were, while still alive, Catholic priests. The heroic role Larkin accorded earlier generations of priests in bringing the mass to the masses resonated with these men and many others who devoted their lives to the church. What they took for granted as priests, the importance of the mass, was reinforced by what they read in Larkin, which is doubtless why they found his ideas congenial.

For the diverse ways in which playwrights and politicians have presented the 1916 Rising, see James Moran, *Staging the Easter Rising: 1916 as Theatre* (Cork: Cork University Press, 2005). Different persons perceive even a solid object like Fr Mathew's Temperance Medal differently. Whether the horizontal line in the shield is seen as an altar is a matter of perception, which in turn is shaped by one's experience and social situation. Professor Jim Donnelly, who first drew my attention to the medal, said it instantly reminded him of the Knock scene. In contrast two recent historians, John Quinn and Paul Townend mention the lamb, cross and angels but not the altar in describing the medal. My initial perception was like Donnelly's. Presumably the Fr Mathew scholars, Quinn and Townend, were not preoccupied with Knock as Donnelly and I were, who have studied the apparition for years. The letters, IHS, beneath the line also reinforced for me this perception since these are often found on the front of an altar. Scholars' preconceptions influence what they perceive even in the same medal; what is in their minds shapes what they see, and thus how they respond.

2   Clifford Geertz, *The Interpretation of Cultures: Selected Essays* (New York: Basic, 1973), pp. 3–30, quoted at pp. 20, 29. Interpretations are contestable when they are made by insiders not to mention by 'outsiders' such as scholars, see Robert Orsi, *The Madonna of 115th Street: Faith and Community in Italian Harlem, 1880-1950*, 2nd edition (New Haven: Yale University Press, 2002) and John Comaroff and Jean Comaroff, *Ethnography and The Historical Imagination* (Boulder: Westview, 1992), p. 27. But not all social scientists agree with Geertz's emphasis on understanding from within a culture. For example, in developing his cognitive theory of religious transmission, Whitehouse pointed to the 'methodological sloppiness of interpretivism' and even the 'vagueness or pretentious obfuscation of some scholars (some of the time)' as obstacles in developing a general theory applicable to all religions. Still he recognised the challenge of explaining episodes like the Knock apparition. 'Miraculous healings, sudden conversions, visitations, possessions, and many other epiphanic episodes not only are widespread in religions of all kinds [but they provoke those involved to try to explain what they experience]. But when these sorts of experiences occur in the context of a routinized tradition, the episodic memories they evince are contaminated by standard interpretive schemas . . . The *experience*, in other words, is somewhat obscured by standardized *stories about* the experience.' Harvey Whitehouse, *Modes of Religiosity: A Cognitive Theory of Religious Transmission* (New York: Altamira, 2004), pp. 29, 124. Such relatively rare episodes typically 'evoke abundant inferences, producing a sense of multivalence and multivocality of religious imagery, experienced as personal and unmediated inspiration', ibid., p. 72. Thus, in so far as the Knock seers' stories were

filtered through the investigating commission of priests the accounts were standardised toward the priests' model.

3 James C. Scott, *Domination and the Arts of Resistance: Hidden Transcripts* (New Haven: Yale University Press, 1990), p. 19.

4 Geertz, *The Interpretation,* p. 30. Among many who recognise this see Sherry B. Ortner, *High Religion: A Cultural and Political History of Sherpa Buddhism* (Princeton: Princeton University Press 1989), p. 12.

5 Compare Christian's comment that by the early twentieth-century, 'the search for a Spanish Lourdes was on', and Blackbourn's statements about Marpingen in the 1870s being regarded as the German Lourdes. William Christian, *Moving Crucifixes in Modern Spain* (Princeton: Princeton University Press, 1992), p. 10; David Blackbourn, *Marpingen: Apparitions of the Virgin Mary in Bismarckian Germany* (Oxford: Clarendon Press, 1993).

6 Hugh F. Kearney, '1875: Faith or Fatherland? The Contested Symbolism of Irish Nationalism', in *'Christianity in Ireland: Revisiting the Story,* eds Brendan Bradshaw and Daire Keogh (Dublin: Columba Press, 2002), p. 74; James S. Donnelly, Jr, 'The Marian Shrine at Knock: The First Decade', *Eire/Ireland* 28, 2 (1993), pp. 61–2.

7 Peter O'Dwyer, *Mary: A History of Devotion in Ireland* (Dublin: Four Courts Press, 1988), p. 265.

8 Fr C. Caddell, 'From the Grotto of Lourdes', *Irish Monthly* (July 1877), p. 471.

9 Lisa Godson, 'Catholicism and Material Culture in Ireland 1840–1880', *Circa,* 103 (Spring 2003), p. 43.

10 Mary P. Magray, *The Transforming Power of the Nuns: Women, Religion, and Cultural Change in Ireland, 1750–1900* (New York: Oxford University Press, 1998), p. 91.

11 H. B., 'Our Lady of Lourdes', *The Irish Ecclesiastical Record* [New series] (May 1870), pp. 447–58.

12 CT, 13 February and 31 May 1879. This Mr Bull was likely a Dubliner since a 'Mrs Bull, Dublin' contributed a prize for a similar fundraising effort for the Castlebar Mercy Convent. CT, 7 February 1880.

13 CT, 23 September 1876. What apparently was the same pilgrimage was estimated at 100,000 in a report in *The Nation,* 8 July 1876.

14 [Thomas Sexton], *The Illustrated Record of the Apparitions at Knock: The Depositions of the Witnesses, Lists of the Alleged Miraculous Cures . . . (reprinted from the "Weekly News")* (Dublin: T. D. Sullivan, [1880]), p. 27; T. O'C[onnor], *A Visit to Knock* (Limerick: T. O'Connor, 1880), p. 15.

15 *The Nation,* 26 June 1880.

16 The sympathies of the Irish laity were overwhelmingly on the French side as proven by their financial support. The *Irishman* newspaper noted 'Ireland has contributed more to the relief of French soldiers in one month, than all Ireland and Irishmen all over the world had subscribed in five years of the Fenian prisoners' funds. This is indeed eloquent testimony', quoted in R. V. Comerford, *The Fenians in Context* (Dublin: Wolfhound Press, 1985), pp. 183–4. 'It is clear that the sympathy expressed for France went much deeper and extended over a much wider spectrum of Irish society than, say sympathetic feelings for the fenian prisoners did. To put the matter plainly, the Irish Catholic community identified wholeheartedly with France in the war of 1870–1 . . . because [France] appeared as the Catholic champion facing the protestant Bismarck.' ibid., p. 183; Marie Corkery, 'Ireland and the Franco-Prussian War', *Etudes Irlandaises,* 7 (1982), pp. 127–44.

17 Donnelly, 'Marian Shrine', pp. 66–7.

18 Liam Ua Cadhain, *Knock Shrine* (Galway: O'Gorman Printing House, 1935), p. 85.

19 Sexton, *Illustrated History,* p. 8.

20 Sisters of Mercy, Claremorris, *Hymn to Our Lady of Knock* (Dublin: Piggott and Co., [1881?]), verse 2.

21 Donnelly 'Marian Shrine', p. 92.

22 The nearness of other worlds so obvious in pre-famine Knock as described by Daniel

Campbell was paralleled elsewhere. Local sacred sites were common, an estimated 3,000 holy wells across the whole country, for example, and maybe 40,000 fairy forts. Reports of interactions across the boundaries of the worlds such as stories like the 'Friars of Urlaur' or of dead priests returning to seek mass servers were also widely found. Lady Augusta Gregory, *Visions and Beliefs in the West of Ireland* (Gerrard's Cross: Colin Smythe, 1970 [1920]) took hundreds of pages to even briefly describe the numerous visionary phenomena she heard about from local people.

23 James Berry, *Tales from the West of Ireland* (Dublin: The Dolmen Press, 1966), p. 118.

24 Daithi Ó h-Ógáin, *The Hero in Irish Folk Poetry* (Dublin: Gill and MacMillan, 1985), pp. 254–5.

25 Anne O'Connor, *The Blessed and the Damned: Sinful Women and Unbaptised Children in Irish Folklore* (New York: Peter Lang, 2005), pp. 126–30.

26 Pádraig Ó Héalaí, 'Moral Values in Irish Religious Tales', *Béaloideas,* 42–44 (1974-1976), p. 184; Ó Héalaí, 'Priest Versus Healer: The Legend of the Priest's Stricken Horse', *Béaloideas,* 62/63 (1994–5), pp. 171–88.

27 'Oral tradition, by its nature, is various, uncentralized, polysemic, and often contradictory.' Angela Bourke, 'Irish Stories of Weather, Time and Gender: Saint Brigid', in *Reclaiming Gender: Transgressive Identities in Modern Ireland,* eds Marilyn Cohen and Nancy Curtin (New York: St Martin's Press, 1999), p. 14.

28 Breandán Ó Buachalla, *Cathal Buí: Amhráin* (Dublin: An Clóchomhar, 1975), pp. 99–101; Ó h-Ógáin, *The Hero,* p. 255.

29 Tim Robinson, *Camchuairt Chonamara Theas: A Twisty Journey, Mapping South Connemara* (Dublin: Coiscéim, 2002), pp. 156–8.

30 ibid., p. 52.

31 The locally documented visions included one with a different mode of criticising the failure of particular priests, that of the long dead priest returning to seek somebody to serve his mass.

32 More than one writer has pointed out that Knock has been presented as a model of submissive women. Marina Warner is careful to recognise that the image of Mary at Knock could well have been used in other ways, including for example calling for the priesthood of women. Warner, 'What the Virgin of Knock Means to Women', *Magill* (September 1979), pp. 30–9. Later interpretations of the apparition have to be understood in terms of the times and social contexts in which they are made. Like Warner, Niamh O'Sullivan argues that the silence of the Virgin at Knock has been used to keep women silent as well as submissive: Niamh O'Sullivan, 'The Iron Cage of Femininity: Visual Representations of Women in the 1880s Land Agitation', in *Ideology and Ireland in the Nineteenth Century,* eds Tadhg Foley and Seán Ryder (Dublin: Four Courts Press, 1998), p. 181–96. But her evidence is a 1979 article (Warner's) and references to the French Revolution. Her illustrations are from London and Paris. To understand the original apparition we have to understand things in Knock (not London or Paris) and in 1879, not 1789 or 1979.

33 This is 'essentially contestable' as Geertz recognised of any ethnographic assertion or indeed any historical or social science interpretation, though it does not follow that one opinion is as good as any other.

34 Scott, *Domination,* p. 18–19 and passim.

35 CT, 1 November 1880.

36 In his *Mass in a Connemara Cabin,* first exhibited in 1884, Aloysius Kelly painted the priest as very young, even boyish. O'Sullivan argues that the piece, which depicts the final blessing at the mass rather than the theologically central moment of consecration, shows the priest giving his blessing to the peasants during the Land War. Niamh O'Sullivan, '*Mass in a Connemara Cabin*: Religion and the Politics of Painting', *Eire/Ireland,* 40, 1/2 (Spring-Summer 2005), pp. 126–39.

37 Blackbourn, *Marpingen,* p. 47. See also Marina Warner, *Alone of All Her Sex: The Myth and the Cult of the Virgin* Mary (New York: Knopf, 1976); Orsi, *Madonna,* p. xlvii and passim.

38 Pádraig Ó Baoill, *Glórtha Ár Sinsear: Béaloideas Oirdheisceart na Gaillimhe* (Dublin: Coiscéim, 2005), p. 20.

39 Gearóid Ó Crualaoich, *The Book of the Cailleach: Stories of the Wise-Woman Healer* (Cork: Cork University Press, 2003), p. 24.

40 See Comaroff and Comaroff, *Ethnography*, p. 27. Orsi claims it is impossible to exhaust the meanings of a popular religious symbol (*Madonna*, p. xlvii).

41 Earlier in the decade, there had been what one scholar and believer called an 'alleged apparition of Mary' in Savoie in France which condemned the clergy as sinners and forced an elderly bishop to resign: Cheryl Porte, *Pontmain, Prophecy and Protest: A Cultural-Historical Study of a Nineteenth-Century Vision* (New York: Peter Lang, 2005), p. 70. It is unlikely that this case was known in Knock.

42 John J. White, *The Knock Apparitions and Pilgrimage: Popular Piety and the Irish Land War* (Unpublished PhD Dissertation in History, Boston College, 1999), pp. 49, 52.

43 Warner, 'What the Virgin of Knock Means', p. 36.

44 9 January 1880; MacPhilpin, *The Apparitions*, p 14; Sexton, *The Illustrated History*, p. 10; Sr Mary Francis Clare, *The Life of the Blessed Virgin Mary, Mother of God* (Dublin: Gill and Son, 1880), p. 734.

45 CT, 17 April 1880.

46 Scott, *Domination*, p. 4. One colleague who read this was sceptical. He pointed out that land demonstrators in Mayo at the time were not unduly deterred by the threat of clerical power. However, there is a world of difference between joining a public mass demonstration in opposition to priests on the land issue, on the one hand, and facing a group of priests as an individual condemning the clergy's use of their religious power, on the other.

47 Such a pattern of recounting, I suggest is best seen as hedging of one's bets and as analogous to the pervasive 'peasant prevarication' that drove outsiders to distraction, especially those with power or authority and/or those who assumed themselves to be superior in nineteenth-century Ireland. As noted earlier, such behaviour is not a pathology of personality but a weapon of the weak. Lay people were not beyond such behaviour in front of priests. See Cara Delay, 'Confidantes or Competitors? Women, Priests, and Conflict in Post-Famine Ireland', *Eire/Ireland*, 40, 1/2 (Spring-Summer 2005), pp. 106–25. The Jesuit priest's report from Knock that the locals lit mid-summer bonfires in honour of St Aloysius is likely another instance.

48 John MacPhilpin, *The Apparitions and Miracles at Knock. Also, The Official Depositions of the Eye-Witnesses* (Dublin: Gill and Son, 1880), p. 37. For various reasons detailed above, the published explanation of how Mary Beirne came to this insight is implausible.

49 In a divided body of priests in the diocese those investigating Knock included the archbishop's nephew, Canon Ulick Bourke, whom his critics berated as a tool of his uncle, and Fr Cavanagh who, too, was likely close to MacHale. MacHale 'who never placed his honours lightly' had recently given Cavanagh the purely honorific title of Archdeacon. Ua Cadhain, *Archdeacon Cavanagh*, p. 18, says this was in 1875, but the *Irish Catholic Directory* in 1877 lists the position of Archdeacon as vacant in the arch-diocese, while in 1878 it lists Fr Cavanagh with the title. Typically only one priest at most in a diocese held this title.

50 It may be significant that the six were curates, four of them subject to the three known panel members. If some original senior priest members of the commission either did not take part or chose not to be associated with the later publication of the evidence, what White suggests makes sense, 'the priests who were proponents of Knock prob-ably sought to give added weight to the devotion by creating the appearance of clerical approval of the developing cult and pilgrimage by means of a show of clerical numbers; thus, the large number of priests who "assisted"': White, *The Knock Apparitions*, p. 88.

51 One of the priests who assisted was Fr James Corbett, a curate in Claremorris. He was quite able to recognise the way domination affected what people did in other social situations. In referring to a landlord's claim — supported by documents — of

fairness toward tenants, Corbett wrote in the press that 'like all rent-office documents, concocted and signed in the presence and under the eye of the landlord, this
mysterious agreement will be taken for all it is worth' (Letter to editor, CT, 8 August
1880).

52   Even if not initially, the seers must have considered the possibility the bishop figure
was indeed MacHale, if for no other reason than other people in the area would suggest
it. Though the seers could not acknowledge it, it would make sense that the other male
figure seen bowing toward the Virgin could be read as Fr Cavanagh rather than St
Joseph. (He could also be read as representing the laity as opposed to the clergy.) There
is not a shred of evidence in the published testimony, however, to support this view. Yet
I suggest that this is not a completely implausible interpretation. We would not expect
the witnesses to directly voice such a position even if they suspected it. In the case of
the bishop figure they could, and did, convey hints while preserving their ability to
deny any criticism. But the priest was altogether more directly involved in their lives.
He was parish priest for all but one of the witnesses and was the employer of one of the
most important. He was the clergyman on whom they had to rely most directly for the
sacraments. He was the man chairing the panel of priests before whom in person they
had to testify. The evidence we have shows the seers likely were clerical partisans;
perhaps criticism of him would not even have entered their consciousness. However,
their dependence on him very likely affected their evaluation of him. Just as 'loyalty
displays' for landlords actually reflected the tenants' powerlessness, so failure to overtly
criticise priests cannot be read as evidence of satisfaction with their behaviour.
'Deference [to landlords] had rarely in Ireland been much more than hostility repressed
or delayed' (K. Theodore Hoppen, *Elections, Politics, and Society in Ireland, 1832–1885*
(Oxford: Clarendon Press, 1984), p. 137. Contradictory and very changeable thinking
and feeling is the hallmark of underdog experiences, especially where the authority
system is under overt threat. Even hagiographical treatments of Cavanagh have persons
who were critics later apologising to him (Ua Cadhain, *Archdeacon Cavanagh*, p 84.
Rynne, *Knock*, p. 83). As Freire put it, 'The oppressed . . . are at one and the same time
themselves and the oppressor whose consciousness they have internalized': Paulo
Freire, *Pedagogy of the Oppressed* (Harmondsworth: Penguin, 1977), p. 32. John
Gaventa, *Power and Powerlessness: Quiescence and Rebellion in an Appalachian Valley*
(Urbana: University of Illinois Press, 1980) penetratingly analyses similar situations in
late nineteenth-century Appalachian coal mining communities. For an application of
Gaventa's framework to a 1980s' conflict in a small town in the US Midwest, see
Eugene Hynes, 'Elite Control and Citizen Mobilization in a Small Midwestern Town',
Critical Sociology, 17 (Spring, 1990), pp. 81–98. Social and economic dependence
skews people's thinking and emotions in ways that normally reproduce inequality.
Challenges to the hegemony of the powerful, however, can emerge and when they do
they follow predictable trajectories that involve stages of reinforced dependence, and
contradictory and confused ideation easily susceptible to manipulation or redirection.

53   [Sexton], *Illustrated Record*, p. 4. There were other, organisationally-important reasons
for the priests to discourage early media reports, such as waiting to see if the official
church authorities accepted the apparition as supernatural. However, these reasons were
still in place when the priests did in fact launch extensive publicity in the newspapers.

54   The priests did not include any witness statements that went beyond description to
interpretation. Mary Beirne was later reported as understanding the apparition as due to
Fr Cavanagh's holiness; if they did not include such positive claims (from a clericalist
standpoint) we can understand why they would not have included any claims to the
contrary, even if they had heard them from witnesses. More interesting than the silence
of the heavenly figures is the silence of the seers (in their published testimony) about
what they understood by the apparition. Perhaps the panel of priests did not press very
much to elicit answers they suspected could be far from music to their ears.

55   Far from admitting any criticisms of Fr Cavanagh, promoters went out of their way to
stress the esteem in which everyone held him. 'Like Pastor, Like Flock', wrote

MacPhilpin (in Latin) stressing the simple devotional religiosity of both (*The Apparitions*, p. 20). Attempts to positively spin Cavanagh's reputation persisted later. Ua Cadhain's 1953 study is as much hagiography as biography and his list of criticisms, largely taken without acknowledgement from the Nun of Kenmare in her early Knock promoting period, is disingenuous: 'The only word of blame or disapproval expressed against the priest was that he was too devout to the Blessed Virgin; that he lived very much in contemplation; nor was he as practical as he might be in worldly matters of business, and, perhaps, worst of all, that he was a man who was never known to take a holiday' (*Archdeacon Cavanagh*, p. 42–3). This is palpably misleading. If it were true, even in Ua Cadhain's mind, there would be no reason for anyone to threaten to maim him. The Nun of Kenmare quickly changed her judgment of Cavanagh. Ua Cadhain also claims there were no public houses in the whole parish when Fr Cavanagh became parish priest of Knock, and that as a remarkable fact, it was ten years after the apparition before the first licensed house sold drink in Knock (ibid., p. 41). Daniel Campbell recalled that nearly every house in the village sold unlicensed drink in pre-famine days and we have little reason to believe this was to change. Moreover, Campbell recalled the Beirne family ran the 'second public house' in the village. We have direct evidence of a pub in the early 1880s: the *Connaught Telegraph* of 2 October 1880 reported that Martin Hughes and John Killeen of Churchfield had applied for a licence to sell alcohol, which they obviously obtained. When the Nun of Kenmare set up a convent in Knock in 1881–2 she rented part of a house owned by the Kelly family at Churchfield, while others ran a 'public tap' in the other part of the house. Cusack complained to Fr Cavanagh about how drinkers there disturbed the nuns and felt his friendship with the Kellys was the reason he refused to intervene. Additionally, according to Cusack, workers hired by the contractor building her new convent spent a lot of time at that very establishment rather than doing their job. We cannot rely on Ua Cadhain's work for evidence of the period around the apparition.

56   *The Apparitions*, p. 10. The first recorded cure, ten days after the apparition, was of Delia Gordon; it is likely not a coincidence that her father was a leader of the land agitation and among those Fr Cavanagh attacked (perhaps not by name) from the altar a few months earlier. Men in his situation would easily see the Virgin's visit as condemnation of the priest. No wonder his wife took Delia out of mass and used mortar from the gable to ease her ear-ache.

57   Ua Cadhain, *Archdeacon Cavanagh*, pp. 82–3, apparently relying on local memories in the Knock area. Since early 1950s' promoters used the Virgin appearance to argue for the recognition of Fr Cavanagh's virtue we can safely assume that the idiom of Virgin appearance as commentary on priestly behaviour was indeed understood in 1879.

58   Pádraig Ó Baoighill, *Nally As Mayo* (Dublin: Coiscéim, 1998), p. 140.

59   CT, 21 February 1880.

60   Ua Cadhain, *Archdeacon Cavanagh*, p. 18.

61   Three centuries earlier difficulties in Episcopal succession in the adjacent diocese of Elphin had precipitated 'marvels and prodigies': Bernadette Cunningham and Raymond Gillespie, *Stories from Gaelic Ireland: Microhistories from the Sixteenth Century Irish Annals* (Dublin: Four Courts, 2003), pp. 134–54. Though William Christian has identified centuries-long traditions of apparitions in Spain, I cannot similarly document any connection between the events of 1588 and 1879. The 1858 Lourdes apparition also was of a type long recognised in the Pyrenees: Ruth Harris, *Lourdes: Body and Spirit in the Secular Age* (New York: Viking, 1999), p. 14.

62   Sean Connolly, 'The "Blessed Turf": Cholera and Popular Panic in Ireland, June 1832', *Irish Historical Studies,* xxiii, no. 91 (1983), pp. 214–232.

63   Connolly, 'Blessed Turf', p. 222.

64   Thomas McGrath, *Religious Renewal and Reform in the Pastoral Ministry of Bishop James Doyle of Kildare and Leighlin, 1786–1834* (Dublin: Four Courts, 1999), p. 187.

65   Connolly, 'Blessed Turf', p. 239.

66   McGrath, *Religious Renewal*, p. 201.

67 Just how seriously this could be taken may be judged from the fact that the assassination of a Limerick magistrate around the same time was ascribed to the hatred he engendered by requiring the same thing: Stephen Gibbons, *Captain Rock, Night Errant: the Threatening Letters of Pre-Famine Ireland* (Dublin: Four Courts Press, 2004), p. 18.

68 McGrath *Religious Renewal*, p. 203.

69 Personal communication from Thomas McGrath, 12 May 1997.

70 ibid., p. 203–4; also see Sean Connolly, *Priests and People in Pre-Famine Ireland* (Dublin: Gill and MacMillan, 1982), pp. 129, 229–30.

71 Connolly, *Priests and People*, p. 250; John C. MacTernan, *Olde Sligo: Aspects of Town and County Over 750 Years* (Sligo: Avena Publications, 1995), pp. 300–305.

72 *Béaloideas*, 1942, p. 205. This was another way of invoking the Virgin to criticise the clergy.

73 Even among people we might expect to be more orthodox in their religious practice we find evidence of resistance to priests on this matter. In 1878, at a meeting of the Ballinasloe Total Abstinence Society, 'a majority of those present' resigned and walked out when the priest in charge introduced new rules prohibiting any member from speaking at meetings or participating in excursions who were in any way connected to Fenianism: CT, 8 June 1878.

74 Daly reprinted his side of the exchange, originally in the *Mayo Examiner*, in his own paper on 14 and 28 December 1878.

75 Curry had spent a year in prison on Spike Island where reportedly his health suffered.

76 Of course, the clergy themselves were not of one mind. Even when the hierarchy and most priests refused Fenians the sacraments, some priests were always available to minister to their spiritual needs. Bishops sometimes found it necessary to deny Jesuit priests permission to hear confessions at parish missions precisely because they knew that Fenians would get absolution from them: Kevin Laheen, SJ, 'Jesuit Parish Mission Memoirs, 1863–1876', Part 1, *Collectanea Hibernica*, 39–40 (1997–1998), p. 290. Fr James Anderson was one priest who never refused to grant absolution to Fenians: 'They were men who fought and suffered for Ireland, they believed in the justice of their cause and in conscience I could never refuse them absolution', quoted in Catherine Mary O'Dwyer, 'James Augustine Anderson, OSA', *Seánchus Árd Mhacha*, 7 (1974), p. 219.

77 Ó Baoighill, *Nally*, pp. 79–81.

78 Daly also highlighted another criticism of Fr Gibbons that is useful in considering the position of Fr Cavanagh at Knock, where the chapel at the time of the apparition had no seating except for a few private pews as in pre-famine days. In Balla, Fr Gibbons not only retained similar pews reserved for the use of their 'owners', but he periodically auctioned off that ownership, thereby, according to Daly, reinforcing unchristian distinctions among his parishioners. This was another example of Gibbons' 'shameful greed for money' and lack of charity going hand-in-hand. In Knock, Fr Cavanagh chose to spend money on additions or devotional items (belfry, stained glass windows, and statues) as opposed to pews in the church. We have no evidence that he did anything about the pews, itself of interest since such private pews were controversial. If Fr Gibbons in Balla was at one extreme, Fr James Anderson in Ballyhaunis was near the other end of the spectrum. For St Mary's, Anderson bought pews that he declared open to all on a first-come, first-served basis. Previous 'owners' had no priority. They neither owned any pew nor had any preferential right to sit in the 'place' where 'their' erstwhile pews had been located. Anderson, Prior from 1874 to 1879, wrote a note warning his successors to be alert to possible attempts by the former pew-owners to claim some sort of privileged treatment and public recognition of their status: O'Dwyer, 'James Augustine Anderson, OSA', p. 241. If Fr Cavanagh did not evince the level of avarice that Fr Gibbons did in Balla, neither did he challenge the social inequality among his parishioners that was manifested and sustained by the pew system, as did Fr Anderson in Ballyhaunis.

79 In a letter to the editor, a Mayo priest referred to Daly's paper the *Connaught Telegraph* as 'that fearless uncompromising organ of faith and fatherland', CT, 14 July 1877.

80 That Delia's mother even thought of applying the cement is evidence of how steeped she was in the traditional taken-for-granted understanding of material as having miraculous curative powers. Yet in many ways Mrs Gordon was a very modern woman. Her husband was a political activist and so was she. She made the famous 'The Land for the People' banner displayed at the first land demonstration meeting in Irishtown and apparently accompanied her husband to the various land meetings, and was later prominent in the Ladies' Land League. Despite her significance, researchers have been unable to even learn her given or maiden name: Patrick Maume 'Rebel on the Run: T. J. Quinn and the IRB/Land League Diaspora in America', in Patrick Maume and Marguerite Quintelli-Neary, *19th-Century Irish and Irish-Americans on the Western Frontier* (Working Papers in Irish Studies, 00–1 Nova Southeastern University, 2000), p. 9, n. 12, cites a newspaper obituary to say her maiden name was either Prendergast or Heavey, while Ó Baoighill, *Nally*, p. 109, writes that she was the daughter of a Tuam bootmaker named Thomas Martin who was 'out' in 1867.

81 On Knock and Gordon, see Paul Bew, '"A Vision to the Dispossessed"? Popular Piety and Revolutionary Politics in the Irish Land War, 1879–82', in *Religion and Rebellion*, eds Judith Devlin and Ronan Fanning (Dublin: University College Dublin Press, 1996), pp. 137–51. Bew mischaracterised Gordon as a 'bitter anticlerical'.

82 Maume, 'Rebel on the Run', p. 1; Gerard Moran, *A Radical Priest in Mayo: The Rise and fall of an Irish Nationalist, 1825–1882* (Dublin: Four Courts, 1994), p. 147; Donald Jordan, Jr, *Land and Popular Politics in Ireland: County Mayo From the Plantation to the Land War* (Cambridge: Cambridge University Press, 1994), pp. 326-7.

83 CT, 31 May 1879. He continued such support in later years: White, *The Apparitions*, p. 59.

84 CT, 14 October 1875, 14 October 1876, and 4 August 1877.

85 CT, 13, 20, and 27 May 1876.

86 Maume, 'Rebel on the Run', pp. 2, 5.

87 *Daily News,* 2 March 1880.

88 Sexton, *Illustrated Record*, p. 11.

89 Maume, 'Rebel on the Run', p. 3, citing *Mayo News*, 16 June 1931, p. 7.

90 I am well aware that, as Kenneth Clarke wrote about the construction of Chartres Cathedral, 'like most miracles, this one can be explained in material terms which, in fact, do not explain it at all' (*Civilization*, p. 59). The question arises, 'explain for whom — insiders or outsiders?'

91 CT, 6 July 1878.

92 Sr Mary Frances Clare [M. F. Cusack] *Three Visits to Knock, with the Medical Certificates of Cures and Authentic Accounts of Different Apparitions* (New York: P. J. Kennedy, [1882] 1904), pp. 67–8.

93 CT, 4 May 1878. Churchfield House was but one of his homes, Cusack: *Three Visits*, p. 68.

94 £2, CT, 13 March 1880.

95 £1, CT, 6 July 1878.

96 Mary Francis Cusack, *The Nun of Kenmare: An Autobiography* (Boston: Ticknor, 1889), pp. 275–6, 291–3; M. F. Cusack, *The Story of My Life* (London: Hodder and Stoughton, 1891), p. 10.

97 Cutting from unidentified contemporary newspaper, copy sent to me by Fr John O'Connor.

98 CT, 2 September 1877.

99 CT, 2 September 1876.

100 CT, 31 August 31 1878.

101 CT, 2 September 1876.

102 Ruth Harris, *Lourdes: Body and Spirit in the Secular Age* (New York: Viking, 1999), pp. 210–1, 220, 402, n. 24.

103 White, *The Knock Apparitions* pp. 82–3.

104 Harris, *Lourdes,* p. 16. The Sacred Heart devotion was being promoted in Ireland long before this and the Irish bishops had formally dedicated the country to the Sacred

Heart in 1873: R. Burke-Savage, 'The Growth of Devotion to the Sacred Heart in Ireland', *Irish Ecclesiastical Record*, cx (1968), p. 185.
105 White, *The Knock Apparitions*, p. 236.
106 Sr Mary Francis Clare, *The Life of the Blessed Virgin Mary, Mother of God* (Dublin: Gill and Son, 1880), p. 723.
107 For an early photograph of the scene, see Fr John O'Connor, OSA, ed., *The Ballyhaunis Friary (in Black and White)* (Ballyhaunis: GREENSprint, 1996), p. 13, a detail of which is shown on page 237.
108 Their familiarity with statues is evidence that the seers were influenced by 'modern' religious material culture but they were not so familiar with them as to be able to comfortably and easily identify the figures represented.
109 Knock Museum employee James Campbell told me in 2003 that local people who were 'serious' about their religion or felt the need to do some powerful praying would do a novena or attend mass at the Ballyhaunis Abbey.
110 *The Connaught Telegraph* referred to the artist both as Mr Bennet and Barratt, of Edinburgh. The *Post Office Edinburgh and Leith Directory* for years between 1856 and 1921 identifies such a business. The first mention was in 1856, a 'glass stainer' by the name of Francis Barnet, 8 Kirkgate, Leith (house: 49 Charlotte Street, Leith). By 1867, the firm was known as Francis Barnett, 101 Constitution Street, and by 1887 it was Barnett and Son, stained glass artists, still at 101 Constitution Street; it was still there in 1921 when this Directory series ends.
111 Fr John O'Connor, OSA, Unpublished notes on St Mary's (1997). I thank Fr O'Connor for sending me a copy.
112 CT, 9 March 1878.
113 MacPhilpin *The Apparitions*, p. 37.
114 Sexton, *Illustrated Record*, p. 23; for slightly different wording see MacPhilpin, *The Apparitions*, p. 46.
115 O'C[onnor], *Visit*, p. 21.
116 I saw the window in 2003, after the chapel was closed following the departure of the last Augustinians. The window was so close above it that decorative wooden scroll-work along the back edge of the altar obscured the bottom few inches.
117 John F. Quinn, *Fr Mathew's Crusade: Temperance in Nineteenth-Century Ireland and Irish America* (Amherst: University of Massachusetts Press, 2002), p. 64; Paul A. Townend, *Fr Mathew, Temperance and Irish Identity* (Dublin: Irish Academic Press. 2002), p. 22–4. The shield is flanked by two figures depicting a husband and wife bearing flags carrying Mathew's message of Temperance. The man carries 'Prosperity' while the woman carries 'Domestic Comfort' while two children sit in front of the shield (at the foot of the altar which is also at the parents' feet). The medal is also pictured in Revd Patrick Rogers, *Fr Theobald Mathew, Apostle of Temperance* (Dublin: Browne and Nolan, 1943), p. 153, and in Townend, *Fr Mathew*, p. 23.
118 In theory every person who took the pledge was given a medal but in practice that did not happen. Estimates of the numbers who took the pledge reach three to five million. When Mathew ran into financial difficulties because of the cost of the medals he explained that he had sent 'hundreds of thousands' to every part of the country without being paid, so an estimate of over a million medals is not fanciful: Townend, *Fr Mathew*, pp. 1, 72; Quinn, *Fr Mathew's Crusade*, p. 117.
119 Townend, *Fr Mathew*, pp. 47, 131; Quinn, *Fr Mathew's Crusade*, p. 80; William Le Fanu, *Seventy Years of Irish Life* (London: Edward Arnold, 1893), p. 114.
120 'May' is the operative word here. The information we have is not only post-apparition but it comes from sources committed to promoting both the apparition and Fr Cavanagh's role in it. Mary Beirne's published evidence does not include this claim. The focus on the mass also contrasts with Cavanagh's well documented faith in the miracle working power of the cement, even above the canonical sacraments.
121 Of the group of visionaries at the church gable that night, only Mary McLoughlin, Bridget Trench, Judith Campbell and the 'serving boy' John Durkan were not kin to

the Beirnes, and they came either with Mary or Dominick: Marina Warner, 'What the Virgin of Knock Means to Women', *Magill* (September 1979), p. 36. The ability of three of these to act autonomously must be questioned. Durkan at age 24 was called a 'servant boy' by eleven to fourteen-year-old Pat Hill, Trench 'depended on the charity of neighbours', and McLoughlin was the priest's housekeeper.

122   There may or may not have been other original priest members but if there were, they had little to do with publicising the apparition. As noted earlier a Jesuit priest in the area early on reported there were four priest members of the original commission. Several pieces of circumstantial evidence point to the fourth being Fr Peter Gerathy, Parish Priest of Bekan. First, when MacEvilly wrote MacHale appointed the members he said they were 'canons', and even though he was generally known as 'Fr Peter', Gerathy was in fact a canon. Second, like the other two canons we know were members, Bourke and Waldron, Gerathy was conveniently close as parish priest in an adjoining parish. If their proximity was a reason for the selection of the first two then Gerathy would be a logical choice as the third member to join Fr Cavanagh. Thirdly, the Jesuit listed Fr Gerathy as a member of the Commission in his 26 June 1881 letter to the editor of *Ave Maria*. (See sources cited in Notes 13, 15 and 23 to chapter 9.) We also have reason to suspect why Fr Gerathy would not be likely to endorse the published claims of miracles. He was popularly believed to be able to cure both animals and humans and people resorted to him for cures from even beyond his own parish, but he discouraged credulity. One story told about a woman in his parish who had such faith in Fr Gerathy's power that when she was ill every day she asked her husband to get a bottle of medicine (holy water?) from the priest. Fr Gerathy, however, told the man to save himself the long walk and get water from a stream near home that would be as good a medicine. Without telling his wife, after that the man always filled his bottle at the stream and 'the wife swore that was the only medicine that seemed to relieve her.' Fr Gerathy would likely not be impressed with reports of the miracle working powers of the cement from the apparition gable. Michael Higgins, 'In Bekan Long Ago', in Fr Michael Comer and Nollaig Ó Muraíle, *Béacán/Bekan: Portrait of an East Mayo Parish* (Privately published by Comer, 1986), p. 93.

123   Fr Bourke had already been the target of disruptive challenges to his authority. While Daly berated him in the press, in private his crops and fields were damaged, and the Fenians had used the cover of a land meeting in Claremorris to convene a meeting of their own. Lay people on the platform adamantly defied his attempts to get the Claremorris meeting he 'chaired' to endorse resolutions he favoured.

124   Fr James Anderson's devotion to the Virgin is evident in several of his actions. He kept a scrapbook of newspaper cuttings that interested him, including several items of Marianism such as a poem on 'Mary Immaculate, Mater Admirabilis' and a report about Welsh Catholic Folklore on devotion to the Virgin. (CT, 28 May and 11 June 1938). An undated cutting in the scrapbook says that the Society of the Pious Union of Our Lady of Good Counsel was first introduced to Ireland by Anderson on his return from Rome in 1878. He later introduced this devotion to Drogheda. In Ballyhaunis, Fr Anderson installed a large stained glass window to Our Lady of Consolation. Even though he served in Ballyhaunis for only five years, Fr Anderson made a big impact. Not only did he renovate the monastery but attendance there and money collected increased dramatically when he was scheduled to say mass. When he revisited Ballyhaunis years later he was given a rapturous reception (scrapbook). (His original 'Scrapbook' has deteriorated to being of little use to researchers. The glue has come unstuck and most cuttings have disappeared. Some, perhaps most of the scrapbook, however, was serialised in 1938 by 'Antiquarian' in the pages of the *Connaught Telegraph*.)

125   Of course, this is why the official church looks sceptically at any claims of direct apparitions.

126   Sexton, *Illustrated Record*, p. 15.

127   *The Irish Times*, quoted in *The Nation*, 3 April 1880; O'C[onnor], *Visit*, pp. 14–5, 18; Donnelly summarises numerous newspaper accounts of the issue, 'Marian Shrine', pp. 75–7.

128 Gallogly, *Diocese of Kilmore*, pp. 348–9; Stiofán Ó Cadhla, *The Holy Well Tradition: The Pattern of St Declan, Ardmore, County Waterford, 1820-2000* (Dublin: Four Courts Press, 2004), pp. 24–5; Caesar Otway, *A Tour of Connaught, Comprising Sketches of Clonmacnoise, Joyce Country, and Achill* (Dublin, 1839), p. 75; S. C. Hall, and A. M. Hall, *Ireland: Its Scenery, Character, Etc*, Volume 1 (London: 1841), p. 284.

129 Donnelly, 'Marian Shrine', p. 97, n. 173; Fr Augustine, *Footprints of Fr Mathew, OFM Cap., Apostle of Temperance* (Dublin: Browne and Nolan, 1947), pp. 544–8; James Coombes, 'Fr John Power (1764–1831): The Man and the Legend', *Seánchas Chairbe*, 1 (1982), 8–13. There is evidence of much later devotion at the graves of dead priests in Mayo and elsewhere. Foxford born Fr Joseph Foy (1841–1918), ordained for Killala in 1871, was suspended by his bishop in 1890 for drunkenness and a fight with a poteen maker. Widely believed to have miracle-working powers, during the rest of his life he was sought out by pilgrims seeking favours and his grave in the cathedral grounds in Ballina became a site of devotion. In 2003, a reporter noted bouquets, medals and other tokens on the grave, including such recent items as a video sleeve: 'Fr Foy – One of the Roving Kind', *Western People*, 15 October 2003. Gallogly, *Kilmore*, p. 349, reported devotion 'still current' [in 1999] at a long dead priest's grave.

130 *Daily News*, 28 February 1880; White, *The Knock Apparitions*, p. 259.

131 O'C[onnor], *Visit*, p. 12.

132 *Daily News*, 28 February 1880.

133 *Weekly News*, 28 August 1880; Tom Neary, *I Saw Our Lady* (Published by the Custodians of Knock Shrine, 1977), p. 68.

134 Andrew Dunlop, *Fifty Years of Irish Journalism* (Dublin: Hanna and Neale, 1911), p. 241.

135 *The Irish Times*, 12 October 1880; Neary, *I Saw*, p. 72.

136 Neary, *I Saw*, p. 67; *The Nation*, 26 June 1880.

137 *Weekly News*, 28 August 1880; Neary, *I Saw*, p. 67; *Daily News*.

138 N.K. B. 4, in Padraig Ó Tuairisc, *Árd-Dheoise Thuama agus Cartlann Choláiste Na nGael sa Roimh san 19ú Aois Déag* (MA Thesis in History, University College, Galway, 2000), p. 562. Fr Cavanagh had told a journalist about two Abbeyfeale men who had miraculous cures of leg ailments, but gave their names as O'Connor and Culhane: *Daily News*, 1 March, 1880.

139 Sexton, *Illustrated Record*, p. 14; Blackbourn, *Marpingen*, p. 148 and chapter 6.

140 Michael Carroll, *Irish Pilgrimage: Holy Wells and Popular Catholic Devotion* (Baltimore: Johns Hopkins University Press, 1999); White, *The Knock Apparitions*, chapter 4.

141 Hoppen, *Elections*, p. 216.

142 Patricia Lysaght, 'Attitudes to the Rosary and its Performance in Donegal in the Nineteenth and Twentieth Centuries', *Béaloideas*, 66 (1998), p. 54.

143 Sister Mary Francis Clare, *The Life of the Blessed Virgin Mary, Mother of God* (Dublin: Gill and Son, 1880), p. 727.

144 Patrick Logan, *The Holy Wells of Ireland* (Gerrard's Cross: Colin Smythe, 1980), p. 117.

145 Mary Douglas, 'Introduction to the Second Edition', in her *Purity and Danger* (New York: Routledge, 2002), p. xii-xiii; Hynes, 'The Great Hunger and Irish Catholicism', *Societas*, 8 (1978), pp. 150–1.

146 Campbell noted that this corroboration would be provided by some woman. If this was the common pattern, then the whole explanatory framework can be understood as one weapon of the weak, here women vis-à-vis men, who provide each other defences against possible charges of child murder. See page 18 above.

147 Michael Higgins, 'In Bekan Long Ago', in *Béacán/Bekan: Portrait of an East Mayo Parish*, eds Fr Michael Comer and Nollaig Ó Muraíle (Privately published, 1986), p. 101.

148 Warner, 'What the Virgin of Knock Means', p. 36-7.

149 *The Knock Apparitions*, p. 94.

150 Angela Bourke, 'More in Anger than in Sorrow: Irish Women's Lament Poetry', in *Feminist Messages: Coding in Women's Folk Culture*, ed. Joan N. Radner (Urbana: University of Illinois Press, 1993), p. 180, n. 38; Seán Ó Coileáin, 'The Irish Lament: An Oral Genre', *Studia Hibernica*, 24 (1984–1988), pp. 97–117.

151 Helen Litton, 'The Famine in Schools', in *Irish Hunger: Personal Reflections on the Legacy of the Famine,* ed. Tom Hayden (Dublin: Wolfhound Press, 1997), p. 61; Angela Bourke, *The Burning of Bridget Cleary: A True Story* (New York: Viking, 1999), p. 112.

152 Cavanagh sent a telegram to Fr Christopher Carton, St Stanislaus' College, Tullamore. Since the telegram is not available we have to infer his question from Fr Carton's letter in reply. Carton to Cavanagh, 13 April 1880, ACSJP, Series 1A, 245. The famous twentieth-century Jesuit writer on Marian apparitions, Herbert Thurston, was especially sceptical of the evidence for Knock cures as is clear from material in the 'Knock' folder among his papers in the archives of the British Province of the Society of Jesus, London.

153 *Daily News,* 1 March 1880; Dunlop, *Fifty Years,* p. 241.

154 Maria Wall, Carrig, Birr, to Venerable Archdeacon Kavanagh (sic), ACSJP, Series 1A 245.

155 Donnelly, 'The Marian Shrine'; White, *The Knock Apparitions.*

156 There is a huge literature on Medjugorje. For good anthropological accounts see Mart Bax, *Medjugorje: Religion, Politics, and Violence in Rural Bosnia* (Amsterdam: VU Uitgeverij, 1995) and Elizabeth Claverie, *Les guerres de la Vierge: Une anthropologie des apparitions* (Paris: Gallimard, 2003). Paolo Apolito, *The Internet and the Madonna: Religious Visionary Experiences on the Web,* trans. by Antony Shugaar (Chicago: University of Chicago Press, 2005), pp. 36–48, explores the wider context for the appeal and the impact of this set of apparitions.

157 James S. Donnelly, Jr, 'The Revival of Knock Shrine', in *History of the Public Sphere: Essays in Honour of John A. Murphy,* eds Tom Dunne and Laurence Geary (Cork: Cork University Press, 2005), pp. 186–200, 259–63.

158 *Daily News,* 20 January 1880.

159 Harris, *Lourdes,* pp. 210–45.

160 Lawrence Taylor, '"Peter's Pence": Official Catholic Discourse and Irish Nationalism in the Nineteenth- Century', *History of European Ideas* 16 (1993), pp. 103–107.

161 Christian, *Moving Crucifixes,* p. 14.

11 CONCLUSION

1 Mary Douglas, *Purity and Danger: An Analysis of the Concepts of Pollution and Taboo* (New York: Praeger, 1966), p. 58.

2 John P. Jordan, 'Notes on the Parish of Aghamore', retrieved 22 March 2005 from www.aghamoregaa.com/society/historical.htm.

3 Gearóid Ó Crualaoich, *The Book of the Cailleach: Stories of the Wise-Woman Healer* (Cork: Cork University Press, 2003), p. 22.

4 Catherine Rynne, *Knock 1879–1979* (Dublin: Veritas, 1979), p. 17.

5 Michael Allen, *Ritual, Power and Gender: Explorations in the Ethnography of Vanuatu, Nepal and Ireland* (New Delhi: Manohar, 2000), pp. 346–67.

6 Niall Ó Ciosáin, 'Gaelic Culture and Language Shift', in *Nineteenth-century Ireland: A Guide to Recent Research,* eds Laurence Geary and Margaret Kelleher (Dublin: University College Dublin Press, 2005), p. 151; Sheridan Gilley, 'Catholicism in Ireland', in *The Decline of Christendom in Western Europe, 1750–2000,* eds Hugh McLeod and Werber Ustorf (Cambridge: Cambridge University Press, 2003), p. 106.

7 My thanks are due to Grace Mulqueen, Curator of Knock Museum, for sending me copies of the School Inspectors' Reports.

8 Of course, the Virgin elsewhere was competent to operate in linguistically difficult terrain. In the Alpine village of La Salette in 1840s' France she spoke alternately in the local patois and standard French even though neither of the two child seers knew more than a word or two of the latter: Richard Burton, *Holy Tears, Holy Blood: Women, Catholicism, and the Culture of Suffering in France, 1840–1970* (Ithaca: Cornell University Press, 2004), pp. 1–19. In Lourdes, only Bernadette Soubirous and nobody else present saw or heard her speak, and she used the local patois, a usage significant in French state and Church politics. Elsewhere where the witnesses heard

no words, as in Pontmain in 1871, the 'silent' Virgin still conveyed her message, spelling out her message on scrolls visible in the sky, appropriately for eight-year-olds just learning to read and write in school: Cheryl Porte, *Pontmain, Prophecy and Protest: A Cultural-Historical Study of a Nineteenth-Century Vision* (New York: Peter Lang, 2005), p. 21.

9 One relief agency estimated that 2,500 of the approximately 3,200 people in the parish of Knock were receiving emergency relief in early 1880 and characterised the position of the parish as 'terrible destitution; people half-starved.' *Proceedings of the Mansion House Committee for Relief of Distress in Ireland During the Months of January and February* (Dublin: Mansion House, March 1880), p. 34.

10 T. O'C[onnor], *A Visit to Knock* (Limerick: T. O'Connor, 1880), p. 17.

11 CT, 21 February 1880.

12 William Butler Yeats, *The Wind Among the Reeds* (London: Elkin Matthews, 1899), pp. 95–6.

13 Fr Dan Gallogly, *Sliabh an Iarainn Slopes: History of the Town and Parish of Ballinamore, County Leitrim* (No publisher given, 1991), pp. 78, 145–6.

14 Catherine Rynne, *Knock 1879–1979* (Dublin: Veritas, 1979), p. 29.

15 ibid., pp. 30–1.

16 ibid., p. 179;*Weekly News*, 21 February 1880; Sexton, *Illustrated Record*; O'C[onnor], *Visit*, p. 18.

17 Rynne, *Knock,* p. 45.

18 See Note 134 to Chapter 9. Proinsias Ó Maolmhuaidh, *Uilleog de Burca* (Dublin: Foilseacháin Naisiúnta Teoranta, 1981), pp. 185–6, n.58.

19 The Beirne family itself seemed caught between the two modes of farm-family succession. In the stem family system the cultural blueprint called for one son, the chosen heir, to be married to a daughter of some other family. In the case of the Beirnes, however, while one son inherited the family land and got married (as was the new expectation and practice) shortly after the apparition, at least two daughters were married, one of them, Eliza, long enough to have an eight-year-old daughter, the apparition witness Catherine Murray. Was Eliza's marriage more along the lines of the older practice? Eliza's sister Mary was to marry a few years after the apparition.

20 Joseph Lee, *The Modernisation of Irish Society 1848–1918* (Dublin: Gill and MacMillan, 1973), p. 66.

21 David Fitzpatrick, 'Ireland since 1870', in *The Oxford Illustrated History of Ireland,* ed. Roy F. Foster (Oxford: Oxford University Press, 1989), p. 213.

22 Patrick Maume 'Rebel on the Run: T. J. Quinn and the IRB/Land League Diaspora in America', in Patrick Maume and Marguerite Quintelli-Neary, *19th-Century Irish and Irish-Americans on the Western Frontier* (Working Papers in Irish Studies, 00–1 Nova Southeastern University, 2000).

23 Terence McGrath, *Pictures From Ireland,* 6th edition (London: Kegan Paul and Trench, 1888), p. 123.

24 John MacPhilpin, *The Apparitions and Miracles at Knock. Also, The Official Depositions of the Eye-Witnesses* (Dublin: Gill and Son, 1880), p. 3.

25 John J. White, *The Knock Apparitions and Pilgrimage: Popular Piety and the Irish Land War* (Unpublished PhD Dissertation in History, Boston College, 1999), p. 270.

26 The P.J. Kenedy edition was in 1880 while the Kelly edition is undated but appears to be 1880 also: Sr Mary Frances Clare, [M. F. Cusack] *Three Visits to Knock, with the Medical Certificates of Cures and Authentic Accounts of Different Apparitions* (New York: P. J. Kennedy, [1882] 1904), pp. 1–16.

27 Letter in *Ave Marie*, xvii, 1 (1 January 1881).

28 Lynch to Bishop Walsh of London, Ontario, 13 June 1882, ARCAT, L AGO3.11; Fr Cavanagh to Archbishop Lynch, 9 June 1884, ARCAT, L AGO3. 02. For Lynch's views on Lough Derg see two letters he wrote from there, one to his Vicar General on 13 August 1879 which was published in the *Irish Canadian*, 10 September 1879, and another dated 14 August 1879 published in the *Irish Canadian*, 17 September 1879.

29 John Higgins to Fr Daniel Hudson, CSC, 3 December 1884, UNDA X-2-n-A.L.S.
30 Patrick Hayes, 'Massachusetts Miracles: Controlling Cures in Catholic Boston, 1929–1930', in *Saints and Their Cults in the Atlantic World*, ed. Margaret Cormack (Columbia: University of South Carolina Press, 2007), pp. 111–27.
31 Emmet Larkin, 'The Devotional Revolution in Ireland, 1850–1875', *American Historical Review*, 77 (1972), pp. 625–52; the illustration was reproduced on the cover of the whole journal issue.
32 T. K. Hoppen, *Ireland Since 1800: Conflict and Conformity* (London: Longman, 1989), p. 152.
33 James S. Donnelly, Jr, 'The Marian Shrine at Knock: The First Decade', *Eire/Ireland*, 28, 2 (1993), pp. 54–99.
34 Patrick Nold, *The Knock Phenomenon: Popular Piety and Politics in the 'Modern' Ireland* (Undergraduate Thesis, University of Michigan, 1993), p. 38.
35 White, *The Knock Apparitions*, pp. 8 (quotation), 10, 17.
36 Sean Connolly, 'The Moving Statue and the Turtle Dove: Approaches to the History of Irish Religion', *Irish Economic and Social History*, XXI (2004), p. 15.
37 It is difficult to make precise arguments using imprecise terms. Accepting Larkin's framework, White, for example, is led to categorise the use of Knock mortar as part of the new devotionalism, and even though he argued that the bishop figure in the apparition was John MacHale, he also argued that the saints who appeared in Knock were not specifically Irish or local but ones 'whose appeal was universal within Christendom'. *Knock Apparitions*, p. 9. MacHale's fame did not extend that far!
    That early pilgrims came by train, that the apparition was reported in the newspapers, that businessmen sold photographs and prints of the scene — these are evidence of the use of modern technologies but in themselves say nothing about how 'modern' were the religious understandings of those involved.
    Donnelly points out that even the successful revival of pilgrimage and devotion in the 1930s can well be read as evidence of the failure rather than the success of the devotional revolution, since it indicated that lay people were not satisfied with the various religious observances at the parish level, which after all was supposedly the intent of Trent. 'Insofar as the "devotional revolution" put the parish unit, the priest as pastor, and the sacraments at the centre of religious life' the extra-sacramental and extra-parochial flowering of Marianism indicated that 'the Tridentine system was not answering (at least not fully) the spiritual needs of large numbers of Irish Catholics,' James S. Donnelly, Jr, 'The Peak of Marianism in Ireland, 1930–60', in *Piety and Power in Ireland 1760–1960: Essays in Honour of Emmet Larkin*, eds Stewart J. Brown and David W. Miller (Note Dame: Notre Dame University Press, 2000), pp. 282–3.
38 Emmet Larkin, *The Roman Catholic Church and The Creation of the Modern Irish State, 1878–1886* (Philadelphia: American Philosophical Society, 1975), p. 24.
39 T. W. Moody, *Davitt and Irish Revolution 1846–82* (Oxford: Clarendon Press, 1982), p. 338.
40 Mary Heimann, *Catholic Devotion in Victorian England* (Oxford: Clarendon Press, 1995) has made the same point with extensive documentation in the case of England.
41 Lee, *Modernisation*, p. 69.
42 Tom Inglis, *Moral Monopoly: The Catholic Church in Modern Irish Society* (Dublin: Gill and MacMillan 1987), and a revised 2nd edition subtitled *The Rise and Fall of the Catholic Church in Modern Ireland* (Dublin: University College Dublin Press, 1998).
43 Cara Delay, 'The Devotional Revolution on the Local Level: Parish Life in Post-Famine Ireland', *US Catholic Historian*, 22 (Summer 2004), pp. 41–60, and 'Confidantes or Competitors? Women, Priests, and Conflict in Post-Famine Ireland', *Eire/Ireland*, 40, 1/2 (Spring-Summer 2005), pp. 106–25.
44 Tomás de Bhaldraithe, *The Diary of an Irish Countryman 1827–1835: A Translation of Cín Lae Amhlaoibh* (Cork: Mercier Press, 1979), p. 120; Joseph Robins, *The Miasma: Epidemic and Panic in Nineteenth-Century Ireland* (Dublin: Institute for Public Administration, 1995), p. 105.

45 See note 66 to chapter 6.

46 www.irishplayography.com/search/play.asp?play_id=2092 accessed 12 December 2007; *Western People,* 20 September 2006.

47 Richard Werbner, *Ritual Passage, Sacred Journey: The Process and Organization of Religious Movement* (Washington, DC: Smithsonian, 1989), pp. 301–2.

48 William Christian, *Moving Crucifixes in Modern Spain* (Princeton: Princeton University Press, 1992), p. 8.

49 Harris, *Lourdes,* p. 90.

50 White, *The Knock Apparitions,* pp. 270–1.

51 Penny Edgell Becker, '"Rational Amusement and Sound Instruction": Constructing the True Catholic Woman in the *Ave Maria*, 1865–1889', *Religion and American Culture*, 8, 1 (Winter 1998), p. 59.

52 Here I am adapting Guy Beiner's formulation on the relationship between local memories and 'national' history that he documented in the case of 1798, *Remembering the Year of the French: Irish Folk History and Social Memory* (Madison: University of Wisconsin Press, 2007), p. 169.

53 Gerard Moran, 'James Daly and the Rise and Fall of the Land League in the West of Ireland, 1879–1882', *Irish Historical Studies,* xxix (1994), pp. 186–207.

54 Recent studies include Fergus Campbell, *Land and Revolution: Nationalist Politics in the West of Ireland* (New York: Oxford University Press, 2005); Michael Wheatly, *Nationalism and the Irish Party: Provincial Ireland, 1910–1916* (Oxford: Oxford University Press, 2006); Marie Coleman, *County Longford and the Irish Revolution, 1910–1923* (Dublin: Irish Academic Press, 2003); and Michael Farry, *The Aftermath of Revolution: Sligo 1921–23* (Dublin: University College Dublin Press, 2000).

55 Christian, *Moving Crucifixes*, p. 14.

56 David Blackbourn, *Marpingen: Apparitions of the Virgin Mary in Bismarckian Germany* (Oxford: Clarendon Press, 1993).

57 One critic of a later proposal to have Tuam town's official advertising in Irish and English pointed out that MacPhilpin was incapable of translating any submitted material to Gaelic. Marie-Louise Legg, *Newspapers and Nationalism: The Irish Provincial Press 1850–1892* (Dublin: Four Courts, 1999), p. 155.

58 John Gaventa, *Power and Powerlessness: Quiescence and Rebellion in an Appalachian Valley* (Urbana: University of Illinois Press, 1980), p. 10ff; Steven Lukes, *Power: A Radical View* (London: MacMillan, 1974).

Bibliography

Archives

Archives of the Congregation of the Sisters of St Joseph of Peace, Washington, DC

Pre-Foundation Papers
(Original materials that I consulted here directly related to Knock have since been given to the Knock Museum where they are being prepared for on-line access. I understand that copies have been retained. The entire archive has been relocated to the offices of the St Joseph Province of the Order in Eaglewood Cliffs, New Jersey.)

University College, Dublin

National Folklore Collection
(Cited as NFC followed by the volume number and page number; the 1936–7 Schools Folklore Project is cited as NFCS followed by the volume and page numbers.)

Archives of the Archdiocese of Tuam

Records of the Second Commission of Inquiry on Knock

Irish Augustinian Archives, Dublin

Anderson Scrapbooks
Ballyhaunis Housebook

Notre Dame University Archives

Hudson Papers

Oxfordshire County Record Office

Dillon Papers, DIL. XII/B/7

Dublin City Library

P.W. Joyce Ballad Collection

Irish College, Rome, Archives

Kelly Papers
Kirby Papers

(I did not consult these archives but I have used letters in them as transcribed in Padraig Ó Tuairisc, *Ábhar a Bhaineann le Árd-Dheoise Thuama sa 19ú Aois i gCartlann Choláiste Na nGael sa Roimh, curtha in eagar, Maille le Réamhra agus Notaí* (MA Thesis, University College, Galway, 1982), giving the original archive reference for the benefit of other researchers as well as the Ó Tuairisc page number.)

Society of Jesus, British Province Archives, London.
'Knock' folder in the *Thurston Papers*

Catholic Archdiocese of Toronto Archives
Archbishop Lynch Papers

Newspapers cited in short title form
CT *Connaught Telegraph*
N *The Nation*

Unpublished Sources

Daniel Campbell, Untitled Memoir, catalogued as *Typescript copy of a manuscript history of the parish of Knock, Co. Mayo; transcribed by Revd John Baptist Byrne 1900?* (sic), Copies in the National Library of Ireland, Dublin, Manuscripts Collections, ms 31,718, and in Knock Museum.
Fr John O'Connor, OSA, Personal communication, enclosing his unpublished 1997 notes on St Mary's Augustinian Abbey, Ballyhaunis

Theses
Almquist, Eric, *Mayo and Beyond: Land, Domestic Industry and Rural Transformation in the West of Ireland* (Boston University, PhD thesis, 1977)
Boltúin, Antoine, *MacHeil agus an Ghaeilge: A Shaothar agus a Dhearcadh* (Ph.D. Thesis, Department of Modern Irish, University College Galway, 1992)
Brennan, P. A., *Aspects of the Fenian Movement in Kilkenny, 1858–1870* (MA Thesis, St Patrick's College, Maynooth, 1979)
Nold, Patrick, *The Knock Phenomenon: Popular Piety and Politics in the 'Modern' Ireland* (Undergraduate Thesis, University of Michigan, 1993)
Ó Tuairisc, Pádraig, *Ábhar a Bhaineann le Árd-Dheoise Thuama sa 19ú Aois i gCartlann Choláiste Na nGael sa Roimh, Curtha in Eagar, Maille le Réamhra agus Notaí* (M.A. Thesis in History, University College, Galway, 1982)
Solan, John, *Religion and Society in the Ecclesiastical Province of Tuam before the Famine* (MA thesis, University College, Galway, 1989)

Internet Sources

Clive Gillis, 'Rome Harnesses Folk Superstition to Revolutionize the Religion of Ireland', Posted 12 April 2005 on www.ianpaisley.org/article, accessed 12 November 2005
John P. Jordan, 'Notes on the Parish of Aghamore', Retrieved from http://www.aghamoregaa.com/society/historical.htm, accessed 22 March 2005

Stephen Josten, 'Ballinsmale Carmelite Abbey, 1288-1870' (1985), accessed 28 February 2005 at http://carmelites.ie/Ireland/ballinsmale.htm
www.from-ireland.net/diocs/archtuam.html accessed, 13 February 2003

Published Works

'A Loss to Catholicity: The Late Archdeacon B. A. Cavanagh, P.P., V.F., Knock, Ballyhaunis, Co. Mayo', *The Lamp*, L1V, No. 315 (1898?), 17–20
A New Song on the Wonderful Apparitions, of the Blessed Virgin, St Joseph, and St John, in Knock Chapel County Mayo (Dublin: Nugent and Co., no date), available in the P. W. Joyce Collection, Book 11, Dublin City Library
Acheson, Alan, *A History of the Church of Ireland, 1691–1996* (Dublin: Columba Press, 1997)
Allen, Michael, *Ritual, Power and Gender: Explorations in the Ethnography of Vanuatu, Nepal and Ireland* (New Delhi: Manohar, 2000)
Anderson, James, 'Rundale, Rural Economy and Agrarian Revolution: Tirhugh 1715–1855', in *Donegal History and Society: Interdisciplinary Essays On the History of an Irish County*, eds William Nolan, Liam Ronayne and Mairead Dunleavy (Dublin: Geography Publications, 1995), pp. 447–69
Andrews, Hilary, *The Lion of the West: A Biography of John MacHale* (Dublin: Veritas, 2001)
'Antiquarian', 'Fr Anderson's Scrap-Books: Famous Augustinian Patriot', Series of 14 articles incorporating reprints in *Connaught Telegraph*, 23 April 1938 and weekly thereafter except 18 June until 30 July 1938.
Apolito, Paolo, *Apparitions of the Madonna at Oliveto Citra: Local Visions and Cosmic Drama*, trans. by William Christian (University Park: Pennsylvania State University Press, 1998)
Apolito, Paolo, *The Internet and the Madonna: Religious Visionary Experiences on the Web*, trans. by Antony Shugaar (Chicago: University of Chicago Press, 2005)
Arensberg, Conrad and Solan T. Kimball, *Family and Community in Ireland*, 3rd edition with a new introduction by Anne Byrne, Ricca Edmondson and Tony Varley (Ennis: CLASP, 2001)
Armstrong, Karen, *A History of God: The 4000-Year Quest of Judaism, Christianity and Islam* (New York: Gramercy, 1993)
Augustine, Fr, *Footprints of Fr Mathew, O.F.M. Cap., Apostle of Temperance* (Dublin: Browne and Nolan, 1947)
Austin, J. L. *How To Do Things With Words* (Cambridge: Harvard University Press, 1962)
Bane, Liam, *The Bishop in Politics: The Life and Career of John MacEvilly* (Westport: Westport Historical Society, 1993)
Barr, David, 'George Henry Moore and His Tenants, 1840–1870', *Cathair na Mart: Journal of the Westport Historical Society*, 8 (1988), pp. 66–79
Bax, Mart, *Medjugorje: Religion, Politics, and Violence in Rural Bosnia* (Amsterdam: VU Uitgeverij, 1995)
Becker, Bernard H., *Disturbed Ireland: Being Letters Written During the Winter of 1880–81* (London: MacMillan, 1881)
Becker, Penny Edgell, '"Rational Amusement and Sound Instruction": Constructing the True Catholic Woman in the Ave Maria, 1865–1889', *Religion and American Culture*, 8, 1 (Winter 1998), pp. 55–90

Beiner, Guy, *Remembering the Year of the French: Irish Folk History and Social Memory* (Madison: University of Wisconsin Press, 2007)

Bell, Catherine, *Ritual: Perspectives and Dimensions* (New York: Oxford University Press, 1997)

Berman, David, 'The Knock Apparition: Some New Evidence', *The New Humanist*, 102, 4 (December 1987), pp. 8–10

Berman, David, 'Papal Visit Resurrects Ireland's Knock Legend', *The Freethinker*, 99 (1979), pp. 145–147, 160

Bernstein, Basil, *Class, Codes and Control*, vol 1 (London: Paladin, 1971)

Berry, James, *Tales from the West of Ireland* (Dublin: The Dolmen Press, 1966)

Bew, Paul, *Land and the National Question in Ireland, 1858–82* (Dublin: Gill and MacMillan, 1978)

Bew, Paul, 'A Vision to the Dispossessed? Popular Piety and Revolutionary Politics in the Irish Land War, 1879–82', in *Religion and Rebellion*, eds Judith Devlin and Ronan Fanning (Dublin: University College Dublin Press, 1996), pp. 137–51

Blackbourn, David, *Marpingen: Apparitions of the Virgin Mary in Bismarckian Germany* (Oxford: Clarendon Press, 1993)

Bourdieu, Pierre *Outline of a Theory of Practice* (New York: Cambridge University Press, 1977)

Bourke, Angela, 'The Virtual Reality of Irish Fairy Legend', *Eire/Ireland*, 31 (1996), pp. 1–25

Bourke, Angela, 'The Irish Traditional Lament and the Grieving Process', *Women's Studies International Forum*, 11 (1988), pp. 287–290

Bourke, Angela, 'More in Anger than in Sorrow: Irish Women's Lament Poetry', in *Feminist Messages: Coding in Women's Folk Culture*, ed. Joan N. Radner (Urbana: University of Illinois Press, 1993), pp. 160–82

Bourke, Angela, 'Irish Stories of Weather, Time and Gender: Saint Brigid', in *Reclaiming Gender: Transgressive Identities in Modern Ireland*, ed. by Marilyn Cohen and Nancy Curtin (New York: 1999), pp. 12–31

Bourke, Angela, The *Burning of Bridget Cleary: A True Story* (New York: Viking, 1999)

Bourke, Angela, 'Legless in London: Padraic Ó Conaire and Eamon A Burc', *Eire/Ireland*, 38 (Fall/Winter 2003), pp. 54–67

Bourke, Canon Ulick J., *Life and Times of the Most Rev. John MacHale, Archbishop of Tuam and Metropolitan* (Dublin: Gill and Son, 1882)

Bourke, Ulick, *A Plea for the Evicted Tenants of Mayo* (Dublin: Brown and Nolan), 1883)

Bowen, Desmond, *Souperism: Myth or Reality?: A Study in Souperism* (Cork: Mercier, 1970)

Bowen, Desmond, *The Protestant Crusade in Ireland, 1800–1870: A Study of Protestant-Catholic Relations Between the Act of Union and Disestablishment* (Montreal: McGill-Queen's University Press, 1978)

Bowen, Desmond, *Paul Cullen and the Shaping of Modern Irish Catholicism* (Dublin: Gill and MacMillan, 1983)

Boyle, J. W., 'A Marginal Figure: The Irish Rural Labourer', in *Irish Peasants: Violence and Political Unrest, 1790–1914* eds Samuel Clark and James S. Donnelly (Madison: University of Wisconsin Press, 1983), pp. 311–38

British Parliamentary Papers, *Mayo Election. Minutes of Evidence Taken Before the Select Committee on the Mayo County Election Petition; with the Proceedings of the Committee, and an Index* (House of Commons, 182, Session 2, 15 July 1857)

Brown, Malcolm, *George Moore: A Reconsideration* (Seattle: University of Washington Press, 1995)

Brown, Stewart J., Book Review (of Whelan 2005) *American Historical Review*, 112, 1 (2007),

Brown, Terence, Ireland: *A Social and Cultural History, from 1922 to the Present* (Ithaca, Cornell University Press 1985)

Burke, Oliver J., *The History of the Catholic Archbishops of Tuam, from The Foundation of the See to the Death of the Most Rev. John MacHale D.D. A. D. 1881* (Dublin: Hodges, Figgis and Co, 1882)

Burke-Savage, Roland, 'The Growth of Devotion to the Sacred Heart in Ireland', *Irish Ecclesiastical Record*, cx (1968), pp. 185–208

Burton, Richard, *Holy Tears, Holy Blood: Women, Catholicism, and the Culture of Suffering in France, 1840–1970* (Ithaca: Cornell University Press, 2004)

Buttimer, Neil, 'Pláig Fhollasach, Pláig Choimhtheach: "Obvious Plague, Strange Plague"', *Journal of the Cork Historical and Archaeological Society* 102 (1997), pp. 41–68

Cadhain, See Ua Cadhain

Caddell, Fr C., 'From the Grotto of Lourdes', *Irish Monthly*, 5 (July 1877), pp. 470–2

Campbell, Fergus, *Land and Revolution: Nationalist Politics in the West of Ireland* (New York: Oxford University Press, 2005)

Carbery, Mary, *Mary Carbery's West Cork Journal 1898–1901, or 'From the Back of Beyond'*, ed. Jeremy Sandford (Dublin: Lilliput Press, 1998)

Carey, F. P., *Knock and its Shrine* (Dublin: Office of the 'Irish Messenger', 1946)

Carleton, William, *The Works of William Carleton*, 2 Volumes (Freeport, New York: Books for Libraries Press, 1970 reprint of 1881 edition)

Carlyle, Thomas, *Reminiscences of My Irish Journey in 1849* (London: Sampson Low, Marston, Searle and Rivington, 1882)

Carroll, Michael P., *The Cult of the Virgin Mary: Psychological Origins* (Princeton: Princeton University Press, 1986)

Carroll, Michael P., *Irish Pilgrimage: Holy Wells and Popular Catholic Devotion* (Baltimore: Johns Hopkins University Press, 1999)

Cashman, D. B., *The Life of Michael Davitt, with a History of the Rise and Development of the Irish National Land League* (Boston: Murphy and McCarthy, 1881)

Cawley, Mary, 'Aspects of Continuity and Change in Nineteenth-Century Rural Settlement Patterns: Findings from County Roscommon', *Studia Hibernica*, 22–23 (1982/1983), pp. 106–27

Christian, William, Jr, *Person and God in a Spanish Valley* (New York: Seminar Press, 1972)

Christian, William, Jr, 'Tapping and Defining New Power: The First Month of the Visions at Ezquioga, July 1931', *American Ethnologist*, 14 (1987), pp. 140–166

Christian, William, *Moving Crucifixes in Modern Spain* (Princeton: Princeton University Press, 1992)

Christian, William, *Visionaries: The Spanish Republic and the Reign of Christ* (Berkeley: University of California Press, 1996)

Clare, Sr Mary Francis, *The Life of the Blessed Virgin Mary, Mother of God* (Dublin: Gill and Son, 1880)

Clare, Sr Mary Francis, *Three Visits to Knock, With the Medical Certificates of Cures and Authentic Accounts of Different Apparitions* (New York: P. J. Kenedy, 1904 [1882])

Claregalway Parish History 750 Years (Ireland: Claregalway Historical and Cultural Society, 1999)

Clark, Kenneth, *Civilisation: A Personal View* (New York: Harper and Row, 1969)

Clark, Samuel, *Social Origins of the Irish Land War* (Princeton: Princeton University Press, 1979)

Claverie, Elizabeth, *Les guerres de la Vierge: Une anthropologie des apparitions* (Paris: Gallimard, 2003)

Coleman, Marie, *County Longford and the Irish Revolution, 1910–1923* (Dublin: Irish Academic Press, 2003)

Comaroff, John and Jean Comaroff, *Ethnography and The Historical Imagination* (Boulder: Westview, 1992)

Comer, Fr Michael and Nollaig Ó Muraíle, eds, *Béacán/Bekan: Portrait of an East Mayo Parish* (Privately published by Comer, 1986)

Comer, Fr Michael, 'Schools in Bekan Parish', in *Béacán/Bekan: Portrait of an East Mayo Parish*, ed. by Fr Michael Comer and Nollaig Ó Muraíle (Privately published by Comer, 1986), pp. 86–7

Comerford, R. V., *The Fenians in Context* (Dublin: Wolfhound Press, 1985)

Concannon, Mrs Thomas, *The Queen of Ireland: An Historical Account of Ireland's Devotion to the Blessed Virgin* (Dublin: Gill and Son, 1938)

Concannon, Helena, 'Canon Ulick J. Bourke (1829–1887)', *Irish Ecclesiastical Record* (May 1950), pp. 405–17

Connell, K. H., *Irish Peasant Society: Four Historical Essays* (Oxford, Clarendon Press, 1968)

Connell, Paul, *The Diocese of Meath Under Bishop John Cantwell 1830–1866* (Dublin: Four Courts Press, 2004)

Connolly, Sean, 'The "Blessed Turf": Cholera and Popular Panic in Ireland, June 1832', *Irish Historical Studies*, xxiii, no. 91 (1983), pp. 214–32

Connolly, Sean, *Priests and People in Pre-Famine Ireland* (Dublin: Gill and MacMillan, 1982; second edition, Dublin: Four Courts, 2001)

Connolly, Sean, 'The Moving Statue and the Turtle Dove: Approaches to the History of Irish Religion', *Irish Economic and Social History*, XXI (2004), pp. 1–22

Coombes, James, 'Fr John Power (1764–1831): The Man and the Legend', *Seánchas Chairbre*, 1 (1982), pp. 8–13

Corkery, Marie, 'Ireland and the Franco-Prussian War', *Études Irlandaises*, 7 (1982), pp. 127–44

Corish, Patrick J., 'Irish College, Rome: Kirby Papers', *Archivium Hibernicum*, 30 (1972), pp. 29–116

Corish, Patrick, *The Irish Catholic Experience: A Historical Survey* (Dublin: Gill and MacMillan, 1985)

Correll, Timothy C., 'Believers, Skeptics, and Charlatans: Evidential Rhetoric, the Fairies, and Faith Healers in Irish Oral Narrative and Belief', *Folklore*, 116 (April 2005), pp. 1–18

Coulter, Henry, *The West of Ireland: Its Existing Condition and Prospects* (Dublin: Hodges and Smith, 1862)

Cousens, S. H., 'The Regional Variations in Population Changes in Ireland, 1861–1881' *Economic History Review*, 2nd series, 17 (1964), pp. 301–321

Cragoe, Matthew, 'Conscience or Coercion?: Clerical Influence at the General election of 1868 in Wales', *Past and Present*, No. 149 (1995), pp. 141–169

Crawford, E. M., 'Indian Meal and Pellagra in Nineteenth-century Ireland', in *Irish*

Population, Economy and Society: Essays in Honour of the Late K. H. Connell, eds J. M. Goldstrom and L. A. Clarkson (Oxford: Clarendon Press, 1981)

Cullen, L. M., 'The Politics of Clerical Radicalism in the 1790s', in *Protestant, Catholic, Dissenter: The Clergy and 1798*, ed. Liam Swords (Dublin: Columba Press, 1997), pp. 274–309

Cunningham, Bernadette and Raymond Gillespie, *Stories from Gaelic Ireland: Microhistories from the Sixteenth Century Irish Annals* (Dublin: Four Courts, 2003)

Cusack, Mary Francis, *The Nun of Kenmare: An Autobiography* (Boston: Ticknor, 1889)

Cusack, M. F., *see* Clare, Sister Mary Francis

Daly, Kieran Anthony, *Catholic Church Music in Ireland, 1878–1903* (Dublin: Four Courts Press, 1995)

D'Alton, E. A., *History of the Archdiocese of Tuam. 2 vols.* (Dublin: Phoenix Publishing Co., 1928)

Darnton, Robert, *The Great Cat Massacre and Other Episodes in French Cultural History* (New York: Random House, 1985)

Davis, Philip H. and Jacqueline Boles, 'Pilgrim Work: Symbolization and Crowd Interaction When the Virgin Appeared in Georgia', *Journal of Contemporary Ethnography* 32, 4 (August 2003), pp. 371–402

Davitt, Michael, *The Fall of Feudalism in Ireland: or The Story of the Land League Revolution* (London: Harper and Brothers, 1904)

de Bhaldraithe, Tomás, *The Diary of an Irish Countryman 1827–1835: A Translation of Cín Lae Amhlaoibh* (Cork: Mercier Press, 1979)

Delay, Cara, 'The Devotional Revolution on the Local Level: Parish Life in Post Famine Ireland', *US Catholic Historian*, 22 (Summer 2004), pp. 41–60

Delay, Cara, 'Confidantes or Competitors? Women, Priests, and Conflict in Post-Famine Ireland', *Eire/Ireland*, 40, 1/2 (Spring-Summer 2005), pp. 106–25

Denvir, Gearóid, *Litríocht agus Pobal* (Indreabhán: Cló Iar-Chonnachta, 1997)

Dillon, Gerald, 'The Dillon Peerages', *The Irish Genealogist* 3 (1958), pp. 87–100

Donnelly, James S. Jr, 'Pastorini and Captain Rock: Millenarianism and Sectarianism in the Rockite Movement in East Munster, 1821–4', in *Irish Peasants: Violence and Popular Unrest 1780–1914*, eds Samuel Clark and James S. Donnelly (Madison: University of Wisconsin Press, 1983), pp. 102–39

Donnelly, James S., Jr, 'The Marian Shrine at Knock: The First Decade', *Eire/Ireland*, 28, 2 (1993), pp. 54–99

Donnelly, James S. Jr, 'The Peak of Marianism in Ireland, 1930–60', in *Piety and Power in Ireland 1760–1960: Essays in Honour of Emmet Larkin*, eds Stewart J. Brown and David W. Miller (Note Dame: Notre Dame University Press, 2000), pp. 252–83

Donnelly, James S. Jr, *The Great Irish Potato Famine* (Stroud, UK: Sutton Publishing, 2001)

Donnelly, James S. Jr, 'The Revival of Knock Shrine', in *History of the Public Sphere: Essays in Honour of John A. Murphy*, eds Tom Dunne and Laurence Geary (Cork: Cork University Press, 2005), pp. 186–200

Donnelly, James S. Jr, 'Captain Rock: Ideology and Organization in the Irish Agrarian Rebellion of 1821–24', *Éire/Ireland*, 42, 3/4 (Winter 2007), pp. 60–103

Donohue, Tony, ed, *Local Songs, Poems and Ballads From the Shadow of Nephin* (Ballina, no date)

Dooley, Terence A. M., 'Landlords and the Land Question, 1879–1909', in *Famine, Land and Culture in Ireland*, ed. Carla King (Dublin: University College Dublin Press, 2000), pp. 116–39

Dorian, Hugh, *The Outer Edge of Ulster: A Memoir of Social Life in Nineteenth-Century Donegal*, eds Breandán Mac Suibhne and David Dickson (Dublin: Lilliput Press, 2000)

Douglas, Mary, *Purity and Danger: An Analysis of the Concepts of Pollution and Taboo* (New York: Praeger, 1966)

Douglas, Mary, *Natural Symbols: Explorations in Cosmology* (London: Barrie and Rockliff, 1970)

Douglas, Mary, 'Introduction to the Second Edition', in her *Purity and Danger: An Analysis of the Concepts of Pollution and Taboo* (New York: Routledge, 2002)

Doyle, David N., 'Knock 1879: Message to a Deprived People', *Doctrine and Life*, 30, 2 (Feb 1980), pp. 69–79

Dun, Finley, *Landlords and Tenants in Ireland* (London: Longman, Green and Co., 1881)

Dunlop, Andrew, *Fifty Years of Irish Journalism* (Dublin: Hanna and Neale, 1911)

Dwyer, Catherine Mary, 'James Augustine Anderson, OSA', *Seánchus Árd Mhacha*, 7 (1974), pp. 215–58

Emmerson, Richard K., 'The Secret', *American Historical Review* 104, 5 (December 1999), pp. 1603–14

Erikson, Kai, *Wayward Puritans: A Study in the Sociology of Deviance* (New York: Wiley, 1966)

Erikson, Kai, *Everything in its Path: The Destruction of Community in the Buffalo Creek Flood* (New York: Simon and Schuster, 1978)

Ewick, Patricia and Susan Silbey, 'Narrating Social Structure: Stories of Resistance to Legal Authority', *American Journal of Sociology*, 108 (May 2003), pp. 1328–72

Farry, Michael, *The Aftermath of Revolution: Sligo 1921–23* (Dublin: University College Dublin Press, 2000)

Fennell, Thomas, *The Royal Irish Constabulary: A History and Personal Memoir* (Dublin: University College Dublin Press, 2003)

Fenning, Hugh, OP, *The Undoing of the Friars of Ireland* (Louvain: Publications Universitaires de Louvain, 1972)

Fenning, Hugh, OP, 'A Time of Reform: From the "Penal Laws" to the Birth of Modern Nationalism, 1691–1800', in *Christianity in Ireland: Revisiting the Story*, eds Brendan Bradshaw and Daire Keogh (Dublin: Columba Press, 2002), pp. 134–43

Fentriss, James and Chris Wickham, *Social Memory* (Oxford: Blackwell, 1992)

Fingall, Elizabeth, Countess of, *Seventy Years Young: Memories of Elizabeth, Countess of Fingall* (London, 1937; reprint Dublin: Lilliput Press, 2006)

First Report of the Commissioners of Public Instruction, Ireland (London: Printed by William Clowes and Sons for His Majesty's Stationery Office, 1835)

Fish, Stanley, *Is There a Text in This Class? The Authority of Interpretive Communities* (Cambridge: Harvard University Press, 1980)

Fitzpatrick, D., '"A peculiar tramping people": the Irish in Britain, 1801–70', in *A New History of Ireland, Vol 5 Ireland Under the Union 1, 1801–1877*, ed. W. E. Vaughan (Oxford: Clarendon Press, 1989)

Fitzpatrick, David, '"A Share of the Honeycomb": Education, Emigration and Irishwomen', *Continuity and Change*, 1, 2 (1986), pp. 217–34

Fitzpatrick, David, 'The Modernisation of the Irish Female', in *Rural Ireland 1600–1900: Modernisation and Change*, eds Patrick O'Flanagan, Paul Ferguson and Kevin Whelan (Cork: Cork University Press, 1987), pp. 162–80

Fitzpatrick, David, 'Ireland since 1870', in *The Oxford Illustrated History of Ireland*, ed. Roy F. Foster (Oxford: Oxford University Press, 1989), pp. 213–74

Flanagan, Bernadette, *The Spirit of the City: Voices from Dublin's Liberties* (Dublin: Veritas, 1999)

Flanagan, T. P., 'Fr Jarlath Ronayne', in *Béacán/Bekan: Portrait of an East Mayo Parish* Comer, eds Fr Michael Comer and Nollaig Ó Muraíle (Privately published by Comer, 1986), pp. 164–7

Flynn, John S., *Ballymacward: The Story of an East Galway Parish* (Privately published, 1991)

Foster, George M., 'Peasant Society and the Image of Limited Good', *American Anthropologist*, 67 (April 1965)

Foster, Roy F., 'Ascendancy and Union', in *The Oxford Illustrated History of Ireland*, ed. Roy Foster (New York: Oxford University Press, 1989), 161–211

Friere, Paulo, *Pedagogy of the Oppressed* (Harmondsworth, Penguin, 1977)

Full Report of the Visitation of the Blessed Virgin, St Joseph, St John in Knock Chapel, Co. Mayo (Dublin: Nugent and Co., [1880?])

Gallagher, John, *A Look into Our Past: Our Irish Heritage* (Knock: Knock Shrine Society, 1990)

Gallogly, Daniel, *The Diocese of Kilmore, 1800–1950* (Cavan: Breiffne Historical Society, 1999)

Gallogly, Fr Dan, *Sliabh an Iarainn Slopes: History of the Town and Parish of Ballinamore, Co Leitrim* (No publisher given, 1991)

Gaventa, John, *Power and Powerlessness: Quiescence and Rebellion in an Appalachian Valley* (Urbana: University of Illinois Press, 1980)

Geary, Lawrence M., 'Prince Hohenloe, Signor Pastorini and Miraculous Healing in Early Nineteenth-Century Ireland', in *Medicine, Disease and the State in Ireland, 1650–1940*, eds Greta Jones and Elizabeth Malcolm (Cork: Cork University Press, 1999), pp. 40–58

Geary, Laurence M., 'Anticipating Memory: Landlordism, Agrarianism and Deference in Late-Nineteenth-century Ireland', in *History and the Public Sphere: Essays in Honour of John A. Murphy*, eds Tom Dunne and Laurence M. Geary (Cork: Cork University Press, 2005), pp. 127–39

Geertz, Clifford, *The Interpretation of Cultures: Selected Essays* (New York: Basic, 1973)

Gibbons, James Cardinal, 'Archbishop MacHale — An Appreciation', *Tuam Herald*, 15 July 1916, reprinted in *Glimpses of Tuam Since the Famine*, ed. John A. Claffey (Tuam: Old Tuam Society, 1997), pp. 122–7

Gibbons, Stephen, *Captain Rock, Night Errant: the Threatening Letters of Pre-Famine Ireland* (Dublin: Four Courts Press, 2004)

Gilley, Sheridan, 'The Background to Knock', *The Tablet*, 18 September 1979

Gilley, Sheridan, 'Catholicism in Ireland', in *The Decline of Christendom in Western Europe, 1750–2000*, eds Hugh McLeod and Werber Ustorf (Cambridge: Cambridge University Press, 2003)

Godson, Lisa, 'Catholicism and Material Culture in Ireland 1840–1880', *Circa*, 103 (Spring 2003), pp. 38–45

Goffman, Erving, *Frame Analysis: An Essay on the Organization of Experience* (New York: Harper and Row, 1974)

Golway, Terry, *Irish Rebel: John Devoy and America's Fight for Irish Freedom* (New York: St Martin's Press, 1999)

Gregory, Lady Augusta, *The Kiltartan History Book* (Dublin: Maunsel and Company, 1909)

Gregory, Lady Augusta, *Visions and Beliefs in the West of Ireland, with Two Essays and Notes by W. B. Yeats* (London: Putnam, 1920; reprinted London: Colin Smythe Ltd., 1970)

Griffin, Brian, 'Social Aspects of Fenianism in Connacht and Leinster, 1858–1870', *Eire/Ireland*, 21 (Spring 1986), pp. 16–39

Guinness, Selina, 'Visions and Beliefs in the West of Ireland: Irish Folklore and British Anthropology, 1898–1920', *Irish Studies Review* 6, 1 (1998), pp. 37–46

Gusterson, Hugh, *Nuclear Rites: A Weapons Laboratory at the End of the Cold War* (Berkeley: University of California Press, 1996)

Gutman, Herbert G., *Slavery and the Numbers Game: A Critique of* Time on the Cross (Champaign: University of Illinois Press, 1975)

Hall, S. C. and Hall, A. M., *Ireland: Its Scenery, Character, Etc*, Volume 1 (London: 1841)

Halbwachs, Maurice, *Les cadres sociaux de la mémoire* (Paris: Alcan, 1925)

Harbison, Peter, *Pilgrimage in Ireland: The Monuments and The People* (London: Barrie and Jenkins, 1991)

Hardiman, James, *The History of the County and the Town of Galway from the earliest period to the Present Time, 1820* (Galway, 1858)

Hardy, Philip Dixon, *The Holy Wells of Ireland* (Dublin 1836)

Harris, Marvin, 'Cultural Materialism is Alive and Well and Won't Go Away Until Something Better Comes Along', in *Assessing Cultural Anthropology*, ed. by R. Borofsky (New York: McGraw-Hill, 1994)

Harris, Ruth, *Lourdes: Body and Spirit in the Secular Age* (New York: Viking, 1999)

Harris, Ruth-Ann, *The Nearest Place That Wasn't Ireland: Early Nineteenth-Century Irish Labour Migration* (Ames: University of Iowa Press, 1994)

Harris, Ruth-Ann M., 'Negotiating Patriarchy: Irish Women and the Landlord', in *Reclaiming Gender: Transgressive Identities in Modern Ireland*, eds Marilyn Cohen and Nancy J. Curtin (New York: St Martin's Press, 1999), pp. 207–25

Hayes, Patrick, 'Massachusetts Miracles: Controlling Cures in Catholic Boston, 1929–1930', in *Saints and Their Cults in the Atlantic World*, ed. Margaret Cormack (Columbia: University of South Carolina Press, 2007), pp. 111–27

Hayes, Richard, *The Last Invasion of Ireland: When Connacht Rose* (Dublin: Gill and Son, 1937)

H. B., 'Our Lady of Lourdes', *The Irish Ecclesiastical Record* [New series] (May 1870), pp. 447–58

Healy, John, *Nineteen Acres* (Galway: Kenny's, 1978)

Heimann, Mary, *Catholic Devotion in Victorian England* (Oxford: Clarendon Press, 1995)

Higgins, Aidan, *Donkey's Years: Memories of Life as Story Told* (London: Secker and Warburg, 1995)

Higgins, Michael, 'In Bekan Long Ago', in *Béacán/Bekan: Portrait of an East Mayo Parish*, eds Fr Michael Comer and Nollaig Ó Muraíle (Privately published, 1986), pp. 93–107

Hill, Christopher, *England's Turning Point: Essays on Seventeenth-Century English History* (London: Bookmarks, 1998)

Hinchman, Lewis and Sandra Hinchman, *Memory, Identity, Community: The Idea of Narrative in the Human Sciences* (Albany: State University of New York Press, 1997)

Hoff, Joan and Marian Yeates, *The Cooper's Wife Is Missing: The Trials of Bridget Cleary* (Oxford: Basic Books, 2000)

Hogan, Patrick, 'The Migration of Ulster Catholics to Connaught', *Seánchas Árdmhacha*, 9, 2 (1978–79), pp. 286–301

Hogan, Patrick M., 'From Reaction to Reform: The Mellowing of a Connacht Squire, The Right Hon. Denis Browne, MP (1763–1822)', *Journal of the Galway Archaeological and History Society*, 57 (2005), pp. 29–37

Hoppen, K. T., 'Landlords, Society and Electoral Politics in Mid-nineteenth-century Ireland', *Past and Present*, 75 (1977), pp. 62–93

Hoppen, K. T., 'National Politics and Local Realities in Nineteenth–Century Ireland.' in *Studies in Irish History Presented to R. Dudley Edwards*, eds Art Cosgrove and Donal McCartney (Dublin: University College Dublin, 1979), pp. 190–227

Hoppen, K. Theodore, *Elections, Politics, and Society in Ireland, 1832–1885* (Oxford: Clarendon Press, 1984)

Hoppen, K. Theodore, *Ireland Since 1800: Conflict and Conformity* (London: Longman, 1989)

Horan, Monsignor James, *Memoirs 1911–1986*, ed. Fr Michael MacGreil (Dingle: Brandon Books, 1992)

Houston, Mrs [Matilda], *Twenty Years in the Wild West, or Life in Connaught* (London: John Murray, 1879)

Howes, Marjorie, 'William Carleton's Literary Religion', in *Evangelicals and Catholics in Nineteenth-Century Ireland*, ed. James H. Murphy (Dublin: Four Courts Press, 2005), pp. 107–22

Hyde, Douglas, *The Religious Songs of Connacht*, 2 vols (Dublin: Gill and Son, no date)

Hyde, Douglas, *Abhráin atá Leagtha ar an Reachtuire: Songs Ascribed to Raftery* (Shannon: Irish Academic Press [1903] 1973)

h-Íde, Dubhglas de (An Craoibhín), [Douglas Hyde], *An Sgealuidhe Gaedhealach (Sgeálta as Connachta)* (Dublin: Institiút Béaloideasa Éireann, 1933)

Hynes, Eugene, 'The Great Hunger and Irish Catholicism', *Societas*, 8 (1978), pp. 137–155

Hynes, Eugene, 'Family and Religious Change in a Peripheral Capitalist Society: Mid-Nineteenth-Century Ireland', in *The Religion and Family Connection: Social Science Perspectives*, ed. Darwin Thomas (Provo, Utah: Brigham Young University Religious Studies Center, 1988), pp. 161–74

Hynes, Eugene, 'Nineteenth-Century Irish Catholicism, Farmers' Ideology, and National Religion: Explorations in Cultural Explanation', in *Sociological Studies in Roman Catholicism: Historical and Contemporary Perspectives*, ed. Roger O'Toole (Lewiston, New York: Edwin Mellen Press, 1989), pp. 45–70

Hynes, Eugene, 'A Chalice in a Bog, or Fool's Gold?', *History/Ireland*, v, 1 (Spring 1997)

Hynes, Eugene, 'Elite Control and Citizen Mobilization in a Small Midwestern Town', *Critical Sociology*, 17 (Spring, 1990), pp. 81–98

Hynes, Eugene, 'The Construction of Insiders as Outsiders: Catholic Accounts of Protestant Converts in Pre-famine Mayo', *Cultural and Social History*, 6, 2 (2009), pp. 195–209.

Hynes, Eugene, 'Making Sense of "Mistakes" in Oral Sources', in *Anáil an Bhéil Bheo: Orality and Modern Irish Culture*, eds Nessa Cronin, Seán Crossan and John Eastlake (Cambridge: Cambridge Scholars Press, 2009), pp. 149–58.

Inglis, Tom, *Moral Monopoly: The Catholic Church in Modern Irish Society* (Dublin: Gill and MacMillan 1987), and a revised 2nd edition subtitled *The Rise and Fall of the Catholic Church in Modern Ireland* (Dublin: University College Dublin Press, 1998)

Jennings, J. J., *The Big Rock* (Privately published, 1989)

Jenkins Richard P., 'Witches and Fairies: Supernatural Aggression and Deviance among the Irish Peasantry', *Ulster Folklife*, 23 (1977), pp. 33–56, reprinted in *The Good People: New Fairylore Essays*, ed. Peter Narvaez (New York: Garland Publishing, 1991), pp. 302–35

Johnson, Allan G., *The Forest and the Trees: Sociology as Life, Practice and, Promise* (Philadelphia: Temple University Press, 1997)

Johnston-Liik, Edith M., *History of the Irish Parliament 1692–1800: Commons, Constituencies and Statutes*, 6 Vols (Belfast: Ulster Historical Foundation, 2002)

Jones, David Seth, *Graziers, Land Reform, and Political Conflict in Ireland* (Washington DC: The Catholic University of America Press, 1995)

Jones, David S., 'The Cleavage Between Graziers and Peasants in the Land Struggle, 1890–1910', in *Irish Peasants and Political Unrest 1780–1914*, eds Samuel Clark and James S. Donnelly, Jr (Madison: University of Wisconsin Press, 1983), pp. 373–417

Jacobs, Nancy, 'The Great Bophuthatswana Donkey Massacre: Discourse on the Ass and the Politics of Class and Grass', *American Historical Review*, 106, 2 (April 2001), pp. 485–507

Jordan, Donald, Jr, *Land and Popular Politics in Ireland: County Mayo From the Plantation to the Land War* (Cambridge: Cambridge University Press, 1994)

Joyce, James, *Dubliners* (New York: Viking, 1967)

Joyce, P. W., *Irish Music and Song* (Dublin: Gill, 1903)

Kane, Anne, 'Theorizing Meaning Construction in Social Movements: Symbolic Structures and Interpretation during the Land War, 1879–1882', *Sociological Theory*, 15 (1997), pp. 249–76

Kane, Paula M., 'Marian Devotion Since 1940: Continuity or Casualty?', in *Habits of Devotion: Catholic Religious Practices in Twentieth-Century America*, ed. James O'Toole (Ithaca: Cornell University Press, 2004), pp. 89–129

Kearney, Hugh F., '1875: Faith or Fatherland? The Contested Symbolism of Irish Nationalism', in *Piety and Power in Ireland 1760–1960: Essays in Honour of Emmet Larkin*, eds Stewart J. Brown and David W. Miller (Belfast: Institute of Irish Studies, Queen's'University, 2000), pp. 65–80

Keenan, Desmond, *The Catholic Church in Nineteenth-Century Ireland: A Sociological Study* (Dublin: Gill and MacMillan, 1983)

Kelly, Michael, 'The Bekan Area in the Year of the French', in *Béacán/Bekan: Portrait of an East Mayo Parish*, eds Fr Michael Comer and Nollaig Ó Muraíle (Privately published by Comer, 1986), pp. 146–7

Kennedy, Liam, 'Profane Images in the Irish Popular Consciousness', *Oral History*, 7 (1979), pp. 42–7

Kennedy, Liam, Paul S. Ell, E. M. Crawford and L. A. Clarkson, *Mapping the Great Irish Famine* (Dublin: Four Courts Press, 1999)

Kerr, Donal A., *Peel, Priests, and Politics: Sir Robert Peel's Administration and the Roman Catholic Church in Ireland, 1841–1846* (Oxford: Clarendon Press, 1982)

Kerr, Donal, 'Priests, Pikes and Patriots: The Irish Catholic Church and Political Violence from the Whiteboys to the Fenians', in *Piety and Power in Ireland 1760–1960: Essays in Honour of Emmet Larkin*, eds Stewart J. Brown and David W. Miller (Belfast: Institute of Irish Studies, Queens' University, 2000), pp. 16–42

Kerr, Donal, 'The Catholic Church in the Age of O'Connell' in *Christianity in Ireland: Revisiting the Story*, eds Brendan Bradshaw and Daire Keogh (Dublin: Columba Press, 2002), pp. 164–85

Kselman, Thomas, *Miracles and Prophecies in Nineteenth Century France* (New Brunswick: Rutgers University Press, 1983)

King, Carla, 'Introduction', in *George Moore, Parnell and His Island* (Dublin: University College Dublin Press, 2003)

Knott, John William, 'Land, Kinship and Identity: The Cultural Roots of Agrarian Agitation in Eighteenth- and Nineteenth-Century Ireland', *Journal of Peasant Studies*, 12 (1884), pp. 93–108

Knowlton, Steven, *Popular Politics and the Irish Catholic Church: The Rise and Fall of the Independent Irish Party, 1850–1859* (New York: Garland, 1991)

Ladurie, Emmanuel LeRoy, *Montaillou: The Promised Of Error* (New York: Braziller, 1978)

Laheen, Kevin, 'Jesuit Parish Mission Memoirs, 1863–1876, Part 1', *Collectanea Hibernica*, 39–40 (1997–1998), pp. 272–311

Laighléis, Tomás, *Seánchas Thomáis Laighléis*, ed. Tomás de Bhaldraithe (Dublin: An Clóchomhar, 1977)

Larkin, Emmet, 'The Devotional Revolution in Ireland, 1850–1875' *American Historical Review*, 77 (1972), pp. 625–52

Larkin, Emmet, *The Roman Catholic Church and The Creation of the Modern Irish State, 1878–1886* (Philadelphia: American Philosophical Society, 1975)

Larkin, Emmet, *The Historical Dimensions of Irish Catholicism* (Washington: Catholic University of America Press, 1976; reprint with new introduction, 1984)

Larkin, Emmet, *The Roman Catholic Church and the Home Rule Movement in Ireland, 1870–1874* (Dublin: Gill and MacMillan, 1990)

Larkin, Emmet, *The Roman Catholic Church and the Emergence of the Modern Irish Political System, 1874–1878* (Washington: Catholic University of America Press, 1996)

Larkin, Emmet, 'The Rise and Fall of Stations in Ireland, 1750–1850', in *Chocs et ruptures en historie religieuse: fin XVIIIe–XIXe siecles*, ed. Michel Lagree (Rennes: Presses Universitaires de Renne, 1998), pp. 19–32

Larkin, Emmet, 'Cardinal Paul Cullen', in *Varieties of Ultramontanism*, ed. by Jeffrey von Arx, SJ (Washington, DC: The Catholic University of America, 1998), pp. 61–84

Larkin, Emmet, Book Review, *Catholic Historical Review*, 86, 3 (2000), pp. 514–6

Larkin, Emmet, Book Review [of Swords, *Dominant Church*] *Catholic Historical Review*, 91.2

Larkin, Emmet, 'The Parish Mission Movement, 1850–1880', in *Christianity in Ireland: Revisiting the Story*, eds Brendan Bradshaw and Daire Keogh (Dublin: The Columba Press, 2002), pp. 195–204

Larkin, Emmet, 'John MacHale', *Oxford Dictionary of National Biography*, 2004

Larkin, Emmet, 'Before the Devotional Revolution', in *Evangelicals and Catholics in Nineteenth-Century Ireland*, ed. James H. Murphy (Dublin: Four Courts Press, 2005), pp. 15–37

Larkin, Emmet, *The Pastoral Role of the Roman Catholic Church in Pre-Famine Ireland, 1750–1850* (Dublin: Four Courts Press, 2006)

Lee, Joseph, 'The Railways in the Irish Economy', in *The Formation of the Irish Economy*, ed. L. M. Cullen (Cork: Mercier Press, 1969)

Lee, Joseph, *The Modernisation of Irish Society 1848–1918* (Dublin: Gill and MacMillan, 1973)

Lee, Richard B., 'Eating Christmas in the Kalahari', *Natural History*, 78, 10 (December 1969), pp. 1–3

Le Fanu, William, *Seventy Years of Irish Life* (London: Edward Arnold, 1893)

Legg, Marie-Louise, *Newspapers and Nationalism: The Irish Provincial Press 1850–1892* (Dublin: Four Courts, 1999)

Lenihan, Edmund, *In Search of Biddy Early* (Cork: Mercier Press, 1987)

Liffey, Michael, 'The 1872 By-Election', in *The District of Loughrea, Vol 1: History 1791–1918*, eds Joseph Forde, Christina Cassidy, Paul Manzor and David Ryan (Loughrea: Loughrea History Project, 2003), pp. 326–48

Litton, Helen, 'The Famine in Schools', in *Irish Hunger: Personal Reflections on the Legacy of the Famine*, ed. Tom Hayden (Dublin: Wolfhound Press, 1997), pp. 56–65

Loewen, James, *Lies My Teacher Told Me* (New York: Simon and Schuster, 1995)

Logan, Patrick, *The Holy Wells of Ireland* (Gerrard's Cross: Colin Smythe, 1980)

Luach, 'St Patrick in Mayo', *Knock Shrine Annual 1961*, pp. 28–32

Ludwig, Dean and Clinton Longnecker, 'The Bathsheba Syndrome: The Ethical Failure of Successful Leaders', *Journal of Business Ethics*, 12 (1993), pp. 265–73

Lyons, John, 'John MacHale, Archbishop of Tuam', *Journal of the Westport Historical Society*, IV (1984), pp. 37–50

Lysaght, Patricia, 'Fairylore from the Midlands of Ireland', in *The Good People: New Fairylore Essays*, ed. Peter Narvaez (New York: Garland Publishing, 1991)

Lysaght, Patricia, '"Is there Anyone Here to Serve My Mass?": the Legend of the "the Dead Priest's Midnight Mass" in Ireland', *Arv*, 47 (1991), pp. 193–208

Lysaght, Patricia, 'Attitudes to the Rosary and its Performance in Donegal in the Nineteenth and Twentieth Centuries', *Béaloideas*, 66 (1998), pp. 9–58

MacDiarmid, Lucy and Maureen Waters, 'Introduction', in their edited volume, *Lady Gregory: Selected Writings* (New York: Penguin, 1995), pp. xi–xliv

McCann, Sr Mary Agnes (Contributor), 'Documents. Bishop Purcell's Journal, 1833–36', *The Catholic Historical Review*, 5 (1919), pp. 239–56

McDermott, Vera, *The Woodlands of Loughglynn.* (Privately published by Mrs C. V. Brookes, 1998)

McDonagh, Marian, 'An Early Victorian Scrapbook', in *The District of Loughrea. Vol 1: History 1791–1918*, eds Joseph Forde, Christina Cassidy, Paul Manzor and David Ryan (Published by Loughrea History Project, 2003), pp. 143–88

McGahern, John, *That They May Face the Rising Sun* (London: Faber and Faber, 2001)

McGoff-McCann, Michelle, *Melancholy Madness: A Coroner's Casebook* (Cork: Mercier Press, 2003)

McGrath, Terence [pseudonym for Sir Henry A. Blake], *Pictures From Ireland.* 6th edition (London: Kegan Paul and Trench, 1888)

McGrath, Thomas, 'The Tridentine Evolution of Modern Irish Catholicism, 1563–1962: A Re-Examination of the "Devotional Revolution" Thesis', *Recusant History*, 20 (1991), pp. 512–23

McGrath, Thomas, *Politics, Interdenominational Relations and Education in the Public Ministry of Bishop James Doyle of Kildare and Leighlin, 1786–1834* (Dublin: Four Courts, 1999)

McGrath, Thomas, *Religious Renewal and Reform in the Pastoral Ministry of Bishop James Doyle of Kildare and Leighlin, 1786–1834* (Dublin: Four Courts, 1999)

McGrath, Thomas, 'James Warren Doyle (1786–1834)', *Oxford Dictionary of National Biography*, 2004

McGuire, Meredith, 'Linking Theory and Methodology For the Study of Latino Religiosity in the United States', in *An Enduring Flame: Studies on Latino Popular*

Religiosity, eds Anthony M. Stevens-Arroya and Ana Maria Diaz-Stevens (New York: Bildner Centre, 2004), pp. 191–203

McKenna, Malachy, 'A Textual History of *The Spiritual Rose*', *Clogher Record*, 14 (1991), pp. 52–73

McKenna, Malachy, ed., *The Spiritual Rose* (Dublin: Institute for Advanced Studies, 2001)

MacLaughlin, Jim, 'The Politics of Nation-Building in Post-Famine Donegal' in *Donegal History and Society: Interdisciplinary Essays on the History of an Irish County*, eds William Nolan, Liam Ronayne and Mairead Dunleavy (Dublin: Geography Publications, 1995)

McLeod, Hugh, 'Popular Catholicism in Irish New York, c1900', in *The Churches, Ireland and the Irish*, eds W. J. Shields and Diana Woods (Published for the Ecclesiastical History Society by Basil Blackwell, 1989), pp. 353–73

MacHale, Edward, '*Aguisín* 1: John MacHale 1791–1881' in *Leon an Iarthair: Aisti ar Shean Mac Héil*, ed. Áine Ní Cheannain (Dublin: An Clóchomhar, 1983)

MacManus, Dermot, *The Middle Kingdom: The Faerie World of Ireland* (Gerrard's Cross: Colin Smythe, 1973)

MacPhilpin, John, *The Apparitions and Miracles at Knock. Also, The Official Depositions of the Eye-Witnesses* (Dublin: Gill and Son, 1880) [For other editions of MacPhilpin's book see Note 37 to chapter 9]

MacTernan, John C., 'The Rout of the Penny Boys', in his *Olde Sligo: Aspects of Town and County Over 750 Years* (Sligo: Avena Publications, 1995), pp. 300–5

Magray, Mary P., *The Transforming Power of the Nuns: Women, Religion, and Cultural Change in Ireland, 1750–1900* (New York: Oxford University Press, 1998)

Mahon, William J. (Editor and Translator), *Doctor Kirwan's Irish Catechism by Thomas Hughes* (Cambridge, Mass: Pangur Publications, 1991)

Mason, W. Shaw, *A Statistical Account or Parochial Survey of Ireland*, 4 vols (1814–19)

Maume, Patrick , 'Rebel on the Run: T. J. Quinn and the IRB/Land League Diaspora in America', in Patrick Maume and Marguerite Quintelli-Neary, *19th-Century Irish and Irish-Americans on the Western Frontier* (Working Papers in Irish Studies, 00–1 Nova Southeastern University, 2000), pp. 1-12

Maxwell, W(illiam) H., *Wild Sports of the West* (New York: Frederick Stokes Company, [1832] 1915)

Meehan, Rosa, *The Story of Mayo* (Castlebar: Mayo County Council, 2003)

Memmi, Albert, *The Colonizer and the Colonized* (Boston: Beacon Press, 1967)

Miller David, 'Irish Catholicism and the Great Famine', *Journal of Social History*, 9 (1975), pp. 81–98

Miller, David W., 'Irish Presbyterians and the Great Famine', in *Luxury and Austerity: Historical Studies 21*, eds Colm Lennon and Jacqueline R. Hill (Dublin: 1999), pp. 164–81

Miller, David, 'Mass Attendance in Ireland in 1834', in *Piety and Power in Ireland, 1760–1960: Essays in Honour of Emmet Larkin*, eds Stewart J. Brown and David W. Miller (Belfast: Institute for Irish Studies, Queen's University, 2000), pp. 158–79

Miller, David, 'Landscape and Religious Practice: a Study of Mass Attendance in Pre-Famine Ireland', *Eire/Ireland* 40, 1/ 2 (Spring/Summer 2005), pp. 90–106

Miller, Kerby, *Emigrants and Exiles: Ireland and the Irish Exodus to North America* (New York: Oxford University Press, 1985)

Mitchell, Claire, 'Catholicism and the Construction of Communal Identity in Northern Ireland', *Irish Journal of Sociology*, 14, 1 (2005), pp. 110–30

Mitchell, Claire, *Religion, Identity and Politics in Northern Ireland: The Limits of Belonging* (Aldershot: Ashgate, 2005)

Mokyr, Joel, *Why Ireland Starved: a Quantitative and Analytical History of the Irish Economy, 1800–1850* (Boston: 1983)

Moody, T. W., *Davitt and Irish Revolution 1846–82* (Oxford: Clarendon Press, 1982)

Moore, George, *Parnell and His Island*, ed. Carla King (Dublin: University College Dublin Press, 2004)

Moran, Gerard, '"A Passage to Britain": Seasonal Migration and Social Change in the West of Ireland, 1870–1890', *Saothar*, 13 (1988), pp. 22–31

Moran, Gerard, 'Famine and the Land War: Relief and Distress in Mayo, 1879–1981', *Cathair na Mart*, 5 (1981), p. 111

Moran, Gerard, *The Mayo Evictions of 1860: Patrick Lavelle and the 'War' in Partry* (Westport: 1986)

Moran, Gerard, 'James Daly and the Rise and Fall of the Land League in the West of Ireland, 1879–1882', *Irish Historical Studies*, xxix (1994), pp. 186–207

Moran, Gerard, *A Radical Priest in Mayo: Fr Patrick Lavelle, The Rise and Fall of an Irish Nationalist, 1825–1882* (Dublin: Four Courts, 1994)

Moran, James, *Staging the Easter Rising: 1916 as Theatre* (Cork: Cork University Press, 2005)

Morash, Chris, 'Literature, Memory, Atrocity', in *'Fearful Realities': New Perspectives on the Famine*, eds Chris Morash and Richard Hayes (Dublin: Irish Academic Press, 1996), pp. 110–8

Mulroy, Sheila, 'The Clergy and the Connacht Rebellion', in *Protestant, Catholic and Dissenter: The Clergy and 1798*, ed. Liam Swords (Dublin: Columba Press, 1997), pp. 253–73

Mulveen, Jack, 'Tóchar Phádraic: Mayo's Penitential and Sculptured Highway', *Journal of the Galway Archaeological and Historical Society*, 51 (1998), pp. 167–81

Murphy, Clare, 'Varieties of Crowd Activity from Fenianism to the Land War, 1867–79', in *Crowds in Ireland, c. 1720–1929*, eds Peter Jupp and Eoin Magennis (New York: St Martin's Press, 2000), pp. 173–88

Murphy, Ignatius, *Before the Famine Struck: Life in West Clare 1834–1845* (Dublin: Irish Academic Press, 1996)

Murphy, James H., 'The Role of the Vincentian Parish Missions in the "Irish Counter-Reformation" in the Mid-Nineteenth Century', *Irish Historical Studies*, 24 (1984), pp. 152–71

Murphy, Joseph, *The Redingtons of Clarenbridge: Leading Catholic Landlords of the 19th Century* (Privately published, 1999)

Murphy, Michael J., *Now You're Talking* (Belfast: Blackstaff Press, 1975)

Nabhan-Warren, Kristy, *The Virgin of El Barrio: Marian Apparitions, Catholic Evangelizing, and Mexican-American Activism* (New York: New York University Press, 2005)

Neary, Tom, *I Saw Our Lady* (Published by the Custodians of Knock Shrine, 1977)

Neary, Tom, *'Ould Acquaintance': A Guide to Knock Folk Museum* (Knock, 2nd ed., 1980)

Neary, Tom and Seán Egan, eds, *Knock Parish Church 1828–2006* (No publisher given)

Ní Liatháin, Íde, *The Life and Career of P. A. McHugh, A North Connacht Politician 1859–1909* (Dublin: Irish Academic Press, 1999)

Nichols, Aidan, OP, *Holy Order: The Apostolic Ministry from the New Testament to the Second Vatican Council* (Dublin: Veritas, 1990)

Nicholson, Asenath, *The Bible in Ireland* (New York: The John Day Company, 1927)

Ó Baoighill, Pádraig, *Nally As Mayo* (Dublin: Coiscéim, 1998)

Ó Baoill, Pádraig, *Glórtha Ár Sinsear: Béaloideas Oirdheisceart na Gaillimhe* (Dublin: Coiscéim, 2005)

Ó Buachalla, Breandán, *Cathal Buí: Amhráin* (Dublin: An Clóchomhar, 1975)

Ó Cadhain, Mairtín, *Tone Inné agus Inniú* (Dublin: Coiscéim 1999)

Ó Cadhla, Stiofán, *The Holy Well Tradition: The Pattern of St Declan, Ardmore, County Waterford, 1820–2000* (Dublin: Four Courts Press, 2004)

Ó Catháin, Séamus and Patrick O'Flanagan, *The Living Landscape: Kilgannon, Erris, County Mayo* (Dublin: Comhairle Bhéaloideasa Éireannn, 1975)

Ó Cathaoir, Brendan, *Famine Diary* (Dublin: Irish Academic Press, 1999)

Ó Ciosáin, Niall, 'Famine Memory and Popular Representation of Scarcity', in *Memory and Commemoration in Irish History*, eds Ian McBride and D. G. Boyce (Cambridge University Press, 2001), pp. 95–117

Ó Ciosáin, Niall, 'Gaelic Culture and Language Shift', in *Nineteenth-century Ireland: A Guide to Recent Research*, eds Laurence Geary and Margaret Kelleher (Dublin: University College Dublin Press, 2005), pp. 131–52

Ó Coileán, Seán, 'The Irish Lament: An Oral Genre', *Studia Hibernica*, 24 (1984–1988), pp. 97–117

O'Connor, Anne, *The Blessed and the Damned: Sinful Women and Unbaptised Children in Irish Folklore* (New York: Peter Lang, 2005)

O'Connor, Fr John, OSA, ed., *The Ballyhaunis Friary (in Black and White)* (Ballyhaunis: GREENSprint, 1996)

O'C[onnor], T., *A Visit to Knock* (Limerick: T. O'Connor, 1880)

Ó Crualaoich, Gearóid, *The Book of the Cailleach: Stories of the Wise-Woman Healer* (Cork: Cork University Press, 2003)

Ó Crualaoich, Gearóid, 'Reading the *Bean Feasa*', *Folklore*, 37, 3 (April 2005), pp. 37–50

Ó Cuív, Brian, 'An Irish Tract on the Stations of the Cross', *Celtica*, 11 (1956), pp. 1–29

Ó Dónail, Niall, ed., *Foclóir Gaeilge-Béarla* (Dublin: An Gúm, 1977)

O'Donnell, Martina, 'Settlement and Society in the Barony of East Inishowen, c.1850', in *Donegal History and Society: Interdisciplinary Essays on the History of an Irish County*, eds William Nolan, Liam Ronayne and Mairead Dunleavy (Dublin: Geography Publications, 1995), pp. 509–46

O'Dowd, Anne, *Spalpeens and Tattie Hokers: History and Folklore of The Irish Migratory Agricultural Worker in Ireland and Britain* (Dublin: Irish Academic Press, 1991)

Ó Duigneáin, Proinnsíos, *The Priest and the Protestant Woman* (Dublin: Irish Academic Press, 1997)

O'Dwyer, Catherine Mary, 'James Augustine Anderson, OSA', *Seánchus Árd Mhacha*, 7 (1974), pp. 215–58

O'Dwyer, Peter, *Mary: A History of Devotion in Ireland* (Dublin: Four Courts Press, 1988)

O'Ferrall, Fergus, *Catholic Emancipation: Daniel O'Connell and the Birth of Irish Democracy, 1820–30* (Dublin: Gill and MacMillan, 1985)

Ó Gadhra, Nollaig, 'Gaeltacht Mhaigh Eo', in *Mayo: Aspects of its Heritage*, ed. Bernard O'Hara (Galway: Regional Technical College, 1986), pp. 123–51

Ó Giolláin, Diarmuid, *Locating Irish Folklore: Tradition, Modernity, Identity* (Cork: Cork University Press, 2000)

Ó Giolláin, Diarmuid, 'Revisiting the Holy Well', *Eire/Ireland*, 40, 1–2 (Spring/Summer 2005), pp. 11–41

Ó Gráda, Cormac, 'Seasonal Migration and Post-Famine Adjustment in the West of Ireland', *Studia Hibernica*, 13 (1971)

Ó Gráda, Cormac, *An Drochshaol: Béaloideas agus Amhrain* (Dublin: Coiscéim, 1994)

Ó Gráda, Cormac, *Black '47 and Beyond: The Great Irish Famine in History, Economy, and Memory* (Princeton, Princeton University Press, 1999)

O'Hara, Bernard, ed., *Mayo: Aspects of its Heritage* (Galway: Regional Technical College, 1986)

O'Hara, Bernard, *Davitt* (Castlebar: Mayo County Council, 2006)

Ó Héalaí, Pádraig, 'Moral Values in Irish Religious Tales', *Béaloideas* 42–44 (1974–1976), pp. 176–212

Ó Héalaí, Pádraig, 'Cumhacht an tSagairt sa Béaloideas,' *Leachtaí Cholm Cille*, 8 (1977), pp. 109–131

Ó Héalaí, Pádraig, 'Priest Versus Healer: The Legend of the Priest's Stricken Horse', *Béaloideas*, 62/63 (1994–5), pp. 171–88

Ó h-Ógáin, Daithi, *The Hero in Irish Folk Poetry* (Dublin: Gill and MacMillan, 1985)

Ó Laighin, Pádraig, *Eadbhard Ó Dufaigh, 1840–1868* (Dublin: Coiscéim, 1994)

Ó Laighin, Pádraig G., *Bánú Phartraí agus Thuar Mhic Éadaigh* (Dublin: Coiscéim, 1997)

Oldridge, Darren, *Strange Histories: The Trial of the Pig, the Walking Dead, and other Matters of Fact from the Medieval and Renaissance Worlds* (London: Routledge, 2005)

Ó Maolmhuaidh, Proinsias, *Uilleog De Búrca: Athair na hAthbheochana* (Dublin: Foilseáchain Naisiúnta Teoranta, 1981)

Ó Móráin, Padraig, *An tAthair Mánus Mac Suibhne, Sagart ó Mhaigh Eo in Éirí Amach 1798/ Fr Manus Sweeney, A Mayo Priest in the Rebellion of 1798*, ed. and trans. by Sheila Mulloy (Westport Historical Society, 1999)

Ó Muirithe, Diarmuid, 'O'Connell in Irish Folk Tradition', in *Daniel O'Connell: Portrait of a Radical*, eds Kevin B. Nowlan and Maurice R. O'Connell (Belfast: Appletree Press 1984), pp. 509–46

Ó Muraíle, Nollaig, 'A Glimpse of Bekan During The Great Famine', in *Béacán/Bekan: Portrait of an East Mayo Parish*, eds Fr Michael Comer and Nollaig Ó Muraíle (Privately published, 1986)

Ó Muraíle, Nollaig, 'Landlord and Tenant', in *Béacán/Bekan: Portrait of an East Mayo Parish*, eds, Fr Michael Comer and Nollaig Ó Muraíle (Privately published, 1986), pp. 149–51

O'Neill, Tim P., 'Famine Evictions', in *Famine, Land and Culture in Ireland*, ed. Carla King (Dublin: University College Dublin Press, 2000), pp. 29–70

O'Reilly, Bernard, *John MacHale, Archbishop of Tuam: His Life, Times and Correspondence*, 2 Vols. (New York and Cincinnati: Fustet, 1890)

O'Riordan, S., CSsR, 'Book Review', *The Irish Ecclesiastical Record*, 89, Series 5 (1958), pp. 141–7

O'Rourke, Brian, 'Mayo in Gaelic Folksong', in *Mayo: Aspects of Its Heritage*, ed. Bernard O'Hara (Galway: Regional Technical College, 1986), pp. 153–200

Orser, Charles, 'Symbolic Violence, Resistance and the Vectors of Improvement in Early Nineteenth-Century Ireland', *World Archaeology*, 37 (2005), pp. 392–407

Orsi, Robert, *The Madonna of 115th Street: Faith and Community in Italian Harlem, 1880–1950*, 2nd edition (New Haven: Yale University Press, 2002)

Ortner, Sherry B., *High Religion: A Cultural and Political History of Sherpa Buddhism* (Princeton: Princeton University Press, 1989)

O'Sullivan, Niamh, 'The Iron Cage of Femininity: Visual Representations of Women in the 1880s' Land Agitation', in *Ideology and Ireland in the Nineteenth Century*, eds Tadhg Foley and Seán Ryder (Dublin: Four Courts Press 1998), pp. 181–96

O'Sullivan, Niamh, '*Mass in a Connemara Cabin*: Religion and the Politics of Painting', *Eire/Ireland*, 40, 1/2 (Spring-Summer 2005), pp. 126–39

Ó Súilleabháin, Seán, *Irish Wake Amusements* (Cork: Mercier Press, 1967)

Ó Tuathaigh, Gearóid, 'The Folk-hero and Tradition', in *The World of Daniel O'Connell*, ed. Donal McCartney (Dublin: Mercier Press, 1980), pp. 30–42

Otway, Caesar, *A Tour of Connaught, Comprising Sketches of Clonmacnoise, Joyce Country, and Achill* (Dublin: William Curry Jun. & Co., 1839)

Pagliaroli, Jessy, 'Kodak Catholicism: Miraculous Photography and its Significance at a Post-Conciliar Marian Apparition Site in Canada', *Historical Studies*, 70 (2004), pp. 71–96

Parliamentary Gazette of Ireland 1844

Partridge, Angela, 'Caoineadh na dTrí Muire agus an Chaointeoireacht', in *Gnéithe Den Chaointeoireacht*, ed. by Breandán Ó Madagáin (Dublin: An Clóchomhar, 1978), 67–81

Partridge, Angela, 'Wild Men and Wailing Women', *Éigse*, 28 (1980), pp. 25–37

Peregrinus, Laicus, 'Knock and the Nun of Kenmare', Cutting from unidentified newspaper (undated but c. 1920), in ACSJP, Series 3A 289

Perry, Nicholas and Loreto Echeverria, *Under the Heel of Mary* (New York: Routledge, 1988)

Pethica, James L and James C. Roy, 'Introduction' in Henry Stratford Persse, *'To the Land of the Free from this Island of Slaves': Henry Stratford Persse's Letters from Galway to America, 1821–1832*, eds James L. Pethica and James C. Roy (Cork: Cork University Press, 1998), pp. 1–59

Persse, Henry Stratford, *'To the Land of the Free from this Island of Slaves': Henry Stratford Persse's Letters from Galway to America, 1821–1832*, eds James L. Pethica and James C. Roy (Cork: Cork University Press, 1998)

Pessar, Patricia, *From Fanatics to Folk: Brazilian Millenarianism and Popular Culture* (Durham: Duke University Press, 2004)

Pleamonn, Liam, 'Seán Mac Haeil, Árd-Easbog Thuama', *An Stoc agus an Chearnóg* (July/August 1927), p. 3

Pope, Barbara Corrado, 'Immaculate and Powerful: The Marian Revival in the Nineteenth Century', in *Immaculate and Powerful: The Female in Sacred Image and Social Reality*, eds Clarissa W. Atkinson, Constance H. Buchanan and Margaret R. Miles (Boston: Beacon Press,1984), pp. 173–200

Porte, Cheryl, *Pontmain, Prophecy and Protest: A Cultural-Historical Study of a Nineteenth-Century Vision* (New York: Peter Lang, 2005)

Power, John O'Connor, 'The Irish Land Agitation', *The Nineteenth Century*, VI, xxxiv (December 1879), pp. 953–67

Proceedings of the Mansion House Committee for Relief of Distress in Ireland During the Months of January and February (Dublin: Mansion House, March 1880)

Prost, Joseph, CSsR, *A Redemptorist Missionary in Ireland, 1851–1854: Memoirs of Joseph Prost, CSsR*, Translated and edited by Emmet Larkin and Herman Freudenberger (Cork: Cork University Press, 1998)

Prunty, Jacinta, *Margaret Aylward, 1810–1889: Lady of Charity, Sr of Faith* (Dublin: Four Courts, 1999)

Purcell, Mary, 'Our Lady of Silence, Knock 1879', in *A Woman Clothed With the Sun*, ed. John Delaney (Garden City: Hanover House, 1960), pp. 129–51

Quinn, Deirdre, 'Mayo Women and the Politics of the Land in the Latter Half of the Nineteenth Century, Part 1', *Cathair na Mart: Journal of the Westport Historical Society*, 16 (1997), pp. 91–111

Quinn, J. F., *History of Mayo* (Ballina: Brendan Quinn, Vol I and II, 1993; Vol III, 1996, Vol IV, 2000, Vol V, 2002)

Quinn, John F., 'The "Vagabond Friar": Fr Mathew's Difficulties with the Irish Bishops, 1840–1856', *The Catholic Historical Review*, 78 (October 1992), pp. 542–56

Quinn, John F., *Fr Mathew's Crusade: Temperance in Nineteenth-Century Ireland and Irish America* (Amherst: University of Massachusetts Press, 2002)

Rafferty, Oliver, Book Review, *Journal of Ecclesiastical History*, 49/3 (1998), pp. 582–83

Rafferty, Oliver P., 'Carleton's Ecclesiastical Context: The Ulster Catholic Experience', *Bullaun* 4, 2 (Winter 1999/2000), pp. 105–24

Redpath, James, *Talks About Ireland* (New York: P. J. Kenedy, 1881)

Reed, Jean-Pierre, 'Emotions in Context: Revolutionary Accelerators, Hope, Moral Outrage, and Other Emotions in the Making of Nicaragua's Revolution', *Theory and Society*, 33 (2004), pp. 653–703

Rhodes, Rita M., *Women and the Family in Post-Famine Ireland: Status and Opportunity in a Patriarchal Society* (New York: Garland Publishing, 1992)

Robertson, James, *The Holy Ground: Mary's Knock* (Knock: Custodians of Knock Shrine, 1975)

Robins, Joseph, *The Miasma: Epidemic and Panic in Nineteenth Century Ireland* (Dublin: Institute for Public Administration, 1995)

Robinson, Tim, *Camchuairt Chonamara Theas: A Twisty Journey, Mapping South Connemara* (Dublin: Coiscéim, 2002)

Rogers, The Revd Patrick, *Fr Theobald Mathew, Apostle of Temperance* (Dublin: Browne and Nolan, 1943)

Rooper, George, *A Month in Mayo: Comprising Characteristic Sketches (Sporting and Social) of Irish Life, With Miscellaneous Sketches* (London: Hardwicke, 1876)

Rosaldo, Renato, *Ilongot Headhunting, 1883–1974: A Study in Society and History* (Stanford: Stanford University Press, 1980)

Ryan, Meda, *Biddy Early* (Dublin: Mercier Press, 1978)

Rynne, Catherine, *Knock, 1879–1979* (Dublin: Veritas, 1979)

Rynne, Etienne, 'The Round Tower, "Evil Eye" and Holy Well at Balla, Co. Mayo', in *Dublin and Beyond the Pale: Studies in Honour of Patrick Healy*, ed. Conleth Manning (Bray, Ireland: Wordwell, 1998)

Sayers, Peig, *An Old Woman's Reflections: The Life of a Blasket Island Storyteller* (Oxford: Oxford University Press, 1962)

Scally, Robert J., *The End of Hidden Ireland: Rebellion, Famine, and Emigration* (New York: Oxford University Press, 1995)

Scott, James C., *Domination and the Arts of Resistance: Hidden Transcripts* (New Haven: Yale University Press, 1990)

Sewell, William H. Jr, 'The Concept(s) of Culture', in *Beyond the Cultural Turn: New Directions in the Study of Society and Culture*, eds Victoria Bonnell and Lynn Hunt (Berkeley: University of California Press, 1999), pp. 35–61

Sexton, Seán, ed., *Ireland in Old Photographs* (New York: Little Brown, 1994)

[Sexton, Thomas], *The Illustrated Record of the Apparitions at Knock: The Depositions of the Witnesses, Lists of the Alleged Miraculous Cures . . . (reprinted from the "Weekly News")* (Dublin: T. D. Sullivan, [1880]). Published without an author being listed, this work is widely wrongly ascribed to T. D. Sullivan.

Shand, Alexander I., *Letters from the West of Ireland, 1884* (Edinburgh: Blackwood, 1885)

Sharp, John, *Reapers of the Harvest: The Redemptorists in Britain and Ireland, 1843–1898* (Dublin: Veritas, 1989)

Sirr, Joseph D'Arcy, *A Memorial of the Honourable and Most Reverend Power le Poer Trench, Late Archbishop of Tuam.* (Dublin: William Curry, Jun. and Co., 1845)

Sisters of Mercy, Claremorris, *Hymn to Our Lady of Knock* (Dublin: Piggott and Co., No Date)

Slater, Eamonn and Terrence McDonough, 'Bulwark of Landlordism and Capitalism: The Dynamics of Feudalism in Nineteenth Century Ireland', *Research in Political Economy* 14 (1994), pp. 63–118

Smith, Alfred P., *Faith, Famine and Fatherland in the Nineteenth-Century Irish Midlands: Perceptions of a Priest and Historian Anthony Cogan 1826–1872* (Dublin: Four Courts Press, 1992)

Smith, Angèle, 'Landscape Representation: Place and Identity in Nineteenth-Century Ordnance Survey Maps of Ireland', in *Landscape, Memory and History: Anthropological Perspectives*, eds Pamela Stewart and Andrew Strathern (London: Pluto, 2003), pp. 71–88

Smith, Brian, *A Guide to Your Mayo Ancestors* (Dublin: Flyleaf Press, 1997)

Solan, John, *Religion and Society in the Ecclesiastical Province of Tuam before the Famine* (MA thesis, University College, Galway, 1989)

Somerville-Large, Peter, *The Irish Country House: A Social History* (London: Sinclair-Stevenson, 1995)

Stack, Carol, *All Our Kin: Strategies for Survibal in a Black Community* (New York: Harper and Row, 1974)

Steinbeck, John, 'Preface', in John Greenway, *American Folksongs of Protest* (University Of Pennsylvania Press, 1953)

Steinbeck, John, 'Foreword' in *Hard Hitting Songs for Hard-Hit People*, eds Alan Lomax, Woody Guthrie and Pete Seeger (New York: Oak Publications; Reprint Lincoln: University of Nebraska Press, 1999)

[Swinford Historical Society], *An Gorta Mór: Famine in the Swinford Union* (No publisher or date given)

Swords, Liam, ed., *Catholic, Protestant and Dissenter: The Clergy and 1798* (Dublin: Columba, 1997)

Swords, Liam, *In Their Own Words: The Famine in North Connacht 1845–1849* (Dublin: The Columba Press, 1999)

Swords, Liam, *A Hidden Church: The Diocese of Achonry, 1689–1818* (Dublin: Columba Press, 1999)

Swords, Liam, *A Dominant Church: The Diocese of Achonry 1881–1960* (Dublin: Columba Press, 2004)

Taves, Ann, *The Household of Faith: Roman Catholic Devotions in Mid-Nineteenth-Century America* (South Bend: Notre Dame University Press, 1986)

Taylor, Lawrence, *Occasions of Faith: An Anthropology of Irish Catholics* (Dublin: Lilliput Press, 1985)

Taylor, Lawrence, 'Bás i n-Éireann: Cultural Constructions of Death in Ireland', *Anthropological Quarterly*, 62 (October 1989), pp. 696–712

Taylor, Lawrence, '"Peter's Pence": Official Catholic Discourse and Irish Nationalism in the Nineteenth-Century', *History of European Ideas*, 16 (1993), pp. 103–07

Tonkin, Elizabeth, *Narrating Our Pasts: The Social Construction of Oral History* (New York: Cambridge University Press, 1992)

Tonna, Charlotte Elizabeth, *Irish Recollections*, ed. Patrick Maume (Dublin: University College Dublin Press, 2004 [1841])

Townend, Paul A., *Fr Mathew, Temperance and Irish Identity* (Dublin: Irish Academic Press, 2002)

Turner, Michael, 'Rural Economies in Post-Famine Ireland, c. 1850–1914', in *A Historical Geography of Ireland*, eds B. J. Graham and L. J. Proudfoot (New York: Academic Press, 1993), chapter 9

Tynan, Michael, *Catholic Instruction in Ireland 1720–1985* (Dublin: Four Courts Press, 1985)

Ua Cadhain, Liam, *Knock Shrine* (Galway: O'Gorman Printing House, 1935)

Ua Cadhain, Liam, *Cnoc Mhuire in Picture and Story* (Galway: O'Gorman, 1945)

Ua Cadhain, Liam, *Venerable Archdeacon Cavanagh, Pastor of Knock Shrine, 1867–1897* (Boyle, Co. Roscommon: Trustees of Knock Shrine, 1953)

Ui Ógáin, Ríonach, *Immortal Dan: Daniel O'Connell in Irish Folklore* (Dublin: Geography Publications, 1995)

Vansina, Jan, *Oral Tradition: A Study in Historical Methodology* (London: James Currey, 1985 [1965])

Vaughan, W. E., *Landlords and Tenants in Mid-Victorian Ireland* (Oxford: Clarendon, 1994)

Vesey, Patrick, 'I Flatter Myself We Have Strangled the Evil In the Bud' in *Hanging Crimes: When Ireland Used the Gallows*, ed. Frank Sweeney (Cork: Mercier Press, 2005), pp. 22–47

Veyvoda, Kathleen, '"Too Much Knowledge of the Other World": Women and Nineteenth-Century Irish Folktales', *Victorian Literature and Culture*, 32 (2004), pp. 41–61

Waldron, Fr Ciaran, 'Memories of Willie Kelly', in *Béacán/Bekan: Portrait of an East Mayo Parish*, eds by Fr Michael Comer and Nollaig Ó Muraíle (Privately published, 1986), pp. 167–9

Waldron, Rev Jarlath, 'The 1857 Mayo Election', in *Mayo: Aspects of its Heritage*, ed. Bernard O'Hara (Galway: Regional Technical College, 1986), pp. 102–21

Waldron, Kieran, 'The Churches of the Archdiocese of Tuam', *Cathair na Mart*, 18 (1998), pp. 162–8

Walker, Brian, *Parliamentary Election Results in Ireland, 1801–1922* (Dublin: Royal Irish Academy, 1978)

Walsh, Brendan, 'Marriage Rates and Population Pressure: Ireland 1871 and 1911', *Economic History Review*, second series, 23 (1970), pp. 148–62

Walsh, Fr Michael, *The Apparition at Knock: A Survey of Facts and Evidence* (Tuam: St Jarlath's College, 1955; second edition, 1959)

Warner, Marina, *Alone of All Her Sex: The Myth and the Cult of the Virgin Mary* (New York: Knopf, 1976)

Warner, Marina, 'What the Virgin of Knock Means to Women', *Magill* (September 1979), pp. 30–9

Weber, Eugen, 'Fairies and Hard Facts: The Reality of Folktales', *Journal of the History of Ideas*, XLII (1981), pp. 93–113

Weber, Max, *Economy and Society: An Outline of Interpretive Sociology*, eds Guenther Roth and Claus Wittich (New York: Bedminster Press, 1968)

Westlander, F., *A Memoir of William Moore, Late Scripture Reader in the Province of Connaught* (London: J Nisbet and Co., 1843)

Wheatly, Michael, *Nationalism and the Irish Party: Provincial Ireland, 1910–1916* (Oxford: Oxford University Press, 2006)

Whelan, Irene, *The Bible War in Ireland: The "Second Reformation" and the Polarization of Protestant-Catholic Relations, 1800–1840* (Madison: The University of Wisconsin Press, 2005)

Whelan, Kevin, 'The Catholic Village, the Catholic Chapel and Village Development in Ireland', *Irish Geography*, 16 (1983), pp. 1–15

White, John J., *The Knock Apparitions and Pilgrimage: Popular Piety and the Irish Land War* (Ph.D. Dissertation in History, Boston College, 1999)

White, Richard, *Remembering Ahanagran: Storytelling in a Family's Past* (New York: Hill and Wang, 1998)

Whitehouse, Harvey, *Modes of Religiosity: A Cognitive Theory of Religious Transmission* (New York: Altamira Press, 2004)

Wilde, Lady, *Ancient Legends of Ireland* (London: Ward and Downey, 1887; reprint, New York: Sperling Publishing Company, 1991)

Wilde, William, *Irish Popular Superstitions* (Totowa, New Jersey: Rowman and Littlefield, 1973 [1852])

Wojcik, Daniel, '"Polaroids from Heaven": Photography, Folk Religion, and the Miraculous Image Tradition at a Marian Apparition Site', *Journal of American Folklore*, 109 (Spring 1996), pp. 129–48

Yager, Tom, 'What Was Rundale and Where Did It Come From?', *Béaloideas*, 70 (2002), pp. 153–86

Yates, Nigel, *The Religious Condition of Ireland 1770–1850* (Oxford: Oxford University Press, 2006)

Yeats, William Butler, ed, *Irish Fairy and Folk Tales* 1993 reprint

Yeats, William Butler, *The Book of Fairy and Fairylore: Folk Tales of Ireland* (London: Octopus Publishing Group, 1994; Bounty Paperback, 2004) [Reprint of originally separate volumes *Fairy and Folk Tales of the Irish Peasantry* (1888) and *Irish Fairy Tales* (1891)]

Index